# Calendar of State Papers Domestic Series of the reign of Edward VI 1547-1553

preserved in the
PUBLIC RECORD OFFICE

Revised Edition

Edited by
C.S. KNIGHTON

HMSO: LONDON

© *Crown copyright 1992*

*Applications for reproduction should be made to HMSO*

*First published 1992*

ISBN 0 11 440237 X

M023 6514 BU

British Library Cataloguing in Publication Data
A CIP catalogue record for this book is available from the British Library


Printed on acid-free paper

# CONTENTS

# PREFACE

This volume is a revised edition of the first part of the *Calendar of State Papers, Domestic Series, 1547-1580*, as explained in detail in the Editorial Note immediately following. Both text and index are the work of Dr C.S. Knighton, who has also (with Dr A.S. Bevan) seen the volume through the press.

Dr Knighton wishes to record his indebtedness to many individuals and institutions in the preparation of this volume. He has derived much assistance from officers of the Public Record Office, and also from the authorities of the British Library, the House of Lords Record Office, The Library of the Inner Temple, Cambridge University Library, the Library of Corpus Christi College, Cambridge, and the Library of the Most Honourable the Marquess of Salisbury at Hatfield House. For advice on subjects within their several special spheres, thanks are due to Mr N.H. Bennett, Mr J.P.B. Brooke-Little, C.V.O., the Reverend Professor H. Chadwick, K.B.E., Dr C.E. Challis, Dr P. Chaplais, Dr N.G. Cox, Mr I.D.D. Eaves, Miss B.F. Harvey, Dr D.E. Hoak, Mr P.A. Kennedy, Dr C.J. Kitching, Dr S.J. Lander, Mrs H. Lockwood, Dr D.M. Owen, Professor T.B.W. Reid, Dr G.J. Walker, Mr C. Webster and Miss P.J. White. Professor Sir Geoffrey Elton has been a constant source of assistance and encouragement throughout the making of this volume. The editor also acknowledges with gratitude the financial assistance of the British Academy.

# EDITORIAL NOTE

This volume was conceived as the first stage in the replacement of the *Calendar of State Papers, Domestic Series, 1547-1580*, compiled by Robert Lemon and published in 1856 as the earliest product of the amalgamation two years earlier of the State Paper and Public Record Offices. Lemon's work has remained for over a century the only printed guide to the principal government records of the reigns of the children of Henry VIII. But it is far from being a calendar as that term has come to be understood, and would now be known as a descriptive list. Indeed, Lemon found it necessary to explain the term calendar in the introduction to his first volume. His second, covering the years 1581-1590, was fuller. But although his work was generally accurate within the limited framework which was offered, he tended to shy away from manuscripts which presented palaeographical or linguistic problems, and in general to take note only of the opening and closing sentences of letters, or merely to copy the endorsements to the originals. The inadequacies of this approach were criticised by M.A.E. Green in the introduction to the first of her own much more useful calendars. Since that time the conventions of calendaring have, to a large extent, been standardized. It is therefore appropriate that the domestic state papers of the mid sixteenth century should have as ample a calendar as do those of earlier and later years.

This new calendar does not include descriptions of the Edwardine documents in the State Papers Domestic: Addenda, Edward VI to James I (SP 15), as they were well and fully described by M.A.E. Green in the *Calendar of State Papers, Domestic Series, 1601–1609; with addenda, 1547–1565* (London, 1870). Most of the addenda for the reign of Edward VI came from two previously discrete series, Scottish border papers and Channel Islands papers, but some general papers were also included.

A particular concern in producing this new calendar has been for the physical condition of the documents in the class State Papers Domestic: Edward VI (SP 10) which, because described so sparingly, have been consulted with a much greater frequency than would have been necessary had the requirements of scholars been at least partially satisfied by a comprehensive calendar and index. It is hoped that the provision of the present volume will greatly reduce the number of occasions on which the originals have to be produced. It is therefore an attempt to fulfil the directions of Royal Commissioners appointed in 1764 for the making of 'exact calendars and indices' by presenting in précis form all the documents in the main series of letters and papers in SP 10 (excluding, that is, four volumes from the series which comprise individual works), along with those few papers from three other classes in the Public Record Office – State Papers Domestic: Williamson Collection, Pamphlets, and Miscellaneous (SP 9), State Papers Domestic: Mary I (SP 11) and Signet Office: Docquets (formerly State Papers Domestic: Docquets) (SP 38) – which were treated by Lemon in the original calendar. It was not thought appropriate to cast a wider net. But a certain amount of re-arrangement in the order of the calendared entries was necessary, to take account of the re-dating of some of the papers. In the main Lemon's dates have been found to be accurate; but where a date he assigned or suggested has been proved wrong and another shown to be correct, the location of the calendar entry is amended accordingly. If, however, a date offered by Lemon is now in question, but without a more accurate one having been found, the item retains its original position. Since Lemon's publication, two documents have been found not to belong to the reign of Edward VI and have therefore been removed from SP 10 to other classes: the former SP 10/18, no. 20 is now SP 16/523, no. 119, and SP 10/18, no. 43 is now MPF 161.

No re-arrangement of the manuscripts was made during the preparation of the present calendar; the opportunity was taken, however, to re-mark the item numbers on the manuscripts, and it is to these numbers rather than the foliation that reference should be made. The SP 10 volumes carry a variety of sometimes contradictory foliations, some of which have been cited in publications. To assist identification a concordance of item numbers and foliations is included as part of the critical apparatus of this volume. The preferred form of citation is SP 10/1, no. 1 (for the first item in the first volume of the series); SP 10/2, no. 1(i) indicates an item enclosed with a preceding document.

The calendar attempts to include the names of all persons and places occurring in the originals – a rule waived in two instances: SP 10/3, no. 10 (a muster roll) and SP 10/10, no. 7 (a manorial account). Place names are given in the text in their modern form, unless this cannot be established; all manuscript variants are given in the index. Surnames of well known persons and titles are given in the modern form; otherwise the manuscript spellings of surnames (which may vary within a single entry) are used.

Dates assigned to documents are as given on the original manuscripts or their endorsements unless qualified by the use of square brackets. Accounts are generally assigned to their terminal dates, which may of course not be the days on which the documents were written.

The number of pages is given for only the longer pieces.

Many of the documents here calendared have been printed elsewhere in whole or part. It was felt that the balance of the volume and the usefulness of the index would suffer if such items were not covered as fully as the rest. Reference is given to material in print, and also (where known) to manuscript originals of which the SP 10 papers are copies, but not generally to other contemporary copies.

# LIST OF CLASSES

# LIST OF ABBREVIATIONS

Anderson      J. Anderson, *Ladies of the Reformation* (1855).

*APC*      *Acts of the Privy Council of England*, ed. J.R. Dasent, n.s., 32 vols (1890–1907).

BL      British Library.

Burnet      G. Burnet, *History of the Reformation of the Church of England*, ed. N. Pocock, 7 vols (Oxford, 1865).

Bush      M.L. Bush, *The Government Policy of Protector Somerset* (1975).

Cardwell      E. Cardwell, *Documentary Annals of the Reformed Church of England*, 2 vols (Oxford, 1839–44).

*CJ*      *Journals of the House of Commons.*

Cornwall, *Revolt of the Peasantry*      J. Cornwall, *Revolt of the Peasantry 1549* (1977).

*CPR*      *Calendar of the Patent Rolls preserved in the Public Record Office. Edward VI.* 6 vols (1924–9). Cited by years: vol. i, 1547–8; vol. ii, 1548–9; vol. iii, 1549–51; vol. iv, 1550–3; vol. v, 1553.

*CSPD*      *Calendar of State Papers, Domestic Series, of the reigns of Edward VI, Mary, Elizabeth 1547-1580, preserved in the State Paper Department of Her Majesty's Public Record Office*, ed. R. Lemon (1856).

Ellis, *Original Letters*      H. Ellis, *Original Letters, illustrative of English History*, 1st series, 3 vols (1824).

Emmison, *Tudor Secretary*      F.G. Emmison, *Tudor Secretary. Sir William Petre at Court and Home* (1961).

*Facsimiles of National MSS*      *Facsimiles of National Manuscripts from William the Conquerer to Queen Anne*, 3 parts (Ordnance Survey, Southampton, 1865–8).

fig.      figurative (usage).

Goff      C. Goff, *A Woman of the Tudor Age* (1930).

Green      M.A.E. Wood (afterwards Green), *Letters of Royal and Illustrious Ladies of Great Britain, from the commencement of the twelfth century to the close of the reign of Queen Mary*, 3 vols (1846).

*HBC*      *Handbook of British Chronology*, ed. F.M. Powicke and E.B. Fryde (Royal Historical Society Guides and Handbooks, no. 2, 2nd edn, 1961).

Heinze, *Proclamations*      R.W. Heinze, *The Proclamations of the Tudor Kings* (Cambridge, 1976).

HLRO      House of Lords Record Office.

| | |
|---|---|
| *HMC Salisbury MSS* | *Calendar of the Manuscripts of the Most Hon. the Marquis of Salisbury, K.G., etc., preserved at Hatfield House, Hertfordshire,* 18 vols (Historical Manuscripts Commission, 1883–1940). |
| Hoak | D.E. Hoak, *The King's Council in the reign of Edward VI* (Cambridge, 1976). Also (where specified) the same author's unpublished Cambridge Ph.D. dissertation of the same title (1971). |
| joc. | jocular (usage). |
| Jordan, i | W.K. Jordan, *Edward VI: the Young King. The Protectorship of the Duke of Somerset* (1968). |
| Jordan, ii | W.K. Jordan, *Edward VI: the Threshold of Power. The Dominance of the Duke of Northumberland* (1970). |
| K.B. | Knight of the Bath. |
| K.G. | Knight of the Garter. |
| Kt | Knight, knighted. |
| Lamond, *Discourse of the Common Weal* | *A Discourse of the Common Weal of this Realm of England*, ed. E. Lamond (Cambridge, 1929). |
| LP | *Letters and Papers, Foreign and Domestic, of the Reign of Henry VIII, preserved in the Public Record Office, the British Museum, and elsewhere in England*, ed. J.S. Brewer, J. Gairdner and R.H. Brodie, 23 vols in 38 (1862–1932). Cited by entry numbers. |
| Muller | *Letters of Stephen Gardiner*, ed. J.A. Muller (Cambridge, 1933). |
| n.s. | new series. |
| Nicholas, *Remains* | *Literary Remains of King Edward VI*, ed. J.G. Nichols, 2 vols (Roxburghe Club, 1857). |
| Pocock, *Troubles* | *Troubles connected with the Prayer Book of 1549*, ed. N. Pocock (Camden Society, n.s., xxxvii, 1884). |
| PRO | Public Record Office. |
| Read | C. Read, *Mr Secretary Cecil and Queen Elizabeth* (1955). |
| Rose-Troup, *The Western Rebellion* | F. Rose-Troup, *The Western Rebellion of 1549* (1913). |
| Russell, *Kett's Rebellion* | F.W. Russell, *Kett's Rebellion in Norfolk* (1859). |
| Rymer | *Foedera, conventiones, litterae, et cujuscunque generis acta publica, inter reges Angliae et alios imperatores, reges, pontifices, principes, vel communitates, ab ineunte saeculo duodecimo, viz. ab anno 1101, ad nostra usque tempora, habita aut tractata; ex autographis infra secretiores archivorum regiorum thesaurarias, per multa saecula reconditis, fideliter exscripta. In lucem missa de mandato nuperae reginae. Accurante Thoma Rymer*, 20 vols (1727–35). |

| | |
|---|---|
| ser. | series. |
| *SR* | *The Statutes of the Realm, from original records and authentic manuscripts,* [ed. A. Luders, T.E. Tomlins, J. France, W.E. Taunton and J. Raithby], 11 vols in 12 (1810–28). |
| *STC* | *A Short-Title Catalogue of books printed in England, Scotland and Ireland, and of English books printed abroad, 1475-1640,* ed. A.W. Pollard and G.R. Redgrave (1946). Revised edn by W.A. Jackson, F.S. Ferguson and K.F. Pantzer, 2 vols (1976–86). |
| Strype, *Cranmer* | *Memorials of the Most Reverend Father in God, Thomas Cranmer, sometime Lord Archbishop of Canterbury,* ed. J. Strype, 3 vols (Oxford 1848–54). |
| Strype, *Ecclesiastical Memorials* | *Ecclesiastical Memorials, relating chiefly to religion, and the reformation of it, and the emergencies of the church of England under King Henry VIII, King Edward VI, and Queen Mary I,* ed. J. Strype, 6 vols (Oxford, 1822). |
| temp. | time of. |
| Townsend, *The writings of John Bradford* | *The writings of John Bradford,* ed. A. Townsend, 2 vols (Parker Society, Cambridge, 1848–53). |
| *Tudor Economic Documents* | *Tudor Economic Documents,* ed. R.H. Tawney and E. Power, 3 vols (1924). |
| *Tudor Royal Proclamations* | *Tudor Royal Proclamations,* ed. P.L. Hughes and J.F. Larkin, 3 vols (New Haven, 1964–9). |
| Tytler | P.F. Tytler, *England under the Reigns of Edward VI and Mary, illustrated in a series of original letters never before printed with historical introductions and biographical notes,* 2 vols (1839). Transcripts in modernised spelling. |
| UV | ultra-violet. |
| *VCH Bedfordshire* | *The Victoria History of the County of Bedford,* ed. W. Page, 3 vols (1904–12). |
| *VCH Hertfordshire* | *The Victoria History of the County of Hertford,* ed. W. Page, 4 vols (1902–14). |
| Wilkins | *Concilia Magnae Britanniae et Hiberniae . . . 466-1718,* ed. D. Wilkins, 4 vols (1737). |

The place of publication of printed works is London unless otherwise stated.

# CONCORDANCE OF ITEM NUMBERS AND FOLIATIONS

| Volume | Item no.* | New calendar no. | Fo. | Microfilm fo. |
|---|---|---|---|---|
| SP 10/1 | 1 | 1 | 1–2v | 1–2v |
| | 2 | 2 | 3–4v | 3–4v |
| | 3 | 3 | 5–6v | 5–6v |
| | 4 | 4 | 7–7v | 7–7v |
| | 5 | 5 | 8–9v | 8–9v |
| | 6 | 6 | 12–13v | 10–12Bv |
| | 7 | 7 | 14–25v | 13–24v |
| | 8 | 8 | 26–26v | 25–25v |
| | 9 | 10 | 27–36v† | 25A–25Fv‡ |
| | 10 | 11 | 37–38v | 26–27v |
| | 11 | 12 | 39–40v | 28–29v |
| | 12 | 13 | 41–50v | 30–39v |
| | 13 | 14 | 51–65v | 40–54v |
| | 14 | 15 | 66–66v | 55–55v |
| | 15 | 805 | 67–68v | 56–57v |
| | 16 | 806 | 69–70v | 58–59v |
| | 17 | 16 | 71–86v | 60–75v |
| | 18 | 17 | 87–87v | 76–76v |
| | 19 | 18 | 88–89v | 77–78v |
| | 20 | 19 | 90–91v | 79–80v |
| | 21 | 628 | 92–92v | 81–81v |
| | 22 | 20 | 93-94v | 82–83v |
| | 23 | 21 | 95–101v | 84–90v |
| | 24 | 22 | 102–102v | 91–91v |
| | 25 | 23 | 103–106v | 92–95v |
| | 26 | 24 | 107–108v | 96–96v |
| | 27 | 25 | 109–110v | 98–99v |
| | 28 | 26 | 111–112v | 100–101v |
| | 29 | 27 | 113–114v | 102–103v |
| | 30 | 28 | 115–116v | 104–105v |
| | 31 | 29 | 117–118v | 106–106v |
| | 32 | 30 | 119–122v | 107–110v |
| | 33 | 31 | 123–123v | 111–111v |
| | 34 | 32 | 124–124v | 112–112v |
| | 35 | 33 | 125–125v | 113–113v |
| | 36 | 34 | 126–131v | 114–119v |
| | 37 | 35 | 132–133v | 120–121v |
| | 38 | 36 | 134–135v | 122–123v |
| | 39 | 37 | 136–137v | 124–125v |
| | 40 | 38 | 138–139v | 126–127v |
| | 41 | 39 | 140–141v | 128–129v |
| | 42 | 40 | 142–143v | 130–131v |

\*    The number used in the old calendar
†    Subsequently re-bound
‡    Incompletely stamped

| Volume | Item no.* | New calendar no. | Fo. | Microfilm fo. |
|---|---|---|---|---|
| SP 10/1 | 43 | 41 | 144–145v | 132–133v |
| *contd.* | 44 | 42 | 146–147v | 133A–134v |
| | 45 | 43 | 148–148v | 135–135v |
| SP 10/2 | 1 | 44 | 1–4v | 1–3Av |
| | 2 | 45 | 5–5v | 4–4v |
| | 3 | 46 | 6–7v | 5–6v |
| | 4 | 47 | 8–9v | 7–8v |
| | 5 | 48 | 10–11v | 9–10v |
| | 6 | 49 | 12–13v | 11–12v |
| | 7 | 50 | 14–23v | 13–22v |
| | 8 | 51 | 24–24v | 23–23v |
| | 9 | 52 | 25–37v | 24–36v |
| | 10 | 53 | 38–38v | 37–37v |
| | 11 | 54 | 39–39v | 38–38v |
| | 12 | 55 | 40–42v | 39–41v |
| | 13 | 56 | 43–54v | 42–53v |
| | 14 | 57 | 55–56v | 54–55v |
| | 15 | 58 | 57–58v | 56–57v |
| | 16 | 59 | 59–62v | 58–61v |
| | 17 | 60 | 63–66v | 62–65v |
| | 18 | 61 | 67–67v | 66–66v |
| | 19 | 62 | 68–68v | 67–67v |
| | 20 | 63 | 69–70v | 68–69v |
| | 21 | 167 | 71–82v | 69A–80v |
| | 22 | 64 | 83–84v | 81–82v |
| | 23 | 65 | 85–86v | 83–84v |
| | 24† | 66 | 87–88v | 84A–84Bv‡ |
| | 25† | 67 | 89–90v | 84C–84Dv‡ |
| | 26 | 68 | 91–92v | 85–86v |
| | 27 | 69 | 93–94v | 87–88v |
| | 28 | 70 | 95–96v | 89–90v |
| | 29 | 71 | 97–108v | 91–102v |
| | 30 | 778 | 109–109v | 103–103v |
| | 31 | 786 | 110–111v | 104–105v |
| | 32 | 72 | 112–119v | 106–113v |
| | 33 | 73 | 120–121v | 114–115v |
| | 34 | 74 | 122–122v | 116–116v |
| SP 10/3 | 1 | 75 | 1–1Av | 1–2v |
| | 2 | 76 | 2–2v | 3–3v |
| | 3 | 77 | 3–8v | 4–9v |
| | 4 | 78 | 9–9v | 10–10v |
| | 5 | 79 | 10–11v | 11–12v |
| | 6 | 80 | 12–13v | 13–14v |
| | 7 | 9 | 14–17v | 15–18v |
| | 8 | 81 | 18–23v | 19–24v |
| | 9 | 82 | 24–43v | 25–44v |

\*    The number used in the old calendar
†    Removed to Safe Room
‡    Not stamped

| Volume | Item no.* | New calendar no. | Fo. | Microfilm fo. |
|---|---|---|---|---|
| SP 10/3 | 10 | 83 | 44–93v | 45–95v |
| *contd.* | 11 | 84 | 94–95v | 96–96v |
|  | 12 | 85 | 96–96v | 97–97v |
|  | 13 | 86 | 97–97v | 98–98v |
|  | 14 | 87 | 98–98v | 99–99v |
|  | 15 | 88 | 99–99v | 100–100v |
|  | 16 | 89 | 100–113v | 101–115v |
|  | 17 | 90 | 114–125v | 116–127v |
|  | 18 | 91 | 126–137v | 128–139v |
|  | 19 | 92 | 138–143v | 140–145v |
|  | 20 | 93 | 144–145v | 146–147v |
|  | 21 | 94 | 146–146Av | 148–149v |
|  | 22 | 95 | 147–152v | 150–155v |
| SP 10/4 | 1 | 96 | 1–2v | 1–2v |
|  | 2 | 97 | 3–4v | 3–4v |
|  | 3 | 98 | 5–5v | 5–5v |
|  | 4 | 99 | 6–7v | 6–7v |
|  | 5 | 100 | 8–8v | 8–8v |
|  | 6 | 101 | 9–10v | 9–10v |
|  | 7 | 102 | 11–12v | 11–12v |
|  | 8 | 103 | 13–13v | 13–13v |
|  | 9 | 104 | 14–24v | 14–24v |
|  | 10 | 105 | 25–26v | 25–26v |
|  | 11 | 106 | 27–27v | 27–27v |
|  | 12 | 107 | 28–29v | 28–29v |
|  | 12(i) | 108 | 30–33v | 30–33v |
|  | 13 | 109 | 34–34v | 34–34v |
|  | 14 | 110 | 35–36v | 35–36v |
|  | 15 | 111 | 37–37v | 37–37v |
|  | 16 | 112 | 38–38v | 38–38v |
|  | 17 | 113 | 39–40v | 39–40v |
|  | 18 | 114 | 41–41v | 41–41v |
|  | 19 | 115 | 42–43v | 42–43v |
|  | 20 | 116 | 44–45v | 44–45v |
|  | 21 | 117 | 46–46v | 46–46v |
|  | 22 | 118 | 47–47v | 47–47v |
|  | 23 | 119 | 48–48v | 48–48v |
|  | 24 | 120 | 49–49v | 49–49v |
|  | 25 | 121 | 50–50v | 50–50v |
|  | 25(i) | 122 | 51–52v | 51–52v |
|  | 26 | 123 | 53–54v | 53–54v |
|  | 27 | 124 | 55–56v | 55–56v |
|  | 28 | 125 | 57–58v | 57–58v |
|  | 29 | 127 | 59–59v | 59–59v |
|  | 30 | 128 | 60–60v | 60–60v |
|  | 31 | 129 | 61–62v | 61–62v |
|  | 31(i, ii) | 130, 131 | 62 | 62 |
|  | 32 | 132 | 63–63v | 63–63v |

\* The number used in the old calendar

| Volume | Item no.* | New calendar no. | Fo. | Microfilm fo. |
|---|---|---|---|---|
| SP 10/4 | 33 | 133 | 64–65v | 64–65v |
| *contd.* | 34 | 134 | 66–66v | 66–66v |
| | 35 | 135 | 67–68v | 67–68v |
| | 36 | 136 | 69–70v | 69–70v |
| | 37 | 138 | 71–71v | 71–71v |
| | 38 | 139 | 72–73v | 72–73v |
| | 39 | 140 | 74–76v | 74–76v |
| | 40 | 141 | 77–80v | 77–80v |
| | 41 | 143 | 81–82v | 81–82v |
| | 42 | 142 | 83–83v | 83–83v |
| | 43 | 144 | 84–86v | 84–86v |
| | 44 | 145 | 87–88v | 87–88v |
| | 44(i) | 146 | 89–89v | 89–89v |
| | 45 | 147 | 90–91v | 90–91v |
| | 46 | 148 | 92–93v | 92–93v |
| | 47 | 149 | 94–95v | 94–95v |
| | 48 | 432 | 96–96v | 96–96v |
| SP 10/5 | 1 | 150 | 1–2v | 1–2v |
| | 2 | 151 | 3–3v | 3–3v |
| | 3 | 152 | 4–5v | 4–5v |
| | 3(i) | 153 | 6–6v | 6–6v |
| | 3(ii) | 154 | 7–7v | 7–7v |
| | 3(iii) | 155 | 8–8v | 8–8v |
| | 4† | 156 | 9–10v | 8A–8AAv‡ |
| | 5† | 157 | 11–12v | 8B–8BAv‡ |
| | 6 | 158 | 13–14v | 9–10v |
| | 7 | 159 | 15–26v | 11–22v |
| | 8 | 419 | 27–33v | 23–29v |
| | 9 | 160 | 34–35v | 30–31v |
| | 10 | 161 | 36–37v | 32–33v |
| | 11 | 162 | 38–38v | 34–34v |
| | 12 | 163 | 39–40v | 35–36v |
| | 13 | 164 | 41–44v | 37–40v |
| | 14 | 165 | 45–46v | 41–42v |
| | 14(i) | 166 | 47–47v | 43–43v |
| | 15 | 169 | 48–56Av | 44–52v |
| | 16 | 170 | 57–58v | 53–54v |
| | 17 | 137 | 59–71v | 55–67v |
| | 18 | 171 | 72–83v | 68–79v |
| | 19 | 172 | 84–123v | 80–119v |
| | 20 | 173 | 124–129v | 120–125v |
| | 21 | 174 | 130–131v | 126–127v |
| | 22 | 168 | 132–146v | 128–141v |
| | 23 | 845 | 147–148v | 142–143v |
| | 24 | 594 | 149–153v | 144–148v |
| | 25 | 784 | 154–155v | 149–150v |

\*    The number used in the old calendar
†    Removed to Safe Room
‡    Not stamped

| Volume | Item no.* | New calendar no. | Fo. | Microfilm fo. |
|---|---|---|---|---|
| SP 10/6 | 1 | 176 | 1–2v | 1–2v |
| | 2 | 177 | 3–4v | 3–4v |
| | 3 | 178 | 5–10v | 5–10v |
| | 4 | 179 | 11–14v | 11–14v |
| | 5 | 180 | 15–15v | 15–15v |
| | 6 | 181 | 16–17v | 16–17v |
| | 7 | 182 | 18–21v | 18–21v |
| | 8 | 183 | 22–22v | 22–22v |
| | 9 | 184 | 23–23v | 23–23v |
| | 10 | 185 | 24–28v | 24–28v |
| | 11 | 186 | 29–32v | 29–32v |
| | 12 | 187 | 33–34v | 33–34v |
| | 13 | 188 | 35–38v | 35–38v |
| | 14 | 189 | 39–40v | 39–40v |
| | 15 | 190 | 41–42v | 41–42v |
| | 16 | 191 | 43–46v | 43–46v |
| | 17 | 192, 193 | 47–48v | 47–48v |
| | 18 | 194 | 49–50v | 49–50v |
| | 19 | 195 | 51–52v | 51–52v |
| | 20 | 196 | 53–54v | 53–54v |
| | 21 | 197 | 55–56v | 55–56v |
| | 22 | 198 | 57–59v | 57–59v |
| | 23 | 199 | 60–61v | 60–61v |
| | 24 | 200 | 62–65v | 62–65v |
| | 25 | 201 | 66–67v | 66–67v |
| | 26 | 202 | 68–68v | 68–68v |
| | 27 | 203 | 69–71v | 69–71v |
| | 28 | 204 | 72–73v | 72–73v |
| | 29 | 205 | 74–75v | 74–75v |
| | 30 | 206 | 76–76v | 76–76v |
| | 31 | 207 | 77–77v | 77–77v |
| | 32 | 208 | 78–78v | 78–78v |
| | 33 | 209 | 79 | 79 |
| | 34 | 210 | 79v–80v | 79v–80v |
| | 35 | 211 | 81–81v | 81–81v |
| | 36 | 212 | 82–83v | 82–83v |
| SP 10/7 | 1 | 213 | 1–2v | 1–2v |
| | 2 | 214 | 3–4v | 3–4v |
| | 3 | 215 | 5–5v | 5–5v |
| | 4 | 216 | 6–7v | 6–7v |
| | 5 | 217 | 8–8v | 8–8v |
| | 6 | 218 | 9–20v | 9–20v |
| | 7 | 219 | 21–32v | 21–32v |
| | 8 | 220 | 33–36v | 33–36v |
| | 9 | 221 | 37–38v | 37–38v |
| | 10 | 222 | 39–40v | 39–40v |
| | 11 | 223 | 41–42v | 41–42v |
| | 12 | 224 | 43–44v | 43–44v |

\*        The number used in the old calendar

| Volume | Item no.* | New calendar no. | Fo. | Microfilm fo. |
|---|---|---|---|---|
| SP 10/7 | 13 | 234 | 45–46v | 45–46v |
| *contd.* | 14 | 236 | 47–48v | 47–48v |
| | 15 | 235 | 49–50v | 49–50v |
| | 16 | 237 | 51–52v | 51–52v |
| | 17 | 238 | 53–54v | 53–54v |
| | 18 | 242 | 55–56v | 55–56v |
| | 19 | 243 | 57–58v | 57–58v |
| | 20 | 244 | 59–60v | 59–60v |
| | 21 | 249 | 61–61v | 61–61v |
| | 22 | 250 | 62–63v | 62–63v |
| | 23 | 251 | 64–65v | 64–65v |
| | 24 | 255 | 66–67v | 66–67v |
| | 25 | 256 | 68–69v | 68–69v |
| | 26 | 257 | 70–71v | 70–71v |
| | 27 | 258 | 72–73v | 72–73v |
| | 28 | 265 | 74–80v | 74–80v |
| | 29 | 271 | 81–82v | 81–82v |
| | 30 | 272 | 83–84v | 83–84v |
| | 31 | 273 | 85–85v | 85–85v |
| | 32 | 274 | 86–86v | 86–86v |
| | 33 | 277 | 87–88v | 87–88v |
| | 34 | 276 | 89–90v | 89–90v |
| | 35 | 280 | 91–91v | 91–91v |
| | 36 | 281 | 92–93v | 92–93v |
| | 37 | 282 | 94–95v | 94–95v |
| | 38 | 283 | 96–97v | 96–97v |
| | 38(i) | 284 | 98–99v | 98–99v |
| | 38(ii) | 285 | 100–101v | 100–101v |
| | 39 | 286 | 102–102v | 102–102v |
| | 40 | 287 | 103–108v | 103–108v |
| | 41 | 288 | 109–110v | 109–109Av |
| | 42 | 289 | 111–112v | 110–111v |
| | 43 | 290 | 113–114v | 112–113v |
| | 43(i) | 291 | 115–116v | 114–115v |
| | 44 | 292 | 117–117v | 116–116v |
| | 45 | 293 | 118–119v | 117–118v |
| | 46 | 294 | 120–120v | 119–119v |
| | 47 | 295 | 121–126v | 120–125v |
| | 48 | 296 | 127–132v | 126–131v |
| SP 10/8 | 1 | 297 | 1–1v | 1A–1Av |
| | 2 | 298 | 2–5v | 2–5v |
| | 3 | 300 | 6–7v | 6–7v |
| | 4 | 301 | 8–11v | 8–11v |
| | 5 | 302 | 12–16v | 12–16v |
| | 6 | 303 | 17–22v | 17–22v |
| | 7 | 304 | 23–24v | 23–24v |
| | 8 | 305 | 25–26v | 25–26v |
| | 9 | 306 | 27–30v | 27–30v |

\*    The number used in the old calendar

| Volume | Item no.* | New calendar no. | Fo. | Microfilm fo. |
|---|---|---|---|---|
| SP 10/8 | 10 | 307 | 31–31v | 31–31v |
| *contd.* | 11 | 308 | 32–32v | 32–32v |
| | 12 | 309 | 33–33v | 33–33v |
| | 13 | 310 | 34–34v | 33–34v |
| | 14 | 311 | 35–35v | 35–35v |
| | 15 | 312 | 36–36v | 36–36v |
| | 16 | 313 | 37–37v | 37–37v |
| | 17 | 314 | 38–38v | 38–38v |
| | 18 | 315 | 39–39v | 39–39v |
| | 19 | 316 | 40–40v | 40–40v |
| | 20 | 317 | 41–41v | 41–41v |
| | 21 | 318 | 42–42v | 42–42v |
| | 22 | 319 | 43–43v | 43–43v |
| | 23 | 320 | 44–44v | 44–44v |
| | 24 | 321 | 45–46v | 45–46v |
| | 25 | 322 | 47–47v | 47–47v |
| | 26 | 323 | 47A–47Av | 48–48v |
| | 27 | 324 | 48–48v | 49–49v |
| | 28 | 325 | 49–49v | 50–50v |
| | 29 | 326 | 50–50v | 51–51v |
| | 30 | 327 | 51–51v | 52–52v |
| | 31 | 328 | 52–53v | 53–54v |
| | 32 | 329 | 54–55v | 55–56v |
| | 33 | 330 | 56–57v | 57–58v |
| | 34 | 331 | 58–59v | 59–60v |
| | 35 | 332 | 60–61v | 61–62v |
| | 36 | 333 | 62–65v | 63–66v |
| | 37 | 334 | 66–69v | 67–70v |
| | 38 | 335 | 70–71v | 71–72v |
| | 39 | 336 | 72–72v | 73–73v |
| | 40 | 337 | 73–73v | 74–74v |
| | 41 | 338 | 74–75v | 75–76v |
| | 42 | 339 | 76–77v | 77–78v |
| | 43 | 340 | 78–79v | 79–80v |
| | 44 | 341 | 80–81v | 81–82v |
| | 45 | 342 | 82–82v | 83–83v |
| | 46 | 343 | 83–83v | 84–84v |
| | 47 | 344 | 84–85v | 85–86v |
| | 48 | 345 | 86–86v | 87–87v |
| | 49 | 346 | 87–88v | 88–89v |
| | 50 | 347 | 89–90v | 90–91v |
| | 51 | 348 | 91–91v | 92–92v |
| | 52 | 349 | 92–94v | 93–95v |
| | 53 | 350 | 95–96v | 96–97v |
| | 54 | 351 | 97–97v | 97A–97Av |
| | 55 | 352 | 98–99v | 98–99v |
| | 55(i) | 353 | 100–101v | 100–101v |
| | 55(ii) | 354 | 102–102v | 102–102v |

\*　　The number used in the old calendar

| Volume | Item no.* | New calendar no. | Fo. | Microfilm fo. |
|---|---|---|---|---|
| SP 10/8 | 56 | 356 | 103–104v | 103–104v |
| *contd.* | 57 | 355 | 105–106v | 105–106v |
| | 58 | 357 | 107–108v | 107–108v |
| | 59 | 358 | 109–109v | 109–109v |
| | 60 | 359 | 110–111v | 110–111v |
| | 61 | 360 | 112–113v | 112–113v |
| | 62 | 361 | 114–114v | 114–114v |
| | 63 | 363 | 115–116v | 115–116v |
| | 64 | 362 | 117–118v | 117–118v |
| | 65 | 364 | 119–120v | 119–120v |
| | 66 | 365 | 121–122v | 121–122v |
| | 67 | 366 | 123–124v | 123–124v |
| | 68 | 367 | 125–125v | 125–125v |
| SP 10/9 | 1 | 368 | 1–2v | 1–2v |
| | 2 | 369 | 3–3v | 3–3v |
| | 3 | 370 | 4–4v | 4–4v |
| | 4 | 371 | 5–5v | 5–5v |
| | 5 | 372 | 6–6v | 6–6v |
| | 6 | 373 | 7–7v | 7–7v |
| | 7 | 374 | 8–8v | 8–8v |
| | 8 | 375 | 9–9v | 9–9v |
| | 9 | 376 | 10–10v | 10–10v |
| | 10 | 377 | 11–11v | 11–11v |
| | 11 | 378 | 12–12v | 12–12v |
| | 12 | 379 | 13–13v | 13–13v |
| | 13 | 380 | 14–14v | 14–14v |
| | 14 | 381 | 15–15v | 15–15v |
| | 15 | 382 | 16–16v | 16–17v |
| | 16 | 383 | 17–18v | 18–19v |
| | 17 | 384 | 19–19v | 20–20v |
| | 18 | 385 | 20–21v | 21–22v |
| | 19 | 386 | 22–23v | 23–24v |
| | 20 | 387 | 24–24v | 25–25v |
| | 21 | 388 | 25–26v | 26–27v |
| | 22 | 389 | 27–28v | 28–29v |
| | 23 | 390 | 29–30v | 30–31v |
| | 24 | 391 | 31–32v | 32–33v |
| | 24(i) | 392 | 33–34v | 34–34Bv |
| | 25 | 393 | 35–36v | 35–36v |
| | 25(i) | 394 | 37–38v | 37–38v |
| | 26 | 395 | 39–40v | 39–40v |
| | 27 | 396 | 41–41v | 41–41v |
| | 28 | 397 | 42–43v | 42–43v |
| | 29 | 398 | 44–44v | 44–44v |
| | 30 | 399 | 45–46v | 45–46v |
| | 31 | 400 | 47–48v | 47–48v |
| | 31(i) | 401 | 49–49v | 49–49v |
| | 32 | 402 | 50–51v | 50–51v |

\*     The number used in the old calendar

| Volume | Item no.* | New calendar no. | Fo. | Microfilm fo. |
| --- | --- | --- | --- | --- |
| SP 10/9 | 33 | 403 | 52–56v | 52–56v |
| *contd.* | 34 | 404 | 57–58v | 57–58v |
| | 35 | 405 | 59–61v | 59–61v |
| | 36 | 406 | 62–63v | 62–63v |
| | 37 | 407 | 64–65v | 64–65v |
| | 38 | 408 | 66–67v | 66–67v |
| | 39 | 409 | 68–69v | 68–69v |
| | 40 | 410 | 70–71v | 70–71v |
| | 41 | 411 | 72–81v | 72–81v |
| | 42 | 412 | 82–83v | 82–83v |
| | 43 | 413 | 84–85v | 84–84Av |
| | 44 | 414 | 86–86v | 85–85v |
| | 45 | 415 | 87–87v | 86–86v |
| | 46 | 416 | 88–88v | 87–87v |
| | 47 | 417 | 89–90v | 88–89v |
| | 48 | 418 | 91–95v | 90–94v |
| | 49 | 420 | 96–97v | 95–96v |
| | 50 | 421 | 98–99v | 97–98v |
| | 51 | 422 | 100–100v | 99–99v |
| | 52 | 423 | 101–102v | 100–101v |
| | 53 | 424 | 103–104v | 102–103v |
| | 54 | 425 | 105–110v | 104–109v |
| | 55 | 426 | 111–112v | 110–111v |
| | 56 | 427 | 113–113v | 112–112v |
| | 57 | 428 | 114–115v | 113–114v |
| | 58 | 429, 430 | 116–117v | 115–116v |
| | 59 | 843 | 118–119v | 117–118v |
| SP 10/10 | 1 | 433 | 1–1v | 1–2v |
| | 2 | 435 | 2–3v | 3–4v |
| | 3 | 436 | 4–5v | 5–6v |
| | 4 | 437 | 6–7v | 7–8v |
| | 5 | 438 | 8–8v | 9–9v |
| | 6 | 439 | 9–10v | 10–11v |
| | 7 | 440 | 11–18v | 12–18v |
| | 8 | 441 | 19–20v | 19–20v |
| | 9 | 442 | 21–22v | 21–22v |
| | 10 | 443 | 23–24v | 23–24v |
| | 11 | 444 | 25–25v | 25–25v |
| | 12 | 445 | 26–27v | 26–27v |
| | 13 | 446 | 28–28v | 28–28v |
| | 14 | 447 | 29–31v | 29–31v |
| | 15 | 448 | 32–35v | 32–35v |
| | 16 | 449 | 36–39v | 36–39v |
| | 17 | 450, 451 | 40–47v | 40–47v |
| | 18 | 452 | 48–49v | 48–49v |
| | 19 | 453 | 50–50v | 50–50v |
| | 19(i) | 454 | 51–52v | 51–52v |
| | 20 | 455 | 53–54v | 53–54v |

\*    The number used in the old calendar

| Volume | Item no.* | New calendar no. | Fo. | Microfilm fo. |
| --- | --- | --- | --- | --- |
| SP 10/10 | 21 | 456 | 55–55v | 55–55v |
| *contd.* | 22 | 457 | 56–57v | 56–57v |
| | 23 | 458 | 58–59v | 58–59v |
| | 24 | 459 | 60–61v | 60–61v |
| | 25 | 460 | 62–62v | 62–62v |
| | 26 | 461 | 63–64v | 63–64v |
| | 27 | 462 | 65–66v | 65–66v |
| | 28 | 463 | 67–67v | 67–67v |
| | 29 | 464 | 68–69v | 68–69v |
| | 30 | 465 | 70–70v | 70–70v |
| | 31 | 466 | 71–71v | 71–71v |
| | 32 | 467 | 72–72v | 72–72v |
| | 33 | 468 | 73–74v | 73–74v |
| | 34 | 469 | 75–76v | 75–76v |
| | 35 | 470 | 77–77v | 77–77v |
| | 36 | 471 | 78–79v | 78–79v |
| | 37 | 472 | 80–81v | 80–81v |
| | 38 | 473 | 82–82v | 82–82v |
| | 39 | 474 | 83–84v | 83–84v |
| | 40 | 477 | 85–85v | 85–85v |
| | 41 | 476 | 86–86v | 86–86v |
| | 42 | 475 | 87–87v | 87–87v |
| | 43 | 478 | 88–88v | 88–88v |
| | 44 | 479 | 89–90v | 89–90v |
| | 45 | 480 | 91–91v | 91–91v |
| | 46 | 481 | 92–93v | 92–93v |
| | 47 | 482 | 94–95v | 94–95v |
| | 48 | 483 | 96–97v | 96–97v |
| | 49 | 484 | 98–99v | 98–99v |
| SP 10/11 | 1 | 485 | 1–1v | 1–1v |
| | 2 | 486 | 2–3v | 2–3v |
| | 3 | 487 | 4–5v | 4–5v |
| | 4 | 488 | 6–6v | 6–6v |
| | 5 | 489 | 7–10v | 7–10v |
| | 6 | 490 | 11–11v | 11–11v |
| | 7 | 491 | 12–12Av | 12–12Av |
| | 8 | 492 | 13–13v | 13–13v |
| | 9 | 493 | 14–15v | 14–15v |
| | 10 | 494 | 16–17v | 16–17v |
| | 11 | 495 | 18–19v | 18–19v |
| | 12 | 496 | 20–21v | 20–21v |
| | 13 | 497 | 22–23v | 22–23v |
| | 14 | 498 | 24–25v | 24–25v |
| | 15 | 499 | 26–27v | 26–27v |
| | 16 | 500 | 28–29v | 28–29v |
| | 17 | 501 | 30–110v | 30–109v |
| SP 10/12 | – | 502 | – | – |
| SP 10/13 | 1 | 503 | 1–1v | 1–1v |

\* The number used in the old calendar

| Volume | Item no.* | New calendar no. | Fo. | Microfilm fo. |
|---|---|---|---|---|
| SP 10/13 | 2 | 504 | 2–7v | 2–6v |
| *contd.* | 3 | 505 | 8–9v | 7–8v |
| | 4 | 506 | 10–11v | 9–10v |
| | 5 | 507 | 12–13v | 11–12v |
| | 6 | 508 | 14–15v | 13–14v |
| | 7 | 509 | 16–17v | 15–16v |
| | 8 | 604 | 18–18v | 17–17v |
| | 9 | 510 | 19–22v | 18–21v |
| | 10 | 600 | 22A–22Av | 22–22v |
| | 10(i) | 599 | 23–23v | 23–23v |
| | 11 | 601 | 24–25v | 24–25v |
| | 12 | 603 | 26–27v | 26–27v |
| | 13 | 511 | 28–29v | 28–29v |
| | 14 | 512 | 30–31v | 30–31v |
| | 15 | 513 | 32–33v | 32–33v |
| | 16 | 514 | 34–35v | 34–35v |
| | 17 | 515 | 36–36v | 36–36v |
| | 18 | 516 | 37–38v | 37–38v |
| | 19 | 517 | 39–40v | 39–40v |
| | 20 | 518 | 41–42v | 41–42v |
| | 21 | 519 | 43–43v | 43–43v |
| | 22 | 520 | 44–45v | 44–45v |
| | 23 | 521 | 46–47v | 46–47v |
| | 24 | 522 | 48–49v | 48–49v |
| | 24(i) | 523 | 50–51v | 50–51v |
| | 25 | 524 | 52–53v | 52–53v |
| | 26 | 525 | 54–55v | 54–55v |
| | 27 | 526 | 56–57v | 56–57v |
| | 28 | 527 | 58–59v | 58–59v |
| | 29 | 528 | 60–61v | 60–61v |
| | 30 | 529 | 62–63v | 62–63v |
| | 31 | 530 | 64–65v | 64–65v |
| | 32 | 531 | 66–67v | 66–67v |
| | 33 | 532 | 68–69v | 68–69v |
| | 34 | 533 | 70–70v | 70–70v |
| | 35 | 534 | 71–72v | 71–72v |
| | 36 | 535 | 73–75v | 73–75v |
| | 37 | 536 | 76–77v | 76–77v |
| | 38 | 537 | 78–79v | 78–79v |
| | 39 | 538 | 80–81v | 80–81v |
| | 40 | 539 | 82–83v | 82–83v |
| | 41 | 540 | 84–85v | 84–85v |
| | 42 | 541 | 86–87v | 86–87v |
| | 43 | 542 | 88–89v | 88–89v |
| | 44 | 543 | 90–90v | 90–90v |
| | 45 | 544 | 91–91v | 91–91v |
| | 46 | 545 | 92–92v | 92–92v |
| | 47 | 546 | 93–94v | 93–94v |

*       The number used in the old calendar

| Volume | Item no.* | New calendar no. | Fo. | Microfilm fo. |
|---|---|---|---|---|
| SP 10/13 | 48 | 547 | 95–95v | 95–95v |
| contd. | 49 | 548 | 96–97v | 96–97v |
| | 50 | 549 | 98–98v | 98–98v |
| | 51 | 550 | 99–100v | 99–100v |
| | 52 | 551 | 101–102v | 101–102v |
| | 53 | 552 | 103–104v | 103–104v |
| | 53(i) | 553 | 105–106v | 105–106v |
| | 54 | 554 | 107–108v | 107–108v |
| | 55 | 535 | 109–110v | 109–110v |
| | 56 | 556 | 111–112v | 111–112v |
| | 57 | 558 | 113–113v | 113–113v |
| | 58 | 559 | 114–116v | 114–116v |
| | 59 | 560 | 117–117v | 117–117v |
| | 60 | 561 | 118–118v | 118–118v |
| | 61 | 562 | 119–119v | 119–119v |
| | 62 | 563 | 120–121v | 120–121v |
| | 62(i) | 564 | 122–122v | 122–122v |
| | 63 | 565 | 123–123v | 123–123v |
| | 64 | 566 | 124–125v | 124–125v |
| | 65 | 567 | 126–127v | 126–127v |
| | 66 | 568 | 128–129v | 128–129v |
| | 67 | 569 | 130–131v | 130–131v |
| | 68 | 570 | 132–132v | 132–132v |
| | 69 | 571 | 134–134v | 134–134v |
| | 70 | 572 | 135–137v | 135–137v |
| | 71 | 579 | 138–141v | 138–141v |
| | 72 | 573 | 142–142v | 142–142v |
| | 73 | 574 | 143–143v | 143–143v |
| | 74 | 577 | 144–145v | 144–145v |
| | 75 | 578 | 146–147v | 146–147v |
| | 76 | 575 | 148–149v | 148–148Av |
| | 77 | 576 | 150–150v | 149–149v |
| | 78 | 580 | 151–152v | 150–151v |
| | 79 | 598 | 153–153v | 152–152v |
| | 80 | 581 | 154–155v | 153–154v |
| | 81 | 582 | 156–157v | 155–156 |
| | 82 | 583 | 158–159v | 157–158v |
| SP 10/14 | 1 | 584 | 1–1v | 1–1v |
| | 2 | 587 | 2–5v | 2–5v |
| | 3 | 585 | 6–6v | 6–6v |
| | 3(i) | 586 | 7–8v | 7–8v |
| | 4 | 588 | 9–9v | 9–9v |
| | 5 | 591 | 10–10v | 10–10v |
| | 6 | 792 | 11–12v | 11–12v |
| | 7 | 608 | 13–13v | 13–13v |
| | 8 | 609 | 14–14v | 14–14v |
| | 9 | 602 | 15–15v | 15–15v |
| | 10 | 592 | 16–17v | 16–17v |

*        The number used in the old calendar

| Volume | Item no.* | New calendar no. | Fo. | Microfilm fo. |
|---|---|---|---|---|
| SP 10/14 | 11 | 593 | 18–19v | 18–19v |
| *contd.* | 12 | 595 | 20–20v | 20–20v |
| | 13 | 596 | 21–22v | 21–22v |
| | 14 | 597 | 23–23v | 23–23v |
| | 15 | 605 | 24–25v | 24–24Av |
| | 16 | 607 | 26–27v | 25–26v |
| | 17 | 606 | 28–29v | 27–28v |
| | 18 | 610 | 30–30v | 29–29v |
| | 19 | 611 | 31–31Av | 30–31v |
| | 20 | 590 | 32–62v | 31A–62v |
| | 21 | 612 | 63–63v | 63–63v |
| | 22 | 613 | 64–64v | 64–64v |
| | 23 | 614 | 65–66v | 65–66v |
| | 24 | 615 | 67–68v | 67–68v |
| | 25 | 616 | 69–69v | 69–69v |
| | 26 | 617 | 70–70v | 70–70v |
| | 27 | 618 | 71–71v | 71–71v |
| | 28 | 619 | 72–72v | 72–72v |
| | 29 | 620 | 73–74v | 75–76v |
| | 30 | 621 | 75–76v | 73–74v |
| | 31 | 622 | 76A–76Av | 77–77A |
| | 32 | 623 | 77–78v | 78–79v |
| | 33 | 624 | 79–79v | 80–80v |
| | 34 | 625 | 80–81v | 81–81Av |
| | 35 | 626 | 82–83v | 82–83v |
| | 36 | 627 | 84–84v | 84–84v |
| | 37 | 629 | 85–86v | 85–86v |
| | 38 | 630 | 87–88v | 87–88v |
| | 39 | 631 | 89–90v | 89–90v |
| | 40 | 633 | 91–92v | 91–92v |
| | 41 | 663 | 93–94v | 93–94v |
| | 42 | 664 | 95–96v | 95–96v |
| | 43 | 668 | 97–97v | 97–97v |
| | 44 | 665 | 98–98v | 98–98v |
| | 45 | 666 | 99–100v | 99–100v |
| | 46 | 667 | 101–102v | 101–102v |
| | 47 | 669 | 103–104v | 103–104v |
| | 48 | 682 | 105–105v | 105–105v |
| | 49 | 683 | 106–107v | 106–107v |
| | 50 | 684 | 108–109v | 108–109v |
| | 51 | 685 | 110–111v | 110–111v |
| | 52 | 686 | 112–113v | 112–113v |
| | 52(i) | 687 | 114–115v | 114–114Av |
| | 53 | 688 | 116–123v | 115–122v |
| | 54 | 689 | 124–125v | 123–124v |
| | 54(i) | 690 | 126–126v | 125–125v |
| | 55 | 691 | 127–128v | 126–127v |
| | 56 | 692 | 129–130v | 128–129v |

\*     The number used in the old calendar

| Volume | Item no.* | New calendar no. | Fo. | Microfilm fo. |
| --- | --- | --- | --- | --- |
| SP 10/14 | 57 | 693 | 131–132v | 130–131v |
| contd. | 58 | 694 | 133–134v | 132–133v |
| | 59 | 695 | 135–136v | 134–135v |
| | 60 | 696 | 137–138v | 136–137v |
| | 61 | 697 | 139–139v | 138–138v |
| | 62 | 698 | 140–141v | 139–140v |
| | 62(i) | 699 | 142–143v | 141–142v |
| | 62(ii) | 700 | 144–145v | 143–144v |
| | 63 | 701 | 146–147v | 144A–144Bv |
| | 64 | 702 | 148–148v | 145–145v |
| | 65 | 703 | 149–149v | 146–146v |
| | 66 | 704 | 150–151v | 147–148v |
| | 67 | 705 | 152–153v | 149–150v |
| | 68 | 706 | 154–155v | 151–152v |
| | 69 | 707 | 156–157v | 153–154v |
| | 70 | 708 | 158–159v | 155–156v |
| | 71 | 709 | 160–163v | 157–160v |
| | 72 | 710 | 164–165v | 161–162v |
| SP 10/15 | 1 | 711 | 1–2v | 1–2v |
| | 2 | 712 | 3–4v | 3–4v |
| | 3 | 713 | 5–6v | 5–6v |
| | 4 | 714 | 7–7v | 7–7v |
| | 5 | 715 | 8–9v | 8–9v |
| | 6 | 716 | 10–10v | 10–10v |
| | 7 | 717 | 11–12v | 11–12v |
| | 8 | 718 | 13–14v | 13–14v |
| | 9 | 719 | 15–16v | 15–16v |
| | 10 | 720 | 17–17v | 17–17v |
| | 11 | 721 | 18–29v | 18–29v |
| | 12 | 722 | 30–30v | 30–30v |
| | 13 | 723 | 31–32v | 31–32v |
| | 14 | 724 | 33–33v | 33–33v |
| | 15 | 725 | 34–35v | 34–35v |
| | 16 | 726 | 36–36v | 36–36v |
| | 17 | 727 | 37–38v | 37–38v |
| | 18 | 728 | 39–39v | 39–39v |
| | 19 | 729 | 40–41v | 40–41v |
| | 20 | 730 | 42–42v | 42–42v |
| | 21 | 731 | 43–47v | 43–47v |
| | 22 | 732 | 48–48v | 47A–47Av |
| | 23 | 733 | 49–50v | 48–49v |
| | 24 | 734 | 51–52v | 50–51v |
| | 25 | 735 | 53–54v | 52–53v |
| | 26 | 736 | 55–56v | 54–55v |
| | 26(i) | 737 | 57–58v | 56–56Av |
| | 27 | 738 | 59–59v | 57–57v |
| | 28† | 739 | 60–66v | 60–66v |

\*      The number used in the old calendar
†      A letter of 8 March 1851 relating to piece no. 28 occupies fos. 58–59v of the microfilm foliation

| Volume | Item no.* | New calendar no. | Fo. | Microfilm fo. |
|---|---|---|---|---|
| SP 10/15 | 29 | 740 | 67–67v | 67–67v |
| *contd.* | 30 | 741 | 68–69v | 68–69v |
| | 31 | 742 | 70–71v | 70–71v |
| | 32 | 743 | 72–73v | 72–73v |
| | 32(i) | 744 | 74–75v | 73A–74v |
| | 33 | 745 | 76–77v | 75–76v |
| | 34 | 746 | 78–79v | 77–78v |
| | 35 | 747 | 80–81v | 79–80v |
| | 36 | 748 | 82–83v | 81–82v |
| | 37 | 749 | 84–84v | 83–83v |
| | 38 | 750 | 85–86v | 84–85v |
| | 39 | 751 | 87–88v | 86–87v |
| | 40 | 752 | 89–90v | 88–89v |
| | 41 | 753 | 91–92v | 90–91v |
| | 42 | 754 | 93–93v | 92–92v |
| | 43 | 755 | 94–95v | 93–94v |
| | 44 | 756 | 96–97v | 95–96v |
| | 45 | 757 | 98–99v | 97–98v |
| | 46 | 758 | 100–100v | 99–99v |
| | 47 | 759 | 101–102v | 100–101v |
| | 48 | 760 | 103–104v | 102–103v |
| | 49 | 761 | 105–106v | 104–105v |
| | 50 | 762 | 107–107v | 106–106v |
| | 51 | 763 | 108–109v | 107–108v |
| | 52 | 764 | 110–111v | 109–110v |
| | 53 | 765 | 112–112v | 111–111v |
| | 54 | 766 | 113–114v | 112–113v |
| | 55 | 767 | 115–118v | 114–117v |
| | 56 | 768 | 119–120v | 118–119v |
| | 57 | 769 | 121–122v | 120–121v |
| | 58 | 770 | 123–124v | 122–123v |
| | 59 | 771 | 125–125v | 124–124v |
| | 60 | 772 | 126–127v | 125–126v |
| | 61 | 773 | 128–129v | 127–128v |
| | 62 | 774 | 130–131v | 129–130v |
| | 63 | 775 | 132–133v | 131–132v |
| | 64 | 776 | 134–135v | 133–134v |
| | 65 | 777 | 136–137v | 135–136v |
| | 66 | 779 | 138–139v | 137–138v |
| | 67 | 780 | 140–141v | 139–140v |
| | 68 | 781 | 142–143v | 141–142v |
| | 69 | 782 | 144–144v | 143–143v |
| | 70 | 783 | 145–146v | 144–145v |
| | 71 | 787 | 147–148v | 146–147v |
| | 72 | 788 | 149–149v | 148–148v |
| | 73 | 789 | 150–151v | 149–150v |
| | 74 | 790 | 152–153v | 151–152v |
| | 75 | 791 | 154–155v | 153–154v |

\*  The number used in the old calendar

| Volume | Item no.* | New calendar no. | Fo. | Microfilm fo. |
|---|---|---|---|---|
| SP 10/15 | 76 | 785 | 156–157v | 155–156v |
| *contd.* | 77 | 793 | 158–163v | 157–162v |
| | 78 | 431 | 164–179v | 163–178v |
| | 79† | 794 | 180–181v | 178A–178AAv |
| | 79(i)† | 795 | 182–183v | 178B–178BAv |
| | 79(ii)† | 796 | 184–185v | 178C–178CAv |
| SP 10/16 | – | 797 | – | – |
| SP 10/17 | – | 798 | – | – |
| SP 10/18 | 1 | 799 | 1–2v | 1–2v |
| | 2 | 800 | 3–4v | 3–4v |
| | 3 | 802 | 5–6v | 5–6v |
| | 4 | 801 | 7–8v | 7–8v |
| | 5 | 803 | 9–10v | 9–10v |
| | 6 | 804 | 11–12v | 11–12v |
| | 7 | 807 | 13–14v | 13–14v |
| | 8 | 808 | 15–16v | 15–16v |
| | 9 | 809 | 17–18v | 17–18v |
| | 10 | 810 | 19–19v | 19–19v |
| | 11 | 811 | 20–20v | 20–20v |
| | 12 | 812 | 21–22v | 21–22v |
| | 13 | 589 | 23–24v | 23–24v |
| | 14 | 816 | 25–26v | 25–26v |
| | 15 | 817 | 27–28v | 27–28v |
| | 16 | 818 | 29–29v | 29–29v |
| | 17 | 819 | 30–31v | 30–31v |
| | 18 | 820 | 32–33v | 32–33v |
| | 19 | 821 | 34–35v | 34–35v |
| | 20‡ | – | – | – |
| | 21 | 822 | 36–36v | 36–36v |
| | 22 | 823 | 37–38v | 37–37Av |
| | 23 | 824 | 39–39v | 38–38v |
| | 24 | 825 | 40–41v | 39–40v |
| | 25 | 827 | 42–43v | 41–42v |
| | 26 | 828 | 44–45v | 43–44v |
| | 27 | 826 | 46–47v | 45–46v |
| | 28 | 829 | 48–48v | 47–47v |
| | 29 | 830 | 49–52v | 48–51v |
| | 30 | 831 | 53–53v | 52–52v |
| | 31 | 832 | 54–54v | 53–53v |
| | 32 | 813 | 55–56v | 54–55v |
| | 33 | 814 | 57–57v | 56–56v |
| | 34 | 815 | 58–59v | 57–58v |
| | 35 | 833 | 60–60v | 59–59v |
| | 36 | 834 | 61–61v | 60–60v |
| | 37 | 835 | 62–63v | 61–62v |
| | 38 | 836 | 64–65v | 63–64v |

\*  The number used in the old calendar
†  Removed to Safe Room.
‡  Removed to form SP 16/523, no. 119

| Volume | Item no.* | New calendar no. | Fo. | Microfilm fo. |
|---|---|---|---|---|
| SP 10/18 | 39 | 837 | 66–67v | 65–66v |
| *contd.* | 40 | 838 | 68–73v | 67–72v |
| | 41 | 839 | 74–77v | 73–76v |
| | 42 | 840 | 78–79v | 77–78v |
| | 43† | – | – | – |
| | 44 | 841 | 81–84v | 79A–82v |
| | 45 | 842 | 85–94v | 83–92v |
| SP 10/19 | – | 844 | – | – |

\*    The number used in the old calendar
†    Removed to form MPF/161

# PROVISION OF COPIES OF DOCUMENTS

The Public Record Office can supply microfilm copies of the documents calendared in this volume, or electrostatic prints from microfilm, which take the form of xerox copies.

There is a minimum charge for microfilm orders, so if only a limited number of copies is required, it may prove to be less expensive for electrostatic prints from microfilm to be made.

Requests for estimates should be sent to the Photo-Ordering Section at the Public Record Office, Chancery Lane, London WC2A 1LR, quoting the relevant volume (e.g. SP 10/1) and the appropriate microfilm folio numbers as shown in the Concordance (e.g. 1–2v for item no. 1 of SP 10/1).

# TEXT

**1.** 1547. January 29, between 3 and 4 a.m. Enfield. Edward [Seymour], earl of Hertford to Sir William Paget, principal secretary.

I received your letter between 1 and 2 this morning and much liked the first part, that the will should [not] be opened until further consultation, and that it might be well considered how much ought to be published. For divers respects I think it not convenient to satisfy the world. In the meantime I think it sufficient, when you publish the king's death at the times and places you have appointed, to have the will with you, showing it to be the will and naming the executors whom the king specially trusted, and the councillors. The contents at the breaking up thereof shall be declared to them on Wednesday morning in parliament. In the meantime we should meet·and agree so there may be no controversy hereafter. For the rest of your appointments, the keeping of the Tower and the king's person, do not be too hasty. *Postscript.* I have sent you the key of the will.

*Endorsed*: Post haste, with all diligence, for your life.
*Holograph.*
*Printed*: Tytler, i, 15–16.                                       SP 10/1, no. 1

**2.** January 30, 11 p.m. Enfield. The earl of Hertford and Sir Anthony Browne, master of the horse, to the council.

I, Hertford, have received your letter concerning a pardon, desiring our opinions. We doubt whether our power is sufficient to answer the present king when he shall call us to account. In case we do have authority, in our opinions the time will serve much better at the coronation than at present; if it were granted now the king could show no such gratuity to his subjects when the time is most propitious. His father, whom we doubt not to be in heaven, would take the credit from him who has more need of it. We intend the king shall be in the saddle by 11 tomorrow morning, and so at the Tower by 3. Lady Anne of Cleves should be told of the king's death.

*Endorsed*: Post haste, for your life.
*Hertford's holograph.*
*Printed*: Tytler, i, 17–18.                                       SP 10/1 no. 2

**3.** [?February 3]. Memoranda of business for the coronation.

Appointment of high steward* and high constable.† Writs of proclamation for those with £40 lands or rents to take knighthoods; commissions for compounding with thóse preferring fines. Commission to appoint knights of the Bath, to determine claims, for mizes and tallage in Wales. Patents of earl marshal‡ and chief butler.§  SP 10/1, no. 3

**4.** February 4. Proclamation announcing court of claims for coronation services.

The king has appointed Lord Wriothesley, K.G., lord chancellor, Francis [Talbot], earl of Shrewsbury, William [Parr], earl of Essex, John [Dudley], Viscount Lisle, high admiral, Sir Richard Lister, chief justice of England and Sir Edward Montague, chief justice of

*     Hertford.
†     Marquess of Dorset.
‡     Earl of Arundel deputised for Hertford at the ceremony.
§     Earl of Arundel [see below, no. 7].

common pleas, or three of them, to be commissioners to begin his court on Monday 7 February in the white hall of the palace of Westminster, there to hear and determine claims of service by reason of tenure to be done at the coronation, to be on February 20. All having business before the commissioners shall attend that day.

*17th cent. copy.*

*Printed*: *Tudor Royal Proclamations*, i, 383, no. 277 (from BL Harleian MS 353, f.1v).

SP 10/1, no. 4

**5.** February 5. Southwark. Stephen [Gardiner], bishop of Winchester to Sir William Paget.

I sent you my servant yesterday, having redress by your advice. I now write in greater matter. Tomorrow the parishioners here and I have agreed to have solemn *dirige* for our late sovereign, and certain of [the earl of] Oxford's players intend to have, as they say, a solemn play, on the other side of the borough. It seems a marvellous contention that some should profess mirth and some sorrow at one time. I follow the common determination to sorrow until our late master is buried. What these lewd fellows mean in the contrary I cannot tell and reform, and therefore write to you who, by means of the lord protector, may procure uniformity in the commonwealth. I have spoken with [Sir Robert] Acton, justice of the peace, whom the players smally regard, and pressed him to answer whether he dare let them play or not. To the play he answers neither yes or no, but to the assembly he pleads no to the players until he has contrary command. But his no is not much regarded, mine less. If you will not meddle, send word and I will myself sue the protector.

*Holograph.*

*Printed*: Muller, 253–4. Tytler, i, 21–2 (part).

SP 10/1, no. 5

**6.** [February 7]. Table of cases before the court of claims for the coronation.

*With folio references to the following document.*

SP 10/1, no. 6

**7.** [February 7].* Statement of claims to perform services at the coronation, heard before the court of claims, stating the nature of the services and the customary fees.

Earl of Shrewsbury: to provide the right glove and support the king's hand while holding the sceptre (allowed). Viscount Lisle: to be a panter (allowed). Earl of Arundel: to be chief butler (allowed). Earl of Sussex: to be sewer (allowed). Lord Abergavenny: to be larderer (allowed, but being the king's ward the service to be performed by a deputy, the fees to remain in the king's hands). Sir Ralph Warren: to be larderer (claim but no suit). Sir Edward Dymmocke: to be king's champion (allowed). Mayor of London: to serve the king with wine after dinner and to nominate other citizens of London to assist the chief butler (allowed). Sir Giles Allington: to serve the king with the first cup of silver and gilt (allowed). Barons of the Cinque Ports: to bear the canopy and sit on the right side at dinner (allowed). Robert Asplond: to hold the towel before the king before dinner (allowed). Nicholas Leghe: to make a mess of pottage called *degeront* (allowed; Brickhed, the king's master cook deputed to do the service). John Wintershall: to be usher in the king's chamber (allowed). Thomas Hussey and William Clopton: to make wafers (allowed). Thomas Gainsforde: to be marshal of the king's hall (not allowed). Robert Puttenham: to be marshal of the whores, to drive out all harlots in the king's house, to dismember all malefactors adjudged and measure all gallons and bushels in the king's house (not allowed). Warden of the Fleet: to be keeper of the palace and hall (service found to be local and not only at coronation). Earl of Oxford: to serve the king with water before and after dinner (allowed). Lord Bray, Lord Latimer and Sir John

---

\* This was the date on which the court met [cf. no. **4** above] but some of the peerages and offices mentioned were granted between that date and that of the coronation on February 20.

Gascoigne, William Gostweek: to be almoner (Latimer and Bray chosen as chief almoners, Gascoigne and Gostweek as under almoners). Earl of Derby, as lord of Man and holder of the isle and Peel ('Pelham') castle: to present the king with two falcons (allowed), to be cupbearer (refused), to bear the sword curtana (allowed). Bishops of Durham and Bath: to assist the king (no proof given save the allegation of an old book remaining in Westminster* which is of no record: verdict deferred). Lord Grey of Wilton: to be falconer (deputy appointed). Mayor of Oxford: to aid the chief butler in service of ale at the bar (allowed). Officers of Westminster church: to have for their labour 100 breads and 88 gallons of wine; the sextons to have the king's outer clothing and all carpets; the vergers and sextons to have scarlet gowns (allowed). Items carried by nobles: the crown – the duke of Somerset; the orb – the duke of Suffolk; the sceptre – the marquess of Dorset; carver, and to assist the great chamberlain† in carrying the train – the marquess of Northampton; the rod – the earl of Oxford; to sustain the king going to coronation – the earl of Shrewsbury; the spurs – the earl of Rutland; sewer – the earl of Huntingdon; sword – Lord St John, then lord great master; sword – Lord Russell, then lord privy seal; sword in scabbard – the earl of Southampton, then lord chancellor; to assist the lord chamberlain in and out – Lord Seymour of Sudeley.

*This and no. **6** in a later hand.* SP 10/1, no. 7

**8.** February 8. Portsmouth. Edward Vaughan, captain of Portsmouth to Sir William Paget.

As promised I have sent you these two poor bearers whom I trust you will find as honest and faithful servants as they have been in my house. The mayor [of Portsmouth] has gone to London on the affairs of the town. He is the lord chancellor's servant and thinks to make great friends. I trust you will not forget that I was of your preferment hither and will not see me put out of reputation with a sort of beer brewers. Help me to become a justice of the peace as you promised. If you get my licence of leather and wheat there will be some commodity to you. Tell me your pleasure for the £100 about which I wrote and it will be with you within three or four days.

*? Holograph.* SP 10/1, no. 8

**9.** February 12. Account of gold, rings and precious stones removed from the king's secret house at Westminster.

20 January 1547: gold &c. removed by [Sir Anthony] Denny, [Sir William] Herbert and [Sir John] Gates and partly delivered to Everard Everdayce, goldsmith, for garnishing a porcelain cup and a gripe's egg for Henry VIII. 8 and 12 February 1547: gold and jewels delivered by the duke of Somerset for making and garnishing the crown for Edward VI. SP 10/3, no. 7

**10.** [February 13]. Order of service for the coronation of Edward VI.

This day the lord protector and other executors of Henry VIII resolved that as divers of the old coronation ceremonies should be corrected, lest their tedious length should weary the king, being yet of tender age, and as many points were such as by the laws of the realm at present were not allowable, the coronation should be celebrated on Shrove Sunday next [February 20] in Westminster Cathedral after the order ensuing.

The order of service follows, describing the parts to be played by the archbishop of Canterbury, the bishops of London and Winchester, the dean of Westminster (in the absence of the bishop), the lord great chamberlain,‡ Sir Anthony Denny, Sir William Herbert, the lord protector and the lord chancellor.

---

\* The *Liber Regalis*, Westminster Abbey Library MS 38.
† Hertford was lord great chamberlain on February 7 but was succeeded by Warwick before the coronation.
‡ Warwick by February 20.

*8 small pp.*
*Copied signatures of*: the archbishop of Canterbury, the lord chancellor, Lord St John, Lord Russell, Viscount Lisle, the bishop of Durham, Sir Anthony Browne, Sir William Paget, Sir Anthony Denny and Sir William Herbert.
*Copy*: from PC 2/2, pp. 48–56.
*Printed*: *APC*, ii, 29–33 (where the signatures appear after other entries).

SP 10/1, no. 9

**11.** [February 14]. Westminster. Inspeximus of commencement and ending of enrolment of the will of Henry VIII, naming as executors Lord Wriothesley, lord chancellor, Lord St John, master of the household, the earl of Hertford, lord [great] chamberlain, Lord Russell, lord privy seal, Viscount Lisle, lord admiral, the bishop of Durham, Sir Anthony Browne, master of the horse, Sir Edward Montague, [chief] justice of common pleas, [Sir Thomas] Bromley, [puisne] justice of king's bench, Sir Edward North, chancellor of the court of augmentations, Sir William Paget, secretary, Sir Anthony Denny, Sir William Herbert, Sir Edward Wotton and Dr [Nicholas] Wotton.
*Copy*: from E 23/4. *Latin and English.*

SP 10/1, no. 10

**12.** [February 15]. List of promotions to dignities*
The earl of Hertford: to be treasurer and earl marshal and duke of [Somerset, Exeter or]† and his son earl of Wiltshire (if he is duke of Hertford) with [£600]† £800 lands a year (£200 of the next bishop's lands). The earl of Essex: to be marquess of Essex with [£200]† £100 lands a year. Viscount Lisle: to be great chamberlain and earl of [Leicester]† Coventry with £200 lands a year. [Lord Russell: to be earl of Northampton with £200 lands a year. Lord St John: to be earl of Winchester with £200 lands a year]. Lord Wriothesley: to be earl of [Chichester]† Winchester with £200 lands a year. Sir Thomas Seymour: to be [Lord Seymour of (*blank*)]† and admiral of England with £300 lands a year. Sir Richard Rich: to be a baron with £66.13.4 lands a year. [Sir Thomas Arundel].† Sir John St Leger, Sir William Willoughby, Sir Edmund Sheffield and Sir Christopher Danby: to be barons. Sir Philip Hoby: to be master of the ordnance [with £66.13.4 lands a year].† The lord privy seal [Lord Russell]: to have £100 lands a year. Lord St John: £100 lands a year. [Sir John] Gates and [Sir Thomas] Cawarden: 100 marks lands a year each. [Sir Anthony] Denny: £200 lands a year, Bungay [priory] &c. [Sir William] Herbert: 400 marks lands a year. [The earl of Essex: £100 a year].† The master of the horse: £100 lands a year. Sir Thomas Paston: steward of the duchy of Lancaster and keeper of Rising chase. Sir Thomas Darcy: steward of the liberties of Bury and all the duke of Norfolk's lands and those of the bishop of Norwich in Suffolk, and keeper of Framlingham castle and park. Lord Wentworth: stewardship of all the bishop of Ely's lands and master of his game in Norfolk, Suffolk and Cambridgeshire. [*Indecipherable*]: 'Mr Goderk' [? Richard Goodrich]. Sir William Petre: to have £100 of the bishop of Winchester. Sir Richard Southwell: keeper of Kenninghall house and park and steward of the duke of Norfolk and the bishop of Norwich in Norfolk. Stewardship of the bishop of Lincoln's lands. Sir William Goring and Sir Ralph Vane: Sheffield house and park, Worth forest, Horsham house and park, Sedgewick park, Bewbush park, St Leonards forest and park. Knepp park to Sir John Mason.

SP 10/1, no. 11

**13.** [February 15]. Preamble of grant by the king to the duke of Somerset of certain [*unspecified*] properties.
Henry VIII had intended to augment the recently depleted numbers of the nobility,

---

\*    Probably drawn up in late December 1546 and amended by Paget in early January 1547 [see H. Miller, 'Henry VIII's unwritten will: grants of lands and honours in 1547' in *Wealth and Power in Tudor England*, ed. E.W. Ives, R.J. Knecht and J.J. Scarisbrick, (1978), 88–91].
†    Deleted.

both as a means of good governance and also to reward faithful councillors and servants, and to endow them with lands to maintain their positions, but was prevented by his death. In particular he named the then earl of Hertford to be duke of Somerset, with suitable endowments. The king has raised him to the dukedom on the occasion of his coronation, and now grants certain lands to the value of [*blank*].

　　*Draft. Latin. Mutilated.*　　　　　　　　　　　　　　　　　SP 10/1, no. 12

**14.** [February 15]. English translation of the above, but not wholly in accordance with it. Accompanied by other draft notes in Latin and English which refer specifically to the will of Henry VIII* in relation to the execution of the promised grants.†

　　*Mutilated. Bound in wrong order.*　　　　　　　　　　　　　SP 10/1, no. 13

**15.** [February 15]. Minute of the styles and titles of the duke of Somerset, earl of Hertford, Viscount Beauchamp, Lord Seymour, governor and protector of the king, lieutenant general of his majesty's land and sea armies, treasurer and high marshal of England, governor of Jersey and Guernsey, K.G.　　　　　　SP 10/1, no. 14

[For SP 10/1, nos. 15, 16 see nos. **805, 806** below.]

**16.** [February 15]. Order of ceremonies to be observed at the funeral of Henry VIII, in conveying the body from Westminster Palace to Windsor.

　　Lord Scrope. Lord Lumney.‡ Lord Chidiock [Paulet]. Lord Giles [Paulet]. Lord Thomas Howard. Lord Mountjoy.

　　Proceeding with the body from Westminster Palace to Windsor. To see the way clear, with no overhanging boughs or broken bridges. Order to all men with baggage or carriage to remain at the appointed place out of the way. Command to be made to the dean of the king's chapel to find priests and clerks to follow the cross. Carts to carry torches to be borne and lighted at all times when they come through towns or villages. 250 poor men in black gowns and hoods to be numbered and billed. Two conductors to be named to carry black staves before the cross and see order kept in the way.

　　250 men in black gowns. Two conductors with black staves. The cross. Priests and clerks. Great torches borne by poor men in black gowns and hoods. Standard of the dragon. Gentlemen, two by two. Esquires. Chaplains without dignity. Gentlemen ushers. Officers of the household. Standard of the greyhound. Knights banneret. Chaplains of honour and dignity. Knights of the Garter. [The chief justices and master of the rolls].§ Standard of the lion. Lords spiritual and temporal. Head officers of the household. The treasurer and comptroller. Viscounts, earls, marquesses and dukes. Ambassadors and foreigners, as Duke Philip. Embroidered banner of the king's arms, borne by a baron. The helm and crest. The targe. The sword. The king's embroidered coat of arms. Banners of the king and Queen Catherine, the king and Queen Jane, March and Ulster, Richmond and Holland, Somerset and Beauchamp, Lancaster with the marriage, York with the marriage, Somerset and Richmond, Henry VII and his marriage, Edward IV and his marriage, St Edmund, St Edward, [Henry VI, saint],¶ St George and St George and the king, surrounding eight chariot horses with arms on black velvet. Bannerol of the king's arms. The corpse, attended by gentlemen ushers. Banners of [Our Lady, the Trinity],¶ Henry VII and his wife, Henry VIII and his wife. The chief mourner. Torches. Other mourners. The lord chamberlain. The master of the horse, leading a courser. The nine henchmen. The captain of the guard. Noblemen's servants.

*　　　E 23/4 (*LP* XXI, ii, 634).
†　　　Cf. grant of 23 July 1547 [C 66/802, mm. 42–50 (*CPR* 1547–8, 124–33)].
‡　　　John Lumley: not officially recognised as Baron Lumley until 1 Edward VI c.17.
§　　　Deleted: 'spared for the law in the term tyme'.
¶　　　Deleted.

Provisions prepared at Windsor Castle by command of the lord great master and others of the council. The way cleared of superfluous boughs &c., and for bridges. Hangings of black, escutcheons and tapers in the church. A chariot. On Sunday 13 February and the day before the removing three solemn masses – of Our Lady, the Trinity and the requiem – were sung. A proclamation was made in London and Westminster that all men having black livery were to be at Charing Cross on Monday next at 7 a.m. to attend the corpse to Syon that night. After dinner a solemn dirge was executed and watch kept. Very early next morning the chariot to the court, and the body brought to it. A robed effigy was carried. At the head of the corpse were Sir Anthony Denny and Sir William Herbert.

The order in proceeding. Conductors (John Herde and Thomas Martin, the king's porters). The cross. 46 of the king's chapel, priests and clerks. 250 poor men with torches (ordered by [the earl of] Worcester). Carts with torches and escutcheons to give to churches. To go a good way before the cross (Ralph Walker and Peers Sleen, appointed by Lord Worcester). Standard of the dragon (Thomas Abrugh, esq.). Gentlemen. Esquires. Chaplains without dignity. Ambassadors' servants being gentlemen. Officers of the household not knights. Standard of the greyhound (Sir Nicholas Sturley). Aldermen of London. Knights banneret. Chaplains with dignity. The king's head officers, being knights. Protestants, if they go, and other notable strangers, if any. Standard of the lion (Lord Burgh or Lord Windsor). All councillors not of the privy council. Barons. Viscounts. Earls. Bishops. The privy council. Marquesses. Dukes. Ambassadors. The ambassador of Venice. Ambassadors' attendants. The emperor's ambassador, with the archbishop of Canterbury. The French ambassador. Duke Philip [of Burgundy]. Embroidered banner of the king's arms (Lord Talbot or Lord Conyers). The helmet and crest (Norroy king of arms). The sword and targe (Clarenceux king of arms). The coat of arms (Garter king of arms). Banners of the king and Queen Catherine (Leonard Chamberlein), the king and Queen Jane (George Harper), March and Ulster (Sir Edward Willowghby), Richmond and Holland (Sir William Barington), Somerset and Beauchamp (Sir Philip Draycot), Lancaster with the marriage (Sir John Markeham), York with the marriage (Sir Fulk Grevell), Somerset and Richmond (Sir Nicholas Poyninges), Henry VII and his marriage (Sir Anthony Hungerford), Edward IV and his marriage (Sir John Harcot), St Edward (Edward Lytleton), St Edmund (George Blunt), King Henry the Saint (Sir William Woodhous), St George (Sir Thomas Cleere). The corpse. Banners of Our Lady (Sir Francis Dawtrye), the Trinity (Sir Michael Lister). Assistants (Sir Thomas Henage, Sir Thomas Paston, Sir Thomas Speke, [Sir John] Gates, [? Sir Thomas] Darcye, [Sir Maurice] Barcleye). 50 or 60 grooms and pages bearing torches about the corpse, sorted by the vice-chamberlain. [Gentlemen ushers to kneel in the chariot and have charge thereof with 14 bannerols of descents (William Rainsford and John Norys)].* To appoint six children of honour to ride on six chariot horses with bannerols of ancient arms, and six others to lead the horses, at the appointment of the master of the horse. The chief mourner (the marquess of Dorset). Mourners (the lord president of the council, the earl of Oxford, the earl of Shrewsbury, the earl of Derby, the earl of Sussex, Lord Morley, Lord Dacre, Lord Ferrers, Lord Clinton, Lord [Grey of] Powis, Lord Scrope, Lord Herbert). The lord chamberlain. The master of the horse (Sir Anthony Browne), with a spare horse royally apparelled. The master of the henchmen (Sir Francis Briane). Henchmen (J. Sturton, Edward Ychingham, T. Lestraunge, George Denis, Richard Browne, Roger Armor, T. Brown, Richard Cotton, Patrick Barnaby [Barnaby Fitzpatrick]) with bannerols of ancient arms. The captain of the guard (Sir Anthony Wingfeld). The guard, in black, halberds reversed. Serjeants of arms, heralds and pursuivants to give order before the corpse from standard to standard, as placed by Garter.

Prelates to execute and meet the corpse at Syon and Windsor: the bishop of Winchester

* Deleted.

to execute. The bishops of London, Durham, Ely, Worcester, Bangor, Bristol and Gloucester. The bishop of Rochester to preach.

To appoint the doles in London and Windsor and for the king's alms to churches: the bishop of Worcester and his ministers. To appoint 16 to bear the corpse from the chariot to the hearse. A canopy to be borne by Lords Abergavenny, Conyers, Latimer, Fitzwalter, Bray and Cromwell. Offerings of palls: a marquess 3, an earl 3, a viscount 2, a baron 1. Serjeants of arms: John Buckeworthe, Lewes ap Watkyn, Nicholas Jackson, Richard Raynshaw, William Clerke, John Smythe, Hugh Mynors, John Curwyn, John Knottysford, Robert Everys, Piers Mutton, John Seint John.

*29 pp.*

On the cover of the MS is written 'Garter' and 'Gilbert Dethicke.' Dethicke was promoted from Richmond herald to Norroy king of arms in January 1547 before Henry VIII's death, but the appointment was repeated on 16 August 1547. He did not succeed Christopher Barker (Kt March 1547) as Garter king of arms until 29 April 1550 [*LP* XXI, ii, 770(3). *CPR* 1547–8, 101; 1549–51, 195].

SP 10/1, no. 17

**17.** [February 15]. Account of cloth of gold, satin, velvet, banners and other furnishings provided for the funeral of Henry VIII.            SP 10/1, no. 18

**18.** February 16, 11 p.m. Portsmouth. Edward Vaughan, captain of Portsmouth to the council.

At 8 tonight I received the king's commission to levy 200 men in Surrey and Berkshire, and at once sent my brother and two men there, trusting the men will be in Portsmouth on February 24 as appointed in your letter. I do not doubt you will consider the state of this town, how it lies open so that at low water men may come in although thirty in rank. The gates at the water side are so weak that three or five men with a piece of timber may lay them on the ground. With the recent frost the walls begin in many places to fall away into the ditches. The fields beside the ditches grow full of bushes and furzes, which ought to be made plain for the surety of the town: but I doubt to do it without your command. For setting on 100 of the 200 men to work as labourers I lack tools, carriages, timber and many other things. I have not yet heard anything of the captain of Wight [Richard Worsley] touching the £200 which I should receive of him. I have therefore given my brother £20 to be given to them in prest until the king's money comes – trusting you will speedily order how they shall be paid from time to time. Gunners are also lacking for the great ordnance in the town, there being only fifteen, and seventeen pieces of brass and forty-eight of iron, as declared in the enclosed list. The ships with the king's victuals are not yet gone, having put back again with a contrary wind. This afternoon two Spanish ships came into the roads saying they dare not pass homewards for fear of six tall ships, Scots or Frenchmen, on the south part of Wight within sight of land. I have no doubt I will render you a good account of the king's town, or lay my bones here.            SP 10/1, no. 19

**19.** February 16. Ordnance mounted for the defence of Portsmouth.

In the bastillion between [John] Ridley's tower and the town: 1 brass culverin with forelock. On the great platform of the town walls: 1 brass double culverin, Arcanes making; 1 French brass cannon; 1 Scotch brass double culverin; 1 brass saker with rose and garter; 1 cast iron saker, Parson Levett's making; 4 iron bombards with chambers. In Green bulwark under Windmill Hill: 1 brass cannon, Peter Bawdes making; 1 brass culverin with forelock, Peter Bawdes making; 1 French brass demi-cannon; 1 French brass saker; 1 iron demi-sling with 2 chambers; 2 iron flankers with 4 chambers; 1 iron port piece with 2 chambers. In the new mount at the end of the four brewhouses: 3

iron fowlers of 1 chamber. In Davy Savor's bulwark: 2 cast iron sakers with 2 chambers, Parson Levett's making; 1 whole iron sling. In the bastillion at the gate: 1 cast iron saker, Parson Levett's making; 1 iron fowler with chamber. On the mount at the gate: 1 brass saker with rose and garter; 2 brass falconets; 1 cast iron demi-culverin, Parson Levett's making; 1 iron quarter sling with 2 chambers; 5 iron flankers with chambers. At the wall end by the town gate: 1 broken brass saker with rose and garter; 2 iron flankers with a chamber. In the new bastillion towards Kingston: 3 iron flankers with chambers. In the bulwark towards Kingston: 1 brass saker with rose and garter; 1 brass falconet with rose; 1 iron quarter sling with 2 chambers: 3 iron flankers with chambers. On the wall towards the docks: 1 cast iron saker, Parson Levett's making; 1 cast iron saker, Flanders making. In the bulwark at the mill bridge towards the docks: 1 brass double culverin, Peter Bawdes making; 2 cast iron sakers, Parson Levett's making; 1 iron sling; 4 iron flankers with chambers. On the green before God's House gate: 2 cast iron sakers, 1 Parson Levett's making, 1 Flanders; 2 iron serpentines with chambers; 1 iron port piece without chamber. In God's House: 1 brass falconet. Total: brass – 17 pieces; iron – 48 pieces; sum – 65. SP 10/1, no. 20

[For SP 10/1, no. 21 see no. **628** below.]

**20.**   [? February]. List of the king's blockhouses of Mersea, St Osyth, Middle house, Hill house and Tower at Harwich, Landguard point and Landguard road, Essex, with salaries of their captains, lieutenants, porters, gunners and soldiers, amounting to £784.15.0 a year. SP 10/1, no. 22

**21.**   February 27. Instructions from the council to Andrew Dudley, appointed admiral of the fleet with command of all ships at Harwich, both of war and victuals.

Dudley is to go first to Harwich, taking personal command of the *Pauncy* and sending other captains to the remaining ships of war – the *Mynyon*, the *Hart*, the *Jenet*, the *Lyon*, the *Dragon* and the *Trego Reneger*. He is to set a straight course for [Holy Island]* the north, leaving the provision ships there and moving on with the warships to the Scottish seas, and to take advantage of any Scots he may meet. He is to have special watch for a fleet of 18 vessels, some furnished for war, which the council hears is on its way to France. He is not to let it pass untouched, but to endeavour to match himself with it and so take advantage of it in passage. He is also to look out for ships coming from France into Scotland, some of which, the council is informed, are charged with munitions. Any such Frenchmen or Scots he is to board quietly, or by force if they cannot be brought to the next port, and unload such munitions as are unnecessary for the furniture of the ship, and then dismiss them. Otherwise all Frenchmen and foreigners are to be treated respectfully. Dudley is to keep close watch for the passage of ships, and sometimes to show himself before St Andrews to the terror of our enemies and the comfort of our friends. He is to contact the latter to receive any letters or other things for the council, which are to be forwarded with his own letters through the officer at the nearest port, telling the council from time to time of his proceedings. He is to remain there with his whole fleet until he has exhausted his supplies, and then to sail to [Holy Island]* the north coast for refreshments; or, of necessity, to take shelter in Harwich or another port, by the order of Lord St John, great master of the household. After refreshment he is to stay at sea for the above purposes until his charge is revoked. SP 10/1, no. 23

**22.**   March 1. Grant by the king to the dean and chapter of St Paul's Cathedral of a faculty for the exercise of their ancient ecclesiastical jurisdiction within the cathedral church and in all peculiars pertaining to them, including probate and administration of

*        Deleted.

wills, presentation to all ecclesiastical benefices, visitation of clergy, people and churches, inquisition into all offences against the ecclesiastical law and the punishment of offenders against the same.

*Parchment. Latin. Seal* ad causas (*missing*). SP 10/1, no. 24

**23.**   March 1, afternoon. Southwark. The bishop of Winchester to Sir William Paget.

I write for the favourable expedition of the commissions, as you promised. Today I saw your addition, by which we [bishops] are called 'delegates' rather than 'ordinaries', which I do not like. Bishops cannot be a match for diplomats and lawyers in making and interpreting words. A bishop who was not an ordinary could not exercise visitation and would have less authority than an archdeacon. Nowadays those with office to order the people should have more committed to them, not less. No man would be foolish enough to exceed the limit of his commission. There is no advantage to be had in curbing the bishops. We have lived long enough to know the state of the world and how soon it is altered. Happy is the man who knows himself and can think of any day as the last of his honour as it may be of his life. I thank God I was versed in this philosophy when I was in your position. Whatever men said, I was never a persecutor – and no persecution has yet prevailed against me. It is not so easy to do good as ill. Since all is uncertain it would be bad policy – less than I would wish in you – to cause through the commission a bishop to take offence, which remains in memory when benefits vanish. I write not in my own cause, in which I think you will make no difficulty, but for all, especially [the bishop of] London, with whom I believe you are offended. Whatever the case I would wish you did the best for yourself, which is to love your enemies. For you have passed the state of wrangling and revenging and are in the age that should desire love and tranquillity. In this love bishops should have a part – according to some they should be served last. Such people are few, I trust, or have little consideration of the state and establishment of the realm, which has hitherto not stood without them. It would be a new experience if they were done away with. There is someone who boasts he would have given away his lands, were it lawful, to kill me. Whatever he says, let our commission be well written, expressing all that we may do and denying what we may not – including receiving convicts. Last Thursday in the courts, if I could receive convicts or not, I had to pay £1,000 if I did not receive them. Such is the world, which I pray you temper, that we may live quietly, without snatching. I wish we would wreak our anger on the Scots and French, if men must be at variance with men, and Englishmen love and agree together, wherein is our strength. Therefore let me have my commission friendly, that I may have full authority to do what I must. I will not deal in wordly matters, but use this opportunity to do something else. Now that I see you stay the fondness of the world against God and his law I will occupy myself awhile in man's law, as I studied originally. I will not be idle, though not best occupied.

*Holograph.*
*Printed*: Muller, 268–72. SP 10/1, no. 25

**24.**   March 2. Westminster. Sir William Paget to the bishop of Winchester.

Thank you for your advice in your letter. Whatever some shall say, I neither mean to nip or snatch anyone, nor to usurp greater power than I have (which is not great) when I could restrain myself from all I might have used, with the consent of him from whom all our powers are derived, often provoked by him to use it, and having his promise to be maintained in the same. In the late king's reign I never did what I might have done. I never loved extremes, nor hindered any to him but notable malefactors. I will not allow private concerns to hinder the public cause, and have always dealt in public affairs according to my conscience. I do not malign bishops, but wish they were to the glory of God and the benefit of the realm. Much less do I malign you, but wish you well. If the estate of bishops shall be reformed, I wish you were no bishop, or so pliable as to bear reformation thought meet for the quiet of the realm. You shall have your commission in as ample a manner as I have authority to make it out, ampler than before.

*Holograph.*

*Printed*: Tytler, i, 24–6.                                                      SP 10/1, no. 26

**25.**   March 4. Licence to the lord chancellor to issue free pardons to all subjects who sue for them within a specified time, in conformity with a general free pardon issued at the coronation, and considering that a copy of the original pardon under the great seal would be too expensive for many.

*Draft in Paget's hand. Form of pardon given in full.*                           SP 10/1, no. 27

**26.**   March 5. Durham Place. Francis Knollys to Sir William Paget.

Do not judge me greedy because I write now in sickness as I spoke in health. My craving arises from necessity. Forbearing to ask my master who is now dead, but of whose benevolence I never despaired, I served his majesty since I was nine, without recompense of office, land or fee, save a reversion of land given me after my mother, and which I had to buy since of [Sir Francis] Inglefield by reason of a former grant made to his father, and save my office in the pensioners' room. Lack of aid was very costly, especially during wars and above all the journey off Landrecies. I have decayed and sold £54 a year of my own lands, and have remaining only 50 marks a year to find myself and my wife. Now through the advancement lately come to me by the lord protector's goodness the charges of my preparation and servitude for my office have brought me £180 in debt, £100 to you and £80 to Mr Inglefield. I do not fear the goodness of the protector or any of the council, but have written to you because of your kindness and influence. I will be content with a small stipend.

*Holograph.*                                                                     SP 10/1, no. 28

**27.**   March 12. Harwich. Andrew Dudley to [Thomas, Lord Seymour of Sudeley], lord admiral.

I have sent you by this bearer more letters which I found among the rude mariners; many were torn and cast into the sea because of the greediness of the spoil, but I have searched as well as I can for letters, and do still. Let me know what I shall do with all the prisoners here and with the victuallers. The *Pauncy* needs more munitions – bows, arrows, pikes, powder, shot, and two new anchors as we had two broken with shot at the boarding of the *Lyon*. Be good to John Rybowde, Hankin, Wilhelmus Tolle and Ryseley, for they have done the king honest service. I am sorry that I am no more able to do them good than I am, for little is yet come to light of so rich a prize. By the confession of the gentlemen and others that were in the ship there were 7,000 or 8,000 crowns, besides jewels. I have been very ill used by the captain of the *Hart* and the master, trusting you will see me right. Written in haste when I came with all the ships.

*Endorsed*: Post haste, for your life.                                           SP 10/1, no. 29

**28.**   March [24]. John [Dudley], earl of Warwick to Sir William Paget.

Some may allege considerations concerning the non-assignment of the lordship of Warwick, saying it is a stately castle, a goodly park and a great royalty. But the castle is of itself unable to lodge a good baron with his train; all one side, with the dungeon tower, is in ruins; the late king sold all the principal manors belonging to the earldom and castle, so that now only the rents of some houses in the town and meadows in Wedgnock park belong to it. I am constable, high steward and master of the game of the castle, park and town, with herbage of the park for life. Because of the name and my descent from one of the daughters of the rightful line I am the more desirous to have the thing. I will rebate [part of] * my fees in my portion to have the castle, meadows and park. Move the rest of the lords to this effect and be friendly to [Sir Anthony] Denny, according to his desire for the site and remains of Waltham with certain other farms adjoining Cheshunt. I suppose it will be good for the neighbourhood to let him have Waltham. In case they will not allow me the lordship of Warwick let me have Tonbridge and Penshurst, Buckingham's lands in Kent, as part of my portion, with [High] Halden, which was my own. Whether I have one or other, let Canonbury be part. The master of the horse would gladly have the lordship in Sussex that was Lord De La Warr's; it were better bestowed on him or such as would keep it up and serve the king by maintaining a household in the country than to let it fall into ruin as with many other houses – a great pity and at length a loss to the king and realm.

    *Holograph.*

    *Printed*: Tytler, i, 28–9.

    For the subsequent grant see *CPR* 1547–8, 252–7.            SP 10/1, no. 30

**29.**    March 31. Indenture of all gold and silver bullion minted into coinage by Sir William Sharington, under treasurer of the royal mint at Bristol Castle, from 1 May 1546 to 31 March 1547.

    Monthly totals signed by Sharington, R[oger] Wigmore and Thomas Marshall.

    *Parchment. Mutilated.*                          SP 10/1, no. 31

**30.**    March 31. Account of Sir William Sharington of all bullion minted into coinage, according to the above indenture, from 1 May 1546 to 31 March 1547, certified by Roger Wigmore, comptroller and Thomas Marshall, assaymaster.

    Gold: 20 carat fine and 4 oz. alloy: 213 lb. 10 oz. Charges: £1,051.11.11. Allowances: £75.15.2. Profit: £975.16.9. Silver: 4 oz. fine and 8 oz. alloy: 16,833 lb. Charges: £25,421.1.0. Allowances: £870.2.7. Profit: £24,550.18.5. Harp groats for Ireland: 3,657 lb. Charges: £6,399.15.0. Allowances: £190.6.1. Profit: £6,209.9.11. Further charges: £116.0.0. Total profit: £31,852.5.11. Allowances sought for wages and fees: William Sharington, under treasurer – £133.6.8; Roger Wigmore, comptroller and surveyor – £40; Thomas Marshall, assaymaster – £40; James Paget, teller £26.13.4; John Barnes, surveyor of the melts – £26.13.4; Giles Evenet, graver (by patent) – £20; John Ellys, finer – £20; George Knight, clerk of the irons and the house – £20; William Goldsmith, porter – £10; William Redferne, chief melter – £13.6.8; George Dabram [and John Bankes],† labourers in the melting house, at £10 – £20; Roland Tuttell, blancher – £13.6.8; Thomas Petit, blancher – £13.6.8; William Hudson, labourer in the firing house – £10; John Robson, labourer in the blanch house – £10; William London, labourer to the graver – £10; total – £426.13.4. Allowances for copper alloys: £300.17.6. Paid in cash to Sir Edmund Peckham, high treasurer of the mints: £14,000.0.0. Total payments: [*blank*]. Arrears remaining March 31: [*blank*].

    *Signed.*                                        SP 10/1, no. 32

**31.**    April 6. Indenture between Sir William Sharington, under treasurer and Roger Wigmore, comptroller and surveyor of the royal mint at Bristol Castle of money delivered by Sharington to Wigmore for necessaries of the mint from 5 April to 5 September 1547, totalling £268.11.10.            SP 10/1, no. 33

**32.**    April 8. Acknowledgement by Thomas Shipman, merchant, of Bristol, minister to the heirs of Nicholas Thorne and company of the receipt of 300 fodder of lead, worth £1,500 from [Sir] William Sharington of Lacock, Wiltshire, the sum to be invested in

  *        Inserted.

  †        Deleted.

the joint stock of the company and there to appear in the ledger book at the end of the following August, for a period of four years.    SP 10/1, no. 34

**33.**   April 8. Similar acknowledgement for £500 received by Shipman from Sharington for investment as above.    SP 10/1, no. 35

**34.**   April 16. The king to commissioners of musters in all shires.

Preparations for war are made by the Scots by sea and land, as also in France and all Christendom. Although England is now at peace (save for the Scots) her subjects are more secure if the defences are put in order. You are therefore to survey the numbers of arrows, bows, pikes and hand guns, and see that those with a legal obligation to maintain weapons do so, and render account of the same. Noblemen and others bound to maintain great horses, with a proportionate number of men and armaments, are to hold them at one hour's readiness after May 20. Those who are not furnished with demilances and harnesses for great horses may obtain them for £2 from Sir Richard Gresham, alderman of London. The declarations are to be returned by [*blank*] May.

*Draft.*    SP 10/1, no. 36

**35.**   April 20. The captain's house, St Michael's Mount. Lord Seymour, lord admiral to the duke of Somerset.

I received your letter this morning and, as soon as wind will serve, will see Scilly, where I am sure to land safe as the *Galle*, the *Greyhound* and the rest of her fellows are there. That done, I will take such order with the ships as you have appointed for their return to Portsmouth, and will repair to you. Commendations to my sister.*

*Endorsed*: Post haste.    SP 10/1, no. 37

**36.**   April 24, afternoon. St John's. Princess Mary to the duchess of Somerset.

Desiring to hear of the amendment of your health, I remind you of my old suit concerning Richard Woode, who was my mother's servant when you were one of her maids and, as you know by his supplication, has sustained great losses without recompense. I thank you for your previous good answer, desiring you to renew the matter to your husband. The poor man is unable to stay long in the city. Again I must trouble you with George Brickhouse, an officer in my mother's wardrobe, of the beds, since my father's coronation, whose only desire is to be one of the knights of Windsor, or to have the next reversion.

*Holograph.*

*Printed*: Tytler, i, 51–2.    SP 10/1, no. 38

**37.**   Copy of the above.    SP 10/1, no. 39

**38.**   April 30. Declaration of fees paid by royal warrant out of the Exchequer to foreigners.

Duke Philip [of Burgundy] – £1,666.13.4, during pleasure. Philip Pyne – £75, for life. Alnixo, John, Anthony, minstrels – £183.16.[. . .]. Francis Pyssher – [. . .], for life. William Denv [. . .]. William Trosshes – [. . .], for life. Jeronimo Prane – £25, for life. Hans de Fremunt – £25, for life. Garfido Harman – £36.10.0, for life. Joachim Guydelfynger – £50, for life. Hans Hardigon – £40 during pleasure. John *alias* Hans Hunter – £17.5.0, for life. Alan Bawdson – £12, for life. Albert Bisshoppe – £50, for life. Nicholas Taphorne – £40, during pleasure. John Barnardino – £75, for life. Petro de Bidotio – £75, for life. John Ribalt – £75, for life. [. . .] – £18.5.0, for life. [. . .] – £150, during good behaviour. [W]illiam Dansell – £40, for life. Angelo de Marianis – £150, during good behaviour.

*    See note to no. **39** below.

Popino Sibraunt – £75, during pleasure. Francisco Barnard – £250, for life. Petro Gambo – £250, for life. Ludovico Nogera – £75, for life. Alonsino de Villa Serga – £100, for life. Petro Nigro – £100, for life. Juliano Romere – £150, for life. Christopher Dyas – £100, for life. Petro Van and Nicholas Rustico – £26.13.4, for life. James Granado – £50, for life. Justinian Bustian – £62.10.0, during pleasure. Total – £4,[. . .].

*Latin. Mutilated.*                                                            SP 10/1, no. 40

**39.**   May 17, midnight. St James's. Lord Seymour to Queen Catherine.

Last night I supped at my brother Herbert's and received from my sister your commendations.* She touched my being with you at Chelsea, which I denied, but [said] I went by the garden as I went to the bishop of London's house. To this I adhered until she told me further tokens which made me change my colours. Remembering what she was, and knowing how well you trusted her, [I] examined her whether these things came from you or were feigned: she answered that they came from you, for which I thank you. By her company, in default of yours, I shall shorten the weeks here. Also I may tell you by her how I proceed in my matter, although I should lack my old friend Walter Erell. I have not yet attempted my suit, for I would first be thoroughly in credit here. Let me not use my suit that they should think and hereafter say that by their suit I attained your good will: hitherto I am out of all their danger for any pleasure they have done for me. I mean only to use their friendship to bring our purpose to pass. Let me receive a letter from you every three days. I beg one of your small pictures, which will remind me of the cheer I shall have at the end of my suit. *Postscript.* I wrote you a key in my last letter that [the duke of] Somerset was going to that shire. He has been sick, but will go tomorrow.

*Holograph.*
*Printed*: Tytler, i, 64–7 (omitting postscript).                              SP 10/1, no. 41

**40.**   Copy of the above.                                                   SP 10/1, no. 42

**41.**   [? May]. St James's. Lord Seymour to Queen Catherine.

Thank you for committing me one of your councillors. I am glad you have been wearied and that you should think on the two years you wrote of in your last letter. My advice for Vastern [park] is to tell my lord that it has not been had from him according to your determination for your house. You have commanded your officers to grow to some point with [Sir Henry] Long for the patent he has of you, by whom you understand he has office during your pleasure – but you do not mean to take it off him unlawfully or without recompense. There is sufficient pasture in the parks to fat all your provision and my lord's – which, being in your hands, you would be loath to deny my lord. Ask him not to meddle, for you will take wrong at his hands rather than claim your right against his pleasure. If you find him, stick fast to Mr Long's interest. Say that if he has such interest as his lordship declares, anything you should grant is not worthy of thanks. Until you know certainly what interest you have you will not part with it; knowing, you will make him a satisfactory answer. I wrote to you of this yesterday, taking the letter to my brother Herbert to be delivered to his wife who, I think, knows of our matter – but not by me. None shall save those you appoint, until it is further forth. I perceive I have [the duchess of] Suffolk's good will touching my desire of you: she told my friend Sir William Sharington she wished me to be married to their mistress – as would I. To bring it sooner to pass I shall set my lord and you at a game, that you weary of your matters and commit them to me to answer for us both.

*Holograph.*                                                                   SP 10/1, no. 43

*        Sir William Herbert married Anne Parr, sister of the queen, whom Seymour himself had secretly married.

**42.** [After June 20]. Particulars of hearse cloths and other furnishings given in rewards to the heralds at the obsequies of [Mary Tudor], queen of France in Westminster Abbey on 11 July 1533, of Isabella, widow of the emperor Charles V in St Paul's Cathedral on 6 June 1539 and of [Francis I], king of France in St Paul's on 20 June 1547; with note that the velvet cushion and carpet for offering is customarily given to the gentleman usher. Examined by A. Walker. SP 10/1, no. 44

**43.** June 27. Hedingham Castle, [Essex]. Sir Thomas Darcy to [? William Cecil].

According to my late communication with you in the [duke of Somerset's] gallery at Westminster I have by all means enquired of the matter between [the earl of] Oxford and Mistress Dorothy, late woman to Lady Katherine his daughter, with whom he is in love. From communication with them both I have found them to be in the same case that they were in when Lord Oxford was before my lord's grace, save that the banns of matrimony between them were twice proclaimed in three days. Other communication between them has only been in secret. If my lord's grace's pleasure is to have the matter further stayed, which I think very expedient, tell me. Have his grace send his letters to Edward Grene of Sampford, in whose house Dorothy continues, commanding him to prevent her and Lord Oxford meeting or exchanging messengers. On instruction from his grace I will negotiate with Lord Wentworth for a marriage between Lord Oxford and one of his daughters. Let me know by this bearer of your motion to his grace concerning the matter.

*Printed*: G.J. Townsend, *History of the Great Chamberlainship of England*, (1934), 100. *The Ancestor*, iv, (Jan. 1903), 24–5. SP 10/1, no. 45

[For grant of arms to Robert Knight, erroneously dated 14 July 1547 in *CSPD*, 4 see no. **126** below.]

**44.** July 15. List of those who furnish great horses.

The lord great master – 10. The lord privy seal – 10. Marquess of Dorset – 6. Marquess of Northampton – 15. [Earl of] Arundel – 10. [Earl of] Oxford – 6. [Earl of] Shrewsbury – 5. [Earl of] Derby – 5. [Earl of] Huntingdon – 5. [Earl of] Westmorland – 5. [Earl of] Cumberland – 5. [Earl of] Southampton – 5. [Earl of] Sussex – 5. The lord admiral – 8. Lord Dacre – 3. Lord Scrope – 3. Lord Latimer – 2. Lord Conyers – 2. Lord Willoughby – 2. Lord Sheffield – 2. Lord Wentworth – 3. Lord Burgh – 3. Lord Morley – 2. Lord Mordaunt – 3. Lord Cromwell – 2. Lord Ferrers – 3. Lord Windsor – 3. Lord Rich – 5. Lord Zouche – 2. Lord Monteagle – 2. Archbishop of Canterbury – 15. Archbishop of York – 10. Bishop of Durham – 5. Bishop of Carlisle – 3. Bishop of Worcester – 5. Bishop of Lichfield – 5. Bishop of Ely – 5. Bishop of Norwich – 3. Bishop of London – 5. Bishop of Peterborough – 2. Bishop of Chichester – 3. Bishop of Winchester – 10. Bishop of Salisbury – 5. Sir John Williams – 6. Sir Thomas Cheyne – 10. Sir John Gage – 2. Sir Anthony Browne – 10. Sir William Paget – 10. Sir Anthony Wingfield – 2. Sir Anthony Denny – 6. [Sir William Herbert – 6].* Sir John Baker – 4. Sir Edward North – 8. Sir Ralph Sadler – 10. Sir Richard Southwell – 4. Sir Edmund Peckham – 2. Sir Robert Southwell – 4. Sir Thomas Pope – 4. Sir Arthur Darcy – 2. Sir William Sydney – 2. Sir Richard Gresham – 4. Sir William Cavendyshe – 3. Sir William Shelley – 1. Sir John Gresham – 2. Sir Rowland Hill – 2. Sir Martin Bowes – 4. Sir Roger Cholmeley – 2. Sir Edmund Mountague – 2. Sir Richard Lyster – 2. Sir Giles Capell – 2. Sir John Raynsford – 2. Sir John Wentworth – 2. Sir Richard Alee – 2. Sir [Ralph] Rowlett – 2. Sir Henry Parker – 1. Sir Robert Lytton – 1. Sir Giles Alington – 2. Sir Humphrey Browne – 2. Sir Wymond Carew – 2. Sir Thomas Moyle – 2. *Bedfordshire*. Sir Francis Bryan – 4. Sir John StJohn – 2. Sir Thomas Rotherham – 1. Sir Michael Fyssher – 1. Sir John Gascoyn – 1.

* Deleted.

Sir Uryan Brireton – 2. Francis Pygot – 1. *Buckinghamshire*. Sir Robert Dormer – 2. Sir Anthony Lee – 2. Henry Bradshaw – 1. Richard Grenwey – 1. Arthur Longvile – 1. Sir Robert Drury – 1. Robert Cheynye – 1. *Berkshire*. Sir William Essex – 2. Sir John Norreis – 2. Sir Humphrey Foster – 2. Richard Brudges – 1. John Welsborne – 1. Sir Alexander Upton – 2. Alexander Fetyplace – 1. Sir Francis Engleffeld – 2. John Wynchecombe – 2. William Hyde – 1. *Kent*. Sir John Hynde – 1. Sir Robert Payton – 1. John Hoddelston – 1. Robert Chester – 1. Thomas Hutton – 1. *Derbyshire*. Sir Henry Sacheviell – 1. Sir William Bassett – 1. Sir James Fulgeam – 1. Sir George Grysley – 1. Sir Thomas Coken – 1. Sir Peter Threshewell – 1. Sir Humphrey Brandbourne – 1. Sir George Vernon – 2. Sir John Porte – 1. Sir Thomas Fitzherbert – 1. *Essex*. Sir John Mordaunte – 1. Sir William Stafford – 1. Sir George Norton – 1. Sir Anthony Coke – 1. Sir William Walgrave – 1. Sir Henry Tyrrell – 1. Sir Thomas Jossolyn – 1. William Harrys – 1. Robert Mordaunte – 1. Thomas Myldmay – 1. *Gloucestershire*. Sir Anthony Kingston – 2. Sir Anthony Hungerford – 2. Sir Walter Dennys – 2. Sir Richard Ligon – 1. Sir Walter Buckler – 1. John Barlowe – 2. *Huntingdonshire*. Sir Robert Kyrkham – 1. *Hertfordshire*. Sir John Perient – 1. William Barlowe – 1. John Broket – 1. George Hyde – 1. *Kent*. Sir William Fynche – 2. Sir John Guldford – 2. Sir Edward Bowton – 2. Sir Henry Isley – 2. Sir Reynold Scote – 2. Sir Percival Harte – 2. Sir George Harper – 2. William Repes – 1. Sir Walter Henley – 2. Sir James Hales – 2. Sir Maurice Denys – 2. Sir Anthony Aucher – 4. William Waller – 1. Edward Thwaytes – 1. Edward Monyng – 1. Thomas Harlakynden – 1. Thomas Hardes – 1. Anthony Sandes – 1. Thomas Roydon – 1. John Culpeper – 1. Thomas Robertes – 1. *Lincolnshire: Kesteven*. Sir John Thimbleby – 2. Sir Thomas Wymbushe – 2. John Hastinges – 1. Richard Cycell – 1. Sir Thomas Brudnell – 1. Austin Porter – 1. *Lincolnshire: Lindsey*. Sir Thomas Henneage – 4. Sir William Skipwith – 2. Sir John Coupeldick – 1. Sir Francis Askew – 2. Sir Edward Dymoke – 2. William Monson – 1. John Henneage – 1. *Leicestershire*. Mr Manners – 6 demilances, 10 light horses. Sir Thomas Turkevyll – 1. John Beamont – 1. Francis Pultney – 1. *Middlesex*. Sir Philip Hobbye – 2. Hugh Losse – 1. *Northamptonshire*. Sir Thomas Tresham – 2. Sir Thomas Gryffen – 2. Sir Richard Catesby – 2. Sir Humphrey Stafford – 2. Valentine Knightley – 2. *Nottinghamshire*. Sir Urian Stapleton – 2. Sir John Byron – 2. Sir John Markham – 2. Sir Henry Sutton – 2. Sir John Chaworthe – 2. Sir John Harcye – 1. Sir Gervase Clyfton – 2. Sir Anthony Nevell – 2. Sir William Hollys – 1. *Norfolk*. Sir Roger Townesend – 2. Sir William Paston – 2. Sir John Heydon – 2. Sir Edmund Bedingfeld – 2. Sir Edmund Knyvet – 2. Sir William Fermor – 2. Sir Edmund Wyndham – 2. Sir Francis Lovell – 2. Thomas Tyndall – 1. Robert Holdiche – 1. Sir John Robster – 1. Sir John Clere – 6, 4 light horses, 6 footmen. *Oxfordshire*. Sir William Barington – 2. Sir John Browne – 1. Sir Anthony Cope – 1. Leonard Chamberlaine – 2. *Rutland*. Sir John Harrington – 2. *Surrey*. Lord William Howard – 2. Sir Thomas Camden – 4. Sir Matthew Browne – 1. Sir Roger Copley – 1. *Staffordshire*. Sir John Gyfford – 1. Sir George Gryffethe – 1. Sir Philip Draycot – 1. Sir John Harcourte – 1. Sir Edward Aston – 1. *Shropshire*. Sir Richard Manwayring – 1. Sir John Blounte – 2. Sir Robert Nedham – 1. *Hampshire*. Sir William Berkley – 1. Sir Michael Lyster – 2. Sir Francis Dawtrey – 1. Thomas Whyte – 1. John Mylles – 1. *Suffolk*. Sir William Drurye – 1. Sir Arthur Hopton – 1. Sir William Walgrave – 2. Sir Thomas Tyrrell – 1. Sir John Jermy – 2. Sir John Jermingham – 1. Sir Thomas Jermyn – 2. Sir Anthony Heningham – 2. Sir John Spring – 2. Sir George Colt – 2. *Somerset*. Sir Hugh Pawlet – 2. Sir John Seyntclo – 2. Sir John Luttrell – 2. Sir John Wyndham – 2. *Sussex*. Sir Anthony Wyndsor – 1. John Sakvyle – 1. Nicholas Pellam – 1. *Worcestershire*. Sir John Talbot – 2. Sir John Russell – 1. Sir John Pakington – 2. *Warwickshire*. Sir George Throgmorton – 2. Sir Fulk Grevill – 2, 8 light horses. Sir William Felding – 1. Sir Walter Smithe – 1. Sir John Grevill – 1.

The earl of Warwick – 40 demilances, 60 light horses. The pensioners – 150. The men-at-arms – 80. Boulogne – 51 demilances, 91 light horses. Lord Grey – 50. Wanting: Sir Ralph Bulnede, George Dalkyns, [Sir Francis] Egglefeld, Lord Nevill, Sir George

Coniers – 100 light horses each. At Newcastle August 24. Coloured. Sir George Blount – 4 demilances, 10 light horses. George Rawley – 2 demilances, 4 light horses. Sir William Pickering – 5 light horses. [Sir John Lutterell on foot with (*blank*)].* Lord Fitzwalter to have charge of 100 demilances with those provided by the earls of Southampton and Sussex July 27. Sir William Pickering – 5 light horses. Earl of Shrewsbury in person. Sir Francis Bryan. 200 men of Essex and 200 of Suffolk to be at Harwich August 10.

SP 10/2, no. 1

**45.** July 18. Hampton Court. The king to Sir Ralph Vane, lieutenant of his gentlemen pensioners.

Being informed that our ancient enemies the Scots assemble great numbers for war, although we have not yet certain knowledge how they will employ them but minding to defend our realm, and having had relation of your activity and courage in our father's service, we have appointed you among others to serve on horse. Put yourself in order for this purpose and bring as many able men from your servants and others under your command as can conveniently be horsed and armed. Be ready with them at Newcastle on August 24, where you will receive money for their coats and conduct, and be told of our pleasure for your service and theirs. Their coats are to be red. In the meantime signify to us the numbers you will be able to bring.

*Signature by stamp.*
*Countersigned by* : the duke of Somerset. SP 10/2, no. 2

**46.** July 22. Sir Edward North, [chancellor of the court of augmentations] to William Cecil.

You may like to know [the duke of Somerset's] pleasure for [William] Fitzwilliams, who formerly had by [the duke's] letters a lease of all the lands and corn belonging to Chertsey Abbey as Sir Anthony Browne late held, paying the usual rents. There are several manors in [Browne's lease] besides the rent corn, as the enclosed particulars show. Where Browne paid a yearly rent of £272.16.5½d., it now appears by the survey that he raised the rents to £294.3.4¼d., above the profits of the courts and other things there. Let [the duke] know the truth, and favour Fitzwilliams with as much expedition as you can, and upon your answer I shall have all the expedition I dare.

*Holograph.* SP 10/2, no. 3

**47.** July 25. Horsley. Lady Elizabeth Browne to William Cecil.

I understand the lord protector has appointed certain gentlemen and others to serve the king in Scotland, and have written to his grace to appoint my brother† to be among them. Supposing he does not know my brother, please prefer his suit that he may deliver my letter to his grace.

*Printed*: Tytler, i, 73–4. SP 10/2, no. 4

**48.** July 25. Offington. Thomas [West], Lord De La Warr to William Cecil.

Today I received a letter from the king and another from the lord protector commanding me with other gentlemen of this county to provide certain horses as the king appointed in former letters. I am appointed for two demilances, and they are ready. I doubt not that the rest of the gentlemen are ready also. The king appoints us to be at Newcastle on August 12, but not who shall be their captains, to whom they shall report – which will be a great business to the poor men, ignorant and inexperienced – how they should order themselves on the way, or whether I should give them their coats in Newcastle. I do not know what livery colours the king wishes us to provide. We shall

---

\*  Deleted.
†  Edward FitzGerald.

send over forty men, mostly horsekeepers. For lack of a ruler or captain they may misorder themselves. Let me know [the protector's] pleasure in these and such other things as my servant this bearer shall mention which are too long to write.

SP 10/2, no. 5

**49.** [? July]. Prayer for peace, particularly between England and Scotland, that the two nations might be united by the marriage of the king and the queen of Scots, to which promises and agreements have been firmly made.

*Endorsed*: The common prayer.

*Printed*: Richard Grafton, (1548). [Unique copy in Magdalene College, Cambridge, Pepys Library 1976(2). *STC* 16503]. SP 10/2, no. 6

**50.** August 30. Westminster. Grant by the king in perpetuity to John Lyon and Alice his wife of certain [*unspecified*] properties formerly belonging to Abingdon Abbey worth £57.5.9½d. a year, and one tenement or curtilage called Buckhurst or Monkhill in the parishes of Woodford and Chigwell, Essex, formerly belonging to the monastery of Stratford Langthorne, Essex, now or late in the tenure or occupation of Ralph Johnson, and one grove or wood called Monksgrove worth £13.8.8 a year.

*Extract*: from C 66/800, mm. 33–5 (*CPR* 1547–8, 39–42). SP 10/2, no. 7

**51.** September 30. Recognisance of William Lanway to the king for £40 against taking excessive toll of those resorting to his mill to grind corn, on the joint surety of Henry Prince and Walter Hackeman.

*Latin and English. Three marks of assent.* SP 10/2, no. 8

**52.** [September 30]. Royal commission to William Paulet, K.G., Lord St John, president of the council and great master of the household, Sir William Petre, principal secretary of state, Sir Walter Mildmay, one of the general surveyors of the court of augmentations, and Robert Keyllewey, surveyor of liveries, to examine the states of the courts of exchequer, the duchy of Lancaster, first fruits and tenths, augmentations and wards and liveries, and to ascertain what yearly revenues do or ought to go to them, and what goods or chattels remain due to the courts and to the executors of the will of Henry VIII. With power to examine all officers of the courts and any others, who are to certify the full extent of royal revenues at Michaelmas 1546 and 1547, and all cash, debts or bonds remaining in their hands on January 28 last and not since discharged. Officers of the court of augmentations and the duchy of Lancaster are to certify how much lead and bells came or ought to have come to Henry VIII by the surrender of religious houses, and how much has been disposed of, to whom and for how much. The commissioners are to make certificate of all the premises with convenient speed.

*Copy*: from C 66/801, mm. 25d–26d (*CPR* 1547–8, 93), n.d., del. November 26.

SP 10/2, no. 9

**53.** September 30. Indenture of all gold and silver bullion coined in the office of Sir William Sharington, gentleman of the privy chamber and under treasurer of the mint at Bristol Castle, with avouchments by Roger Wigmore, comptroller and Thomas Marshall, assaymaster, from 1 April to 30 September 1547. Totals: gold – 204 lb. 4 oz.; silver – 7,838 lb.

*Parchment. Monthly figures specified.* SP 10/2, no. 10

**54.** Duplicate of the above.

*Parchment.* SP 10/2, no. 11

**55.** September 30. Account of Sir William Sharington, under treasurer of the mint at Bristol Castle of silver and gold bullion coined from 1 April to September 30 1547, with avouchments by Roger Wigmore, comptroller and Thomas Marshall, assaymaster.

Gold (20 carat fine and 4 oz. alloy): clear gain – £200.12.6. Silver (4 oz. fine and 8 oz. alloy): clear gain – £9,031.19.10½d. Total – £9,231.12.4½d. [*sic*]. Allowances: fees, wages and necessaries – £496.18.6. Arrears remaining – £8,748.13.10½d.

SP 10/2, no. 12

**56.** [? October]. Book of memoranda and assessments concerning the rates and subsidies on wools.

(1) Comparison of the profits of custom and subsidy of wools, fells and cloths, and the alnage thereof in 28 Edward III [1354/5] and 38 Henry VIII [1546/7]. King Edward had £55,202.8.3 a year more by customs than King Henry, besides other subsidies. (2) Remembrances to the lord protector explaining the terms and accounting methods used. (3) Three rates of a subsidy to be granted by the king, stating contributions from sheepmasters, clothiers, merchants, graziers and tanners.

*Printed*: *Tudor Economic Documents*, i, 178–84 (some omissions).    SP 10/2, no. 13

**57.** [? October]. Memoranda concerning wool: the units of its measurement, the local names of sorts of wool which used to be shipped to the staple, cost of carriage, packing and freight to Calais, and customs charges.    SP 10/2, no. 14

**58.** [? October]. Memoranda concerning quantities of wool brought to the staple of Calais, and the customs, freight, packing and other charges thereby incurred; quantities of wools exported from various specified areas of England, amounting to £39,929.6.8, with explanatory notes and observations.    SP 10/2, no. 15

**59.** [? October]. Table of weights of wool in todds, nails, ounces, pounds and other measures, according to the manner of the Calais staple.    SP 10/2, no. 16

**60.** [? October]. Similar table of English weights of wool.    SP 10/2, no. 17

**61.** [? October]. Tabular synopsis of the statute laws of England, classified as causes royal, military, ecclesiastical, popular and criminal; with lists of types of legal proceedings, secular and ecclesiastical.*    SP 10/2, no. 18

**62.** [? October]. Extract from statute 1 Edward VI [c. 5] allowing the warden of the Cinque Ports to give no more than six horses or geldings in any year to persons in friendly foreign ports.

Extracts from statutes 1 Henry IV [c. 6] and 6 Henry VIII [c. 15] to the effect that whoever asks of the king what was formerly granted to another shall make his own grant void.    SP 10/2, no. 19

**63.** November 3. Westminster. Letters patent appointing the duke of Somerset, lord protector, to enjoy a seat of honour in parliament, sitting in the middle of the bench on the right hand of the throne, and to enjoy all privileges formerly made to the uncles of sovereigns or to any protectors, the statute for placing the lords in parliament of 31 Henry VIII [c. 10] notwithstanding.

*Copy*: from C 66/805, m. 49 (*CPR* 1547–8, 217).
*Printed*: Rymer, xv, 164.    SP 10/2, no. 20

[For SP 10/2, no. 21 see no. **167** below.]

---

\*    Cf. *The Chronicle and Political Papers of King Edward VI*, ed. W.K. Jordan, (Ithaca, 1966), 43–4: John Cook, master of requests and other lawyers appointed to prepare such a list for the council, 13 August 1550.

**64.** December 12. Newcastle. George Revelay to [the duke of Somerset].

After the king's ships had arrived in the haven at Berwick it was twenty-eight days before they could be made ready and have wind to come out again; all the beer was removed and filled up again, with thirty tons' leakage. We left the haven on the 3rd of the next month and went to sea as far as Scarborough, and then met the southerly wind with snow and rain, so that we were driven back to Holy Island, and likely to have been put into the Firth. We came out within six days and went to sea again as far as Flamborough Head, and were then driven back to Tynemouth haven. We stayed there three days, and went to sea again as far as Humber, but put back again to Tynemouth, and were scattered by weather, not meeting again for two days, where we remain. Our tackle is spoilt. The beer leaked because of the weather, so that some ships have to take ballast. Part of the beer is bad – some of it so before it came at Berwick, and I think it worse now. *Postscript.* The admiral's ship, the *Lewis*, having sixty men with their captain for three months' wages amounts to £21.17.8. The *Francis*, with the same number of men, £21.7.8; the *Hoobarke*, wages for twenty men a month, £9.1.8. There are four other ships freighted with the king's beer which need half freight to victual them and buy tackle, amounting to £30. The whole sum will amount to £82.19.0.     SP 10/2, no. 22

**65.** December 14. Newcastle. Robert Heylord, captain of the *Lewis* to [the duke of Somerset].

The king's ships are at Shields because of the wind and weather, their victuals spent and their month over on Tuesday. We desire a warrant for money to discharge our victuals and wages, as Captain Rewley will certify to you, until we come near London. For favour the victuallers here in our company have spent all the money they received at Berwick and are without victuals and money. Let them have some money until they come to their ports.                                     SP 10/2, no. 23

**66.** December 28. Beeleigh. Princess Mary to the duke of Somerset.

Thank you for your gentleness touching my requests, of which I have been told by Mr Comptroller.* Although I will not trouble you now with all my requests, I signify my desire for those who have served me very long and have no certain livings. Let them have pensions as others of my servants have. I fear they shall not live long to enjoy them.

*Holograph.*

*Printed*: Tytler, i, 60–1. *Facsimiles of National MSS*, ii, 68 (facsimile no. XXXVIII).
                                          SP 10/2, no. 24

**67.** [? December]. Sunday. Cheshunt. Princess Elizabeth to Queen Catherine.

I was sorry to leave you in your doubtful health. Although I answered little, I weighed more deeply your saying that you would warn me of all evils that you should hear of me. I thank God for your friendship and wish such friends long life. Although I have plenty of matter, here I will stay, for I know you are not quiet to read.

*Holograph.*

*Printed*: Tytler, i, 70. *Facsimiles of National MSS*, ii, 69 (facsimile no. XXXIX). Facsimile also in C.J. Kitching (ed.), *Tudor Royal Letters: the family of Henry VIII*, (PRO Museum Pamphlets, no. 2, HMSO 1972), no. v.                 SP 10/2, no. 25

**68.** [? 1547]. Petition from Henry Pony of the city of London, alebrewer, to the duke of Somerset, lord protector.

The petitioner was leased a tenement and brewhouse called the Pye in Smithfield in the suburbs of London, by indenture for eighty years by Swithun Skarne, esq., deceased,

---

\*     Sir William Paget, comptroller of the household.

of Kingston upon Thames, Surrey. The petitioner also, with John Fynkell of London, cooper, at the petitioner's request, became bound to Thomas Cressell of Wargrave, Berkshire, for £40 for the debt that Thomas Walden of Warfield, Berkshire owed to Cressall. After payment of £20 of the £40 Walden, being in poverty, fled the country. So the petitioner and Fynkell were wholly burdened with payment of the other £20. Since Fynkell became surety at the petitioner's request and was a poor man without substance, the petitioner delivered him his said lease, giving him power for payment of the £20 to Cressell, Fynkell receiving the £3 yearly value of the lease until the £20 was repaid, which was in seven years following. During his life Fynkell, and after him his wife Alice, now Alice Dacres, widow, had for twenty-one years and still has the said brewhouse, and so has had £148 over the £20, all quit rents discharged. Not thus contented, Alice has sold lead and other implements belonging to the brewhouse, and a horse mill, valued at their entry at £74. The petitioner is poor, with a wife and children. He has often required Alice Dacres, being rich, to restore his lease and implements, but she has refused. He therefore petitions the protector to summon her to bring her lease for examination that recompense may be given him.

*Parchment. Mutilated.*                                                                    SP 10/2, no. 26

**69.**  [?]. Dorothy Wingfield, widow to the duchess of Somerset.

I was bold to be your suitor as a means to the lord protector for favour concerning the livelihood I have by the king's gift. I understand there is a new commission for the sale of certain of the king's abbey lands.* Move the protector to make no grant or sell the reversion of the late priory of Woodbridge, Suffolk or anything belonging to it until they know his further pleasure, for I know of an intention to purchase some part of it.

SP 10/2, no. 27

**70.**  [?]†. Petition from Vincent Bellacio, Italian gentleman, to the duke of Somerset, lord protector.

It may be seen by the letters from M. Barbanson to the duke and from Sir Philip Hoby to Secretary [Thomas] Smith, that the petitioner, as of accustomed desire, has willed to serve the king and duke, not doubting to receive sufficient entertainment; but the duke has not appointed his sustenance. The petitioner asks to serve with the duke's company of servants and horses in the king's affairs in Scotland, and to be entertained according to his service and deserts.                                             SP 10/2, no. 28

**71.**  [?]‡. Persons certified by the sheriffs to possess £40 or more yearly who have not compounded for their fines for knighthood.

*London.* William Ha[...]ng. John Clerc. Robert Warnor. Dominic Lumleyn. Nicholas Sympson. William Berners, auditor. Robert Haymond, woodmonger. Arthur Devonshire. William Crompton. Roger Moore, serjeant of the bakehouse. Christopher Barker *alias* Garter. [John Crooke].§ Thomas Berthelet. Edward Elrington. William Garrard. Richard Duke. Dr Richard Barthelet. Steven Vaughan. Oliver Leader. *Gloucester.* George Guyes. Arthur Porter. *Newcastle upon Tyne.* James Lawson. Edmund Lawson. Robert Lewen. *York.* William Thwaytes. *Caernarvonshire.* Rice Gruffith. Thomas Moston. *Anglesey.* Roland Gruffith. *Carmarthenshire.* James Williams. James Reade. Rice William. Walter Vaughan. Henry Barret. *Denbighshire.* John Salesbury junior. John Lloid of Yale. Tuder ap Robert.

---

*        ? 27 April 1548 [*CPR* 1548–9, 57].

†        Some time in or after April 1548, when Hoby was appointed ambassador in Germany and Smith made
         secretary.

‡        A commission for distraint of knighthood was issued on 15 February 1547 with extent to 2 February
         1548 [*CPR* 1547–8, 185–6]. Several of those in this list appear as knights in no. **44** above (July 1547); at
         least five were knighted on 22 February 1547 in the coronation honours.

§        Deleted.

*Pembrokeshire.* John Aphilleps. James Williams. Lewes Watkyns. *Flintshire.* Thomas Ranscrofte. *Glamorganshire.* James Thomas. William Mathewe of 'Castle Menetes'. Walter Herbert. *Kent.* James Hale, serjeant at law. George Harper. Anthony Auchar. Maurice Denys. John Norton. Henry Cutt. Reginald Pekham. William Harman. Robert Fynche. Thomas Wyldforde. George Blage. Thomas Cokkes. Thomas Digges. Thomas Swan. William Culpeper. William Oxenden. John Lucas. William Everenden of Benenden wood. Robert Edolf. William Parys. *Monmouthshire.* Walter Herbert. Charles Herbert. David Ellmer Morgan. *Cornwall.* John Wynslade. Humphrey Trevilian. Thomas Arrundell of 'Lee'. John Canynowe senior. John Raskynner. *Lancashire.* Gervase Midleton. Richard Towneley. Thurston Tyldesley. Henry Halsall. Peter Standley. Henry Kighley. Richard Kyrkby. Hugh Flemyng. Thomas Barton. John Talbot. Ralph Bradshawe. James Skaresbrik. Adam Hulton. Thomas Caterall. James Standisshe. Thomas Egleston. William Westbye. Henry Byrom. Robert Holt. *Somerset.* William Portman, justice [of king's bench]. John Wyndham. John Kenne. Humphrey Keynes. Thomas Payne. Giles Hyll. John Ogan. Thomas Newton. Henry Chamneys. John Bonvyle. Richard Marshall. Thomas Dyer. Richard Cupper. *Bedfordshire.* Uryan Brereton. Anthony Dukkett. Thomas Forster. William Markham. *Huntingdonshire.* Robert Bulkeley. *Cambridgeshire.* Philip Parys. John Hudleston. Robert Chapman. *Hampshire.* Richard Pexall. Thomas White. Richard Waller. William Moore. John Brewen. Thomas Cooke. John Samborn. Thomas Windesor. John SeyntJohn. George Dabriscourt. John Newes. John Dowce. John Pescod. *Derbyshire.* Thomas Fitzherbert. Ralph Leeke. *Nottinghamshire.* Edmund Molyneux, serjeant at law. William Holles. *Herefordshire.* Richard Walwyn. Richard Inkpenne. Roland Moreton. Richard Palmer. James Vaughan. Gregory ap Harry. *Oxfordshire.* William Fermor. James Langston. Thomas Pygott. Richard More. William Davers. Thomas Penyston. John Osbaston. William Dormer. John Oglesthorp. John Foxe. John More. John Carleton. Richard Gunter. *Warwickshire.* John Grevile. John Spencer. George Rawley. Alverd Trussell. Giles Forster. John Fissher. *Leicestershire.* Thomas Nevell. Bertyn Hasilrigg. William Villers. *Wiltshire.* Silvester Davers. John Hungerford. Edmund Mompesson. Henry Clifford. John Thynne. Thomas Stanter. Charles Bulkeley. John Merven. Henry Bruncker. Walter Skilling. William Webbe. *Hertfordshire.* John Cokk. John Knyghton. Humphrey Fitzherbert. Edward Leventhorp. John Carye. William Barley. William Gerye. Robert Chester. Edward Capell. James Orwell. John Kechyn. William Ipgrave. John Penne. Edmund Burdolf. Richard Harvy. *Staffordshire.* George Audeley. Thomas Skrymshere. *Westmorland.* Walter Stryklande. Anthony Dukkett. Thomas Sandford. Thomas Blynkensop. Thomas Warcop. Lancelot Lancastr. John Preston. Christopher Crakenthorp. Richard Dudley. James Pikering. *Gloucestershire.* Nicholas Wikes. John Butler. David Broke. Edmund Abridge. Giles Poole. Roland Moreton. John Palmer. Henry Tracye. Robert Cassey. Henry Brayne. *Cumberland.* Cuthbert Huton. William Penyngton. John Leight. Richard Egleffeld. Thomas Dawlston. Thomas Salkeld. William Huton. John Thwaites. John Skelton. *Shropshire.* Edward Rawley. Richard Horde. William Foxe. Thomas Kylmerston. Richard Mytton. Fulk Crompton. *Buckinghamshire.* Henry Bradshawe. Thomas Gyfford. Edmund Wyndesor. Robert Latymer. Nicholas Purfray. William Byrt. *Berkshire.* Francis Egleffeld. Richard Bruges. Thomas Essex. John Latton. John Coope. Thomas Yate. Thomas Ogle. Reginald Williams. *Northamptonshire.* Humphrey Stafford. Richard Cecyll. Valentine Knyghtley. John Rodney. Francis Quarles. Robert Browne. William Dudley. Robert Wingfeld. John Hartwell. John Fermor. William Gyfford. John Worley of Dodford. *Norfolk.* John Rosbart. Roger Woodhous. Nicholas le Straunge. John Holles. Robert Holdiche. Robert Hoggam.* Thomas Woodhous. Edmund Beawpre. John Rippes. John Dedyk. Edmund Thursby. John Woodhous. George Haydon. William Elverton. John Gray. John Castell. William Buttes. Anthony Gorney. Christopher Coote. Edmund Billingford. Clement Pagrave. Henry Spilman. John

*　　　Deceased.

Harward. Fermyn Rockwoode. Thomas Hubbert. Roger Rokwoode. Anthony Thwaites. Edward Blomvile. John Sturges.* John Calybutt. William Bromefeld. *Cheshire.* Thomas Aston. Robert Dukkenfeld. *Middlesex.* William Belamy. Robert Cheseman. Alan Nycholas. Richard Peksall. Thomas Burbage. *Essex.* William Stafford. Eustace Sulierd. Humphrey Tirrell of South Ockenden. Francis Clovell. John Cornewall. William Payne. William Browne. Clement Smyth. Thomas Audeley. Thomas Clovell. Ralph Nalinghurst. Francis Smythe. Marrelyn Hales. Richard Sampford. William Wentworthe. Thomas Cornewall. Thomas Sysselden. William Mores. John Franke. Edward Bugges. Nicholas Colyn. *Lincolnshire.* John Reade. Thomas Wymbisshe. Thomas Husey. Thomas Fokingham. John Hasilwoode. James Harrington. John Hargrave. Nicholas Jakson. William Ermyn. Thomas Horseman. Charles Sutton. Thomas Keyme. William Sandon. John Broxholme. Austin Massingberd. John Langham. Oliver Wotherwik. Richard Welbe. Edward Forsett. John Langton. Arthur Dymmok. Philip Bleysbye. John Barnardiston. Thomas Mounson. William Hatclif. *Yorkshire.* Thomas Markenfeld. John Burnand. William Hungate. [Walter Pullen].† Vivian Staneley. Thomas Slynsbye. Henry Arthyngton. John Vanesure of Weston. John Gascoigne. Steven Tempest. Walter Hawkeswoorthe. Thomas Draxe. Charles Jakson. Christopher Hopton. Robert Roose. Nicholas Womwell. Charles Moreton. Geffrey Leigh. John Vanesure. Thomas Goldesburgh of Goldsborough. George Brigham. Thomas Grymston. William Hothom. Robert Normavile. William Clapham. John Lambert. Richard Smetheley. John Barton. Richard Sigewike. William Conyers of Marske. Richard Bowes. William Catherik. Charles Dransfeld. Symond Conyers. Christopher Brugh. Thomas Gore of Picton. Thomas son of James Craythorn. Christopher Conyers of Danby Wiske. George Conyers. Thomas Bilbe. Christopher Thomlynson. *Cinque Ports.* John Theccher. John Sleverik. *Suffolk.* Edward Walgrave. Robert Garnysshe. John Sulyerd. John Tyrrell. Richard Freston. William Duke. Edmund Rous. Thomas Rous. Robert Downes. Christopher Platter. John Barney of Reedham. Alexander Newton. Francis Barnard. Robert Wetherby. Thomas Arnott. [Thomas Goldbold].† Thomas Godbold senior. William Waller. *Dorset.* Thomas Pullett. John Tregonwell. John Wadeham of Catherston. Henry Uvedall. Edward Twynowe. Thomas White of Poole. Christopher Claverell. Oliver Laurence. George Turbervile. Robert Temmes. Roger Clavell. *Devon.* Henry Beaumonte. Walter Raleigh. William Holland. Henry Waldron. Nicholas Assheford. John Drewe of Kenn. John Seyntclere. Thomas Kirkham. William Hoddy. Otho Gylbert. Thomas Gybbes. Richard Hales. Thomas Fortescue. William Coole. Anthony Buttukeshier. Hugh Preist. Robert Yeoo. John Kelleigh. William Bedlowe. Alexander Wollacombe. John Cruse. Anthony Harvy. Rober Gy[f]ford. John Barnehous. William Hawkyns. Laurence Prowse. *Surrey.* Thomas Lussher. William Saunders. James Skynner. Thomas Gaynsforth. John Carleton. Robert Curson. Thomas Edgarr. Henry Goodyere. John Scott of Camberwell. Steven Bekingham. [*blank*] Brewen of Farnham. William Udall. Richard Udall. *Sussex.* Richard Sakvile. William Cheyney. Nicholas Pelham. Thomas Morley. Thomas Th[...]eill. Richard Bellingham. John Culpepe[r]. John Owen. Thomas Mych[ell]. William Shurleigh. Edward Lew[ken]or. Henry Husey. Edward Shelley. Thomas Prestall. John Janne. Thomas Devenysshe. *Worcestershire.* Roland Moreton. William Gowar of Wood Hall. Richard Muklowe. Richard Calowhill.                                                            SP 10/2, no. 29

[For SP 10/2, nos. 30, 31 see nos. **778, 786** below.]

**72.** [January x April 1547]. Petition from William Parr, marquess of Northampton to the king.

\*     Deceased.
†     Deleted.

The petitioner once married Lady Anne Bowsar [Bourchier], who has confessed to and been found guilty of adultery, bearing a bastard son declared illegitimate by act of parliament* and an ecclesiastical court for the divorce of the said lady. He asks the king's consideration for his present state, desiring marriage for the honour of God and the procreation of an heir. The late king shortly before his death intended to appoint a commission of learned men to determine whether in this case the petitioner might marry another in the lifetime of Lady Anne, but the king's death prevented further proceeding. He asks the king to appoint a similar commission.† SP 10/2, no. 32

**73.** [1547]. Account of John Cumberworthe *alias* Smythe, bailiff of Sempringham, part of the ministers' accounts for the lands of the late priory of Sempringham, Lincolnshire for 1 Edward VI, the first year of account to the king after the erection of the court of augmentations.

Farms of the rectories of Stow with Birthorpe chapel (£4.6.8), Billingborough (£6.13.4) and Walcot (£12.19.5); total – £23.19.5. Leased to Lord Clinton by seal of the court of augmentations 10 December 1538 for 21 years. SP 10/2, no. 33

**74.** [July 1547 x ? September 1548]. Names of those licensed to preach under the great seal since July 1547.‡

Baldwin Norton, D.D. [? Matthew] Parker, D.D. Richard Queene. Dr [Henry] Eglyambye. William Leremount, chaplain to Lady Anne of Cleves. John Whitehedde, B.D. William Chamberlaine. Richard Wilkes, B.D. Edward Robynson, M.A. John Bythe, M.A., Scotsman. Hugh Sewell, M.A. Gilbert Barkeley. Henry Parrye. Thomas Beaton [Becon]. Edmund Allen. [John Taylor *alias*] Cardemaker. Hugh Latimer, D.D. Rowland Taylor, LL.D. William Byll, D.D. Godfrey Gilpin, B.D. Christopher Thredder, vicar of [Saffron] Walden. Dr [? Richard] Coxe. [Bernard] Gilpin, M.A. Leonard Coxe. Thomas Roose. John Gybbes, B.D. Robert Horne, B.D. Thomas Levar, M.A. Thomas Brickhedd, B.D. Edwin Sandes. William Rede, vicar of Grantham. William Claybourghe, D.D. Robert Watson, D.D. John Ruthe, Scotsman. Henry Parrye. Alexander Logen, M.A. James Pylkyngton, M.A. John Whitewell, B.D. John Keyron, M.A. Thomas Gilham, B.D., Scotsman. Stephen Clercke. John Madewe, M.A. Thomas Bayley, B.D. Matthew Parker, D.D. Andrew Perne, B.D. Henry Wilshawe, B.D. Robert Leighborne, B.A. Richard Coxe, D.D. Thomas Cottesforde, student in divinity. Lawrence Taylor, king's chaplain. Henry Kinge, D.D. Henry Sydall, B.D. Christopher Threader, student in dvinity. Robert Banckes, M.A. John Appelbye. William Hutton, M.A. Edmund Perpoincte, B.D. William Cholwell, student in divinity. Lawrence Saunders, D.D. Robert Kinge, D.D. Richard Hide, M.A. William Torner, student in divinity. Henry Marshall, M.A. John Knoxe, Scotsman. John Macbraier, M.A., Scotsman. Nicholas Daniell, M. A. John Bradforde. Thomas Buarde. Edmund Gest, B.D. John Willocke, M.A. James Haddon, M.A. William Huett, M.A. Launcelot Thexton, M.A. Thomas Sampson. John Jewell. Adam Shepparde, B.D. Alexander Nowell. Richard Tavernor. Henry Hamilton. Edmund Gryndall, B.D.

*Printed*: R.W. Dixon, *History of the Church of England from the abolition of the Roman Jurisdiction*, (Oxford, 1878–1902), ii, 485–6. SP 10/2, no. 34

**75.** 1548. January 8. Ely Place. The earl of Warwick to the duke of Somerset.

The bishop of Worcester has a manor joining my lands and I have lands lying as commodious for him. We shall, I think, conclude an exchange, that the king's licence and your grace's to us both may be obtained. In the meantime, if you will write favourably to the bishop he will show me more friendship. This is the first exchange I ever desired

---

* HLRO, Original Acts, 34 & 35 Henry VIII no. 39.
† Appointed 19 April 1547 [*CPR* 1547–8, 137].
‡ Preaching was further limited in September 1548 [*Tudor Royal Proclamations*, i, 432–3, no. 313]; but this list was perhaps drawn up to assist distribution of a circular from the protector and council to licensed preachers, dated 23 May 1548 [Burnet, v, 193–6].

at any of [the bishops'] hands and shall be the last. I desire no disprofit to the bishop; I am sure he is satisfied.

*Signed.*                                                                    SP 10/3, no. 1

**76.**   January 9. Hampton Court. The duke of Somerset to the town of Cambridge.

The university of Cambridge has sued us for confirmation of certain privileges and for new royal grants. Since you have begged us stay these requests, without explanation, we have sent them for perusal. Return any contrary reasons in writing before the 18th of this month, or we shall grant or deny them as we think convenient.

*Copy.*

*Printed*: J. Lamb (ed.), *A collection of letters ... illustrative of the University of Cambridge*, (1838), 87, from another copy in Corpus Christi College, Cambridge MS 106, no. 78, p. 243.                                                                    SP 10/3, no. 2

**77.**   [? January]. Answers of the mayor, bailiffs and burgesses of Cambridge to the privileges claimed by the university.

1. The claim of the university to use civil law in all personal actions involving a scholar or a scholar's servant is inconvenient but the town will accept it at the protector's pleasure. The chancellor of the university or his deputy should not have jurisdiction in mayhem or felony, which he never had. The court should meet at an approved time – henceforth once a week – and in a specified place. All suits should be put in writing, so that every party may have a copy of the actions, as in the king's courts. No scholar or scholar's servant should take over another man's debts and commence action thereupon.

2. Many of the ancient liberties of the university, especially those given in the time of Edward II by procurement of Hugh Spencer the younger and [Robert] Baldocke were so unreasonable as to be inadmissible – as the king's prohibition not to have place in a personal action before the chancellor: if a freeman of the town hurts a scholar the freeman is imprisoned until he makes recompense, but if a scholar hurts a freeman he is imprisoned only until the vice-chancellor requires him to be released, without any recompense; if a freeman's servant grievously hurts or kills a scholar and flees his master is bound to seek him in peril of standing in judgement for him. If this article is allowed a composition between the town and university for appeasing divers variances between them will be made void.

3. The kind of victuals which the university desires to search and view should be specified: no such view should be taken in daytime by the vice-chancellor or proctors, and the wardens of the same occupations. They are not to take as forfeited anything but such victuals as are corrupt or for sale. Twelve men on oath should find the defaults and assess the amercements.

4. The mayor, bailiffs and burgesses ought to have all forfeitures of merchandise in Stourbridge fair, in consideration of their fee farm, which the university has usurped under pretence of a commandment by Richard II after the grant made to them of assize of bread and ale, made on a surmise that they could not be suffered to use the authority of the assize, affirming that the fair was within the suburbs, and that false weights and measures were used there. Therefore they were commanded to search all weights and measures in the fair as they did in the town; they have no title for other searches. Since then they have encroached more and more on the liberties of the town, so that yearly on the day after the Nativity of Our Lady [September 9] the university commissary, with four bedels, two proctors, two taskers, with their servants and common crier and sixteen men in harness come to the fair, about a mile outside the town, and make solemn proclamations, without any authority, as if the lawful owners of the fair. The commissary then keeps a court in the form of the civil law, and convenes all persons for all injuries and personal actions, wherever committed. The proctors search all merchandise – except

leather and sackcloth – and seize as forfeited all that pleases them, to the manifest wrong of the mayor and bailiffs in their lawful franchise. The taskers take 4d. of every cart laden with oatsheaves and 1d. for every bushel of mustard seed, over and above great fines of persons keeping victualling booths within the fair for dispensing bread, wine, ale, &c., up to 1s. 8d., and taking 4d. of divers men for the sign poles of their ale house booths, and other notable exactions. About fifteen years ago the town complained to the king's council and order was taken by the archbishop of Canterbury, the late duke of Norfolk and others that all victuals be searched indifferently by two of the university and two of the town, and all forfeitures be kept until the council determined which of the two parties should enjoy them. The mayor and bailiffs beg that the charters of the university be examined, and that they may be ordered to use and have those things which of right it ought to have.

5. Concerning the expulsion of bawds and common women from the university and town: the university ought not to deal with them, as their desire is, and as they have lately usurped, for the authority thereof is committed to the mayor by charters granted to the university, considering that such business is not agreeable to their study. According to the charters, on notification from the chancellor or his deputy, the mayor is to issue a proclamation that all such lewd persons avoid the university and town, on pain of punishment if they tarry. For the better execution thereof, at a yearly meeting called the black assembly the vice-chancellor and proctor administer an oath to two aldermen, four burgesses and two of every parish to search by day and night for vagabonds, lewd and suspect persons; this the aldermen and others have attempted to do and have sustained much displeasure, sometimes being put in danger of their lives, by the scholars, who will not permit them to do their duties. The townsmen desire either to be allowed to perform these duties or to be released from their oaths.

The answer of the mayor, bailiffs and burgesses to the new requests made by the university.

1. If the king grants to the university that no common taker or purveyor shall by virtue of any commission take any victuals in Cambridge market or within five miles, the town prays that this shall not be prejudicial to any burgess or other person residing within five miles of the town for dealing in any kind of victuals or merchandise.

2. The town will accept the protector's pleasure that horses of all masters of colleges, halls and hostels, resident students and doctors of medicine should not be taken to ride post; but they desire that horses of householders in the town and suburbs that bear the name of scholars' servants may be taken for this purpose and other royal business.

3. The town never intended that any musters should be taken of scholars, doctors of medicine or their household servants, or of the bedels, cooks, manciples or butlers of any college, hostel or hall; but that all other inhabitants of the town should be so liable, and be charged according to composition between the town and university, and the doctors of medicine, bedels, cooks and manciples, being householders, to be chargeable accordingly.

4. If the vice-chancellor and masters of colleges and their successors were justices of peace, and had the only order of scholars and their servants, it is to be feared that there would be very much inconvenience between the said bodies, as frays, breaking up of houses in the night, and other notable offences, and little punishment. The town therefore prays that justices of the peace and gaol delivery, being temporal offices, should be appointed from time to time by the king's commission, as in the rest of the country. But if it is thought convenient that the university should have justices of the peace and gaol delivery within themselves, let it also have its own prison and not meddle with that belonging to the mayor and bailiffs. Nor let it have power to call anyone to its sessions other than scholars and their servants – for if they did, the townsmen would be driven away.

[5]. Tradesmen and householders of the town, some of whom are very rich men, who are made launderers of colleges – formerly poor women's offices – or else admitted to some other small offices in the colleges or university, and thereby becoming scholars' servants in order only to be privileged in all things by the university and discharged of financial obligations to the town, should not be recognised as scholars' servants as they have been lately – whereby the town has been disturbed and its estate much decayed, and in a few years will be undone thereby, unless the protector and council take some order for the same.                                                                         SP 10/3, no. 3

**78.**   January 12. Account by John Bird, bishop of Chester, in accordance with the orders of the lord protector, of the sale of church goods within the diocese of Chester, and of the appropriation thereof.

   *Deanery of Richmond.* Churches and chapels of Richmond, Romaldkirk, Croft, Ainderby [Steeple], Easby, South Cowton, Marske, Melsonby, Barton, Middleton [Tyas], Rokeby, [Kirkby] Ravensworth, [Kirkby] Wiske, Forcett, Barningham, Bowes, Manfield St John, Grinton, Startforth, [West] Gilling, [Great] Langton, Brignall, Marrick, Catterick, Hunton, Danby [Wiske], [Great] Smeaton, Wycliffe, [East] Cowton: nothing alienated or sold. *Deanery of Catterick.* Bedale: chalice sold for 40s. for repair of the church, by Marmaduke Paris, William Clapam, John Webstare and Richard Lumley, churchwardens. Well: vestments and cope [*described*] sold by James Lambert, Cuthbert Andreson and Richard Willson, churchwardens. Other churches and chapels (Hornby, Masham, Coverham, Patrick Brompton, [Thornton] Watlass, Pickhill, Thornton Steward, Fleetham, Middleham, [West] Tanfield, Burneston, Aysgarth, Scruton, Wath, Spennithorne, Fingall): nothing alienated or sold. *Deanery of Copeland.* Churches and chapels of Ponsonby, St Bridget [Beckermet], Harrington, Lamplugh, Arlecdon, Dean, Egremont, 'Crudall', St Bees, Millom, Cleator, Drigg, Irton, Cockermouth, Lorton, Brigham, Gosforth, Haile, Bootle, 'Wicliff', Corney: nothing alienated or sold. *Deanery of Furness.* Churches and chapels of Pennington, Cartmel, Ulverston, Dalton, Kirkby Ireleth, Aldingham: nothing alienated or sold. *Deanery of Amounderness.* Broughton: two chalices sold for £4 to Messrs Singleton and Barton, for building the rood loft. Preston: silver cross sold to Oliver Brevis for £3.6.8, for church repairs, by Roger Aston, William Sindall, Richard Thornboror and Alex Hogekynson, churchwardens. Lancaster: two chalices sold for £5 by the parishioners to the hands of Richard Burton, Richard Dowson and others, churchwardens, kept for payment of debts. Chipping: their one chalice laid in gage to Robert Sherburn to maintain the churchwardens' suit against Dr [George] Wolfitt the parson. Kirkham: silver cross pledged for £20 for repair of rood loft, by George Sharpuls and Richard Browne, churchwardens. Poulton [le Fylde]: chalice pledged for £1.13.4 to George Kyghley, for repair of the church. Stalmine: two chalices pledged for needs for the church. St Michael's [on Wyre]: two chalices sold to Mr Kyrkbe and William Easton for repair of the church and bells. Ribchester: nothing alienated or sold. *Deanery of Lonsdale.* Sedburgh: a cross was bought by James Cowes, but the church masters [*sic*] are not certain whether he gave it to the church or not. Caton: chalice sold for 5 marks [£3.6.8] for building a schoolhouse. Other churches and chapels (Clapham, Tatham, Bentham, Ingleton, Thornton, 'Singham', Melling, [Kirkby] Lonsdale, Tunstall, Claughton, Whittington): nothing alienated or sold. *Deanery of Kendal.* Hevershsham: two chalices sold for £9 for church repairs. Kendal: not yet certified. Warton: churchwardens allege they have made their certificate to the king's visitors. Other churches and chapels (Bolton [le Sands], Burton, Beetham, Heysham): nothing alienated or sold. *Deanery of Boroughbridge* : nothing alienated or sold. *Deanery of Malpas.* Churches and chapels of Malpas, Aldford, Handley, Tilston, Coddington, Tattenhall: nothing alienated or sold. *Deanery of Chester.* St Peter's: silver cross sold for £4.12.6 for a side aisle, by William Brasse and Ranulph Cune, churchwardens. St Michael's: silver cross of 82 oz. @ 5s. the oz. sold for coverings of the church and other repairs, by Robert Percevall, Thomas Monkisfeld and others, churchwardens. *Deanery of Wirral.* Churches and chapels of Eastham, Bromborough, Heswall, Neston, Backford, Stoke, Bebington, Woodchurch, Upton, Shotwick, Burton, Wallasey, West Kirby, Bidston: nothing alienated or sold. *Deaneries of Middlewich, Macclesfield and Bangor.* Churches and chapels of Middlewich, Davenham, [Church] Lawton, Brereton, Sandbach, Goostrey, Holmes Chapel and Swettenham, Astbury, Bangor, Hanmer, Macclesfield, Prestbury, Wilmslow, Northenden, Cheadle, Stockport, Mottram, Taxal, Gawesworth, Pott, Mobberley, Alderley: nothing alienated or sold. *Deanery of Nantwich.* Audlem: chalice sold for £6.15.4 for lead to cover the church, by Hugh Bolton, Thomas Eyton and others, churchwardens. [Church] Minshull: chalice, cope and vestment sold to Thomas Walker for 10 marks [£6.13.4] by Laurence Holfelde and Roger Knyght, churchwardens. Wybunbury: cross and two silver cruets sold for £19 for the church, in great decay, by Edward Picton and William Clutton, churchwardens. Other churches and chapels: nothing alienated or sold. *Deanery of Frodsham.* Rostherne: cross sold for £15 and chalice for 4 marks [£2.13.4] to Jenkin Broke, for maintaining the church, yet in building. Other churches and chapels: nothing alienated or sold. *Deaneries of Manchester, Leyland and Blackburn*: nothing alienated or sold. *Deanery of Warrington.* Childwall: chalice sold for 40s. bestowed on the bells, by William Crosse and others, churchwardens. Wigan: three chalices sold for £8.18.9 bestowed on payment for bells bought of the king, by James Anderton and Robert Chalnor, churchwardens. Warrington: nothing alienated or sold, but bill of goods delivered to John Rigewaye and others, churchwardens. Other churches and chapels: nothing alienated or sold.

*Parchment, with tag for seal (missing). Partly in Latin.*

*Signed by*: the bishop.                                            SP 10/3, no. 4

**79.** January 19. [Penzance]. Examination and confession of John Lodwyke *alias* Gonner of Bristol before John Mellyton, esq., sheriff of Cornwall, John Godolhan, esq., Richard Gayre, gent., John Arscott, priest, Henry Kelevas, gent., Michael Vyvyan, gent., and others.

Lodwyke, who arrived in Penzance on January 16, said that the captain of the *Xpofer* of Leith in Scotland confessed to him in the ship at sea, being taken prisoner with him, that on Thursday before Christmas last there arrived in Dumbarton haven in Scotland seven French ships, wherein was young Garrett of Kildare [Gerald FitzGerald] with forty or fifty French captains. The captain of the *Xpofer* said that Kildare should marry the Scots queen and so raise all Ireland for them against England in a short time; and further, that before Easter there would be a battle in England between us and them, that all England should rue it. Moreover they confessed that fifteen or more Scots had landed in Ireland at the Skerries at Portrush, and from there have subdued all the coast to Strangford. At the departure of the captain of the *Xpofer* from the coast on January 14 they had taken Strangford and remained there. Lodwyk is master of the *Kateryne Sumpter* of Bristol, which was owned by Leonard Sumpter and which was taken with the *Xpofer* off Land's End on January 15. Leonard Sumpter and two others remain prisoners with the captain of the *Xpofer*.

*Signed by*: Lodwyke.

Thomas Verdon of Dundarave in Ireland, mariner, says he was taken with others by the *Xpofer* on Christmas Eve in the bark *Patrycke* of Dundarave in 'Knockefergos' bay and carried to Dumbarton haven. There he saw the said seven ships and spoke with several mariners who showed him that they had brought young Garrett and had put him ashore, and said that he should be king of Scotland, &c. From there the *Xpofer* departed and sailed to Strangford, where he went ashore with the captain and saw the fifteen Scots land, as above said; and also how they came to Strangford, and spoke with the captain of the Scotsmen, James Maconyll of the outer isles.

*Signed by*: Verdon.                                                    SP 10/3, no. 5

**80.** February 1. Ely Place. The earl of Warwick to William Cecil.

This bearer, my servant, will explain that I write at the request of my neighbours concerning a free school where poor folk are found, to obtain the protector's favour for its preferment, which they would keep in the same foundation. In this he would act charitably, and your furtherance will be honestly considered by them.

*Holograph.*                                                           SP 10/3, no. 6

[For SP 10/3, no. 7 see no. **9** above.]

**81.** February 20. Aylesbury. Certificate of musters for the three hundreds of Aylesbury, Buckinghamshire, taken by Sir Anthony Lee, Richard Grenewaye, William Dormer and John Babham, esquires, appointed by commission dated February 4 and received February 11.

*Aylesbury.* Archers – 2; billmen – 14; almain rivets – 6 pairs for billmen, 2 pairs for archers. *Aston Clinton.* Archer – 1; billmen – 4; almain rivets – 1 pair for billman. *Monks Risborough.* Billmen – 5; almain rivets – 1 pair for billman. *Little Kimble.* Billman – 1; almain rivets – 1 pair for billman. *Bledlow.* Archer – 1; billmen – 5; jacks – 1 for archer, 1 for billman. *Little Missenden.* Archer – 1; billman – 1; almain rivets – 1 pair for billman. *Cuddington.* Billmen – 6; almain rivets – 1 pair for billman. *Hulcott.* Billman – 1; almain rivets – 1 pair for billman. *Great Missenden.* Archer – 1; billmen – 7; jacks – 1 for archer, 1 for billman. *Stoke [Mandeville].* Horseman – 1; almain rivets – 1 pair for billman. *Walton.* Billman – 1; almain rivets – 3 pairs for billmen. *Wendover 'foren' and 'burgus'.* Archers – 2; arquebusier – 1; billmen – 15; almain rivets – 1 pair for archer, 1 pair for billman. *Bierton with Broughton.* Archer – 1; billmen – 9; almain rivets – 1 pair for archer, 1 pair for billmen. *Ellesborough.* Archer – 1; billman – 1; almain rivets – 1 pair for billman. William Hawtrey, gent., servant to Sir Edmund Peckham: horse – 1. *Princes Risborough.* Archer – 1; billmen – 6; almain rivets – 1 pair for archer. *Haddenham.* Horeseman – 1; archers – 2; billmen – 8; almain rivets – 1 pair for archer, 1 pair for billman. Edmund Astell, gent. and William Clarke, servant to Sir Robert Dormer: light horses – 2. *Brondes. Lee.* Billmen – 2; almain rivets – 1 pair for billman. *Buckland.* Billmen – 4; almain rivets – 1 pair for billman. *Stone.* Billmen – 5; jack – 1 for billman. *Weston Turville. [North] Lee.* Billmen – 3; jack – 1 for archer; almain rivets – 1 pair for billman. *Hartwell cum [Little] Hampden.* Billmen – 2; almain rivets – 1 pair for billman. *Dinton. Upton.* Archer – 1; billmen – 2; almain rivets – 3 pairs for billmen. *Halton.* Archer – 1; billmen – 2; jack – 1 for billman. *Great Hampden.* Billman – 1; almain rivets – 1 pair for billman. House of Sir John Hampden: archer – 1; horseman – 1; harnesses – 1 for horseman, 1 for archer; horses – 2. *Horsenden.* House of Sir Edward Dune: archer – 1; billmen – 3; almain rivets – 2 pairs for billmen. *Great Kimble.* Billmen – 2; almain rivets – 1 pair for billman. Griffith Rychard, esq.: almain rivets – 2 pairs for archers; bows – 3; sheaves of arrows – 3; bills – 3. House of Sir Anthony Lee: light horsemen – 4; arquebusier – 1; archers – 4; billmen – 9; almain rivets – 2 pairs for archers, 4 pairs for billmen; trotting horse furnished for a demilance – 1; light geldings furnished for light horsemen – 2. House of Richard Greneway: archers – 2; arquebusiers – 2; billmen – 8; almain rivets – 2 pairs for archers, 2 pairs for billmen.

*Total men*: 161 (light horsemen – 7; arquebusiers – 4; archers – 23; billmen – 127). *Total arms*: 58 (jacks – 3, harnesses for archers – 16, for horseman – 1, for billmen – 41). Great horses – 4; light geldings – 4.

*Names specified.*

*Signed and sealed by*: Lee and Greneway.                              SP 10/3, no. 8

**82.** February 27. Holmes Chapel. View of musters for the hundred of Northwich,

Cheshire taken by Sir William Brereton, Sir Thomas Venables and William Moreton, esq.

*Archers.* Cranage – 1. Tetton – 1 (with jack, sallet and splints). Bradwall. Hollins [Green] – 1. Arclid – 1 (with sallet). Sandbach – 1. Witton. Cross – 4. Lostock Gralam – 2 (with jacks, sallets, bows and arrows). Nether Peover – 1 (with jack, sallet, bows and arrows). Leftwich – 1 (with harness). Lees – 1. Total -14. *Billmen.* Holmes Chapel – 6 (with 3 jacks, 1 sallet, 2 bills, 2 [pairs of] splints. Cranage – 10 (with 3 jacks, 2 sallets, 1 stole, 1 [pair of] splints). Tetton – 3 (with 2 jacks, 2 sallets, 3 [pairs of] splints, 3 bills). Moston – 3 (with 3 jacks, 2 sallets, 2 bills, 1 [pair of] splints). Elton – 4 (with 3 jacks, 3 sallets, 1 bow, 1 [pair of] splints). Warmingham – 4 (with 2 jacks, 2 sallets, 1 [pair of] splints, 2 bills). Bradwell. Hollins [Green] – 8 (with 1 jack). Wheelock – 3 (with 3 jacks, 3 sallets, 2 [pairs of] splints, 3 bills). Arclid – 2 (with 1 jack, 1 sallet, 1 [pair of] splints, 1 axe). Sandbach – 12 (with 9 jacks, 9 sallets, 8 [pairs of] splints, 7 bills, 2 bows). Brereton – 8 (with 3 jacks, 3 sallets, 2 [pairs of] splints, 3 bills). Swettenham – 4. Hulme Walfield – 3 (with 3 jacks, 3 sallets, 3 bills). Astbury – 5 (with 1 jack, 1 sallet). Davenport – 1. Kermincham – 3. Buglawton – 9 (with 1 sallet, 2 bills). Somerford – 3 (with 1 jack, 1 harness for a footman). Newbold – 6 (with 1 harness for a footman). Moreton [cum] Alcumlow – 3 (with 1 harness for a footman, 1 jack). [Odd] Rode – 7 (with 4 harnesses for footmen). Smallwood – 5 (with 2 harnesses for footmen, 1 bill, 1 sallet). Church Lawton – 8. Congelton – 17. Total – 136. *Billmen with harness.* Witton. Cross – 15 (with 15 jacks, 15 sallets, 12 [pairs of] splints, 8 bills, 5 poleaxes). Northwich – 4 (with 4 jacks, 4 sallets, 4 [pairs of] splints, 4 bills). Middlewich – 2 (with 2 jacks, 2 sallets, 2 bills and 1 [pair of] splints). Allostock – 5 (with 5 jacks, 5 sallets, 5 bills, 5 [pairs of] splints). Lostock Gralam – 14 (with 14 jacks, 14 sallets, 14 bills, 13 [pairs of] splints). Nether Peover – 4 (with 4 jacks, 4 sallets, 4 bills). Newton – 1 (with jack, sallet and bill). Waverton – 5 (with 5 jacks, 5 sallets, 5 bills, 2 [pairs of] splints. Bostock – 6 (with 6 jacks, 6 sallets, 6 bills, 3 [pairs of] splints). Stanthorne – 5 (with 5 jacks, 5 sallets, 5 bills, 5 [pairs of] splints). Rudheath – 2 (with 2 jacks, 1 sallet, 1 steel cap, 1 [pair of] splints, 2 bills). Yatehouse – 1 (with jack, sallet, bill and splints). Davenham – 2 (with 2 jacks, 2 sallets, 2 bills, 2 [pairs of] splints). Leftwich – 3 (with 3 jacks, 3 sallets, 3 bills, 3 [pairs of] splints). Whatcroft – 1 (with jack, sallet, bill and splints). Eccleston – 1 (with jack, sallet, bill and splints). Hulse – 1 (with jack, sallet, bill and splints). Sutton – 1 (with jack, sallet, bill and splints). Total 209. *Able men lacking harness.* Witton. Cross – 9. Northwich – 22. Allostock – 20. Lostock Gralam – 15. Middlewich – 35. Kinderton – 19. Nether Peover – 11. Newton – 11. Wanerton – 10 (with 1 poleaxe, 2 jacks). Bostock – 8. Shurlach – 4. Stanthorne – 5. Minshull Vernon – 6 (with 1 jack, 2 [pairs of] splints). Shipbrook – 4. Clive – 5 (with 3 jacks, 1 sallet). Rudheath – 9 (with 2 jacks, 1 bill). Yatehouse – 9 (with 1 jack, 2 sallets). Davenham – 2. Leftwich – 10 (with 5 jacks, 2 sallets, 2 bills). Whatcroft – 1 (with jack and stole). Wimboldsley – 9 (with 1 poleaxe). Eaton – 3. Eccleston – 5. Hulse – 3. Sutton – 3. Lach Dennis – 3. Goostrey – 19 (with 8 jacks, 2 sallets, 7 bills). Twemlow – 6 (with 6 jacks, 1 sallet, 1 bill). Lees – 7 (with 3 jacks, 1 sallet, 4 bills). *Men unable to serve, with harness.* Witton. Cross – 4 (with 4 jacks, 2 sallets, 2 [pairs of] splints, 2 poleaxes). Northwich – 3 (with 3 jacks, 2 sallets, 1 stole, 1 bill, 1 poleaxe, 1 [pair of] splints. Middlewich – 2 (with 2 jacks, 2 sallets, 2 bills, 2 [pairs of] splints). Lostock Gralam – 6 (with 6 jacks, 6 sallets, 6 bills, 6 [pairs of] splints). Nether Peover – 5 (with 5 jacks, 3 sallets, 3 bills, 1 [pair of] splints). Newton – 3 (with 3 jacks, 3 sallets, 3 bills, 3 [pairs of] splints). Wanerton – 2 (with 1 jack, 1 bill, 2 [pairs of] splints). Bostock – 5 (with 4 jacks, 3 sallets, 2 bills). Rudheath – 4 (with 2 jacks, 1 sallet, 1 steel cap). Yatehouse – 1 (with jack). Davenham – 4 (with 4 jacks, 1 sallet, 2 bills, 1 [pair of] splints). Leftwich – 1 (with jack). Whatcroft – 3 (with 3 jacks, 3 sallets). Wilmboldsley – 1 (with sallet and bill). Eaton – 2 (with 2 jacks, 2 sallets, 1 bill). 'Mooton' – 3 (with 2 jacks, 1 sallet, 1 bill, 1 [pair of] splints, 2 poleaxes). Croxton – 4 (with 4 jacks, 4 sallets, 4 bills, 4 [pairs of] splints). Hulse – 2 (with 2 jacks, 1 sallet, 1 [pair of] splints). Sutton – 1 (with jack and sallet). Lach

Dennis – 2 (with 2 jacks, 2 sallets, 2 bills, 2 [pairs of] splints). Goostrey – 1 (with jack, sallet, bill and splints). Twemlow – 3 (with 3 jacks, 2 sallets). Holmes Chapel – 7 (with 7 jacks, 6 sallets, 6 bills, 1 [pair of] splints). Cranage – 8 (with 7 jacks, 6 sallets, 3 bills, 1 [pair of] splints, 1 stole). Tetton – 3 (with 3 jacks, 2 sallets, 2 [pairs of] splints, 2 bills). Moston – 5 (with 4 jacks, 5 sallets, 1 [pair of] splints, 4 bills). Elton – 7 (with 7 jacks, 6 sallets, 5 [pairs of] splints, 4 bills). Warmingham – 3 (with 3 jacks, 3 sallets, 2 [pairs of] splints, 3 bills. Bradwall. Hollins [Green] – 9 (with 9 jacks, 3 sallets, 2 [pairs of] splints, 2 bills). Wheelock – 3 (with 2 jacks, 3 sallets). Arclid – 3 (with 3 jacks, 1 sallet, 1 bill). Sandbach – 9 (with 9 jacks, 8 sallets, 6 [pairs of] splints, 6 bills, 1 stole). Brereton – 16 (with 16 jacks, 15 sallets, 8 bills, 10 [pairs of] splints). Swettenham – 6 (with 4 jacks, 1 sallet, 1 bill, 1 horse and harness for man). Hulme Walfield – 6 (with 5 jacks, 4 sallets, 4 bills, 1 [pair of] splints. Astbury – 1 (with bill). Davenport – 1 (with harness for a footman). Kermincham – 9 (with 1 harness for a footman, 4 jacks, 2 [pairs of] splints, 2 bills, 1 sallet). Buglawton – 23 (with 9 harnesses for footmen, 12 jacks, 3 sallets, 5 bills). Somerford – 8 (with 1 horse and harness for man, 2 harnesses for footmen, 3 jacks, 1 sallet, 3 bills, 1 [pair of] splints). Newbold – 20 (with 9 jacks, 9 harnesses for footmen, 1 sallet, 5 bills, 1 [pair of] splints, 2 bows). Moreton [cum] Alculmow – 7 (with 6 jacks, 1 [pair of] splints, 1 harness for a footman). [Odd] Rode – 15 (with 10 harnesses for footmen, 2 jacks, 3 sallets, 1 bill, 1 [pair of] splints). Smallwood 17 (with 6 harnesses for footmen, 7 jacks, 3 sallets, 3 bills, 1 [pair of] splints). Church Lawton – 18 (with 12 harnesses for footmen, 2 jacks, 3 sallets, 2 bills, 1 [pair of] splints, 1 dagger). Congleton – 14 (with 1 horse and harness for man, 5 harnesses for footmen, 7 jacks, 4 sallets, 1 [pair of] splints).

Totals given: archers – 14; able billmen – 389; total men – 403.

*Names specified.*

*Signed by*: the commissioners.                                    SP 10/3, no. 9

**83.** February 29. York. Certificate of musters for the city of York and the wapentake of Ainsty and the liberties thereof taken by Robert Paycok, mayor, Sir William Fairfax, Sir Robert Stapleton, John North, Robert Elwald, Robert Heckylton, Peter Robynson, John Beane and William Holme, aldermen, and Thomas Standevyn and James Symson, sheriffs.

[*City of York*]. *Walmgate Ward. St Michael Ousebridgend.* Archers – 18 (equipped – 18; horses – 6; coats of plate – 6; jack – 1; white harnesses – 2; bows – 18; sheaves of arrows – 7 and 11 halves; sallets – 5). Billmen – 37 (equipped – 21, of whom 1 not able; horses – 7; white harnesses – 6; sallets – 5; battle axes – 6; bills – 15; jacks – 4; coat of plate -1). *St Peter le Willows.* Billmen – 10 (equipped – 10, of whom 2 not able; horse – 1; harness – 1; jack – 1; bills – 9). *St Peter the Little.* Archers – 10 (equipped 10; horses – 4; coat of plate – 1; jack – 1; bows – 10; sheaves of arrows – 5 and 5 halves; sallets – 2). Billmen – 3 (equipped – 3; jack – 1; bills – 3). *St Denys.* Archers – 2· (equipped – 2; horse – 1; jack – 1; bows – 2; sheaves of arrows – 1 & ½). Billmen – 26 (equipped – 22, of whom 2 not able; horses – 7; coats of plate – 3; jacks – 12; sallets – 11; battle axe – 1; bills – 14; lead malls – 2; eyelet coat – 1; pair of splints – 1). *Micklegate Ward. St John [at] Ousebridgend.* Archers – 14 (equipped – 10; horses – 6; coats of plate – 2; almain rivets – 1; jacks – 6; bows – 9; sheaves of arrows – 9; sallets – 7; pairs of splints – 5). Billmen – 17 (equipped – 14, of whom 2 not able; horses – 8; harness – 1; jacks – 7; almain rivets – 3; sallets – 8; bills – 12; pairs of splints – 6; coats of plate – 2). *[Holy] Trinity.* Archers – 5 (equipped – 3, of whom 1 not able; horses – 2; eyelet coat – 1; coat of plate – 1; jack – 1; sallets – 3; bows – 3; sheaves of arrows – 2 & ½). Billmen – 24 (equipped – 20; horses – 6; jacks – 8; steel coat – 1; sallets – 4; pairs of splints – 3; bills – 18; battle axe – 1). *All Saints, North Street.* Archers – 4 (equipped – 1; jack – 1). Billmen – 17 (equipped – 15, of whom 1 not able and 1 a widow; horses – 5; white harnesses – 2; jacks – 6; almain rivets – 1; sallets –

6; pairs of splints – 6; bills – 12; battle axe – 1). *Bishophill Senior.* Billmen – 11 (equipped – 6; horses – 2; jacks – 3; almain rivets – 1; sallets – 3; pair of splints – 1; pairs of chains – 2; bills – 6). *Clementhorpe.* Billmen – 5 (equipped – 1; jack – 1; sallet – 1; bill – 1). *Bishophill Junior.* Archer – 1 (equipped – 1; coat of plate – 1; bow – 1; sheaf of arrows – ½). Billmen – 8 (equipped – 2, of whom 1 not able; jacks – 2; sallet – 1; bills – 2). *St Gregory.* Billmen – 11 (equipped – 4; coat of plate – 1; almain rivets – 1; jack – 1; bill – 1). *St Martin.* Archers – 12 (equipped – 3; horses – 2; steel coats – 2; jack – 1; sallets – 3; bows – 3; sheaves of arrows – 2 & ½). Billmen – 17 (equipped – 11; horses – 2; jacks – 7; sallets – 3; pairs of splints – 2; bills – 11). [*Another, untitled*]. Billmen – 16 (equipped – 16; jack – 1; sallets – 2; bills – 16). *St Crux.* Archers – 13 (equipped – 13; horses – 8; coats of plate – 6; jacks – 2; sallets – 7; pairs of splints – 2; bows – 13; sheaves of arrows – 10 and 3 halves). Billmen – 34 (equipped – 31; horses – 14; coats of plate – 4; almain rivets – 1; white harness – 1; jacks – 9; sallets – 8; pairs of splints – 4; bills – 31). *St Lawrence.* Archers – 9 (equipped – 9, of whom 1 not able; horses – 2; coats of plate – 2; white harness – 1; jack – 1; sallets – 2; pair of splints – 1; bows – 9; sheaves of arrows – 3 and 6 halves). Billmen – 11 (equipped – 11; horse – 1; sallet – 1; bills – 11; jack – 1). *All Saints Pavement.* Archers – 7 (equipped – 7; horses – 2; coat of plate – 1; jacks – 3; sallets – 4; bows – 7; sheaves of arrows – 5 and 2 halves). Billmen – 15 (equipped – 15; horses – 5; white harness – 1; coat of plate – 1; jacks – 7; sallets – 7; pairs of splints – 3; pairs of chains – 3; bills – 13; battle axes – 2). *St Margaret.* Archers – 15 (equipped – 11; horse – 1; jacks – 2; bows – 11; sheaves of arrows – 2 and 9 halves). Billmen – 21 (equipped – 21; horses – 3; white harness – 1; jacks – 8; coat of plate – 1; sallets – 2; bills – 20; lead mall – 1). Man with javelin – 1. Gunner with hand gun – 1. *St Mary Castlegate.* Archers – 5. Billmen – 3 (equipped – 3; horses – 3; white harnesses – 2). *Bootham Ward. St Helen Stonegate.* Archers – 7 (equipped* – 5; horse – 1; almain rivets – 1; sallet – 1; pair of splints – 1; harness – 1; bows – 3; sheaves of arrows – 3 halves). Gunner with hand gun – 1. Billmen – 26 (equipped * – 19; horses – 2; jacks – 10; sallets – 9; pairs of splints – 4; pair of chains – 1; bills – 15; lead mall – 1). *St Michael le Belfry.* Archers – 15 (equipped * – 5; horses – 4; coat of plate – 1; white harness – 1; sallet – 1; bow – 1; sheaf of arrows – 1). Billmen – 49 (equipped 31, of whom 2 not able; unequipped – 18, of whom 1 not able; horses – 19; coats of plate – 16; white harnesses – 7; almain rivets – 2; jacks – 4; sallets – 14; pairs of splints – 4; bills – 23). Gunners with arquebuses – 3. *St Olave.* Constables – 2. Archers – 7 (equipped * – 2; coat of plate – 1; harness – 1; sallet – 1; pair of splints – 1; bow – 1; sheaf of arrows – 1). Billmen – 19 (equipped * – 5; coats of plate – 2; harness – 1; jacks – 2; sallets – 3). Gunner with hand gun – 1. *St Martin, Coney Street.* Archers – 11 (equipped – 10, of whom 1 not able; horses – 2; coats of plate – 4; harness – 1; sallets – 4; steel bonnet – 1; bills – 2; halberd – 1; pairs of splints – 3; bows – 11; sheaves of arrows – 9). Billmen – 29 (equipped – 28, of whom 1 not able; horse – 1; breast plates – 2; back plates – 2; coats of plate – 2; white harness – 1; pair of splints – 1; sallets – 8; jacks – 3; bills – 25; battle axes – 3). *St Wilfred.* Constables – 2. Archers – 2 (equipped – 2; jacks – 2; sallets – 2; bows – 2; sheaves of arrows – 2; pair of splints – 1). Billmen – 9. *Monks Ward. Holy Trinity, Goodramgate.* Archers – 3 (equipped – 2; horse – 1; bows – 2; sheaves of arrows – 2). Billmen – 13 (equipped – 13, of whom 2 not able; horses – 4; coat of plate – 1; jacks – 5; sallets – 7; battle axes – 1; bills – 10; lead malls – 2; pair of splints – 1. Man with great horse for demilance and harness – 1. *St Saviour.* Archers – 6 (equipped – 4; jack – 1; sallet – 1; bows – 4; sheaves of arrows – 1 and 3 halves). Billmen – 15 (equipped – 6; jacks – 6; sallets – 6; pairs of splints – 4; bills – 6). *St Helen on the Walls.* Archer – 1 (equipped – 1; jack – 1; sallet – 1; bow – 1; sheaf of arrows – 1). Billmen – 9 (equipped – 2; coat of plate – 1; jack – 1; sallets – 2; bill – 1; battle axe – 1). *St Andrew.* Billmen – 5. Gunner – 1 (equipped – 1; horse – 1; coat of plate – 1; hand gun – 1). *St Mary Layerthorpe.* Archer – 1 (equipped – 1; bow – 1; sheaf of arrows – 1). Billmen – 3 (equipped – 3; bills – 3). *Christ's.*

*      Including men listed as 'without harness' but with some items of armour or weapons.

Archers – 10 (equipped – 5; horses – 3; coats of plate – 4; buff coat – 1; sallets – 5; bows – 5; sheaves of arrows – 5). Billmen – 31 (equipped* – 19; horses – 12; jacks – 14; sallets – 10; pairs of splints – 3; bills – 14; coat of plate – 1). *St Morys*. Billmen – 20 (equipped – 2; horse – 1; jacks – 2; bills – 2). Unable men – 2 (equipped – 2; jacks – 2; sallets – 2; bills – 2). *St John del Pyke*. Archer – 1 (equipped – 1; white harness – 1; bow – 1; sheaf of arrows – 1). Billmen – 8 (equipped – 3; jack – 1; sallet – 1; bills – 3). Gunner with gun – 1. Unable man – 1 (equipped – 1; sallet – 1; bill – 1; pair of splints – 1). *St Sampson*. Archers – 12 (equipped – 5; horses – 2; coats of plate – 3; sallets – 3; bows – 5; sheaves of arrows – 3 and 2 halves). Billmen – 16 (equipped – 5; horses – 3; sallets – 4; jacks – 3; pairs of splints – 3; bills – 5). Unable men – 2 (equipped – 2; coat of plate – 1; sallet – 1; jack – 1; bills – 2; pair of splints – 1). Musters taken on 28 February 1548. *Ainsty*. *[Long] Marston*. Constable – 1 (not able; jack – 1). Archers – 5 (equipped – 3; horses – 3; sallet – 1; harnesses – 2). Billmen – 22 (equipped – 12, of whom 3 not able; horses – 4; coat of plate – 1; jacks – 5; sallets – 7; bills – 2; pair of splints – 1). *Colton*. Constable – 1. Archers – 2 (equipped – 1; jack – 1). Billmen – 11 (equipped – 5, of whom 1 not able; jacks – 5; sallets – 3). *Moor Monkton*. Constable – 1. Billmen – 10 (equipped – 8, of whom 2 not able; jacks – 7; sallets – 4; pair of splints – 1; bills – 2). *Walton*. Constable – 1. Archers – 6 (equipped – 5; horses – 2; harnesses – 2; jack – 1; bows – 2; sheaves of arrows – 2). Billmen – 6. *Appleton [Roebuck]*. Constable – 1. Archer – 1. Billmen – 17 (equipped – 9; horse – 1; harnesses – 3; coat of plate – 1; jacks – 5; sallet – 1; pair of splints – 1). *Bickerton*. Archers – 2 (equipped – 1; jack – 1; sallet – 1). Billmen – 8 (equipped – 5; jacks – 5; sallets – 3; pair of splints – 1). *Hessay*. Archer – 1. Billmen – 8 (equipped – 4; jacks – 3; sallets – 3; bill – 1; black bills – 3). *Thorp Arch*. Constable – 1. Archer – 1 (equipped – 1; horse – 1; jack – 1; sallet – 1; bow – 1; sheaf of arrows – 1). Billmen – 12 (equipped – 3; horses – 3; jacks – 3; sallets – 3; steel cap – 1; bills – 3). *Bilbrough*. Billmen – 10 (equipped – 7, of whom 1 not able; horse – 1; jacks – 2; sallet – 1; bills – 6). Spearman – 1 (equipped – 1; horse – 1; harness – 1). *Dringhouses*. Constable – 1. Archers – 2 (equipped – 2; bows – 2). Billmen – 5 (equipped – 4, of whom 1 not able; jacks – 4; sallets – 4; bills – 4). *Tockwith*. Archers – 4 (equipped – 4, of whom 1 not able; harness – 1; coat of plate – 1; jacks – 2; sallets – 2; bows – 2; sheaves of arrows – 2). Billmen – 9 (equipped – 9, of whom 3 not able; horse – 1; harnesses – 2; jacks – 6; sallets – 6; bills – 6). Spearman – 1 (equipped – 1; harness – 1). *Bolton Percy*. Constable – 1. Archers – 2 (equipped – 2; coat of plate – 1; jack – 1; sallet – 1; bows – 2). Spearman – 1 (equipped – 1; horse – 1; harness – 1). Billmen – 8 (equipped – 5; harness – 1; coat of plate – 1; jacks – 2; sallets – 3; bills – 4). *Askham Richard*. Constable – 1. Archer – 1. Billmen – 9 (equipped – 6, of whom 2 not able; horse – 1; coat of plate – 1; jacks – 3; sallets – 3; bill – 1; lead mall – 1). *Copmanthorpe*. Constable – 1. Billmen – 12 (equipped – 10, of whom 2 not able; horse – 1; harness – 1; jacks – 3; sallet – 1; bills – 9). Archer – 1 (equipped – 1; bow – 1; sheaf of arrows – 1). *Askham Bryan*. Archers – 3 (equipped – 2; bows – 2; sheaf of arrows – ½). Billmen – 21 (equipped – 7, of whom 2 not able; jacks – 6; sallets – 2; pair of splints – 1; bill – 1). *Acaster Malbis*. Archers – 6 (equipped – 6; jacks – 2; sallets – 2; bows – 6; sheaves of arrows – 4). Billmen – 14 (equipped – 12; horses – 4; jacks – 9; sallets – 9; pair of splints – 1; bills – 6; battle axe – 1; lead mall – 1; sheaf of arrows – 1). Unable men – 4 (equipped – 4; jack – 1; sallets – 2; bills – 3). *Stutton*. Spearman – 1 (equipped – 1; horses – 2; coat of plate – 1; spear – 1). Archers – 2 (equipped – 2; coats of plate – 2; sallets – 2; bows – 2). Billmen – 4 (equipped – 4; coats of plate – 4; sallets – 4; bills – 4). *Bilton*. Constable – 1. Archers – 7 (equipped – 3; horses – 3; harnesses – 2). Billmen – 6 (equipped – 5; horses – 5; sallets – 2; jacks – 4; bills – 2). Able men – 2 (equipped – 2; horses – 3; harnesses – 2; coat of plate – 1; sallet – 1). Unable man – 1 (equipped – 1; horse – 1; sallet – 1, jack – 1; bill – 1). *Acomb 'in Holegait'*. Archers – 6 (equipped – 2; horse – 1; harness – 1; bows – 2; sheaves of arrows – 2). Billmen – 14 (equipped – 8; horse – 1; jacks – 7; sallets – 3; bills – 3). Unable man –

---

*        Including men listed as 'without harness' but with some items of armour or weapons.

1 (equipped – 1; horse – 1; jack – 1; sallet – 1). *Holgate*. Constables – 2. Unable man – 1. *Wighill Hall and the township*. Archers – 9 (equipped – 8; horses – 2; coats of plate – 8; bows – 8; sheaves of arrows – 8). Billmen – 14 (equipped – 7; coat of plate – 1; jacks – 6; sallets – 6; bills – 6). *Bishopthorpe*. Constable – 1. Archers – 6 (equipped – 4; jack – 1; sallet – 1; bows – 2). Billmen – 8 (equipped – 4; jacks – 4; sallets – 2). Unable man – 1 (equipped – 1; jack – 1; sallet – 1). *Nether Poppleton*. Archer – 1 (equipped – 1; horse – 1; harness – 1; bow – 1). Billmen – 11 (equipped – 5; horses – 2; harnesses – 2; jacks – 2; sallet – 1; bills – 2). Unable men – 4 (equipped – 4; horses – 3; jacks – 2; sallet – 1; bills – 2). *Over Poppleton*. Billmen – 19 (equipped – 17; horses – 3; jacks – 4; sallets – 3; bills – 17). Unable men – 3 (equipped – 3; horse – 1; jack – 1; sallets – 3; bills – 3). *Middlethorpe*. Archer – 1. Billmen – 5 (equipped – 1; jack – 1; bill – 1). *Knapton*. Billmen – 11 (equipped – 6; horse – 1; jacks – 3; sallets – 2; bills – 5). *Hutton. Wandesley. Angram*. Archers – 5 (equipped – 2; horse – 1; jack – 1; sallet – 1; bow – 1). Billmen – 16 (equipped – 5; jacks – 5; sallets – 2; bill – 1; lead mall – 1; halberd – 1). Unable men – 2 (equipped – 2; horse – 1; jacks – 2; sallet – 1; bills – 2). *Healaugh. Catterton*. Spearmen – 2 (equipped – 2; horses – 2; coats of plate – 2; sallets – 2). Archer – 1 (equipped – 1; sallet – 1; bow – 1; sheaf of arrows – 1). Billmen – 19 (equipped – 8; horse – 1; jacks – 4; sallets – 2; bills – 7; lead mall – 1). *Rufforth*. Constable – 1. Billmen – 22 (equipped – 12; horses – 2; harnesses – 2; jacks – 7; pair of splints – 1; bills – 6; sallets – 2). Unable man – 1 (equipped – 1; bill – 1). *Acaster Selby*. Constable – 1 (equipped – 1; sallet – 1). Archers – 4 (equipped – 2; horses – 2; harnesses – 2). Billmen – 22 (equipped – 7; jacks – 3; sallets – 3; bill – 1; sheet of mail – 1; lead mall – 1). Unable men – 3 (equipped – 3; horses – 3).

*Totals*.* Light horsemen and spearmen with able horses – 8. Archers with harness and hosting horses – 55. Archers with harness and no horses – 53. Archers without horse or harness – 141. Billmen with harness and hosting horses – 136. Billmen with harness and no horses – 199. Billmen without horse or harness – 453. Unable men with harness and hosting horses – 14. Unable men with harness and no horses – 34. Men with able horse and no harness – 14. Able horses with harness for demilance – 1. Gunners with arquebuses and hand guns – 8.

*Names specified.*

*Signed by*: the commissioners.                                                    SP 10/3, no. 10

**84.** February 29. Certificate of the territorial responsibilities of the commissioners of musters for Cambridgeshire appointed by commission dated February 1 and delivered to the bishop of Ely on February 14.

*Isle of Ely.* Thomas [Goodrich], bishop of Ely; Henry Goderick, arm.; Richard Wylkes, clerk; Thomas Rudston. *Hundreds of Staine, Staploe and Flendish.* Sir Robert Peyton; George Frevyle, arm.; Thomas Rudston; William Walpole. *Hundreds of Papworth, Northstow and Chesterton.* Sir John Hynd; Sir John Cutte; William Cooke, serjeant at law; Thomas Hutton, arm.; Christopher Burgoyn; William Malorye. *Hundreds of Radfield, Cheveley, Chilford and Whittlesford.* John Cotton, arm.; John Huddleston, arm.; James Dyer, arm.; Robert Lokton; John Milsent. *Hundreds of Armingford, [Long]stow, Wetherley and Thriplow.* Thomas Hutton, arm.; Henry Pygott, arm.; Thomas More, arm.; Richard Bury; Richard Warde; Thomas Wendy. *Town of Cambridge.* William Cooke, serjeant at law; Thomas Hutton, arm.; Thomas Wendy; William Bill, clerk.

*Parchment.*

*Signed by*: the bishop of Ely, Sir John Hynde, Sir Robert Peyton, Thomas Hutton, Thomas Rudstone.                                                    SP 10/3, no. 11

**85.** February. Certificate of John Cotton, John Huddyllston, esquires, James Dyer and Robert Lockton, gentlemen, commissioners of musters assigned to the hundreds of

---

*      Totals as given in the MS, not wholly accurate.

Radfield, Cheveley, Chilford and Whittlesford, Cambridgeshire.

*Hundred of Radfield. Balsham.* Archer – 1, billmen – 11, horse – 1, harnesses – 4. *West Wratting.* Archers – 2, billmen – 5, harness – 1. *Weston [Colville].* Billmen – 4, harnesses – 3. *Carlton. Willingham.* Billmen – 2, harness – 1. *Brinkley.* Archers – 3, billmen – 4, harnesses – 3. *Burrough.* Archer – 1, billmen – 4; harnesses – 2. *Westley [Waterless].* Archer – 1, billmen – 3, harnesses – 2. *Dullingham.* Archer – 1, billmen – 5, harnesses – 2. *Stetchworth.* Billmen – 4, harnesses – 3. *Hundred of Cheveley. [Wood] Ditton.* Archers – 2, billman – 1, harnesses – 2. *Cheveley.* Billmen – 4, harnesses – 2. *Kirtling.* Billmen – 5, harnesses – 3. *Ashley.* Billman – 3, harnesses – 2. *Newmarket.* Archer – 1, billmen – 3, harnesses – 3. *Sum of two hundreds.* Men – 71, harnesses – 33. *Hundred[s] of Chilford and Whittlesford. Horseheath.* Billmen – 4, harness – 1. *Pampisford.* Billmen – 5, harness – 1. *Great Abington.* Archer – 1, billmen – 4, harnesses – 2. *Little Abington.* Billmen – 3, harness – 1. *Castle Camps.* Billmen – 5, harnesses – 2. *Babraham.* Billmen – 4, harnesses – 2. *Hildersham.* Billmen – 5, harness – 1. *Bartlow.* Archer – 1, billman – 1, harness – 1. *Wickham.* Billmen – 5, harness – 1. *Linton.* Archer – 1, billmen – 6, harnesses – 3. *Township of Shudy Camps.* Visited by the plague. *Whittlesford.* Archers – 3, billmen – 5, harnesses – 3. *Hinxton.* Billmen – 8, harnesses – 3. *Sawston.* Billmen – 6, harnesses – 4. *Duxford.* Billmen – 7, harnesses – 3. *Ickleton.* Archers – 2, billmen – 6, harnesses – 3. *Total of four hundreds.* Men – 155, harnesses – 67. The countess of Oxford – 3 horses for demilances.

*Parchment.*

*Names specified.*

*Signed by*: the commissioners.                                        SP 10/3, no. 12

**86.**    February. Certificate of Thomas Hutton, Henry Pygot and Richard Ward, esquires, commissioners of musters assigned to the hundreds of Armingford, Long [stow], Wetherley and Thriplow, Cambridgeshire.

*Hundred of [Long]stow. Little Gransden.* Billmen – 3, harnesses – 1 for archer, 1 for billman. *Croxton.* Billmen – 3, harnesses – 2 for billmen. *Caldecote.* 0. *Caxton.* Archer – 1, billmen – 3, harnesses – 2 for billmen. *Toft.* Billmen – 3, harnesses – 2 for billmen. *Hardwick.* Billman – 1, harness – 1 for archer. *Eversden.* Archer – 1, billman – 1, harnesses – 2 for billmen. *Kingston.* Billmen – 2, harnesses – 2 for billmen. *Eltisley.* Billmen – 5, harnesses – 3 for billmen. *[Long] Stowe.* Billman – 1, harnesses – 2 for billmen. *Bourn.* Billmen – 5, harnesses – 1 for archer, 3 for billmen. *Gamlingay.* Archers – 2, billmen – 3, harnesses – 1 for archer, 2 for billmen. *East Hatley.* Billman – 1, harness – 1. *Total.* Archers – 4, billmen – 32, harnesses – 28. *Hundred of Wetherley. Harlton.* Billman – 1, harnesses – 2 for billmen. *Comberton.* Billmen – 2, harnesses – 2 for billmen. *Grantchester.* Archers – 2, billmen – 2, harnesses – 2 for billmen. *Haslingfield.* Archers – 3, billmen – 5, harnesses – 3 for billmen. *Barton.* Archers – 2, billman – 1, harnesses – 2 for billmen. *Coton.* Archer – 1, billmen – 3, harnesses – 1 for archer, 1 for billman. *Shepreth.* Billmen – 2, harnesses – 1 for archer, 1 for billman. *Barrington.* Billmen – 4, harnesses – 1 for archer, 2 for billmen. *Arrington.* Archers – 3, billmen – 2, harnesses – 1 for archer, 1 for billman. *Orwell. Malton.* Archers – 2, billmen – 7, harnesses – 3 for billmen. Total: archers – 13, billmen – 31, harnesses – 23. *Hundred of Thriplow. Stapleford.* Archers – 3, billmen – 2, harnesses – 1 for archer, 2 for billmen. *Little Shelford.* Billmen – 2, harness – 1 for billman. *Great Shelford.* Archer – 1, billmen – 6, harnesses – 1 for archer, 3 for billmen. *Trumpington.* Archers – 2, billmen – 5, harnesses – 1 for archer, 2 for billmen. *Newton.* Billmen – 4, harnesses – 2 for billmen. *Thriplow.* Archer – 1, billmen – 7, harnesses – 1 for archer, 2 for billmen. *Harston.* Billmen – 5, harnesses – 1 for archer, 2 for billmen. *Fowlmere.* Billmen – 6, harnesses – 1 for archer, 2 for billmen. *Hauxton.* Archers – 2, billmen – 3, harnesses – 2 for billmen. *Foxton.* Archers – 2, billmen – 2, harnesses – 1 for archer, 1 for billman. Total: archers – 11, billmen – 43, harnesses – 26. *Hundred of Armingford. Abington [Pigotts].* Archer – 1, billmen – 2, harnesses – 2 for billmen. *Melbourn.* Archers – 5, billmen – 4, harnesses – 2 for archers, 2 for billmen.

*Guilden Morden.* Billmen – 3, harnesses – 3 for billmen. *Tadlow.* Billmen – 2, harness – 1 for billman. *Royston.* Archers – 3, billmen – 3, harnesses – 1 for archer, 1 for billman. *Meldreth.* Billmen – 6, harnesses – 3 for billmen. *Whaddon.* Billmen – 5, harnesses – 1 for archer, 1 for billman. *Litlington.* Billmen – 4, harnesses – 1 for archer, 1 for billman. *Bassingbourn.* Archers – 2, billmen – 8, harnesses – 2 for archers, 2 for billmen. *Steeple Morden.* Billmen – 7, harnesses – 1 for archer, 2 for billmen. *Wendy. Shingay.* Archer – 1, billmen – 5, harnesses – 1 for archer, 1 for billman. *Croydon.* Billmen – 5, harnesses – 1 for archer, 1 for billman. *Kneesworth.* Archer – 1, billmen – 3, harness – 1 for archer. Total: archers – 13, billmen – 59, harnesses – 31. Total of four hundreds: men – 206 (archers – 41, billmen – 165), harnesses – 108 (for archers – 26, for billmen – 182).

 *Parchment.*
 *Names specified.*
 *Signed by*: the commissioners.          SP 10/3, no. 13

**87.** February 29. Certificate of Sir Robert Peyton, Thomas Rudston and William Walpole, commissioners of musters assigned to the hundreds of Staine, Staploe and Flendish, Cambridgeshire.

 *Hundred of Staine. Bottisham.* Archers – 3, billmen – 6, harnesses – 7, bills – 6 , bows – 4, sheaves of arrows – 2, swords – 4, daggers – 10. *Swaffham Prior. Reach.* Archers – 4, billmen – 9, harnesses – 6, bills – 6, bows – 2, sheaf of arrows – 1, swords – 2, daggers – 2. *Little Wilbraham.* Billmen – 3, harnesses – 2, bills – 3, bow – 1, sheaf of arrows – 1. *Stow cum Quy.* Archer – 1, billmen – 2, harnesses – 2, bills – 3, bow – 1, sheaf of arrows – 1. *Great Wilbraham.* Archers – 2, billman – 1, harnesses – 3, bills – 4, bows – 2, sheaf of arrows – 1, swords – 2. *Swaffham Bulbeck.* Pikeman – 1, billmen – 3, harnesses – 3, bills – 4, bows – 2, sheaves of arrows – 2, swords – 2, pikes – 2. *Hundred of Flendish. Fulbourn.* Archers – 2, billmen – 4, harnesses – 8, bills – 10, bows – 3, sheaves of arrows – 3, swords – 4, daggers – 4. *[Cherry] Hinton.* Archers – 2, billmen – 2, harnesses – 3, bills – 6, bow – 1, sheaf of arrows – 1, swords – 2, daggers – 2. *Horningsea.* Archers – 2, billmen – 2, harnesses – 2, bills – 4, bow – 1, sheaf of arrows – 1, sword – 1, dagger – 1. *Fen Ditton.* Billmen – 3, archer – 1, harnesses – 3, bills – 6, bow – 1, sheaf of arrows – 1, swords – 2, daggers – 2. *Teversham.* Billmen – 2, harnesses – 2, bills – 2, bow – 1, sheaf of arrows – 1, sword – 1, daggers – 2. *Hundred of Staploe. Soham.* Archers – 2, billmen – 12, harnesses – 14, bills – 20, bows – 4, sheaves of arrows – 4, swords – 6, daggers – 6. *Fordham.* Archers – 2, billmen – 6, harnesses – 8, bills – 10, bows – 2, sheaves of arrows – 2, swords – 3, daggers – 3. *Snailwell.* Archer – 1, billman – 1, harnesses – 2, bow – 1, sheaf of arrows – 1, bills – 4, swords – 2, daggers – 2. *Burwell.* Archers – 2, billmen – 7, harnesses – 6, bills – 8, bows – 2, sheaves of arrows – 2, swords – 4, daggers – 4. *Chippenham.* Archers – 2, billmen – 4, harnesses – 3, bills – 6, bows – 2, sheaves of arrows – 2, swords – 2, daggers – 2. *Kennett.* Archers – 2, harness – 1, bills – 2, sword – 1, dagger – 1. *Landwade.* Billman – 1, bow – 1, sheaf of arrows – 1. *Wicken.* Billmen – 2, harnesses – 2, bills – 4, bow – 1, sheaf of arrows – 1, swords – 2, dagger – 1. *Isleham.* Archer – 1, billmen – 3, harnesses – 5, bills – 6, bows – 2, sheaves of arrows – 2, swords – 2, daggers – 2. Total: men – 101 (archers – 27, billmen – 74), harnesses – 82, bills – 114, bows – 33, sheaves of arrows – 29, swords – 42, daggers – 42, horses – 0.

 *Parchment.*
 *Names specified.*
 *Signed by*: the commissioners.          SP 10/3, no. 14

**88.** February 28. Certificate of Thomas [Goodrich], bishop of Ely, Harry Goderyck and Thomas Rudston, esquires and Richard Wylkes, clerk, commissioners of musters in the Isle of Ely.

 *Ely.* Archers – 3, billmen – 8, harnesses – 13, bows – 4, sheaves of arrows – 4, bills –

18. *[Little] Downham.* Archers – 2, billmen – 2, harnesses – 3, bills – 6, bow – 1, sheaf of arrows – 1. *Littleport.* Archer – 1, billmen – 2, harnesses – 3, bills – 6, bow – 1, sheaf of arrows – 1. *Witchford.* Billmen – 2, harness – 1, bills – 3. *Coveney. Manea.* Billmen – 2, harnesses – 2, bills – 4. *Wentworth.* Billman – 1, harness – 1, bills – 2. *Witcham.* Billmen – 2, harness – 1, bills – 2. *Sutton.* Archers – 2, billmen – 3, harnesses – 3, bow – 1, sheaf of arrows – 1, bills – 12. *Mepal.* Archer – 1, harness – 1, bill – 1. *Haddenham.* Archers – 2, billmen – 4, harnesses – 4, bows – 2, sheaves of arrows – 2, bills – 10. *Stretham. [Little] Thetford.* Archers – 3, billmen – 3, harnesses – 3, bills – 8, sheaf of arrows – 1. *Wilburton.* Billmen – 2, harnesses – 3, bills – [8], sheaf of arrows – 1. *Chatteris.* Archers – 2, billmen – 2, harnesses – 5, bows – 2, sheaves of arrows – 2, bills – 12. *March.* Billmen – 5, harnesses – 3, bills – 5, sheaves of arrows – 2, bows – 2. *Doddington. Wimblington.* Archer – 1, billmen – 3, harnesses – 3, bills – 8. *Whittlesey.* Archers – 2, billmen – 6, harnesses – 6, bills – 14, bows – 2, sheaves of arrows – 2. *Wisbech.* Archers – 3, billmen – 8, harnesses – 10, bows – 4, sheaves of arrows – 4, bills – 20. *Elm.* Billmen – 3, harnesses – 2. *Newton.* Archer – 1, billmen – 2, harnesses – 2, bills – 6, bow – 1, sheaf of arrows – 1. *Leverington.* Archer – 1, billmen – 3, harnesses – 3, bills – 12, bow – 1, sheaf of arrows – 1. *Tydd.* Archer – 1, billmen – 2, harnesses – 2, bills – 6, bow – 1, sheaf of arrows – 1. *Upwell. Outwell.* Billmen – 4, harnesses – 3, bills – 7. Bishop of Ely: great horses for demilances – 5. Dean of Ely: great horse for demilance – 1. Total: men – 93 (archers – 25, billmen – 68), harnesses – 76, bows and sheaves of arrows – 25, bills – 172, great horses – 6.
*Parchment.*
*Names specified.*
*Signed by*: the commissioners.                                                                SP 10/3, no. 15

**89.**    February 20 x 23. Certificates of musters for Surrey.
  1. Certificate of Lord William Howard, Sir Thomas Cawarden, James Skynner, John Skynner and Thomas Yngler, commissioners of musters for the hundreds of Tandridge and Reigate, taken 23 February 1548. *Hundred of Tandridge. Lingfield.* Archers – 12, billmen – 26, harnesses – 4 for archers, 4 for billmen. *Limpsfield.* Archers – 3, billmen – 24, harnesses – 3 for archers, 4 for billmen. *Tandridge.* Archers – 7, billmen – 13, harnesses – 3 for archers, 2 for billmen. *Crowhurst.* Archers – 3, [billmen] – 12, harnesses – 2 for archers, 3 for billmen. *Oxted.* Archers – 9, billmen – 17, harnesses – 5 for archers, 3 for billmen. *Blechingley.* Archers – 16, billmen – 6, harnesses – 5 for archers, 4 for billmen. *Horne.* Archers – 3, billmen – 9, harnesses – 1 for archer, 3 for billmen. *Godstone.* Archers – 15, billmen – 25, harnesses – 4 for archers, 3 for billmen. *Titsey.* Archers – 4, billmen – 4, harnesses – 2 for archers, 1 for billman. *Tatsfield.* Billmen – 5, harness – 1 for archer. *Chelsham.* Archers – 2, billmen – 6, harnesses – 3 for archers, 2 for billmen. *Farleigh.* Archer – 1, billmen – 3, harnesses – 1 for archer, 1 for billman. *Warlingham.* Archers – 3, billmen – 3, harnesses – 1 for archer, 1 for billman. *Woldingham.* Archers – 2, billmen – 3, harnesses – 1 for archer, 1 for billman. *Caterham.* Archers – 2, billmen – 5, harnesses – 1 for archer, 3 for billmen. Total: men – 246 (archers – 82, billmen – 164), harnesses – 72 (for archers – 37, for billmen – 35). *Hundred of Reigate. Horley.* Archers – 3, billmen – 10, harnesses – 4 for archers, 4 for billmen. *Charlwood.* Archers – 2, billmen – 18, harnesses – 3 for archers, 3 for billmen, horse – 1. *Leigh.* Archers – 5, billmen – 6, harnesses – 4 for archers, 3 for billmen, horse – 1. *Newdigate.* Archer – 1, billmen – 3, harness – 1 for billman. *Betchworth.* Archers – 12, billmen – 6, harnesses – 4 for archers, 2 for billmen. *Buckland.* Billmen – 5, harnesses – 1 for archer, 2 for billmen. *Burstow.* Archers – 2, billmen – 5, harnesses – 3 for archers, 3 for billmen. *Merstham.* Archers – 2, billmen – 6, harnesses – 2 for archers, 2 for billmen. *Nutfield.* Archers – 7, billmen – 13, harnesses – 4 for archers, 4 for billmen. *Chipstead.* Archers – 8, billmen – 4, harnesses – 2 for archers, 2 for billmen. *'Burgus' of Reigate.* Archers – 6, billmen – 16, harnesses – 3 for archers, 2 for billmen. *'Foren' of Reigate.* Archers – 4, billmen – 25, harnesses – 3 for archers, 8 for billmen. *Kingswood.* Billmen –

2. Total: men – 179 (archers – 52, billmen – 127), harnesses – 69 (for archers – 33, for billmen – 36).

*Signed by*: the commissioners.

2. Certificate of Sir Thomas Cawerdon, William Sawnders and John Skynner, commissioners of musters for the hundreds of Kingston and Elmbridge, taken 21 February 1548. Able men – 237 (archers – 46, gunners – 7, billmen – 183), harnesses – 49 (for archers – 12, for billmen – 37), horses – 0.

*Signed by*: Sawnders and Skynner.

3. Certificate of Sir Matthew Brown, William Sawnders, William Sakvild and John Skynner, commissioners of musters for the hundreds of Copthorne and Effingham, taken 22 February 1548. Able men – 163 (archers – 24, gunners – 5, billmen – 134), harnesses – 46 (for archers – 12, for billmen – 34), horses – 0.

*Signed by*: Sawnders and Skynner.

4. Certificate of John Scott, Nicholas Leigh and William Heron, commissioners of musters for the hundred of Wallington, taken at Croydon on 20 February 1548. Able men – 110 (archers – 20, billmen – 90), harnesses – 40, horses – 0.

*Signed by*: the commissioners.

5. Certificate of Sir Matthew Brown, Sir Christopher More, Harry Polsted, Thomas Saunders, Richard Bedon, Lawrence Stowghton, William Sakvild, William Creswell, William More and Thomas Stowghton, esquires, commissioners of musters appointed by commission received February 12 for the hundreds of Woking, Godley, Farnham, Godalming, Blackheath and Wotton, taken at several days and places in February 1548. *Hundred of Woking*. Archers – 75, billmen – 125, harnesses – 51. *Hundred of Godley*. Archers – 55, billmen – 95, harnesses – 22. *Hundred of Farnham*. Archers – 49, billmen – 106, harnesses – 30. *Hundred of Godalming*. Archers – 77, billmen – 128, harnesses – 50. *Hundred of Blackheath*. Archers – 76, billmen – 139, harnesses – 32. *Hundred of Wotton*. Archers – 34, billmen – 76, harnesses – 21. Total: men – 1,035 (archers – 366, billmen – 669), harnesses – 106, horses – 0.

*Signed by*: the commissioners.

6. Certificate of Sir Thomas Pope, Robert Curson, baron of the exchequer, John Skott and Henry Mannock, esquires and John Eston, gent., commissioners of musters appointed by commission dated 4 February 1548 for the borough of Southwark and the hundred of Brixton, taken 21 and 22 February 1548. *Borough of Southwark*. Archers – 20, billmen – 65, gunners – 10, pikemen – 5, harnesses – 100 pairs. *Hundred of Brixton*. Archers – 30, billmen – 78, gunners – 10, pikemen – 2, harnesses – 40 pairs, horses – 0.

*Names specified.*

Many able men have been lately taken from the borough of Southwark to serve the king on the seas and beyond. We fear that if more were taken we would be unable to furnish the number above certified, unless we levied two strangers to one Englishman, which would not be convenient.

*Signed by*: Pope, Curson and Eston.                                        SP 10/3, no. 16

**90.** February 23. Certificate of Thomas West, Lord De La Warr, Edward Shelleye, John Shelley, John Ledes and John Apslee, esquires, commissioners of musters for the rape of Bramber, Sussex, appointed by commission dated February 4.

*Hundred of Brightford. Household servants of Lord De La Warr.* Archers – 17, billmen – 14, great horses – 3, harnesses for demilances – 3, harnesses – 70, bows – 24, sheaves of arrows – 24, bills – 46. *Tithing of Lancing*. Archers – 3, billmen – 5, harnesses – 6, bows – 10, sheaves of arrows – 5½, bills – 28. *Tithing of Sompting*. Archers – 2, billmen – 3, harnesses – 9, bows – 10, sheaves of arrows – 6, bills – 19. *Tithing of Broadwater*. Archer – 1, billmen – 4, harnesses – 6, bows – 5, sheaves of arrows – 3, bills – 8. *Tithing of Worthing*. Archers – 4, billmen – 6, harnesses – 7, bows – 6, sheaf of arrows – 1, bills – 21. *Tithing of*

*Durrington.* Archers – 0, billmen – 2, harnesses – 4, bows – 5, sheaf of arrows – 1, bills – 10. *Tithing of Clapham.* Archers – 0, billmen – 0, harnesses – 3, bows – 4, sheaves of arrows – 3, bills – 8. *Household servants of Sir William Shelleye.* Archers – 3, billmen – 6, great horses – 0, harnesses for demilances – 0, harnesses – 30, bows – 12, sheaves of arrows – 12, bills – 20. *Tithing of Heene.* Archers – 0, billmen – 3, harnesses – 4, bows – 6, sheaves of arrows – 2, bills – 16. *Tithing of Findon.* Archers – 2, billmen – 4, harnesses – 4, bows – 6, sheaves of arrows – 3, bills – 15. Total: archers – 32, billmen – 46, great horses – 3, harnesses for demilances – 3, harnesses – 143, bows – 88, sheaves of arrows – 60½, bills – 186. *Hundred of Tarring. Township of [West] Tarring.* Archers – 3, billmen – 9, harnesses – 4, bows – 12, sheaves of arrows – 5, bills – 17. *Tithing of Salvington.* Archer – 1, billmen – 0, harness – 1, bows – 5, sheaf of arrows – 1, bills – 9. *Tithing of Patching.* Archers – 0, billmen – 2, harnesses – 5, bows – 13, sheaf of arrows – 1, bills – 9. Total: archers – 4, billmen – 11, harnesses – 10, bows – 30, sheaves of arrows – 7, bills – 35. *Half hundred of Fishersgate. Tithing of Kingston by Sea.* Archers – 2, billmen – 2, harnesses – 7, bows – 7, sheaves of arrows – 5½, bills – 8. *Tithing of Southwick.* Archers – 2, billmen – 3, harnesses – 2, bows – 7, sheaves of arrows – 3½, bills – 8. *Borough of New Shoreham.* Archers – 5, billmen – 11, harnesses – 4, bows – 7, sheaves of arrows – 5½, bills – 16. *Borough of Old Shoreham.* Archers – 2, billmen – 2, harnesses – 4, bows – 8, sheaves of arrows – 5, bills – 8. Total: archers – 10, billmen – 19, harnesses – 17, bows – 29, sheaves of arrows – 19½, bills – 40. *Hundred of Steyning. Tithing of Wiston.* Archer – 1, billmen – 3, harnesses – 4, bows – 8, sheaves of arrows – 3½, bills – 16. *Household servants of William Sherleye.* Archers – 3, billmen – 3, great horse – 1, harness for demilance – 1, harnesses – 4, bows – 2, sheaves of arrows – 2, bills – 2. *Tithing of Coombes.* Archers – 0, billmen – 2, harnesses – 2, bows – 4, sheaves of arrows – 2, bills – 3. *Tithing of Washington.* Archers – 2, billmen – 4, harnesses – 7, bows – 14, sheaves of arrows – 6, bills – 14. *Tithing of Charlton.* Archers – 3, billmen – 3, harnesses – 6, bows – 7, sheaves of arrows – 15, bills – 12. *Tithing of Annington.* Archer – 1, billmen – 2, harnesses – 4, bows – 5, sheaves of arrows – 3½, bills – 5. Total: archers – 10, billmen – 17, harness for demilance – 1, harnesses – 27, bows – 40, sheaves of arrows – 21½, bills – 52, great horse – 1. *Borough of Steyning and Bramber. Steyning.* Archers – 6, billmen – 10, gunner – 1, harnesses – 4, bows – 8, sheaves of arrows – 3, bills – 16. *Bramber.* Archer – 1, billmen – 0, gunner – 1, harnesses – 2, bows – 2, sheaves of arrows – 2, bills – 8. Total: archers – 7, billmen – 10, gunners – 1 [*recte* 2], harnesses – 6, bows – 10, sheaves of arrows – 5, bills – 24. *Hundred of Tipnoak. Tithing of Henfield.* Archers – 10, billmen – 14, harnesses – 10, bows – 10, sheaves of arrows – 5, bills – 24. *Tithing of Blackstone.* Archers – 3, billmen – 8, harnesses – 2, bows – 4, sheaves of arrows – 2, bills – 10. *Tithing of Albourne.* Archers – 2, billmen – 6, harness – 1, bows – 4, sheaves of arrows – 0, bills – 11. Total: archers – 15, billmen – 28, harnesses – 13, bows – 24, sheaves of arrows – 7, bills – 45. *Half hundred of [East] Easewrithe. Tithing of Warminghurst.* Archers – 5, billmen – 6, harnesses – 3, bows – 5, sheaves of arrows – 2, bills – 14. *Household servants of Edward Shelleye.* Archers – 2, billmen – 6, harnesses – 4, bows – 4, sheaves of arrows – 4, bills – 6. *Tithing of Thakeham.* Archers – 2, billmen – 7, gunners – 2, harnesses – 9, bows – 10, sheaves of arrows – 3, bills – 23. *Household servants of Mr Apsleye.* Archers – 2, billmen – 3, harnesses – 3, bows – 3, sheaves of arrows – 3, bills – 3. *Tithing of Disenhurst.* Archer – 1, billmen – 2, gunners – 2, harnesses – 3, bows – 4, sheaves of arrows – 3, bills – 6. *Tithing of Sullington.* Archers – 3, billmen – 5, harnesses – 7, bows – 6, sheaves of arrows – 4, bills – 15. *Tithing of [West] Chiltington.* Archer – 1, billmen – 3, harnesses – 2, bows – 4, sheaves of arrows – 2, bills – 4. Total: archers – 16, billmen – 27, gunners – 4, harnesses – 31, bows – 35, sheaves of arrows – 20, bills – 71. *Hundred of Burbeach. Tithing of Beeding.* Archers – 3, billmen – 4, harnesses – 3, bows – 5, sheaves of arrows – 1½, bills – 8. *Tithing of Horton.* Archers – 2, billmen – 3, harnesses – 4, bows – 5, sheaves of arrows – 2, bills – 6. *Tithing of Edburton.* Archers – 4, billmen – 5, harnesses – 4, bows – 8, sheaves of arrows – 3, bills – 10. *Tithing of Ifield.* Archers – 4, billmen – 6, harnesses – 3, bows – 6, sheaves of arrows – 2, bills – 12. Total: archers – 13, billmen – 18, harnesses – 14, bows – 24, sheaves of arrows – 8½, bills – 36. *Hundred of [West] Grinstead. Tithing of [West] Grinstead.* Archers – 2, billmen – 6, harnesses – 5, bows – 5, sheaves of arrows – 2, bills – 12. *Tithing of Apsley.* Archers – 5, billmen – 15, gunners – 2, harnesses – 5, bows – 7, sheaves of arrows – 3, bills – 30. *Tithing of Ashurst.* Archers – 2, billmen – 11, harnesses – 2, bows – 3, sheaves of arrows – 2, bills – 20. *Tithing of Bines [Green].* Archers – 4, billmen – 5, harnesses – 2, bows – 3, sheaves of arrows – 2, bills – 20. *Tithing of Wakeham.* Archer – 1, billmen – 3, harnesses – 2, bows – 8, sheaf of arrows – 1, bills – 6. *Household servants of Mr Leedes.* Archers – 2. billmen – 3, harnesses – 3, bows – 3, sheaves of arrows – 2, bills – 3. Total: archers – 16, billmen – 43, hand gunners – 3, harnesses – 23, bows – 23, sheaves of arrows – 12, bills – 86. *Half hundred of Wyndham. Tithing of Wyndham and Ewhurst [Manor].* Archers – 9, billmen – 18, harnesses – 7, bows – 6, sheaves of arrows – 4, bills – 28. *Borough of Horsham.* Archers – 5, billmen – 28, gunners – 3, harnesses – 2, bows – 6, sheaves of arrows – 3, bills – 36. *Hundred of Singlecross. Tithing of Warnham.* Archers – 4, billmen – 13, harnesses – 8, bows – 10, sheaves of arrows – 6, bills – 22. *Household servants of [John] Carrell.* Archers – 2, billmen – 2, great horse – 1, harness for demilance – 1, harnesses – 4, bows – 2, sheaves of arrows – 2, bills – 2. *Tithing of Washington in the Wold.* Archer – 1, billmen – 2, harnesses – 3, bows – 4, sheaves of arrows – 2, bills – 8. *Tithing of Shortsfield.* Archers – 3, billmen – 5, harness – 1, bows – 3, sheaf of arrows – 1, bills – 15. *Tithing of Coombes in the Wold.* Archers – 2, billmen – 4, harness – 1, bows – 3, sheaves of arrows – 2, bills – 11. *Tithing of Sedgewick.* Archers – 3, billmen – 6, harness – 1, bows – 4, sheaf of arrows – 1, bills – 18. *Tithing of Marlpost.* Archers – 2, billmen – 13, harnesses – 3, bows – 3, sheaf of arrows – 1, bills – 19. Total: archers – 15, billmen – 47, great horse – 1, harness for demilance – 1, harnesses – 29, bows – 29, sheaves of arrows – 14, bills – 95. Sum total: archers – 150, billmen – 307, gunners – 12, great horses – 5, horses for demilances – 5, harnesses – 322, bows – 340, sheaves of arrows – 182½, bills – 734.

*Signed and sealed by*: the commissioners. SP 10/3, no. 17

**91.** February 19 x 22. Certificate of John Gunter and John Stanney, esquires, commissioners of musters for the rape of Chichester, Sussex.

*Hundred of Bosham. Tithing of Bosham.* Archers – 3, billmen – 4, harnesses – 6, bows – 7, sheaves of arrows – 5, bills – 22. *Tithing of Chidham.* Archer – 1, billmen – 3, harnesses – 3, bows – 6, sheaves of arrows – 3, bills – 15. *Tithing of [West] Stoke.* Archers – 0, billman – 1, harness – 1, bows – 2, sheaf of arrows – 1, bills – 8. *Tithing of Funtington.* Archer – 1, billman – 1, harnesses – 2, bows – 4, sheaf of arrows – 1, bills – 8. *Tithing of West Ashling.* Archers – 0, billmen – 2, harness – 1, bows – 2, sheaf of arrows – 1, bills – 12. *Tithing of East Ashling.* Archers – 0, billman – 1, harnesses – 0, bows – 2, sheaf of arrows – 1, bills – 7. Total: archers – 5, billmen – 12, harnesses – 13, bows – 23, sheaves of arrows – 12, bills – 22. *Hundred of Manhood. Tithing of West Wittering.* Archers – 0, billmen – 2, harnesses – 2, bows – 3, sheaves of arrows – 2½, bills – 16. *Tithing of 'Thirlewood'.* Archer – 1, billmen – 2, harnesses – 2, bows – 4, sheaves of arrows – 1½, bills – 5. *Tithing of Birdham.* Archer – 1, billmen – 2, harnesses – 2, bows – 9, sheaves of arrows – 5, bills – 10. *Tithing of Sidlesham.* Archer – 1, billmen – 4, harnesses – 7, bows – 12, sheaves of arrows – 5, bills – 21. *Tithing of Selsey.* Archers – 0, billmen – 2, harnesses – 5, bows – 12, sheaves of arrows – 5, bills – 16. *Tithing of Bracklesham.* Archers – 0, billmen – 2, harnesses – 2, bows – 4, sheaves of arrows – 3, bills – 3. *Tithing of Almodington.* Archer – 1, billman – 1, harnesses – 4, bows – 8, sheaves of arrows – 4, bills – 10. *Tithing of Somerley.* Archer – 1, billman – 1, harnesses – 2, bows – 7, sheaves of arrows – 2, bills – 12. Total: archers – 5, billmen – 16, harnesses – 26, bows – 59, sheaves of arrows – 28, bills – 93. *Hundred of Aldwick. Tithing of East Lavant.* Archers – 0, billmen – 2, harnesses – 4, bows – 7, sheaves of arrows – 2, bills – 12. *Tithing of Slindon.* Archers – 2, billmen – 7, harnesses – 2, bows – 6, sheaves of arrows – 2, bills – 12. *Tithing of Bersted.* Archers – 2, billmen – 3, harnesses – 2, bows – 12, sheaves of arrows – 4, bills – 11. *Tithing of Tangmere.* Archers – 0, billmen – 2, harnesses – 2, bows – 3, sheaves of arrows – 2, bills – 4. *Tithing of Pagham.* Archers – 2, billmen – 4, harnesses – 7, bows – 8, sheaves of arrows – 3, bills – 24. Total: archers – 6, billmen – 18, harnesses – 17, bows – 36, sheaves of arrows – 13, bills – 63. *Hundred of Westbourne and Singleton. Tithing of Westbourne.* Archers – 0, billmen – 3, gunner – 1, harnesses – 2, bows – 4, sheaf of arrows – 1, bills – 8, gun – 1. *Tithing of Prinsted.* Archer – 1, billmen – 4, harnesses – 4, bows – 5, sheaf of arrows – 1, bills – 12. *Tithing of Compton.* Archer – 1, billmen – 2, harnesses – 2, bows – 4, sheaf of arrows – 1, bills – 6. *Tithing of Walderton.* Archers – 0, billmen – 1, harness – 1, bows – 6, sheaves of arrows – 3, bills – 8. *Tithing of Stoughton.* Archer – 1, billmen – 0, harnesses – 2, bows – 2, sheaf of arrows – 1, bills – 5. *Tithing of North Marden.* Archers – 0, billman – 1, harness – 1, bows – 2, sheaf of arrows – 1, bills – 3. *Tithing of East Marden.* Archers – 1, billman – 1, harnesses – 2, bows – 3, sheaf of arrows – 1, bills – 4. *Tithing of Up Marden and West Marden.* Archer – 1, billmen – 0, harnesses – 2, bows – 4, sheaves of arrows – 2, bills – 5. *Tithing of East Dean.* Archers – 2, billman – 1, harnesses – 3, bows – 3, sheaves of arrows – 2, bills – 12. *Tithing of Singleton.* Archer – 1, billmen – 0, harnesses – 4, bows – 3, sheaf of arrows – 1, bills – 5. *Tithing of Mid Lavant.* Archer – 1, billman – 1, harnesses – 2, bows – 2, sheaf of arrows – 1, bills – 7. *Tithing of Binderton.* Archer – 1, billman – 1, harnesses – 2, bows – 3, sheaves of arrows – 2, bills – 5. *Tithing of West Dean.* Archers – 2, billman – 1, harnesses – 3, bows – 5, sheaves of arrows – 2, bills – 12. Total: archers – 12, billmen – 17, harnesses – 30, bows – 46, sheaves of arrows – 19, bills – 93. *Hundred of Dumpford. Tithing of West Harting.* Archers – 2, billmen – 4, harnesses – 2, bows – 4, sheaf of arrows – 1, bills – 16. *Tithing of East Harting.* Archers – 0, billmen – 2, harnesses – 2, bows – 4, sheaves of arrows – 2, bills – 15. *Tithing of South Harting.* Archers – 0, billmen – 2, harness – 1, bows – 3, sheaves of arrows – 2, bills – 9. *Household of Sir Anthony Wyndsor.* Archer – 1, billman – 1, great horse – 1, harness for demilance – 1, harnesses – 4, bows – 3, sheaves of arrows – 3, bills – 6. *Tithing of Didling.* Archers – 0, billmen – 3, harness – 1, bows – 2, sheaves of arrows – 2, bills – 8. *Tithing of Chithurst.* Archer – 1, billman – 1, harnesses – 0, bows – 3, sheaf of arrows – 1, bills – 2. *Tithing of Trotton.* Archers – 0, billman – 1, harness – 1, bows – 3, sheaf of arrows – ½, bills – 8. *Household servants of Richard Lewkenor, esq.* Archer – 1, billman – 1, great horse – 1, horse for demilance – 1, harnesses – 3, bows – 3, sheaves of arrows – 3, bills – 5. *Tithing of Elsted.* Archer – 1, billman – 1, harnesses – 2, bows – 2, sheaf of arrows – 1, bills – 6. *Tithing of Rogate.* Archers – 0, billmen – 2, harnesses – 3, bows – 2, sheaf of arrows – 1, bills – 12. Total: archers – 6, billmen – 21, great horses – 2, harnesses for demilances – 2, harnesses – 16, bows – 28, sheaves of arrows – 16, bills – 87. *Hundred of Box and Stockbridge. Tithing of Southgate.* Archers – 0, billmen – 2, harnesses – 2, bows – 3, sheaves of arrows – 2, bills – 2. *Tithing of Eartham.* Archers – 2, billmen – 0, harnesses – 2, bows – 4, sheaf of arrows – 1, bills – 6. *Tithing of [New] Fishbourne.* Archers – 6, billmen – 3, harnesses – 2, bows – 2, sheaf of arrows – 1, bills – 12. *Tithing of Aldingbourne.* Archers – 2, billmen – 6, harnesses – 2, bows – 6, sheaves of arrows – 4, bills – 14. *Tithing of Rumboldswyke.* Archers – 0, billmen – 4, harness – 1, bows – 0, sheaves of arrows – 0, bills – 9. *Tithing of Strettington.* Archers – 0, billmen – 1, harness – 1, bows – 2, sheaf of arrows – 1, bills – 4. *Tithing of Runcton.* Archer – 1, billmen – 2, harness – 1, bows – 4, sheaves of arrows – 2, bills – 6. *Tithing of Merston.* Archer – 1, billmen – 2, harnesses – 0, bows – 3, sheaf of arrows – 1, bills – 7. *Tithing of Boxgrove.* Archer – 1, billmen – 2, harness – 1, bows – 3, sheaves of arrows – 3, bills – 4. *Tithing of Halnaker.* Archers – 2, billmen – 0, harnesses – 2, bows – 4, sheaves of arrows – 2, bills – 3. *Tithing of Westgate.* Archer – 1, billmen – 2, harnesses – 2, bows – 3, sheaves of arrows – 2, bills – 7. *Tithing of Westerton.* Archer – 1, billmen – 2, harnesses – 4, bows – 2, sheaves of arrows – 2, bills – 4. *Tithing of Drayton.* Archers – 0, billman – 1, harnesses – 2, bows – 2, sheaf of arrows – 1, bills – 3. *Tithing of Colworth.* Archers – 0, billmen – 2, harness – 1, bows – 2, sheaves of arrows – 2, bills – 9. *Tithing of Woodcote.* Archers – 0, billmen – 2, harnesses – 2, bows – 2, sheaves of arrows –

2, bills – 6. *Tithing of Hunston.* Archer – 1, billmen – 3, harness – 1, bows – 3, sheaf of arrows – 1, bills – 10. *Tithing of Oving.* Archer – 1, billman – 1, harness – 1, bows – 4, sheaf of arrows – 1, bills – 10. *Tithing of Appledram.* Archers – 0, billmen – 2, harnesses – 3, bows – 3, sheaves of arrows – 2, bills – 9. *Tithing of Donnington.* Archers – 0, billmen – 2, harnesses – 3, bows – 5, sheaves of arrows – 2, bills – 5. *Tithing of Mundham.* Archer – 1, [billmen – 0], harnesses – 3, bows – 6, sheaves of arrows – 2, bills – 10. Total: archers – 14, billmen – 41, harnesses – 36, bows – 63, sheaves of arrows – 34, bills – 133. *City of Chichester. East Street.* Archers – 2, billmen – 6, harnesses – 5, bows – 12, sheaves of arrows – 7, bills – 12. *South Street.* Archers – 2, billmen – 3, harnesses – 7, bows – 8, sheaves of arrows – 4, bills – 8. [Household servants of]* Robert Peterson, treasurer of Chichester [Cathedral]. [Archer – 1, billmen – 2, gunner – 1],* great horse – 1, harness for demilance – 1, [harnesses – 2],* bows – 2, sheaves of arrows – 2, [hand gun – 1].* *North Street.* Archer – 1, billmen – 4, gunners – 2, harnesses – 8, bows – 10, sheaves of arrows – 6, bills – 14, guns – 2. *West Street.* Archer – 1, billmen – 3, gunner – 1, harnesses – 8, bows – 6, sheaves of arrows – 4, bills – 14, gun – 1. *Tithing of the Pallant.* Archers – 2, billman – 1, harness – 1, bows – 3, sheaf of arrows – 1, bills – 16. Total: archers – 9, billmen – 19, great horse – 1, harness for demilance – 1, harnesses – 31, bows – 38, sheaves of arrows – 23, bills – 69, hand guns – 4. *Hundred of Easebourne. Tithing of Graffham.* Archers – 2, billmen – 0, harnesses – 0, bows – 2, sheaf of arrows – 1, bills – 14. *Tithing of Cocking.* Archers – 2, billmen – 2, harnesses – 5, bows – 5, sheaves of arrows – 3, bills – 14. *Tithing of Iping and Woolbeding.* Archer – 1, billmen – 2, harness – 1, bow – 1, sheaf of arrows – 1, bills – 15. *Tithing of Heyshott.* Archers – 2, billmen – 0, harness – 1, bows – 3, sheaf of arrows – 1, bills – 6. *Tithing of Selham.* Archers – 2, billman – 1, harnesses – 2, bows – 2, sheaf of arrows – 1, bills – 6. *Tithing of Easebourne.* Archers – 0, billmen – 5, harness – 1, bows – 2, sheaf of arrows – 1, bills – 22. *Tithing of Stedham.* Archer – 1, billmen – 3, harness – 1, bows – 4, sheaf of arrows – 1, bills – 12. *Tithing of Bepton.* Archer – 1, billmen – [2], harnesses – 0, bows – 2, sheaf of arrows – 1, bills – 8. *Borough of Midhurst.* Archers – 3, billmen – 10, harnesses – 5, bows – 12, sheaves of arrows – 5, bills – 24. Total: archers – 14, billmen – 25, harnesses – 16, bows – 33, sheaves of arrows – 15, bills – 121. Sum total: archers – 71, billmen – 145, gunners – 8, great horses – 3, harnesses for demilances – 3, harnesses – 186, bows – 326, sheaves of arrows – 150, bills – 680, hand guns – 5.

SP 10/3, no. 18

**92.** [? February]. Certificate of Edward Vaughan, Thomas Uvedale and John White, esquires, commissioners of musters for the hundreds of Portsdown, Bosmer, Titchfield, Fareham, Hambledon and the town of Havant, [Hampshire], taken at Portsdown.

*Hundreds of Portsdown and Bosmer. Southwick.* Archers – 8, billmen – 28, harnesses with bows and arrows – 7, harnesses with bills – 9. *West Boarhunt.* Archers – 5, billmen – 4, harnesses with bows and arrows – 2, harnesses with bills – 3. *Porchester.* Archers – 10, billmen – 20, harnesses with bows and arrows – 6, harnesses with bills – 3. *Wymering. Hilsea.* Archers – 3, billmen – 4, harnesses with bows and arrows – 8, harnesses with bills – 10. *Walsworth. Widley.* Archers – 5, billmen – 6, harnesses with bows and arrows – 2, harnesses with bills – 4. *Drayton. Farlington.* Archers – 5, billmen – 3, harnesses with bows and arrows – 4, harnesses with bills – 5. *Bedhampton.* Archers – 4, billmen – 2, harnesses with bows and arrows – 4, harnesses with bills – 5. *Warblington. Emsworth.* Archers – 3, billmen – 8, harnesses with bows and arrows – 2. *South Hayling ('Southwood'). North Hayling ('Northwood').* Archers – 12, billmen – 17, harnesses with bows and arrows – 4, harnesses with bills – 2. *Havant.* Archers – 19, billmen – 34, harnesses with bows and arrows – 3, harnesses with bills – 9. *Portsea.* Archers – 7, billmen – 16, harnesses with bows and arrows – 8, harnesses with bills – 4. *Kingston.* Archers – 5, billmen – 9, harnesses with bows and arrows – 6, harnesses with bills – 4. *Portsmouth.* Archers – 11, arquebusiers – 4, billmen –

*      Deleted.

46, harnesses with bows and arrows – 17, harnesses with bills – 23. Total: men – 298, harnesses – 154. *Hundred of Fareham.* Archers – 10, billmen – 21, harnesses with bows and arrows – 8, harnesses with bills – 26. *Hundred of Titchfield. Town of Titchfield.* Archers – 5, billmen – 12. *Crofton and the barony.* Archer – 1, billmen – 6. *Chark. Lee Markes.* Archers – 2, billmen – 7. *Hook. Swanwick.* Billmen – 7. *Stubbington. Rowner.* Archers – 3, billmen – 4. *Wickham.* Archers – 7, billmen – 24. Total: men – 78, harnesses – 48. *Hundred of Hambledon. Hambledon.* Archers – 3, billmen – 7. *Denmead...[indecipherable].* Archers – 3, billmen – 8. *Glidden. Chidden.* Archers – 4, billmen – 14. Total: men – 39, harnesses -17. Sum total: men – 446, harnesses – 253.

    *Names specified.*

    *Signed by* : Vaughan and White.                            SP 10/3, no. 19

**93.**   [? February]. Certificate of the ships of Whitby.

    The *Margeret*, 28 tons, owner – Richard Chameley, master – William Kendall, with 4 men. The *Hyell*, 16 tons, owner – James Stranquyshe, master – Richard Stabill, with 4 men. The *Xpoffer*, 26 tons, owner – Richard Browne with Richard Clarke, master – John Wryght, with 4 men. The *Mary John*, 30 tons, owners – Richard Browne and Robert Bushell, master – Richard Watesone, with 5 men. The *Xpoffor*, 60 tons, lacking cables, mast and all things belonging to her, which will not be ready before Easter, owner – Matthew Wilson. The *Michael*, 50 tons, owner – Matthew Wilson, master – Robert Peche, with 6 men. The *Mary James*, 36 tons, owner – Matthew Wilsone, master – William Burton, with 6 men.                                  SP 10/3, no. 20

**94.**   [? February]. Certificate of the ships of Scarborough.

    The *John Baptiste*, 80 tons, owner – William Lokwode, master – John Gray, with 10 men [*named*]. The *Mare Grace*, 55 tons, owner – William Girdler, master – Thomas Shakills, with 7 men [*named*]. The *Mare Kateryn*, 50 tons, owners – Robert Neightgaill, William Kenros and Robert Banke, master – Robert Banke, with 7 men [*named*]. The *Mare James*, 58 tons, owner – William Kenros, master – Lawrence Bedon, with 8 men [*named*]. The *Mary Sithe*, a little work ship, 26 tons, owner and master – Nicholas Clarke, with 3 men [*named*]. Fishing boats which cannot sail to any ports without pilots but only to the fishing seas. The *Gabrell*, 50 tons, owners – William Percy and Richard Denande, master – Richard Denande, with 6 men [*named*]. The *Blithe*, 40 tons, owners – William Kenros and John Stephenson, master – John Stephenson, with 6 men [*named*]. The *George*, 40 tons, owners – John Herwood and William Kenros, master – John Bedom, with 5 men [*named*]. The *Bartholomew*, 55 tons, owner – Richard Conyers, master – John Beforde, with 6 men [*named*]. The *Cudbarte*, 40 tons, owner – William Lokwood, master – Robert Craill, with 6 men [*named*]. The *James of Barwike*, 20 tons, owner – Sir William Eure, captain of Berwick, master – John Batte, with 6 men [*named*]. The *Thomas*, 40 tons, owners – William Kenros and Uxor Bedom, master – Thomas Londe, with 6 men [*named*]. The *Trynitie*, 50 tons, owners – Francis Kyldaill, Robert Banke and William Stoxley, master – John Osten, with 6 men [*named*]. The *Cristofer*, 50 tons owners – Robert Rawghton and Thomas Browne, master – Robert Shipperde, with 5 men [*named*].           SP 10/3, no. 21

**95.**   [? February].* Estimates laid before the king showing comparative charges for sending an army to Scotland by land and sea.

    Estimate for an invasion by sea with an army of 15,000 footmen, without accounting for the furniture of the army. Coats – £2,500. Conduct money, six days outward and six days home – £4,500. Conduct money for the chief captains, captains of hundreds and petty captains – £560. One month's (28 days) wages for the chief captains, captains of hundreds and petty captains – £2,250. One month's wages for 15,000 men at 6d. a day

---

\*    Assigned to February in *CPSD*, 7; but April or May is more likely [Jordan, i, 251 n. 1].

– £9,500. Hire of tonnage for one month at 4s. a ton – £2,000. Charges of 1,000 men with their wages, coats and conduct money, lying over the border for two months – £2,500. Total – £23,810. This leaves all chances, which may make the charges greater, which would not be if the army went by land.

Estimate for an army of 4,000 horsemen and 14,000 footmen to invade by land. Coats – £3,060. Conduct money for twelve days outward and homeward – £6,010. Wages for 4,000 horsemen at 8d. a day for 28 days – £3,733.6.8. Conduct of the chief captains, captains of hundreds and petty captains for twelve days – £560. Wages of the chief captains, captains of hundreds and petty captains for 28 days – £1,250. Wages for 14,000 footmen at 6d. a day for 28 days – £9,500. Total – £24,153.6.8.

Difference – £343.

Estimate of victuals for 20 days. Eight days' biscuit for 18,000 a day, taking in white meal – 144,000 lb. 400 quarters. 110 tons of wine at 200 gallons a ton. Provender for horses and beasts – 1,420 quarters. All which is ready at Berwick save the wine and baking the biscuit. The wine must be sent to Berwick and bakers for the biscuit. A similar proportion must be sent to the Firth [of Forth] for 20 days. Biscuit – 360,000 lb. Sweet wine – 220 tons. Provender – 3,510 quarters. Meat shall be taken out of the carriages. Carriages to be provided by the king for victuals, provender and ordnance – 262 carts, which may be well purveyed in Yorkshire, where there are the greatest oxen and the best carts. All the biscuit will take 1,500 quarters of the largest wheat at 13s. 4d. a quarter for 28 days – £1,000. Sweet wines – 560 butts at 120 gallons a butt and £5 a butt – £2,800. Carriage – 262 carts at 2s. a cart per day for 50 days coming and going – £1,310. Total – £5,110.

Whereof must be received for 18,000 men at 2d. a day for bread and drink – £4,200; and at 2½d. a day for a man for bread and drink – £4,914; and at 3d. a day – £5,944. So that at 2d. a man the victual is more than the receipt by £910, at 2½d. by £196 and at 3d. there will be more received than the victuals draw unto towards the charges of bringing the victuals by sea – £834. Charges of the provender: 4,930 quarters at 4s. a quarter – £986. Whereof there shall be received again for the horsemen's horses and for the provender of the beasts of carriage: 2,790 quarters – £558. So the provender shall cost more than shall be received because of the provender spent by the beasts of carriage – £428. So that at 3d. a man there shall be saved but £406. Also, for 2 lb. of meat, 1½d., and so every soldier shall have for his 4½d. 1 lb. of biscuit, a bottle of drink and 2 lb. of meat. The 30 carts for ordnance are among the 262 mentioned; in addition 400 draught horses must be provided.

To come to Berwick. Bakers for biscuit to teach others, for there are few skilled here, to serve for the first eight days, for which there is enough ready ground meal. 140 tons of sweet wines for making drink at 200 gallons a ton. There is enough oats for provender for the eight days. More ordnance for battery and the field, and all things belonging, according to the rate in my former book, and all necessary for the lack of ordnance and artillery here.

To be sent by sea to the Firth. 360,000 lb. of biscuit, 600 tons of beer, 140 tons of sweet wine at 200 gallons a ton – the beer to serve the army if it lies at Edinburgh so long, which will save 210 tons of sweet wines, which will cost £2,000 here, and the beer not above £600. The other 140 tons of sweet wine to serve for the eight days homeward. 3,550 quarters of oats, barley, or both, for provender. All which to be in the Firth before the army enters Scotland. In my opinion you shall not send a main army far into Scotland and remain any while without revictualling by sea, for the great abundance and excess of carriage, especially at this time of year. An army coming in by land and the navy coming by sea will put the Scots in no small dread. This way the army will not lack victuals or provender although they found none in Scotland.          SP 10/3, no. 22

**96.**   March 11. Certificate of George Mathew, esq., commissioner of musters for the hundred of Llantrisant, Glamorganshire.

Able men [*named*]: Llantrisant – 42, Ystrad – 16, Llanwonno – 19, Aberdare – 14, 'Lanylltyd' – 7, Pentyrch – 5. Total – 103. In harness, i.e. coats, skulls, daggers and swords – 42. Harnesses upon gentlemen: George Mathew, esq. – 8, William Mathewe – 2. Bills – 42, pikes – 10. Total harnesses – 52. No horses or geldings meet for demilances or light horsemen. Bills and glaives ready at one hour's notice for the rest of the unarmed men.

*Signed.*                                                                                            SP 10/4, no. 1

**97.**   March 15. The council to the bishops.

Parliament lately established that, according to the use of the primitive church, communion should be distributed under both kinds. The king, with the advice of the lord protector and council, caused some of his most learned prelates and others to confer, and after long deliberation they have agreed on an order for the distribution, of which we send a copy. We are sure you will dutifully publish this order; but, remembering the devil's craftiness and considering that many curates cannot or will not be so ready to employ it, have the books delivered to every parson, vicar and other curate in your diocese, that they may have time to instruct themselves and their unlearned parishioners before Easter. The order is published so that in all the realm one uniform prayer should be quietly used.

*Signed by*: the archbishop of Canterbury, Lord Rich, the earl of Arundel, Lord St John, Lord Russell, Sir William Petre, Sir Edward North, Sir Edward Wotton.

*Printed*: Wilkins, iv, 31–2. Cardwell, i, 72–4.                                         SP 10/4, no. 2

**98.**   March 26. Newcastle. Thomas Wyndam to the duke of Somerset.

In my last letter I advised that the king's navy should remain at berth, the more to disconcert the enemy. Considering the command of your last letter that I should be at Newcastle with the whole navy by the end of this month: the winds at Sir Thomas Palmer's departing being fair and the tides at the best of the spring for entering Newcastle with the great ships, and being forced for lack of victuals, especially beer, I came out on the 23rd in the bark *Ager* with the *Mary Hanbrow*, the *Phenexe*, the *Dowbull Roysse* and the *Marlen*, which all came to this haven on the 23rd. In all we had not three pipes of beer, because we left all the victuals we could in the castle and fort; yet they have not beyond one week's dinner. I sent the factor to conduct over the victuallers, at present at Holy Island. The *Mary Henbrow* is weak and leaking, her hold needing much repair. The sea was so great in our passage that the *Phenexe*, lately repaired at Newcastle, was so leaky that she was brought here with much pain: she must be where she may be bound with stays and footwales. Command these poor men their pay for their great pains. Many are very sick and weak because of ill victuals and lack of money. I received £100 from Sir Andrew Dudley, and since my arrival £400 of Master Woodwale's treasure in prest. The whole pay of the navy is about £2,000, above the reward promised for their labour in the castle and fort. Tell us your pleasure for our departing to sea. Let 200 replacement men be sent from Hull or London. I have spoken here with [Robert] Horsley, one of the victuallers, who says that the whole provision of victuals is ready at Berwick and Holy Island: on our arrival here no victuals were provided.

*Endorsed*: Post haste, for your life.                                                   SP 10/4, no. 4

**99.**   March [31].* Indenture of all gold and silver bullion coined in the office of Sir William Sharington, under treasurer of the mint at Bristol, between 1 May 1547 and [31]* March 1548.

Gold – 213 lb. 10 oz. Silver – 16,333 lb. Harps and groats – 2,657 lb.

*          Date on analogy of previous year's indenture, no. **29** above.

*Parchment. Mutilated.*
*Signed by*: Roger Wigmore, [comptroller and surveyor] and Thomas Marshall, [assaymaster].      SP 10/4, no. 3

**100.** April [? 11]. Obligation given to Lazarus Toucher securing the payment of 167,218 florins lent by him to the king.
*Latin.*
*Badly mutilated.*
*Signed by*: the duke of Somerset, the archbishop of Canterbury, Lord St John, Lord Russell.      SP 10/4, no. 5

**101.** April 14. London. R[obert] Goche, at his house there, to William Cecil.
I was to speak with you, and heard you were sick. I wished to take my leave of you and tell you of a letter sent to me from Mr Chancellor [of augmentations] for the bailiwick of Weston, which my servant has occupied since the death of William Reisbie, bailiff since the suppression – not a weighty thing, but some increase of living to my poor man. Serving the king honestly, I have small commodity or profit, but when any bailiwick falls vacant my few poor servants sometimes desire my help. Having nothing to gratify them with, I help them to the same, thinking they will not be supplanted if they serve honestly. But a year ago your servant [Richard] Trowghtone forcibly took a bailiwick from one to whom I had given it, lewdly speaking behind my back. Because he was your servant I never spoke of it. Now this other bailiwick, which my servant has occupied a year or more, is sought by you – the rather, I think, because he is my man. If you will have it I will not stick with you in that or anything. But I would be grateful for the continuance of my servant in what I promised for him.
*Holograph.*      SP 10/4, no. 6

**102.** April 19. Extract from chantry certificate for the dean and chapter of St Paul's Cathedral, London.
There are forty-seven chantries in the cathedral, including those of Fulk Povell and John Brayforde, founded in 1298 and 1275 and since united, of which the present incumbent is Alexander Smithe, who has a house and sustenance to the net annual value of £14.1.1½d. [*items specified*] and £1.13.4 for an obit.
*Signed by*: William May, [dean], John Reston, William Ermysted and Gabriel Dune, [canons of St Paul's].      SP 10/4, no. 7

**103.** May 10. Westminster. Lord Seymour, [lord admiral] to all vice-admirals, mayors, sheriffs, bailiffs, constables and other royal officers concerned.
Complaint has been made to me on behalf of several London merchants who freighted sundry merchandise at London and Rye in French ships to be transported to Rouen and Dieppe. The vessels were apprehended at sea and boarded by Englishmen who robbed and spoiled them. Repair to the ports within your offices and immediately examine all vessels arriving, and sell any wares suspected to belong to the merchants. On further examination attach the ships and the parties, committing them to safe custody, seizing the goods and as much of them as was spoiled and unbarked. Search the premises and report to me.      SP 10/4, no. 8

**104.** [May]. Instructions to Lord Clinton, appointed admiral of the fleet.
Since the Scots and French are known to be assembling large forces by land and sea the king has decided to arm a navy and appoints you admiral, with authority to commandeer supplies from any of the king's ports. Go first to Harwich, entering the ship of your choice and placing captains in the others, namely the *Greate Barke*, the *Peter*,

the *Pauncye*, the *Jesus of Lubeck*, the *Swepstak*, the *Ane Gallant*, the *Antelop*, the *Harte*, the *Greate Gallee*, the *Greate Mistress*, the *Mary of Hamburgh*, the *Lesse Galey*, the *Salamander*, the *Grehounde*, the *Barke Aucher*, the *Saker*, the *Fenix*, the *Marlyon*, the *Poplin*, the *Sonne* and the two new pinnaces. Sail north, without waiting for victuals but appointing them to follow; endeavouring on your way and while there to take advantage of all Scots and Frenchmen you meet, men of war, merchants and others, forcing them to yield and disposing of them to the king's best uses. Passing Tynemouth and Holy Island take with you such other ships and victuallers as intend to augment your force; the taking of smaller vessels is left to your discretion, with the advice of the officers of the admiralty. Sir Thomas Palmer is to accompany you from Holy Island to the mouth of the Forth, being specially instructed to advise you. If you discover the French and Scots navies have entered the mouth you shall lie with a convenient part of your fleet before it and do your best to keep them in, to have command of the whole sea, to prevent them receiving victuals or coming out to meet you, leaving a convenient wind to close them in. Go with Sir Thomas Palmer to Burntisland and Inchkeith and make fortresses there according to our specific verbal instructions to you and him. The commanders are to keep that passage and prevent the coming of foreign victuals from the Fife side. You will thus have a force to devastate that part and you have permission to land men for that purpose, leaving the ships adequately defended. Take advantage of their victuals about Leith if you think fit. Send some of your shallops for their victuals at Aberlady. You are allowed discretion to amend these instructions as convenient, on the advice of Sir Thomas Palmer and the others. We believe the prescribed course will be the best.

Speak gently with the ships of the emperor and other friendly nations – all, that is, except the Scots and the French. If they bring munitions or victuals for the enemy, hold them: otherwise let them proceed unless you need any of their supplies, in which case you may gently take them by indented bill and we will defray the charges.

If you learn that, because of the time of year or otherwise, the French and Scots ships are laid up or otherwise unable to annoy your fleet, go to Broughty [Craig]. Learning from Sir John Luttrell the names of those who have been disloyal, prosecute them, their lands and friends to their devastation, as you may also do to Fife side. When the Germans come we will give you further order for their employment. We have in the meantime by [*indecipherable*] of the offer made by the master of Ruthven to practise by his father the delivery of St Johnstoun [Perth] and also that Melvile, a Scotsman sent down to Berwick, may do some credit in Fife. Take them aboard with Sir Thomas Palmer and use them well. When you come to land where they are to serve, let them disembark. When Germans come by sea to your service use them as you think best by the advice of Lord Grey and Sir Thomas Palmer.

Take special order with the captains of every ship, pursers and other officers for victuals, regarding the preservation of the cask which is to serve for special purposes and cannot be recovered for money when need requires, and also for the distribution and preservation of victuals, so that in time of need they are fully furnished without having to wait for the tide. You will receive from Sir Richard Southwell and John Riche the numbers of men allotted to the ships under your charge; consider what numbers are furnished and let us know. On your arrival inform Lord Grey and Sir Thomas Palmer of the state of the country. Send us frequent and diligent information by small vessels or by land.

*20 pp.*

*Corrected draft; some passages partly indecipherable.*          SP 10/4, no. 9

**105.** [? May]. The king to sheriffs and justices of the peace.

We have ordered the justices of the peace of coastal shires to erect their beacons for warning the inland shires to assemble for defence, as necessary. Thinking that the inland shires should be ready, you are to confer, according to your orders in the late king's time and since, to direct beacons to be set up and watched in the places they were last in, and that the force of the shire may be ready to march under suitable captains for the defence of such places as the beacons of other counties give warning. Follow your previous rules, setting forward the most able men, well armed, with eight days' victuals or money for that time. In the meantime have special regard to the doings of the common people; in case of any misdemeanours, unlawful assemblies, riots and breaking of the peace, order the stay and reformation of the same with all diligence. See that clothiers, other artificers and others with servants by covenants or otherwise keep them in labour, good order and obedience.

*Unfinished draft.*                                          SP 10/4, no. 10

**106.** June 4. Ely Place. The earl of Warwick to William Cecil, with the lord protector.

Thank you for your friendly remembrance of my suit to [the lord protector] and your news of the sequel, which I trust will succeed, of which all my lord's friends will receive the best for the king's honour and his own.

*Holograph.*                                              SP 10/4, no. 11

**107.** June 5. The council to justices of the peace.

We expect you have done the king's pleasure for ordering and watching beacons and putting able men in readiness with able captains in every hundred. To avoid confusion on the landing of enemies you and the whole force of that shire and other shires mentioned shall attend only to the defence of the coasts of the counties of [*blank*] and not elsewhere without special command. In case of landing the lord protector has appointed Lord [*blank*] to be lieutenant for the repulse of the enemies and the order of the county. We have informed you so that if you repair thither with the force of the shire you shall obey his order. In a postscript to our last common letters to sheriffs and justices of the peace we required that, in case of the setting forward of the force of the shire, all commissioners of musters should go in person. But since order will be needed for those remaining behind, some gentlemen should remain also. We have chosen certain whose names appear in an enclosed schedule [*which follows*] – all or so many of whom as are resident in the shire may be left at home. Take order with them and inform the rest of the justices.

*Signed by*: the duke of Somerset, Lord St John, Lord Russell, the earl of Arundel, Lord Seymour, Sir Thomas Cheyne, Sir Anthony Wingfield, Sir William Petre.

                                                 SP 10/4, no. 12

**108.** [June 5. Enclosed with the above]. Names of those appointed to remain at home in case of invasion.

*Worcestershire.* Bishop of Worcester. Sir John Pakington. Sir Roland Moreton. [David Brooke].* George Willoughby. *Warwickshire.* William Willington. George Willoughby. William Lucy. *Northamptonshire.* Bishop of Peterborough. Sir Edward Mountaigue. [Edward] Saunders, serjeant at law. Edward Griffen. Francis Morgan. Robert Catlyn. *Nottinghamshire.* Sir Edmund Molineux. Sir John Chaworth. [Lord Burgh].* *Norfolk.* Sir William Paston. Sir John Haydon. Sir Nicholas Hare. Sir Edmund Bedingfeld. [Sir Richard Gresham. Henry Godericke].* Osbert Moundford. Edmund Beaupree. Thomas Gawdey. John Corbet senior. [Richard Fulmerston].* Richard Catlyn. Paul Gressham. *Oxfordshire.* Sir Walter Stoner. Henry Bradshaw. [John] Pollard, serjeant at law. William Fermor. Roger More. Thomas Wayneman. *Rutland.* Lord Zouche. Richard Cecyll. Edward Griffyn. *Surrey.* Sir Thomas Pope. Sir John Gresham. Sir Matthew Brown. Sir Christopher More.

\*       Deleted.

Robert Curson. Griffin Leyson. [John Carell].* Richard Godericke. *Hampshire.* Lord Audley. Sir Richard Lister. Sir Edmund Mervyn. [Sir John Paulet].* Sir William Berkeley. Sir William Giffard. Richard Worseley. Edward Vaughan. John Mues. *Suffolk.* Lord Burgh. Sir Thomas Turrell of Gipping. Sir Edmund Bedingfeld. Sir John Jermingham. Nicholas Bacon. John Gosnold. Lionel Talmage. [Henry Godericke].* Robert Brown. *Somerset.* Bishop of Bath. Sir William Porteman. David Broke. Thomas Clerke. William Hargill. John Wadham. William Vowell. John Mawdelyn. *Sussex.* Bishop of Chichester. Sir William Shelley. Sir Christopher Moore. John Carell. John Covert. John Stanney. John Apseley. *Wiltshire.* Bishop of Salisbury. Sir Henry Long. John Erneley. Edmund Mountpesson. Charles Bulkeley. William Stumpe. Richard Woodcocke. *Herefordshire.* [Bishop of Coventry and Lichfield].* Bishop of Hereford. [Sir Robert Tonshend. Sir John Pakington].* Sir John Price. Sir John Pilston. [Sir Rowland Moorton].* Sir Adam Mytton. Hugh Coren, clerk. [Richard Hassall].* George Willoughby. John Warmecombe. *Kent.* Sir John Baker. Sir Edward Wotton. Sir Walter Hendley. Sir Humphrey Style. Sir Martin Bowes. Sir James Hales. William Roper. Edward Thwaytes. Edward Monyng. Thomas Harlakynden. Thomas Roydon. William Goldwell. William Boyse. Anthony Sandes. *Lincolnshire. Kesteven.* Lord Burgh. Sir Thomas Hennage. [Sir Thomas Brudenell].* John Tayler, clerk. Richard Cycill. Richard Ogle. John Dyon. Richard Panell. [*Lindsey*].* [Lord Burgh].* Richard Godericke. Matthew Sentpole. William Dalyson. Richard Welby. John Broxholme. Robert Gouche. [*Holland*].* Anthony Eyrby. Nicholas Robertson. Thomas Holland. [William (? Cecil)].* Richard Goding. Thomas Paynell. *Leicestershire.* Edward Griffen. John Beamont. George Vincent. Francis [Cave]. Robert [Catlyn]. *Middlesex.* Sir Roger Cholmeley. Sir Edmund Peckham. Sir Ralph Waren. Sir Richard Gresham. Sir Martin Bowes. Sir Rowland Hill. Sir Wymond Carew. Dean of Westminster. Richard Godericke. William Locke. Robert Brooke. [William Roper].* Richard Duke. Robert Chydley. [John Gosnold].* John Tawe. John Bowes. John Yorke. Randal Cholmeley. *Dorset.* Sir Thomas Trenchart. Richard Duk. Richard Philippes. John Willyams. William Thornehyll. John Aylworth. John Lewson. *Essex.* Lord Morley. Sir Humphrey Brown. Sir Giles Capell. Sir John Mordaunt. Sir Walter Myldmay. Sir Clement Smyth, Sir Anthony Cook. Sir W[illiam] Roch. Guy Crayford. John Lucas. Edmund Mordaunt. Anthony Brown. Thomas Myldmay. William Bradbery. George Hadley. John Wyseman. William Chyshull. William Bernars. Richard Genor. John Danyell. Alexander Chyborn. John Corbett. [Henry Polstede].* John Cooke. John Hamond. William Caudenall. *Gloucestershire.* Bishop of Gloucester. [Sir John Pakington].* David Broke. [Richard] Morgan, serjeant at law. George Throgmerton. Arthur Porter. Richard Bray. [Richard Hassall].* Richard Tracy. *Huntingdonshire.* Bishop of Ely. Sir John Hynde. Sir Laurence Taylord. [Nicholas Luke].* [William] Coke, serjeant at law. Henry Godericke. Robert Aprice. Oliver Leder. Robert Druell. Thomas Fitzhugh. Thomas Wawton. William Laurence. Robert Rowley. *Hertfordshire.* Lord Morley. Sir William Candisshe. Sir John Perient. John Cocke. George Eliot. Thomas Hemmyng. John Kechyn. John Seymour. *Bedfordshire.* Lord Mordaunt. Sir Michael Fysshar. Nicholas Luke, baron of the exchequer. Francis Pigott. Thomas Dycons. Nicholas Harding. Thomas Fitzhue. John Colbeck. William Smyth. Richard Durye [Bury]. *Buckinghamshire.* Sir Edmund Peckham. Henry Bradshaw. John Crock. Edmund Wyndsor. Paul Darell. Anthony Cave. John Babam. John Goodwyn. Christopher Wescott. John Seymour. *Berkshire.* [Sir] William Essex. William Brunsopp. John Wynchcombe. Thomas Vachell. William Hide. John Knight. Robert Gayer. *Cornwall.* Thomas Trefrye. William Carneshew. John Aylworth. Thomas St Abyn. William Bere. Hugh Buscawen. *Cambridgeshire.* Bishop of Ely. Sir Edward North. Sir John Hynd. William Cocke, serjeant at law. Nicholas Bacon. Thomas Hutton. Henry Goodryk. Thomas Wendye. John Frevill. Richard Wilkes. William Byll. Henry Pygott. Richard Ward. Thomas Weston. *Devon.* Sir Thomas Denys. Simon Heyns. John Harryes, serjeant at law. John Whyddon, serjeant at

*       Deleted.

law. Richard Hales. George Rolles. Richard Duk. Humphrey Prydaux. John Aylworth. John Hull. Anthony Bery. John Rydgeway. Nicholas Bydwell. William Rope. Edmund Stur.

*Some names supplied from the commissions of the peace [CPR 1547-8, 85].*

SP 10/4, no. 12(i)

**109.** June [5]. The earl of Warwick to William Cecil.

Tell [the lord protector] that today a poor merchant who trades out of Sussex to Dieppe and Newhaven [Ambleteuse] told me that, being at Dieppe within the last fortnight, the Scotsmen inhabiting the town enticed him to remain with them and not return to England. To hear more of their meaning he pretended not to dislike their advice. He learnt that the Frenchmen mean suddenly to attack Pevensey Castle in Sussex because it is so ill guarded. I have stayed the man till I know if his grace will speak with him. He can show little else concerning the French preparations, save of [. . .] ships he saw at Newhaven ready to depart for a month past and much munition on the wharf ready to be shipped.

*? Holograph.*

*Printed*: L.F. Salzman, 'Documents relating to Pevensey Castle', *Sussex Archaeological Collections*, xlix, (1906), 26–7.

SP 10/4, no. 13

**110.** June 9. Westminster. Lord Seymour to Queen Catherine.

I have been worried that I should not have justice from those I thought would be partial. But your letter revived my spirits, because I see your patience, however the matter will weigh, and chiefly because I hear my little man shakes his head – trusting that if he lives as long as his father he will revenge such wrongs as we cannot now. Just before receiving your letter I spoke with my lord [? Somerset] who is somewhat qualified: I am in no hope, but no despair. I also told him of your mother's gift: he replied that at the end of your matter you should have yours again or some recompense. He was sorry to hear of your going to the country on Monday, trusting I would be here tomorrow to hear what the Frenchmen will do. On Monday at dinner I trust to be with you. I do not expect the Frenchmen will prevent my going with you this journey or my continuance with you. Keep the little knave lean with good diet and walking that he may be small enough to creep out of a mousehole.

*Holograph.*

*Printed*: Tytler, i, 102–4.

SP 10/4, no. 14

**111.** June 11. The earl of Warwick to William Cecil.

I have received my lord [protector]'s letters, being glad he accepts my offer to serve, which is but my duty: for his friendship I would do more if I could. I am glad that the meaning of the Frenchmen's enterprise northward is now so well known as their passing with their navy has declared, trusting they will have an ill journey.

*Holograph.*

SP 10/4, no. 15

**112.** [June 12]. Tuesday night, late. The earl of Warwick to William Cecil.

On behalf of Browne, in whose suit he desires Cecil's aid as a means to the lord protector's favour.

*? Holograph.*

*Badly mutilated.*

SP 10/4, no. 16

**113.** June 14. Ely Place. The earl of Warwick to William Cecil.

I write to ask if [the lord protector] has proceeded with the arrogant bishop* according

* Stephen Gardiner, bishop of Winchester.

to his deservings. I heard he was to be before my lord's grace and the council yesterday, but had it been so I suppose it would have been more spoken of. I fear his accustomed wiliness and the persuasions of his friends will again let the fox deceive the lion. Tell me something of the matter. Remind my lord about the navies. I hoped to take [John] Gosnold with me into the marches but am told that Townsend has his office for life; when I move he retreats, so I would be loath to be with him. I will not sue out that commission until my lord's grace hears of his demeanour, which I am loath he should do from me, for then the man would be more discredited. He cannot be removed without a great cause and I will not advise my lord to break any of the king's grants by letters patent, for the same may happen to me and others afterwards. *Postscript*. There is a rumour of some business in Ireland. Let me have news when you can.

    *Holograph.*                                                        SP 10/4, no. 17

**114.** June 14. Westminster. Licence from the king to John [Veysey], bishop of Exeter, by consent of the dean and chapter of Exeter, to grant the hundred, fee, borough and manor of Crediton and the manor of Morchard Bishop, Devon, the mansion house of Crediton, with all natives and villeins and their followers, with all their rights and appurtenances, and all other possessions there, with all tithes, fairs and markets in Crediton and all tolls, customs and other profits pertaining to the premises, and also the advowsons of the rectory of Morchard Bishop and the vicarage of Crediton *alias* the rural deanery of Crediton, which are held of the king in frankalmoin, to Sir Thomas Darcy, his heirs and assignees for ever, by fine or otherwise, reserving to the bishop and his successors an annual rent of £40, with clause of distraint. Without fine or fee in the hanaper. Similar licence to Sir Thomas Darcy to hold the premises, and to the bishop to receive the rent, notwithstanding the statute of mortmain or any other, or the absence of any writ *ad quod damnum* or any other writ.

    *Parchment.*
    *Latin.*
    *Pen portrait of Edward VI in initial letter.*
    *Enrolled*: C 66/812, m. 27 (*CPR* 1548–9, 16).                        SP 10/4, no. 18

**115.** June 18. Sudeley. Lord Seymour to William Cecil.

    You know I moved [the lord protector] in favour of Busshe, to whom I sold Yanworth manor, Gloucestershire. Thomas Culpeper, esquire, claims it and certain manors sold and exchanged by the late king to my use and to the warden and fellows of Winchester College, to Richard Tracy and others. The manors were given to Culpeper by way of remainder in consideration that the manor of Bedgebury, Kent should have been assured to Thomas Culpeper the younger, attainted of high treason, and his heirs, which was not assured, nor any other recompense (as far as I know) given to the late king. Lest the present king be called upon for recompense of the manors if they should be recovered, use the matter so that I have no cause to be further troubled to sue for any recompense on behalf of Busshe, and discharge the king of £3,000.         SP 10/4, no. 19

**116.** July 1. The council to the ambassadors.

    Knowing that the recent committal of the bishop of Winchester to the Tower will be diversely reported in many places we thought good to inform you of some of the matters for which he is committed and the favour shown to him. The king, with our advice, thinking a general visitation necessary, did about ten months ago, by the advice of bishops and other learned men, address commissions and appoint general orders and injunctions for the reformation of abuses and the good governance of the realm. These were obediently observed by all save this man who, by conference with others and open protests and letters, showed such wilful disobedience that, had it not been quickly spied, might have bred much trouble. Being sent for and charged before the whole council, he was thought to deserve the sharpest punishment. But considering the position he had held, he was only sequestered to the Fleet where he remained at ease. Within a short time, on promise of conformity, he was released and licensed to remain within his diocese. As soon as he was home he forgot his promise and began to set forward matters again which bred more contention in one small city and county than in the whole realm. To withstand those whom he thought we sent he had all his servants secretly armed and harnessed. We sent for him again and charged him; but upon a second promise made released him, only requiring him to remain at his London house because we thought best to sequester him from his diocese for a time. He soon began to meddle in matters in which he had no commission or authority, and touching the king's right. Again admonished by the lord protector, he promised to conform in all things like a good subject. Because he understood he was diversely reported of, and offended many, he offered to declare his conformity in an open sermon affirming satisfaction with the king's proceedings. But at the appointed day he spoke most arrogantly and disobediently of certain matters, contrary to express command, and in the rest of the articles to which he had agreed used such seditious speech in the presence of the king, us and a great audience, that he was very likely even then to have stirred a great tumult. He spoke of certain great matters touching our policy that we are sure he shows himself an open great offender and a very seditious man.

*Draft.*                                                                SP 10/4, no. 20

**117.**   July 2. Barnet. The earl of Warwick to William Cecil.

This poor man, having often asked me to write to you for him, met me today near Barnet and renewed his old suit with such lamentation of his necessity that I was moved to commend his case to you. The duke of Norfolk did him great wrong. The late king, being told the truth, commanded him to be restored to his office, but it was so soon before his death that it served the man nothing, who is now old and poor.

*Holograph.*                                                            SP 10/4, no. 21

**118.**   July 2. Canonbury. The earl of Warwick to William Cecil.

I have left this bearer my servant to solicit my causes, principally to know my lord [protector]'s resolution concerning the commission of marches. If my liveries will serve me I will serve [wherever] he decides. Without honest and sound associates the president* will be able to do little good with the forward and ignorant.

*Holograph.*
*Spoiled by damp.*                                                      SP 10/4, no. 22

**119.**   [July 2]. Indenture begun 1 February 1548 between Sir Edmund Peckham, high treasurer of all mints and Sir William Sharington, under treasurer of the mint at Bristol Castle, of all sums received by Peckham to the king's use of the profits of Bristol mint.

February 3 – £339.13.6. February 21 – £4,000. April 6 – £2,000. April 18 – £1,200. July 1 – £110.6.8. July 2 – £804.6.2½d. *Postscript memorandum.* To enter £5,000 received on June 14 into the counterpart of his indenture.

*Parchment. Mutilated.*
*Signed by*: Peckham.                                                   SP 10/4, no. 23

**120.**   July 4. [? Hampton] Court. John Cheke to William Cecil, concerning his suit to the lord protector for some benefice.†

*    Of the Council in Wales [i.e. Warwick himself].
†    Perhaps in connection with the grant to Cheke of the site of Stoke College, Suffolk, made 21 October
     1548 [*CPR* 1548–9, 284].

*Holograph (signature missing).*
*Torn in half, left side only remaining.*                                    SP 10/4, no. 24

**121.**   July 6. Sir Edward North, [chancellor of the court of augmentations] to William
Cecil.
   I enclose the draft of a lease in reversion of the manor of Hotham, Yorkshire, according
to the lord protector's command, as you shall see from [Sir Michael] Stanhope's letter,
also enclosed [*which follows*]. Help the matter with your favour and expedition. Although
called a manor it is but a farm, having no tenants.
   *Partly holograph.*                                                       SP 10/4, no. 25

**122.**   June 27 [enclosed with the above]. St James's. Sir Michael Stanhope to Sir Edward
North, chancellor of the court of augmentations.
   You know that the lord protector has granted a lease in reversion of the manor of
Hotham, Yorkshire to my servant Richard Maunsell in lieu of another thing. He has no
cause to remain here but the suit of the lease, and wishes to depart to do my business
in the country, so I commend the expedition of his suit to you.    SP 10/4, no. 25(i)

**123.**   July 7. Pendley. The earl of Warwick to William Cecil.
   I see by your letter that [the lord protector] does not wish to displace any officer. I
first wanted a new justice associated with me and you sent me word that my lord allowed
my choice of [John] Gosnold. After that it was altered and not thought right Townsend
should leave his office. But, being slandered that he and his wife take all that comes,
besides his corrupt judgement, it was thought (although Townsend continued) that some
others should be displaced and then that none should be lest they blame me. I wrote to
my lord again and he sent you to me to know which I would have out. I sent you the
names of the commissioners – [Sir John] Pris, [David] Broke and one or two others –
whom I thought might best be spared. I had answer that my lord would wait, not seeming
to disapprove, but was finally told that he is hardly bent to remove any. By whose
persuasion this happens I know not, but am sure I have base friends who smile to see
me so used. But I trust, despite my charges and pains, I have made my provision there.
Despite mockery I shall be as ready to serve as those who have now won their purpose,
not the first or last to be worked with my lord. If they work no more displeasure I will
be more willing to forgive.
   *Holograph.*                                                              SP 10/4, no. 26

**124.**   July 13. Southwark. Sir Anthony St Leger to William Cecil, master of requests.
   Late yesterday evening I received your letter of the 12th, perceiving that [the lord
protector] wishes my brother to repair to him to answer a stranger's old charges. Although
I think him very ill to travel (as you partly know) and poor to sustain the charge I shall
send to him, forty miles away, to obey my lord who will, I trust, weigh his long, painful
and chargeable service. Remember my suit for licence to exchange with the archbishop
of Dublin, the dean of Christ Church or the bishop of Meath such benefices I have in
Ireland for temporal lands worth £50 a year which I may sell to pay my debts. Accept
this token of a dozen marten skins for a remembrance until better comes. I would have
attended myself, but my lord's grace licensed me to repair to my house where I have
not been ten days in ten years.                                             SP 10/4, no. 27

**125.**   July 13. London. The chancellor and council of the court of augmentations to
William Cecil, secretary to the lord protector.
   Suit is made to us for a commissaryship and registrarship of certain exempt and private
jurisdictions within the dioceses of York, Lincoln, London and Westminster (which

remain at the king's disposition) as his highness has lately done for the jurisdictions of St Albans and Bury. As it shall be much quietness to the inhabitants to have officers to hear their causes at home as before the dissolution of such places, and because commodities will come to the king as previously to the monasteries, you are to further the suitors (whom we think apt) to have the king's bill assigned to us to pass under the seal of the court of augmentations.

*Signed by*: Sir Edward North, [chancellor]. Sir Walter Mildmay, Richard Goodrich, John Gosnold, John Arscot. SP 10/4, no. 28

**126.** July 14. London. Grant of arms by Thomas Hawley, Clarenceux king of arms to Robert Knyght, gentleman, of Bromley, Kent.
*Illuminated parchment. Two seals.*
*Printed*: *Miscellanea Genealogica et Heraldica*, ed. W.B. Bannerman and A.H. Hughes Clarke, 5th ser., i, (1916), 287 and discussed in R. Griffin, 'A note on two grants of arms,' *Archaeologia Cantiana*, xxxiii, (1918), 153–5. Both articles contain facsimiles of the arms. SP 9/1/5

**127.** July 15. Eton. Thomas Smith, principal secretary to William Cecil, master of requests.
The dean of Peterborough, who is mortally ill with a palsy, was content to resign a prebend to [Edward] Gascoigne of Queens' College, once my pupil. I would rather he had the whole deanery and dare answer for his wit and judgement. He will commune with you: further him as much as you can. You may count on me if you think right, as I do, to ask [the duchess of Somerset's] help. Thus, as I think, imprisoned without cause, will [the lord protector] come here.
*Holograph.* SP 10/4, no. 29

**128.** July 16. Pendley. The earl of Warwick to William Cecil.
I am urgently written to by a lady who, having been destroyed by bad London surgeons, has been eased by the surgeon of Boulogne. Please have my lord [protector] let him remain or she may lose a leg. *Postscript.* My lord's token or command to the deputy of Boulogne will serve.
*Holograph.* SP 10/4, no. 30

**129.** July 19. Hampton Court. John Fowler, [groom of the privy chamber] to Lord Seymour.
Thank you for your letter of the 15th which I showed to the king. In my last letter I told you that if he had time he would write to the queen and you, but he begs your pardon for he is not half a quarter of an hour alone. He has written the enclosed commendations [*which follow*], willing me to tell you he is bound to remember you always. I have no news but that we hope Haddington will be able to abide this great brunt. The king looks every day for good news; [the lord protector] sends him the letters as they come. [The duchess] of Somerset has had a goodly boy: I trust the queen shall have another. The king will christen my lord's son, but I cannot tell whether he will go to Sheen himself. The lord protector has given me the keeping of the great park of Petworth or Woolavington. On Monday I intend to go to Sussex and see them. Let any letters be delivered to myself. See that this tells no more tales after your reading. Now I write at length because I am promised a trusty messenger. *Postscript.* I forgot to tell you about the money you would my friend should have: when he has need I shall be bold to send.
*Holograph.*
*Printed*: Tytler, i, 110–2. SP 10/4, no. 31

**130.** July 18 [enclosed with the above]. Hampton Court. The king to [Lord Seymour].
Thank you and commend me to the queen.
*Holograph.*
*Printed*: Tytler, i, 112. SP 10/4, no. 31(i)

**131.** [July 18. Enclosed with no. **129** above]. [Hampton Court]. The king to Lord Seymour.
Send me as much as you think good for [Hugh] Latimer and deliver it to Fowler.
*Holograph.*
*Printed*: Tytler, i, 112. SP 10/4, no. 31(ii)

**132.** July 21. Pendley. The earl of Warwick to William Cecil.
My servant Cuthbert Musgrave, this bearer, has made a suit or renewed an old one to [the lord protector]. I would help him for he is my kinsman, but I was not privy to his suit. He is bold but indiscreet: help him as you can. *Postscript.* After writing this I received a letter from Sir Anthony Lee about the bad behaviour of a priest belonging to Lord Windsor, to whom I wrote since my coming to the country after complaints from the mayor and best inhabitants of Chipping [High] Wycombe, Buckinghamshire. If Lord Windsor had some sharp letter or command from my lord he would do much good, for he is the chief ringleader of all who serve in this county.
*Holograph.* SP 10/4, no. 32

**133.** July 24. Windsor. John Hales to the duke of Somerset.
I do not intend flattery if my information pleases you. The people in all the circuit we have passed* and now almost finished for the first time, although suspected of disobedience, we found tractable and quiet. If they had justices of the peace and preachers devoted to God and the king all these suspicions of sedition would be proved utterly false. The people thank God for so good a king and perceive your zeal and love for them. If the thing goes forward – without which the country will soon be in misery – no king will have more faithful subjects. The people will embrace God's word only when they see it bears good fruit. Although it may be thought a money matter, I believe you that, despite selfishness, it will proceed to the common good and concord. Because the commissioners are not heard of elsewhere we thought men only intend displeasure there. If the rest might proceed we would avoid slander. Being done before parliament, all might know what damage has happened, and what will follow if it is not resisted. We did not think it right to send you details until we have received the presentments in our next circuit, for hitherto we have only given them their charge. But we hear of great efforts to corrupt jurors, and much money offered to men to sue to be sheriffs next year – so that if anything is now presented, friendly sheriffs may give friendly inquests. If the matter is handled as in the past in the exchequer, that the king's attorney and solicitor may put in and out, do and undo what they wish, your intent will be frustrated and our labours in vain.
*Holograph.*
*Printed*: Tytler, i, 113–7. SP 10/4, no. 33

**134.** July 26. Pendley. The earl of Warwick to William Cecil.
Dr [Nicholas] Ridley, bishop of Rochester has a prebend in Canterbury Cathedral and receives the profits for a time by the lord protector's grant to help pay the first fruits of his bishopric. This bearer, my chaplain, is honest and learned; recommend him to the lord protector for the next voidance, trusting that the bishop might soon afterwards let him take possession.

\* On a commission for enclosures.

*Holograph.* SP 10/4, no. 34

**135.** July 27, 4.30 a.m. Waltham. Thomas Fisher to William Cecil.

Although I hurried to leave London, where I was last night before 8, because of the sloth of the post and lack of horses it was 3 this morning before I passed Shoreditch. I searched London for horses like a hunting spaniel; without [Richard] Palady's help I would have been there till now. Tell [the duke of Somerset] when I left. I do not know how I shall ride but will do my best to accomplish my charge.

*Holograph.*
*Endorsed*: Haste, haste. SP 10/4, no. 35

**136.** July 27, 4 p.m. Stamford. Thomas Fisher to William Cecil.

I have been badly handled by post horses and by the post at Royston, about whom I said I would complain to the master of the posts. Let [Sir John] Mason upbraid him in his next despatches; unless he and others are sometimes reminded by the master, travellers will be unable to make necessary speed. I arrived here about 2 this afternoon. Much rain fell last night, impairing the way and discomforting my man, the guide and myself. Within four miles of this town we were trapped for more than three hours by rain and great hail, sheltering under the lord privy seal's hedges at Thornhaugh. I had to change here, as did my servant, who is so covered in rain and dirt that I fear I shall leave him here or at Grantham. Your country lacks neither thunder, hail, rain nor lightning. I am ready to leave. My friend Mr Trige tells me your father, mother and son are well. *Postscript.* Commendations to your wife, Mr Steward, Jenkyn, [John] Seymour and my old wedlock Winifred and the rest.

*Holograph.*
*Endorsed*: Post haste with all diligence.
*Printed*: Tytler, i, 117–9. SP 10/4, no. 36

**137.** [July].* Light horses and demilances to be furnished by taxation. [Numbers of light horses given first, numbers of demilances (if any) second].

*Lords and other privy councillors.* Lord protector – 20 & 20. Archbishop of Canterbury – 10 & 10. Lord chancellor [Lord Rich] – 10 & 10. Lord great master [Lord St John] – 10 & 10. Earl of Warwick – 10 & 10. Lord privy seal [Lord Russell] – 12 & 8. Earl of Arundel – 12 & 8. Lord admiral [Lord Seymour of Sudeley] – 12 & 8. Treasurer [of the household] [Sir Thomas Cheyne] – 10 & 10. Comptroller [Sir William Paget] – 10 & 10. Vice-chamberlain [Sir Anthony Wingfield] – 4 & 2. [Sir Anthony] Denny – 6 & 6. [Sir William] Herbert – 6 & 6. [Sir Edward] North – 6 & 6. Chancellor of [first fruits and] tenths [Sir John Baker] – 2 & 2. Secretary [Sir William] Petre – 2 & 2. [Sir Ralph] Sadler – 4 & 2.

*Privy chamber and certain of the council at large.* Sir Michael Stanhope – 6 & 4. Sir Edward Rogers – 4. Sir Francis Bryan – 6 & 4. Sir Thomas Cawarden – 6 & 4. Sir John Gates – 4 & 2. Sir Thomas Paston – 4 & 2. Sir Thomas Darcy – 4 & 2. Sir Thomas Speke – 4 & 2. Sir Maurice Barklay – 3 & 1. Sir John Williams – 10 & 6. Sir Thomas Pope – 4 & 2. Sir Richard Southwell – 4 & 2. Sir Thomas Moyle – 3 & 1. Sir Walter Myldmay – 2 & 1. Sir Robert Southwell – 4 & 2. Sir Arthur Darcy – 4 & 2. Sir Wymond Carew – 4 & 2. Sir Anthony Aucher – 3 & 3. Sir William Candisshe – 4 & 2. Sir Edmund Peckham – 4 & 2. Lord chief baron [Sir Roger Cholmeley] – 4 & 2. Sir John Gressham – 2 & 2. Sir Richard Gressham – 2 & 2. Sir Rowland Hill – 2 & 2. Sir Ralph Waren – 2 & 2. Sir Martin Bowes – 2 & 2.

*Lords.* Marquess Dorset – 0 & 5. Marquess of Northampton – 0 & 5. Earl of Oxford – 0 & 5. Earl of Huntingdon – 0 & 5. Earl of Southampton – 0 & 5. Earl of Sussex – 0

* Assigned to or about this month by Hoak, 46, 287 n. 58.

& 2. Earl of Rutland – 0 & 3. Lord Wentworth – 0 & 2. Lord Burgh – 0 & 2. Lord Morley 0 & 2. Lord De La Warr – 0 & 2. Lord Mordaunt – 0 & 2. Lord Cromwell – 0 & 2. Lord Windsor – 0 & 2. Lord Zouche – 0 & 2.

*London.* 100 & 100.

*Middlesex.* Robert Chidley – 0 & 1. William Stamford – 1. Thomas Rolf – 1. Thomas Burbage – 1. John Rowley – 1. John Edgose – 1. John Bowes – 1. William Goddard – 1. Thomas Hayes – 1. William Edwardes – 1. Henry Toppes – 1. William Rigges – 1. Robert Morton – 1. Ralph Parker – 1. William Belamy – 1. Alan Nycoll – 1. Edward Stokwood – 1. John Leeke – 1. Sir Thomas Wrothe – 1. Edward Taylor – 1. Thomas Hemyng – 1. Bishop of London – 2 & 3. Dean of St Paul's – 1. Archdeacon of Essex – 1. Archdeacon of Colchester – 1. Dean of Westminster – 1. Archdeacon of Middlesex – 1.

*Surrey.* Sir Christopher Moore – 2. Sir Robert Acton – 2. Henry Goodyere – 0 & 1. Henry Leyke – 1 & 1. Henry Vyne – 1. Lady Knyvet – 0 & 2. Lady Weston – 1. John Wyntershull – 1. Henry Polstede – 1. Sir Matthew Brown – 0 & 1. Robert Curson – 1. John Scot – 1. [*blank*] Woodcock – 1. Henry Mannockes – 1. Ambrose Wolley – 1. [Margaret] Whorwood – 1. William Saunders – 1. Alan Horde – 1. Thomas Liste – 1. Thomas Gaynsford – 1. Lady Dannet – 1. Archdeacon of Surrey – 1.

*Sussex.* Sir William Goring – 1 & 1. John Covert – 1. Sir William Shelley – 1 & 1. Lady Sherley – 1. William Sherley – 1. John Apslee – 1. John Carrell – 1. Nicholas Pelham – 1. Thomas Darrell – 1. Thomas Morley – 1. John Sakvile – 0 & 2. John Culpeper – 1. Richard Covert – 1. Nicholas Gaynsford – 1. Richard Bellingham – 1. Sir John Gage – 1 & 2. Robert Oxenbridge – 2. Richard Sakvile – 1. John Aysshbournham – 1. Ralph Johnson – 1. William Wyborn – 1. William Cheyne – 1. Anthony Pelham – 1. John Palmer – 1 & 1. Sir John Dawtrey – 2. Thomas Devenisshe – 1. Sir Geoffrey Poole – 1. [Sir] Henry Hussey – 1. Sir Anthony Windsour – 1. Edmund Forde – 1. Bishop of Chichester – 1 & 3. Dean of Chichester – 1. Archdeacon of Lewes – 1. Archdeacon of Chichester – 1.

*Lincolnshire.* Sir Thomas Hennage – 2 & 2. Sir William Skipwith – 1 & 1. Henry Portington – 1. Sir John Candisshe – 1. Lord Sheffield – 1 & 1. William Mounson – 1. Matthew St Poole – 1. John Torney – 1. Lady (Elizabeth) Askue – 1. Robert Brokilsbee – 1. John Bellow – 1. Sir Thomas Myssendyn – 1. Sir Edward Madyson – 2. Sir Robert Turwhit – 0 & 2. Sir Francis Askue – 2. Richard Bolles – 1. Arthur Dymmock – 1. Matthew Thymbelby – 1. John Hennage – 1. Sir Thomas Massingberd – 1. Sir John Copledike – 2. Thomas Lytelbury – 1. Leon Godericke – 1. Vincent Grantham – 1. Richard Wolmer – 1. Thomas Wymbisshe – 1 & 2. Mary Wymbisshe – 1. Lady Hussey – 1. Richard Dysney – 1. Richard Markham – 1. Nicholas Jakson – 1. Sir John Thymbelby – 1 & 1. Godfrey Colvyle – 1. Boston town – 0 & 2. Richard Ogle – 1. Henry Tofte – 1. Anthony Irby – 1. Bishop of Lincoln – 1 & 2. Dean of Lincoln – 1. Archdeacon of Lincoln – 1. Archdeacon of Huntingdon – 1. Archdeacon of Buckingham – 1. Archdeacon of Leicester – 1.

*Oxfordshire.* Sir William Barantyne – 0 & 2. William Farmor 1 & 1. Antony Brigham – 1. Sir Walter Stoner – 1 & 1. Humphrey Aysshfeld – 1. John Croker – 1. Thomas Gibbons – 1. Thomas Briges – 1. William Dormer – 1. Thomas Lentall – 1. Sir John Brome – 2. Richard Fenys – 1. [Thomas] Weyman – 1 & 1. Leonard Chamberlayn – 1 & 1. Sir William Raynsford – 1. Bishop of Oxford – 1 & 2. Dean of Oxford – 1. Archdeacon of Oxford – 1.

*Wiltshire.* Henry Bramker – 1. Edmund Mompesson – 1. William Grene – 1. Silvester Davers – 2. Edward Dayberde – 1. Richard Scroupe – 1. Sir John Marvyn – 1. Sir William Wroughton – 1. John Goddard senior – 1. Sir Edmund Darrell – 1. John Chocke – 1. Ambrose Dauntesey – 1. John Erneley – 1. Andrew Baynton – 1 & 1. William Webbe – 0 & 1. William Bryan – 1. Bishop of Salisbury – 1 & 3. Dean of Salisbury – 1. Archdeacon of Berkshire – 1. Archdeacon of Wiltshire – 1.

*Hampshire.* Sir Richard Lister – 2 & 2. Thomas Whyte – 0 & 1. George Paulet – 1. Nicholas Ticheborn – 1. John Samebourn – 1. John Whyte – 1. William Wayte – 1. John Broume – 1. Sir William Barkley – 2. John Abarrough – 1. John Foster – 1. John Cooke – 1. Austin Whytehed – 1. Richard Waller – 1. Sir Michael Lister – 1 & 1. John Kyngesmele – 2. Sir Edmund Mervyn – 1 & 1. William Moore – 1. Sir William Gifford – 1. William Warham – 2. Thomas Welles – 1. William Thorpe – 1. John Mylle – 1. Thomas Pace – 1. Sir Francis Dawtrey – 1. Dean of Winchester – 1. Archdeacon of Winchester – 1.

*Northamptonshire.* Sir Edward Mountague – 2 & 1. Richard Humphrey – 1. John Barnard – 2. Richard Wake – 1. Antony Catesby – 1. Thomas Brudenell – 2. Simon Norwiche – 1 & 1. Edward Watson – 1. Edward Griffyn – 1. Francis Coniers – 1. Sir Robert Kyrkham – 1. Sir William Fitzwilliam – 1. Robert Wingfeld – 1. John Leveson – 1. Thomas Lovet – 1. Francis Tanfeld – 2. John Cope – 1 & 1. Giles Poulton – 1. Sir Thomas Tresham – 1 & 1. Sir Thomas Griffyn – 0 & 2. Edward Saunders – 2. Edward Osbourn – 1. John Hasylwood – 1 & 1. Roger Knolles – 1. Thomas Cave – 0 & 2. Richard Burnby – 1. Sir Robert Stafford – 1. Sir Valentine Knightley – 1 & 1. Thomas Andrewes – 1. Richard and Anthony Andrewes – 0 & 1. Sir Thomas Newneham – 1. Bishop of Peterborough – 2 & 2. Dean of Peterborough – 1. Archdeacon of Northampton – 1.

*Leicestershire.* Sir Richard Manners – 0 & 2. Sir Thomas Nevell – 1 & 1. Brian Cave – 1. Bartholomew Haselbrigge – 1. Richard Nevell – 1. Sir William Turvile – 1. George Sherrard – 1. John Dygby – 1. Francis Keble – 1. William Skevington – 1. John Beamont – 1 & 1. Francis Shyrley – 0 & 2. Francis Cave – 1. William Lee – 1.

*Warwickshire.* Sir George Throgmerton – 1. Sir Fulk Grevill – 0 & 2. Sir Richard Catesby 1 & 2. William Stoke – 1. Sir John Willoughby – 1. Henry Willoughby – 1. Sir Humphrey Ferrys – 2. Edmund Odingsall – 1. William Clopton – 1. William Lucy – 1. Thomas Verney – 2. William Willington – 1. Bishop of Lichfield and Coventry – 2 & 2. Dean of Lichfield – 1. Sir Marmaduke Constable – 1. Sir Walter Smyth – 1. Robert Myddelmore – 1. Robert Burdyd – 1. Edward Gryvell – 1. Thomas Marrow – 1. Humphrey Dymmock – 1. Thomas Shuckborow – 1. John Somerfelde – 1. Edward Ferrys – 1. William Wigston – 1. John Hicforth – 1. Giles Foster – 1. Edward Pye – 1. Thomas Boughton – 1. John Dyckeswell – 1.

*Huntingdonshire.* Oliver Leder 1 & 1. Robert Aprice – 1 & 1. Thomas Hall – 1. Sir Lawrence Taylord 1 & 1. Miles Forrest – 1. Thomas Cotton – 1.

*Rutland.* Sir John Harrington – 1 & 2. Andrew Nowell – 1. Kellam Dygby – 1.

*Cambridgeshire.* Sir John Hynde – 1 & 1. Sir Robert Peyton – 1 & 1. William Mallory – 1. Thomas Hutton – 1. Richard Everard – 1. Geoffrey Colvill – 1. John Cotton – 1 & 1. [James] Dyar – 1 & 1. Thomas Rudston – 1. Thomas Bolles – 1. Thomas Moore – 1. Thomas Lyn – 1. Bishop of Ely – 1 & 4. Dean of Ely – 1. Francis St George – 1. Thomas Chicheley – 1. John Huddeston – 1 & 1. Philip Parrys – 1. Sir Giles Allington – 1 & 2.

*Kent.* Sir John Guldford – 2. Sir Walter Hendley – 1 & 2. Thomas Roberthe – 1. Peter Carrthop, servant to the lord admiral – 1. Richard Carrthop, servant to the lord admiral – 0 & 1. Walter Mayne – 1 & 1. John Lucas – 1. Thomas Horden – 1 & 1. John Mayne – 0 & 2. Herbert Fynche – 1. Thomas Culpeper – 1 & 1. Paul Sydnour – 1. Sir Ralph Vane – 1 & 2. George Fane – 1 & 1. Thomas Roydon – 1. George Whetenhall – 1 & 1. John Dramer – 1. Peter Hayman – 1. Sir Raynold Scot – 1 & 1. John Honywood – 1. Robert Edolf – 1. Sir Thomas Kemp – 1. William Twisden – 2. Walter Moyle – 1. Edward Thwaytes – 2. William Fyneox – 1. Edward Isacke – 1. Sir James Hales – 1. William Boyce – 1. Edward Moyning – 1. John Byar – 1. John Leonard – 1. William Roper – 2. Sir Percival Hart – 2. William Sidley – 1. Sir Maurice Denys – 1. Robert Knight – 1. Sir Edmund Walsingham – 2. Thomas Grene – 1. Anthony Sandes – 1. Sir Anthony St Leger – 2. Sir Henry Isley – 1. [Thomas Spilman].* Sir William Fynche – 1. Thomas Harlakenden

*      Deleted.

– 1 & 1. Archdeacon of Canterbury – 1. Bishop of Rochester – 2. Dean [? of Canterbury *or* Rochester] – 1.

*Norfolk.* Sir Roger Townsend – 1 & 2. Sir Edmund Knevet – 1 & 2. Sir Francis Lovell – 1 & 2. Sir John Robesart – 1. Roger Wodhouse – 1. Sir Edmund Windham – 1 & 1. Sir John Haydon – 1 & 1. Sir James Bulloyn – 2. Henry Hubbard – 1 & 1. George Ogard – 1. John Reps – 1. William Hunston – 1. Humphrey Carvill – 1. Edmund Thursby – 1. Sir Thomas Holles – 1. Edmund Beauprey – 1. Thomas Dereham – 1. Thomas Waters – 1. Thomas Guiborn – 1. Sir William Fermor – 1 & 1. Robert Holdiche – 1. William Yelverton – 1. Sir John Clere – 1 & 1. Sir Thomas Clere – 1 & 1. Sir William Paston – 2 & 1. Bishop of Norwich – 1. Archdeacon of Norwich – 1. Archdeacon of Suffolk – 1. Archdeacon of Sudbury – 1.

*Suffolk.* Sir Thomas Jermyn – 1 & 1. Thomas Eden – 1. Thomas Danyell – 1. William Marnocke – 1. Richard Martyn – 1. Robert Spring – 1. William Rysbey – 1. Sir William Walgrave – 1 & 2. Antony Walgrave – 1. Lionel Talmage – 1. Francis Jenney – 1. Antony Henningham – 1 & 1. Sir Arthur Hopton – 1 & 1. Sir Henry Doyle – 2. Thomas Tylney – 1. William Forth – 1. Walter Clerke – 1. John Clerke – 1. Robert Weysey – 1. Clement Higham – 1. Thomas Lucas – 1. John Harvey – 1. Sir William Drury – 0 & 2. Thomas Heigham – 1. John Gettor – 1. Sir Philip Calthrop – 2. John Brens – 1 & 1. William Rede – 1. Christopher Playter – 1. Sir John Jermy – 1 & 1. George Colte – 1. Henry Turnor – 1. Francis Clopton – 1. Richard Codington – 1. Thomas Bacon – 1. John Drury – 1. Ralph Chamberlayn – 1. Edward Glenham – 1. Robert Downes – 1. John Croftes – 1 & 1. Robert Ayshefeld – 1. Richard Freston – 1. Henry Bedingfeld – 1. Thomas Cornewales – 1. Sir Edmund Bedingfeld – 1 & 2.

*Essex.* Thomas Eggelfeld – 1. Giles Bridges – 1. Richard Stapleton – 1. Sir William Stafford – 1 & 2. William Strangman – 1. William Harrys – 1 & 1. William Brown – 2. William Pawne [Payne] – 1. John Pastall – 2. William Barners – 2. Francis Clovell – 1. Thomas Brokeman – 1. Alexander Frognall – 1. John Alen – 1. William Aylef – 1. Sir Anthony Cooke – 1. Sir Henry Tyrrill – 1 & 1. James Baker – 1. Sir John Mordaunt – 1 & 1. Stephen Bekingham – 1. Thomas Darcy – 2. Humphrey Tirrell of [South] Ockenden – 1 & 1. Ralph Lathom – 1. John Danyell – 1. Sir Thomas Nevell – 2. George Forster – 1. [*blank*] Abell – 1 . Peter Cut – 1. Sir John Raynsford – 2 & 1. William Cardynall – 1. Edward Brigges – 1. James Morrice – 1. Edward Grene – 1. Robert Mordaunt – 2. Sir George Norton – 2 & 2. Thomas Crawle – 1. Sir William West – 1. [*blank*] Colyn of Broxted – 1. John Smyth – 1. George Stonard – 0 & 1. William Shelton – 1. John Whright – 1. John Brown – 2. Sir John Wentworth – 2 & 1. William Wilford – 1. Sir Giles Capell – 2 & 1. Francis Jobson – 1. John Christmas – 1. Thomas Audley – 1. John Lucas – 1. Richard Joynor – 1. John Wiseman – 1. William Fiches – 1. Sir Thomas Josseleyn – 1. John Coker – 1.

*Bedfordshire.* Sir John St John – 0 & 2. Sir Thomas Rothoram – 2. Sir Henry Gray – 1. William Gostwike – 1. Nicholas Luke – 1. Sir Michael Fyssher – 2. Sir John Gaskoyn – 1 & 1. Sir Urian Brereton – 2. Lewes Dyve – 1. Edmund Conquest – 1. Gerard Harvie – 1. Edmund Harvie – 1. Richard Snowe – 1. Thomas Dikons – 1. [*blank*] Cary – 1. [*blank*] Foster – 1. [*blank*] Butler – 1. Francis Pigot – 1. [*blank*] Luson – 1.

*Buckinghamshire.* Sir Robert Dormer – 1 & 2. Henry Bradshawe – 1. Sir Anthony Lee – 2 & 1. Thomas Gyfford – 1. Paul Darrell, for his own lands and his wife's – 1. John Croke – 1. Sir John Hamden – 0 & 1. Sir Robert Drury – 2. Arthur Longvile – 2. George Gifford – 1. John Godwyn – 1 & 1. William Hugon – 1. Robert Cheney – 1. [*blank*] Pagington – 1. Edmund Windesor – 1. [*blank*] Falkenor – 0 & 1. William Hawtry – 1. [*blank*] Langfore – 1. [? Leonard] Rede – 0 & 1.

*Berkshire.* Sir William Essex – 2 & 1. Sir Humphrey Foster – 2 & 1. Sir John Norres – 1 & 1. Richard Bridges – 1 & 1. John Winchcomb – 1 & 1. Sir Francis Inglefeld – 2. William Hyde – 1. Dean of Windsor – 0 & 1.

*Hertfordshire.* Sir Richard Lee – 1 & 2. [*blank*] Franklyn – 1. Sir John Peryent – 0 & 2. Ralph Rowlet – 1. Sir John Brocket – 1. John Hayworth – 1. Robert Warner – 1. Richard Ranshaw – 1. [*blank*] Dockrey – 1. Nicholas Bristowe – 1. Robert Chester – 1. Sir Robert Lytton – 2. Francis Southwell – 1. John Knighton – 1. John Cocke – 1. John Caree – 1. Sir Henry Parker – 1. William Barley – 1. Edmund Bardolf – 1. [*blank*] Horsey – 1. [? John] Newporte – 1. George Hide – 1. William Copwood – 1. William Gurrey – 1. John Kichin – 1.                                                                                           SP 10/5, no. 17

**138.**  August 3. Lord De La Warr, at his house, to William Cecil.

Help my brother Sir Anthony Sayntmond, this bearer, deliver my letter to [the duke of Somerset]. He has much to tell his grace about the king's causes in ordering his people, which I am unable to do without his grace's help.                                    SP 10/4, no. 37

**139.**  August 6. Hampton Court. The duke of Somerset to Lord Seymour.

We see from your letters your good bearing of the last evil chance in Scotland, which was not as bad as we first thought. No more than sixty were killed and none of note taken except [Sir Robert] Bowes and [Sir Thomas] Palmer. Lord Grey thinks most, with their horses and harnesses, will be delivered by their takers, the assured Scots. The news is not yet returned which will, we trust, countervail the former. The French have fired cannon at Boulogne pier for three days, with little gain but breaking down some [*blank* ]. They claim to break no peace but only annoy us for proceeding further with the pier. God knows what will happen, so do well.

*Endorsed*: Post haste.                                                                SP 10/4, no. 38

**140.**  [August 7]. The council to Lord Seymour.

We have lately heard in letters from Boulogne that the French, claiming our building of the mole to be a fortification, requested the council there by M. de l'Ange to have further building stayed and the existing work dismantled. Although the French king allowed it as long as it was thought only a wall to improve the harbour, because of the flank and the placing there of ordnance and soldiers, he will now impede its progress. The council replied that the men were only to guard our workmen, as they guard theirs, and the ordnance was put there because they had killed two of our workmen. If they impeded the building the council would make necessary provisions. Next day, seeing our building continued, they shot at the pier, to Boulogne, the base town and all our other positions, and we returned fire. We wished to inform you of our terms with the French, who still profess friendship. They have lately raided the king's pales in several places, spoiled many and killed some, claiming to act only in revenge for robberies done by our men. Their northbound navy took five of our crayers, burnt three and committed their men to the galleys. They took a ship laden with island [Newfoundland] fish, ransomed some of the men and put the rest to the galleys. Pietro Strozi, being told by the merchant that we had peace with France, replied that he and the rest were, for the time of their stay there, Scots. A pinnace of theirs lying at [Le] Portel took three or four of our victuals. The lord protector has spoken several times with the French ambassador and our ambassador has spoken to the French king, but we cannot obtain justice. Since a great fleet of theirs laden with island fish shortly returns, and many westerners have sued to send ships at their own risk, they shall be free to go to sea. Because complaints have previously been made of spoils of the king's friends, we have devised orders for you to execute with all speed.

*Signed by*: the duke of Somerset, Lord St John, Lord Russell, Sir William Petre, Sir Anthony Denny.

[1]. It is to be declared that the ships appointed to go to sea are armed and sent only against the Scots, pirates and the king's other enemies.

[2]. The owners and captains of all ships are to be bound as mentioned hereafter, with your vice-admiral, in the presence of the mayor and officers of their home ports, to behave honestly towards the king's subjects and friends, and to answer any complaints from them.

[3]. A book is to be kept of all ships with licence to go to sea, stating their burdens, ports, owners, captains and masters, with copies of the bonds or obligations for good behaviour. A copy of this book is to be sent to us.

[4]. The owners, captains and masters are to be told secretly that, besides Scots and pirates, they may stay the French fleet with the Newfoundland fish and any other French ships, saying that they have previously been spoiled by Frenchmen and could have no justice, or pretending that victuals or munitions in any such French ships were sent to aid the Scots. They must bring such ships as they take to an English port and have inventories and valuations made before the officers there, with whom the inventories, or copies, must remain.

[5]. The captains, owners and masters must also be told that since there is no open war with France, the inventories are taken so that, if peace continues and the French redress wrongs done to the king's subjects, their goods or their value may be restored. If war follows the goods shall remain to the use of the takers.

[6]. If peace continues and the Frenchmen's goods are ordered to be restored, order will be given for the charges of the takers.

[7]. Because the matter is of very great weight we have appointed Sir Thomas Denys and Sir Richard Grenefeld to act in Devonshire and Sir Hugh Trevanyan and Sir William Godolphyn in Cornwall. Your vice-admiral shall join them to see this order executed.

[8]. This commission for sending ships to sea is to be addressed only to Devonshire and Cornwall unless you think ships should go from Bristol or any other port.

*Signatures as before.*                                                                    SP 10/4, no. 39

**141.** August 9. Sudeley Castle. Lord Seymour to Sir Peter Carew [vice-admiral], Sir Thomas Dennys and Sir Richard Grenfelde (for Devonshire), John Grenefelde [vice-admiral], Sir Hugh Trevanyan and Sir William Godolphan (for Cornwall).

It is better to be prepared against a suspicious friend. The French have lately taken five of our crayers, burnt three and sent the men to the galleys. They have also taken a ship laden with island fish, putting some of the men to ransom and the rest to the galleys. Pietro Strozi, at sea, being told by the merchant that we were at peace with France, answered that during their abode in Scotland they were Scots. But they still profess friendship. A great fleet of theirs will shortly return from Newfoundland with fish, with whom we wish you to meet to requite some of these wrongs. By consent of the lord protector and council I shall licence as many ships in that shire as are willing, to go to sea at their own risk to take this fleet and any other Frenchmen they can. But because such liberty has previously brought complaints to the council they have prescribed certain orders which I enclose [*which follow*]. You may be surprised that Sir Thomas Dennys and Sir Richard Grenefelde / Sir Hugh Trevanian and Sir William Godolphan* are involved. But remembering the weight of the matter and the trust of the lord protector and council in your secrecy and circumspection I do not doubt your willing co-operation. So that I can report your activity, I wish Sir Peter Carowe / John Grenefelde,* my officer there, to send the information required by the instructions and anything else thought appropriate.

*Instructions follow*: as in no. **140** above, items 1 to 6.

*16th cent. copy.*                                                                    SP 10/4, no. 40

*        To be inserted as appropriate for Devon and Cornwall respectively.

**142.**    August 10.* Sudeley Castle. Lord Seymour to the duke of Somerset.

By your separate letter you told me that our recent loss in Scotland was not as great as first reports suggested. With you, I expect some good news. By other letters from you and the rest of the lords I understand the wrongs of the French and our doubtful terms with them. You wished me to order ships of Devon and Cornwall to go to sea at their own risk to distress the island fleet and other Frenchmen. I immediately wrote to the gentlemen you named and my vice-admirals, sending them copies of the instructions, which I required them to execute. I approve of our readiness against suspicious friends.

*16th cent. copy.*                                            SP 10/4, no. 42

**143.**    August 11. Sudeley Castle. Lord Seymour to the lord protector and council.

I learnt from your letters of the 7th of the French quarrel over our fortification on the mole at Boulogne, their cannon fire at it and our other positions there, their open enmity at sea and their feigned profession of friendship since communications between your grace and their ambassador and our ambassador and the French king. Since you have decided to meet their injuries by ordering me to send ships to distress their fleet of Newfoundland fish and any others they meet, I wrote immediately to the gentlemen of Devonshire whom you recommended and my own vice-admirals there to execute your instructions, of which I sent several copies. I shall follow these instructions if I decide to send more ships from Bristol or hereabouts.

*16th cent. copy.*                                            SP 10/4, no. 41

**144.**    August 13. Oatlands. The duke of Somerset to Lord Seymour.

We have received your letters, including one to me on behalf of Thomas Agarde for prosecution of a bargain made to him by Leche for lands worth about £50 a year. You note the evil demeanour of Leche's wife and claim the bargain was corrupt. We find for the plaintiff, without searching the private life of those before us. After further examination we think Agarde has abused you by not declaring his case truly, and if he does not immediately accomplish our order he shall know the price. We find that the bargain made by Leche should not disinherit the succession to that land so as all parties should attain their own, and first had promise from Agarde to cease to profit the bargain by fine. After we had given order, with considerations to save the inheritance, Agarde had the fine to convenient uses. We maintain our order to the impartial relief of all parties, leaving Agarde to follow our command, which otherwise we cannot see will bear towards him. *Postscript.* We enjoined Agarde to meddle no further with the bargain. Then Leche showed him to be so desperate that he would needs sell it. To save the inheritance we appointed Agarde's bargain to proceed by fine, that assurance might be made to give every man his own money and to keep the inheritance, which could not have been done otherwise. Leche did not respect the succession.

The captain of Haddington,† whom you know to be honest and modest, writes that during five days' skirmish he has killed a good number of his neighbours, many of them notable, and retains a good prisoner. Lord Grey and others write the same, adding that a notable man in a gilt harness was blown to pieces out of the town with a great gun, and there is a good prisoner in the town. The French ship *Grete Cardynale* perished on a rock and our ships sank a galley near Tantallon, apparently forced by our pursuit. Jernyngham reports that on Sunday as he went with a Scotsman, his taker, he saw many slain and hurt carried away with great lamentation, including five or six notable men in wooden biers, one a great personage followed by captains and an ensign of weeping

---

\*      So dated in the text. August 11 is given in the endorsement, in the same hand in which the whole letter is copied, and this was followed in *CSPD*, 10.

†      Sir James Wilford.

footmen. He dare not ask then, but the Scot afterwards told him they had been killed and hurt the day before, and the French had lost thirty dead and others hurt to a total of eighty. Ten or [? eleven] of ours were killed. The poor townsmen are busy with them when they skirmish. You may use this information at your discretion.

SP 10/4, no. 43

**145.**　August 13. The court at Oatlands. Lord Russell to Lord Seymour.

Thank you for your letters of the 11th with the warrant for two bucks at Enfield chase. You rejoice at the honesty of our assured Scots. They were faithful and honest and I trust will still be, for we are told they are very weary of the French. One of the galleys chased by our ships was sunk by artillery. At the same time the French admiral struck a rock and sank. The galleys retired to a place between Tantallon and the land where our ships cannot go. Our fleet is now in the mouth of the Firth [of Forth], of which we are still masters. Last week sixteen ships came from Scotland towards France; seeing them, those of the French sort came to the shore and rejoiced at the safe return of their ships. Of our men only Chamberlayne was abroad, with a further vessel, who set on them courageously and in front of 500 Frenchmen took four of their best vessels at [Le] Portel, putting the rest to flight, whom he says he would easily have taken with two or three more vessels. The four he keeps as a good outset. Our western men took three Breton vessels laden with salt, which are also stayed. The Scots begin to fortify Leith, with 500 men at work daily. Lord Shrewsbury will fortify at Pease [Sands] and Musselburgh if possible. The French camp is not yet moved. Their neighbours of Haddington are in a good state, wanting nothing more than powder. They trust to keep it until Christmas with pike and sword. At Boulogne we and the French, forgetting the treaty, have shot at and killed each other to renew acquaintance. [Sir John] Walloppe killed twelve or thirteen of them, putting the rest to flight. About the same time about 500 Frenchmen came to the mole nearby: we slew many and the rest fled. The shooting has now ceased after communication between the captains.

You have in the parish of [North] Mimms, Hertfordshire [recte Middlesex] two capital messuages, Potwells and Boltons, of £9.13.4 rent, unlet, of which I enclose details [which follow]. My secretary John Gale wishes to be your tenant and would pay the customary rents and any reasonable fine. I would be glad he should be there because he would be within six miles of his brother-in-law Sir John Butler and near my house at Chenies. Let him have at least one of the messuages, without favour, unless in the fine. Please answer in your next letters. Commendations to the queen, praying for her good deliverance.

We have received further news from Scotland that our men have had successful skirmishes with the French, killing many including one presumed from his gilt harness to be of note. Another of note is taken, with gilt harness and sumptuous apparel, who is within Haddington, which is made five times stronger than at the arrival there of the French.

*Postscript.* Francis* wishes to see you this summer and has written. I do not know what his enclosed letter will be.

SP 10/4, no. 44

**146.**　[August 11. Enclosed with the above]. Particulars of the messuages of Potwells (£3.13.4) and Boltons (£6) in the parish of [North] Mimms, Hertfordshire [recte Middlesex], of a total annual rent of £9.13.4.

SP 10/4, no. 44(i)

**147.**　August 16. Sheen. The duke of Somerset to Lord Seymour.

This bearer, Matthew Hulle, because of merchandise freighted in his ship which the owner fraudulently insured for four times its value, afterwards attempting to have it and the ship cast away, complains that his freight is detained and he is troubled in the

---

\*　　Sir Francis Russell, son and heir of Lord Russell.

admiralty court as if he would have cast his own ship and goods away. As you know your judge of the admiralty [Anthony] Hussey has not been upright in this matter, or in others with which we may charge him before you. Order him to see Hulle reasonably answered for his freight and other duties without delay and to proceed uprightly in this matter which will otherwise be sought at his hands. SP 10/4, no. 45

**148.** August 19. Sudeley Castle. Lord Seymour to the duke of Somerset.
Your letter of the 13th answered mine on behalf of Francis Agarde, my man. Although I was not fully informed of your pains to order the matter between Leche and his father, upon intimation of the lewdness of Leche's wife and his intention to part with the land rather than let bastards be his heirs, I besought you that the bargain already made should be lawfully enjoyed. The man at whose request I wrote is honest and deserved help.

I lately apprehended Walter ap John and John ap Thomas here for counterfeiting the king's coin. They will not confess to being the principal workers but say Jeyne Goughe, a smith of 'Llandylo,' Monmouthshire delivered them the money, about £3 of various sorts, of which I enclose examples. I immediately sent for his arrest but he had fled. I have caused the sheriff of Monmouthshire [and some of my servants there]* to search and bring him to me. The other two confessed that after Goughe had cast the money they rounded it by scraping on a rough stone delivered to them for the purpose. They are both now in Gloucester gaol where they will stay until I am told if you wish them sent to you or tried where they committed this treason. My thanks for your good news.
*16th cent. copy.* SP 10/4, no. 46

**149.** August 23. Lacock. Lord Seymour to the duke of Somerset.
I have received your letters of the 16th, but not by the named bearer, Matthew Hull, whose conscience is unclear. He is ashamed to appear as I know so much of his evil dealing with Kelley, Kelley's letters and his own confession to his condemnations. You wished me to write to [Anthony] Hussey (whom you call my judge of the admiralty, but is only my minister, Dr [Griffin] Lyson being judge) to see Hull answered for his freight and other charges without delay, and to proceed uprightly. Although I do not satisfy the first part of your request, when I have told you at my coming all I know in the matter you will judge that Hull ought to sue the king and you for a pardon for piracy rather than for recompense of freight. Three or four days after you examined the matter in Chelsea garden I told you that he was the principal in the piracy, confederate with Kelley, which I shall prove at our next meeting. I have written to Hussey to use only upright justice. If ever I found the contrary (as I never did) I would have been the first to procure his punishment. Do not be offended with him in this matter, in which a dishonest man is his accuser in an unjust suit.
*16th cent. copy.* SP 10/4, no. 47

[For SP 10/4, no. 48 see no. **432** below.]

**150.** September 1. Syon. The duke of Somerset to [Lord Seymour], lord admiral.
We have no time to reply to your long letter of August 27. We are sorry that just complaints have been made against you, which it is our duty to receive. In the case of Sir John Brigges and the other, avoid extreme judgements. If the complaints are true, redress them. *Postscript.* We wrote to you before on behalf of Matthew Hull and other sailors in the same ship, that the ship should be delivered and they answered of their freight. It now appears that the ship's goods were not piratically taken but carried up and down to deceive the assurers, and ought to be the king's. Hull and the others did only their duty in bringing them to light. The goods should therefore be put in safe

* Deleted.

custody until it is known if they are pirates' goods. Taking sureties of Hull should anything be hereafter proved against him, dismiss him and the other sailors, seeing them recompensed of their goods for their freight. *Further postscript (holograph)*. We have now received letters from Boulogne, as before from Dr [Nicholas] Wotton, that there will be an insurrection in Brittany. Wotton's letters speak of 10,000, these of 50,000 who, having made a fort, have either with their garrisons or by their camp defeated 400 French men at arms. The matter seems hot, for Châtillon, against these reiters, is to send Germans, thought to be those about St Etienne. This news, with that of [Sir James] Wilford and Mr Luttrel as worth reading, was not to be omitted but sent for your comfort.

    *Printed*: Tytler, i, 120–3 (less postscripts).                    SP 10/5, no. 1

**151.**   September 1. Syon. The duke of Somerset to Lord Seymour.

    We are glad by your letter that the queen your bedfellow has made you father of so pretty a daughter. Although it would have been to us, as we suppose also to you, more joy and comfort if it had been a son; yet the escape of the danger, and the prophecy and promise of sons to come, which as you write we trust to be true, is no small joy to us.

    *Printed*: Tytler, i, 123–4.                    SP 10/5, no. 2

**152.**   September 7. Fowey. John Grenefeld to [Lord Seymour], lord admiral.

    On August 25 my bark and three others of Looe and Millbrook, of 65 tons apiece, left Cornwall and arrived on the coast of Brittany, where we split up to seek our separate ventures, which caused much trouble and often drove us to chase one another. But command was given to keep together. On August 30* I, being alone within half a league of Penmarc'h, discerned a fleet of twenty-two sail of Normans and Bretons. Although our power was small we let twelve pass and set on the thirteenth. After he had challenged us with six pieces of ordnance we drove him to the shore and left him rolling on the terrible waves. In the same way we drove two other ships into the bay of Audierne; when we were thus in chase one of the fleet windward of us mustered his men and with their swords and flag washed us under their lee, to whom we made, and suddenly boarded them. The ship was 95 tons, with twenty-four men besides the captain and master that was slain in the boarding. Certain prisoners remaining with us confessed that the fleet came from Scotland and had served there six months. They had 120 pieces of ordnance and 1,100 men from Scotland, besides three Scots gentlemen who were appointed to be captains for [? provisioning] the fleet shortly appointed to go to the vintage in Bordeaux. They confessed further that 300 sail are appointed to go out of Penmarc'h, Bénodet, 'Blewet' and Le Croisic to the said vintage, for beverage and victuals for furnishing great armies and powers prepared by the French king to make war at the beginning of next year. The prisoners were encouraged at their departure from Scotland that they should shortly have greater aid from 'Martelly' from where nine galleys would come, or next March, at whose coming they were commanded to make entertainment. Six great ships are appointed to pass through the north coast into Scotland very shortly with victuals. There are lacking two or three good ships of 140 or 160 tons to be resident in the west, for their trade now is much [*indecipherable*] the sea. There are three or four Scotch rovers that often come and take their prey between Scilly and Land's End, 90 sail of which passed that way homewards from Scotland in the past twelve days. On September 3 I and my company aboard brought into the haven of Looe, Fowey and Millbrook ten sail of Bretons, Frenchmen and Normans, two ships, three barks and five badges, mostly laden with salt. We discharged their company, saving two or three of a vessel, and told them that they should travail with their king that we might have restitution and justice at his hands, considering that there is no war between us. Certain of the prisoners told

\*    Or 31.

us that twelve days ago four galleys and two great ships came out of Scotland on the North Sea, in one of which was a great number of ladies and gentlemen, which arrived at St Pol de Leon, six miles out of Morlaix, and one of our Bretons said plainly that the Scots queen was among them. It is further said by credible persons that [*indecipherable*] of Bilbao that Poitou and Gascony are risen against their king because of his demand of the gabelle of salt. If you will consult with the protector concerning the stay of the vintage fleet it will much hinder the French king's proceedings next year. It is thought that six good ships of the east parts, with the ships of Devon and Cornwall, being in order at Belle Ile [en Mer] about All Saints would bring most of them to England, if it might be secretly wrought – for the men of this country are so expert on that coast; they only lack gunpowder. The stay of this vintage will prevent much bloodshed. I pray to know your pleasure as to the Normans we have in keeping. I send you certain bills [*which follow*] I found in the ship I took for provision of their service in Scotland. All the time I was at sea I met no Newfoundland ships. Many of that country are returned home with loss of voyage because they went out so late. There are now eight good ships out of Cornwall to wait for those coming home.

    *Holograph.*

    *Some mutilations.*                                                    SP 10/5, no. 3

**153.** [? April. Enclosed with the above]. Certificate from Mathieu Dennar (?), captain La Garde and Jehan de Kaneton, seigneur de la Roche, deputy commissioners to Petre Stroccy [Pietro Strozzi], *chevalier de l'order du roi*, captain general of the army of Provence and colonel of the Italian infantry, and to Charles de Moy, seigneur de la Milleraye [Charles de Mouy, seigneur de la Mailleraye], vice-admiral of France and captain of fifty armed men, of the unloading from *Lestienne de Plenmarg* (master, Guillaume Steve[n]) of [*stated*] quantities of wine, beef, (?) eggs and candles delivered to Captain Harenbure for his [three]* two galleons; butter and fat bacon delivered to the master of *Lesperit de La Rochelle*; and further bacon and oats disembarked.

    *French.*

    *Signed by*: Kaneton and Lagarde.                                SP 10/5, no. 3(i)

**154.** [? April. Enclosed with the above]. Certificate of *Lestienne de Penmard* (Guillaume Stepha[n], master). Marines 20, servants ... (?) Rations [*stated*] of biscuit, wine, beef or herrings, bacon, butter, candles and vinegar for each marine to be distributed by the captain or master. By command of the king's lieutenants.

    *French.*

    *Signed by*: [Antoine de] Noailles.                                  SP 10/5, no. 3(ii)

**155.** April 20. Brest. [Enclosed with the above]. Licence from Merry de Seopys, *chevalier*, seigneur of the same, vicomte de Clignon, *conseiller, maistre d'hostel ordinaire du roy*, vice-admiral of Brittany to Guillaume Steven, master, to press sailors from the coast of Brittany to serve aboard his ship *Le Steven de Pennemare*, requisitioned for the king's service. He shall put to sea as soon as weather permits to execute orders to be given. The sailors, under penalty of hanging, shall obey the order immediately to embark and prepare the ship. All *justiciers*, officers and subjects shall give Steven all assistance. By command of Vice-Admiral Maillard [Mailleraye].

    *French.*

    *Signed.*                                                          SP 10/5, no. 3(iii)

**156.** [? September]. Friday. Cheshunt. Princess Elizabeth to the duke of Somerset.

    Many lines are not enough for the thanks you have deserved of me, especially for

\*     Deleted.

your care for my health, by writing and by sending your physicians, including Dr [Thomas] Bill, whose diligence has been a great part of my recovery, and who can tell you of my state of health. Thanking you for the expedition of my patent.          SP 10/5, no. 4

**157.** October 1. Lady Jane Grey to Lord Seymour, lord admiral.

Thank you for your letter and your great goodness from time to time. You have become a loving father to me, whom I shall always obey.

*Holograph.*

*Printed*: Tytler, i, 133. Green, 198. *Facsimiles of National MSS*, ii, 75 (facsimile no. XLII).                    SP 10/5, no. 5

**158.** October 2. Bradgate. Frances [Grey], marchioness of Dorset to [Lord Seymour], lord admiral.

I perceive from your letter your good will to my daughter,* and am bound to you for desiring her to continue with you. I trust that at our next meeting which, according to your appointment will be shortly, we shall make a satisfactory arrangement.

*Holograph.*

*Printed*: Tytler, i, 134–5.                    SP 10/5, no. 6

**159.** October 17. Hackney. Grant to Thomas Hayberne of London, cooper and Stephen Andrewes of London, draper, for £890.5.0 paid to the court of augmentations, of messuages and tenements then or late in the separate tenures of Ulstan Wynne, Thomas Lucas, Robert Hayes, John Lewes, Thomas Clayton, Thomas Shottesham, John Morton, Thomas Moore and Ellen Evingar in the parish of St Mary at Hill, London, and two messuages and tenements then or late in the separate tenures of Joan Goodwyn and Richard Eve in the parish of St Mary at Hill, to their heirs and successors in perpetuity, in free burgage of the city of London and not in chief. With issues since the previous Easter, without any rent and quit of all charges to the crown or any other persons, except an annual rent of 13s. 4d. of the tenement then or late in the tenure of Ulstan Wynne to the master of the Bridgehouse, London, and of an annual rent of 18s. 4d. from the messuage &c. then or late in the tenure of George Litlecote, Roland Staper and Sir Ralph Sadler.

*Latin.*

*Extract*: from C 66/814, m. 35 (*CPR* 1548–9, 130–1).                    SP 10/5, no. 7

[For SP 10/5, no. 8 see no. **419** below.]

**160.** October 26. John Yong to [Michael] Throgmerton.

Having received licence of the lord protector to write to you I told [him] how much you regretted that the cardinal's letters could not be received here, what you told me on the cardinal's behalf concerning the emperor's pretence of quarrel to the king and realm for religion, and how you persuaded me of the affection the cardinal bears towards his native country. The protector replied that he had heard of no letters sent privately by the cardinal, though he had heard of some that should have come to him by a public messenger or legate of the pope. He was surprised that the cardinal should think his letters acceptable, the pope's authority being (as you know) long abolished here. But since the cardinal offers his assistance the protector will receive and consider private letters from him, as is his custom. So, whenever the cardinal will write privately and send you or Dr [Richard] Hyllyard or another, so that he is one of our men, make the bearer stay in Flanders or France until I have word, and then I will arrange the protector's safe conduct. Since he has agreed to the hearing, I trust the cardinal's business proves as

*          Lady Jane Grey.

honourable as you have persuaded me it is.
*Holograph.*
*Partly indecipherable.*              SP 10/5, no. 9

**161.** [? October]. Names of prisoners in the Tower [of London], with the causes of their imprisonment as far as known to the lieutenant.

Thomas, duke of Norfolk. Edward Courtenay. Robert, Lord Maxwell ('Maxfelde'). The laird of Panmure ('Palmure'). Davy Dowglas, James Dowglas, William Foster, Scotsmen. Anthony Foskew. Sir John Rybald. Francis Purlam, Frenchman; suspected a spy [Marshalsea].* William Pecok, priest; refused to sign certain articles before the visitors and still is of a corrupted judgement [King's Bench].* Henry Yelverton, of Gray's Inn; would have slain his father [King's Bench].* Sawey Deshennes, Italian; taken for a spy [Marshalsea].* M. Carsey, Frenchman; sent by Lord Grey from Broughty Craig. John Edmonston, Scots servant and kinsman to Lord Bothwell; what is laid against him I know not. The bishop of Winchester. Robert Alen; for calking certain figures and prophesying [Marshalsea].* Thomas Morgayne; upon information given against him by Undrell [Marshalsea].* Julius [de Carcano], Italian; sent by the lord great master, I suppose, for circulating counterfeit testons. John Hychecokes [to Newgate or Marshalsea],† John Bradston [King's Bench],* Richard Harwarde, Luce [? Grene], Edward Havers; for robbing Vyner, a clothier, in Wiltshire. M. Trasy, Frenchman; for murders [King's Bench; to have law].* Humfrey Nelson, priest; Mr Horner, the protector's servant, knows best [King's Bench].* William West, gent.; intended to poison Lord De La Warr. James Noble, Patrick Barron, Scotsmen; of those who broke out of Colchester Castle.

             SP 10/5, no. 10

**162.** November 2. William [Paulet], Lord St John, lord great master to the lord protector.

To answer your letter concerning the coining of testons to groats, in which you doubt there may be disaster in debasing the king's coin from standard; no man may depress from the standard. Therefore every man that has testons or receives them must stand to the danger of loss [if] they are counterfeit. The officers of the mint must take heed what they receive for in receipt of counterfeits. I told them they shall not charge the king for it.

*Holograph.*              SP 10/5, no. 11

**163.** November 8. Oxford. The president and fellows of Magdalen College to the lord protector.

Some fellows of Magdalen have submitted to you that the president dissuaded them from accomplishing the tenor of your letters for redress of religion as used in the King's College, Oxford.‡ They complained that [the president] saw your letters as an innovation to dissolve our foundation, perjure us and have our lands from us. We, fellows and officers of the college, testify to the president's proceedings. [The president] said then that [he] would rather receive an order from you and the council than alter that to which we are bound by oath and statute, having as yet received no dispensation or express prohibition in your letters. But [the president] was and shall be bound by you for obedience sake and because you would order nothing which is not godly. [The president] received the Order of Communion as used in the king's chapel, willingly ministered it [him]self and caused it to be used ever since in place of high mass, contrary to the complaint of them to you. Nor has [he] expelled any fellow or scholar or complained of them to their friends. We have redressed matters on contemplation of your letters,

\*      Inserted.
†      Inserted then deleted.
‡      Christ Church.

as this bearer can tell. Do not tender the complaints against [the president] but take order by visitation, commission or otherwise for the furtherance of learning and God's honour.

*Signed by*: Owen Oglethorpe [president], William Redinge, John Wyman, Thomas Caponhurst, Simon Parrett, Thomas Gardner, James Bond, William Standishe, John Redmayn, Richard Slythurst, William Webbe, Robert Bede, Robert Haslape, William Gilbert, Thomas Godwyn, Richard Huys, John Slade, Thomas Coveney, James Goode.

*Printed*: J.R. Bloxam (ed.), *Register of Magdalen College, Oxford,* (1853–85), ii, 303–4.

SP 10/5, no. 12

**164.** November 12. Westminster. Royal commission to Thomas [Goodrich], bishop of Ely, Nicholas [Ridley], bishop of Rochester, councillors, Sir William Paget, K.G., comptroller of the household, Thomas Smith, secretary, John Cheke, the king's tutor, William May, LL.D., master of requests and Thomas Wendy, M.D., the king's physician, to visit the university of Cambridge and Eton College, in head and members to inquire into the state of learning there, and the quality of those residing, and to punish faults, by deprivation, sequestration or otherwise; to restrain the rebellious by ecclesiastical and temporal censures; to convert moneys spent in obsequies and feasts, or public or private lectures, to other uses; to convert money spent on choristers, chanters or other daily ecclesiastical services, or on grammar scholars, to the support of scholars in literature and philosophy; to expel any who are unworthy; to replace any who resign; to unite any two or more colleges of the university, of the king's or any other foundation, if it seems advantageous to the university; to change all chantries and assign the profits to the exhibition of scholars; to examine all statutes, accounts and other muniments; to change the terms of divine offices, disputations, lectures and degree ceremonies, and to substitute others more reasonable; to publish such injunctions in the king's name as they think convenient, and to abolish all statutes and ordinances repugnant thereto; to exact the oath of obedience to the king and his heirs, and repudiation of the bishop of Rome, as required by law; to summon congregations and convocations of heads and members for the execution of the premises and any urgent business; to dissolve two or more colleges and erect and endow in the king's name a college of civil law; to convert one of the existing colleges into a medical college, making its fellows fellows of the king's medical college or, if they are unwilling or unsuitable, translating them to other colleges or assigning them pensions.

*17th cent. copy*: from C 66/810, m. 19d (*CPR* 1547–8, p. 369).

*Printed*: Rymer, xv, 178–80.

*Summarised*: C.H. Cooper, *Annals of Cambridge,* (Cambridge, 1843), ii, 23–5.

SP 10/5, no. 13

**165.** [? November]. Sir Richard Hosyer to [? the council].

Item I made means to Sgr Martyn, a Venetian, about the peace between the kings of England and France. I often pursued Lord Poynings by his tabors and trumpets coming for prisoners to Montreuil. Also to [Leonard] Garton and a cousin of Mr Genynges, both prisoners, who can inform you of the pleasure I did them there, trusting by their means to have been restored to my country. Being in Rouen sundry times I pursued merchants and servants or Mr Knevett. One of them, whose name is unknown to me, is with Mr Comptroller Paget. At my first coming to Scotland I wrote to Lord Grey desiring him that I might with the king's favours be restored to my country. He replied full of hope, but would have had me advertise him from time to time the secrets of our camp, which I thought too vile and against my honesty: for whosesoever money I take, him will I serve and have ever done so.

At the return of Lord Bowes* and [Sir James] Wylford (which I trust will not be long) you will perceive the pleasures and services I did to the English prisoners there, and the means that I made to them for my restitution. Mr Dakyns, taken by the lord of 'Wasston'† can inform you what means I made to him to purchase my grace. He promised he would do his best. John Bryan, who served under Cruese, captain of 'Fernharse', whom I pledged of the Frenchmen's hands, promised to cause the general of Roxburgh to write to the lord protector for my pardon. Mosgrave, servant to [the earl of] Warwick can also witness the services and pleasures done to Englishmen there and the means I made for my coming home, and many more.

For nine years I have haunted the wars among all people – French, Italian, German, Spanish and Scots – and have seen many things which might well serve my prince and country. I know you have many captains in this realm who have seen much, but there is none in England of my years who has seen so many battles, skirmishes, sieges and action. If you put in execution the things that I have seen to your comforts, you shall think my life well given wherever you employ me by sea or land against all men.

That you shall be out of all doubt for my truth, my eldest brother may spend £100 lands, another 100 marks, and another 40 marks of lands, who will be bound in all that they have that I will serve you faithfully.

Beseeching your pity, considering the imprisonment and miseries I sustained in Paris for nine years may somewhat qualify my former lewd life, and promising to serve you with my life.

*Holograph.*
*Rough notes, the first page apparently missing.*                    SP 10/5, no. 14

**166.** [? November. Enclosed with the above]. Men willing to be sureties for Sir Richard Hosyer.

Edward Hosyer, gent., of £100 worth of lands and £500 worth of goods. John Makeworthe, gent., of £30 worth of lands and 500 marks worth of goods. Geoffrey Hosyer, merchant, of £500 worth of goods. John Hosyer, of £20 worth of land and £100 worth of goods. Robert Yerlande, merchant, of £500 worth of goods. Richard Whittakers, merchant, of 500 marks worth of goods, being gentlemen and young brethren. All of Shrewsbury, Shropshire.                   SP 10/5, no. 14(i)

**167.** [? November].‡ Parliamentary bill to curb dearth resulting from overbreeding of sheep.

The private gain to be had from sheep and wool and the fattening of oxen, runts and other animals, and consequent decline in breeding calves, beasts and milch kine has led to a scarcity of beef, butter and cheese. Cattle are smaller than they were. Prices are so risen that those keeping households are burdened and some made destitute. Therefore, all who after May 1 keep over 120 sheep, besides those used in their own houses during one year, are to keep for every fifty sheep one milch cow, and for every two kine to rear one calf, on forfeit of 10s. for every month in which they do not do so.§ No such calf is to be killed or disposed of before it is one year old, on forfeit of 10s., half of which to go the the king and half to any party bringing a suit in the king's courts or before justices of the peace. But if a cow being seasoned with a bull does not take it, or if the calf dies, the forfeiture is to be waived, on the oath of the owner to two justices to that effect. The act shall not extend to any who keep sheep only for their own households, unless they have sheep going on the commons, for one year's expense of

---

*     Sir Robert Bowes, lord warden of the east and middle marches.
†     Patrick Hepburn, laird of Waughton, Roxburghs.
‡     For dating see Jordan, i, 432 n. 2 and Bush, 50 n. 62.
§     This provision was originally drafted to the effect that all who after Michaelmas kept sheep were to keep one milch cow and one calf for every twenty sheep.

their households. Justices of the peace shall have authority to deal with matters in this act. Parish officers shall make yearly surveys and before Michaelmas make certificate of all cattle in their parishes to the justices, on forfeit of £10. Concealments by justices to bring a forfeiture of £20.

*Corrected draft.*                                                                                    SP 10/2, no. 21

**168.**   [? November]. Parliamentary bill against monopoly of farms.

Since the beginning of this parliament the king has received complaints against the ignorance of God's word and the destruction of corporate towns. Complaint is now made against the destruction of country towns and villages, dearth and the decay of people generally, chiefly caused by neglect by the nobility of their duties and their becoming graziers and sheepmasters, having pulled down many townships. This has caused decline in population and rise in prices so that labourers cannot live on the wages regulated by law and artificers cannot make or sell their works for a reasonable price, but are forced to forsake their occupations and leave the towns desolate. Let it be enacted that none holding property worth 100 marks [£66.13.4] a year after Michaelmas 1548 shall by any deceit occupy any property in which they have a private interest on forfeiture of £10 for every month's wrongful occupation, except those occupying land for the maintenance of their households, feeding horses, mules and asses. None having property worth 100 marks to occupy more than one farm, on the same pain. None to keep in his own occupation any more of his own lands to graze with any beast than of the annual value of £100 according to the usual rent (or, if it is not rented, to be so assessed), on forfeiture of 1s. for every acre so offending, provided that the soil of woods is not included. Everyone keeping 1,000 sheep shall yearly before May 6 put 200 of them into common fields, and 200 for each further 1,000, to remain until Michaelmas, unless two honest parishioners think it too dangerous for them to remain so long, on forfeiture of 40s. a week for every 200 sheep not so placed.

A statute of 27 Henry VIII [c. 28] for dissolution of religious houses worth £200 ordained that those receiving sites of monastic houses and their demesnes should be bound to keep continual hospitality there and to occupy as much of the demesnes in ploughing and tillage as so used by their monastic predecessors within twenty years before the act, on forfeiture of £6.13.4 for every month's offence. Since then divers other religious houses, colleges, chantries and hospitals have come to the king by surrender and attainder, in which hospitality was formerly maintained, and the price of victuals much less than now. Let it be enacted that all who since 27 Henry VIII have received demesnes of religious houses, colleges, &c., or any other property, or who hereafter shall receive such, shall continually occupy them in ploughing and tillage as used within thirty years of this act, or in planting oak, chestnut, walnut, beech or other wood suitable for building, on forfeiture of £6.13.4 for every month so offending. One part of all forfeitures mentioned to go to the king, the other to be divided between the poor of the parish in which the offence is committed and he who presents the offender. All justices of assize and of the peace in their sessions, all mayors, sheriffs, bailiffs and other municipal officers to have full authority to enquire (on pain of £20 for every failure to do so) of all offences in this and the previous act, by oaths of twelve men or otherwise at their discretion, and to proceed against any presented by verdict of twelve men, as commonly used in judgements of trespass. Any person presented and afterwards committed by confession or otherwise to forfeit no less than mentioned in this act. Every lease of demesnes of any manor of £5 yearly rent or above, and every lease of a parsonage or tithes worth 20 marks [£13.6.8] a year or above, and every lease of free land, not copyhold, on which ought by law to be one mansion house and to which two ploughs and sufficient feeding for one bull and twelve cattle belong, in several or common, shall be considered as a farm for the purpose of this act.

*15 pp.*

*Printed*: E. Lamond (ed.), *A Discourse of the Common Weal of this Realm of England*, (Cambridge, 1929), pp.xlv–liii.        SP 10/5, no. 22

**169.** [December]. Monthly accounts of ingots, black plates, sizel &c. received at the mint for coinage, with waste, from April 1547 to December 1548; and of gold ingots from 15 January to 23 February 1548.

    *20 pp. (11 blank).*                  SP 10/5, no. 15

**170.** [? 1548]. Petition of Sir William Drury and Elizabeth, Lady Drury his wife, Sir John Constable and Jane, [Lady] Constable his wife, daughters and heirs of Henry Sotehill, esq., son and heir of John Sotehill, esq., son of Henry Sotehill, esq., to the duke of Somerset, lord protector.

Whereas Henry Sotehill father of John was lawfully seised in his demesne as of fee tail of the manor of Wrenthorpe, Yorkshire, granted to him by John Manyngham and Edith his wife, and being so seised, made a feoffment in fee to certain persons unknown to the petitioners in order that four priests should sing within the church of Wakefield, Yorkshire, and pray for the souls of Henry and his parents for ever; by reason of which feoffment the profits of the manor have been employed to the finding of the priests for sixty years and above; so it is that the petitioners in the right of their wives have divers times sued for recovery of the said tail in the manor by force of the gift entail, in the time of Henry VIII, so that long before the late king's death and at the time of his decease there was a form pending in the court of common pleas at Westminster. The process was discontinued at the king's death. Now, by act of parliament in the first year of the present reign concerning colleges and chantries the manor is come to the king's possession. Although the title of strangers is saved by the act, because the petitioners in the right of their wives are the founders of the services of the profits, their title to the manor is not saved, so that they and their heirs are barred for ever by the act. In consideration whereof, and of the services done by the petitioners to the king at home and in foreign wars, [they ask] that the manor be restored to them.     SP 10/5, no. 16

[For SP 10/5, no. 17 see no. **137** above.]

**171.** [? 1548]. Book of assessment for light horses and demilances from the city of London. [Individual valuations (in goods unless stated otherwise) are followed by the numbers of light horses and then of demilances, if any, (0 denoting blank) and finally by any marginalia: counties and other places indicate where some individuals are charged].

[*Tower Ward*].* John Pope (£700) 1 & 1. [Domenico Heriso and company (£700) 1 & 1. Leonard Shore and company in the house sometime Onaister Fermore's (£400) 0 & 1].* George Rolle (£267) 1: Devonshire. Thomas Blower (£300) [1]* 0 & 1. Robert Lorde (£200) 1. [Sir [Thomas]Wyat (£300 lands and fees) 1 & 2].* William Robyns (£667) 1 & 1. [Walter Myldemaye (£167 fees) 1 & 1: council book].* Sir John Champneyes (£1,000) 1 & 1. Sir William Denham (£1,600) 1 & [2]* 1. [Thomas a Woode (£300) 0 & 1: deceased].* Rowland Dee (£200) 1. Thomas Bacon (£200) 1. Thomas Laughton (£267) 1. Thomas Constable (£200) 1. Richard Tate (£100 lands and fees) 1. Thomas Burnell (£200) 1. Thomas Pyke (£1,100) 2 & 1. Henry Hardson (£200) 1. [[Sir Percival] Harte (£200 lands and fees) 0 & 1: Kent. Benjamin Gonson (£200) 1 & 1: Kent].* Edmund Lomner, surveyor of the custom house (£400) 0 & 1. [William] Abbot, serjeant of the cellar (£134 lands and fees) 1 & 1. Christopher Draper (£250) 1. [Sir John Allen's legacy to his bastards Christopher and Lanfrarus (£1,000) 1 & 1].* *Cordwainer Street Ward.*

---

\*      Deleted in whole or part.

Thomas Parcey (£200) 1. Walter Yonge (£300) 1. Sir William Laxton (£1,100) 2 & 1. Thomas White, alderman (£1,400) 2 & 1. William Graye (£400) 0 & 1. Robert Dawbney (£300) 1. Harry Suckeley (£1,000) 1 & 1. Ralph Davenet (£500) 0 & 1. William Woodlyfe (£80 lands) 1. Joan Wilkenson, widow (£500) 0 & 1. Katherine Adington, widow (£667) [1 & 1].* William Lambert (£300) 1. William Parker (£200) 1. [Robert Chester (£100 lands): Hertfordshire].* Thomas Pykeman and Ellis Wymarke (£200) 1. Mr Tuston (£120 lands) [2]*: Kent, within age. [Sir Ralph Warren (£1,600) 0 & 2; council book].* Roland Shakerley (£667) 1 & 1. [William Gresham (£400) 0 & 1: deceased].* Thomas Jennyns (£200) 1. Richard Jervies, alderman (£1,600) 0 & 2. William Locke, alderman (£1,000) 1 & 1. Anthony Marler (£300) 1. George Elyot (£200) 1. *Broad Street Ward.* John Wylforde, alderman (£1,000) 1 & 1. George Barne, alderman (£1,400) 2 & 1. Richard Tull (£600) 1 & 1. Thomas Goodman (£250) 1. John Whyte (£267) 1. Francis Lambert (£200) 1. John Cosowarthe (£200) 1. Sir William Roche, alderman (£1,100) 2 & 1. William Watson (£267) 1. Ralph Foxley (£400) 0 & 1. Roger More, serjeant of the buttery (£100 lands, fees) 1. John Quarles (£267) 1. Thomas Stacye (£200) 1. Robert Chapman (£200) 1. Dego de Astoldilo and his company (£300) [1].* William Garrard (£500) 0 & 1. William Crompton (£200) 1. Bartholomew Campaine (£400) [0 & 1].* Robert Farmor (£500) 0 & 1. [Charles Tuke (£200 lands) 1 & 1: deceased].* John Ascue (£500) 0 & 1. *Billingsgate Ward.* Thomas Clayton (£300) 1. John Byrde (£400) 0 & 1. Thomas Malby (£400) 1[& 1].* [William Burnyngyll (£200) 1: deceased].* Thomas Nycholson (£300) 1. [Thomas Knight (£134 lands and fees) 0 & 0].* Robert Lyves (£400) 0 & 1. Emmanuel Lucar (£200) 1. Harry Austen (£300) 1. Nicholas Ravell (£300) 1. Owen Cluner (£200) 1. Lady Forman (£500) 0 [& 1].* John Charleye (£260) 1. Nicholas Wylford (£460) 0 & 1. *Walbrook Ward.* Bartholomew Averrel (£320) 0 & 1. William Burry (£200) 1. [Henry Becher (£180) 0 & 0].* Robert Crane (£100 lands) 1. Roger Pynchester (£400) 0 & 1. John Clerke (£400) 0 & 1. [Sir Rowland Hill (£1,500) 2 & 1: council book].* John Yorke (£134 lands and fees) 1 & 1. Francis Flemynge (£80 lands and fees) 1. William Bayswyke (£200) 1. Bernard Jenyns (£700) 1 & 1. Harry Richardes (£200) 1. John Rogers (£250) 1. *Coleman Street Ward.* Richard Poynter (£200) 1. John Thrushe (£300) 1. [William Barnyshe, auditor (£300) 1: Essex].* John Sadelor (£600) 1. John Osborne (500 marks [£333.6.8] lands) 1. Thomas Leighe (£300) 0 & 1. *Bread Street Ward.* [Anne, Lady Purgetory (£1,000) 1 & 1].* Richard Reede (£300) 1. John Cockes (£250) 1. William Tucker (£450) 0 & 1. Robert Mellishe (£700) 1 & 1. William Harper (£500) 0 & 1. Lawrence Wythers (£600) 1 & 1. Thomas Rowe (£350) 0 & 1: [Devonshire].* William Bower (£200) 1. William Goone (£200) 1. Robert Horton (£220) 1. William Tyllesworthe (£200) 1. [Ralph Allen's widow (£300) 1].* Richard Dobbes, alderman (£1,334) 2 & 1. William Mounslowe (£350) 0 & 1. [Lady Askewe (£500) 0 & 1].* John Haulse (£500) 0 & 1. John Smythe (£500 lands) 1. Edmund Askewe (£250) 1. Richard Holte (£667) 1 & 1. [John Scutte (£500) 0 & 1: Somerset ].* John Brydges (£200) 1. [Robert Harry's widow (£334) 0 & 1. Salters' Company (£75.10.0) 1].* *Bassishaw Ward.* [Lady Herforde (£267) 1].* [*blank*] Olyver, keeper of Blackwell Hall (£300) 1. Humfrey Pakington (£500) 0 & [1]:* Worcestershire. *Bishopsgate Ward.* Robert Wryght (£500) 0 & 1. Harry Fysher (£267) 1. John Richemonde (£1,200) [2 &] 1*. Adam Wynthrop (£300) 1. John Lambe (£300) 1. John Kyddermyster son of John Kyddermyster, deceased (£50 lands) 1. Harry Polsted (£200) 1. [Edward Altham (£900) 1 & 1: deceased].* Andrew Judde, alderman (£1,334) 2 & 1. William Gurlee (£300) 1. [William Shelton (£80 lands and fees) 1: Essex].* Mr Ryde (£134 lands and fees) 1 [& 1].* Thomas Bisshop (£50 fees) 1. Peter Smythe (£50 lands and fees) 1: Isle of Wight. [Sir Ralph Bulnede (£200 lands) 1 & 1. Lady Clifford (£80 lands) 1: directed both. Lady Baynton (£200 lands) 1 & 1. Edward Vaughan (£100 lands and fees) 1: Portsmouth. Anthony Bonvyx (£1,334) 2 & 1].* *Aldgate Ward.* [Sir Gawen Carowe (£134 lands and fees) 1 & 1: Devonshire].* Robert Hennage (£200 lands

*    Deleted in whole or part.

and fees) 1 & 1. Sir George Blagge (£70 lands and fees) 1. Thomas Offley (£700) 1 & 1. [Thomas Eden (£100 lands and fees) 1: Suffolk].* Mr Barnardiston (£134 lands and fees) [1 &]* 1. Mr Pykeringe (£134 lands and fees) [1 &]* 1. *Cheap Ward*. John Hare (£500) 0 & 1. Stephen Vaughan (£667) [1 &]* 1. John Egleston (£200) 1. [Francis Edwarde and Anthony Bosome (£200) 1: deceased].* Robert Longe (£200) 1. Richard Greves (£634) 1 & 1. Humphrey Luce (£400) 0 & 1. John Gremes (£400) 0 & 1. Thomas Eton (£200) 1. Christopher Dauntseye (£200) 1. Leonard Barker (£200) 1. Robert Downes (£500) 0 & 1. Stephen Cobbe (£400) 0 & 1. Arthur Devenshyre (£300) 1. Cuthbert Bystone (£300) 1. Anthony Totehyll (£200) 1. Bartholomew Barons (£750) 1 & 1. [Nicholas, John and Jane, children of John Malby (£534) 1 & 1].* Mercers' Hall (£104.5.0 lands) [2].* [John Myller (£500) 0 & 1: deceased].* William Hobson (£500) 0 & 1. [William Merye (£667) 1 & 1: deceased].* William Butler (£667) 1 & 1. [William Brothers (£450) 0 & 1].* Richard Wadington (£400) 0 & 1. Harry Mylles (£200) 1. Harry Barrowes (£450) 0 & 1. Edward Moreton (£460) 0 & 1. John Lyan, alderman (£750) 1 & 1. Robert Riche (£70 lands and fees) 1. Ralph and Thomas Bodenham (£350) 0 & 1. William Lane (£200) 1. [Widow of Thomas Marbury (£200) 1: country].* John Maynarde (£650) 1 & 1. *Farringdon Without Ward*. Reynold Conygrave (£200) 1. [Alice Dacres, widow (£200) 1: Middlesex. Mrs Garrard, widow (£334) 0 & 1].* Thomas Richardes (£250) 1. William Peyghen (£200) 1. William Wyggeston (200 marks: [£133.6.8] lands) 2. [John Connyngsbye (200 marks [£133.6.8] lands) 2: Hertfordshire, deceased. Sir Morris Barkeleye (300 marks [£200] lands) 1 & 1: council book. John Croke (£200 lands and fees) 1 & 1: Buckinghamshire].* Richard Tonge (£300) 1. [Leonard Chamberlayne (400 marks [£266.13.4] lands) 1 & 1: Oxfordshire].* Thomas Fachell (200 marks [£133.6.8] lands) [2]:* Berkshire. Richard Morresson (£200) 1. John Hale (£200) 1. [Sir Richard Page (400 marks [£266.13.4] lands) 0 & 0: deceased].* William Buttes (£100 lands) 1. Edward Horne (100 marks [£66.13.4] lands) 1. George Blunte (£100 lands) 1. Nicholas Bacon (£200 lands and fees) 1 [& 1].* [Richard Snowe (£200) 1: Bedfordshire].* Thomas Barthelet (£400) 0 & 1. Richard Clarke, executor of John Harrison (£200) 1. Thomas Babington (£100 lands and fees) 1. Nicholas Spakeman (£500) 0 & 1. Richard Allen (£500) 0 & 1. George Allen (£250) 1. John Wishe (£400) 0 & 1. Richard Modye, auditor (£100 lands and fees) 1. Dr [Richard] Barthelet (£200) 1. Richard Duke (£200 lands and fees) 1 & 1. [Sir Philip Draycote (£127 lands) 2: in the north. Robert Chydleye (£200) 1: Middlesex. Thomas Whyte (£150 lands and fees) 1 & 1: Hampshire. Sir John Parte (£120 lands and fees) 1 & 2: Derbyshire].* *Bridge Ward*. John Dawes (£250) 1. Thomas Anslowe (£400) 0 & 1. John Cowper (£400) 0 & 1. William Turke (£200) 1. Thomas Taylor (£247) 1. John Lane (£400) 0 & 1. Richard Turke, alderman (£900) 1 & 1. [Sympson's widow (£450) 0 & 1: deceased].* John Sympson, her son (£250) 1. Harry Brayne (£200) 1. Symonde Lowe (£200) 1. Thomas Dichefelde (£300) 1. Nicholas Barker (£200) 1. John Jeralde and Bartholomew Fortune and company (£300) [1].* Fishmongers' Company [(£188.10.0 lands) 1 & 1].* John Gardenor (£500) 0 & 1. Harry Amcottes, alderman (£1,000) 2 & 1. John Swyngfeld (£300) 1. Thomas Pawleye (£300) 1. Harry Cholmeley (£200) 1. John Thomas (£200) 1. John Core (£400) 0 & 1. John Essex (£200) [1].* Thomas Blanke (£1,000) 2 & 1. John Farthynge (£200) 1. Robert Warner (£500) 0 & 1. *Cornhill Ward*. John Towles, alderman (£1,000) 2 & 1. John Jakes (£400) 0 & 1. Richard Stanefeld (£350) 0 & 1. Thomas Hunte (£200) 1. Philip Gunter (£300) 1. Thomas Lodge (£650) 1 & 1. George Forman (£200) 1. William Hynton (£300) 1. *Cripplegate Ward*. Dame Margaret Longe [(500 marks [£333.6.8] lands) 2 & 2: Suffolk].* John Calthrop (£267) 1. William Hardinge (£200) 1. Nicholas Rosse (£250) 1. Thomas Loune (£240) 1. William Knight (£50 fees) 1. John Knotting (£200) 1. William Byllingsleys (£67 fees) [1].* [Clement Paston (£200) 1].* Robert Chertsaye, alderman (£1,200) 2 & 1. [Sir

---

\*     Deleted in whole or part.

Richard Gresham (700 marks [£466.13.4] lands and fees) 2 & 2: council book].* Roger Storkeye's widow (£350) [1].* Lady Dormer, widow (£800) [1 & 1].* Margaret Parke, widow (£350) [1].* John Blundell (£300) 1. John Dormer (£400) 0 & 1. Vincent Randall (£450) 0 & 1. John Browne (£500) 0 & 1. Richard Butle (£500) 0 & 1. Dr [George] Owen (£300) 1. John Lambard, alderman (£700) 1 & 1. William Rawlens (£400) 0 & 1. George Medley (£200) 1. Augustine Hynde, alderman (£1,200) 1 & 1. John Machell (£700) [1 &]* 1. Richard Fulkes (£200 lands) 1. Morgan Wolfe (£500) 0 & 1. [Sir John Wylliams (£600 lands and fees) 1 & 1: referred to the council].* John Beaumonde (£700) [1: Leicestershire].* John Hall (£200) 1. John Cowper (£200) 1. [Thomas Hayes (£100 lands) 1: Middlesex].* *Dowgate Ward.* Paul Wythpoll (£600) [1 & 1: deceased]. * [Cornelius Hayes (£200) 1: deceased. Anthony Guerras and company (£300) 1: in Spain. Skinners' Hall (*blank*) 0 & 0].* *Queenhithe Ward.* Richard Townesende (£200) [1: deceased].* Thomas Kyrrdye (£250) 1. William Bhellout (£250) 1. William Berde (£300) 1. Thomas Lowyn (£450) 0 & 1. Christopher Allen (£1,000) 1 & 1. *Candlewick Street Ward.* John de Swygo and company (£200) [1].* Sir Humfrey Browne (£334 lands and fees) 2 & 2. Hamond Amcotes (£400) 0 & 1. William Hewet (£667) 1 & 1. [Giles Brygges (£300) 1: Essex].* John Wiseman (£200) 1. John Lewen (£500) 0 & 1. James Apott (£500) 0 & 1. *Langbourn Ward.* [Sir Martin Bowes (£1,334) 1 & 1: council book].* Thomas Bowdde (£400) 0 & 1. James Staveleye (£400) 0 & 1. Benedict Gondolowe and company (£200) [1].* Nicholas de Nalo and company (£200) [1].* Thomas Curtayes (£600) [1 &]* 1. William Chester (£400) 0 & 1. Nicholas Symson (£50 lands and fees) 1. Sir William Sheryngton (£200 lands and fees) [1 & 1]:* Bristol. George Eton (£200) 1. John Hethe (£300) 1. Asselyn de Salvago and company and Maryson de Maryno (£200) [1].* Peter Anthony Ardison and company (£200) [1].* *Farringdon Within Ward.* Richard Mallorye (£250) 1. Alexander Avenan (£250) 1. William Calton (£200) 1. John Jarmyn (£200) 1. William Ettes (£200) 1. William Mathewe (£200) 1. Sir Miles Parteriche (£100 lands and fees) 1. Anthony Husye (£234) 1. Christopher Barker *alias* Garter (£400) 0 & 1. William Wolbarde (£250) 1. John Bannyster (£100 lands and fees) 1. John Talkerne (£300) 1. [Alice Barker, widow (£200) 1. Lady Pecoke (£300) 1: Middlesex].* Mr Wellesbourne (£134 lands and fees) 1 & 1. [Mr Lucas (£100 lands and fees) 1: Essex].* William Lucye (£120 lands and fees) 1. Richard Fynes (£100 lands) [1]:* Oxfordshire. Thomas Calton (£500) 0 & 1. Robert Spendleye (£300) 1. [Nicholas Aldwyn (£400) 0 & 1: deceased].* Robert Hartope (£260) 1. Robert Ashehurst (£240) 1. Nicholas Bull (£330) 0 & 1. *Portsoken Ward.* Sir Anthony Darcye (£300 lands and fees) 1 & 2. Harry Goodere, alderman (£900) 1 & 1. John Frankes (£600) 1 & 1. Giles Harryson (£350) 0 & 1. *Lime Street Ward.* Lady Bowyde (£400) 0 [& 1].* Stephen Kyrton (£850) 1 & 2. [William Browne (£667) 1 & 1: Essex].* Denise Laveson, widow (£550) [1 & 1].* Edward Elderton (£100 lands and fees) 1. John Lewson jnr (£300) 1. Harry Judde (£100) 1. Thomas Spylman (£120 lands and fees) 1. David Woodruse (£500) 0 & 1. *Aldersgate Ward.* John Maye (£200) 1. [Sir Thomas Holtcrofte (£100 lands and fees) 1].* Robert Trappes (£1,800) 0 & 2. Thomas Cowper (£200) 1. Elizabeth Onely, widow (£500) 0 [& 1].* Roger Taylor (£200) 1. Richard Dauntseye (£134 lands and fees) 1 & 1. Lady Fitzwilliams (£100 lands) [1].* Richard Strowde (£140 lands) [1 & 1]:* Devonshire. [Sir Richard Southwell (*blank* lands): council book. Sir William Cavendishe (£100 lands and fees: council book)].* Mr Isham, who married Lady Pollard (referred to the council) [1].* [Mr Yonge, the king's servant (referred to the council) (*blank*)].* Goldsmiths' Company (£217) [1].* *Castle Baynard Ward.* [Dame Agnes Smythe, widow (£100 lands and tenements) 2].* William Ibgrave (£550) 1 & 1. Matthew Coltehurst, auditor (£400) 0 & 1. Robert Hamonde (£200) [1]:* Hampton Court. Sir Nicholas Poynctes (£200 lands and fees) [1 & 1]:* Gloucestershire. Clement Smyth (£134 lands and fees) 1 & 1: Essex. Sir John Mason (£100 lands and fees) 1: Hampshire. Sir John Godsalve (£150 lands and fees) 1: Norfolk. Hugh Losse (£100

---

\* Deleted in whole or part.

lands and fees) 1: Middlesex. *Vintry Ward*. William Brownesope (£100 lands and fees) 1. [George Pollerd's widow (£100 fees) 1].* Thomas Myldemay (£500) 0[& 1]:* Essex. [Oliver Leder (£150 lands and fees) 1 & 1: Bedfordshire. Sir Robert Turwyt (£134 lands and fees) 1 & 1].* Alexander Karlell (£200) 1.            SP 10/5, no. 18

**172.** [1547 or 1548]. Certificates of churchwardens and others in the diocese of London for church goods sold or pledged within their respective parishes; stating the items so disposed of, by whom, for how much, and to what uses the proceeds were employed. [The following summary gives the names of the wardens or others making the certificate; the names of any others stated to have sold the goods; the total sums realised; the destination of the money where other than the general funds of the parish or the repair of the churches].

*City of London. St Martin, Iremonger Lane.* Edmund Brydges, John Platte, wardens; £23.10.0. *All Hallows, Honey Lane.* John Eccleston, Thomas Cole, wardens; £43.15.0; to houses belonging to the church, a law suit and the church debt. *St Peter, Paul's Wharf.* John Rowllysley, Robert Turnor, wardens; goods sold by William Haddon and Nicholas Pyggott; £18.5.0. *St Martin Vintry.* Robert Day, John Hyckeson, wardens; £22.3.0; to repair of houses belonging to the church. *St Benet Sherehog.* John Lyen, James Hall, wardens; £33.7.6. *St Michael Queenhithe.* Thomas Brooke, John Lounsdyn, John Cockes, Thomas Lieghe, wardens; £33.17.8; to glazing and white limning the church and repair of tenements which belonged to a brotherhood there. *St Olave, Hart Street.* Thomas Burnell, Robert Newton, Alexander Haynes, parishioners; £76.6.1½d.; for making a well in the churchyard, the residue to three young men of the parish. *St Lawrence Jewry.* Nicholas Bacon, Robert Whetston, wardens; goods sold by James Browne, former warden, in 1545; £5.6.2; to tenements belonging to the church. *St Katherine Coleman.* Robert Jugliger, John Cauper, wardens; £28.2.6. *St Edmund, Lombard Street.* John Royse, William Chester, wardens; [£63.2.0]; for building a new aisle and other repairs. *St Matthew, Friday Street.* Richard Doo, Thomas Lewyes; goods sold by Doo and Thomas Porter; £31.16.5. *St Anthony.* John Bolthar, Thomas Mydleton, Henry Shusshe, wardens; goods sold by Bolthar and William Lamberte; £80 and odd money. *St John Zachary.* Richard Kynwelmarshe, Richard Lowde, wardens; £45. *Guildhall College.* Roger Asshe, warden, John Rychardeson, chaplain; [102 oz.]; for repairs to and new building of tenements belonging to the college. *St Giles, Cripplegate.* John Sheffeelde, John Garrett, Robert Langley, Richard Hyll; goods sold by John Hall, John Helde, John Sheffelde, John Garratt, Robert Langley and Richard Hill; [£291.11.8]; for rebuilding the church after a fire in September 1545. *St Nicholas Acons.* Thomas Hawke, Edward Cowke, wardens; goods sold by Robert Kinge and Ralph Barnard, wardens in 1545; £21.14.0. *St Alban, Wood Street.* Richard Maynard, William Raynton, parishioners; £15.18.9½d. *St Martin Orgar.* Robert Westmor, Thomas Hubberde, Thomas Gyllett, parishioners; goods sold by Gyllett as warden in 1545; £19.3.6; for making a wharf called Black Raven. *St Mildred, Bread Street.* William Boxe, William Fleton, wardens; goods sold by William Ustewayte and Clement Kyllingworthe, wardens in 1544; £41.6.5½d. *St Peter, West Cheap.* Richard Malory, George Sympson, Richard Folkes, parishioners; £31.10.8; to tenements called the Old Swan in Thames Street £22, &c. *St Magnus.* Roger Wolhowse, Thomas Clerke, parishioners; goods sold by William Lyvers and John Cowper, wardens in 1544; £102.9.2½d; to repair of waterwork called Churchyarde Alye. *All Hallows, London Wall.* Thomas Whytebrooke, Richard Logston, wardens; goods sold by Henry Wylkockes and William Stookes, former wardens; £27.19.4; for building the steeple, &c. *St Swithin, London Stone.* William Borne, John Parpoynte, wardens; £25.17.9. *All Hallows, Barking.* Nicholas Mynchell, John Hancockes; goods sold 4 September 1547; £77. *St Gregory.* Thomas Jackett, John Wylkynson, wardens; goods sold 21 September 1547; [£15.0.4]. *All Hallows the Great, Thames Street.* Nicholas Bell,

*     Deleted in whole or part.

Edmund Key, wardens; goods sold by consent of John Weele, parson, Richard Elrycke and Nicholas Bell, wardens; £67.5.0. *St Olave, Silver Street.* William Assheton, parson, Richard Rydge, Matthew Woodde, Thomas Mawnde, Richard Wylson; £8. *St Peter le Poer.* John Dalton, parson, John Quarles, William Watson, wardens; £3.15.0. *St Mary Woolchurch.* Geoffrey Jones, parson, William Bennyng; goods sold 10 October 1547; £41.10.8. *St Mary Colechurch.* Robert Hobby, John Murfyn, wardens; [£13.9.6]; for repair of church and steeple. *Holy Trinity, Old Fish Street.* Gervase Walter, James Castelyn, wardens; goods sold by them and Henry Robertes, John Robynson, Hugh Gryffyn; £9.9.8. *St Martin Outwich.* John Brewe, John Warryn, Henry Townesende, Richard Davye; 8s. *St Botulph without Bishopsgate.* Matthew Whyte, Robert Woodde, wardens; goods sold by John Howell and Robert Warner, wardens c. 1545; £8.2.0; for tiling and other church repairs. *St Stephen, Coleman Street.* John Wystone, Hugh Reede, Richard Poynter; £24.18.9; for making new pews and other repairs. *St Andrew, Holborn.* Nicholas Burton, parson, Richard Hunte, William Bowbye, wardens; [£27.1.1]; for paving the church £10, the rest needed for repairing church walls. *St Michael le Querne.* William Smythe, Thomas Kinge, wardens; £4.19.0 and £10 in pawn; for leading, tiling &c. *St Dunstan in the West.* Henry Lee, William Rydgeley, wardens; [£52.19.8]; to a new tenement belonging to the church. *St Bride.* John Taylor, vicar, John Hulston, Walter Childerhouse, wardens; £28.14.8; for white limning and new painting the church. *St Alphage.* Robert Martyn, parson, Christopher Hole, James Sweteman, Thomas Baxter, Thomas Reeve, Christopher Wotton, parishioners, George Foyster and Thomas Hudson, wardens; laid in gage for £40 paid to the late king for the church and bells of the dissolved priory of Elsing Spital. *St Botulph without Aldersgate.* Robert Owen, Thomas Rutter; [*no sums given* ]. *St Helen.* Andrew Judde, Anthony Bonvyce, Guy Crayford, Thomas Colshill, Jerome Shelton, Richard Pryor, parishioners; £41.16.6 in gage. *St Benet Gracechurch.* Richard Hunte, Ralph Clarvyes, John Starky, Edward Braynewall, parishioners; [*no sums given*]. *St Sepulchre.* Richard Browne, Humfrey Aleyn, Anthony Sylver; £6. *Deanery of Barking [Essex].* '.. .inforde' [? *Chingford*]. Nicholas Cotten, Thomas Thunder, wardens; goods sold by Richard Munnes and Roger Gandy, wardens in 1547; in pawn [*no sums given*]; for new roof and repairs. *Waltham Holy Cross.* James Sutton, Edward Stacye, Oliver Rigsbye, John Pecocke; goods sold in 1547; 13s. 4d. *West Ham.* Richard Bawdewyn, Richard Angere, Geoffrey Porter, wardens, Robert Clerke, John Warner, John Shypman, William Meryton, John Moll, John Clerke, John Keynett, Thomas Coll, parishioners; goods sold by John Collyns, Thomas Gorley and John Lorde, wardens in the previous year; [*no sums given*]; £10.13.3½d. removed from the church box; £15 received of Geoffrey Porter for a house in Stratford Langthorne and lands belonging; £8.6.8 received from Mr Brigges for lease of six acres belonging to the church; for making a new aisle. *Deanery of Rochford, [Essex].* *Shopland.* John Thorneton, John Marchaunte, wardens; £3. *Rayleigh.* John Bover, John Love, John Bullocke, wardens; goods sold by Henry Boode, John Hasteler, Robert Clerke and John Bover, wardens; £9.3.8; Thomas Alen sold two bells and other matter from the little chapel. *Great Stambridge.* Thomas Dayes, Richard Dryver, wardens; [£4.6.8]; for repairs of highway and the church. *Eastwood.* John Noble, John Chyche, John Bennett, Stephen Keyle, William Burne; £2.2.0. *Prittlewell.* William Salmon, William Morecocke, John Nell, Marmaduke Myddellwoodde; goods sold by Salmon and Morecocke with John Bradcock and John Harryes, also of the parish; [£44.17.0]. *Rochford.* John Freborne, John Meeke, Thomas Tyler, John Crymbill, parishioners; 12s.; to the poor. *Leigh.* William Aston, curate, John Pope; £4.16.8; for redeeming men of the parish taken prisoner in France 17s. 10d., the rest on repairs to the church and highways. *Hadleigh.* John Wade, Thomas Edwardes, Thomas Cookes; £1.13.4. *Canewdon.* James Anderkyn, John Mychell, wardens; goods sold by Anderkyn and John Eckeforthe, wardens; [£21.6.5]. *Deanery of Barstable, [Essex].* *Nevendon.* John Hagbye, John Sandyll, wardens; goods sold by Thomas Browne and John Tenderinge; £2.10.0. *Orsett.* John Broughton, William Chyrrye, wardens; £19.3.4. *North*

*Benfleet*. John Stryckeland, John Hyde, wardens; £2.4.0. *South Benfleet*. John Camber, Thomas Lutton, wardens; £3.6.8; partly for repairing the church, partly for sending soldiers to the king's wars. *Horndon [on the Hill]*. John Shawarden, John Marshall, wardens; goods sold by Marshall and William Clerke; [*no sums given*]. *Hutton*. John Smythe, Bernard Roos, wardens; goods sold by Roos and John Hatter, wardens; £6. *Basildon*. William Erwoodde, Laurence Fraunces, wardens; £2.6.8. *Bowers Gifford*. Richard Pryor, Thomas Dyryvall; [*no sums given*]. *Great Burstead*. William Harryes, John Bowchor, wardens; goods sold by Thomas Wattes and Thomas Wolnner, February 1545; £12.13.4. *Little Burstead*. John Dyer, Thomas Jenner, wardens; goods sold by Jenner and John Stewarde; £3.9.9; residue given to the poor. *Deaneries of Ongar, Chafford, Chelmsford* and Dengie, [Essex]. *Chigwell*. Robert Woode, Lawrence Mundes, wardens; 18s. *Great Warley*. Robert Marrown, parson, Richard Neeson, warden, Richard Brighte; £1.9.2. *Cricksea*. Thomas Gelder, Robert Daye, wardens; £4; John Bridge gave a house and land to the church for an obit which Hugh Bridge, son and heir, sold to Stephen Tedyner for £8. *Great Baddow*. Richard Hyckes, Lawrence Spylman, wardens; goods sold by Robert Kinge, James Deylande, John Pastall and Robert Sturgeon; [£23.7.6]. *Great Leighs*. John Englande, George Osborne, wardens; goods sold by James Spylman and John Danyell; 4s. 6d.; to the poor. *Chelmsford*. Geoffrey Skotte, William Nooke, wardens; goods sold by them and Roger Platte; [£2.9.2]; for washing the church with lime, writing scripture about the church and removing images. *Woodham Ferrers*. Robert Styleman, Richard Newton, wardens; goods sold by John Sandes and William Pirrs; £20; for a new frame in the steeple and for shingling the church. *Danbury*. Thomas Emery, Richard Roolf, wardens; £9.0.10. *Bradwell [juxta Mare]*. Thomas Butler, William Page, wardens; 10s. 8d. *Norton [Mandeville]*. John Whytinge, warden; 1s. 8d. *Stowe Marys*. John Latcheler, John Grygges, wardens; [£4.5.11]. *St Peter's, Maldon*. Richard Collett, John George; £6.10.4 in pledge. *Margaretting*. Robert Taber, William Dawson; 4s. '...ghe'. William Wayleman, Thomas Thrustell, wardens; 1s. 8d.; to the poor. *North Fambridge*. Peter Draper, warden; goods sold by James Osborne; 10s. *Deaneries of Sampford and Newport, [Essex]*. *[Saffron] Walden*. Robert Turnor, John Hubberde, wardens, Thomas Boyton, John Cotten, John Smythe jnr, James Williamson, John Dowson, parishioners; [£82.6.8]; for relief of the poor, maintenance of the free school and other charitable uses. *Newport Pound*. Henry Douham, Thomas Marten, wardens; goods sold by Ralph Stanmore, Thomas Cole, John Brande, John Coles, Richard Grace and Richard Stanys; £28.3.6. *Little Bardfield*. Thomas Perry, warden; [18s. 6d]. *Birchanger*. William Thorowgoode, Thomas Ramsey, wardens; £7 lands. *Elsenham*. James Waylott, Nicholas Thorowgod; 2s. 8d. *Little Sampford*. John Fynche, John Sulivan, wardens; £5.18.4; for repair of the steeple. *Manuden*. Robert Dane, Richard Bull, wardens; 4s. and £1.6.8 in pawn. *Little Saling*. William Parmeter, Thomas Pollarde, wardens; £3; spent in lawsuit with the vicar of Great Bardfield concerning tithes demanded by him. *Wendon Lofts*. John Collyns, warden; 1s. 4d. *Great Chishall*. John Prentyce, Robert Hagger, wardens; £1. *Great Sampford*. Richard Petytt, John Mylner, wardens; [17s. 6d]; for casting a new bell 10s., the rest for the church and churchyard. *Heydon*. John Colte, William Moll, wardens; £2.13.4. *Takeley*. John Norrell, Robert Franke; £2.5.0; for repair of church walls. *Henham*. Robert Smythe, John Wylde, wardens; 10s. *Clavering*. John Hagger, William Bell, wardens; goods sold by Robert Cotten and John Hagger snr; £5.6.8; to Thomas Barnarde, sometime clerk there £2, towards finding a poor child 10s., legal expenses with the vicar £1.6.8., &c. *Great Bardfield*. William Benlowes, William Borleley, Thomas Botulphe, John Smythe, parishioners; [£17.6.8]; for repair of bells and their frames. *Great Chesterford*. Thomas Rayner, Robert Barker, wardens; £1.4.0 in pawn for payment of the clerk's wages. *Deaneries of Lexden and Tendring, [Essex]*. *Great Clacton*. Thomas Gardener, Thomas Westeborne, wardens; £14.10.0; for making stools and a pulpit in the church, and repairs. *West Donyland* [alias *Berechurch*]; five bells given by Mr Audeley sold and the proceeds given to the new church; [*wardens not named and sums not given*]. *All Hallows,*

*Colchester*. [*Wardens not named*]; 18s.; on a hutch with locks and keys bought for 3s. 4d. *Great Bentley*. John Hawen, John Orves, wardens; goods sold by Thomas Westeman; [£24.10.0]; for repairing highways and dangerous bridges £7, on other bridges, in alms and on almshouses £1.6.0, for mending the church 11s. 4d. *St Mary's, [Colchester]*. John Wells, John Parke, wardens; [£22] and 26¼ oz.; for casting a great bell, distribution to the poor, whitening the church and aisle with scriptures, glazing and defacing the church windows, and for a chest. *Thorrington*. John Cawton, warden; goods sold by John Clare and William Colman; £30.8.6; for repair of the church and building Boreflett bridge. *Alresford*. Stephen Gardener, Robert Anderton, wardens; £8.5.4; glazing for a hutch and for a pulpit. *Peldon*. William Hoy, Gregory Sakes, parishioners; £15.3.4; for repair of highways and bridges. *St James, Colchester*. John Lucas, Robert Pytte, wardens; [£2.1.9]; for glazing, whitening and panelling the church. *Great Horkesley*. John Noothe, Reynold Welne, wardens; £2.8.0. *St Leonard, Colchester*. John Cooke, Robert Lambert, wardens; £3.6.8. *St Runwald, Colchester*. Nicholas Wylbore, Robert Buxton, wardens; goods sold by Robert Myddleton and Thomas Symell, parishioners; [£12.16.0]; for a pair of organs £6.6.8, & c. *Great Bromley*. [*Wardens not named*]; goods sold by John Munte and John Lytleburye, parishioners; £20; highways £8, residue and 30 yards of linen to the poor. *Fordham*. William Swanne, John Cockrell, wardens; 12s. *East Donyland*. John Dorrell, Richard Hampkyn, wardens; 15s. 4d. *Mistley*. Thomas Polley, John Aunger, wardens; £2.5.4. *Manningtree*. Henry Warmynham, John Browne, wardens; 9s. 7½d. *St Martin, Colchester*. John Gylder, Thomas Dybney, wardens; [£6.6.4]. *Marks Tey*. Robert Peverell, John Damyan, wardens; £4; for repairs of the church and casting a new bell. *Dedham*. [*Wardens not named and sums not given*]; partly to build a grammar school, to repair the church and build a bridge. *St Botulph, Colchester*. William Smythe, Thomas Radeley, wardens; [£4.18.5]; for repairs of the church and a lawsuit against the parson of All Hallows over tithes claimed by him. *Mile End*. Thomas Gye, John Knyghte, wardens; [£1.1.6]; for repairs of the church, the poor, and debts. *West Mersea*. John Wylson, Robert Feelde, wardens; £4.6.8. *St Giles, Colchester*. Richard Stampe, John Thompson, John Bowyers, wardens; 9s.; for whitening the church. *Chiche Regis* [alias *St Osyth*]. Edward Shorte, Richard Duke, wardens; £40.18.6; for covering and repairing the church. *Frating*. Thomas Stevyn, Elyze Churche, wardens; 10s; for a pulpit and a hutch for the church. *St Nicholas, Colchester*. William Blotte, George Harryson; £3; for trimming the church. *Abberton*. Thomas Lyvinge, John Thymble, wardens, David Bennett, parson, Thomas Lyving, parishioner; £2.0.4. *Great Oakley*. [*Wardens not named*]; 10s.; to the poor. *St Peter, Colchester*. Robert Maynerde, John Robertes, wardens; £8.15.0. *Dovercourt*. Robert Sale, Christopher Alen, John Alen, parishioners; £22.5.0; spent on suing the king and council concerning the benefice. *Tendring*. John Busshe, Richard Dyxe, wardens; 8s. 7d.; for making a pulpit and a hutch, and repairs. *Lawford*. [*Wardens not named*]; 18s.; for the church and the poor. *Brightlingsea*. Thomas Spysall, John Hubbarte, wardens; [£55.5.4]; for repairing the steeple and two aisles and mending two bridges, and defending a suit concerning a chantry. *Wix*. Nicholas Stewarde, John Batemen, wardens; 6s. 8d. *Ardleigh*. John Fynche, warden; £38.4.2. *Ramsey*. Robert Mervyn, John Wyckes, wardens; £9; for repairing a bridge. *Elmstead*. William Payne, John Chace, wardens; 10s.; for making a pulpit and a hutch. *Little Clacton*. Philip Stubbes, Richard Harwye, wardens; £8.11.4. *Harwich*. Thomas Rychemonde, John Sake, wardens; [£22.6.4]; for the town quay £5, for the town charter £8. *Earls Colne*. George Beeston, Nicholas Garrarde, wardens; [£11.3.0] and odd money; for repairs of the steeple £8.10.0, and for church debts. *Corpus Christi Guild, [Great] Coggeshall*. Clement Sutton, John Crane, wardens; £13.19.6 and plate. *Aldham*. William Draper, Richard Twyde, wardens; [£1.2.4]; for sending soldiers 6s., for glazing the church 9s. *White Colne*. John Warde, John Potter, wardens; [£1.17.0]; given in exchange with their bells for those of Earls Colne ('Colne Pryors'). *Deanery of Witham, [Essex]*. *Feering*. John Borowe, John Wyndwell, wardens; £17.6.8; for glazing the church £1.5.6.

*Guild of Our Lady, Ulting.* Thomas Russell, warden; goods sold by Mr Church of Maldon and Mr Blake of Danbury, masters of the guild; £18. *'Wyteley' [? White Notley].* [*Wardens not named*]; [£4.7.3]. *Witham.* Andrew Weston, William Haywarde, wardens; [£16.17.0]. *Bradwell [juxta Coggeshall].* [*Wardens not named*]; £3.8.9. *Langford.* Thomas Prynde, warden; goods sold by Thomas Sames; £1.14.11; for tiling the church, and debts. *Great Totham.* [*Wardens not named*]; £1.6.8 pledged. *Castle Hedingham* in Hedingham deanery. William Sadlington, warden; £5.6.8. *Deanery of Hedingham, [Essex]. Pentlow.* Robert Chryshall, John Chryshall, wardens; £6. *Steeple Bumpstead.* Thomas Loude, warden; £9. *Halstead.* William Fuller, parishioner; £7; for making a bridge. *Great Yeldham.* Thomas Freeman, parishioner; £7.18.0. *Braintree.* Robert Haynes, John Tendringe, John Pryor, wardens; £42.16.2; for repairs £8.18.2, in subsidies to Henry VIII £3.14.8, in contributions £1.13.4, residue in hands of John Godday, William Gegill, Richard Skynner, Robert Haynes, John Pouder, Richard Buckeforde and John Tendringe. *Deanery of Dunmow, [Essex]. Great Dunmow.* William Glastocke, William Dente, Thomas Colfelde, John Turnour, wardens; £54.2.4. *Stebbing.* John Greene, Thomas Panell, wardens; £10. *High Easter.* John Cavyll, John Alen, wardens; goods sold by them and Richard Croor, Richard Barde and Robert Alen; £18.8.3. *Shellow Bowells.* [*Wardens not named*]; goods sold by Richard Sampforde; £1.17.4. *Thaxted.* John Smythe, William Longe, wardens; £43.15.8; repairs £33, remainder in hands of John Gate and William Spilman. *Deanery of Braughing, [Hertfordshire]. Great Hadham.* Thomas Newes, parishioner; £19.5.0; in hands of Sir Henry Parker, Aldreede of 'Dainton' and Newes. *Cheshunt.* John Clare, Edward Holder, George Jackeson, wardens; £3; to church houses. *Little Hadham.* William Harvie, [*blank*] Solles, wardens; £5.6.8. *Standon.* John Lamkyn, Nicholas Barr, wardens; £1.9.8. *[Bishops] Stortford.* John Bayforde, Edward Wylley, wardens; £38.17.9; on repairs £1.15.0, remainder with Sir Henry Parker. *Thorley.* William Osborne, John Payton, wardens; 8s. *Ware.* Thomas Leonarde, Michael Mede, Robert Poininge, Richard Cassum, wardens; £2.12.3.

*79 pp.*

Printed: E.P. Dickin, 'Embezzled Church Goods of Essex', *Transactions of the Essex Archaeological Society*, n.s., xiii, pt iii (1914), 157–71 (Essex parishes only).

SP 10/5, no. 19

**173.** [?]. Memorandum on the causes of dearth.

There are three causes of the universal dearth of victuals in the country: lack of breeding of cattle and poultry, regrating by a few, and the king's provisioning from the poor, which discourages breeding and increases prices. The danger from purveyance is not caused by lack of good laws, but because they cannot be executed for lack of money. The king must have more money to meet his increasing charges. His predecessors had greater income, albeit without monastic and chantry lands: the exchequer records show that Edward III had £55,202.8.4 more revenue from the custom of the staple than the late king had from all cloth customs. It is unnecessary to show the hurt done by purveyance to the poor: the purveyor allows for a lamb worth 2s. only 1s.; for a capon worth 1s. only 6d., and so on. The poor sometimes have to sue at length and great cost for their money, and sometimes never have it; and so have to sell dearer to the king's subjects.

It would be better for men to give a certain amount yearly, say 1d. for every sheep kept in the common fields, 2d. for every ewe and lamb kept in several pasture, and 1½d. for every shearing sheep in pasture. If there were 3,000,000 sheep in the country, of which 1,500,000 were on the commons at 1d. each, it would give £6,250; 750,000 ewes with lambs at 2d., £6,250, and 750,000 other pasture sheep at 1½d., £4,687.10.0, totalling £17,187.10.0, which would do something for the provision of the king's household.

Kings used to have great revenues from the export of unwrought wool, and the people were less charged with subsidies. An imposition should be put on the clothiers who now manufacture cloths in this country of 5s. for a broad cloth and 1s. 8d. for a kersey, and of double custom on the merchants who export them.

The tenant in chief cannot lose by payment for sheep used in his houses, for he shall be allowed as much in respite of homage. If he pays £1 a year in respite of homage at 1d. a sheep he may kill 240 sheep and pay no more than before. The clothier cannot lose, as he will recover it in his sale as 2d. in a yard of cloth; purchasers may easily bear this light burden. If the merchants have the cloth justly made they will be great gainers, as shall the wearers; for well made garments will last twice as long as those made now.

Therefore, let it please the king that after Christmas his officers shall take nothing without paying the market price in cash. All carriages, by sea and land, shall be rated at the prices his subjects pay, at the assessment of two justices of the peace and twelve men of the hundred with carriages of their own; also, that the sheriffs may be discharged on their accounts of all farms and rents not leviable; that all cities, boroughs and towns may be discharged of their fee farms and rents for their liberties paid to the king, and that the profits from them be applied to a stock occupied by the inhabitants in setting their poor to work, according to the orders to be set out by the king's commissioners; also that no money shall be paid in the exchequer or elsewhere for respite of homage, and that no process shall be made against anyone to do homage; these articles to be in force until the end of the next parliament to be held after the king comes of age.

*6 pp.*
*Draft. Probably by John Hales.*
*Printed*: Lamond *Discourse of the Common Weal*, (Cambridge, 1929), pp.xliii–xlv. *Tudor Economic Documents*, ii, 219–22.                                      SP 10/5, no. 20

**174.**   Fair copy of the above.
*3¹/₂ pp.*
*Some corrections and re-arrangements.*
*Printed*: Tytler, i, 367–72, (ascribed to 1551).                          SP 10/5, no. 21

[For SP 10/5, no. 22 see no. **168** below.]

**175.**   Lands sold by Sir Richard Lee. This document (SP 10/5, no. 23) is now known to be temp. Elizabeth I and is calendared as no. **845** below.

[For SP 10/5, no. 24 see no. **594** below.]

[For SP 10/5, no. 25 see no. **784** below.]

**176.**   1549. [January 11]. Friday.* Lord Seymour, from his house, to the duke of Somerset.

Mr [*blank*], your servant, just now asked me to come to you. Excuse me until tomorrow at the parliament chamber or at Westminster in the afternoon, so that the council may be present. Wishing you well, although you should do me wrong.
*Holograph.*                                                         SP 10/6, no. 1

**177.**   January 18. Instructions from the council to Sir Hugh Pawlett, Sir Thomas Chaloner and John Yernley, esq.

They are to go as soon as possible to the lord admiral's house at Bromham, Wiltshire, and tell his officers and servants of his committal and their own charge from the king and council. They shall make those with charge of plate, jewels, specialties or moveables

*          Thursday deleted.

declare their responsibilities. They shall call for the keys of the jewel houses, closets and other places where the most important things are kept and make inventories of all household stuff, implements, plate, jewels, chattels, specialties and other moveables in the house and grounds. They shall have this inventory copied, signed by themselves and the chief officers, and brought to the protector and council. They shall search for letters and other writings, putting anything important in custody. They shall instruct the officers to keep the other servants and family in good order. They shall note the proceedings of those with whom they deal, learn all they can, and then commit the house and its contents to the officers, if suitable, or appoint one or more local gentlemen to take charge.

SP 10/6, no. 2

**178.** January 20. Inventories of goods and chattels of Lord Admiral Seymour in Chesworth manor and park and his other offices in Sussex, taken by Sir Thomas Cawarden and Sir William Goring by virtue of a commission of assistance and instructions delivered by the lord protector and council on January 18.

Chesworth manor. Hangings, carpets, beds, bedding, napery, 21 boxes of evidences, chapel cloths and furnishings (including 1 chasuble, 1 siver gilt chalice, 1 mass book, 1 sacring bell, 3 pewter cruets), tables, cupboards, candlesticks, plates, chests, pots. Smith's forge: bellows, irons, anvil, sledge, hand-hammers, tongs, pliers, stamp, punch, horse shoeing equipment. Bakehouse: baskets, pales, pans, &c. Brewhouse: copper, vats, kettles and equipment. Slaughter house: bedsteads, ropes and pins, scales, axe &c. Kitchen and pantry: utensils. Scullery: chargers, dishes &c. Barns: hay, bricks.

Chesworth park. Cattle, horse, oxen lately sold to Richard Waller of Shipley, deer, fatting oxen lately driven towards London by a servant of William Clerk, the admiral's servant, dwelling at Tottenham, since stayed and remaining at Nonsuch. Knepp park. Fatting oxen, cow, fatting sheep, geldings, hay. Sedgewick park. Pigs, deer. Bewbush and Shelley park. Deer. The agistment of the park for which William Clerk stands accountant to my lord's use. Little park in the forest. Deer.

Barony of Lewes, borough of Lewes with Lentall's part for Lord Seymour. Clayton manor, Middleton manor, Allington manor, Bramber barony, Chesworth manor, Knepp manor, Grinstead manor, Kings Barn manor, Bramber borough, Shoreham borough, Horsham borough, bailiff errant's office, St Leonards forest: all unaccounted for for one year ending Michaelmas 1548.

Chesworth house and park. Henry Foyce, keeper, at £6.1.8 and £2 as under steward, a year. Barony of Bramber and Lewes. Henry Foyce, receiver, at £2 a year, with herbage of 14 beasts, 2 horses and 2 horses found in my lord's stable. Knepp park. William Skoterell, keeper, at my lord's pleasure, with herbage of 14 beasts, 2 horses and 10 hogs; George Barnard, under keeper, with the going of 6 beasts or nags and 6 hogs. Sedgewick park. William Barwyke, keeper, at £14.11.3 a year and the rate of 8 oxen, 12 kine, 6 mares and geldings and 16 swine. Bewbush and Shelley park. John Berde, keeper, at £6.1.8 a year, 6 cattle and 20 horses. Little park in the forest. John Myles, keeper, at £3 a year and the going of certain cattle. John Roosse, water bailiff, at £1.6.7. Thomas Bradbrige, bailiff errant, at £4. John Carell, esq., high steward of the barony of Bramber, for counsel £3.6.8. Edmund Mychell, gent., steward of the barony of Lewes, at £2. Richard Gybson, aged 80, has enjoyed an almshouse at Shoreham about 16 years, worth 4 marks yearly to him, having no other recompense for 50 years' service to the late duke of Norfolk and his ancestors. William Barrow, bailiff of Shoreham, at £3.10.0 a year.

*Fully itemised.*

*Signed by*: Cawarden and Goring.

*Printed*: H. Ellis, 'Inventories of goods ... belonging to Lord Admiral Seymour, at the time of his attainder, taken 1549', *Sussex Archaeological Collections*, xiii, (1861), 120–6.

SP 10/6, no. 3

**179.** January 21-2. Inventories of the goods and chattels of Lord Admiral Seymour taken by Sir Thomas Cawarden and Sir William Goring by virtue of a commission of assistance and instructions delivered by the lord protector and council on January 18.

January 21. Sheffield manor, Sussex. In charge of John Sherief, clerk, servant to the lord admiral. Oxen, hay, iron furnace and equipment, coal, raw iron, ore, forge and equipment, raw iron, iron bars, coal, wood (some delivered to the White Hart, Southwark, midsummer 1548). Some iron delivered to Cornelius Smithe of the Strand, midsummer 1547, and to Smartwhode of Bow Lane, midsummer 1548. 33 workmen hired by rate and 3 yearly.

January 22. Worth forest, Sussex. Double furnace for ordnance, shot or raw iron with equipment, raw iron, ordnance (some carried to Southwark), shot, ore, wood, forge and equipment, raw iron, iron bars (some carried to the White Hart), blooms, coal, wood. 33 workmen hired by rate, 1 yearly. All committed to John Sherief and Henry Foyce.

Estimated values: iron bars – £497.15.0; ordnance – £620; shot – £76; raw iron – £251; wood – £42.5.0; coal – £84; ore – £359; blooms – £27; oxen – £23.6.8; implements – £10; owed by Parson Levett for shot delivered 1547 – £77. Total – £2,077.6.8. For wages due to gunfounders and other workmen – £160. Remainder – £1,917.6.8.

Memoranda: to know if the gunfounders shall cast any more ordnance and shot, and of what kind; John Sherief has not accounted for the furnace and mills of Sheffield since 1 November 1546, nor for those of Worth since Christmas, and wishes to do so now.

Worth forest and park. Thomas Michell, ranger, at £3.0.10 a year, has the herbage and pannage by patent for life. Robert Moncke and Robert Cowstock, keepers, have £2 each yearly. Thomas Cowstock, bailiff of the barony of Lewes for the lord admiral's part has £1.15.0 fee a year.

*Fully itemised.*

*Signed by*: Cawarden, Goring, Sherief and Foyce.

*Printed*: *Sussex Archaeological Collections*, xiii, (1861), 127–31.                    SP 10/6, no. 4

**180.** January 28. London. William Gyffard to Laurence Lee.

I am commanded by commission from the master* and surveyor† of the king's woods to sell certain woods in the manor of Collyweston and elsewhere in [Northamptonshire] and thirty acres in Tomlin wood in the manor of Apethorpe, part of your office. My servant will allow your firewood there for last year and this, and any other lawful request.

                                                                                    SP 10/6, no. 5

**181.** January 31. Hatfield. Sir Robert Tyrwhit to the duke of Somerset.

I have received your letters of the 29th. [Princess Elizabeth] received your instructions kindly but will as yet acknowledge no more than she has already written to you. She will write from time to time as she remembers. She now confesses that she commanded the cofferer‡ to tell [Katherine] Ashley what he told her about marriage with the lord admiral, saying she would hear no such thing, but that Ashley should know it, as she was made her mistress by the king her father. He promised to do so. Because Ashley said nothing of it that night [the princess] asked the cofferer next day if he had told Ashley. He said he had, and that she had replied she would not speak of it without more authority. Her grace will not confess that before or afterwards Ashley spoke to her about the marriage – which I think untrue, and see she will no more accuse Ashley than herself, and cannot now abide anybody who disapproves of her doings. For her desire to see the king, she confesses that her pallet was removed from her bedchamber because it was so small at Chelsea. But four of her gentlewomen confess that Ashley first removed Lady Troy,

*           Sir Thomas Pope.
†           Sir Geoffrey Gates, surveyor south of the Trent.
‡           Thomas Parry, cofferer to the princess.

who has lain there continually for about two years, and then her successor [Blanche] Parry, and could abide nobody there but herself. After they came to the Grayne, in her absence, Mistress Norwege, her maid, lay with her grace. If you knew all my persuasions with her, weighing her honour and safety and the danger to the country, you would marvel that she will not cough out more. Her love for Ashley is to be wondered at, and must be for ill. But if Ashley would confess any of the things with which she is filled, that she might see some of it, I would hope to make her cough out all.

*Holograph.* SP 10/6, no. 6

**182.** [? January]. Depositions of Henry Grey, marquess of Dorset.

1. Immediately after the king's death [John] Harrington, the lord admiral's servant, came to my house at Westminster and showed me that the admiral was likely to come to great authority and, as the king's uncle, might do me much pleasure, advising me to report to him and enter more into his friendship. 2. He advised me to allow my daughter Jane to be with the admiral, saying he would have her married to the king. 3. Within a week I went to the admiral's house at Seymour Place where he persuaded me to send for my daughter, who remained there until the queen's death. 4. I then sent for her and she remained at my house. Shortly afterwards the admiral came and persuaded me to have her return, renewing his promise for her marriage to the king, adding that if he might once get the king at liberty he dared warrant it. Sir William Sharington spoke as earnestly to my wife. After long debate we agreed to her return and she remained at his house until his coming to the Tower. 5. The admiral told me last December and at other times and places that he in no way liked the doings of the lord protector and council. In the gallery of his London house he said he did not love the protector, and would have the king have the honour of his own things as he was wise and learned, and said he would achieve this in three years. 6. When I was with the admiral at Sudeley at the end of the summer and at my house after Michaelmas he asked me what friends I had in the country. He said it was well I had divers servants who were gentlemen, able to live of themselves, but told me not to trust them too much as they have something to lose. He advised me rather to make much of the head yeomen and franklins, especially the ringleaders, for they are best able to persuade the multitude and bring the number. He would that I went to their houses with wine and venison, being familiar, making them love me and have them at my command – as he intended to do himself. 7. The admiral also advised me to keep my house in Warwickshire, as it is a county full of men, chiefly to match Lord Warwick. I replied that my house was almost down and I was unable to repair it. I had stone, brick and wood, but lacked provision for keeping my house at Bradgate, sixteen miles away. He said that was nothing, and wished me to settle in Warwickshire. 8. He told me when I came first to this parliament that the king often complained to him that Somerset dealt very hardly with him and he could not have money at will, but that the admiral sent it to him. Harrington also reported this. 9. Hearing me complain of debt, the admiral offered to lend me £2,000. He sent me £500 of this when I sent my daughter to him last, saying he would keep her in gage instead of a bond. 10. At the first session of this parliament he said, Lord Clinton being behind me, that they spoke of a black parliament, but that if he were thus used he would make it the blackest ever. Lord Clinton answered that we would lose the protector and undo himself. The admiral turned and said he would live better without the protector than the protector would without him. 11. On the day of his committal, as we came from parliament together towards Lord Huntingdon's house for dinner, he told me that the earl of Rutland had accused him to the council. After dinner Lord Huntingdon, my brother Thomas, Sir Nicholas Poyntz and I came with him to his house. Walking in his gallery he spoke at length of what had been between Lord Rutland and himself, being

much afraid to go to the council, and would not go unless he might have Mr Comptroller*
for a pledge to remain in custody until his return. My brother answered that as he knew
himself to be true and his brother merciful he should go; for if he would have him, that
house could not keep him, even though he had ten times more men. During this Mr
Secretary Smith and [Sir John] Baker came, and I went to my chamber. 12. The admiral
told me soon before his arrest that he had heard a subsidy would be granted to the king
in this parliament of 2d. for every sheep a man had, which he would never grant. I told
him he had better grant such a subsidy than one from his lands; he replied he would
not.

   *Signed.*
   *Printed*: Tytler, i, 137–41 (omitting articles 7–10, 12). Russell, *Kett's Rebellion*, 15 (article
6).                                                                              SP 10/6, no. 7

**183.**  [? January]. Depositions of Edward Rous.
   About November 24 last the lord admiral commanded me that sixty tons of beer
should be brewed at Hailes, Gloucestershire, to be ready by April 15 or 18, and carried
to Tewkesbury and thence by water to Bewdley, Shropshire, where he intended to keep
household from the beginning of May for most of the summer. He also commanded
me to prepare all the houses of office there, saying he would keep as great a house there
as he did in the queen's life, despite the charge, in order not to be bullied out of his
own.
   *? Holograph.*
   *Slightly mutilated.*                                                    SP 10/6, no. 8

**184.**  [? January]. Depositions of Sir Richard Cotton.
   Pigot, the admiral's servant, told his sister, Cotton's maid, that he had heard the admiral
say to Sir William Sharington after the queen's death that it would be strange to some
when his daughter came of age, taking place above [the duchess of] Somerset, as a queen's
daughter, not his. He would wear black for one year, and would then know where to
have a wife.
   *Signed.*                                                              SP 10/6, no. 9

**185.**  [? January]. Depositions of John Fowler.
   1. At St James's, where the king was, the lord admiral called me to his chamber. After
dismissing his servants he enquired after the king and if he lacked anything. I said not.
He asked if the king ever asked for or about him: I said he would sometimes ask for
him, but nothing else. I asked him what the king should ask and he said nothing unless
why he did not marry. I said I never heard him ask such questions. He paused and asked
me, if I had communication with the king soon, to ask him if he would be content he
should marry, and if so whom. I agreed, and that night when the king was alone I said
I marvelled that the admiral did not marry. He said nothing. I asked him if he was
content he should do so and he agreed. I asked him whom and he said Lady Anne of
Cleves, and then he said no, but he should marry his sister Mary, to turn her opinions.
So he went away. 2. Next day the admiral came again to St James's and called me to
him in the gallery. I told him all the king had said. He laughed and asked me to ask the
king if he would be content for him to marry the queen and if he would write in his
suit. I agreed and did so that night. Next day the admiral came to the king: I cannot tell
what communication they had, but the king wrote a letter to the queen and the admiral
brought one back from her. 3. Shortly afterwards the admiral came to St James's and,
meeting me in the gallery, went into the inner chamber and talked with [Sir Thomas]
Wroth, the king being at school. When he came out I followed him into his chamber.

  *    Sir William Paget.

He dismissed his men and asked me whether his brother had been there since he last was himself. I said not. He told me that the protector had fallen out with him concerning the admiralty, and took his part before his. I prayed him bear with his brother, but he said the protector would have his head under his girdle. I protested: he paused and said we should do well enough for all this. He asked me to tell the king or [John] Cheke, or he would tell him himself, lest the protector should do so. He said if the protector told him he would be impartial and say that the two should agree as brothers. I said I would tell the king, and did so. The admiral said he would pray Mr Cheke to do the same, as I think he did, also Mr Wroth. 4. Shortly before going into the country with the queen the admiral came to court at Westminster and called me to his chamber. He said that since he would do nothing to which the king was not privy, he prayed me tell him he would sue the protector for certain jewels which the late king gave the queen, including her wedding ring, which he thought legally hers. I lamented that jewels or worldly muck should begin a new matter with his brother. He trusted the protector would be content. Then he called for boats to Hanworth, bidding me send to him and nobody else if the king lacked anything. He often wished me to remind the king of him. 5. Since his last coming to court he frequently came to the privy buttery to drink alone and ask me whether the king spoke of him. I answered not. He would wish the king were five or six years older. He often asked me to tell him when the king was rising, which I did. 6. When the king was at St James's (I am unsure if it was the last time or not) the admiral came about 9 a.m. into the gallery where I was playing the lute. He said there was slender company about the king – no-one in the presence chamber and not a dozen in the whole house. I thanked God we were in a quiet realm and the king loved, or a hundred men could make foul work. He replied that a man might steal away the king now, for he came with more men than were in the house. He went into the inner gallery and thence to the king, with whom he talked for a while (of what I know not) and went home for dinner, saying he had guests. 7. After Mr Sharington was arrested I came at night to the admiral's chamber at court and asked him what he had done. The admiral told me he had heard no great charge yet. Someone had accused him for coining testons since the command to the contrary, but he denied it. He said if Sharington were false he would never trust anyone for his sake. He was sure the late king trusted him. There was, he said, never anyone of the council who spoke for him, but he thought they would take his part. I then reminded him that about a year before he had willed me, if I lacked money for the king, to send in his absence to Mr Sharington. When [the admiral] was at Enfield I had written to [Sharington] for £20; if that letter were found I would be undone, and would need to tell the truth to the protector for my discharge. The admiral doubted if Sharington would have kept the letter. I said I doubted it; that I was once in the protector's displeasure, and if I fell into it again I should never recover his favour. He said I might say he gave it to me. He told me to devise an answer, but I refused and prayed him to devise to save me. He agreed and I left. 8. Four or five nights after New Year's Day he came to the privy chamber after the king was in bed, and took bread and drink. He told [John] Philpot, [Robert] Maddox* and me that he had not remembered us since New Year, but would. 9. When he went to the country he much desired remembrances from the king. I procured the king to write several times, but only two or three lines of recommendation to him and the queen. Sometimes I wrote myself with them for money, and once had answer to receive £40 of [Anthony] Bowcher, the queen's receiver, and so did. Many other times I had answer that if I lacked money I should have £40 of Mr Locke at London, for he had caused Bowcher to write to him to deliver me as much as I sent for. 10. So I confess he made me a minister to allure the king with money and praise of his liberality, to make the king fond of him [and cause the

* Grooms of the privy chamber as was Fowler.

king to do all that he should require the protector to do].* Be a means to the protector to have mercy on me, not justice.

Money received by John Fowler of the lord admiral: at Westminster shortly after the coronation – £10; from [Arthur] Sturton last Lent at Westminster – £20 or £40; at his own house in London – £10; by letter from him to the queen's receiver at Hampton Court at the beginning of the progress – £40; another letter from Hampton Court enclosing a letter from the queen's receiver to Mr Locke of London – £40; from Mr Sharington a week before Christmas a year ago – £20; shortly before parliament, at Hampton Court – £10; since the king's coming to London, from Sturton – £20; at New Year a year ago at Hampton Court – £5; last New Year's Day after breakfast in the privy buttery at Westminster – £3; at Hampton Court, Westminster, St James's and Greenwich – £5, 20 nobles and £10; shortly before his marriage – a cap of aiglets and a brooch.

   *Signed.*                                                                                SP 10/6, no. 10

**186.**  [? January]. Depositions of Lord Clinton.

Riding behind Marquess Dorset from parliament, the lord admiral spoke to us of an act passed the same day repealing another for speaking words, in which the admiral would have had a promise that men should not have liberty to speak against the queen. He said he perceived what was meant; he had heard talk of a black parliament, and was so used that he would make it the blackest ever. I said I was sorry to hear such words, which would hurt him and might utterly lose him the protector's favour. He replied he had no need of it and might better live without the protector than the protector without him. Afterwards he told Dorset that he would take his feast from the best of their ears, from the highest to the lowest, not sparing the protector's. Dorset advised him to be at peace with his brother. The admiral asked why he was made protector, for there was no need of one.

Two or three days before, hearing from Mr Legg that the admiral had commanded him to deliver me a Scottish prize which [the protector] had given me before, and that the admiral had remembered the protector in that behalf, and finding the admiral in the protector's outer chamber, I thanked him for his remembrance to the protector and said I would do him any pleasure. He thanked me and said he would prove me or it before long – which I did not understand, for I did not know then that he was offended with the protector. Two days later, riding to parliament, the admiral told me he intended to introduce a bill, reasonable to all impartial men, for which he asked my support and that of my friends. It was known he was the king's uncle and in what credit the late king had him; yet he perceived he was not meant to have any estimation if some might prevent it, so he intended to prove what would be said to it in parliament. It was easy to see he meant to get some authority that way. I said little, save that the protector and council would gladly grant him what was meet. He said he could not tell me that, and spoke no more until he came to the parliament chamber. After he had been there about an hour he called me out, and after talking with some of the lords, asked me again to consent to the bill and make him as many friends as I could. I said that if he made the protector privy he might be sure to have all the lords' consent to any reasonable matter. He replied he had rather the bill were in the protector's tail than desire his good will in it. I asked him to pardon me for otherwise I would not consent, and so he left me.

   *Signed.*
   *Printed*: Tytler, i, 148–50 (first paragraph only).                        SP 10/6, no. 11

**187.**  [? January]. Depositions of Henry Manners, earl of Rutland.

1. Riding from my mother's house to the Marquess Dorset's at the end of last summer, the lord admiral told me he was my friend and would do me any pleasure. I thanked

---
*    Deleted.

him and asked him if I might sit in parliament without a writ, as I was a ward last year. He said he could not tell and that I were best to take counsel, but was glad I should be in the house, and trusted to have my voice with him. I said I was content my conscience should serve me. 2. He enquired of the state of my living and how I was friended in my country. I told him such friends as I had, and he told me a great number of his friends, and how he was banded in their countries, saying he thought me so friended in my country as I was able to match [the earl of] Shrewsbury. I said I could not tell, but thought my lord would do me no wrong. 3. He advised me to make much of the gentlemen in my country, but more of honest and wealthy yeomen who were ringleaders in good towns; there was no great trust to be had in the gentlemen, but for making much of the others and sometimes dining in their houses I would allure all their good will to follow me. 4. We talked of the queen; I said I thought his power much diminished by her death. He answered that the council never feared him as much as they do now. 5. He showed me his proceedings in the last parliament, and how he was against the bill of patents, at which he burst out and asked me how I would say if in a year or two, or sooner, he were to tell the council that the king (whom he praised very much) was now of some discretion and should have the honour and rule of his own doings – for at present the king bears the charges and the protector receives the honours. He said he did not desire his brother's hurt, but that he should rule just as a chief councillor. 6. I asked him how your grace made of him at his being taken with you after the queen's death; he said very much, but he would beware how he trusted you. 7. At the beginning of parliament, talking with him in his garden concerning a patent that Lord Abergavenny promised him, I willed him to beware whom he trusted. He said he would, as no man should accuse him.

*Signed.*  SP 10/6, no. 12

**188.** [? January]. Depositions of Sir William Sharington.

1. When the admiral was appointed he told me he was as glad of that office as of any in the realm, and no man should take it from him unless he took his life also, since he had the rule of a good sort of ships and men. 2. When the protector went to Scotland the admiral told me he disliked the protector not appointing him to have governance of the king before so drunken a soul as Sir Richard Page. 3. The admiral was always most desirous of stewardships and to entertain gentlemen – to what end I never knew, save to serve the king as he said. 4. He told me that the earl of Warwick would have had the manor of Stratford upon Avon of him and offered him a better thing elsewhere. Although it was out of his way and only beggarly houses he would not part with it, saying it was a pretty town and would make many men. 5. The admiral often showed me on a map of England how strong he was, how many men he was able to make, how far his lands stretched, and how they lay between his houses of Bromham and Holt. 6. He often showed me what shires and places were for him, noting where he was the judge of his friends, and where lay the lands of the protector and Lord Warwick, to whom I know he had no affection. At the beginning of last winter, riding from Marquess Dorset's house, he often showed me the country, saying which there were his friends. 7. He then boasted that as many gentlemen loved him as any nobleman in England, and more than the protector. Besides his friends he could make or bring 200 men of those within his rule and of his tenants and servants, if he were commanded to serve. 8. Another time he asked me what money I could make him if necessary. I said about £4,000, which he said was little. I said it would be very hard to make more suddenly, but if he gave me a little warning I should be able to make as much as I should have stuff of which to make it. He willed me get as much money into my hands as I could, often advising me to have a good mass of money ready. 9. When riding [from Dorset's] he asked me how much would find 10,000 men a month, and calculated that at 6d. a day a man £10,000

would serve. He added that it was good to stop building and always have a good mass of money. 10. At the same time he wished I were able to make £10,000 in ready money. I replied that he should not lack if I were able, and if the mint continued at Bristol, which he trusted it would. 11. Last Christmas week, after my return from Canterbury, suspecting trouble, I went and told the admiral I could not justify my doings in the mint if they were known, but had ordered the matter that no man would be able to accuse me. I had received £1,000 from the admiral when he went to Landrecies, for which I promised him £900 interest. I also received £400 from him for wools, so my whole debt was £2,300, of which I told him I had spent £1,500 on his buildings at Bromham, £1,000 at Sudeley, lent him £900 at the queen's death, paid Marquess Dorset £900 for him, and £600 for building his ship; he admitted he was £2,800 in my debt, but I prayed him take a bill of £2,000 debt to him, with four years' interest totalling £800, lest trouble should happen to me. He accepted the bill, which I think is in his London house. He promised to bear me in anything he could if I were troubled. 12. He said Lady Jane, the marquess's daughter, was a fitter marriage for the king than the protector's daughter. 13. About twelve days before last Christmas the admiral told me in his house that he was not content that he was not placed in the parliament house as one of the king's uncles. 14. He often said that he had given the king £80, which [John] Fowler received and distributed according to the king's pleasure to the pages and other poor waiters. 15. On the first day of this parliament, as I was going there I met Smythweke, who advised me not to go to [Princess] Elizabeth. Hereupon I gathered matter touching the admiral, determining to speak with him when I next met him, but I forgot for more than a week until he came to my house one morning as he was going to his ship. Walking in my garden after breakfast, or before supper, I told him of Smythweke's warning. He said he had nothing to do with it, but asked why the king's daughters should not be married within the realm, which he had said to some of the council, who were able to say little to it. 16. Another time I asked him why he gave himself no better to serve, as every other man so willingly offered himself. He said it was good staying to make merry with country neighbours. I said I thought it would not be well taken, as it was known he could serve well. He would speak no more of it.

*Signed.*                                                                 SP 10/6, no. 13

**189.** [? January]. Depositions of William Parr, marquess of Northampton, commanded by the lord protector and council to show what conference he had with the lord admiral in the previous year.

1. About a year past, supposing I was not content, knowing well why he should think so, the admiral advised me to set up house in the north where my lands lay, so that being loved by my friends and tenants there, I should be stronger to serve the king, whereby the protector and council would be as glad of me as I of them. 2. When the admiral first came to court after the queen's death he showed me suits he had to the protector touching the queen's servants, jewels and other things which he claimed to be hers, for which he would remain at court. If he did not speed well he would return to the country, which life he liked well. He was very friendly in deed and word, promising money or anything he had, and gave me a valuable specialty. 3. When the admiral last came to London he told me in his own gallery that there would be much ado for Lady Jane, Marquess Dorset's daughter, and that the protector and [the duchess of Somerset] would do what they could to obtain her for Lord Hertford. But he said they would not prevail, for the marquess had given her wholly to him on certain convenants. I asked him what he would do if the protector, handling the marquess gently, should obtain his good will; he answered that he would never consent to it. 4. Another time the admiral told me that he had never heard that the protector had said he would clap him in the Tower if he went to [Princess] Elizabeth. I said I thought it but a rumour, but advised

him to break the matter with the protector, to put any suspicion out of his head. He replied that there was no woman he went about to marry, but would shortly go to his house and ask the protector if he would command him any service to Elizabeth, as he would pass Hatfield on his way home. 5. The night before he was committed to the Tower the admiral called me and seemed perplexed, declaring that the council had secret conferences that day in the garden, but he could not learn their effect; he could get nothing of the lord privy seal. He thought they conferred to see if they could get anything against him from Sharington, who was more straitly handled for his sake. But he cared not, for he was able to answer all charges. The protector was in fear of his own estate and was very jealous because the admiral was better furnished with men about him. 6. The day he was committed the admiral said he knew he would be called that day before the council to answer charges from Lord Rutland, who had been examined by the protector very late the night before. He would question Rutland before all the other lords, saying he would answer all things at his liberty, and not be shut up when he should not answer. He would send for and declare his mind to the lord privy seal and Mr Comptroller. At my departing he would have me take a message to the protector to send the lord privy seal and Mr Comptroller.

*Signed.* SP 10/6, no. 14

**190.** [? January]. Depositions of Thomas Wriothesley, earl of Southampton.

During the first session of this parliament the admiral and I were appointed with certain lords and others to dine with Sir John Gresham, then mayor of London, to consider a bill touching weirs and purprestures in the river Thames. On the way the admiral said I had been well handled with my office. I asked him what he meant and said I was glad to be discharged of it. I told him to take heed as I had heard he would contend with his brother and make a party. He said he would have things better ordered. I warned him against attempting violence. He might say he meant well, but would show himself the king's greatest enemy. He might begin a faction and trouble, but could not end it when he would. He said he did not mean that. I said that the world believed so, and he were better buried alive than to attempt it; at which he broke off and never since looked on me. I reported this talk to the protector.

*Signed.*
*Perhaps the final part of a longer statement.* SP 10/6, no. 15

**191.** [? January]. Depositions of Lord Russell, lord privy seal.

Riding behind the protector to parliament, I told the admiral I was sorry to hear rumours that he made means to marry [Princess] Mary or [Princess] Elizabeth, which would be his undoing. I told him I had heard this from some of his near friends; he denied attempting any such thing. Two or three days later, riding from the protector's house to parliament, he said I was very suspicious of him and asked who had told me of the marriage he should attempt. I declined, but advised him against it. He replied that it was convenient for them to marry, and better within the realm than abroad, and why might not he or another made by their father marry one of them. I told him that it would be the undoing of anyone, particularly him who was so near the king. The king might be suspicious like his father and grandfather, and suppose that if the admiral married his sister he wished for his death. He replied that he who married one of them would have £3,000 a year. I said only £10,000 in money, plate and goods, but no lands, which he did not accept, and swore none of us dare say no to it. I swore I would, for it was against the king's will. Another time we spoke of Sharington's matters, as we often did; he said more extremity was showed to him than his offence deserved – he was not allowed to go upon sureties and all his books and writings were taken so he could have nothing to show for himself. I said Sharington's matter touching the king's coin was more heinous than it seemed to him. Another time he showed me Sharington's patent, and seemed to affirm thereby that he might lawfully coin testons and other coins as before. I told him he did not do well to defend Sharington. He would have better opportunity to speak for him when his matter was brought to further trial. Riding another time to parliament, the admiral asked what I would say if he went above me shortly. I said I would be glad of his preferment, and did not care if he took nothing from me. I reported this to the lord chancellor that morning.

*Signed.*

*Printed*: Tytler, i, 142–6 (with omissions). M.L. Bush, 'The Tudors and the Royal Race', *History*, lv, (1970), 38–9 (extract only).                                    SP 10/6, no. 16

**192.**    [? January]. Depositions of Sir George Blagge.

About a year ago the admiral, waving a paper, told me it was a request to have the king better ordered, and not kept so close that no one might see him, which he intended to put into the house, saying he cared not for his brother's friendship. I tried to dissuade him but, seeing my words took small effect, said the protector might commit him to ward. He said he would go if sent for, but that the protector would not be so hasty to send him to prison. This was all our communication, which I so disliked that I never talked with him since.

*? Holograph.*

*Printed*: Tytler, i, 146–8.                                    SP 10/6, no. 17

**193.**    [? January]. Depositions of the earl of Warwick.

At about the same time, hearing of the admiral's motion in the commons, and on being shown a copy of his letter that he would not come to the protector, Warwick said that if the protector knew this he would set the admiral fast in the Tower, as he would do if he were [protector]* as him. The admiral swore he would stab whoever laid hands on him to fetch him to prison.

*Signed.*

*On the same paper as the preceding statement.*                                    SP 10/6, no. 17(i)

**194.**    [?]. Memorandum of causes by which a subject may be liable to forfeit his lands to the king.

1. Lands concealed. 2. Rents concealed. 3. Lands mortgaged. 4. Fee farms reserved to the king. 5. Tenths reserved upon letters patent. 6. Misprision of the writer. 7. Misnaming the corporation. 8. Misnaming the possessions. 9. Leases not recited. 10. Finding of false offices. 11. Granting of lands when they are not in the crown. 12. Attainted lands. 13. Escheated lands. 14. Aliens' purchase. 15. Patents antedated. 16. Advowsons instead of rectories impropriate. 17. Two manors carried away for one. 18. False exchanges. 19. Encroachments. 20. Assarts. 21. Surrendered lands. 22. Entails general and special. 23. Entails upon the king's person. 24. Misprisions in patents where the *habendum* is repugnant to the grant. 25. Resumptions by act of parliament.

SP 10/6, no. 18

**195.**    February 2. Depositions of Katherine Ashley.

Immediately after the death of the queen at Cheshunt when [Princess] Elizabeth was sick, Ashley told her that her old husband, appointed at the king's death, was free again, and she might have him if she wished. She answered no. Ashley said she would not deny it if the protector and council were pleased, and asked why one worthy to match a queen should not marry her. Often at play in drawing hands she saw the admiral and my lord of 'Sarset' [? Somerset] together, and she laughed when she chose the admiral. Ashley

*        Deleted.

would say she wished she would not refuse him if the council were content. At the queen's death it was reported that the admiral was the heaviest man in the world, and Ashley would have had her or her secretary write to comfort him, but she would not lest she be thought to woo him. Upon [Thomas] Parry's letter offering his house and household stuff, Ashley counselled her to refuse both unless [Sir Anthony] Denny advised it. She bade Ashley so write, and she did. Parry sent word that the admiral would see her grace. Ashley wrote again that she would not come until he came to parliament again, and then she would come to London and tell him her mind. About All Hallowtide she asked leave to go to London to speak with the admiral. Her grace refused it for it would be said she did stud her. She was to have begged the gatehouse at Durham Place for she had no [good]* lodging in London.

    *Signed.*
    *Text in the hand of Secretary Smith.*                                    SP 10/6, no. 19

**196.**    February 4. Further depositions of Katherine Ashley.

    She came to London about three weeks or a month before Christmas. She spoke to nobody there except her husband, Lady Berkley, Lady Denny, Parry, William, Mr Ashley's servant, his horsekeeper, Hornbie, yeoman of the chamber and William Russell, gentleman of his grace's chamber. She did not leave Slanynge's house till she went to take horse at Lady Berkley's in Fleet Street with Slanynge's wife. Lady Denny came to her there. She came to London on Tuesday at noon and left the next day at noon. She had no sore arm, but an ache there, and was not bled for it, but pretended to [Princess] Elizabeth and everybody that it was for that cause. In fact it was because there had been a jar between her and her husband. She could not be merry until she had spoken with him, for he had not replied to her letter. She sent for him, and he tarried with her all that night. Her husband and Parry breakfasted with her that morning, and so she went with Slanynge's wife to Lady Berkley's and there took horse. She did not go into the town because she had only a russel night gown, which she has on now in the Tower, or else she would have seen [the duchess of] Somerset – she sent William Russell to her grace with a token from Elizabeth given her by her grace. Gawain and Peter Carew, George Eliot and Archdeacon [George] Carew came to her at Slanynge's. She went away so soon because her errand was done when she and her husband were agreed. She spoke then neither with the admiral nor any of his men. She was never a mile from Elizabeth's house since she was first sick about midsummer; at that time she had no communication with Parry of any matter between Elizabeth and the admiral. On the night that the lord great master† and [Sir Anthony] Denny supped at Hatfield, Lady Foskew, Mr Comptroller's wife‡ and she supped with them. After supper Parry's wife looked on her husband, wept, and told her she was afraid they would send him to the Tower, and of what they would do to him. [Ashley] replied that there was no such cause, but that there was a private communication between him and her, praying her to pray him not to meddle in that, as it did not concern their examination. Parry sent her word again by Lady Foskew that he would be torn to pieces rather than open that matter. When she talked with Parry of speaking to the admiral she forbade him to tell anybody as she feared it should come to her husband; she knew it would displease him as he always said that the admiral's suitors would come to an evil end, and forbade her to meddle in anything concerning him.

    *Signed.*
    *Text in Smith's hand.*                                    SP 10/6, no. 20

---

\*      Deleted.
†      Lord St John.
‡      Thomas Parry had married Anne, widow of Sir Thomas Fortescue.

**197.**   [February 4]. Further depositions [of Katherine Ashley].

Immediately after the queen's coming to Hanworth [when Princess] Elizabeth [was] walking in the garden, the admiral cut her gown in a hundred pieces. I chided with her when she came up so trimmed. She said the queen held her while the admiral 'did so dresse hyt'. I said I wished he would show her more reverence although he was homely with the queen.

*Holograph (unsigned).*

*Minuted by Smith*: To my Lady Elizabeth's grace.                          SP 10/6, no. 21

**198.**   [February 4]. Final depositions of Katherine Ashley.

I never secretly moved [Princess Elizabeth's] affections to [the admiral] or any other, but always counselled her to keep her mind safe and at the council's appointment. I never had letters or tokens from him to her or myself since the queen's death, except three commendations, by Parry, John Seymour and Mary Cheke; her grace never sent to him except the letter for Alan. I told the admiral in St James's park that I had heard it said he should have married my lady. He denied it, saying he loved not his life to lose a wife, and it could not be, but said he would prove to have the queen, which I said was past proof as I had heard he was already married to her. I told her grace she might have the husband appointed her at the king's death. She, sick in bed, said no. I said she should if the council agreed, for he was the noblest man unmarried in this land, but she always said no. When she played at drawing hands she chose the admiral and drove him away. I told her she would not refuse it if the protector and council bade her, and she said yes. I would have had her write to comfort him at the queen's death, but she refused because they would think she wooed him. I told her it was impossible for the admiral to have her until the king came to his own rule. I was sure the protector and council would not allow a subject to have her. I think I said the same to Parry. At the reading of his letter I think I told her not to set her mind on it, seeing its unlikelihood.

I remember no more, and would not hide it if I could. Pity me, Mr Secretary,* and let me change my prison, for it is so cold that I cannot sleep, and so dark that I cannot see by day, for I stop the window with straw as there is no glass. My memory is never good, as my lady, fellows and husband can tell, and this sorrow has made it worse. Move my lord's grace to pity me and forgive my great folly in speaking of marriage to such a person as she. I have suffered punishment and shame. I trust my lord will not deny me for this first fault, and if I were with her grace again (which I do not look for) I would never speak of marriage. I told my lord his boldness in her chamber was complained of to the council, but he would swear, asking what he did and wishing they all saw. I could not make him stop, and at last told the queen, who made little of it and said she would come with him, and did so ever after.

*Holograph.*

*Minuted by Smith*: To my Lady Elizabeth, to Mary Cheke, to Parry, to John Seymour.

SP 10/6, no. 22

**199.**   February 11. Ely Place. The earl of Warwick to William Cecil.

I forgot to sue [the council] in two things. I would be glad to help Henry Makerell, the king's surgeon, who has taken great pains with me. He is cunning and honest, much esteemed by the late king. He has the good will of Vicars to be joint patent with him, for Vicars is old and sick, and can no more give his bounden attendance on the court. Makerell is young and able to take pains. The other matter is for poor Turpyn, my servant, to have in farm some of the poor chantries in Deritend or others. He has done notable service at Boulogne and on the borders. I send the half year's fee of your patent which shows your possession. I trust the matter we communed of will take good effect;

---

*        Smith, presumably.

the other party is well inclined to seek it.

*Holograph.*　　　　　　　　　　　　　　　　　　　　SP 10/6, no. 23

**200.** February 14. Indenture between the king and the mayor and commons of Plymouth, Devon, granting, over and besides much money, timber and other provisions previously paid at the king's charge for making a fort at St Nicholas Island in Plymouth harbour, for the security of the inhabitants and navigation, £23.6.8 for five fodders of lead for covering and other necessaries, and £100 for its completion; also granting [*blank*]* for four resident gunners, one having 8d. a day and the others 6d., to be paid by the customer of Plymouth from customs there, from next Lady Day, half yearly, during pleasure. In consideration the mayor and commons bind themselves to complete the fort, maintain it with munitions and provide the gunners' wages, seeing that three are always present by day and all four by night. If, upon the approach of enemies or for other cause it is necessary for the fort to be better furnished, the mayor and commons will provide sixteen extra men at their own costs. The mayor and another burgess – or two burgesses – shall inspect the fort every week. The king may at all times appoint commissioners to survey it and make other ordinances for its keeping.

*Draft.*　　　　　　　　　　　　　　　　　　　　　　SP 10/6, no. 24

**201.** February 15. The council to justices of the peace in all counties.

The king is informed that many have presumed, contrary to his commands, to sell church vestments, plate, jewels, ornaments, bells and lead, applying the money to their own uses, so causing much contention. He therefore appoints you commissioners for the county of [*blank*]. You are to assemble and assign to yourselves hundreds and quarters of the county. There you shall summon the parson or vicar if resident, or curate and churchwardens with three or four other discreet and substantial men of every parish in your circuit, to make two inventories of the goods of all churches and chapels, signed by you and them, one left in each of the parishes and the other with the *custos rotulorum*. You shall then charge the curates and parishioners on the king's behalf not to alter, sell or give away any of their church goods. If any parishioner attempts such alienation the clergy, churchwardens and other honest men shall notify you the justices of the peace, whereupon you shall take immediate order for the stay of the alienation and imprison the offenders for a convenient time. For every alienation made within one year before this date, unless by the common consent of the parishioners and the money applied to common use, you shall have the goods restored, sending us the names of any who refuse, for whom we may send further order. You may require of the bishop's offices a copy of the inventory previously made for every parish. Send us an abridgement of the inventories, of the plate and bells only, for the whole shire, with a full declaration of your doings.

*Draft.*　　　　　　　　　　　　　　　　　　　　　　SP 10/6, no. 25

**202.** February 20. Depositions of John Cheke.

In the first session of parliament, the king then at Westminster, the admiral came to me with a paper, saying he had a suit to the house of lords and that the king was content to write to them for it, asking me to have him do so. The bill, in the admiral's hand, prayed the lords to favour his suit. I told him the protector had commanded me that the king should sign no bill without his hand on it before, and I dare not let the king write or sign it. He said I might do so as the king had promised him; although he was an ill speaker, if he had the bill he was sure the best speakers in the house would help him prefer it. I refused, and left him. The king later told me in private that the admiral should have no such bill signed or written of him. I heard no more before or since of

*　　　Sum should be £39.10.0.

the admiral's part or this bill.

*Holograph.*

*Printed*: Tytler, i, 154–5.                                                    SP 10/6, no. 26

**203.** February 24. Answers of the lord admiral to articles objected against him by the lord chancellor and other councillors.

1. Last Eastertide he told [John] Fowler he would be glad to have the king in his custody as [Sir Richard] Page had, and thought he might be brought through the gallery to his chamber and so to his house. He spoke merrily, meaning no harm. In the meantime he found that there were once in England a protector,* a regent of France† and the duke of Exeter and bishop of Winchester governors of the king's person. He had thought to sue parliament for that purpose. He had the names of all the lords, and totted those whom he thought he might have to his purpose, to labour them. Afterwards, reminded by Mr Comptroller at Ely Place of his written assent to the lord protector's being the king's governor, he was ashamed and ceased his suit. 2. He gave money to two or three of those about the king. He gave [John] Cheke £40 a year last Christmas when the queen was at Enfield, £20 to himself and the rest for the king to bestow among his servants. Cheke was loath to take it. He gave him no more since the coronation. He has given money to the grooms of the chamber at New Year – he does not remember what. He gave Fowler £20 for the king since the beginning of the last parliament at London. The king often sent to him for money and he sent it. When [Hugh] Latimer preached before him the king wrote to ask what he should give him; he sent him £40 by Fowler, saying that £20 was a good reward for Latimer, and he might bestow the rest among his servants. He does not remember if he gave Fowler any money for himself. 3. He did draw such a bill and preferred it to the king or Cheke. Before that he had Fowler move the king if he could be his governor as [Sir Michael] Stanhope was. He knows not what answer he had, but he drew the bill to the effect that the king was content. He cannot tell what answer he had to the bill, but Cheke can.

The admiral refused to answer the rest of the articles before us.

*Signed by*: Lord Rich, lord chancellor, the earl of Southampton, the earl of Warwick, the earl of Shrewsbury, Sir Thomas Cheyne, Sir Thomas Smith, Sir Anthony Denny and Sir John Baker.                                                    SP 10/6, no. 27

**204.** February 19. List of items from the king's secret houses at Westminster Palace.

August 1547. Taken from the silk house by the [duke] of Somerset: crimson velvet to [cov]er a wagon made for him; taken by his command by George [. . .]stowe, draper: fine red cloths and Irish frieze to line the wagon – £2.13.4 as yet unpaid; black velvet for covering a litter or side saddle; passementerie ('paysmaynes') of gold and silver Venice to garnish the wagon. 1548. Crepons, coifs, sacrament cloths, coverpanes, pillows, wrought with silk and gold, and other things taken trussed in a sheet from the silk house by the [duchess] of Somerset and Sir Michael Stanhope, carried to her chamber and delivered to Mistress Sabcott. June 1548. Taken from the silk house by the [duchess] and Stanhope: tinsel delivered to the yeomen of the robes, the rest to Stanhope for the king's use; tinsel and baudkin carried to [the duchess's] chamber and delivered to Mistress Sabcott. July 1548. Taken by Sir John Thynne who brought the keys of the silk house: silks and satin which [the duke] had appointed for the earl of Ormond, but were carried to Sheen and delivered to Jenkin, the boy of the [duke's] chamber. 6 February 1549. Taken from the jewel house on the great garden side by the [duchess] and Stanhope: a wooden coffer, a desk, a looking glass, an alabaster hour glass and an ebony box; taken by them from the study on the great garden side: a wooden box with silver instruments

---

\*      Humphrey, duke of Gloucester.

†      John, duke of Bedford.

called joints, a desk, 12 pairs of shears, boxes for rings and jewels, a round box, a comb case. February 19. Rob[. . .]dson, Stanhope's servant, carried loads of stuff from the long gallery to his master's chamber, thought to be from the silk house.

　　*Detailed.*　　　　　　　　　　　　　　　　　　　　　　　　　　SP 10/6, no. 28

**205.**　[February]. Estimate of plate, jewels, money and other goods belonging to Sir William Sharington remaining in his houses at his arrest in January.

　　Lacock, Wiltshire. All plate sent to London under charge of John Berwick, sole commissioner, worth at least 1,000 marks [£666.13.4]; ingots [*specified*] probably worth £1,000; napery [*specified*] filling one wagon taken to Berwick's house to the duke of Somerset's use, worth over £300; [Sharington's] wife's jewels, chains and two of [his], taken by Berwick, worth over £200; more old gold, broken silver and money, velvet and silk of [Lady Sharington's] store, delivered by her to Berwick, worth £140 or £160; jewels of [the duchess of] Suffolk, of great value, left with [Sharington] for assurance of £11,000 left to her, delivered to Berwick; all [Lady Sharington's] apparel, inventoried and locked in a chest by Berwick; household goods also inventoried by Berwick and put in charge of one of the servants.

　　Bristol Castle. As much gold and silver as, by word of Thomas Dowrishe, deputy there, would with alloy have made £13,000 or £14,000; £200 in cash; assays of gold and silver; household goods and [Sharington's] clothes; specialties worth over £1,000; £1,500 worth of lead and £500 cash in the hands of the company there; two ships with ordnance and tackle at Bristol quay, given [Sharington] by the lord admiral, worth at least £200.

　　House on Tower Hill, London. Plate, the value of which will appear by Sir Edmund Peckham's books who, with Richard Fulmerston, the duke of Somerset's comptroller, was commissioner there; broken plate of Anne Sharington, [his] sister, worth £50 or £60; cash, with old gold and silver and coins, worth over £3,000; household goods, horse &c., inventoried (except a bed and poor stuff allowed to [Lady Sharington]) and taken away; five chambers hung with tapestry, furnished with down beds and woollen quilts, silk canopies, taken to the duke of Somerset's house; a diamond and a white ruby, worth at least £100, taken by Fulmerston to [the duchess of] Somerset, who afterwards told [Lady Sharington] that they were of no value; a turquoise worth £10; a diamond worth £40; other jewels worth £50, taken from [Sharington's] company house; a casket containing specialties worth £7,000 or £8,000. [Sharington] occupied in Flanders, being free of the company there, having stock of over £2,000.

　　*Written in the first person.*　　　　　　　　　　　　　　　　SP 10/6, no. 29

**206.**　[? March]. Extract from chantry certificate of 2 Edward VI for the master and wardens of the guild [of the Blessed Virgin Mary and St Dunstan] of St Dunstan's [in the West, London].

　　Also they have a lease for 99 years yet to come from the bishop of Chichester for £2.13.4 a year of tenements and gardens and land on which they have set a new frame for tenements in Chancery Lane – which lease, they think, is not given to the king by act of parliament.

　　Rental. A tenement in the tenure of William Ranwicke for years by lease – £1.13.4 (said to be rented at 100 marks [£66.3.4]); 3 tenements in the tenure of John Whytepayne by lease at 13s. 4d. each – £2; a garden in the tenure of John Whytepayne by lease by year – 6s. 8d.; a garden in the tenure of Thomas Harrison, by year – 6s. 8d.; a tenement in the tenure of Thomas Harrison, by year – 6s. 8d.; a tenement in the tenure of Thomas Cooke by lease, by year – £4; a tenement in the tenure of Hugh Ryleighe by lease, by year – £1.6.8; a tenement in the tenure of William Lostyce by lease, by year – £1; a tenement in the tenure of William Yeeo, by year – £4 (by year – £20); a tenement in the tenure of David Morryce, by year – £1; a tenement in the tenure of John Gryffyn, by year – £1; two great gardens in the tenure of Reginald Conygrave by lease, by year – £2.13.4; total – £19.6.8. For 4 new houses worth, if finished – £26.13.4 (these four underneath are rented at £80 a year, enclosed by a brick wall); paid yearly to the bishop of Chichester – £2.13.4; to the exhibition of a scholar at Oxford – £2.13.4; remaining clear – £14.

Extract from royal confirmation of an indenture made 1 April 1542 between Richard [Sampson], bishop of Chichester and Henry Le, draper, master of the guild of St Mary and St Dunstan in the church of St Dunstan on the east of Fleet Street, London, Thomas Harryson, girdler, and Nicholas Mellowe, plumber, citizens of London and wardens of the guild, the bishop having granted to the master and wardens all his property between the messuage and garden belonging to the chamber of London on the north and the king's Rolls house on the south, abutting on Chancery Lane to the east and the Rolls garden and others late of Christchurch Priory, London on the west, and property in the parish of St Dunstan; also four small tenements and gardens adjoining Lincoln's Inn on the north, and tenements lately belonging to the hospital of St John of Jerusalem in England on the south, Fykett's field on the east and Chancery Lane on the west, in the parish of St Dunstan, from Michaelmas 1549 for 99 years, paying £2.13.4 at Lady Day and Michaelmas from Lady Day [1550]. SP 10/6, no. 30

**207.** April 6. Thorpe Mandeville. William Gyffard to William Cecil.

By virtue of Sir Thomas Pope's commission I sold 'Mare sale' copse with four acres adjoining in the manor of Collyweston and Tomlin wood, part of the manor of Apethorpe. Perceiving by his letter of February 18 that [Princess] Elizabeth has the wood as part of her assignment, I am charged to pay the money made to her officers, my reasonable charges allowed. Lawrence Alee tells me you wish him to be charged with the receipt of the money for Tomlin wood and will not allow me to meddle further. I am content to do so if it is your pleasure. *Postscript (? incomplete)*. On Lady Elizabeth's behalf and in the name of the lord protector. SP 10/6, no. 31

**208.** April 6. Rome. Reginald, Cardinal Pole to the earl of Warwick.

I am sending two messengers to the lord protector, and write to you that by your authority in the council my advice may have better effect, which has no special design but the good of all, especially those who now rule. The messengers will explain my information.

*Mutilated.*
*Printed*: Tytler, i, 165–6. SP 10/6, no. 32

**209.** April 9. Syon. The duke of Somerset to the vice-chancellor, proctors and masters, regent and non-regent of the university of Cambridge.

The royal visitation is not more to be encouraged as your private affair than as the concern of the king and whole realm that the universities should be well constituted and governed. They are storehouses or great nurseries of letters and piety from which humane teaching is spread throughout England. We wish your body to be regulated by laws and statutes by which learning shall increase. Nothing grows in the king more than love of letters and all studies; you need fear nothing from him if you nourish letters continually. The visitors will be with you shortly to set all aright.

*Latin.*
*Copy.* SP 10/6, no. 33

**210.** April 10. Westminster. The king to William Bill, vice-chancellor and the proctors of the university of Cambridge.

By commission under the great seal dated 12 November 1548* Thomas [Goodrich], bishop of Ely, Nicholas [Ridley], bishop of Rochester, privy councillors, Sir William Paget, K.G., comptroller of the household, Sir Thomas Smith, secretary, John Cheke, the king's tutor, William May, LL.D., master of requests and Thomas Wendy, M.D., the king's physician, among others, were authorised to visit the university of Cambridge. All its members are therefore cited to appear before the commissioners in the new chapel† of the university on May 6 between 8 and 10 a.m. and thereafter during the visitation. The charters, statutes, registers and all other accounts and writings of the university, colleges, halls and houses of scholars are to be exhibited there and verified. Everything that this visitation requires shall be done and received, on pain of contempt for transgressors from the day of the reception hereof. The full names of all cited shall be clearly certified in your schedules for each college and hall.

*Latin.*

*Seal* ad causas.

*Witnessed by* : the visitors above named.

*Copy.*

*Printed* : J. Lamb (ed.), *A collection of letters . . . illustrative of the University of Cambridge,* (1838), 107–8, from Corpus Christi College, Cambridge MS 106, no. 176, pp. 489–90 (contemporary copy). *Translation printed in*: J. Heywood (ed.), *Collection of Statutes for the University and Colleges of Cambridge,* (1840), 1–3. SP 10/6, no. 34

**211.** [? April 11]. Thursday morning at 6. [The Savoy].‡ Derby Place. R[ichard] Whalley to William Cecil.

I see no likelihood to obtain Wimbledon as you desire (although I can do no more for my father) but the park, with the tithe of Mortlake, Ambrose Wolley's house and other parcels to serve your need will be obtained on your next witty talk with Mr Chancellor [of augmentations], who is now persuaded to use you friendly in the park and lodge for his whole interest there as he has it at [Sir Robert] Tyrwytte's hands. He promised me to speak and conclude with you today. I desire to be at Welbeck with my nurse.

*Holograph.*

*Printed*: Tytler, i, 276–7. SP 10/6, no. 35

**212.** April 12. Leighton [Bromswold]. Sir Robert Tyrwhitt to William Cecil.

I have received the protector's letter and yours for Mortlake lodge and park as he would have you near him. Not twenty [days] before Sir Michael Stanhope wrote to me that the chancellor of augmentations had agreed with [Richard] Whalley for Wimbledon parsonage, desiring me to agree for my farm and office, praying that as he had found him his friend since his trouble, I would let him have them. I replied that I intend either to come or send up to conclude with him after Easter, so my promise is made. But if you can obtain it again of Stanhope I would willingly accomplish the protector's request. Commendations to [the duke and duchess].

*Holograph.* SP 10/6, no. 36

**213.** May 4. Stepney. Mary [Fitz Roy], duchess of Richmond to Sir Thomas Smith, principal secretary.

Ask [the protector] for three licences which this bearer will deliver, that these men's preaching may be of more authority. They are honest and godly; licence has already been given to many less worthy. [John] Hontyngeton and [Thomas] Some are already licensed

---

* No. **164** above.

† That of King's College [cf. no. **222** below].

‡ Deleted.

by the archbishop of Canterbury; the third is Dr [Henry] Kynge of Norwich. Thank you for enabling my cousin Sir William Faremer to purchase lands.

    *Holograph.*
    *Printed*: Green, 201–4.                                          SP 10/7, no. 1

**214.**  Copy of the above.
    *17th cent.*                                                       SP 10/7, no. 2

**215.**  May 5. Stepney. The duchess of Richmond to Sir Thomas Smith.

    Withdraw your evil opinion of Huntyngeton. He is godly, learned and eloquent. It seems a pity that he might not, with the king's and [protector's] authority, preach as well as the others. Remember Dr Kynge of Norwich and Some, who are also godly and honest. I again ask you to solicit my lord's grace.

    *Holograph.*
    *Printed*: Green, 204–5.                                       SP 10/7, no. 3

**216.**  May 5. Eton. William Goldwyn, vice-provost of Eton to Sir Thomas Smith, provost.

    We have chosen [Augustine] Crosse and [William] Dobson bursars, to take account of all rents received since Lady Day, those to be received with arrears, and all remaining store, of which your servant shall have the number and tally to employ to the college's best advantage. As he has been profitable concerning the brewhouse he shall receive the number of all cattle, fish and other things, to show how, where, and of whom they were bought, and how bestowed weekly in the house – so that, thanks to your good device and counsel, all things will content you and profit the college. [William] Boswell told me he had not sold or changed his benefice, as he will write to you himself. The report that the schoolmaster* is a dice and card player, rioter or gamer, not applying his school, is manifestly false. I can find no fault in him. But (as I have honestly told him) he is somewhat too gentle and gives his scholars more licence than they have been used to, of which evil tongued men spread much matter, and defame without care of redress. I trust there is none such in our company.

    *Holograph.*
    *Printed*: H.C. Maxwell Lyte, *A History of Eton College*, (3rd edn, 1899), 133 (last section only).                                    SP 10/7, no. 4

**217.**  May 8. W.P. [Sir William Paget], from his chamber at court, to the duke of Somerset.

    If I did not love you so deeply I might hold my peace as others do; but I am forced to say that unless you show your pleasure more quietly in debate with others and graciously hear their opinions when you require them, there will be sorry consequences, and you will be first to repent. No man dares speak what he thinks, although necessary. Out of the council you hear me very gently; I think I speak mostly without experience and you seldom follow my advice. But in council, as I am freer to speak than others (which I will amend if you dislike it), you sometimes nip me so sharply that, if I did not know you well and were not assured of your favour, I might often have blanched for speaking frankly. If other honest men, not so well acquainted with your nature, say their opinions honestly and are snapped, God knows what you shall lose. I would not write this much if I did not know how many men of service are troubled. Sir Richard Alee, after you had unnecessarily rebuked him this afternoon, came to my chamber weeping, almost out of his mind. The late king once almost killed him in this way. You may think nothing of this but (as I once wrote to you) if you would recall telling those who said

---

\*    William Barker.

opinions contrary to yours that before, if a king or cardinal had spoken to them, it would have pricked them in the stomach, you will realise such words from the lord protector go to a man's heart. You have lately been very angry when contradicted. A king who discourages men from saying their opinions frankly imperils the realm. A subject in great authority as you are, doing so, is likely to endanger himself as well as the commonwealth. Consider this, and when the whole council gives advice (as they lately did for sending men to Boulogne), follow it, and relent sometimes from your own opinions. Your surety will be greater, your burden less.

*Holograph.*

*Printed*: Strype, *Ecclesiastical Memorials*, ii, II, 427–9, from copy in BL Cottonian MS Titus F.3, f. 276v. SP 10/7, no. 5

**218.** [May 8. Westminster]. Commission to John [Dudley], earl of Warwick, Viscount Lisle, great chamberlain, Henry [Holbeach], bishop of Lincoln, Nicholas [Ridley], bishop of Rochester, privy councillors, Sir William Paget, comptroller of the household, Sir William Petre, secretary, Richard Cox, the king's almoner and tutor, Simon Haynes, dean of Exeter, Christopher Nevinson, LL.D. and Richard Morison to visit the king's free chapel and college within Windsor Castle, Winchester College and the diocese and especially the university of Oxford.

In the same terms as the commission for Cambridge and Eton [no. **164** above].

*Latin.*

*Copy*: from C 66/816, m. 22d (*CPR* 1548–9, 251).

*Printed*: Rymer, xv, 183–5. SP 10/7, no. 6

**219.** Another copy of the above. SP 10/7, no. 7

**220.** May 10. London. W[. . .] Wightman to William Cecil, master of requests.

I am innocent of fraud towards the protector. The allegations against me are as false as he* who made them. Although my old master, the master of the horse† was known to dissent from the proceedings in religion, long ago, communing with the protector in the garden at Enfield when the king came from Hertford he consented that he should be protector, thinking it the best kind of government. I never heard him deny this. I never knew or enquired to what sum the protector's lands rose, and I could not have spoken to my master about this. Concerning the abatement of tenths, I heard my master say about the answer to the protector in Bridge's matter, when he was greatly heated, that his brother was keen to help every man to his right save him. He made a great sort to let him have the queen's jewels, legally his, pretending he wished the king should not lose so much. But he made nothing of the king's loss in the court of first fruits and tenths, where his revenue was abated by almost £10,000 a year. I told him it was believed that all lands surrendered since the king's death were far less than that. He said that now no bishopric, deanery or prebend could fall vacant but one of them would have a fleece of it. I agreed, and mentioned the deanery of Wells, the bishopric of Lincoln and others sorely plucked at. He said it did not matter as it would come in again as fast when the king came of age. He would not be in their coats when he heard of it. I told him nothing would discommend him more than his slackness of service at a time when one day's service was worth years'. He answered and I replied as in my former confession. I beg pardon for not mentioning this before. Have pity.

*Printed*: Tytler, i, 168–73. SP 10/7, no. 8

---

\* Lord Seymour.

† Sir Anthony Browne.

**221.**   May 12. Benjamin Gonson, [treasurer of the navy] to Sir William Petre, sending a list of ships and galleys ready to sail by the following Wednesday [May 15], so that the victuallers cause no more delay.

The *Antelope* (Thomas Cotton, vice-admiral, captain), the *Harte* (Richard Bethell, captain), the *Salamonder* (John Wyngfyllde, captain), the *Genet* (William Hall, captain), the *Inglesshe Galley* (Richard Broke, captain), the late *French Galley* (William Terrell, captain), one shallop. *Draft postscript.** Because the soldiers and sailors appointed to serve at sea have lately stolen away, to the great danger of the whole navy and those that remain, the king requires Cotton to keep his men at sea except those appointed to land for necessaries and those licensed to depart for sickness or other reasonable cause.

SP 10/7, no. 9

**222.**   May 14. Cambridge. William Rogers to Sir Thomas Smith.

The first day [of the visitation], May 6, the bishop of Rochester preached at 8 o'clock in St Mary's Church, exhorting the three degrees (as he divided them [*sic*]) of the university to apply the study of wisdom and learning. All the visitors then went to King's College Chapel and sat with the whole university before them. The bishop of Ely took me the commission to read, and when I had read it the vice-chancellor and proctors exhibited their certificate containing the names of the master, fellows, scholars and ministers in each house. I then called, college after college, every man to swear to the renunciation of the usurped power of the bishop of Rome, and obedience to the king. The bishop of Ely declared the king's liberality towards the maintenance of learning and delivered the new book of the statutes to [John] Cheke to read. When he had done so the bishop of Ely gave it to the vice-chancellor, appointing next day to sit at St John's and then at Trinity College, and dismissed the assembly.

Next day at 9 o'clock the visitors met in the chamber of the master of St John's† and called each member of that house individually to declare what ought to be reformed there, as appointed the day before. This kept them until 5 o'clock when they called certain of the company against whom they had to speak, as [Thomas] Crosley, [Alban] Langdale, [Christopher] Browne and others of their faction, and dismissed them with a lesson, leaving further order until they had perused the whole university. On the third day they sat at Trinity in Dr [John] Redman's chamber, viewing first the foundation, proportion and whole state of the college, which they found much out of order, governed at pleasure for want of statutes. They spent much of the day thus, and for the rest examined the fellows, who are mostly bad. They were so troubled with them that they could not go through a quarter, but had to return next day. On the fourth day they had so many grievous complaints that they could not tell where to begin. Such a nest of them cannot be seen in the realm. [John] Yonge, [Thomas] Vavasor, [? Thomas] Peacock, [Thomas] Parker, [Nicholas] Morton, [William] Rudde, [? Henry] Richardson, [Thomas] Atkinson and a great rabble more occupied them all that day – but I dare say they went away the same men as they came. The next three days were also spent at Trinity to induce them to surrender the grammar school and pay £80 to the law college, which they were loath, and to correct other complaints among themselves.

Today they sat at Gonville Hall, taking only void bills of each man, containing nothing but requests for amendment of their commons and such other petitions. To ease the house Dr [Thomas] Wendy bade them to supper at his house. This is all that is done as yet. Tommorrow they go to Trinity Hall, where it is said they have already disposed themselves to ease the visitors' labour, having made havoc of leases and other things there and at Clare Hall. Of men who should have wisdom and discretion I have not see so childish and unadvised. They openly declare the new ordinances to be too extreme,

---

*        A draft of part of the instructions to Cotton found in no. **224** below.
†        Dr William Bill.

but most of them can no more tell what the same require than I know the way to Rome. Stubborn, idle persons lead and the rest follow for company. This morning, the first disputation being appointed for afternoon (to which the visitors had much ado to bring Richardson, whose turn it was to dispute), there was set up on many posts and doors in the town a bill which would have none to begin after this new order, and to fear the beginner. The author is not yet known. Everybody is loath to do anything, especially the seniors. I will inform you of further doings, praying pardon for remaining so long, but the visitors will not now let me depart.

*Holograph.*                                         SP 10/7, no. 10

**223.**   May 15. Cambridge. William Rogers to Sir Thomas Smith.

Since my last letter the visitors have been to Trinity Hall, where they did not find such spoil as was rumoured. They had made no alienations of late or purloined anything. Only three fraudulent leases were made, to three of the young fellows, [Edward] Cantrell, [William] Bulwer and [Henry] Gibbons; they are not delivered but remain in the president's custody, to be allowed or disallowed by the visitors: determination is deferred. All the fellows are content with the union with Clare Hall and rightly take it to be a great furtherance of their legal studies. Two, [Edward] Buckhnam and Cantrell, desire their pensions at once; the first because he is old and out of exercise, the latter because, being unlearned, he knows he is unable to accomplish what shall be required of him. The state of the house was indifferent not long before because of their making a garden between their college and the former Michaelhouse, walling it and buying the ground of the town, which surely cost them much. They have not more than £70 in money, about 100 marks in plate and adequate utensils in the buttery and kitchen.

Today the visitors have been at Clare Hall where nothing is left but bare walls. I cannot tell you all their doings, as we could not learn them all in one day. At last Stourbridge fair [the fellows], hearing of the dissolution of their house, conspired to sell all their plate, worth £16 or above, and share the money among themselves, which they unashamedly claim to have been their right. A salt with cover worth £13 or £14 was stolen last St Martin's night. Since the visitors' coming to Cambridge their library has been utterly spoiled, leaving only a few old law books and others worth nothing; all the doctors, with many godly books, gone, to the estimated value of £15. The dishes and other trinkets in the house are carried away so fast that unless they are locked up there will be none left in two days. Tomorrow an inventory will be taken of all things, which I will copy and send. The fellows will in no case consent to the giving up of the house. The master* said he desired the king to take his pleasure without his consent. He was so content to depart at the visitors' command, but not to give up the house or his voice there. The rest sing the same song, except [Christopher] Carleill and [Thomas] Baillie who simply consented to the king's pleasure. They have a respite until tomorrow. I guess they will not be brought from their old stubbornness.

*Holograph.*                                         SP 10/7, no. 11

**224.**   May 16. Instructions [from the council] to Thomas Cotton, vice-admiral.

The French king, having many subjects fishing for mackerel and other fish, has lately sent four well armed ships which, lying on the coast of Sussex near the fishermen, on the pretence to waste them, have taken many of the king's subjects, merchants and others. The king has therefore appointed Thomas Cotton vice-admiral of the navy presently to be sent to sea to cleanse the coasts of these and other French and Scots ships. Entering the *Antellope* and taking the *Hart*, the *Salamander*, the *Jenet*, the *Englysshe Galley*, the *Frenche Galley* and our shallop, he shall as quickly as possible pass into the narrow seas and make for the coast of Sussex, using his force to take those French

---

\*     Rowland Swynburne.

men-of-war and fishermen and for the continual annoyance of any other French or Scots ships. Having removed the Frenchmen he shall sail to the Isle of Alderney and patrol the seas between there and Portland, between the Poole roads and Wight and further east or west as occasion requires for the defence of the king's subjects and the hindrance of his enemies. He shall endeavour to take any Frenchmen or Scots. It is said the French king makes great naval preparations at Brest and elsewhere; Cotton must seek as much intelligence of this as he can and notify [the council]. He is to take care not to harm the subjects of the emperor and other friendly powers (from whom there have been complaints of injuries done by the king's captains). Offenders will be punished severely.

Because the soldiers and sailors appointed to serve at sea have lately stolen away, endangering the whole navy and those that remain, Cotton shall keep his men at sea as much as he can, allowing ashore only those appointed to fetch necessaries, the sick, or those licensed to depart for some other reasonable cause.

Receiving here two iron sakers with 200 shot, 40 half sakers, half a last of powder and bow strings appointed for Alderney, Cotton shall deliver them to John Aborough there, indenting with him for their receipt; such other munitions as he receives here for the king's forts of Scilly he shall leave either at Falmouth or Dartmouth, and take order for their speedy sending to the captain of Scilly.* Cotton shall use the advice of the captains sent with him, especially Richard Broke and William Tirrell, and not enterprise anything unless they advise he may be able to conduct it to good purpose.

*Corrected draft.*                                                                       SP 10/7, no. 12

**225.**   May 16. Greenwich. Docket of warrant for Sir John Williams to pay Thomas Matson, captain of 100 men, for their coats at 4s. each – £20; their passage at 1s. each – £5. Delivered to him in prest for arms and other necessaries to be deducted from his wages – £120. For himself – 4s. a day; his ensign bearer – 1s.; his drummer – 1s.; sergeant 1s.; 50 arquebusiers at 8d.; 20 pikes at 6d.; 30 bows and bills at 6d. The month to begin May 16.                                                                       SP 38/1, f. 1

**226.**   May 16. Greenwich. Docket of warrant for the treasurer and barons of the exchequer to send £500 to the treasurer of Calais for the king's service.
*Marginal note* : A warrant for £2,000 sent at the same time to Calais.
*Not in CSPD.*                                                                       SP 38/1, f. 1

**227.**   May 16. Greenwich. Docket of warrant to Sir John Williams to pay Captain Petro Zanzy, Albanois, £73 in prest, to be deducted from his and his band's wages, coming from the sales.                                                                       SP 38/1, f. 3

**228.**   May 17. Greenwich. Docket of warrant for Sir John Williams to pay Otto van Brunswick two crowns each for himself and sixteen other lance knights now sent north – £8.10.0, to be taken of the sales.                                                                       SP 38/1, f. 1

**229.**   May 17. Greenwich. Docket of warrant for Sir John Williams to pay Oliver Dawbney for conveying some of the king's treasure from Bristol to Ireland.
                                                                          SP 38/1, f. 1

**230.**   May 17. Greenwich. Docket of warrant for the barons of the exchequer to pay [*blank*] to be conveyed to the treasurer of wars in the north – £5,000.
                                                                          SP 38/1, f. 1

**231.**   May 17. Greenwich. Docket of warrant for Sir John Williams to repay Secretary

*          Sir William Godolphin.

Smith £3 paid to [Sir William] Herbert's man for riding post to and from the commotion in Somerset.          SP 38/1, f. 1v

**232.** May 18. Greenwich. Docket of warrant for Sir Edmund Peckham to pay Edmund Berwick, man-at-arms, £7 in prest, to be deducted from the next money sent north.
         SP 38/1, f. 1v

**233.** May 18. Greenwich. Docket of warrant for Sir John Williams to pay Sir Thomas Woodlock £60 for bringing here pirates taken in Ireland.      SP 38/1, f. 1v

**234.** May 18. Windsor. William Fitzwilliams, [gentleman of the privy chamber] to William Cecil and [Robert] Kellwaye.

I understand that the matter at variance between Mr Hawtrye and my brother-in-law John Danyell, once heard by the lord great master and the comptroller, is now received again and appointed by the protector to the hearing of you and Mr Kellwaye. This is to tell you the truth in the matter in which I was mostly the worker. First, supposing that the office was in Mr Cofferer's* grant, I sued to him in that on my brother's behalf. He gave me his good will, but shortly afterwards I understood Mr Hawtrye made suit to the protector for the same. I desired him to come and commune with me, which he did. After two or three [hours'] communication we were fully agreed, that I should find means that Mr Cofferer should be his friend and grant him another office, and also that my brother should give him £40 and have the whole interest in the office. Mr Cofferer was content Mr Hawtrye should have the office at Michaelmas following. I brought him and Mr Hawtyre together at St James's where the king was and all parties were agreed as before. Mr Hawtrye gave my brother until midsummer to pay the £40 and my brother gave him a bill for the payment. Mr Hawtrye promised that he would cause the gentleman who was a suitor to him in that behalf to withdraw and said he would thank [the duke and duchess of Somerset], saying he was fully satisfied in what he sued for from Mr Cofferer. There were many more words and tokens between Mr Hawtrye and me which I will gladly come and show.          SP 10/7, no. 13

**235.** May 18. Cambridge. The bishops of Ely and Rochester, John Cheke, William May and Thomas Wendy, visitors of Cambridge University to the duke of Somerset.

We have proceeded from college to college and for the last two days have thoroughly perused Clare Hall, one of the chief points in our commission. We called the master and fellows severally before us and told them the king's pleasure in uniting their college with Trinity Hall to make one college of civil law and that we would provide for all members of the house. They were unanimously content and were ready to depart, but would not surrender as they had sworn to maintain their corporation. Unable to persuade them to consent to the alteration, we set a stay on their affairs so that they cannot alter or dispose of anything. We left them in expectation of further order and went to other colleges, desiring your further order on this point.
    *Printed*: A. Townsend (ed.), *The writings of John Bradford*, (Parker Society, Cambridge, 1848–53), ii, 369–70.          SP 10/7, no. 15

**236.** May 18. Cambridge. The bishops of Ely and Rochester, John Cheke, William May and Thomas Wendy, visitors of Cambridge University to Sir Thomas Smith.

We need not write to you of our doings as Mr Rogers by whom we have written to the protector, can tell everything by word of mouth. Let him return as soon as possible to finish what he has begun.          SP 10/7, no. 14

---

\*      John Ryther, cofferer of the household.

**237.**   May 18. Cambridge. The bishop of Rochester to the duke of Somerset.

In addition to our common letters concerning the visitation, I thought it my duty to write to you privately about the uniting of Clare Hall and Trinity Hall. I think it a sore thing and a dangerous example to take a college founded for the study of God's word and use it for students of man's laws, and to take it without the consent of the present possessioners. The story of Naboth's vineyard, which I have often heard preached at court, makes me tremble when I hear anything like. The purpose of the fundatrix* was godly and her means of accomplishment faultless. I also consider what learned men may be brought up there in the future and those who have been already, some of whom it is hard for the whole university to match. I will mention only [Hugh] Latimer, to whom the king, council and realm are bound for his maintenance of God's word when papists and persecution assaulted the godly, as now, by his preaching. Alexander spared a city for Homer's sake: Latimer excels that poet and so shall the king excel that prince by his mercy. I therefore make my petition not so much for the present students (of whom, if the report of some of them is true, I think no loss) as for the continuing study of God's word according to the fundatrix's intention. If you decide otherwise, give me leave to be absent or abstain from the proceedings. I have written thus boldly according to the command you gave me in your gallery at London to write privately when I thought I had just occasion.

*Holograph.*
Printed: Townsend, *The writings of John Bradford*, ii, 370–2.          SP 10/7, no. 16

**238.**   Copy of the above.                                          SP 10/7, no. 17

**239.**   May 20. Docket of warrant for Sir Edmund Peckham to send £5,000 from the mint to the treasurer in the north, allowing [*blank*] for carriage.          SP 38/1, f. 1v

**240.**   May 20. Docket of warrant for Sir John Williams to pay the bearer £3,000 for the king's service in the north.                                         SP 38/1, f. 1v

**241.**   May 21. Docket of warrant for the treasurer and barons of the exchequer to pay £37.10.0 in reward to Andrew Reignhart, chancellor to Duke Otto of Lüneburg.
*Not in CSPD.*                                                         SP 38/1, f. 1v

**242.**   May 22. Proclamation against enclosure rioters.

The king warned offenders against enclosure statutes to make redress or be punished; some have taken the law into their own hands, destroying pales, hedges and ditches. He now forbids all riots or unlawful assemblies; any knowledge of such is to be given to the justices of the peace. Sheriffs and justices are to use force to prosecute offenders and to spoil and rifle the houses and goods of any who have left them to join assemblies. All officers and other subjects are to assist the sheriffs and justices.

*Signed by*: the duke of Somerset, Lord St John, the earl of Shrewsbury, Sir William Paget and Sir Anthony Wingfield.
Printed: *Tudor Royal Proclamations*, i, 461–2, no. 333 (incorrectly cited), where dated May 23. Cf. Hoak, 326–7 n. 57.                                       SP 10/7, no. 18

**243.**   Draft of the above.                                         SP 10/7, no. 19

**244.**   May 25. Rye. The mayor and jurats of Rye to the duke of Somerset.

Because of the scarcity of timber, devoured by the iron mills, we are compelled, as we desire the defence of the town, to make our platform at the strand, our quays and

*     Lady Elizabeth de Burgh, *suo jure* Lady of Clare.

other waterworks, with lime and stone – for lack of which we are unable to do as the present necessity requires. Since at your being here you granted us the mortar and stone at Camber Castle, which decays daily and is unlikely to be occupied for the king's use, we ask to use it for these purposes.                                      SP 10/7, no. 20

**245.** May 26. Greenwich. Docket of warrant for Sir John Williams to pay Robert Wy £20 for leading 200 Italians, and 4 crowns each to Jasparo Como and nine other Italians sent north – £10, in prest of their month's wages, to be taken of the sales.
                                                                            SP 38/1, f. 3

**246.** May 26. Greenwich. Docket of warrant for Sir John Williams to pay Secretary Smith £8.10.0 paid by him to Henry von Brochnson and sixteen other lance knights at 10s. each, for their expenses northwards, coming of the sales.                  SP 38/1, f. 3

**247.** May 27. Greenwich. Docket of warrant for Sir Edmund Peckham to pay Jacob Schult 1,000 thalers lent to [John] Dymok for the king's use.                  SP 38/1, f. 3

**248.** May 27. Greenwich. Docket of warrant for Sir John Williams to pay [*blank*] in prest of the Irishmen's wages for payment of their hosts – £135, coming of the sales.
                                                                            SP 38/1, f. 3

**249.** May 27. Hemingford Abbots. Simon Kent to the bishop of Lincoln.
Last Monday in the open market at St Ives a lewd youth nailed a dead cat upon a post with a paper on its head, like a rood. Some asked him why he had done it, others had sport, but many like me were offended. On Tuesday I heard [Thomas] Hall talk of it at Hunt[ingdon] but I have since heard that Robert Jaye, dwelling with Candelar of Huntingdon, did it. It were well looked into. I hear little as yet of those of Brampton and St Ives who were before you at Buckden but will certify you if I do.
    *Contemporary copy.*                                                    SP 10/7, no. 21

**250.** May [? 28]. The duke of Somerset to the visitors of Cambridge University.
We have received your letters of the 18th and send you the king's and our own thanks for your good proceedings. Seeing you require our advice if, as we hear, the [master and]* fellows of Clare Hall deserve expulsion, you are to proceed according to the law. [If any suitable men will take places in other colleges you should provide them].† Since they have neither master nor fellow who can make election, the college is dissolved by their own default. After pronouncing sentence, provide for uniting the lands of the college to Trinity Hall according to the laws, as the bishop of Ely and the dean of St Paul's can best inform the rest. You need not provide pensions or livings for those to whom you promise future favour. The bishop of Rochester moves to be taken away. If the master or fellows, not consenting when they have deserved expulsion, are ordered according to their deserts, the rest will be dealt with more gently.
    *Substantially corrected draft.*                                        SP 10/7, no. 22

**251.** May 29. Cambridge. William Rogers to Sir Thomas Smith.
I have sent you by this bearer, Mr Holinshed, six pairs of double gloves. I could have sent as many single gloves but did not like them. I sent two pairs of the finest I could get and will provide more if you wish. Today Dr [John] Redman was before the visitors, bringing an interpretation of three sentences from the Homilies, which he trusted to be their only meaning, although the words might strictly be taken otherwise. He was content

*        Inserted.
†        Deleted.

to subscribe, and did so. In other colleges some have refused to subscribe – hanging, it is thought, only on Dr Redman's judgement. I think the rest will now follow him. The visitors are now wholly occupied for orders to be taken in every house; then they intend to go to Clare Hall. I trust at the beginning of next week to be able to certify you of the forwardness of the law college.

*Holograph.*                                                                 SP 10/7, no. 23

**252.** May 29. Docket of warrant for Sir Edmund Peckham to write to Thomas Chamberlayn, under treasurer of Bristol [mint] to pay Rice Amorgan, Philip Lower and Nicholas Buckingham £60, part of the king's reward of £100 here given them for taking [Richard] Cole the pirate.                                             SP 38/1, f. 3v

**253.** May 29. Docket of warrant for Sir John Williams to deliver £40 of the sales to Rice Amorgan and Nicholas Buckingham as part of the king's reward for taking Cole the pirate.                                                              SP 38/1, f. 3v

**254.** May 30. Docket of warrant for Sir John Williams to repay Secretary Smith £2.10.0 of the sales, paid by him to five lance knights sent north to the king's service, for their expenses in the journey.

*Marginal note*: Three lance knights sent there at the same time, paid in this warrant.
                                                                            SP 38/1, f. 3v

**255.** May. Establishment for the college of civilians to attend on the council, the lord chancellor and the king's other business.

President – £40, with the protonotariship of the chancery attached at the next vacancy – 40 marks [£26.13.4].* Vice-president – £20. 11 fellows, doctors of civil law, at 20 marks [£13.6.8] each – £146.13.4.† The vice-president and fellows to be masters of chancery with 20 nobles [£6.13.4] each – [£80].† Steward – £6.13.4. Cook – £6.13.4.† Under cook – £5.† Butler – £6.13.4.† Total – £231.13.4.† Repairs – [*blank*]. Receiver's and other outward officers' fees – [*blank*].

Establishment for the college of civil law to be erected at Cambridge, called King Edward's College.

Master – £20.[32]‡ 33 fellows at 20 nobles [£6.13.4] each – [£133.6.8]‡ £153.6.8. Scholars [or bible clerks]‡ at 5 marks [£3.6.8] each – [£73]‡ £93. Butler – £3.6.8. Cook – £5. Under cook – £4. Porter and barber – £1.6.8. Launderer – £2. Reader – £4.[6.8].‡ Sublector [£2]‡ £3. Examiner – [£1.6.8]‡ £2. Repairs and extraordinary charges – [£41]‡ £40.9.1½d. Total – [£287.13.4]‡ £331.9.1½d. From: Trinity Hall – £119.2.0; Clare Hall – £132.7.1½d; 20 boys from the new college§ – £80; total – £331.9.1½d. The king's lecture of civil law to be appointed to that college.¶

*Corrected draft.*                                                          SP 10/7, no. 24

**256.** Copy of the above, incorporating the corrections and other differences mentioned in the note to the previous entry; King Edward's College detailed first.
                                                                            SP 10/7, no. 25

**257.** May. Assignment of money for the charges of the king's household.

From the court of augmentations: Michaelmas term – £4,000; Hilary term – £3,000;

---

*       Not included in the stated totals.
†       No. **256** has 8 fellows at 20 marks – £106.13.4; cook – £5; under cook – £3.6.8; butler – £4; total – £185.14.4.
‡       Deleted.
§       Trinity, which was compelled to surrender its grammar school [cf. no. **222** above].
¶       Not in no. **256** below.

midsummer term – £3,000; total – £10,000. From the court of the duchy [of Lancaster]: Easter term – £3,000; Michaelmas term – £3,000; total – £6,000. From the exchequer: Michaelmas term – £3,000; Easter term – £3,000; total – £6,000. From the court of first fruits and tenths: Hilary term – £7,000; Easter term – £3,000; midsummer term – £6,000; total – £16,000. Sum total – £38,000. Payments of these charges: in prest, to be delivered before midsummer to pay the quarter's charges until Michaelmas – £9,000; for the charges from Michaelmas to Christmas: augmentations – £4,000; duchy – £3,000; exchequer – £3,000; total – £10,000; for the quarter ending March 31; first fruits – £7,000; augmentations – £3,000; total – £10,000; for the quarter ending June 30: first fruits – £3,000; exchequer – £3,000; duchy – £3,000; total – £9,000; for the quarter ending September 30: augmentations – £3,000; first fruits – £6,000; total – £9,000.

SP 10/7, no. 26

**258.** June 1. Pembroke Hall, Cambridge. The bishop of Rochester to the duke of Somerset.

Even when you blame me I am sure the truth will not displease you. You blame me because I did not show my mind before the visitation began: but I had no knowledge of the union of the two colleges until we were two days into the visitation. A little before Easter, at Rochester, I received letters from Secretary Smith and the dean of St Paul's to come to the visitation of the university and to preach at the beginning. I sent my servant immediately to London to have some knowledge of the things to be done there. From Mr Dean I had a letter telling me only that the visitation was to abolish popish statutes and set forth God's word and good learning.

When I saw the instructions I thought the master and fellows [of Clare Hall] would surrender, but when their consent could not be obtained after two days' work we began to consult secretly (all thinking it best for every man to say his mind, but one way to be taken of all) when it seemed to some we might unite the colleges by the king's power, without their consent. I simply declared my conscience, inoffensively. You suggested that I dishonoured the king and would dissuade others from executing his commission, which is untrue. I was specially moved because you had told me in private letters to open my mind freely to you.

If I did amiss in being ready to grant the execution of the commission before I knew the instructions, I submit to your correction. Your wish that flesh, blood and country might not weigh more with some men than godliness and reason is godly. But in this matter country will not move me: for I am ready to expel those of my country as others. Flesh and blood is a fear of mortal men. I fear my own frailty to confess the truth.

There is no man (save the king) whose favour I seek or displeasure I fear more than yours. I am in most danger to offend you in this. But I pray I act not for favour or fear of men. I therefore ask you not to be offended with the renewal of my suit, that if anything happens in this visitation to which my conscience will not agree I may have your licence to be absent or silent.

*Holograph.*

*Printed*: Burnet, v, 347–50. H. Christmas (ed.), *The works of Nicholas Ridley*, (Parker Society, Cambridge, 1841), 372–30.          SP 10/7, no. 27

**259.** June 2. Docket of warrant for Sir John Williams to repay Secretary Smith £5, paid by the council's order to one used in the king's special affairs.          SP 38/1, f. 5

**260.** June 2. Docket of warrant for Sir John Williams to pay Carlo Dado, Italian, sent north to serve the king, £15 in prest, to be deducted of his wages, of the sales.

SP 38/1, f. 5

**261.** June 2. Docket of warrant for Sir John Williams to pay Vincent Bellachy, two gentlemen and four servants in his company, £20 in prest, to be deducted by the treasurer of the garrisons in the north.                                                                                    SP 38/1, f. 5

**262.** June 3. Docket of warrant for the barons and chamberlains of the exchequer to pay [*blank*] or the bearer £10,000 to be sent to the treasurer in the north, to be of the relief.                                                                                                              SP 38/1, f. 5

**263.** June 3. Docket of warrant for Sir John Williams to pay the bearer £10,000 to be sent to the treasurer of Boulogne, to be taken of the sales.
     *Not in CSPD.*                                                                                              SP 38/1, f. 5

**264.** June 3. Docket of warrant for Sir Edmund Peckham to pay [*blank*] or the bearer £3,000 to be sent to the treasurer in the north, to be taken from the revenues of the mint.                                                                                                            SP 38/1, f. 5

**265.** June 4. Greenwich. The duke of Somerset to Cardinal Pole.
     Having received your letters of May 6 we hoped at last that, seeing Rome's abuses, [its deceit and abominations],* you now had respect to your native country and king and Christ's word here, and had sent your messengers and used the king's pardon to come home. But on reading your instructions we realised there was nothing new to come from Rome. Save that we still supposed you to be sincere, we regretted ever hearing your ministers or reading your letters, which mistake things here. You write as if you were a foreign prince, seeking to meet the king or his commissioners on foreign soil. It is so long since we forsook the usurped power of the bishop of Rome that these things seem very strange.
     You fear because the king is a child. But, with the help of God and faithful councillors and subjects, he has defended his own as none of any age has done before. Josias and Solomon at his best were not old. You mistake Henry VI's reign, whose childhood was more victorious than his manhood. King Edward [IV]'s children would have been no example if their uncle had not been so greedy for the crown. Old kings suffer seditions and murders – Harold [II], Edward II, Richard II, Henry VI – and chronicles would show more old than young ones deposed and murdered. But we trust God will keep our king in childhood and age. Our own private sorrow might have happened at any time; we impute it to the devil and our brother's lack of grace, not to the king's youth. Your discourse on neighbouring rulers is as derogatory to them as the rest is to the king. You appear to have little regard for the emperor's honour if you think that, after so many treaties, he would invade this country; and if he did, would not God overthrow him ? The quarrel of the dowager's divorce is long past. Experience shows nothing lost to us by the open enmity or doubtful friendship of France and Scotland; we are accustomed to fight both and win. Your last fear, of giving a colour to princes by the schism (as you call it) from Rome has been the greatest cause of disobedience among subjects and dissension between princes. We hope all princes will realise their authority and detest Rome's usurped power.
     Your greatest fear, of dissension among our bishops on the main points of religion, is unknown to us. Common agreement has been freely reached by the most learned men, followed by open debate in parliament, concluded with consent of both houses. A form of service has been established by statute and received gladly and quietly. If a bishop or another is dissatisfied in a school point or two that does not derogate the quiet of the country. If any are disobedient they will be apprehended before they make a disturbance. Since you exaggerate public dangers the conference you speak of is unnecessary, and

---

\*         Three lines of invective deleted.

undesirable that the king should go abroad to treat with his subjects. No men can be truly indifferent in religion, or about the pope's temporal power, to which you have sworn. We would rather die than see the king lose any of his authority.

You mention personal dangers and question the king's title to the crown; it is not surprising that the late king hated Rome, as all princes should. We would welcome a universal conference of wise men who followed the gospel, not the bishop of Rome's decrees. Friendship between nations should not be hindered by difference in ceremonies, since we all believe in one God and Christ. Some popes, emperors and kings have been friendly to the Turks.

We would be content to mediate for your return from exile and are sure that if you spoke with the learned men here you would be satisfied. [We are not so set that we would not make any reform you showed to be according to God's word].* *Postscript*. We have given your messengers the Book of Common Prayer and would gladly receive your judgement on it.

*10¹/₂ pp.*
*Draft.*
*Initialled* : E.S.
*Printed* : Pocock, *Troubles*, pp. vi–xiv.                                   SP 10/7, no. 28

**266.** June 5. Docket of warrant for [Sir John] Williams to pay Matthew de Mantua, returning home, £40 of the sales, for services to the king and his father.
                                                                SP 38/1, f. 5v

**267.** June 6. Docket of warrant for [Sir John] Williams to pay Edward Walshe, leader of 200 kern, £39.5.0 of the sales, for their pay to June 25 and to him for leading them, in addition to the sum lately paid him in prest.                    SP 38/1, f. 5v

**268.** June 6. Docket of warrant for [Sir John] Williams to repay Secretary Smith £8 for £5.10.0 paid to Joachim Camerhurst and eleven others and £1.10.0 to three others for their expenses northwards.                                           SP 38/1, f. 5v

**269.** June 7. Docket of warrant for [John] Beaumont, general receiver of wards and liveries, to pay Captain Cunstable £10 for his charges coming from and returning to Scotland.
     *Not in CSPD.*                                                SP 38/1, f. 5v

**270.** June 7. Docket of warrant for [Sir John] Williams to repay Secretary Smith or the bearer £5 of the sales, paid to five German gentlemen commended by Mr Delye for their expenses to the king's service in the north.                         SP 38/1, f. 5v

**271.** June 9. Cambridge. William Rogers to Sir Thomas Smith.
     I have deferred writing in daily hope of something worth writing of. The bishop of Rochester is very loath to proceed against Clare Hall and delays as much as he can. For the last five days [the visitors] have been about to displace the master and fellows but nothing is done except that they have at last agreed, after the holidays and the bishop of Ely's return (he is at Downham for six days) to thrust them all out of the house. The master is very stout, and crakes abroad. He told the visitors they cannot expel them for the sale of the plate, which is the chief thing laid against him, expressly against the statutes – for the greatest penalty is to restore it, which he says he can do. He said he had the advice of the best lawyer in England. This stayed them somewhat, but they are fully resolved not to stick. If you advise the bishop of Ely you will cause them to go

*     Deleted.

through more boldly and speedily. The dean [of St Paul's] is appointed these holidays to prepare orders for each house, in which he is very diligent. [John] Cheke had the bedels' matter to finish. The bishop of Rochester goes to preach at Soham. I trust all will be ended within a week of their meeting again. The bill ratifying the Common Prayer and Homilies is signed by all; after Dr [John] Redman did, no man sticked. Last Thursday, according to the statutes, there was a law disputation, all of which the visitors heard. The conclusions were that a prince may order what none of his predecessors did; that statutes cannot be prorogued without the contempt and pain in them, and that a new statute removes old ones.* Dr [Humphrey] Busby answered, not very doctor-like. Dr [Henry] Harvie, principal of St Nicholas's Hostel and Mr [James] Haddon replied.

*Holograph or contemporary copy.*                                                  SP 10/7, no. 29

**272.**    June 10. Richmond. The duke of Somerset to the bishop of Rochester.

In your letter of June 1, replying to our last, you still ask to absent yourself rather than act against your conscience. We would not wish you to, and you discredit the visitors by supposing they would. The archbishop of Canterbury told us you are troubled by the diminishing of divines. But the union of the two colleges was meant in the late king's time as we are sure you heard and as Sir Edward North can tell; all the law students in the new cathedrals were disappointed of their livings reserved to that civil college. The King's Hall, all canon lawyers, was joined to Michaelhouse and made a college of divines,† increasing their number and diminishing that of civilians. If in all other colleges with lawyers by statute or the king's injunctions you changed them to divines you would have more than before – King's would have six, Jesus four, Queens' and the others one or two each. These are more than the fellows of Clare, and if they are now made divines the number of divinity students will be increased. You know how important the civil law is in foreign treaties and how few now serve the king therein. We wish the increase of divines as well as you; we must maintain that science also. You hinder the visitation and make the master and fellows of Clare more obstinate. Look to the king's honour and the quiet performance of the visitation. We can be content you will act as you think best for quieting your conscience.

*Draft, unsigned.*

*Printed*: Burnet, v, 351–2. H. Christmas (ed.), *The works of Nicholas Ridley*, (Parker Society, Cambridge, 1841), 505–6.                                                  SP 10/7, no. 30

**273.**    June 11. Syon. The duke of Somerset to the marquess of Dorset and the earl of Huntingdon.

In most parts lewd men have attempted to assemble and, seeking redress of enclosures, have in some places, by seditious priests and other evil people, sought restitution of the old bloody laws, and some fall to spoil. Have the enclosure proclamation published by the sheriff,‡ to withstand evil rumours. Be ready with the Leicestershire gentlemen to repress any attempts in the beginning. Lest the people believe by rumours that you would overrun them before they commit evil, keep to your houses; you will thereby be less charged.

*Endorsed*: Haste, for life *(three times)*.

*Printed*: Pocock, *Troubles*, 1–2.                                                  SP 10/7, no. 31

**274.**    June 11. Kew. Dr William Turner to William Cecil.

Thank you for obtaining my licence which, if I had sealed, I would shortly occupy in Yorkshire, for the archbishop of York has written to me to come to him with all speed,

---

*          The heads given in Latin.
†          Trinity College.
‡          Sir Ambrose Cave, sheriff of Leicestershire.

which I would gladly do if I had [the protector's] consent – who (I heard you say) intended me to be occupied at Winchester. I would so gladly if I might have a living for myself and mine, but since another should have the deanery I would only have hope of a prebend. My love to my wife and children will not allow me; my children have been fed so long with hope that they are very lean; I would have them fatter. Discover [the protector's] pleasure: I cannot dwell here all winter. I hear you have some houses to let in London. If they are not all promised let Mistress Auder, my mother-in-law (whom I think you know) have one for as much as you would take of another; she intends to dwell by her children.

*Holograph.*

*Printed*: Pocock, *Troubles*, 3–4.                                      SP 10/7, no. 32

**275.**   June 14. Docket of warrant for the treasurer and chamberlains of the exchequer to pay the bearer £500 to be sent to the treasurer of Calais, to be taken of the relief.

*Not in CSPD.*                                                            SP 38/1, f. 7

**276.**   June 15. Cambridge. The bishop of Ely, John Cheke, William May and Thomas Wendy to Sir Thomas Smith.

We are very sorry that the bishop of Rochester has been called away by [the protector's] letters and to be deprived of his service now that we are ready to finish certain things. We have hitherto worked together, lest the absence of one – much less the bishop, who is one of the chief – might occasion forward people to say he did not consent to what the others did. Have [the protector] allow him remain for six or seven days until the visitation is finished.                                         SP 10/7, no. 34

**277.**   June 15. Cambridge. William Rogers to Sir Thomas Smith.

After sealing their letters the visitors bade me write that the bishop of Rochester is very willing to join in depriving and expelling the master and fellows of Clare Hall but they are uncertain if he will go further. They say that if this may be done while he is here the rest will be easier for them to do after his departure. He must be told of the protector's pleasure by Monday night or he will be gone, for he dare not tarry without licence.

*Holograph or contemporary copy.*                                        SP 10/7, no. 33

**278.**   June 17. Richmond. Docket of warrant for [*blank*] to repay Secretary Smith £6 for £5 paid to Cecase Dattylo, Italian, sent north with four servants, for conduct money, and £1 paid to the keeper of Colchester gaol for his coming to and returning from court with a prisoner for examination.                                        SP 38/1, f. 7

**279.**   June 18. Docket of warrant for [*blank*] to pay Captain [Paolo Baptista] Spinola and his four servants, serving in the north, £5 in prest for wages.        SP 38/1, f. 7

**280.**   June 18. The earl of Warwick to William Cecil.

I enclose a bill sent to the lord great master concerning mares and colts by the person who sowed oats in one of the parks, in fairest pasture which would have borne much hay. He did this although all the neighbours marvelled. He had thirty or forty head of his own cattle in one of the same parks when my officers came there. The foregoing of his yearly profit is the only cause that he stirs so much. Had it not been for my lord's pleasure I would have not let them plough up the fairest ground in the park and use it to their own advantage, however they are placed. This Christopher is the worst of all, having made good gain of his office, not much for the king's advantage. *Postscript.* Mr Skynner and others of the stable, of the late master of the horse's preferment, boast everywhere that they will keep these parks from me and that I shall have other recompense.

*Holograph.*

*Slightly mutilated.* SP 10/7, no. 35

**281.** June 19. London. Oliver Leder to William Cecil.

I have lately received letters from the protector to redress a matter between Edmund Hatley and me. So that the protector may be better informed whether my tenant or I default I send my answer to Hatley's surmise and will give him the whole farm if it is not proved true. The protector's letters restrain me from felling or carrying anything, to my great loss; but I will obey him if I should lose £100. I send my messenger as this journey has wearied me. Release me from this injunction if you can.

*Holograph.* SP 10/7, no. 36

**282.** June 20. Richmond. The king to sheriff, justices of the peace and other gentlemen of Devon.

Some in Devon have rebelled against the proceedings of the last session of parliament at Westminster concerning the Book of Common Prayer, but rather from ignorance than malice. By the advice of our protector and council we pardon all offenders on condition that they return to obedience.

*Draft.*

*Printed*: Pocock, *Troubles*, 4–6. SP 10/7, no. 37

**283.** June 22. Richmond. Sir Thomas Smith to the duke of Somerset.

Immediately after leaving you I wrote to [Sir Edmund] Peckham about all you wished to know of the mint and received the enclosed reply [*which follows*] which shows that the mints have coined and received to be coined this month more than £45,000. Although they may achieve this this month they can do no more until they agree to receive smaller sums – £40, £100, more or less; in this way I reckon they might coin £4,000 or £5,000. This is the chief and last consignment of testons. They coin no gold, which makes short riddance of a great sum. I cannot see that they can keep promise for more this week, by when the month will be ended. If there is urgent need of granting more warrants the other treasurers may help, for there are no more testons brought them. Necessity will empty York and Canterbury mints as well as Bristol unless you have them coin pence, halfpence and twopences from the remainder of the testons, to ease the poor. Bullion is so scarce that I fear the revenue of the mint cannot continue as before unless the consignment I told you of takes place shortly. 4,000 lb. a month is a great quantity of fine silver – a goodly revenue if it may be furnished. But since that is so uncertain, because of the emperor's restraints, and now this half year they have not given £5,000 a month to the king but £3,000 or £4,000 because of testons, of which the chief gain was taken before, I see no great trust of quantity thence, which may yet be helped if some of the mints were called to a reckoning.

Much of the relief is paid, almost all by the laity. You should be certified by next Sunday by Sir John Baker how much is paid, what he has remaining, and how much is unpaid. The subsidy of the clergy is not payable before October, the relief of the sheep not till November – so winter will come before any help from them. Cloth comes at the year's end, which I take to be midsummer next but one. I can see no remedy unless you take some help from the sales, particularly for July, August and September, or make some anticipation or loan, or else determine to prepare bullion by all means and reject all old debts and all other payments which may be spared until winter, when hopefully you will be better able to deal with them. The clergy would not much stick to anticipate payment of their subsidy, which may be done by earnest letters to the bishops – so you might have it by mid August, at least so much as by favour may be obtained, enough to help in August and September. July may be pieced out with the sales, the rest of the relief, and somewhat of the mints.

I have sent your letters of export of corn and victuals to the lord great master, whom I reminded of his promise to redress everything if you committed the matter to him with [Sir Anthony] Aucher. Now he has better matter to work on, and none can learn if the customers allow any export more than his ministers and Mr Aucher's, who are the most offended. I have sent you the commissions for the lord privy seal, according to your instructions, for Cornwall and Devon, with a space for two others if you will have them. The form is very good, and to be used in all such hereafter. I enclose a letter from Mr Comptroller to me, written at Calais but not delivered till now for his man went with him to Bruges: he wishes you to see it. Let me go to Eton for four or five days to rest and to be rid of this ague.

    *Holograph.*

    *Printed*: Hoak, 186 (extract only).                  SP 10/7, no. 38

**284.** June 22 [enclosed with the above]. London. Sir Edmund Peckham, [high treasurer of the mints] to Sir Thomas Smith.

I enclose a certificate [*which follows*] of money paid out of the mints since June 1, of testons received for exchange into current money for the king's affairs, and of payments which must be made before the beginning of next month. You will see that all the officers of the mints have their hands full. Although they had much bullion they now have only what they have melted. I only have a small quantity. I have spoken with the merchants with whom I bargained, who promised me some bullion; they said they had some shipped a long time and more provided, not yet shipped, and know nothing of either, fearing it is not well. If we lack bullion we will have to make groats, which will be averted as long as it may. 4,000 lb. of silver is little enough for one month, which I fear will be very hard to get hereafter. You wrote that the lord great master has warrants for payments from the mints for provision of victuals: it will be hard to do so, whatever the sums. I will pay him £2,000 on receipt of his bullion, as promised, if I have to borrow most of it. [Sir John] York has paid two foreigners of the Steelyard £2,090.8.4 by warrant for the exchange of 8,650 thalers delivered in Flanders to John Dymok at 4s. 10d. the thaler, for repayment of which Lord Southampton prays you obtain a warrant to the exchequer or the court of augmentations, for the mint is unable to bear it. The money to be paid to the treasurer of Boulogne and to be sent north, which is in these mints, will be ready next Tuesday or Wednesday, but I doubt if that at Canterbury and York will be ready for a week as they coin groats for lack of bullion. I have been ill since coming to town, so have not been so often at the mints but I trust the worst is now past.

    *Holograph.*                          SP 10/7, no. 38(i)

**285.** June 22 [enclosed with the above]. Certificate of money paid from the mints on warrants from June 1 to June 22.

To Paulus Finus and Bartholomew Sulsoo, foreign merchants, in exchange for 8,600 thalers delivered by them in Flanders to John Dymocke for the king's affairs there, at 4s. 10d. each – £2,090.8.4.

Testons received into the mints at London to be changed into current money in the same period. Of Anthony Senhowse and Robert Cranwell, to be sent after coining to the treasurers of Boulogne and the north – £10,000; of Benjamin Gonson, for marine causes – £1,500; of Spencer and Baynerd for provision of butter, cheese, &c. – £2,000; of [Richard Worsley], captain of the Isle of Wight, by command of Lord Southampton – £1,260; of Patrick Shurlocke and John Welshe, for the despatch of certain Irishmen –

£558; of Captain Gambolde – £300; of George Maxey, for provision of victuals – £180; of Henry Nedham, to be taken by him after coining to the treasurer of Calais – £500; of Sir Anthony Aucher, for provision of victuals – £2,000, of which £1,000 paid to him; of Mr Cofferer, for expenses of the king's household – £13,000, of which £1,000 paid to him; of Sir Richard Leighe, for various affairs of the king – £850, of which nothing paid to him; of Laurence Bradsha[w], surveyor of the king's works – £1,1000, of which nothing as yet exchanged; total – £20,288.*

Testons received into the mints, not yet exchanged or paid for – £15,150.

Other payments made and to be made before the end of this month. To be paid out of the office and sent north – £3,000; received for payments to Boulogne and to the merchant – £3,460; owing to the merchants, which must be paid – £2,800; to be paid to the lord great master on his warrant for provision of victuals – £2,000; total – £11,260.

*Signed by*: Sir Edmund Peckham.                                                                    SP 10/7, no. 38(ii)

**286.**   June 22. London. Sir Edmund Peckham to [Sir Thomas Smith].

Immediately after finishing my other letters, which I enclose, at about 9 o'clock as I was preparing for bed, not being well, the post brought me your letters, enclosing yours to the lord great master; finding you had answered him very fully I sealed them and delivered them to the post to be taken to him. As you wrote, when he delivered his bullion he demanded no payment but for it and £2,000 monthly for provision of victuals. For his bullion he had £3,000 before Whitsuntide, so that £400 remains, for which shift will be made to pay it. He will also have his £2,000 for his warrant for victuals by the last day of this month, as I wrote in my other letter; but it will be hard for me to do so unless you write to [John] Bowes of Durham Place to pay me the £1,000 he promised you from the profits of his office, of which he has only paid £600 since its erection, so he may well spare £1,000 more.

You write that [the protector] wishes to know what plate of the king's is melted and how much coined. I am unable to tell, but have called on the avouchers to be so certified more than ten times this month; there are so many that it is hard to get them together, but I will continue to call until I am told. As far as I can learn the silver hitherto melted is barely £4,000 of which I have not received above £2,000 which I used to purchase bullion, having little other money for that purpose save what shall always be had again on three days' warning. The rest remains with [Stephen] Vaughan.† It is not yet all reduced to current money, but he will do it out of hand, which shall be ready to be had at all times. The gold of the same plate, which it is thought will come to £2,400 or £2,500, is melted but not touched for coinage, remaining with the avouchers. I have written before what store of bullion I have and what testons the treasurers have to be exchanged for the king's use. I would gladly attend on you at court but have been ill all week with fever and the stone and dare not go out till I recover.

*Holograph.*

*Printed*: H. Symonds, 'Edward VI and Durham House', *Numismatic Chronicle*, 4th ser., xiv, (1914), 146 (extract only).                                                                    SP 10/7, no. 39

**287.**   [June 24]. Instructions [from the council] to Lord Russell, lord privy seal.

The king, by the advice of us the lord protector and council, has appointed Lord Russell to reside for a time in the west for the good governance of Devon, Cornwall, Somerset and Dorset and their defence against any foreign invasions. He shall first summon the justices of the peace and such other great and honest men as he thinks convenient, by whom and by as many other ways as he can he shall inform himself of the state of the shires. Finding them good he shall take further order for the continuance

---

*          Error for £20,388.8.4.
†          Under treasurer of Tower II mint.

thereof. If the people are disobedient he shall inform himself of the causes of their unquietness and work to remedy them and bring them to conformity by gentle persuasions. If they are not reduced by knowledge of their duties he shall by force of the king's commission assemble such men as may repress the obstinate and wilful and bring them to knowledge of their duties as an example to others. In case of any invasion by enemies he shall repulse them and defend the country to the uttermost. He shall order, if not already done, the setting up and watching of beacons in all customary places, especially by the coasts, according to previous orders. To avoid trouble at home he shall give special charge to masters and fathers continually to regard the good governance of their children and servants and for seeing that clothiers, dyers, weavers, fullers and other artificers are kept occupied, and all occasions of unlawful assemblies are avoided. [Any who attempt breach of the laws or use any disorder are to be punished to the example of others].* He shall have special respect to see the king's proceedings in religion well obeyed according to the late order. Because we know that seditious persons have often spread lewd and false rumours, Lord Russell (who will be immediately told by us of all occurrences of importance) shall search out their authors and spreaders, causing them to be apprehended, committed to ward and punished.

*Corrected draft.*

*Printed*: Pocock, *Troubles*, 8–10. SP 10/7, no. 40

**288.** [June 24]. Lord Russell to the duke of Somerset.

Sherborne does not stand on any strait which may with any mean force stay the passage of the rebels eastward; they can only be stopped in that county by an army able to meet them in the face. The river [Frome] through Dorchester is twenty miles from that [the Parrett] through Bridgwater. Men may ride over the river by Dorchester in almost all places. The country from Langport to Bridgwater and down to the sea, almost eight miles, is very strong but is not for horsemen to serve in. Between these two rivers they may pass in all places. Sherborne stands between them, slightly to the east; an army may pass between it and Bruton, through Somerset, or by Dorset between it and the south coast, without any strait to impede them other than the low country of Blackmoor, which extends not above two miles from the town. But the town is a convenient place for a force to lie, for the indifferent stay of Somerset, Wiltshire and Dorset while the rebels do not pass the bounds of Devon. If we are driven to retire, we are as yet uncertain by what quarter we shall best use the same until their intentions appear, but we will omit nothing that may impede them.

*Endorsed*: Answer to instructions for the situation of the country.

*Headed*: Answer to the instructions sent by Mr Dudley and Mr Travers.

*Printed*: Pocock, *Troubles*, 11–12. SP 10/7, no. 41

**289.** June 26. Syon. The council to Sir Thomas Denys, Peter Courteney and Antony Harvy, justices of the peace in Devon.

We understand by your letters of June 24 that those lewd persons of whom you wrote before, once quieted by you, are again assembled in far greater numbers by the persuasion of seditious persons. For remedy, although you may partly understand our mind by our former letters, but considering that such disorders are more easily helped at the beginning and may grow to further inconvenience if the declaration of such matter as we signified you before shall not satisfy them, we require you either openly with all or with the ringleaders to induce them to retire to their houses, especially reminding the chief doers of the unnaturalness of rebellion, the unkindness the king may hereafter conceive of these things attempted in his minority, the dishonour and unsurety of the realm, and the courage that will be given to the French, Scots and other enemies. Remind them that

* Deleted.

obedient subjects first sue for remedy at the king's hands, and do not take upon themselves the sword and authority to redress as they choose; matters established by law cannot be altered except by the law again. If you are unable to satisfy them, yet you shall by these means somewhat mitigate their furore. Use what means you can to stay the coming of greater numbers to them. In the meantime put yourselves with such of your tenants and servants as you trust best secretly ordered to attend such further direction as the lord privy seal, now travelling to you, shall give for execution of the statute. Of sheep and cloth we wrote more amply before.

    *Draft.*

    *Printed*: Pocock, *Troubles*, 12–13.                           SP 10/7, no. 42

**290.**   June 27. Pinchbeck. Richard Ogle to William Cecil.

    I have sent you as near as I can terms of the demesnes of Spalding. I trust you will go forward for you will have few such bargains. Had I been able to ride I would have waited on you to declare my mind. As I wrote, John Wyseman the auditor can tell you of Crowland; if he is absent his son-in-law [Thomas] Everard, also an auditor, knows the truth. Holland, because of the drains that come from Peterborough by Thorney and so to Wisbech by Southeau, a division between Lincolnshire and Cambridgeshire and by a great river called the New River ('New Lene') and others, upon which since the suppression of Thorney no cost was bestowed nor known whether the king or the farmers ought to do it, is likely to be surrounded. If the king and all his tenants in Holland did all they could to cleanse, reed, dyke, scour and bank Southeau, if nothing were done in Cambridgeshire it would be no help. Find a discreet person of the court of augmentations to come down with speed to see both shires and report the danger to the lord protector. The commissioners of sewers in Lincolnshire cannot ease without help of those of Cambridgeshire. The water was not so high at Christmas as now. Write to all the king's bailiffs to see the banks maintained and to be as diligent now as they were in the prior's days, to whom they would crouch and kneel, come and ride. Now none will set his foot further than to receive his rents and attends to his office little or nothing. There are bailiffs in Holland whom I scantly know as officers, for but once a year some of them come to the great Michaelmas court at Spalding and elsewhere. They have great fees and do little. A sharp letter from you will quicken them. I sued for a commission of sewers that is granted, and none will pay for it. I will see it paid if Mr Attorney* will have it delivered.

    *Holograph.*                                           SP 10/7, no. 43

**291.**   [June 27. Enclosed with the above]. Particulars of the lands and demesnes of Spalding.

    The park pasture, 48 acres, let for £12 a year, worth 3s. an acre if converted to tillage – £12. Amber fields, 16 acres – £2 [£7.6.8].† 'Bellesmore', like fen, £2 in the king's book but let for £1.6.8. The farmer bears all charges. Some wood growing. Wheatcroft pasture, 66 acres, let for £6.13.4 [£3.10.0].† 'Saresland' pasture, 57 acres, let for £5 [£3.6.8].† Barrett's close, 40 acres, worth £5 [£2].† 'Shallowe' court, 140 acres, worth £12 [£8].† Sum – £44.

    How much ground Holbeach marsh with one field contains is much to estimate, but with other small onlets is worth £4 or £5. 1,500 sheep are kept there now, which will not be pastured on marsh under £3 the 100, but it is let. For Spalding tithes you must account of one who occupied the profits for Mr Coppes for a short time and will not let men take them. If Pinchbeck tithes are paid by law they are worth as much as Gamble paid and half as much more. He pays tithes only for Crowland marsh, a great profit: for

\*      Richard Goodrich, attorney of the court of augmentations.

†      Inserted.

that he should pay but certain, so did the late abbot and now the parson of Holbeach, and he is in suit for tithes in the spiritual law. As I wrote, Whytwell and the abbot made a lease for the marsh, to be void if the house stood, and if it were suppressed the abbot should have a profit of it. A similar lease was made of Langtoft hall, which Mr Penne had. The covenant being disclosed by me and others, as our duties were, to the king, the abbot, being examined by John Wyseman, auditor, confessed and the leases were made void. Then Dennis Coppes had the lease of that marsh and Mr Penne Langtoft, by exchange agreed between them.

I have certified as much as I can learn, but cannot tell most of the actual value or men but he who occupies it. I know that six years ago the tenant there was not worth £20, but I dare say he is now worth 1,000 marks [£666.13.4]. It appears the farm is good, as I always wrote. Let it not pass you; take the whole, as Dennis Coppes had. One mark is lost by Bellzmore, a small loss considering other gains.

*Richard Ogle's hand.* SP 10/7, no. 43(i)

**292.** June 29. Guildford. Henry [Fitz Alan], earl of Arundel to Sir William Petre.

These parts remain as well as may be in a quavering quiet. The honest promise to serve the king; the rest, I trust, will follow if the devices shall be shortly used. I hear Sir William Goring is out for the commission of oyer and terminer. He is not famous for just administration of justice. I heard this since our departure from [the duke of Somerset]: reveal it to him alone – it were better opened by you my friend than by my own letters.

*Printed*: Pocock, *Troubles*, 14. SP 10/7, no. 44

**293.** June 30. Gray's Inn. William Dalyson to William Cecil.

My thanks for accepting me at my late being at court. Move the protector for the wardship of William, son and heir of my brother George, already granted by the lord great master to [Nicholas] Bacon, attorney of the wards, at my request. My suit is nothing without your help. SP 10/7, no. 45

**294.** [? June]. Petition of the inhabitants of Staines, Middlesex to the council.

They have received command from the lord protector to pull down Staines bridge to safeguard the realm from enemies, which will be the utter undoing of the town and its surroundings. The bridge still stands; the town has promised to send a scout to spy any army coming that way, and prays for further order.

*Printed*: Pocock, *Troubles*, 19–20. SP 10/7, no. 46

**295.** [?]. Eucharistic opinions of Martin Bucer.

1. We should speak plainly of the eucharist, as of all Christ's mysteries, that God's children clearly understand Christ's mind and others find least occasion to obscure His truth. 2–6. This we cannot better achieve than by correctly explaining the words of the Holy Spirit who, by the mouths of Christ and the apostles and by scripture, has given us the mystery of the eucharist, as of other sacraments, by words and form of giving and receiving, showing bread and wine to be symbols of Our Lord's body and blood, confirmation of the new testament and remission of sins, as Christ told His disciples. 7. He defines the right use of this sacrament as that by which we are made one body – that of which Christ is the head, into which we are baptised. 8. In the true eucharist is given that communion with the Father, Son and saints of which the Lord prayed, by which Christ is in us as the Father in Him and we in Them. 9. That communion is the heavenly regeneration of a new creature, of great and divine mystery, which cannot be known except by faith and its effects – judgement, will and new, godlike actions. 10. All worldly feeling must be set apart. 11. The Holy Spirit not only showed that we are endued with Christ's spirit and merit but that we live by His intercession and work; He

dwells in us and is received in communion: these things we must affirm. 12–13. These are metaphors by which we explain regeneration, which man cannot and should not express in natural language. 14. We must not obscure the Lord's command or Christ's sacraments with superstitions or circumlocution. 15, 16. The Word was made flesh that God and man might be of one substance; the incarnation can only be accepted by faith. 17. Christ is God and man, chief of the saints, firstborn of the sons of God; we must not separate the unity of the substance. 18. The scripture is consistent in speaking of Christ among and in us, showing He has left the world and has one body, limited, in heaven. 19–21. Christ's presence with us, by word or sacraments, is spiritual, not sensual or worldly as antichrists make the simple believe, that the accidence should be worshipped. 22. Let the teachable be taught that Christ is present in the supper only in its rightful use and only to be known by faith. Let the rest be left as blind leaders of the blind; those who are not born of God do not hear His word. 23. We must turn from their falsehoods by truly expounding God's word. 24, 25. Good men, imagining some local presence, must be taught that these mysteries cannot be known by reason, only by faith. 26. I dare not reason about the heavens; scripture describes them by God's majesty, not physically. 27. I do not see what more the fathers can tell of the place of Christ's body in heaven than that we should respect His two natures – the divine everywhere, the human limited; this agrees with scripture, although we do not place His body in the heavens of *Physics*, 6.* 28. In such great mysteries my conscience allows the use of sayings, indeed on the authority of the fathers, not taught in scripture. We deplore how Satan and antichrist have led us. 29. Therefore I will respect the sayings of the fathers concerning the changing of signs; but their sayings are too far from God's words. 30. If the fathers write anything of the place of Christ in heaven I will not irreverently reject it, nor contend with anyone of it; I only wish no dogma should be made of it and that I should be left in the simplicity of God's word. 31, 32. Although a man of faith interprets the presence as local, I cannot see how the language of the Holy Spirit should be amended because of our foolishness. 33. Christ said He would be wherever two or three gathered in His name, as we do at the rightful eucharist. Wherever we are in the world Christ is in our hearts although He is not in the world. How can the head be apart from the body ? I therefore define the presence of Christ, however perceived by us, by sacrament or the gospel, to be the apprehension and fruition of Him, living in us. This we can only perceive by faith. 34. His presence, known by faith, is more certain than presence known by sight or sound. 35. Christ and St Paul spoke of His presence in the world, and the fathers teach His presence in baptism and the eucharist, calling it carnal, as opposed to the presence we have by faith. 36. Faith embraces Christ, God and man, holds Him present, and according to His divinity, is not only with His saints, but everywhere. But some are not content unless we say we have His body and blood carnally and substantially present. 37. Ambiguity is always avoided by the wise and much more should be in Christ's mysteries; we should repudiate unscriptural language unless it usefully explains Christ's truth. 38. If we deny Christ is received really and substantially we should seem to declare He is received by fiction and accident. I would rather avoid all such terms. 39. But if they must be used I would have real and substantial presence understood as reception truly by faith; I deny any worldly presence since the Lord has left the world. 40. I will never admit the terms 'carnally' and 'naturally' because they imply sensual reception. 41. We should therefore say, in accord with the Lord, the apostle [Paul] and the early church, that Christ is given by word and sign, received by faith, that we may the more live in Him and He in us. 42. Christ must be received until nothing of ourself remains. The sharing of Christ in baptism is strengthened by the eucharist, as by the gospel. 43. I trust hereby my eucharistic belief may be seen to accord with scripture and the teaching of the early church. 44. Christ is the principal minister of the eucharist,

*      The reference is to Aristotle, but should be to Book 4 rather than Book 6.

as in the gospel and baptism. 45. The bread and wine are signs by which the Lord gives Himself, as He gave the Holy Spirit by His breath and imposition of hands. 46. By faith in the love of the Father we have eternal life. This faith proceeds that Christ, God's son, gives Himself to us for our forgiveness and resurrection. Therefore God gave the meat and drink as signs of our spiritual partaking of Him. 47. The connection between Christ's glorious body in heaven and the bread on earth is as between the water and regeneration of Christ's breath and the Holy Spirit, which I call communion of the covenant. Those who faithfully receive these signs become incorporated with Christ. 48. Whoever uses these signs otherwise than the Lord appointed is idolatrous and receives only damnation. 49. Those with faith, but not rightly judging this food (as some Corinthians blamed by the apostle) receive, but do not eat Christ. 50. Christ's words 'this is My body' mean that to the senses it is bread, to the mind His body, as by the representation of an image. 51. There is no scriptural authority for transubstantiation and therefore it cannot be an article of faith. 52. Three things are received by rightful communicants: bread and wine, in themselves unchanged, made symbols by the Lord's word and ordinance; His very body and blood, to our greater communion and regeneration; and confirmation of the new testament of our forgiveness and adoption as the sons of God. 53. With Iranaeus I call the symbols earthly, the confirmation of the new testament heavenly, to be know only by faith. 54. In bread and wine the body and blood are given, signifying the Lord; some of the fathers have rightly said 'representing'. Most important is the word 'receive'.

*10 pp.*
*Latin.*
*Slightly mutilated.*
*Printed*: in 1557 as *Antidotus Valerandi Pollani Flandri adversus Ioachim Vuestphali consiliũ* Aphorismi D. Martini Bvceri de S.S. Coena Domini, 42–57, and later in Bucer's *Scripta Anglicana*, (Basle, 1577), 538–45, under the title *Exomologesis sive confessio D. Mart. Bvceri de S. Evcharistia in Anglia aphoristicos scripta, anno 1550.*
*Translated*: Strype, *Cranmer*, ii, 855–869, from a MS of John Foxe.
*Summarised*: R.W. Dixon, *History of the Church of England*, (Oxford, 1878–1902), iii, 244n., where the composition is ascribed to 1549 or 1550. There are substantial variants in the SP 10, *Scripta* and Strype texts. The numeration used above is found in the Strype version. See C. Hopf, *Martin Bucer and the Church of England*, (Oxford, 1946), 49 n. 4. SP 10/7, no. 47

**296.** Copy of the above, before mutilation.
*10 pp.*
*Latin.* SP 10/7, no. 48

**297.** July [1]. Richmond. The king to [various lords].
We previously wrote to you to have ready able horsemen and footmen from your tenants, servants and others. Doubting not that you have done so, we require you to repair to Windsor Castle with your men and equipment by the [*blank*] of this month, when you will hear our further pleasure.
*Draft for the signet.* SP 10/8, no. 1

**298.** July 1. Names of those who had letters to come or send to Windsor.
*Essex.* The marquess of Northampton. The lord chancellor. The earl of Oxford. Lord Morley. Sir W[illiam] Petre. [Sir] Humphrey Browne. [Sir] Giles Capell. [Sir] John Mordaunt. [Sir] Thomas Darcye. [Sir] John Gates. [Sir] George Norton. [Sir] John Raynesford. [Sir] Walter Myldmaye. [Sir] Clement Smyth. [Sir] Anthony Cooke. [Sir] Henry Tyrrell. [Sir] Thomas Josselyn. Robert Mordaunt. William Harrys. John Browne. William Bonham. Thomas Mildmaye. Thomas Darcye. William Barners. *Hertfordshire.* Sir

Anthony Denny. Sir Henry Parker. Sir Ralph Sadler. Sir Roger Cholmeley. [Sir] William Cavendish. [Sir] Richard Lee. [Sir] John Peryent. [Sir] Robert Lytton. Sir John Broket. Sir Ralph Rowlet. William Barley. Edmund Bardolph. Robert Chester. Edward Broket. Francis Sowthwel. John Penne. Nicholas Bristowe. Richard Raynshawe. John Newport. John Knighton. Thomas Skipwith. Thomas Hemyng. John Kechyn. *Middlesex.* Sir Anthony Wingfeld. The bishop of London. [Sir Roger Cholmeley].* Sir Ed[mund] Pekham. Sir Ralph Warren. Sir John Gresham. [Sir] Martin Bowes. [Sir] Rowland Hille. [Sir] Wymond Carewe. William Locke. William Roper. Roger More of the privy chamber. Robert Burchier. Richard Morisyn. Richard Duke. Robert Chidley. William Stamppe. John Cocke. Hugh Losse. [John Hales].* John Bowes. John Newdigate. John Marshe. [Robert Curson].* The lord great master [Lord St John]. [John Marshe].* *Surrey.* [Lord Arundel].* Lord William Howard. [Sir John Gage, (Sir) Robert Southwell].* [Sir] Thomas Cawarden. [Sir] Thomas Pope. [Sir] Edmund Walsingham. [Sir] Matthew Browne. [Sir] Christopher More. Robert Curson. John Carrel. Nicholas Leigh of Addington. Henry Polstede. Thomas Sanders. William Sakevile. Richard Tavernour. John Eston. Lawrence Stowghton. John Tyngleden. James Skynner. *Sussex.* [The earl of Arundel].* The bishop of Chichester. Lord De La Warr. Sir John Gage. [Sir Roger (? *recte* Richard) Lyster].* Sir Richard Sackvile. Sir William Goryng. [Sir Christopher More].* Sir Anthony Wyndsor. Sir John Dawtrye. Edward Gage. John Shelley. Edward Shelley. John Covert. Giles Fynes. Nicholas Pelham. Thomas Darrell. John Parkar. William Wiborne. Edmund Ford. John Palmar. Robert Oxebrig. Nicholas Gainsford. *Berkshire.* Sir Thomas Smyth, secretary. Sir William Portman. [John Harrys, serjeant at law].* Sir Humphrey Foster. Sir John Nores. Sir William Penyson. Sir Francis Engleffeld. Richard Bruges. Thomas Weldon. John Cheney. William Brounsop. Reginald Williams. Edward Fetiplace. Thomas Essex. Alexander Fetiplace. John Norres. Thomas Denton. Walter Chalcot. Richard Warde. John Winchecombe. Thomas Vachel. William Hyde. Thomas Bullok. William Gray. Roger Young. John Knight. John Lovelace. Robert Gayne. *Buckinghamshire.* Lord Grey: Wiltshire. Lord Windsor. Sir Anthony Lee. [Sir Edmund Pekham].* Sir Robert Dormer. Sir Francis Russel. Sir Robert Drewry. John Croke. Henry Bradshawe. Thomas Gifforde. Edmund Windesor. Robert Cheney. Robert Peckham. Richard Greneway. Arthur Longvile. George Gifforde. John Bosse. [William Dormer].* Leonard Rede. Edward Chamberlayn. Paul Darell. John Langston. Anthony Cave. William Davers. Edmund Ashefelde. Thomas Pigot. George Wright. Ralph Gifforde. William Wogan. John Goodwyn. William Hawtrye. Christopher Weston. William Tyldesley. William Walter. John Hogan. Roger Lee. Henry Hampden. John Seymur. Thomas Benger. John Cheney of Amersham ('de Agmond'). Ticherus Bold. *Oxfordshire.* [Sir Thomas Pope].* Sir John Williams. Sir Walter Stonor. Sir William Barentyne. Sir John Browne. Sir William Raynsford. Sir Francis Knolles. Leonard Chamberleyn. Richard Fynes. William Dormer. *Kent.* The archbishop of Canterbury. Sir Thomas Cheyney. Sir John Baker. Sir Anthony Sentleger. Sir Robert Southwell. Sir Edward Wotton. Sir Thomas Moyle. Sir Edmund Walsyngham. Sir Walter Hendlye. Sir William Fynch. Sir Percival Harte. Sir John Guldford. Sir Reginald Scott. Sir Humfrey Style. [Sir Anthony Bowes].* Sir Thomas Wyat. Sir Henry Iseley. Sir Ralph Vane. Sir Anthony Aucher. Sir James Hales. Sir John North. Sir George Blage. [William Roper].* Edward Thwaytes. Edward Mony. Thomas Darrell of Scotney. Thomas Harlakynden. John Culpeper. Thomas Hardes. [Thomas Roydon. William Goldwell. Thomas Robartes. Thomas Grene. William Boysse. Anthony Saundes. Walter Mole. John Cooke. Edward Isak. Robert Culpeper. John Derynge. Thomas Culpeper. Paul Sydnor. Herbert Fynche. George Darrell. Robert Rudston. George Fane. Peter Hayman. John Gason].* Lord Abergavenny. Sir Thomas Kempe. [Sir George Harpers. Sir Edward Boughton. William Twynsenden. John Brent of Charing. John Brent of Willesborough. John Mayne. Walter Mayne. (*blank*) Wylloughbe. (*blank*) Clerke of Wrotham. (*blank*) Wombewell. Reynold

\*          Deleted.

Pekham. Thomas Hendle. (Thomas) Engeham of Chart. (? William) Fyneux. Christopher Rooper. John Palmer. William Iden. (*blank*) Watton].*     SP 10/8, no. 2

**299.** July 3. Docket of warrant for [*blank*] to repay Secretary Smith £3.10.0 paid for conduct money to seven Germans sent to serve in the north.     SP 38/1, f. 7

**300.** July 4. Aldingbourne. George [Day], bishop of Chichester to William Cecil.

I hear that [the lord protector] is shortly to come to these parts and to Chichester and I wish him to use my house there. It is as yet unfurnished for any nobleman (I am not yet able to furnish the house I live in), but I will provide for the kitchen, buttery and pantry. I hear he brings his own bed. I will provide six feather beds for those he wishes to have lodged within. There is scarcely room for these beds and his, and for his chamberlains. I have laid in a ton of beer and a hogshead of claret, part of a poor present to the protector. Let me know when he intends to be at Chichester. I have declared my mind to my friend Sir Henry Hussey who has promised to report to the protector.

*Holograph.*     SP 10/8, no. 3

**301.** July 7. Sir William Paget to the duke of Somerset.

Hearing what is said of your government at home and knowing partly before my departure and partly since how things are there, I am most distressed. I see at hand the king's destruction and your ruin. If you love me or value my service since the king's father's death, allow me to write what I think. Remember what you promised me in the gallery at Westminster before the late king died, and immediately afterwards, planning with me for the place you now occupy – to follow my advice before any other. Had you done so things would not have gone as they have. I wrote to you on Christmas Day, or at night on Christmas Eve, telling you the truth, which you did not believe, but now see. The people are out of discipline because of your softness and wish to be good to the poor. I know your good meaning but it is a pity it should have caused the present evil.

Society is maintained by religion and laws: you have neither. The old religion is forbidden and the new not generally imprinted. The law is almost nowhere used: the commons are become king. You should have followed the first stir hotly and used justice to the terror of others, and then granted a pardon. To grant a pardon out of course was as much good as the pardons the bishop of Rome used to grant, giving men more boldness than contrition. They must have what they want – new prices for victuals, wools and cloths and every other thing. You should not put so many irons in the fire as you have this year – war with Scotland and France (though not so termed), commissions, new laws, proclamations. Are enclosures new, or prices high only in England? Victuals are twice as expensive here. Enclosures have been lived with quietly for sixty years. As I told you in the gallery at the Tower the day after the king first came there, the trouble is liberty. Too much gentleness would have been avoided if you had followed my advice. But you have discouraged me in open council. The whole council has disliked your proceedings. You may say you are alone answerable to the king: but so must be those who first consented to your authority.

I know you as well as any man and have been loyal to you. Be no more gentle, for it has been harmful. I write privately: if you dislike my giving my opinions, dismiss me from the council. Having the absolute power of a king, you must act as one; follow the examples of others, of Henry VIII. He kept his subjects in obedience by the maintenance of justice. Force is necessary. In Germany, when similar trouble began, it might have been appeased with the loss of twenty men, or afterwards of one or two hundred. But

*     Deleted.

it was thought nothing and some spiced consciences were unwilling to lose even so many simple, godly folk; by allowing the matter to run so far it cost one or two thousand lives.

Send for all the council not abroad. Because many of the best are absent, take the advice of six of the most experienced. If you cannot deal with the matter with your men of war, send for the German horsemen at Calais, almost 4,000, who may be spared for a little. Have Lord Ferrers and Sir William Herbert bring as many horsemen as they can from Wales and those they trust. Let the earl of Shrewsbury bring the same from Derbyshire, Shropshire, Staffordshire and Nottinghamshire, from his servants and keepers of forests and parks. Send for your own trusty servants. Have the king stay at Windsor with his household, pensioners, men at arms and guard. Go yourself with the German horsemen, noblemen and their companies to Berkshire, appointing the gentry to meet you with their trusty friends and servants. Appoint three or four of the chief justices to go with commission of oyer and terminer to the town nearest to you with justices of the peace of the county, with command to seize twenty or thirty of the rankest knaves of the county. If they come peacefully to justice, let six be hanged in various places and the rest remain in prison. If any rich men have been implicated let the justices take sureties for their good behaviour and appearance in star chamber next term, to wait further order. Let the horsemen lie in the towns which have been busiest, taking enough for their money that the rebels may smart. Deprive offending towns of their liberties, to be restored at your pleasure. Send some of the doers away from their wives, to the north, to Boulogne, to be soldiers and pioneers. Make no promises. Make similar progress through the offending counties during this hot weather.

So you will redress the matter to your great honour abroad. You will not lose the hearts of good people: the evil do not matter. You will be feared, which you are now only of a few honest men. You will give the king an obedient realm, and be able to serve him in office, if you meddle no more with private suits but remit them all to ordinary courses. You will hear poor men's causes when you send them to chancery; to deal with them by letter suggests your favour in the matter. Let enclosure suitors be heard one at a time: the offenders will be punished, the king profit, and the poor be relieved.

I have written frankly: I believe you will take it graciously.

*8 pp.*

*Signed*: W.P.

*? Holograph.*

*Printed*: Strype, *Ecclesiastical Memorials*, ii, II, 429–37, from a copy in BL Cottonian MS Titus F.3, ff. 277–9v.

The last side of this document contains copies of three sets of verses of an amatory nature, in the same hand as that of the main text.                    SP 10/8, no. 4

**302.**   [July (? 8)]. The king's answer to the supplication of his subjects of Devon and Cornwall.*

If you would hear as readily as we have perused your supplication, you would easily return to order and see the difference between an anointed king who rules by counsel and the blind guides of sedition which lead you against your king to your destruction and theirs. You require things by a bill and send a gentleman with your requests to the lord privy seal. What manner is it to come to the king armed? What order would you keep if the French or Scots invaded? Be content: see Devon and Cornwall well ordered; gather the harvest; if laws are to be reformed, parliament is at hand. We have answered most of your supplication in a printed message to the people of Devon, which shows

---

\*   Attributed in *CSPD*, 20, to Cranmer. But the editor's endorsement (to one of the copies, no. **304** below) refers to Burnet, ii, 115 (*sic*, for 118), [ed. Pocock, ii, 209–12] which refers to the much fuller answer to the rebels written by the archbishop printed in Strype, *Cranmer*, ii, 502–62 and elsewhere, from Corpus Christi College, Cambridge MS 102, no. 28, pp. 337–405.

how you are deceived.

You fear your children should be christened only on Sunday – but the priest may christen them at any time, as before.

You do not seem to dislike the order of confirmation, but think your children shall not learn it unless they go to school. The curate is to teach them without their so doing. One child having learnt it, will teach twenty. How did you learn the *Pater Noster*, *Ave* and *Credo*? Cannot your children learn so much in English? The bishop and curate must have discretion to decide if a child's inability to answer comes from malice or impediment of wit.

You seem to require again the Six Articles, the statutes making words treason and other severe laws which were abolished at parliament's request. They thought that before no man was sure of his life, lands and goods. Do you wish us to rule with the same scourge again? Those who most desire it will soonest and sorest repent.

We believe your complaints of the blindness and unwillingness of your curates to set forth our proceedings, and think much of this dangerous stir comes from them.

Does receiving communion make matrimony? Men and women have always received it at the same time, but to their purification, not to licence filthiness.

The abuse of baptism by curates, their refusal to bury, contrary to our orders, and neglect of divine service for forwardness and lack of books are just causes of punishment, but no reasons why you should rise against us.

You say certain Cornishmen are offended because they have no service in Cornish and do not understand English. But there are few or no towns in Cornwall but where more understand English than Latin, and so they are better off.

You object as if these things were done without our knowing: but nothing passes in parliament without our consent. There is nothing in our book of orders for the church which we, despite our youth, are unable to prove to be according to the scriptures.

Lastly you ask for the relief granted us by parliament of cloth and shearing sheep to be remitted, saying we have no need. You do not consider the expenses of wars against France and Scotland now continued for almost eight years. Our father and ourselves have had to keep many armies by land and sea. You do not reckon how many thousand pounds are sent monthly to Boulogne, the ports there and the garrisons in the north. Our father, whom you think so rich, was at no less charge. We marvel that you think so, as he had to take so many loans, subsidies and benevolences, and sell his lands. He left us about £300,000 in debt. You mistrust our officers and those whom you say were appointed by our father: we can call them to account well enough without you. We have no cause against them because some are rich, as we would wish all our subjects.

War and defence consumes our treasure. You double this charge by your rebellion – which we will shortly suppress, if we spend all, even our life. If you will not bear the cost, the rest of the country will. You make us need a double relief.

At the petition of the house of commons we remitted for three years fee farms of towns and other things, worth more than this relief of sheep and cloths. Since the parliament we have granted that this year only those having over a hundred sheep shall pay, and clothiers shall give only notes of the number and valuation of their cloth, until the protector and council take further order.

When Scotland was ready to obey us, the French dare not. Now the French, taking courage from your rebellion, have sent out twelve galleys and many other ships and intend to take the Isle of Scilly or land in Cornwall or Devon and, according to our intelligence, take a gentleman's house that is almost an island. You that should defend it are now against us.

Do you think that if our enemies take advantage of your misrule and plunder our dominions that we shall not ask account of you? They would rob and despoil you as well, but we would reckon it our own loss.

Repent and return home while you have mercy, or you will be punished as a memorial to posterity.

You complain of dearth of victuals and other things. Do you think this is the way to make plenty? You spoil grass, corn, hay and all other things. Our force against you must use much victual. You bring with you those who should mow grass and harvest corn and keep idle those who should make cloth and gather tin. Old stores are wasted and new ones not kept. Last year you said you had a dearth of cattle; now you waste them as though there were a host of enemies in the country. Will rebellion make you wealthy? God will see it revenged.

*8 pp.*

Printed: F. Rouse-Troup, *The Western Rebellion of 1549*, (1913), 432–40. Tytler, i, 178–82 (incomplete). SP 10/8, no. 5

**303.** Copy of the above.

*8pp.* SP 10/8, no. 6

**304.** Fragment of another copy of no. **302**, being the first and last folios only.

SP 10/8, no. 7

**305.** Another fragment, as above. An earlier draft, with an insertion incorporated into the text of all other copies. SP 10/8, no. 8

**306.** [July (? 8)]. Order for repressing any commotions in Oxfordshire, Berkshire and Buckinghamshire.

[1]. Every gentleman to put his servants and tenants in readiness; if any uproar happens they are, on pain of forfeiting their holdings, to wait on their landlords for suppressing the uproars as soon as they can. [2]. All constables, bailiffs and other officers, except mayors, bailiffs, constables and other head officers of market towns, to be ready with their servants to assist the justices of the peace. The constables and other officers of every hundred with their servants and all other subjects to repair to the justices appointed for that hundred. [3]. The mayors, constables and other head officers of market towns to remain in their towns until otherwise commanded. [4]. If there is a rising all gentlemen in every hundred, not justices of the peace, to appear with their whole force before the justice appointed for the hundred. [5]. All justices to resort to an appointed place to take order for repression of the rising. [6]. The constables of every town to view the harness there and take them to the justice appointed for the hundred. [7]. The constables to be charged that the towns are watched nightly, not with light persons, until Michaelmas, according to the law and further order. [8]. The constables to apprehend tale bearers and seditious speakers and bring them to the nearest justice. [9]. Gentlemen to have trusty spies, especially in thoroughfares and market towns. [10]. The gentlemen of Oxfordshire to confer with those of Berkshire and Buckinghamshire to take orders for those counties and, if necessary, to join together. [11]. The justices to meet at least once a fortnight at some gentleman's house. [12]. Any gentleman leaving his house to leave word there where he will be. [13]. Any gentleman leaving the county to leave men and furniture for the county's aid. [14]. At our next meeting four gentlemen of the county to be elected marshals to execute mutineers or rebels, according to [the protector's] letters. [15]. Any mutineer or rebel taken to be brought before the two nearest justices and examined; being found guilty they and their examinations shall be sent to the marshals of that quarter; execution to be done at the nearest market town on the next market day. Record to be indented and kept between the marshal and the justices for their discharge. SP 10/8, no. 9

**307.** July [8]. London. Printed instructions from the king to commissioners for execution of statutes 4 Henry VII [c. 19], 7 Henry VIII [c. 1] and 27 Henry VIII [c. 22], to be enquired of in places named in a [formerly annexed] commission.

To enquire: [1]. What towns, villages and hamlets have been decayed and laid down by enclosures since 4 Henry VII. [2]. What land was in tillage and in pasture at the time of these enclosures. [3]. How many ploughs are decayed and laid down because of these enclosures. [4]. How many messuages, cottages and dwellings are decayed and their inhabitants departed because of enclosures and how much land belonged to them. [5]. If anyone has severed lands from any house of husbandry, making it a cottage, sheep house, dairy house or otherwise. [6]. By whom the enclosures were made and how long ago; if they were made at the same time, and their yearly rents and profits. [7]. How many new parks have been made since the same time. [8]. What arable land was then emparked. [9]. How many parks were enlarged and how much arable ground put in tillage. [10]. How many ploughs, houses and habitations are decayed because of the new emparking. [11]. If anyone has or keeps over 2,000 sheep, besides lambs of one year, in his own right or in the name of his wife, child, kinsman or other person, and whether he has kept them on his own lands, farms or otherwise by fraud, and for how long he has kept them. [12]. How many sheep are necessary for the yearly expenses of such persons' households. [13]. If anyone has let lands by copyhold reserving the sheep pasture to himself, or has taken from others their commons whereby they are unable to breed cattle and maintain husbandry as before. [14]. If anyone has had or occupied more than two houses or tenements of husbandry in any town, village, hamlet or tithing, and for how long. [15]. Whether such persons have taken the same in farm for terms of life, years, at will, by indenture, copyhold or otherwise since Christmas 1545, and where they live. [16]. If any person or corporation that has by gift, grant, lease or demise the site or precinct and demesnes of any religious house dissolved by act of 27 Henry VIII keeps honest continual household there and yearly occupies as much of the demesnes in ploughing and tillage as was used by the monastic owners or their farmers within twenty years before the statute. [17]. The commissioners to take copies of all offices found concerning the premises in 9 or 10 Henry VIII and to summon at all places they think fit six persons of every parish – two freeholders, two farmers and two copyholders or tenants at will – or as many as live there, to swear to all things presentable before them by virtue of this commission. [18]. [To enquire] if anyone has or keeps in one town, parish, lordship or hamlet more than one tenement of husbandry, and by what title. [19]. If any commons or highways have been enclosed or emparked contrary to right and without due recompense, this shall be reformed by the commissioners.

*Printed*: Richard Grafton [*STC* 7825]. *Tudor Royal Proclamations*, i, 471–2, no. 338. [But not in fact a proclamation: see Bush, 46 n. 38 and G.R. Elton, 'Government by Edict', *Historical Journal*, viii, (1965), 268, reprinted in *Studies in Tudor and Stuart Politics and Government*, (Cambridge, 1974), i, 303.]  SP 10/8, no. 10

**308.** July [? 8]. Richmond. The duke of Somerset to the commissioners appointed by the king, with articles [no. **307** above] annexed for redress of unlawful enclosures, decay of houses and reform of other disorders.

Since the matters are of great importance, you are to assemble as soon as possible after receipt of the king's commission. To avoid all suspicion, those of you who are within any of the cases to be reformed should begin with reformation of yourselves, as an example. We trust you will act impartially.  SP 10/8, no. 11

**309–320.** Further copies of the above, without date or place.  SP 10/8, nos. 12–23

**321.** July 10. London. Sir Thomas Darcy and Sir John Gates to William Cecil.

We have perused the commission and instructions to us and others concerning decay of houses and husbandry, enclosures, parks and other articles. Having already worked at this, we take it we cannot redress the same by this commission. Because we cannot deal with matters presented to us, we fear that the people think we delay, and they may be more enraged. Move the protector and council to authorise us to command the sheriff to pull down as much of the king's parks and others as are presented before us for pulling down, and set open commons and highways similarly presented. Let us be allowed to summon those presented for severing lands from houses and having above the prescribed number of sheep or farms, and to order these things by our discretion – without which authority we can set open the highways only, which we think contrary to the meaning of our commission, the expectation of the people, and our previous promise to them.

  *Printed*: Russell, *Kett's Rebellion*, 172–3.        SP 10/8, no. 24

**322.** July 14. Syon. The duke of Somerset to the enclosure commissioners.

  Although the commission allows you to proceed in pairs, it is the king's pleasure that you act jointly, without divisions.        SP 10/8, no. 25

**323–326.** Further copies of the above.        SP 10/8, nos. 26–9

**327.** July 18. The council to Princess Mary.

  You have no doubt heard of seditious assemblies and doings in many places, for stay of which we have done and will do all we may. Certain of your servants are reported to be chief in these commotions: a priest and chaplain of yours, now at Sampford Courtenay, Devon; Pooley, late a receiver, a captain of the worst sort assembled in Suffolk, of such credit elsewhere that his passport alone may give security to come and go even to Devon; your household servant Lyonell is of like credit with the rebels in Suffolk. Although we think you have no certain knowledge of these servants' doings, since your religion is known to be against that of the king and the whole country, encouraging (we fear) these men, we thought necessary to give this notice, praying you [to tell us by this bearer whether your said servants or others have received]* to order the stay of your servants [to tell us your meaning in these matters]* so they would have no occasion to judge that any of yours should so act against the king.

  *Corrected draft in Petre's hand.*

  *The MS was damaged by ink spillage in 1857; SP 10/8, nos. 30–44 were the worst affected. An account of the accident is inserted at the front of the volume.*  SP 10/8, no. 30

**328.** Copy of the above, as corrected.        SP 10/8, no. 31

**329.** July 19. Witney. Order taken by Lord Grey, assisted by the gentlemen of Oxfordshire, for execution of traitors in his absence, being otherwise directed by the king's letters and unable to proceed personally with his commission in Berkshire, Buckinghamshire, Northamptonshire and Oxfordshire.

  The sheriff and gentlemen undermentioned, dividing themselves with their forces, shall have the traitors taken safely to the towns and assist their executions: Sir Anthony Coope, sheriff, Sir John Williams, Sir William Barandyne, Sir William Raynsford, Leonard Chamberlaine, Richard Fynes, William Fermor, Sir John Browne, [John] Pollard, serjeant at law, William Dormor, Humfrey Ashfelde, John Crocker, Vincent Power, Thomas Gibbons, John Denton, Ralph Laughton, John Ogle, John Ardenne. The undermentioned traitors to be hanged immediately or on the next market days, as others have suffered

---

\*  Deleted.

elsewhere; their heads to be set up in the highest places of the towns for the greater terror of evil people: George Raves, * John White of Combe, Richard Tomson, vicar of Duns Tew – at Banbury; Henry Mathew, parish priest of Deddington – at [Bicester]† Deddington; John Brokyns, craftsman – at Islip; William Boolar of Watlington – at Watlington; two of the most seditious not yet apprehended – at Thame; two others of the most seditious – at Oxford; Richard Whyttington of Deddington, weaver – at Bicester; the vicar of Chipping Norton – on the steeple there; John Wade, parish priest of Bloxham – on the steeple there; Bowldry of Haseley – at Oxford.      SP 10/8, no. 32

**330.**  July 19. Eton. Sir Thomas Smith to William Cecil.

Thank you for your letters. I have long lamented the miserable state of our commonwealth. I intended to be at court today, but have not slept for a week and could not stand when I would take horse. If [the protector] would allow one or two men to execute the last proclamation against mutinies, the whole country would be ready to serve the king. I know that those who have anything are weary and would help redress. Proclamations should not be otherwise directed, but letters should be sent to one or two men in each county, to be aided by gentlemen and chief yeomen householders. They should be ready to go by night with sixty or a hundred horse to suppress stirs. Tell [the protector] that the watchmen, formerly well ordered, are now men of nothing and doers of all mischief. I know the uproar they made at [Saffron] Walden and throughout Essex. No man ought to watch without special command from the justices, on pain of death. [Princess] Mary's matter gives me great distress.‡ We can learn nothing certain of Lord Grey's doings. Tell [the protector] to be severe, especially on those coming here from other counties. The despatch of many of the boisterous would be no loss. Tell me some news. Will my man will write secretly. I hope to serve again soon. I would have been with you before, but for these commissions and because I still expected the king here. *Postscript.* Thank you for your gentleness to [Edward] Gascoyn. You will not repent anything you can do for him.

   *Holograph.*
   *Printed*: Tytler, i, 185–9.      SP 10/8, no. 33

**331.**  July 23. The council to Sir William Herbert.

To answer your letters of July 22, we have written to [the earl of] Worcester to aid you with men. You and the lord privy seal will know better what number is necessary. Arrange for them will all speed. We refer to you and him whether they shall have coats. If you think it necessary to prepare cloth for these and other needs, so that [you are not only ready] but marching towards the lord privy seal, we will allow 4 cloths a coat and order payment when you certify your numbers. The lord privy seal knows the wages, about which you asked; horsemen well horsed, with lances, to have 16d. a day, other mounted archers or arquebusiers [9d.]† 10d., footmen 6d.; captains' wages to be as in the lord privy seal's band. He has authority to take what artillery and other munitions he thinks meet. You may take what you please at Bristol, provided the castle is not left unfurnished. The lord privy seal has written for more aid against the rebels and we have appointed you to go to him as soon as you can. Your request from Bromham House is answered; it can do you little pleasure now as you cannot tarry [or we would have lent it].† Devote yourself wholly to this matter with all speed.

   *Corrected draft in Smith's hand.*      SP 10/8, no. 34

**332.**  July 24. Grimsthorpe. Katherine [Brandon], duchess of Suffolk to William Cecil.

* Possibly deleted.
† Deleted.
‡ In Latin.

I have so wearied myself with letters to [the duke and duchess of Somerset] that I have none for you. Another time you will have letters when they have none. I reminded my lady of her promise of some pension for maintaining the late queen's child who, with a dozen others, lies at my chamber. The continuation of this will keep me in debt this year. The marquess of Northampton, to whom I should deliver her, has as weak a back for such a burden as I, and would receive her, but more willingly with the appurtenances. Never a word that I ask you. *Postscript.* Do not forget Corneles.

 *Holograph.*               SP 10/8, no. 35

**333.** August 2. The king to [Edmund Bonner], bishop of London.

 Many in London and elsewhere in your diocese are negligent in attending church and holy communion, at a time when their prayers are most needful. We are sorry that this is generally caused by your own evil example and slackness. You used to preach on all principal feasts, but do so seldom or never since the setting forth of the new order. Many in your diocese frequent foreign rites and masses. Adultery and fornication are openly practised, provoking God's wrath. You have been admonished but have made no redress as your pastoral office requires. We therefore, as supreme head, order you to reform these things, on such pains as our ecclesiastical and temporal laws may inflict, to deprivation. We send instructions. St Paul's and other London churches are more neglected in repairs of glass and other buildings and ornaments than before, and many in the city maliciously deny tithes, so that the curates are less able to do their duties. Reform this. Since these complaints are mostly in London, you are to reside in your house there until otherwise licensed.

 Articles to be treated in your first sermon at St Paul's. Those who resist temporal authority resist God's ordinance, and those who die in rebellion are utterly damned. The rebels in Devon, Cornwall, Norfolk [and Suffolk]* or elsewhere deserve death as traitors and receive eternal damnation with Lucifer, the first rebel, whatever pretence they make of masses or holy water – as Korah, Dathan and Abiram were swallowed alive into hell for rebelling against Moses, although they pretended to sacrifice to God, as Saul was rejected for saving the fat sheep, and Agag for sacrifice. Scripture says obedience is better than sacrifice. In the order of the church and outward rites God requires humility, innocence, charity and obedience. If any man uses the old ceremonies his devotion is made naught by his disobedience, as that of Saul, Korah, Dathan, Abiram and Aaron's two children. It is a foolish, unlearned devotion. God requires the heart rather than the outward act.

 *Corrected draft in Smith's hand.*         SP 10/8, no. 36

**334.** [? August 9]. Articles sent to the bishop of London.

 *Copy of sermon headings, as in no.* **333** *above, with the following subsequent instructions.*

 As an example, a week on Sunday you shall celebrate communion at St Paul's. You will also set forth in your sermon that our royal authority is no less in our youth than that of any of our predecessors, though they were much older, as appears by the example of Josias and other young kings in scripture.

 *Draft of a separate letter from the council.*

 Since God has given the king victory over the traitors, declare the same in your next sermon and add this to your other instructions: God has showed how much he is displeased by rebellion. We shall not now need to read old stories. Devon and Cornwall, where the greatest fountain [of rebellion] was, are now so subdued that none of the leaders is unpunished or unapprehended. In Norfolk, where a more pernicious sort of rebels gathered, showing the fruit of rebellion – spoil, robbery, filthiness and the destruction of themselves and their prince... [*The MS breaks off here*].

\*  In no. **334** only.

*Printed*: Foxe, v, II, 745–6 (the second section of the MS only).    SP 10/8, no. 37

**335.**  August 10, 4 a.m. Warwick. The earl of Warwick to William Cecil.

Thank you for your letter; seeing how we stand with the French, open war seems better than coloured friendship. I wish we had no more to deal with; as it is we must trust in the Lord. With your letter I received a commission to lead the counties of Cambridge, Bedford, Huntingdon, Northampton, Norfolk and Suffolk, for which I am bound to [the protector] and council, but wish they might allow the marquess of Northampton to continue in his commission, or at least [have it] renewed. He has lately had enough misfortune and this might discourage him for ever. I shall be glad to serve with or under him. No one should be discarded for one mischance, which may happen to us all. Explain this to [the protector] and write again. In the meantime I will make these counties ready.

*Holograph.*

*Printed*: Tytler, i, 193–4. Russell, *Kett's Rebellion*, 117–18.    SP 10/8, no. 38

**336.**  August. Westminster. Circular from the council.

The king's letters commanded you to be at London on the [*blank*] of this month with [*blank*] armed men to attend him. You are now to await further order, keeping the men in readiness.

*Signed by*: the duke of Somerset, the archbishop of Canterbury, Lord Rich, Lord St John, the earl of Southampton, Sir William Paget, Sir William Petre, Sir Thomas Smith, Sir Edward North and Sir John Baker.    SP 10/8, no. 39

**337.**  Copy of the above, with the same signatures.    SP 10/8, no. 40

**338.**  August 12. Depositions of Andrew Blakman of Wherwell, Hampshire and Richard Sylver of Clatford, Hampshire, the king's servant, before Sir Henry S[eymour], William Keylwey, John Kyngsmeale, J[ohn] Myll, Thomas Welles and Thomas Pacy, esquires.

On Wednesday morning, August 6, John Garnham of Winchester, carpenter, told Blakman at the Crown in Winchester that they had 10,000 men ready for Flynte would bring many from Sussex; they should have all the bishop's tenants and all the country round about would repair to them. If any of the bishop's servants had 12d. they should have 6d. of it. Bishop's Waltham and Botley looked every day for them to begin, waiting only for answer from Flynte. They would begin their first intrigue at Portsdown at Mr Wayte's. If [Blakman] would come to [Garnham] at Winchester next Sunday they would go to Botley, meet Flynte and know all. It was not feigned. They would all have enough money by aid of the priests in the Close, the warden,* the chancellor† and [Peter] Langriche. They would not part with any until they were all together at Longwood, when they must send to them for two barrels of beer in which would be all the money the priests had. They would have every farmer's cart, go straight to Salisbury and cut off the mayor's head. Then all the villains that were against the western men would flee and they would come over their backs and destroy them, especially [Sir William] Herbert. Garnham appointed Blakman and Sylver to go the following Sunday morning from Winchester to Botley, which they did. On the way Garnham told them he would have a trumpeter among the men and five pieces of ordnance in Selsey church, which he had seen. When they came to Smythe's house at Botley, the Angel, the townspeople and others appointed welcomed him as though he were very honest. Then a farmer's son of Waltham came to him. They two ordered a banner of the Five Wounds with a chalice and host and a priest kneeling. They stayed there that night. Smythe told Garnham it

---

\*    John White.
†    Edmund Steward.

was not well that Flynte did not come, and that they should return home; he would forward the letter and do the business there well enough. So Garnham left and told Smythe he would see all things ready about Winchester.

*Originally endorsed*: Confession of Garnham against the warden of Winchester College.

SP 10/8, no. 41

**339.** August 15. Robert Broke and Richard Goodrich to [the duke of Somerset].

According to your letters we have examined Roger Lansdale of London, surgeon, prisoner in the Counter for felony, accused by John Gyle of London, surgeon. Lansdale says that Gyle and Richard Gyle, priest, his brother, lent him 20 marks and another time John lent him £4. After much circumstance John told him he would be bound to him and it would be worth £100 besides. On July 4 John told him that the matter was for Lansdale to take a good horse of Master Wood of the parish of St Dunstan in the West, London for £7. The next day he should take three letters which were then on the table in John's house. One was delivered by him to his late master the lord admiral, who had wished him to have it delivered to the earl of Angus in Scotland. Another was to tell the earl of the insurrections in England. The third was from Richard, telling the earl that two of the lords of the council had examined [Princess] Mary concerning the new service, and that she had said she would have the old service until the king came of age, and would not obey the protector's laws because he was no king. Because Lansdale refused the message, that night John had him laid in the Counter and charged with felony. Otherwise he would have disclosed the matter to the council immediately. We have also examined John and Richard Gyle in the Tower, secretly and otherwise. They deny all except lending [Lansdale] money. They say he has done many felonies and has accused them because they charged him, wishing them not at liberty to give evidence against him.

SP 10/8, no. 42

**340.** August 16. Westminster. The council to the bishops.

Inhibition was previously made by royal proclamation that none should preach without licence of the king or us until a uniform order of church service was set forth, because of the diversity of preaching by which the people were brought to a marvellous [?destruction]. This cause being now removed by a uniform order in the church made in the last session of parliament, we, the lord protector, there declared the king's pleasure that all as [his highness had called]* were called to be bishops, whom he specially trusted, should now preach and set forth the king's proceedings. Some do not, on pretence of the first inhibition or some other cause. We therefore signify that the king's will is you preach God's word, teach the people obedience to God and the king, preserve peace and unity, and thankfully receive the orders prescribed by king and parliament. In all your sermons and prayers reform the errors and disobedience of the people by wholesome doctrine. If you neglect this, not only God but the king shall ask account of you. Trusting this admonishment will make you more vigilant, and that with your spiritual exhortation you will help the king's temporal sword in reducing the people to due obedience.

*Draft in Smith's hand.*

*Endorsed*: After the book of common prayer passed.

SP 10/8, no. 43

**341.** August 17. Westminster. Fair copy of the above.

SP 10/8, no. 44

**342.** August 19. Dr [Geoffrey] Glyn, [advocate] of the court of arches to Sir Thomas Smith, secretary.

Remember my suit to you for the advocateship of the admiralty, which I have had ever since my coming to London, with 20 nobles' fee – as [the earl of] Warwick, as one

*       Deleted.

that paid me himself, can testify at his return. Mr Clapham, I see from his letters, has obtained his purpose by Mr Cecil. I am glad, but fear that some other man in my absence will disappoint me of my office. If Mr Petre hears that the proctor is sped, he will do all he can to bring the advocateship to some Oxford man, as he has done in all other legal offices. Mr Clapham has now opened the gate for one or other to enter shortly, seeing the proctor is already made advocate. My trust is only in you: speak to no other man. I trust Lord Warwick will at his return thank you for my preferment.

    *Holograph.*                                          SP 10/8, no. 45

**343.**    August 19. The council to the marquess of Dorset.

    We have received your letters of August 17 and thank you for the quietness of Leicestershire and Rutland through your diligence, praying you continue and serve the king well. We would gladly allow your request for the return of your brother Lord Thomas [Grey], but your brother Lord John [Grey] at Newhaven [Ambleteuse] earnestly asked us for him. Since he will comfort and serve Lord John well, with the enemy approaching, we have sent him there with 200 men, besides others we sent before.

    *Draft.*                                               SP 10/8, no. 46

**344.**    August 21. [Westminster]. The council to [Lord Russell], lord privy seal.

    We have received your letters of August 19 and rejoice at your good proceedings. We thank you as the chief; thank those who have not special letters from us. Touching the two points of our former letters of diminishing your numbers and pursuing the rebels, you have taken the best way of accomplishing them. The other parts of your letter, concerning Sir William Herbert's entertainment and money are already answered and, we suppose, received. You do well to search diligently for Sir Thomas Pomerey; send here as soon as you can Sir [*sic*] Humphrey Arundel, Maunder, the mayor of Bodmin* and two or three of the rankest traitors and ringleaders, to be examined and dealt with. Since the pardon you have is general, if you give it soon you might acquit some of the chief rebels. Wait, and pick out the most sturdy and obstinate to be punished as an example of terror. Then promulgate the king's pardon to the others. Those who bring the prisoners here must make account to us, lest any attempt should be made to free them.

    *Corrected draft in Smith's hand.*

    *Printed*: Pocock, *Troubles*, 63–4, from Inner Temple, Petyt MS 538/46, ff. 458–9, a contemporary copy with an additional sentence and postscript, and the supplied signatures of the duke of Somerset, Lord Rich, the archbishop of Canterbury, Lord St John and Sir William Petre.                    SP 10/8, no. 47

**345.**    August 29. Henry Polsted to William Cecil.

    Guildford, Farnham, Godalming, Chertsey and surrounding parishes are weak of worthy men, notably by the death of Sir Christopher More. Move [the protector] to renew the commission for more justices of the peace in this part of Surrey. I recommend William More, son and heir of Sir Christopher, as handsome a gentleman as I knew bred in the county, John Vaughan, who married Lady Knyvett, John Agmondesham, somewhat learned in law, who did much good in these late stirs at Guildford, as [the protector] and council know, and John Byrche of Gray's Inn, very well studied in the law. Tell the protector there is no common gaol in Surrey or Sussex, save such as the sheriff borrows sometimes in the King's Bench or the Marshalsea. Many thieves and others escape unpunished, to the encouragement of malefactors. Some of the fee farm money for these

---

\*    Henry Bray was mayor when the disturbances began, but by the date of this letter had been succeeded by Nicholas Bowyer, who was arrested; it is uncertain if the council was aware of the change [J. Cornwall, *Revolt of the Peasantry 1549*, (1977), 57–8, 202–3].

three years should be spent in making two new gaols in these counties.

SP 10/8, no. 48

**346.**   August 31. Northborough. Alice Browne to William Cecil.

My husband John has long been absent from me and I am told you might work for his pardon. Let me know, for I am with child, as I was at the siege of Boulogne when you wrote to me that he was alive, which has ever since bound me to you. I not only miss him greatly, but have great loss. In my absence my husband's goods were priced at £300, a great deal more than they were worth. The bishop of Peterborough gave me one part and his servant [John] Mountstevyng two parts. After my husband fled Mountstevyng carried away all my household stuff and left me not one bed. He still keeps it, except three beds which my lord gave me, but reserving my best down bed. I have offered Mountstevyng 100 marks to have my goods again, but he will not take it. I could receive no rent for my house at Walcote, where Markeham dwelt, due last Lady Day, whereby he has forfeited his lease. They have done me as much harm as they can, destroying my dovecote and hopyard, beating down my fruit and breaking down my gate there. I would be glad to have my husband home at Michaelmas, to demand his rent and avoid other charges.                    SP 10/8, no. 49

**347.**   August 31. Leeds Castle. Sir Anthony St Leger to William Cecil.

[The lord protector] wrote to the lord warden of the [Cinque] Ports [Sir Thomas Cheyne], Sir Edward Wotton and me to prepare 600 men, who were made ready in this county. 200 were appointed to enter the king's ships at Gillingham, 200 to Sir John Norton, who are already forth, and 200 to Sir Anthony Knyvett, whom we appointed to be levied from the west of the shire by the master of the rolls [Sir Robert Southwell] and his associates. Yesterday I had a letter from him affirming that the hundred of Washlingstone, the town of Shipbourne and the levy of Tonbridge defaulted, the constable alleging they had command from [Sir Ralph] Vane not to appear. The master of the rolls thinks twenty will be lacking and Mr Knyvett disappointed. I have written to the master of the rolls to levy more in other hundreds. If there is any such restraint by order there, let it be advertised, that men may be furnished elsewhere in time. The bishopric of Kildare in Ireland has been vacant half a year, not worth more than 40 marks a year. Move the lord protector to grant it to Lewes Tedder, a poor man, sometime my chaplain, now resident on a benefice in County Wexford. He lately did good service there in preventing the French from landing. Let him retain his small benefice. He is learned and of good condition. I dare offer no pleasure for your pains, hearing of your abstinence in that behalf, but will be bound to you.                    SP 10/8, no. 50

**348.**   [August]. [Westminster]. The king to Princess Mary.

After long conference of learned prelates and others we have, by the advice of the protector, privy council, convocations and parliament, established a uniform order of common prayer. We marvel what grounds you have to mislike or refuse it. But knowing your good nature, we can think it but a grudge of conscience for want of good information or conference with learned men. As we have said before, we would be pleased to [send] any of our prelates or others as are most agreeable to you. In the meantime, in respect of your weakness, we have dispensed you and your chaplains and priests for hearing and saying services other than set forth by our statutes. For fear of seducing others, the services are to be in your private chamber, in the presence of yourself and not more than twenty ladies and gentlemen appointed by you, whose names you shall signify to the protector and council, that order may be given for their discharge.

*Signet (missing).*
*Much mutilated, but lacunae supplied from no. **350** below.*

*Printed*: Green, 213–4.          SP 10/8, no. 51

**349.** Draft of the above.          SP 10/8, no. 52

**350.** Copy of no. **348** above made before its mutilation.      SP 10/8, no. 53

**351.** August. Lord Russell, lord privy seal, Lord Grey and Sir William Herbert to [the council].

Names of prisoners sent from the west: Sir Thomas Pomery, Humphrey Arundell, [John] Winslade the elder, [William] Winslade the younger, Wise, [John] Harryse, Coffyne, [John] Byrry, [Thomas] Holmes, Forteskewe. Castell, Arundell's secretary, sent by compulsion as accuser of Arundell and Coffyne, not as a prisoner. We have found him honest. He came of himself, and in the middle of the hottest stir sent his secret information to [Sir William] Godolphinne and other gentlemen.*     SP 10/8, no. 54

**352.** September 6. Babraham. Sir William Woodhouse to William Cecil.

I received these letters [*which follow*] from my brother on the way into Norfolk. Consider his services and great losses – at this last journey to Yarmouth the charge of a hundred men borne of his own purse. Consider his charity in accusing no man. None has more cause to. He desires a commission for the admiralty: it is very necessary for the sea causes. All mariners be out of order. Move the protector for him. This bearer will wait on you from time to time to remind you.

*Holograph.*          SP 10/8, no. 55

**353.** September 3 [enclosed with the above]. Waxham. Sir Thomas Woodhous to his brother Sir William at Sir Anthony Aucher's house by Tower Hill, London.

[The earl of] Warwick executes many men in Norwich and the gentlemen crave the escheats, daily bringing in men by accusation. I have accused no one, nor asked the gift of any, although I am spoiled of 2,000 sheep, all my bullocks and horses and most of my corn. All the ordnance and spoil taken in the camp is the king's. I moved my lord for two pieces of brass, but cannot have them. Ralph Symondes made great complaint of Turcock to my lord, yet he was in camp but two days in the beginning and then went to Newcastle, not returning home until the battle was done. Nevertheless the sheriff seized all his goods, and had I not made earnest suit to my lord, he would have lost his goods and been in danger of death. Write if you think I should come up. There is a commission of oyer and terminer. We have many prisoners at Yarmouth [which will be ordered by Sir Thomas Clere and me].† The commission includes Lord Willoughby, Lord Wentworth, Sir Edmund Wyndham, Sir John Clere and others, yet I am left out. But there are in my charge at Yarmouth 140 or 160 prisoners. Tell the lord great master I think it not meet. I am sure Danyell told you the truth of the taking of the prisoners: if Gilliote had not been with those who came from London, few would have been taken. Because I went out when others kept within their gates, the town ruffians wrote to Sir Thomas Clere that if he kept my company he would be in danger of his life, for they determined to kill me with half hakes, and the bailiffs. This was on Monday when they thought Warwick had been overthrown. Speak with Mr Cecil, that when any commission or letters are sent here, I am not forgotten and lose my credit in the county. I spoke with Mistress Anne Wotton: she is well. Little Henry is with me at my house.

*Endorsed*: Haste, haste.

*Printed*: Tytler, i, 195–7. Russell, *Kett's Rebellion*, 151–3.     SP 10/8, no. 55(i)

---

\*      For identifications see Rouse-Troup, *The Western Rebellion of 1549* and Cornwall, *Revolt of the Peasantry.*
†      Deleted.

**354.** September 5 [also enclosed with no. **352**]. Norwich. Sir Thomas Woodhows to his brother Sir William in London.

Sue the protector for a commission for the admiralty to deal with goods of those attainted, as of other pirates, of which one was lately taken in Suffolk. I dare not meddle, but my last letter from my lord declared me to be vice-admiral of Norfolk and Suffolk, and I need a patent to keep courts for island ships and other suits from party to party. The sheriffs and others meddle in my office as I have no warrant. Let it be sent down. There are two gunners in Lowestoft: have them placed at Yarmouth, for one was arraigned traitor. They lost all their ordnance to the traitors and we won it again at Yarmouth.

*Endorsed*: Haste.

*Partly indecipherable; synopsis above based on conjectural reading.*

*Printed*: Russell, *Kett's Rebellion*, 153. SP 10/8, no. 55(ii)

**355.** [September 8. Westminster]. Commission by letters patent to [Thomas Cranmer], archbishop of Canterbury, [Nicholas Ridley], bishop of Rochester, [Sir William Petre and Sir Thomas Smith], secretaries of state and [William May], dean of St Paul's.

Whereas on complaint made before us we gave injunction to Edmund [Bonner], bishop of London to be followed and preached in a sermon; notwithstanding, the bishop, in contempt of us, appears to have overslipped and not observed certain of the things ordered and done others intended for reformation perversely and negligently; you are therefore appointed to call him and his denouncers and hear the matter summarily and *de plano* or otherwise. If you find him deserving suspension or deprivation or full absolution, you shall proceed according to justice.

*Copy*: from C 66/825, mm. 28d–29d (*CPR* 1549–50, 166).

*Printed*: Rymer, xv, 191–2. Foxe, v, II, 748–9. Cardwell, i, 80–2. SP 10/8, no. 57

**356.** September 10. Dover. Sir Anthony Aucher to William Cecil.

Last Sunday John Whyte brought me a bill of words spoken by George Flecchar, whom I send with the bill and his answers. Be plain with the protector that under pretence of simplicity may rest much mischief, as I fear does in these men called 'comon welthes' and their adherents. None of the gentlemen dares touch them for some have been sent up and come away unpunished: that 'comen welthe' Latimer* has obtained the pardon of others and I gather some of them are jealous of my lord's friendship. To be plain, I think my lord's grace wishes the decay of gentlemen. Ask him to bear with my boldness, for I write only of duty to the king and him. If words may be treason, none ever spoke so vilely as these 'comon welthes' saying if they have no reformation before St Clement's Day† they will seek another way. I travelled yesterday with the lord warden,‡ who seemed to think the protector took his letters ill because he had not been fully answered concerning seditious persons, doubting if the protector would punish. If he wrote to him he would be fully satisfied. I have written a similar letter to the protector, enclosed; seal and deliver it if you think meet. Be friendly to Flecchar, who has a wife and eight children, trusting he will henceforth be honest.

*Printed*: Russell, *Kett's Rebellion*, 202–3. SP 10/8, no. 56

**357.** September 13. Questions put to the bishop of London.

[1]. Whether you received from the king by the hands of the lord protector and council in the council chamber on August 10 injunctions to be followed and articles to be preached, and whether you accepted and promised to follow them ? [2]. Whether you

---

\*      Not Hugh: see B.L. Beer and R. J. Nash, 'Hugh Latimer and the Lusty Knave of Kent', *Bulletin of the Institute of Historical Research*, lii, (1979), 175–8.

†      November 23.

‡      Sir Thomas Cheyne, lord warden of the Cinque Ports.

fully declared all the articles in you last sermon ? [3]. Whether you wrote your sermon, whether alone or by whose help; who has seen it before and since you preached it ? [4]. Whether you declared in your sermon that old rites now used in disobedience are nothing, although men have devotion to them ? [5]. Whether you declared the king's power in his minority, to refute the evil opinions of the rebels: if so, how ? [6]. Whether you will defend the rebels' opinion ? [7]. Whether you know of any who have heard or celebrated mass or evensong in Latin after the old rite in your diocese after the injunctions were given ? [8]. If you had called any such before you, and to what punishment you subjected them ? [9]. Whether divers rites are used in your diocese, and what you have done for redress; whom you have summoned and corrected ? [10]. Whether you have any church in London unrepaired and the ornaments not looked into; what they are, and what you have done ? [11]. Whether you know of any notable adulterers, incesters, fornicators; whom you have punished, and how ? [12]. Whether you were at the sermon of Dr [Richard] Cox, king's almoner, a year last midsummer, in which he declared the bishop of Winchester's contempt in not observing the injunctions given him, especially that he did not treat, as commanded, of the king's authority in his minority ?

SP 10/8, no. 58

**358.** September 14. Ely Place. The earl of Warwick to William Cecil.

Intercede with [the protector] that this bearer, Thomas Druery, captain of 180 footmen serving the king against the Norfolk rebels for two months since the marquess of Northampton went there, except sixty killed in battle and other skirmishes, for whom he demanded nothing since August 27, [should now be paid] and his band speedily employed or broken up.

*Printed*: Tytler, i, 198. Russell, *Kett's Rebellion*, 157. SP 10/8, no. 59

**359.** September 15. [King's] Lynn. Sir Nicholas Le Strange to William Cecil.

Thank you for my last letter from [the protector] to Lord Willoughby for execution of my office, but its delivery made him hate me. He commanded me from office, against the law and the letter, whereby I have lost not only the commodity but my reputation in my county. Not content, they seek my utter undoing, using Sir Roger Townsend and Sir Edmund Benyngfyld, who before sought to purchase several pieces of my land which lie near them, with which I will not part. Now they seek, I think with the counsel of the shamefaced [? Thomas] Husseye, to obtain the same by craving my blood. They are joined with Sir Thomas Hoolles, who as you know is to be led with every wind. They seek to make me the beginning of the commotion in Norfolk – which, as you know, was begun in two places before I came from Hampshire. If I had intended the commotion I had no need to go by boat to Lincolnshire, or to have craved Lord Willoughby or Husseye to go to Lynn to defend the town and the gentlemen who, sheltering there, were driven out. From there, as you know, I came to London, seeking means at the council to quiet the rebels, of whom I received a letter to declare to them. On their not being contented I came to Lynn and waited on Lord Willoughby with fifty men until the end at Norwich. I refer the manner of my service to the judgement of all who were there and of Sir William Wodhowsse, who was with me. If I am charged with leaving my brother and son as pledges for myself and Sir William Wodhowsse, I thought it better to escape by any means than to remain, having a bill signed by the king and protector for levying the county. If anything of this comes to the protector, have the evil judgement respited until I may be heard. A thousand traitors have been pardoned in Norfolk for the offence of which I am wrongly accused. For three hundred years my ancestors have not been touched with any such charge. The papists, left at Lynn to keep the town, found no time to enquire of any of their own faction nor of the chief or under constable, whereof some never ceased until the last day. *Postscript.* I think Husseye wishes

me troubled so that I might not enquire of his doings. [Sir Michael] Stanhope is his very good master. Make Mr Steward* privy to this letter: I trust he will show me friendship.
*Holograph.*
*Printed*: Russell, *Kett's Rebellion*, 210–13.                                            SP 10/8, no. 60

**360.** August 18. Leighs [Priory]. Lord Rich, lord chancellor, from his house there to William Cecil.

The commissioners of oyer and terminer for Essex sit at Brentwood next Saturday for the arraignment of Essex and Nicholas More, now prisoners in the Tower. Let me know [the protector's] pleasure for sending them down by some of the guard or by the knight marshal's servants, to be at Brentwood on Friday night. Have Essex's boy sent down to give evidence against his master. The jury should hear what the boy can say on oath. [Let me know] my lord's grace's pleasure for the execution of the prisoners. Sir Thomas Darcy and the rest of the commissioners think Essex should suffer at Maldon and More at Braintree.
*Holograph.*
*Printed*: Tytler, i, 199–200.                                                          SP 10/8, no. 61

**361.** September 18. Warwick Lane. Sir Edward Wotton, from his house there to William Cecil.

Further this bearer, my kinsman Hugh Darrell, in his suit to the protector for the bailiwick of certain lands and revenues in Kent that Sir Thomas W[yat], deceased, exchanged with the king, void by the death of [John] Deryng.
*Printed*: Tytler, i, 203.                                                              SP 10/8, no. 62

**362.** September [? 22]. Sunday. Hatfield. Thomas Parry to William Cecil.

I enclose [Princess Elizabeth's] letters† which she wishes you to deliver to [the protector] that she may hear again from him, to whom she refers all, and to know what time he thinks best for her coming. She asks me to send you commendations and say she is grateful for the offer of help in your letter; your request is fully served: let the party make the report. Her hand is weak because of her illness. She does not go to Ashridge for ten or twelve days because of the unreadiness there.
*Holograph.*
*Printed*: Tytler, i, 425–6, where ascribed to September 1551. On various conjectures as to the date of this letter see Read, 64, 473 n. 12.                                    SP 10/8, no. 63

**363.** September 25.‡ Thomas Parry to William Cecil.

The Venetian ambassador came yesterday with letters of commendation from the duke that he, being the king's orator, should also see [Princess Elizabeth] on the duke's behalf. Seeing that [the protector] has spoken with him as he said, he talked with her several times, hunted, and left at night. Her grace commanded me to write to you with all speed to ask [the protector] yourself or in writing if she should herself write of it; not that the talk was important, but she will know or do nothing which seems important without [the protector's] understanding. If you advise her to write, tell his grace. In the meantime she asks you to make him privy. I deferred on this occasion to write of 'Surbury', being then at hand, and thought it enough for Owtrede to tell you what I thought good. I will write next to be certified of next year's wood sale, its setting forward, and suchlike.
*Holograph.*
*Printed*: Tytler, i, 201–2.                                                            SP 10/8, no. 64

---

\*      'Mr Stuard' in the MS most probably refers to Lord St John, lord great master of the household, which office had previously been known as steward.
†      No longer extant.
‡      So dated, but endorsed September 26.

**364.**   September 28, morning. Sir Francis Dawtrey to William Cecil.

I sued the lord protector for a licence of 1,000 tons of wine. He said he had not yet determined to grant any wine licence, but bade me repair to you to have you put me in your book of remembrance for 1,000 tons, saying that if any licence for wine were granted, mine should be first. So my only preferment rests with you.   SP 10/8, no. 65


**365.**   [? September]. The king to special men in shires where risings have occurred.

By the advice of the protector and council we lately gave a free general pardon to many subjects for unlawful assemblies, riots and other disloyal behaviour, and made proclamations for the stay of such assemblies hereafter and the punishment of tale tellers, vagabonds and others going about to raise the people without our command. Despite this many idle, disobedient and godless persons still loiter and use seditious and stubborn talk, refusing to work. Although we have already ordered their punishment by the sheriff and justices of the peace in the county of [*blank*], we thought good, respecting our special trust in you, to charge you to have special regard for the observance of our proclamations and the severe punishment of offenders. Cause the justices and other officers and subjects of the county to make diligent enquiry of those spreading seditious tales or raising the people by bells, trumpets, drums or otherwise, whom you shall apprehend and hang without delay as rebels. Vagabonds and idle persons refusing work are to be similarly executed.

*Draft or minute.*                                                         SP 10/8, no. 66


**366.**   [? September]. Sir Henry Hussey to William Cecil.

I am glad to hear you are merry. My neighbours Richard Cooke and John Fraunces have long been suitors to [the protector] for goods taken from them in France and from ships arrested in England. The first time was at Dieppe for a ship that John of Ry, Frenchman, took. These poor men sued [the protector] who said they should be recompensed if all Frenchmen's goods in England could do so; but they had none. Last year their goods were taken from French ships arrested at Dover and they left them behind. [The protector] again replied that they should have their own goods again or be recompensed of Frenchmen's goods under arrest here. Because of the daily cries of their creditors they came to [the protector] about midsummer and he replied personally that they should return when they heard whether it would be war or peace. They now hear war cried between England and France, and sued for a leather licence, but could not have it. On their return their creditors went mad, for eight of them had lent their chief substance to Cooke and Fraunces, and so deserve pity, having done the king's service and having wives and many children. Help them to have their recompense. I hear there are certain prizes in the Thames of French ships that lie there and do the king no good. Some were first arrested at Dover, in which these men's goods were arrested in France; which, if the protector gives them, are sixteen of them in one or two of the same prizes. Otherwise these men will have to beg or steal.

*Holograph.*                                                              SP 10/8, no. 67


**367.**   [? September]. Petition of Edward Morley to Sir Thomas Smith, secretary.

You helped my wife and me in our suit to the lord protector for a life annuity of £10 granted to my wife by Dr [Thomas] Legh from Sherburn [Hospital], as appeared before you and others of the council by a patent under the convent seal of the house. After Dr Legh's death, Dr [Anthony] Bellasis possessed the house and refused to pay the annuity. On my suit by bill of petition, the lord protector gave us a letter commanding Bellasis to pay the annuity and arrears of £25. Despite this and your letters to Sir Nicholas Hayre and the dean of St Paul's, judges of the white hall, my wife had only £5 a year and £6.13.4 in arrears awarded her, to our great impoverishment.* Considering my charges about the suit and the seven yards of velvet I gave you, thinking I should obtain the arrears and the whole annuity, I refer all to your conscience. With my wife's death I have lost all. Robert Whetley, who was my holder, can show you of my poverty, which forces me to write this petition.                                              SP 10/8, no. 68

**368.** October [5]. Hampton Court. The king to all subjects, to repair armed and with all haste to Hampton Court to defend the king and the lord protector, against whom a most dangerous conspiracy has been attempted.

*Sign manual.*

*Countersigned by* : the duke of Somerset.

*Note* : Received of George Dunstall, the archbishop of Canterbury's servant, between 1 and 2 p.m. on October 6.

*Printed* : Tytler, i, 205. *Tudor Royal Proclamations*, i, 483, no. 351, with reproduction facing p. 484. [But not in fact a proclamation: see Hoak, 327 n. 63, where date is also shown to be October 5 not 1 as given in this MS by a clerk's error].

SP 10/9, no. 1

**369.** October 5. Hampton Court. Certified copy of the above, sent to all justices of the peace, mayors, sheriffs, bailiffs, constables, headboroughs and other royal officers and subjects.

*Printed* : Pocock, *Troubles*, 76.                                              SP 10/9, no. 2

**370.** October 5. Hampton Court. The king to Sir Henry Seymour.

Because we hear of a conspiracy against us, we command you to assemble as many armed men on horse and especially on foot as you can so suddenly, by authority of any commission or office or that of these letters, and bring them here to await further order.

*Signet (missing).*

*King's stamp.*

*Countersigned by* : the duke of Somerset.

*Printed* : Pocock, *Troubles*, 77–8.                                              SP 10/9, no. 3

**371.** October 5. Hampton Court. The duke of Somerset to his servant [Henry] Golding.

Have the earl of Oxford, his servants and forces, ready to serve the king if required. If occasion arises we will write to you. Use all convenient secrecy.

*Printed* : Tytler, i, 212–13. G.J. Townsend, *History of the Great Chamberlainship of England*, (1934), 101.                                              SP 10/9, no. 4

**372.** October 5. Hampton Court. The duke of Somerset to [Lord Russell], lord privy seal and Sir William Herbert.

For the king's surety we are very desirous to have you here, being sure of your affection for us. Mr Herbert can be here more speedily. Order your servants to follow.

*Contemporary copy, or fair copy with signature supplied.*†

*Printed* : Pocock, *Troubles*, 78.                                              SP 10/9, no. 5

**373.** October 6. Hampton Court. The duke of Somerset to [Lord Russell], lord privy seal and Sir William Herbert.

A conspiracy has lately risen against the king and us, as was never seen before. It cannot be maintained without unheard of rumours. They say we have sold Boulogne to

---

\*      REQ 2/17/79.

†      The signatures on this document and nos. **373–6** are in a contemporary hand but not in imitation of the sign manual and Somerset's autograph.

the French and withhold soldiers' wages. The matter is now brought to a marvellous extremity, involving men from whom we and the king rather deserved love. As it is, you are to hasten here for the king's defence with such force as you have, causing the rest to follow. *Postscript.* They are not ashamed to send posts abroad that we are already committed to the Tower and that we would release the bishops of Winchester and London, and bring back the old mass.

> *Contemporary copy (cf. note to no.* **372** *above).*
> *Printed*: Pocock, *Troubles*, 82–3, from Inner Temple, Petyt MS 538/46, ff. 467–467v, where the last sentence of the main text may be summarised as follows: We are sure you will have other letters from them, but you are to make no stay, but repair immediately to Windsor Castle, causing the rest of your force to follow.
>
>               SP 10/9, no. 6

**374.**    October 6. Hampton Court. The duke of Somerset to [Lord Russell], lord privy seal and Sir William Herbert.

Give credit to the communication of this bearer Lord Edward [Seymour] concerning the king's state, and follow his instructions.

> *Contemporary copy (cf. note to no.* **372** *above).*
> *Printed*: Pocock, *Troubles*, 79.             SP 10/9, no. 7

**375.**    October 6. Hampton Court. The king to [Lord Russell], lord privy seal and Sir William Herbert.

To attend immediately with all the force they can raise.

> *In the same terms as no.* **370** *above.*
> *Sign manual.*
> *Countersigned by*: the duke of Somerset.
> *Contemporary copy (cf. note to no.* **372** *above).*       SP 10/9, no. 8

**376.**    October 6. Hampton Court. The king to [Lord Russell], lord privy seal and Sir William Herbert.

A wicked conspiracy is attempted against us and the lord protector, maintained with falsehoods. They rumour that our uncle has sold Boulogne and detains wages, and other tales which we know to be untrue. He never did anything to which the rest of the council did not agree. Repair with all speed for our defence.

> *Sign manual.*
> *Countersigned by*: the duke of Somerset.
> *Contemporary copy (cf. note to no.* **372** *above).*
> *Printed*: Tytler, i, 214. Pocock, *Troubles*, 79–80.      SP 10/9, no. 9

**377.**    October 6. London. Letter from the council.

The king is in danger because of the treason of the duke of Somerset, who now has it rumoured that we of the council intend evil to his highness, hoping to deceive and be aided by the people. For the king's surety we require you to let the people know the truth; and since he already gathers force, to put yourself in order with all the power you can and repair to us for the king's service.

> *Signed by*: Lord Rich, lord chancellor, Lord St John, the marquess of Northampton, the earl of Warwick, the earl of Arundel, the earl of Shrewsbury, the earl of Sussex, Sir Thomas Cheyne and Sir Edward North.
> *Printed*: Pocock, *Troubles*, 80–1.         SP 10/9, no. 10

**378.**    [October]. Henry A. to all true Englishmen.

Be loyal and not deceived by crafty traitors who aim at one target and shoot at others.

They have murdered the king's subjects and now, fearing that the lord protector, according to his promise, would have redressed things in parliament to the ease of the commons, have conspired his death. That done, they will murder the king because of their ambition and to restore popery. Do not be persuaded by their proclamation. If the lord protector did anything unjust, they were all of counsel in the same. They came up lately from the dunghill, and are more meet to keep swine than occupy the offices they do. They conspire to the utter undoing of the commons. They call themselves the body of the council, but lack the head. As for London, faithless Troy, Merlin says that twenty-three of its aldermen will lose their heads in one day, which God grant be shortly.

*Addressed*: Read it and give it forth.

*Endorsed*: A seditious bill found in London.

*Printed*: Tytler, i, 208–10. SP 10/9, no. 11

**379.** [October]. To all true lords and gentlemen and us the poor commons.

Let us rise with all our power to defend the king and lord protector against certain lords and gentlemen who would depose the lord protector and endanger the king. We, being injured by the extortions of these gentlemen, had our pardon this year by the king's mercy and goodness of the protector, who needs no extortion.

*Endorsed*: Copy of the bill sowed amongst the commons.

*Printed*: Tytler, i, 210–11. SP 10/9, no. 12

**380.** [October]. Memorandum to or on behalf of the duke of Somerset.

Let the king write to all the lords, sorrowing at the false and vile reports against the protector, which he is able to answer himself, and willing them to trust his own letter for all true subjects to repair to him in person, without their powers; or else he assumes they seek his own deposition. He bears with them in love only because he sees them blinded.

*Printed*: Tytler, i, 207–8. SP 10/9, no. 13

**381.** Memoranda of recent events and necessary business.

Mr Bowes ... [M]ercers' Hall for th... me against Tuesday at 9 o'clock to ... the king. On Sunday the lord great master entered the Tower of London to the king's use, made [Sir Edmund] Peckham lieutenant and gave him table allowance. The king to write to the mayor, sheriffs and aldermen to be delivered to the messenger by the king's man. A letter to the lords willing as many as were honourable to repair to him against his enemies, or else they sought his blood as well as his uncle's. The protector should send a ship to the French king laden with gold and silver in barrels like gunpowder by Sir Anthony Aucher; which ship was taken. The disobedience of Mr Markeham in his office. Sir Thomas Darcy is laid in the Tower as a traitor. They find themselves aggrieved in bringing up the king, which they will otherwise order. To send word if Lord Harry* is there. To countermand the nobility not to come to or near London. To write to Lord [Warwick]† from the king only. To send home Musthian if he can be spared. Your butler is stayed by the lords in London.

*In the same hand as no.* **380.**

*Mutilated.* SP 10/9, no. 14

**382.** October 7. Windsor Castle. The king to the bailiffs and constables of Uxbridge, Hillingdon and Colham [Green].

Certain lords and their powers conspire against us and the protector fears for our person without the aid of our subjects. By whatever authority you have, or that of this

---

\* Either Sir Henry Seymour (the protector's brother) or possibly Lord Henry Seymour (his younger son).

† Deleted.

letter, assemble the whole force of our subjects and lead them here with all speed, in the best armour, but not leaving behind able men for lack of weapons. They will have armour and weapons here. Give necessary order for bringing victuals, and proclaim in the country that no commands are to be obeyed unless they come directly from us or our uncle.

*Signet (missing).*
*Sign manual.*
*Countersigned by*: the duke of Somerset.                                        SP 10/9, no. 15

**383.**    October 7. Windsor Castle. The duke of Somerset to the councillors in London.

The king, informed that you were assembled as you still are, was advised by us and the other councillors here to send Mr Secretary Petre with a message whereby might have ensued the king's safety, the preservation of the country, and the quiet of ourselves and you. We all marvel much that you still hold Mr Secretary and have not answered the king by him or another. We ourselves are very sorry at your doings, as you should be, bent with violence to bring the king and us to these extremes. If you use violence we intend defence to death. We do not know what you seek, nor whether you intend to hurt the king. You will find us agreeable to any reasonable conditions in all private matters, to avoid bloodshed and preserve the king and his subjects. We value the king and the wealth and peace of the country above all worldly things, even our own life. Send answer by Mr Petre or this bearer.

*Drafted by Secretary Smith.*
*Signed.*
*Printed*: Tytler, i, 214–16. Pocock, *Troubles*, 88–90, from copy in Inner Temple, Petyt MS 538/46, ff. 469–469v.                                        SP 10/9, no. 16

**384.**    October 7. [London]. The councillors in London to the king.

Having received your message by your secretary, Sir William Petre, we were upset that, upon false information, you seemed to doubt our fidelity. [Give no further credit to the duke of Somerset].* As we have always served the king your father and you faithfully, we intend to continue your true servants to death. We have consulted together only for the safeguard of your person and dominions. We have attempted by all gentle means to have the duke of Somerset govern your affairs by our advice and that of your other councillors. Finding him so much given to his own will that he refused to hear reason, and doing things dangerous to the king and country, we thought again to speak with him gently, had he not gathered force about him, so that we could see he was bent on maintaining his own [traitorous]* troublesome doings. For redress of which only we remain here. Almost all your council being here, we caused your secretary to remain. We are concerned only to deliver you from the present peril; nothing else could have made us seem to stand as a party.

*Corrected draft.*
*Printed*: Burnet, v, 273, from the copy as sent, BL Cottonian MS Titus B.2, ff. 36–37v, which is signed by Lord Rich, Lord St John, the earl of Warwick, the earl of Arundel, the earl of Shrewsbury, the earl of Southampton, the marquess of Northampton, Sir Thomas Cheyne, Sir Edward North, Sir John Gage, Sir Ralph Sadler, Sir Edward Montague, Sir Richard Southwell, Dr Nicholas Wotton and Sir William Petre. Registered copy in PC 2/4, p. 5 (*APC,* ii, 333–4)    SP 10/9, no. 17

**385.**    Contemporary copy of the above, as finally corrected.            SP 10/9, no. 18

*        Deleted.

**386.** Another contemporary copy, as above.
*Printed*: Pocock, *Troubles*, 83–5, adding the signatures from the BL copy (see note to no. **384**).                                                                    SP 10/9, no. 19

**387.** October 7. London. The council to [sheriffs].
The duke of Somerset, seeing his detestable treasons detected, levied many men to achieve his devilish purpose, to the great peril of the king and state, and also spreads false rumours against us the king's council assembled here. Publish this in all places within your shrievalty and allow no men to be raised or molested by any orders not from us.
*Signed by*: Lord Rich, lord chancellor, Lord St John, the marquess of Northampton, the earl of Warwick, the earl of Arundel, the earl of Shrewsbury, the earl of Sussex, Sir Edward North and Sir John Gage.                                          SP 10/9, no. 20

**388.** October 7. London. The council to [justices of the peace].
*In the same terms as the above.*
*Signed by*: Lord Rich, Lord St John, the marquess of Northampton, the earl of Warwick, the earl of Sussex, Sir Edward North, Sir John Gage and Sir Edward Montague.                                                                           SP 10/9, no. 21

**389.** October 7. [London]. The councillors in London to those at Windsor.
Learning what false and slanderous bills and rumours are spread about in [almost all]* many places by the duke of Somerset concerning the cause of our assembly, we must assure you of our loyalty to the king and country. If the duke had listened to our advice and to reason we would have quietly communed with him for redress of all things. But, knowing he raised great forces and circulated false reports of us, we also were forced to assemble [great]* some numbers. If the duke, as a good subject, will leave the king and be ordered by reason and justice, and disperse his force, we will gladly commune with him for the king's safety and the order of all other things. But if we see you care more for the maintenance of one man's ill doings than for the execution of the king's laws, we must make other account of you. We are almost the whole council, much bound to the king. If you refuse peaceful agreement, the ensuing disturbances will be of your doing.
*Corrected draft.*
*Printed*: Pocock, *Troubles*, 86–8, adding the signatures of Lord Rich, Lord St John, the marquess of Northampton, the earls of Warwick, Arundel, Shrewsbury and Southampton, Sir Thomas Cheyne, Sir William Petre, Sir Edward North, Sir John Gage, Sir Ralph Sadler, Sir Richard Southwell and Dr Nicholas Wotton from the copy as sent, BL Cottonian MS Caligula B.7, ff. 391–391v (which is printed in Ellis, *Original Letters*, ii, 166–8).                                               SP 10/9, no. 22

**390.** October 8. Andover. Lord Russell and Sir William Herbert to the duke of Somerset.
We have received your letters and lament your dissension with the nobility. You required us to repair to Windsor Castle. As long as we thought the nobility now assembled had conspired against the king, we proceeded with our company. But today we heard from the lords that they are loyal, which we believe, and that this great extremity proceeds only from private causes between you and them. We have therefore decided to levy as great a force as we may for the safety of the king and realm. Let the king not fear, and conform yourself, as these private causes produce universal displeasure. Let bloodshed be prevented by any means. We much dislike your proclamations and bills put about for raising the commons. Evil men will stir as well as loyal subjects. We and other gentlemen

\*        Deleted.

who have served in the counties where they have been published have thereby incurred much discredit.

*Copy. Facsimile signatures.*

*Printed*: Tytler, i, 217–19. Pocock, *Troubles*, 90–2, from copy in Inner Temple, Petyt MS 538/46, ff. 467v–468v, adding signatures from the SP copy. SP 10/9, no. 23

**391.** October 8. Windsor Castle. The king to the councillors in London.

By your letters delivered by our servant William Honynges last night we learned your reasons for your assembly, the staying of Sir William Petre, and your opinion of the lord protector. Moved by the sight of our uncle, councillors and others here, we lament our present danger, and unless you quieten these uproars, will think you forget your duty to us and the benefits given to you all by the late king. You charge our uncle with wilfulness, but we have found him so tractable that we trust you may come to a peaceful agreement. All have faults – he his and you yours. If we weigh yours as rigorously as you intend to purge his, who will be able to stand before us? He intends no personal harm to us. If he has been indiscreet in government, extreme remedy is not required, as you would doubtless counsel if he were another person. We send certain articles [*which follow*] exhibited by our uncle and signed by our hand, and our councillor Sir Philip Hoby: give him credit and return him with your answer.

*Sign manual.*

*Printed*: Tytler, i, 220–3.

*Another copy*: BL Harleian MS 353, ff. 76–7 (later date). SP 10/9, no. 24

**392.** October 8 [enclosed with the above]. Windsor Castle. Articles offered by the lord protector to the king in the presence of the council and others, to be declared to the lords and others of the council in London.

1. I do not, nor did not intend to arrest or otherwise disturb them; but hearing of their meetings and gatherings of horsemen and other force out of several counties, not knowing the cause, and to avoid further danger to the king as was said to be imminent by sundry rumours and intelligence, I was forced to seek this defence, as I first told the king. 2. The force now about the king is only for his defence, and not to hurt those in London in person or goods. [3]. I do not refuse a reasonable agreement with the council. If they send two commissioners I beg the king to appoint two of us to join them, submitting myself to their decision, to be ratified by parliament if necessary. [4]. I beg the king to grant free passage to their two commissioners with twenty servants each.

*Sign manual.*

*Countersigned by*: the duke of Somerset.

*Printed*: Burnet, v, 275–6, from copy in BL Cottonian MS Caligula B.7, ff. 394–394v, collated with the SP original. SP 10/9, no. 24(i)

**393.** Contemporary copy of no. **391**. SP 10/9, no. 25

**394.** Contemporary copy of no. **392**. SP 10/9, no. 25(i)

**395.** October 8. Windsor Castle. The archbishop of Canterbury, Sir William Paget and Sir Thomas Smith to the councillors in London.

We have received your letter of yesterday by [William] Horninges, by which we understand the causes of your assembly, charging the protector with the manner of his government and requiring him to withdraw from the king, disperse the force he has levied, and be ordered with justice and reason. You say you will gladly commune with us for the king's safety and general order. We believe that as rumours that you intended to destroy the lord protector induced him to fly to the defence he has assembled, so your hearing his intention to destroy you has moved you to do as you have done. We beg you to delay, before blood is shed. This is not written for any private fear – but because we hear and know more than you. We are true to God, king and country, and count nothing more. We have communed with the protector, who is content to do what he has often said – let the king and country be otherwise served. He has little regard for his position. He considers he was called to it by the king with your advice and the consent of all the lords, as appears in writing. He thinks it unreasonable to be violently removed. He is here with the king, where his place is, as we are. We hope for a peaceful agreement and that the protector may live in quiet. It is unreasonable for him to put himself simply in your hands without conditions. They say you seek his death; if he is himself driven to extremity, innocent blood on both sides will be on your hands. When you would have him again for service, you will realise your loss. Put any such plan out of your heads and be kind; he has never been cruel to any of you. Credit Sir Philip Hoby and return him with your answer.

    *Printed*: Tytler, i, 223–6.                                      SP 10/9, no. 26

**396.**   October 8. Windsor Castle. Sir Thomas Smith to Sir William Petre.

    Having most acquaintance because of vicinity and office, I am bold to write to you. Now is the time to show the moderation of which you have rightly boasted. By our persuasion the protector is content to refuse no reasonable conditions. He will leave office rather than that matters should come to extremes. I trust no man seeks the blood of him who has been too easy to others. I cannot think you or any of the lords there would require with blood what may be had with persuasion and honour. Join with us in moderation. I am most miserable. I cannot leave the king and him who is my master, from whom I have had all. I cannot deny I disliked some of the things you disliked; but now be charitable, that the country does not have a double tragedy in one year, and become the scorn of the world. *Postscript.* Write, if only two words of comfort to me.

    *Holograph.*

    *Printed*: Tytler, i, 228–30.                                SP 10/9, no. 27

**397.**   October 8. London. The council to sheriffs, justices of the peace, constables, headboroughs and all other royal officers and subjects.

    The duke of Somerset, abusing the king's hand, stamp and signet, and without our consent, has written to levy the king's subjects and disturb the peace for the maintenance of his own outrageous doings only. You should not levy or cause to be levied any men by force of any writing not signed by the majority of the privy council. Remain quietly at your work, without giving credit to any such slanderous rumours spread by the duke to our dishonour.

    *Signed by*: Lord Rich, lord chancellor, Lord St John, the marquess of Northampton, the earl of Warwick, the earl of Arundel, the earl of Shrewsbury, the earl of Southampton, Sir William Petre, Sir Edward Montague, Dr Nicholas Wotton and Sir John Baker.

    *Printed*: Pocock, *Troubles*, 92–3. Hoak, 150 (part only).           SP 10/9, no. 28

**398.**   Another copy of the above.

    *Signed by*: Rich, St John, Northampton, Warwick, Arundel, Shrewsbury, Southampton, Petre and Baker.                    SP 10/9, no. 29

**399.**   October 8. Markshall. [Henry Parker], Lord Morley to the council.

    I have received your letters explaining the dangerous state of the king and country because of the lord protector. As I am bound, I shall put myself and my poor power in one hour's readiness to live and die.

*Holograph.*
*Printed*: Pocock, *Troubles*, 94.                                       SP 10/9, no. 30

**400.** October 9. Wilton. Lord Russell and Sir William Herbert to the council in London.

Immediately on arrival here we received divers letters, of which we enclose copies,* from the king and protector to go to court, especially one from [the protector's] son Lord Edward. We prepared to go with the gentlemen in our company and came as far as Andover with our servants, where we learnt much, for the country was everywhere in a roar and no man knew what to do. The gentlemen had received similar letters from the king. The people had found bills sown abroad to raise them in the king's name and the protector's quarrel. We enclose copies. Had we not arrived 5,000 or 6,000 men would have gone to Windsor, besides the popular disturbance that might have arisen. The local gentry, hearing of our presence, held back and sought our opinions; we satisfied them by letters, of which we enclose copies.† Considering the uncertainty of the country, we sent Lord Edward to the protector with an answer, of which we enclose a copy.‡ We returned to Wilton to stay with the assembly of local gentry and to gather a force to serve us if necessary (which we hope not). We have sent to Bristol for some light ordnance and other necessaries. We have learned ... [? from Windsor] and specially from [Sir Michael] Stanhope's man who was here this morning that if you send thither no great business will be needed, the less if it is well followed. We cannot believe the protector will stand to violence, his quarrel being private. We have stayed all these parts, this part of Hampshire, Wiltshire, Gloucestershire, Somerset, Wales and the west, so that he can draw on nothing to do any hurt. Having a few with him, we marvel that you have not kept free passage between you and us and that we have not had better notice of your proceedings. Nevertheless we endeavour to strengthen ourselves against the worst and will soon be able to keep the highway to you, despite resistance. Let us know what you would have us do, and with what numbers. If we had known what proclamations you had set forth they would have been published here before now. Let us know this and other things by this trusty bearer. I, Sir William Herbert have also received a letter from Sir Michael Stanhope, which I enclose. *Postscript.* Since writing we received your letters by our servants. We had previously heard only from the lord great master, although he made you privy. Tell us what proclamations to publish. We have stayed sending your commission to sheriffs and justices of the peace because your order has been passed to them already.

*Slightly mutilated.*
*Printed*: Tytler, i, 231–5.                                       SP 10/9, no. 31

**401.** October 9 [enclosed with the above]. Wilton. Lord Russell and Sir William Herbert to the sheriff of Gloucestershire.

Because of variance among the king's councillors disquieting rumours have spread, which must be prevented before greater inconveniences follow. Give immediate warning throughout Gloucestershire against the publication of unsubstantiated rumours, on pain of punishment at your discretion. No man is to assemble or raise others, except as appointed by us or by letters signed by the king and six of the council. Many light commands and assemblies have been made to the confusion of the country and dishonour of the king. We have already been commanded by the king to assemble his power for the good order of the whole country. Warn all justices of the peace and other gentlemen to come to us at Wilton with such horsemen as they can, leaving order for their footmen to be in readiness for our further order.

---

\*      Not *all* the stated enclosures are extant, but see nos **372, 373, 374, 375** and **376** above.
†      No. **401** below is the one extant example.
‡      Presumably no. **390** above.

*Contemporary copy.*
*Endorsed*: Similar letters sent to other sheriffs, justices and gentlemen.

SP 10/9, no. 31(i)

**402.** Copy of no. **400** above, supplying some words now missing in the original.

SP 10/9, no. 32

**403.** October 9. The council to Princess Mary and Princess Elizabeth.*

Because the trouble between us and the duke of Somerset may have been diversely reported to you, we should explain how the matter is now come to some extremity. We have long perceived his pride and ambition and have failed to stay him within reasonable limits; but he has laboured to bring the king and country to confusion, continually declaring he meant never to account to any superior. He would reject or pass over in silence the council's advice. We resolved to treat the matter with him. But a few of us had not dined together more than twice when he took the Tower and raised the country about Hampton Court, crying that certain lords had determined to go to court and destroy the king, whom we wish as long life as any of his progenitors. When he had gathered the people at Hampton Court he brought the king into the base court and then to the gate to those outside. Having caused him to pray them to be good to him and his uncle, he said many untruths, especially that we would have him removed from office and your grace made regent with rule of the king's person, adding that it would be dangerous to have you, the next in succession, in that place. This was a great treason. None of us has by word or writing opened such matter. He concluded, most irreverently and abominably, by pointing to the king and saying that if we attempted anything against him, he [the king] should die before him. When we understood this, we thought it neither meet to go to court as we had determined nor to remain unprepared against him. So we have quietly taken the Tower for the king and furnished ourselves with the help of the city of London, which was loyal to the king before the Tower was ours. The matter was so quick and unexpected that we could not report our doings earlier. He has now carried the king to Windsor, in such sort as may show he sets no great store by him. God will, we trust, help us to deliver [the king] from his cruel and greedy hands. If it should come to extremity – which we will work to avoid – we trust you will stand by us.

*Corrected draft.*
*Printed*: Tytler, i, 248–51.

SP 10/9, no. 33

**404.** Later copy of the above.

SP 10/9, no. 34

**405.** October 9. London. The council to the king.

We have received your letters of the 8th by [Sir Philip] Hoby and heard him speak your further pleasure. We are [most]† sorry you are troubled, especially in this kind of matter – the only cause of which, as we can prove, comes from the duke of Somerset. We are grieved you should have been persuaded that we do not have the care we ought for pacifying these uproars; we are as careful as any, and shall not forget the benefits received of your father or our duties, which force us to consult and join. Had we not, you and the whole country would shortly have been imperilled; and if we should not make provision, we would not be answerable to your hereafter. Do not think that we, your whole privy council – one or two excepted – are led by private affections or would presume to write that of which we are not most assured. Think most expedient what is thought by your council, to whom, and to no man, your father appointed care of you and your most weighty affairs. We feel much wronged that you are shut up from us by

\* So addressed, but this version is clearly intended for Mary.
† Deleted.

the duke, to our great heaviness, the fear of your subjects and the wonder of the world. Do not think what your council does or agrees upon to be wilfulness. [It is true, you write, every man has his faults].* We are encouraged by your clemency and that you will approve us and our doings.

If the duke has the respect for your safety which he pretends, the consideration of his duty that his oath demands, remembrance of the performance of your father's will, and the reverence to your laws of a good subject, let him suffer us to be restored to your presence [and for a time withdraw with his family and adherents to any convenient place]* and submit himself to your council and laws. Let the assembled forces be sent away. Then we may do our duty in attending you, and after freer consultation with you, give order for your safety; so your subjects may be quiet and all occasions of stir taken away. If the duke refuses, we must think him [to keep not his oath nor be a good executor or subject]* to remain in his detestable determination [whereby you and the country may come to danger].* The protectorship was not granted by your father's will but only by agreement first among us the executors and after by others. It was committed to him during your pleasure, on condition that he should do all things by the advice of your council. Because he has so many times broken this condition, notwithstanding being often spoken to, without all hope of amendment, we think him most unworthy of those honours and trust. Other things, too many and long to be written now, may at our next access to you be considered for the conservation of your safety and the quiet of your dominions.

*Corrected draft.*

*Printed*: Burnet, v, 277–9, from the registered copy, PC 2/4, pp. 8–10 (*APC*, ii, 337–40), with some collations to the SP draft.　　　　　　　SP 10/9, no. 35

**406.**　Later copy of the above.　　　　　　　　　　　　　　　SP 10/9, no. 36

**407.**　October 9. Westminster. The council in London to the council at Windsor.

We have received your letters by [Sir Philip] Hoby and have heard him speak on the king's behalf and yours. We forbear to repeat our answers, which appear at length in our letters to the king and Mr Hoby's report. But take continual care for the king's surety and do not let him be moved from Windsor Castle, as you will answer for the contrary to your peril. It seems very strange to us and all true subjects that you allow the king to remain guarded by the duke's men, sequestered from his old sworn servants. By our letter to the king things may be soon quietly and moderately compounded. We trust none of you has cause to note one or all of us of the cruelty you often mention. We much marvel that you claim to know more than we. If you have learned of matters touching the king and the state you should have informed us, the whole council.

*Draft.*

*Printed*: Pocock, *Troubles*, 104–6. The copy as sent is in BL Cottonian MS Caligula B.7, ff. 395–396v, signed by Lord Rich, Lord St John, the marquess of Northampton, the earls of Arundel, Shrewsbury and Southampton, Sir Thomas Cheyne, Sir John Gage, Sir William Petre, Sir Edward North, Sir Edward Montague, Sir Ralph Sadler, Dr Nicholas Wotton, Sir Richard Southwell and Sir John Baker, printed in Ellis, *Original Letters*, ii, 169–70. Registered copy in PC 2/4, p. 11 (*APC*, ii, 240–1), printed in Burnet, v, 280–1.　　　　　　　　　　　　　　　　SP 10/9, no. 37

**408.**　Contemporary copy of the above.　　　　　　　　　　　SP 10/9, no. 38

**409.**　October [? 9]. Windsor Castle. Sir Thomas Smith to Sir William Petre, chief secretary.

*　　Deleted.

I thank [the earls of] Warwick and Arundel for allowing my brother George to visit me. Help moderate this tumult and it will be to your greatest honour. I am sorry it is come so far. I am unable to judge your doings, but wish the proclamation had been stayed and made for other matter. The heats of both parties and the rumours have done much hurt, but I trust there is time yet for composition or moderation. If you can, let me know by my brother how I stand. I cannot understand what I should think. I know nothing of which my conscience can accuse me. I trust my tarrying here will not be prejudicial to me, when I cannot leave; and cannot tell what might be said if I could, and left the king. I commit it all to God, and my lords' and your judgements. Tell me if anything is objected, and do for me as you would wish me do for you in like case.

*Holograph.*

*Printed*: Pocock, *Troubles*, 106–8.　　　　　　　　　　　　　　　　SP 10/9, no. 39

**410.** [October 10]. Proclamation against traitorous bills.

Lewd and seditious persons, labouring to maintain the traitorous doings of the duke of Somerset, devise vile, false and traitorous bills, papers and books, strewing them in the streets of London and elsewhere, slandering the king's council and thinking to amaze and abuse the king's good subjects who are ready to join the council for the delivery of the king, remaining to his great peril in the duke's custody, and for restoring order and quietness. The council, to avoid the inconvenience and extreme danger that by these bills might ensue to his majesty, require by his authority all good subjects to search out the writers, devisers, casters and counsellors of such bills, apprehend and present them before the council for punishment. Whoever brings such persons or reports their names and doings, if they are apprehended and their offences proved, shall receive [40]* 100 crowns reward, as shall any who apprehend or report any who by ringing bells, striking drums, proclaiming bills or letters or otherwise stir the people to the danger of the king and the slander of the council.

*Printed*: Pocock, *Troubles*, 108–9.

*Calendared*: *Tudor and Stuart Proclamations, 1485–1714*, ed. R. Steele, (Oxford, 1910), i, no. 374, from a copy printed by Richard Grafton, in the library of the Society of Antiquaries, no. 49 [*STC* 7829]. Other contemporary MS copies are in Corporation of London Record Office, Journal 16, f. 38v and Letter Book R, f. 43 [Hoak, 289 n. 87].　　　　　　　　　　　　　　　　　　　　　　　　　　SP 10/9, no. 40

**411.** October 11. The council to the ambassadors.

By the corrupt government and conspiracies of the duke of Somerset the king was in [some]* great danger and the country brought almost to ruin. We, the whole of the king's privy council consulting together, have hitherto proceeded without great stir or business, and trust to deliver the king from danger and restore the country. Because rumours abroad may be diverse, we signify the whole truth of this matter. Henry VIII obtained by act of parliament† the right to order, by his will or otherwise, the affairs of this and his other realms during the present king's minority. By his will, under the great seal, he gave executors and other councillors governance of the king during his minority and maintenance of all the country's affairs. This was sworn to by the executors [who, after the king's death, assembling in council, resolved to appoint one man their mouthpiece, to hear ambassadors and other suitors, and to answer as the country's affairs should require them]* who, nevertheless, considering it expedient to have one as their mouthpiece, to whom all who had to do with the council might resort, chose the duke of Somerset, then earl of Hertford – partly because he was one of the executors and a man of service, but especially because he was the king's maternal uncle – on condition

---

\*　　　Deleted.

†　　　35 Henry VIII c.1.

that he should do nothing touching the king's affairs without the advice and consent of the rest of the council, which he promised and solemnly swore in open council. But shortly he began to do things of most importance by himself. If he called any man he ordered the matter as he pleased, refusing to hear any man's reason but his own. He became so arrogant as to taunt those who spoke frankly in open council. We, together openly and most of us individually, often gently exhorted him to remember his promise and oath and to stay himself within the bounds of reason. But as we have devised with him for preservation of the king's person and honour, he has laboured to bring his majesty and his whole estate into such confusion as he might dispose of both, declaring that he never meant to account with any superior. No true hearted Englishman does not lament that he ever bore rule, not only for the loss of Ambleteuse, Blackness, Bolemberg and other small members about Boulogne, endangering the chief pieces there – all which might easily have been prevented if his greed to finish his four or five pompous buildings had allowed him to furnish these pieces with men, munitions and money in time – but also for the loss of Haddington in Scotland, all for want of necessaries and money to encourage the poor soldiers whom he left unpaid of notable sums. In the meantime he has entertained the main captains and ringleaders of the commons who have so lately troubled the country, as we have more fully written to you, with gifts and some with annuities. He was indeed the occasion of the tumults, as since has appeared, meaning first to destroy the nobility and other honest persons, then to have aspired to his majesty's place. Nothing else is to be conjectured of his devilish enterprises – conferences with accomplices to make himself strong, replacing honest justices of the peace with his own brood, giving his own men royal offices, and seeking by all means to enrich himself, leaving the king bare.

At length, when we saw counsel would not prevail, but he would either reject it or pass it over in silence, we thought we could suffer no longer – weighing the state of the country, and remembering our duties, unless we would consent with him in his evil doings – so we resolved friendly and quietly to treat the matter with him, and if we might by any means have brought him to reason, to have avoided all trouble and slander. A few of us had not dined above twice together but immediately he took the Tower of London and raised all the country about Hampton Court where the king lay, crying that certain lords meant to repair to court to destroy his highness. When he had gathered his people at Hampton Court he brought the king into the base court and to the gate to those outside. Having had the king pray them to be good to him and his uncle, he spoke, too slanderous and foolish to rehearse, concluding irreverently that the king would die before he were destroyed. When we understood this we thought it neither meet to go to court as we had resolved, nor to rest so unfurnished as he might use his will first upon us and afterwards more easily proceed. So we have quietly obtained the Tower for the king from him and furnished ourselves with sufficient men if need be shortly to deliver the king from danger without bloodshed, establish a better order for his safety, and restore the country to its former honour and reputation.*

We have told you all of this matter, to be declared by you to the senate,† there and otherwise to be opened as you see occasion.

*14 pp.*
*Corrected draft, in Petre's hand.*
*Printed*: Pocock, *Troubles*, 113–18.                                    SP 10/9, no. 41

**412.** October 11. Windsor. The archbishop of Canterbury, Sir William Paget, comptroller of the household and Sir Anthony Wingfield, vice-chamberlain to the council in London.

---

\*      This paragraph is substantially the same as the letter to the princesses, no. **408** above.
†      I.e. of Venice.

I, the vice-chamberlain, arrived here this morning and, according to your instructions, have the duke in my keeping. Because his chamber adjoined the king's he is moved to the lieutenant's tower, next to the gate of the middle ward, where a strong watch will be kept. The rest contained in your billet to me is forthcoming, save [Richard] Whalley, who yesterday, on hope conceived by the duke of [Sir Philip] Hoby's report, was sent by him to comfort the duchess at Beddington. With the duke were his son the earl and his young brother. We have appointed them to stay at the duke's house until your further pleasure is known. The king has a bad cold, partly from riding here by night, increased by the subtlety of the air, and much desires to be away, thinking himself a prisoner. Consider this and give order. I, the comptroller, have ordered provision at Richmond where there are already five tons of beer and four of wine. But the doctor criticises the house and wishes us rather go to Hampton Court or London. The king is well and merry. Today after breakfast he came to the vice-chamberlain and the rest of the gentlemen, whom he welcomed, asking how you were and when he should see you, saying you would be welcome. All the gentlemen kissed his hands.

*Printed*: Tytler, i, 241–3. SP 10/9, no. 42

**413.** Copy of the above. SP 10/9, no. 43

**414.** October 11. London. Letter from the council there.

By our former letters we signified our doings, and upon occasion of assemblies of men made by the duke of Somerset, desired you to repair to us [with as m]any men as you might for the king's surety. The king is now safe, and without any tumult or great business the duke is in custody. Stay your numbers without further travail. Our thanks for your good readiness.

*Signed by*: Lord St John, the marquess of Northampton, the earl of Warwick, the earl of Shrewsbury, the earl of Southampton, Lord Wentworth, Sir John Gage, Sir Edward Montague, Sir John Baker, Dr Nicholas Wotton and Sir Richard Southwell.
*Printed*: Pocock, *Troubles*, 118–19. SP 10/9, no. 44

**415.** October 13. The council to [Sir Edmund Peckham], lieutenant of the Tower of London.

In previous letters we ordered that none should speak with the duke of Somerset or any other prisoner we commit, and think you respect the importance of the matter. Servants attending the duke and other prisoners shall remain continually with their masters, to avoid secret practices and intelligence. Give Tanner and others of the king's servants appointed to attend the duke similar order.

*Draft.*
*Printed*: Pocock, *Troubles*, 120. SP 10/9, no. 45

**416.** October 16. The council to lords lieutenant.

Levy immediately [*blank*] able men in the county of [*blank*] for the king's service in the wars, of which [*blank*] to be archers and the rest pikemen and billmen, appropriately armed, to be at Dover by [*blank*] at the latest, and from there transported to Boulogne. Take the idle and ringleaders in the late sedition. They shall receive money for their coats and conduct at Dover.

*Draft.* SP 10/9, no. 46

**417.** [October 16]. Memorandum of numbers levied [for Boulogne] and ? those who levied them.

Sussex – 150: the earl of Arundel and Lord De La Warr. Hampshire – 150: [Lord St John], lord great master, the earls of Arundel and Southampton. Surrey – 100: the justices.

Kent – 200: the justices. Essex – 150: the earl of Oxford and the justices. Suffolk – 250: Lord Wentworth and the justices.

[Sir Thomas Cheyne], lord warden [of the Cinque Ports] and Dean [Nicholas] Wotton to go to the emperor to explain the removing of the duke of Somerset and the state of Boulogne, and to require 4,000 footmen and 2,000 horsemen at our expense; to levy presently 1,000 men to send to Boulogne from the above shires, especially those busiest in the rebellion.                                                               SP 10/9, no. 47

**418.**   October 22. Report on the prisoners in the Tower, made by [Sir Edmund] Molyneux, king's serjeant at law, and Henry Bradshaw, attorney-general.

Thomas, [d]* late duke of Norfolk: attainted of high treason. Edward Courtenay: by procurement of others broke the prison there. Robert, Lord Maxwell ('Mayfyld'), Scot: has his liberty. Anthony Foscue, late marshal of Ireland: intended to sell his office and to have gone with Geoffrey Poole, his father-in-law, it is supposed – to be examined concerning the king's supremacy: Mr Wotton, Mr Gage and the lieutenant.† The bishop of Winchester: committed by the council for contempt and preaching. Julius de Carcano, Italian: for bringing in counterfeit testons; many times examined, but denies it and there are no witnesses – by Mr Wotton, to be convened and on submission pardoned.† Robert Maule, laird of Panmure, Scot: taken out of his house in Scotland by the king's soldiers during the wars; to be released for redemption of [Sir Andrew] Dudley. David Douglas, earl of Morton, son of Sir George Douglas, Scot, and James, his elder brother: both taken in the wars in Scotland. William West: intended to poison his cousin, Lord De La Warr. James Noble, Scot: taken on the seas; has lands and goods – Worthington.† Patrick Barron, merchant, Scot: taken in the wars; broke Colchester prison; has goods of unknown value – Lambert.† Sir John Rybald of London, Frenchman: served in the king's wars about seven years past in various places; has by the king's patent 500 crowns for life; committed because he was going to Rye to pass into France to see his children, as he says: twice examined by Mr Comptroller; in prison two years; the lieutenant reports him an apt soldier. John Harrington, late servant to the lord admiral: committed at his arrest; examined before the lord great master and the earl of Southampton and other times before Mr Smith – to be discharged.† [Sir William Sharington: attainted of treason]* – p[ardoned].† Semaryall, Mundell le Bois, Andrew Denere, Lemonyall, Peter Longere, Lewis de Vale, Frenchmen: taken on the seas between Scotland and France – to be spoken with by Mr Wotton, Mr Gage and Mr Lieutenant.† William Hychecockes, late of [*blank*], Buckinghamshire, carpenter: committed for conspiracies and seditious words; examined by Mr Comptroller. Richard Coole of 'Mynnyt', Somerset, mariner: pirate for a year; took divers prizes; at last sued to the lord deputy of Ireland, [Sir Edward] Bellingham, to submit himself to the king's mercy; the deputy commanded him to go to Strangford Castle in Ireland, which the Scots had taken; he did, and restored it to its owner, then helped the deputy's servant against Savage, a rebel in Ireland, and the deputy promised him his pardon; he went to the Isle of Man, landed his mate as a pledge, and shortly afterwards was taken by Cornelius and others, of his own good will; in prison since May – to be examined and ordered by the lord admiral's officers.† Robert Bell of Gazeley, Suffolk, labourer: committed on Whitsun eve by Lord Wentworth, who examined him after he and John Fuller sued against Mr Rouse for certain wrongs – to justice.† John Fuller of 'Canon', Suffolk, collarmarker: committed on Whitsun eve by Lord Wentworth's command because he and Robert Capp procured a supplication against Mr Syder and Mr Rowse for certain wrongs and destruction of their corn – to justice.† Robert Capp of 'Canon', Suffolk, labourer: committed on Whit Wednesday by Lord

---

\*        Deleted.
†        Words after the dash are inserted.

Wentworth's command because he, John Fuller, Kynge, Stephenson and Bell made a supplication to the king against Robert Syder and William Rowse for their corn, being every year's land; all examined by Lord Wentworth – to justice.* Thomas Kynge of Gazeley, Suffolk, smith: committed the same Wednesday by Lord Wentworth's command because John Fuller desired him to send for Bell to make supplication and was at no commotion; examined by Lord Wentworth; they all say they gave Thomas Boughton of Bury, learned in spiritual law, four marks to make their supplication and solicit their justice, and he promised to get from the council a commission against Syder and Rowse – justice.* John Stephenson of Bury St Edmunds, Suffolk: arrested by Lord Wentworth's command because he was accused for saying that if John (*sic*) Bell went to execution a hundred men would fetch him away; he denies these words, saying he was in prison on June 12 and in no camp – justice.* James Robet [*corrected to*] Rowett, merchant of Paris: arrested by the mayor of London; brought to London 50 tons of wine sold to Mr Nashe to the king's use, and the money owing to him; has been here two months; never examined: [to speak with the mayor]† – to remain for redemption of some prisoner of ours in France.* John Moreman, D.D., of Exeter: committed for preaching in the west; accused by the dean of St Paul's and other commissioners there; examined by the archbishop of Canterbury; the sermon upon which he is accused is in the Fleet with other stuff of his. Richard Crispyn, M.A., of Exeter: likewise accused and examined. John Feckenham, B.D., late chaplain to the late bishop of London: arrested by Lord Grey in Oxfordshire and sent to London: [committed by the duke of Somerset and (*inserted*: never) examined by Mr Mason]† – to be examined by Mr Wotton & c.* Richard Tomson of Harting, Sussex, tile maker: arrested by Sir Anthony Windsor on the Monday after St James's Day; accused of saying that the king should have trouble before All Hallowtide, which he denied; never examined before; he says Mr Windsor's servants accused him – to justice.* Thomas Rychardson of Plaitford, Hampshire [*recte* Wiltshire], clerk: committed by [John] Kingesmelle for speaking in favour of the western men, which he denies – to justice.* John Unthanke, parson of Hedley, Hampshire: committed at the end of August and examined by the duke of Somerset; came to London on letters from the lord grand (*sic*) master, accused of a vision in his sickness, which he now denies – to be examined by the earl of Southampton.* Robert Kette of Wymondham, Norfolk, tanner – justice.* William Kett, his brother: at large in the Tower – justice.* Sir John Bartylfyld, Frenchman: retained in the king's service with £250 pension under the great seal; never examined but committed to the Tower by Mr Smith. Peter Pawle, Italian, sea diver: committed about five weeks past by the duke of Somerset because he left Portsmouth (where he had taken guns from a sunken ship) towards the earl of Arundel's to take certain of his stuff out of the sea – to be examined by Mr Wotton &c. The lord great master can inform.* Symond Penbroke: committed for coining money; has a signed bill of pardon according to the lieutenant – p[ardoned].* Humphrey Arundell, esq., of Helland, Cornwall: confesses that he and two others fled into a wood for fear of the rebels and there remained two days; afterwards his pregnant wife desired him to come to her, which he did; then a man of Bodmin came and procured him to go with him to the rebels, which he refused; more rebels came and forced him to Bodmin; on the morrow he sent to Sir Hugh Trevanyon to know what he should do; he advised him to tarry with the rebels, to be in their favour and learn their doings; after the rebels made a supplication to which he was privy he feigned sickness and returned home. The rebels forcibly fetched him to go with them again; he stayed divers rebels; at Launceston he fled and declared the matter to Sir Richard Grenfyld and was stayed there; examined by the knight marshal and another time by Mr Smith – justice.* John Burye, gent., of Silverton, Devon, servant to Sir Thomas Denys: came to Exeter to stay there with his

---

\*        Words after the dash are inserted.
†        Deleted.

harness; waited upon his master and returned home, when he was taken by 500 rebels, remained with them until the last fray, and was at the fray at Kingweston, Somerset; examined by the lord privy seal, the lord chancellor and Mr Smith – justice.* John Wyncheland, esq., of Tregarrick, Cornwall: sent for by the rebels' post on pain of burning his house; resorted to them and remained four or five weeks; taken at Bodmin and was there continually, at no fray; examined by the lord privy seal, Lord Grey and Mr Mason – justice.* Thomas Holmes, yeoman of Blisland, Cornwall: went with the parishioners of Blisland to Bodmin and remained with the rebels until the end, against his will; in the field, about a mile from the fray; examined by Mr Herbert and afterwards by Mr North and Mr Mason – justice.* Prisoners lately committed: the duke of Somerset, Sir Ralph Vane, [Thomas] Fisher, Somerset's secretary, John Bowes, treasurer of the mint at Durham Place, Richard Paladye, Somerset's clerk of the works, Sir Michael Stanhope, Sir Thomas Smith, Sir John Thynne, [Edward] Wolf of the privy chamber, William Grey of Reading, [John] Hales.

    *Printed*: Tytler, i, 268–73 (part only). Rouse-Troup, *The Western Rebellion*, 344–6 (part only).                                        SP 10/9, no. 48

**419.**    October 22. Geneva. John Calvin to the duke of Somerset.

    We must thank God for befriending you in setting up the purity and rule of His service in England. But present circumstances, man's nature and the workings of Antichrist put you in need of holy exhortations. Your late troubles were doubtless very hard, especially because many have taken them as an occasion of slander, as they were partly provoked under colour of changing religion. Recall the tribulations of King Ezechias when he purged Judaea of idolatry. Eventually the gospel will pacify men; as in the early days of Christendom its spreading has been followed by universal upheavals. But in feeling the blows we ought to behold the hand of Him who strikes us and His reasons – our slackness is less excusable now that we know His word.

    You have two kinds risen against the king and realm – fantastical people who would set all to confusion under colour of the gospel, and stubborn papists. They all deserve punishment by the sword committed to you, as conspirators against God and the king. Extreme libertarians are set to work by Satan to defame the gospel, as though it engendered nothing but disorder. These and the papists are the scourges of God. Those who profess the gospel, particularly nobles and magistrates, should set an example by their own soberness, taking Christ as their model. Use you position principally to this end, to pursue a full reformation of the church in (1) teaching the people, (2) extirpating abuses, and (3) correcting vices. As to (1), there is no need to tell you true doctrine. But there are in England few sermons, the gospel mostly read in lectures: you do not have enough good preachers, and must guard against foolish fantasies of unlearned speakers. But first there should be an agreed summary of the learning they ought to preach, which all prelates and curates should swear to as a condition of holding any ecclesiastical charge. Secondly, there should be a common form of instruction for children and the ruder sort of people. Catechism is the seed that multiplies from age to age. In the meantime, it is good and necessary to restrict parsons to a written form. Thirdly, the catechism should serve against all curiosity and extravagant invention, as also should the form of the sacraments and public prayers. The reformation will not succeed unless unfolded by preaching.

    (2). The papacy is a bastard Christendom, which God will disavow on the last day, as He has now condemned it by His word. It is not enough, as some propose under shadow of moderation, to uproot only the principal abuses and leave others untouched. Nevertheless we must avoid extremities and accommodate ceremonies to the rudeness of the people. Prepare things for the young king so he has only to maintain an established

---

\*     Words after the dash are inserted.

order. An example of your incomplete reformation is in the prayer for the dead: even though this is not taken as an acknowledgement of purgatory, the Lord's Supper is too holy to be spotted with human inventions. Lesser but still inexcusable offences are the ceremonies of cream* and extreme unction. The apostles used oil to heal by miracles; but when the miracle is ceased, so should the sign. Men should not compromise over spiritual things for the sake of peace with their neighbours, as they may do in worldly affairs. Nothing displeases God more than the modification of His will by human wisdom. The reformation is a work of His hand. If we follow Him we shall more easily avoid temptations which might stop us in the middle way.

(3). Although you doubtless have good laws, the general disorder I see in the world constrains me to pray you take care that men are kept in good discipline. Although violence and theft are punished as they offend other men, drunkenness, adultery and blasphemy are treated less severely, if at all, though they are also offensive to God. Because these sins go unpunished God takes His vengeance on us all.

*13 pp.*

*Contemporary translation.*

*Published*: by Somerset in 1550 [*STC* 4407, 4408].

*Printed*: G.C. Gorham, *Gleanings of a few scattered ears during the period of the Reformation in England*, (1857), 55–71, from another MS. For the dating of this letter see Bush, 110 n. 71.                                                                            SP 10/5, no. 8

**420.**   October 31. Westminster. The council to [Sir William] Godolphin, captain of the Isles of Scilly.

Sir Richard Southwell and Sir Edward North shall receive from you and your officers regular notice of your furniture and wants of men, munitions, victuals and other necessaries for the king's service, to inform the rest of us that by our advice they may order supply of the same. Follow the directions of either of them as if they came from us all.

*Fair copy, unsigned.*                                                                            SP 10/9, no. 49

**421.**   [October 31]. Division of responsibilities among councillors.

Boulogne – [the earl of] Arundel. Calais with the marches – Sir Edward Wotton, Sir John Gage. Ireland – the lord great master [Lord St John], the master of the horse [Sir William Herbert].† The north and its victualling – [the earl of] Shrewsbury, Mr Comptroller [Sir William Paget], Sir Richard Cotton, Mr Cofferer [John Ryther]. Alderney and Scilly – Sir Richard Southwell, Sir Edward North. Isle of Wight and Portsmouth – the earl of Southampton. Victualling the sea – men at the lord admiral's [the earl of Warwick's] appointment.‡ Foresight for money – by weekly treasurer's report. Mints – the earl of Southampton.

*Printed*: Tytler, i, 273–4.                                                                            SP 10/9, no. 50

**422.**   [October]. Duties of the earl of Warwick as constable of Dover [Castle], lord warden and admiral of the Cinque Ports.§

[1]. Within Dover Castle and the Cinque Ports: all whales, goods and chattels of felons, fugitives and outlaws as the king has, as appears by royal letters patent to the earl. [*In margin*: nothing in use but wrecks. To be enquired whether the lord warden or the ports have the most right to the rest within any port]. [2]. Every distress brought into the castle for a night; for every great beast – 1d., for the poll, and for every four sheep – 1d.

---

*     Confirmation.
†     Appointed 2 December 1549.
‡     Re-appointed 28 October 1549.
§     Warwick never took up these offices.

[*In margin*: lost because the castle ward is taken away by act of parliament of Henry VIII*]. [3]. Surplus of all ward money of the castle and amercements for lack of payment remaining clear after the wages and clothing of the castle officers paid. [*In margin*: likewise taken away]. [4]. £4 a year for pasture of the castle, above tithe paid to the church of the same. [*In margin*: long been £6]. [5]. 144 mulvel fish from the inhabitants of the port and town of Faversham at Lammas Day; as appears in the exchequer accounts in the castle, they pay the warden 10 marks for every default. [*In margin*: Faversham to pay or show how it can discharge itself]. [6]. Fines for contempt and disobedience and forfeitures of recognisances entered for breaking the king's peace in the court of conscience at St James's Church, Dover. [*In margin*: still in use, may be good profit]. [7]. All fines and amercements for the court of admiralty belonging to the lord warden there; 1s. 8d. to him for every £1 recovered. [*In margin*: still in force]. [8]. In the sessions of the admiralty of the Cinque Ports, his shares and fines of all trespasses in the same jurisdictions, and all other profits, whales and forfeitures. [*In margin*: still in force, good profit]. [9]. 3s. 4d. from every enemy of the king captured, after ransom paid for safe conduct home. [*In margin* : out of use, but due when occasion shall serve]. [10]. 3s. 4d. at least of the master of every boat of the Cinque Ports for licence of safe conduct to fish at herring time, and as much at mackerel time. If all the fishing boats, or at least 120, fish twice a year, the admiral's duty is at least £40. [*In margin*: not used of late, but may be revived]. [11]. 100 marks for every erroneous judgement given by the mayors and jurats of the Cinque Ports at the high court of Shipway, which may only be held in the lord warden's presence. [12]. 100 marks for every wrongful execution, extortion or oppression by the bailiffs of the Cinque Ports. [*In margin*: in force].                                    SP 10/9, no. 51

**423.** [? October]. Information to the council of embezzling of goods belonging to the late lord protector by his servants, from Syon and Sheen.

Conveyed to [Richard] Whalley's house at Wimbledon on the Monday after the duke of Somerset went from Hampton Court to Windsor at night: two loads of coffers and other stuff. That morning the duchess of Somerset carried openly four square caskets and lighted with them at Mr Whalley's. That night were conveyed to [Sir Michael] Stanhope's house at Beddington: two loads of coffers and other stuff; two loads of coffers were conveyed to Croydon, to what place uncertain, for such scouts were there that no man could see their receipt and unloading. To the house of Ravys, clerk, the duke's comptroller at Roehampton was conveyed one load of stuff the following night. Davy, the duke's porter, that week conveyed to his house at Richmond a coffer with two books, with other stuff often the same week. Walter Blackwell, his footman, dwelling at Richmond, made much conveyance every day and night home to his house of stuff and goods. Halfeld, yeoman of the scullery, conveyed to his house at Richmond many coffers, bedding and other stuff, by day and night, with a bag with two bushels of meal and a square casket. Ruttur in Richmond, carter, conveyed coffers, bedding and other stuff the same week. Another carter, William Smyth, dwelling in Richmond, conveyed coffers and other stuff to his house by night and day. Certain stuff was conveyed by boats at night to Kew, but uncertain where it was laid, save that the duke had three servants dwelling in the town – Sir Miles Partridge, [William] Turner, his physician and Gely, gentleman usher; no man can tell to which the goods were conveyed, because of such scouts as were present on Sunday night that week, who would allow none to look out at his door. Huddy, the duke's surgeon, on Friday that week before day, after the duke went to Windsor, conveyed two geldings from Sheen and his boy rode away with them from Turner's house at Kew before day. The week before he broke open a door at Syon and conveyed to Turner's house three beds and a coffer at night; the bellringer of the works at Syon who kept the water gate let him in and out; being examined he

*       14 & 15 Henry VIII c. 28.

can tell of more conveyance. Wetheredd, surveyor of the works, that week conveyed by carts from Syon bedding, carpets, hangings and other stuff to his house at Isleworth. Springe, bailiff of Syon, sold as much of the duke's wood as he could, all the week the duke was at Windsor, and received much money. James Lawrence of Ham, the duke's warrener, conveyed two beds and other stuff from the duke's warren house that week by night.

    *Printed*: Pocock, *Troubles*, 120–2.                                    SP 10/9, no. 52

**424.**  [? October]. Inventory of the king's goods taken by the duke of Somerset, given in by Sir Walter Mildmay.

    Plate, belonging to the late college of St Stephen, Westminster, delivered to him; rich copes, altar cloths and hangings belonging to the college, of which the duke had the best, Sir Ralph Vane and [Sir John] Thynne the rest. The duke of Norfolk's stuff and jewels delivered by Sir John Gates. The best of [Sir William] Sharington's stuff and jewels at London and Lacock. The admiral's stuff at Bromham and Sudeley. Lead, stone and stuff of Syon, Reading and Glastonbury, of great value. The instalment of the king's alum, sold to the merchants of London for fourteen of fifteen years day of payment, for which the duke, [Sir Thomas] Smith and Thynne had £14,000. 1,000 marks given the king by the city of London at his coronation. The customers' offices in England in which he had by Thynne's practice notable sums. The king's secret houses at Westminster and elsewhere, in which he only was privy half a year after the king's death. The gifts and exchanges passed in his name since the king's death. It is thought much land was conveyed for the duke in trust in the names of Thynne, [Robert] Keleway, [John] Seymour, [John] Berwick, [Matthew] Colthurst and others of his men, that they have made assurance again of all to the duke and his heirs, and that they know best where all evidences of his lands and specialties remain. The duke's diet of 8 marks paid out of the augmentations court.

    *Items not specified.*
    *Printed*: Pocock, *Troubles*, 123–4.                                    SP 10/9, no. 53

**425.**  November [5]. Instructions [from the council] to William Tirrell, sent to survey the Isles of Scilly.

    Taking this memorial and other letters and books prepared, he shall repair to the isles, and by summoning [Sir William] Godolphyn, general captain, and [John] Kyllygrew, surveyor of the fortifications, and otherwise [inform himself]* of the state of things. He shall peruse the whole isle and consider any wants and disorders. He shall immediately have the men mustered and see if their numbers, entertainment and wages agree with those in a book he shall receive from Sir Edward North. He shall cashier and replace those sick or otherwise unable. He may show the soldiers and others that the receiver of the duchy of Cornwall† is ordered to continue payment by warrant dormant of wages due. He shall consider what ordnance, shot, powder, armour, weapons and other munitions furnish the forts and order supplies. He must consider whether the forts are best placed for defence, their strength and, if they are not completed, the charges of finishing them; what store there is, and order further provision as requisite. If the forts are not best placed and are not mostly completed he may order their stay until further order. He shall survey the length and breadth of the isle; how many roads and landing places are about it; how they may be defended; whether the appointed men are sufficient for defence; when the fort is made, and if it is not, what further furniture is requisite; how victualling is made; how it may be continued, and by whom; how many dwell in the country; whether they farm or fish; what land any husbandman has with his house,

<hr/>

\*      Deleted, but still necessary for the sense of the passage.
†      Sir Thomas Arundell.

at what rent, to whom he pays it, and by what grant. If any unlet land requires to be leased, order may be taken by commission from the chancellor of augmentations. Tirrell shall consider whether the isles are sufficient in grain and cattle feed, and enquire for a man of trust and experience dwelling near the isles to take general charge under the appointed commissioners, and have some entertainment. Tirrell shall note all this, and anything worth consideration, order redress and supply in immediate matters, and inform himself thoroughly of all others, that on his return we may be fully advertised. We require him to use all his dexterity, for the place is of such importance.

*6 pp.*
*Draft.* SP 10/9, no. 54

**426.** November 20. Westminster. The council to justices of the peace.
The king is informed that farmers and others having store of wheat and other grain greedily forbear to bring any to market, and themselves buy and engross to make such unreasonable prices as they choose; which, if suffered, would bring great dearth and destruction of many people. The king, minding to provide for this great inconvenience and punish the doers, requires you to assemble to understand his pleasure, and then divide yourselves among the hundreds and parts of the shire, joined by such other upright gentlemen as you think convenient, to search every barn, granary and house of every farmer and others having corn to sell. Order such as may spare it to bring every market day to such markets as you appoint such quantities of wheat, malt, barley and other grain as you shall limit. Allow every man to find for his house, sow his summer corn, pay his corn rent and fulfil bargains you find they have made with noblemen, gentlemen or others for the expenses of their houses. This is to continue until God sends plenty. If any refuse your orders or embezzle or hide their corn, imprison them at your discretion. Let us know if the offence is notable. Search for those having sufficient of their own who regrate and buy to advance the price. Arrest them and commit them to gaol, to remain without bill of mainprize until we give further order.
*Signed by*: Lord St John, Lord Russell, the marquess of Northampton, the earl of Arundel, the earl of Shrewsbury, Lord Wentworth, Sir William Petre, Sir William Herbert, Sir Anthony Wingfield, Sir Richard Southwell and Sir Edward North.
*Postscript*: Give the mayors, bailiffs and other officers of all market towns a list of those appointed to bring grain to the markets, the quantity and sort to be brought, so that any offenders may be punished. SP 10/9, no. 55

**427.** November 27. The council to justices of the peace.
The king's pleasure has been signified by our former letters for levying [*blank*] able footmen in the county of [*blank*] for his service in the wars, to be transported [to Boulogne]* over the seas, with further charge to appoint the greatest doers and ringleaders in the late sedition, all which we understand you have done. We are since informed that many of those appointed, having received their coats and conduct money, are returned without passport [or licence]* of their captain. Search and commit any such to ward, to be ordered according to our laws. If you find any dismissed by the captain with his passport whom you think able to serve as first appointed, examine why he was dismissed, whether he gave or promised the captain or others any reward for the same, with such further matter as you may obtain by any means, informing us of your doings.
*Draft.* SP 10/9, no. 56

**428.** December 25. Westminster. The king to the bishops.
The Book of Common Prayer was set forth by act of parliament and commanded to be used by all in this realm. Nevertheless divers unquiet and evil disposed persons, since

* Deleted.

the apprehension of the duke of Somerset, have rumoured that they should have again their old Latin service, conjured bread and water and suchlike superstitious ceremonies, as though the book had been the act of the duke only. We, by the advice of our privy council, considering the book our act and that of the whole realm in parliament, being scriptural and agreeable to the order of the primitive church and much to the edifying of our subjects, to put away such vain expectation, require you to command the dean and prebendaries of your cathedral church, the parson, vicar or curate and churchwardens of every parish in your diocese, to deliver to you or your deputy all antiphoners, missals, grails, processionals, manuals, legends, pies, portases, journals and ordinals of the Sarum, Lincoln, York, Bangor, Hereford or any other private use, and all other service books which would prevent the use of the Book of Common Prayer. Deface and destroy them, that they may never be hereafter used. Any who refuse to bring such a book commit to ward until you have certified us. Search for hidden books from time to time and deal with them as we have appointed. Since obstinate persons refuse to pay for communion bread and wine, according to the book, so that communion is often omitted on Sunday, convene such before you and admonish them to keep order; if they refuse, punish them by suspension, excommunication or other censures of the church. Fail not, as you will avoid our displeasure.

> *Facsimile signatures*: Sign manual, the archbishop of Canterbury, Lord St John, Lord Russell, Lord Rich, lord chancellor, the marquess of Dorset, the earl of Arundel, the earl of Warwick and the bishop of Ely.
> *Copy*: from BL Stowe MS 142, ff. 16–16v of which a facsimile and transcript appear in W.J. Hardy, *The Handwriting of the Kings and Queens of England*, (1893), 73–9 (where the MS is wrongly cited).
> *Printed* (SP version): Pocock, *Troubles*, 127–9. Wilkins, iii, 37.          SP 10/9, no. 57

**429.**   December 28. Kingston. The duchess of Suffolk to William Cecil.

I received your letter riding to [Martin] Bucer. You encourage me to become as you paint me. You have the excuse why I do not write of my own hand, but it does not suffice me with the hearts of prisoners alone, as though they had nothing else to part with, as you say; it makes me think you have already shifted your apparel, though not your lodging, or else you might have given me 'some quick cataile of your soyle'. If my provision were no better than your presents, my household should 'chewe thankes for chewettes'. But you shall fare thereafter: I have shaped my deserts accordingly. Only I fear lest you call back again for some of your thanks, but that I have matter of record against you. So I beshrew those not merry if it is not I. *Postscript.* For your master's* cause, I am sure he has used deeds not words; for yours, pray Cornelius [Zifridius] that he shall have his money in a fortnight, or a little and [? the rest] later. *Further postscripts.* But it is almost unpardonable of one of my best friends to give such sentence; you might rather have said deeds without words. I cannot say too much of him.

> *Postscripts holograph.*                                                  SP 10/9, no. 58

**430.**   [December]. William Cecil to Dr Cornelius [Zifridius].

Commendations to you and your wife. Heed your diet, that the country may get the praise of your amendment. Our hope comes slowly forward, having the hindrance of heavy adversaries (but I trust the strength of our friends shall prevail in a few days). I have sent this letter to show what the good lady writes of you, to whom I have again made excuses for not writing.

> *On the dorse of the preceding letter.*
> *Printed*: Read, 473 n. 54.                                              SP 10/9, no. 58(i)

---

*       Not Somerset but an unknown patron, according to Read, 59.

[For SP 10/9, no. 59 see no. **843** below.]

**431.** [Before 1550]. Yearly value of all spiritual promotions in England of £50 or above. *Bishoprics.* Canterbury – £3,223.18.6. London – £1,517.8.0. Winchester – £3,885.3.4. Lincoln – £1,962.17.0½d. Salisbury – £1,367.11.8. Norwich – £978.19.4½d. Ely – £2,534.18.5⅛d. Bath and Wells – £1,843.14.5¼d. Worcester – £1,049. Exeter – £1,546.14.5½d. Coventry and Lichfield – £705.5.2⅜d. Durham – £2,831.17.0¼d. York – £2,035.3.7⅜d. Carlisle – £531.4.11½d. Chester – £271.4.8. Rochester – £411.11.0¾d. Chichester – £677.1.3. Hereford – £768.10.10½d. Llandaff – £144.4.1. St Asaph – £187.11.5. St David's – £477.1.10½d. Bangor – £148.6.8. Westminster* – £573.5.6¾d. Peterborough – £410.11.2⅝d. Oxford – £354.16.3¼d. Gloucester – £315.7.2. Bristol – £383.8.4¾d. *Kent.* Archdeaconry of Canterbury – £163.1.10. Vicarage of Ashford – £70.8.2. Rectory of Cliffe – £50. Rectory of Wrotham – £50.8.0. *Calais.* Rectory of La Marque – £56.13.10. Rectory of Oye – £50.7.6. *Sussex.* Deanery of Chichester – £58.11.4. Treasurership of Chichester Cathedral – £62.6.8. *Norfolk.* Archdeaconry of Norwich – £71.1.1½d. Archdeaconry of Norfolk – £143.8.3½d. Archdeaconry of Suffolk – £89.1.11. Archdeaconry of Sudbury – £76.9.4½d. Deanery of Norwich – £102.2.0½d. *Huntingdonshire.* Archdeaconry of Northampton – £107.7.0. Prebend of Leighton Bromswold† – £57.15.1. *Bedfordshire.* Prebend of Leighton Buzzard – £68.15.11. *Northamptonshire.* Rectory of Castor – £52.12.7. *Leicestershire.* Rectory of Bottesford – £51.4.11. Archdeaconry of Leicester – £80.12.4. Rectory of [Market] Bosworth – £55.18.2. *Hertfordshire.* Rectory of [Much] Hadham – £66.13.4. *London and Middlesex.* Deanery of St Paul's – £210.12.1½d. Archdeaconry of Essex – £52. Archdeaconry of Colchester – £50. Archdeaconry of Middlesex – £60. Rectory of St Magnus – £67.12.1. Rectory of St Dunstan in the West – £60. Rectory of St Clement without New Temple [St Clement Danes] – £51. *Essex.* Vicarage of [Saffron] Walden – £53.10.0. *Lincolnshire.* Dean and chapter of Lincoln – £575.7.10¾d., divided among canons residentiary, deanery – £196.10.8, chancellorship – £54.1.6. Prebend of Leighton Buzzard – £68.15.8. College of vicars choral in Lincoln Cathedral – £145.11.2, divided among 25 vicars. Archdeaconry of Lincoln – £179.19.0. Archdeaconry of Huntingdon – £57.14.2. Archdeaconry of Bedford – £57.2.4. Rectory of Algakirk – £50.18.1. *Cambridge colleges.* Christ's – £190.10.10½d. St John's – £507.12.11¾d. Trinity – £1,000. Queens' – £230.15.2½d. Pembroke – £153.17.9. Clare – £84.13.9. Jesus – £87.18.3. Trinity Hall – £72.1.0. Corpus Christi – £83.16.8. Gonville – £99.6.9½d. Peterhouse – £125.7.0¼d. King's – £751.8.1½d. *Oxfordshire.* Archdeaconry of Oxford – £71.6.0. *Oxford colleges.* Merton – £353.12.2½d. The Queen's – £302.3.10. University – £78.14.7. All Souls – £393.2.3½d. Lincoln – £101.8.10. Oriel – £158.15.0. Corpus Christi – £382.8.9½d. Christ Church – £2,000. New College – £887.7.8½d. Exeter – £81.5.0. Balliol – £74.5.0¾d. Brasenose – £111.0.3¼d. Magdalen – £1,066.5.2½d. *Berkshire.* St George's Chapel, Windsor – £1,396.17.1¼d. Archdeaconry of Berkshire – £54.18.4¼d. Prebend of Blewbury – £54. *Wiltshire.* Vicarage of Bradford [on Avon] with chapels of Westwood, [Limpley] Stoke, Winsley, [South] Wraxall, Atworth and Holt – £50.0.6. Rectory of Great Bedwyn – £63.13.4. Deanery of Salisbury – £204.10.0. Precentorship of Salisbury Cathedral – £99.6.8. Chancellorship of Salisbury Cathedral – £56.5.9. Treasurership of Salisbury Cathedral – £101.3.0. Archdeaconry of Dorset – £88.5.4. Archdeaconry of Berkshire – £54.18.4¼d. Archdeaconry of Sarum – £88.5.4. Archdeaconry of Wiltshire with church of Minety – £70.12.2. Prebend of Highworth – £62. Prebend of Kingsteignton – £63.13.4. Hospital of St John, Ansty [with that of] Trebigh, Cornwall –

---

\*    Bishopric dissolved on 1 April 1550 [*CPR* 1549–50, 171–2].

†    There were two prebends of Leighton Bromswold, of the manor and the church, until the alienation of the former on 25 February 1548: R.E.G. Cole (ed.), *Chapter acts of the Cathedral church of St Mary of Lincoln, A.D. 1547–1559*, (Lincoln Record Society, xv, 1920), 19–20. If the document is after this date the prebend referred to is that of Leighton Ecclesia.

£81.8.5½d. *Dorset.* Deanery of Bristol – £100. Hospital of St John Baptist [*unidentified*] – £50.10.4¼d. Prebend of Gillingham – £54. *Yorkshire.* Precentorship of York Minster – £89.10.8. Deanery of York – £308.10.6. Archdeaconry of York – £90.3.0. Chancellorship of York Minster – £85.6.8. Subdeanery of York Minster – £51.10.4¼d. Archdeaconry of the East Riding – £62.14.2½d. Archdeaconry of Nottingham – £61.0.8½d. Archdeaconry of Richmond – £156.8.1½d. Prebend of Wistow – £65.16.0. College of vicars choral [Bedern] – £136.5.5. Wardenship of the fabric – £76.11.6. Hospital of St Leonard, York – £262.11.1½d. Chapel of the Blessed Virgin Mary and Holy Angels by York Minster called [St] Sepulchre's Chapel – £138.19.2½d. Rectory of Spofforth – £73.6.8. Rectory of Darfield – £53.1.8. College or almshouse of Holy Trinity, Pontefract – £182.14.7. Vicarage of Halifax – £84.13.6. Hospital of St James by Northallerton – £56.2.2. *Nottinghamshire.* Archdeaconry of Nottingham – £59.15.4. [*Archdeaconry of] Richmond.* Rectory of Bedale – £89.4.8. Rectory of Warton – £74.10.1. Vicarage of Kendal – £92.5.0. Rectory of Romaldkirk – £58.14.0. *Cumberland.* Vicarage of [Great] Crosthwaite – £58.8.11. *Durham.* Archdeaconry of Durham – £100. Rectory of Houghton [le Spring] – £124. Sherburn Hospital – £135.7.0. Greatham Hospital – £97.6.3. Rectory of Wearmouth Episcopi – £89.7.0. Rectory of Stanhope – £67.6.8. Rectory of Brancepeth – £60.10.4. Rectory of Sedgefield – £73.18.0. Rectory of Haughton [le Skerne] – £53.6.8. Vicarage of Rothbury – £58.6.8. *Lancashire.* Rectory of Wigan – £80.13.4. Rectory of Winwick – £102.9.8. Rectory of Walton [le Dale] – £69.16.10. *Cornwall.* Vicarage of Madron – £50. Rectory of St Columb major – £53.6.8. *Devon.* Deanery of Exeter – £158. Precentorship of Exeter Cathedral – £99.13.4. Chancellorship of Exeter Cathedral – £59. Archdeaconry of Exeter – £60.15.10. Archdeaconry of Cornwall – £50.6.6½d. Hospital of St John within the eastern gate, Exeter – £102.12.11. Rectory of Silverton – £51.8.4. Rectory of Uffculme – £54.0.6. Rectory of South Molton – £67.3.4. Rectory of Chittlehampton – £76.16.10. Rectory of Tavistock – £69.12.1. Rectory of Ilfracombe – £50.4.4½d. Vicarage of Brixham – £52.15.0. Vicarage of Paignton – £52.1.0½d. Vicarage of [West] Alvington – £62.15.10½d. Rectory of Ugborough – £76.11.3. *Worcestershire.* Archdeaconry of Worcester – £58.9.11. Hospital of St Wulfstan by Worcester – £63.18.10. Vicarage of Blockley – £54. Rectory of Tredington – £99.17.4. Rectory of Bredon – £72.11.0. Rectory of Fladbury – £81.0.8. *Gloucestershire.* Archdeaconry of Gloucester – £64.10.0. Rectory of [Bishop's] Cleeve – £84.6.8. *Somerset.* Provostship of Wells Cathedral – £64.19.4. Archdeaconry of Wells – £144.2.11½d. Archdeaconry of Taunton – £83.7.8. Treasurership of Wells Cathedral – £62.2.2½d. Deanery of Wells – £295.13.1. Rectory of Huntspill – £75.15.0. *Surrey.* Archdeaconry of Surrey – £91.3.6½d. Vicarage of Kingston upon Thames – £54.13.4. Hospital of St Thomas, Southwark – £266.17.11. Rectory of St Olave, Southwark – £68.4.9½d. *Hampshire.* Archdeaconry of Winchester – £67.15.2½d. Holy Cross Hospital, Winchester – £84.4.2. Vicarage of Ringwood – £75.5.5. Rectory of Cheriton – £66.2.6. Warwickshire. Hospital of St John, Coventry – £83. Rectory of St Nicholas, Coventry – £50. Rectory of Hampton Episcopi – £51.6.8. *St David's.* Archdeaconry of Menevia – £56.8.6. College [of St Mary or Vicars' College] by St David's Cathedral – £106.3.6. Rectory of Llanfihangel [Cwmdu] – £60.17.8½d. *Llandaff.* Llandaff Cathedral – £87.12.10½d. *Bangor.* Archdeaconry of Anglesey – £58.10.6. Rectory of Towyn, Merioneth – £60.13.4. *St Asaph.* Archdeaconry of St Asaph – £74.15.7. *Cheshire.* Archdeaconry of Chester – £65.10.0. Rectory of Hawarden – £66.6.4. Rectory of St Mary, Chester – £52. Rector of Bangor – £59. Rectory of Astbury – £67.19.8. Rectory of Stockport – £70.6.8.

*Paper book.*                                           SP 10/15, no. 78

**432.** 1550. [February 20].* Duties of Sir Richard Sackville as chancellor of the court of augmentations.

[1]. To rate such gifts as he shall be commanded by at least six of the council; the same for seals of inheritance to pass by the signet, privy seal and great seal, as purchases have been used. [2]. To rate exchanges similarly. [3]. To take lands in recompense for debts, the lands being first surveyed, and to seal longer days, taking sureties. [4]. To recompense the deans of the newly erected cathedrals, colleges and schools that they may have the proportion of their first assignment. [5]. To make stewards of courts, bailiffs and woodwards. [6]. To take surrender of leases and make new leases for twenty-one years to begin immediately, with the assent of at least two of the council and officers of the court. [7]. To authorise others to survey the erection of schools and give allowances for them. [8]. To rate lands to those who have paid money but as yet have no assurance, or repay their money. [9]. To recompense in money purchasers and others that have lands by gift for such lands as shall by just title be recovered from them, being above £200. [10]. To take surrender of the offices and fees of the late courts of augmentations and general surveyors and compound with them. [11]. To recompense in money such as have had lands emparked or enclosed after the rate of twenty years' purchase. [12]. For the better accomplishment of the late chantries' act to order the erection of schools, endowment of vicars, assignment of livings to the poor and to assistants and preachers in great parish churches. To pass the same by signed bill as before. The lands assigned to any one corporation or endowment not to exceed £20 a year.† [13]. To order payment of the late lord admiral's debts and such as shall be appointed to be paid by act of parliament or letter from at least eight of the council, and to sell the debtors' goods. To sell chantry goods towards payment of the debts. [14]. To order the manumission of villeins for the third part of their lands, paying the fees for the great and privy seals customarily paid for making denizens.

*Parchment.*

*Signed by*: Sackville.                                                                     SP 10/4, no. 48

**433.** February 21. Indenture between Sir William Herbert, K.G., master of the horse and John Storye, D.C.L.

Whereas Thomas Darbyshere, prebendary of Tottenhall *alias* Tottenham Court in St Paul's Cathedral, London, by indenture dated 1 August 1549 granted to John Storye the prebend and manor of Tottenhall and all its appurtenances in the parish of St Pancras *alias* Kentish Town, Middlesex, from then for eighty years at an annual rent of £46; Storye, in consideration of £200 paid him by Sir William Herbert, has granted and sold all his interest in the premises until the end of the term of the former indenture, which he will deliver.

*Parchment. No seal (missing).*

*Signed by*: Herbert.                                                                     SP 10/10, no. 1

**434.** March 5. London. Grant of arms by Sir Gilbert Dethick, Garter king of arms‡ to Richard Elken of London, gentleman.

*Illuminated parchment. One seal.*

*Printed*: *Miscellanea Genealogica et Heraldica*, ed. A.H. Hughes Clarke, 5th series, ii, (1916–17), 26, (with illustration).                                           SP 9/1/6

---

\*        Dated 24 August 1548 in *CSPD*, 10, citing Sackville's patent of appointment [C 66/809, m. 4 (*CPR* 1547–8, 297)]. But this document is clearly based on a subsequent commission of 20 February 1550 [C 66/827, mm. 9d–10d (*CPR* 1549–50, 214–16)]. See W.C. Richardson, *History of the Court of Augmentations*, (Baton Rouge, 1961), 191–4.

†        Inserted.

‡        Dethick's patent as Garter is dated 29 April 1550 [*CPR* 1549–51, 195].

**435.** March 25. Kingston. The duchess of Suffolk, from her cottage there, to William Cecil.

The matter between the council and my lord* seems by your letter to differ little from what I heard before, but you have quieted my greatest fear. I never feared so much that wicked tongues should harm him by sowing suspicion against him in the council. I trust my journey will be less needful, for the greatest good I could have done was to have counselled him if he had been impatient at their unkind dealing. I would adventure anything for him, but if I come and am unable to help I would harm him. I will think how I can master my perverse mind before I come, and will not fail to accomplish your desire and mine. Till then I shall lament your wrong, and purge you of slanders if I am given credit. My commendations and excuses to them for not writing, but I have lost my speech and almost my sight by a bad cold. *Postscript.* After writing I had a letter from a friend with the good news and hope that [the duke of] Somerset is to be called to the council very shortly. I am therefore more determined to stay, lest if I come I appear to take away their due thanks. I think thanks, but they must not be spoken until a better time.

*Holograph.*

*Printed*: Green, 251–3. Goff, 189 (part only: mis-dated 1551). Read, 59 (extracts).

SP 10/10, no. 2

**436.** March 25. Salisbury. John [Capon *alias* Salcot], bishop of Salisbury to William Cecil.

I have received your letter in favour of Mr Browne for the grant of the next advowson of the prebend in Salisbury Cathedral of which Edward Welshe his kinsman is incumbent. I am sorry I cannot accomplish your request, having already granted two advowsons, one to Sir William Herbert, master of the horse, of the first void prebend in my gift worth between £20 and £30, and to Dr [Robert] Oking, my chancellor, of the next voidance in my gift of whatever value. These two being served, I shall be glad to serve your friend's turn. If order is not kept for advowsons the contents of the end of your letter may come to pass.

SP 10/10, no. 3

**437.** April 24. London. Sir John Thynne to William Cecil, at Sheen.

This bearer, Mr Lok, one of [the duke of Somerset's] old chaplains, has a suit to his grace concerning the resignation of a benefice he had of him in Somerset to one that he affirms is an honest man. Considering that the suit is of no great importance, further him therein for my sake.

*Holograph.*

SP 10/10, no. 4

**438.** April 27. Kingston. The duchess of Suffolk to William Cecil.

It is doubly thankful that [the duke of Somerset] has remembered and appointed the matter between [Richard] Fulmerston ('Fillington') and [William] Nawneton. I store up thanks for him, but will bestow them sooner than you shall have any for the pains you shall take in hearing the cause. My opinion of you is that affection will turn you to either party from equity as if they were Jews. If you will not break justice's head for friendship, do not look for thanks at your friend's hand.

*Holograph.*

*Printed*: Tytler, i, 281.

SP 10/10, no. 5

**439.** May 9. Kingston. The duchess of Suffolk to William Cecil.

I am sorry that the marquess† follows his good beginning no better: what can I do

---

\*          The duke of Somerset.

†          Northampton [according to Read, 60] but possibly Dorset.

but be sorry for all faults, help them if I can, and otherwise be patient? I have lately written to criticize him again but he answers only that all is well. I think it better to let him alone or forbid it to him. Some men are so stubborn like women to follow their own commodities: they will act much better by friendly exhortation.

[The earl of] Warwick, for better show of his friendship, wished [the duke of] Somerset to have my son for his daughter.* I trust the friendship between my lord Somerset and me has such good assurance simply by our good wills that we need not do anything rashly to make the world believe better of our friendship, or for one of us to think well of the other. No unasked bonds between a boy and girl can give such assurance of good will as has been tried already, nor their marrying by our orders and without their consent or judgement to give it. I cannot tell what unkindness one of us might show the other than to bring our children into so miserable a state as not to choose by their own liking. I have said this for his daughter as well as my son. I know none that I wish my son rather than her, but I do not therefore wish that she should be constrained by her friends to have him whom she might not like. Neither can I yet assure myself of my son's liking, nor greatly mistrust it. If he is ruled by good judgement he shall have no dislike, unless he thinks himself disliked. It is best that we kept our friendship and let our children follow our examples, to begin their loves of themselves without forcing them. Although both might feel bound to their parents' pleasures, the loss of their free choice is enough to break the greatest love. I will therefore make much of his daughter without respect to my son's cause, and wish him to love my son for his mother's sake. God willing, my son and his daughter will much prefer to make up the matter themselves. No good agreement can happen between those we dislike. If it should not happen, none should blame another.

*Holograph.*
*Printed*: Green, 245–8. Goff, 187–8. Anderson, 330–1.    SP 10/10, no. 6

**440.**   May 12. Rental of the manor of Chatham, Kent.
*14 pp.*
*Latin.*
*Giving names of past and present tenants.*    SP 10/10, no. 7

**441.**   May 18. Kingston. The duchess of Suffolk to William Cecil.
I had hoped for letters from you. Edmund Hall wrote that he had opened to you Lord Paget's reply concerning my desire to purchase Spilsby chantry and how he advises me to enter the same. He adds that you promised to write your advice: as it is, I must proceed blindly. With ill will I have written to the council, according to Lord Paget's device. It seems to me readier to have a bill of my suit drawn and presented to the council and to labour my friends with private letters. Devise what you think best – that my letter or a bill of supplication should be delivered. I would have written to [the duke of] Somerset, but my leisure does not serve and his assuredness makes me bolder to wait on others. Tell Edmund Hall how I should begin, and how follow with letters, and my money in the rear. *Postscript.* Your letter arrived when this messenger was about to depart. If you do not like this device, draft a letter and send it for me to sign, for I have none here instructed in the matter. I have also written to [the duke of Somerset] and wish him to see my letter to Lord Paget and the council, that all my doings be privy to him. I neither commanded nor know of any such practising with Lord Paget's seal as Edmund Hall wrote of to me.

*Holograph.*
*Printed*: Tytler, i, 281–2 (except postscript). Goff, 184.    SP 10/10, no. 8

*    Presumably the eldest children (the duke of Suffolk and Lady Anne Seymour) are intended here.

**442.**  June 26. Ware. Richard Whalley to William Cecil.

Last night [the earl of] Warwick, having perused your letters, talked with me at great length about [the duke of Somerset], to whom he seems a faithful friend, being much concerned about his late proceedings – his unadvised attempt to release the bishop of Winchester and the Arundells* and his late conference with [the earl of] Arundel. He told me that the whole council dislikes these things, and partly the rest of his proceedings in council. They all think he aspires to have again the same authority he had as protector. He would harm himself. His late government is still disliked, and he does not stand in the king's best credit as he and others fondly believe. By discretion he might have the king as his good lord, and all he can reasonably desire.

[Warwick] declared his good opinion of you, and would write at length to you in the premises. For my lord's better stay he would have his intended journey to court made with more speed – minding, I judge, to put in ure your articles for the bishop of Winchester, for which he praised you as a faithful servant and most wise councillor to the king.

I cannot serve his grace as I would or should: let your better wisdom consider his preservation. Never leave him until you persuade him to some better consideration of his proceedings, and to concur with Warwick, who will be very plain with him at his coming to court. Otherwise great peril will ensue. His lordship has promised me his help in my suit, which I pray you to remember, and to move Lord Paget, who has promised his assistance. *Postscript.* Tell me by my servant, whom I have appointed to wait on you, if [the duke of Somerset's] journey shall be stayed before my return.

*Holograph.*

*Printed*: Tytler, ii, 21–4 (mis-dated 1551). Read, 60–1 (extracts).    SP 10/10, no. 9

**443.**  June 30. Baston. Randall Lynne to William Cecil.

Do not be displeased because you have not had an answer of my request to you according to my promise and your appointment. I was with your mother on Trinity Sunday.† Being sick, she would not receive my letter, so I delivered it to one whom I trusted, who has since disappointed me. I have declared your pleasure for your chapel to the inhabitants of Baston, and they will be at your service, trusting you will be their good master for the payment of their money which they shall give you for your chapel, that you will give them such assurance as you may of the chapel and help them to have it made their parish church, which they would be unable to do without you. At your coming down they will wait upon you or your father, which they had rather do than come to London, for it would be so costly. I also showed them your request concerning the suit of vestments. They are content that you shall have them, trusting you will allow them to have one of the copes for their church. If it is appointed hereafter that sacraments and services are to ministered without copes, the cope shall also be yours.

*Holograph.*                                                                 SP 10/10, no. 10

**444.**  July 1. Welbeck. Richard Whalley, from his house there, to William Cecil.

Being much troubled by manifold disorders here, concerning much of my best living, I am compelled to desire a much longer time here. Tell me by this bearer as near as you can the time of [the duke of Somerset's] journey to Reading and his circuit westward. I mean, all other business laid apart, not to be absent on that journey. On your advertisement I will be with his grace within a day and a night. I defer coming now because last night friends coming from [the earl of] Shrewsbury told me that his grace's journey was postponed – as some thought, for this year. Not doubting you have remembered my greatest suit left with you: tell me how forward it is.

---

*     Sir John and Sir Thomas Arundell.
†     June 1.

*Holograph.*  SP 10/10, no. 11

**445.** July 8. Thomas Parry to William Cecil.

Being, in the absence of Mr Chamberlain and Mr Comptroller alone occupied with business, I cannot write my full mind, but will send you part by Owtrede and bring part myself before long. [Princess Elizabeth] thanks [the duke of Somerset] for his unexpected remembrance. Touching Hatfield, I am unable to acquit your good will and like opinion of me, but thank you, assuring you that if her grace had not appointed me her keeper, I, inept to have sued for it, would never have taken such an office of unquietness at either of their hands. Your liking of it pleases me more than the thing itself. Saving to do her pleasure, I would refuse it, since you know old Bryce may not be put out. There is no profit. Touching your office of surveyor, her grace remains the same good lady she was, whatever has been said, and is content that your deputy shall travail for you therein. If time had served I would have gone with the king, but I sent a discreet man of mine to be his aid, that they may view things with as new an estimate as possible, and certify what they shall have done as soon as they may before Michaelmas, and do what they can for this time by your advice: such is her grace's pleasure. Of the things found to be in her grace's hands to be now certified, and at the courts to make the grants by your advice at her pleasure – some part to relieve her poor servants and some the poor tenants. Her grace is content to pass your patent under her hand and seal. Make it and send it to me and I will solicit it out.

*Holograph.*  SP 10/10, no. 12

**446.** July 19. Case for legal opinion concerning the lease of a rectory.

The parson of Dale made a lease of the rectory, reserving a rent. The bishop of Dale, being patron and ordinary, was, before the lease was made, sequestered from his bishopric by the king's commission. During the sequestration the bishop confirmed the lease and, the dean being abroad, the chapter confirmed it. Within six months he was deprived and died. The parson died; his successor received the reserved rent, and died. The second successor entered upon the lease. Was the confirmation valid? Does the acceptance of the rent by the first successor make the lease good against the second successor? To find out the commission of sequestration. That commission only lacks.

*Note: Dale is a fictional place, and the case in question was actually related to Gardiner's sequestration. This item and the following are in the same hand and form a single document.*

SP 10/10, no. 13

**447.** July 19. Proceedings in the council for the sequestration of the bishop of Winchester.

Today the council had access to the king for divers causes, but specially for the bishop of Winchester's matter. The council having declared to the king their proceedings with the bishop, he commanded that if he persevered in his obstinacy the council should proceed to the immediate sequestration of his bishopric and consequently to the intimation. The bishop was brought before the council and the articles before mentioned read, to which he refused to subscribe or consent. The sequestration and intimation were read in the following form:–

Where the king has at divers times sent sundry of us to travail with you to conform to the uniformity in religion set forth by acts of parliament and otherwise by his majesty's authority, and has also of late sent by certain of his council articles for you to affirm by subscription and declare yourself content to publish and preach them; because you have refused, to the great contempt of his command and the dangerous example of others, we, having his special commission to hear and determine your contempts and disobedience, again demand if you will obey his majesty's command.

He answered that in all things that his majesty would lawfully command he was ready to obey, but as there were divers things asked of him that his conscience would not bear, he prayed them to have him excused. Mr Secretary Petre, by the council's order, proceeded:–

As the king understands, and it is notorious to us, that his clemency and long sufferance works not in you dutiful humbleness and conformity, and because your first disobediences and misbehaviour for which you were committed to ward have since increased, so that great offence and trouble is risen in many places, and likely to ensue if your offences, being openly known, pass unpunished, we, having his majesty's special commission, for your contumacies and contempts, to eschew slander and offence, and that the church of Winchester may be provided of a good minister, sequester all fruits, revenues and possessions of your bishopric and judge them committed to the custody of such as his majesty shall appoint. We require you to obey his command and declare yourself by subscription content to accept, preach and teach the articles and such other matters as are or shall be set forth by his majesty's authority of supreme head of this church of England, within three months. We appoint one month for the first monition, one for the second, and one for the third and peremptory monition. Within this time you shall have paper, pen and ink when you call for them to declare your conformity. If you refuse, we intimate that the king who, like a good governor, desires to keep his commonwealth quiet and purge it of evil men (especially ministers), intends to proceed against you as an incorrigible person and unmeet minister of this church, to the deprivation of your bishopric.

Nevertheless it was agreed, especially in hope that within his time he might yet be reconciled, that his house and servants should be maintained in their present state until the time of this intimation should expire, and the matter for the meantime to be kept secret.

*Contemporary copy*: from PC 2/4, pp. 89–90 (*APC*, iii, 84–7), made by William Say, registrar; adding two clauses from the royal commission for the bishop's deprivation:–

We have further proceeded to the sequestration of his bishopric and commanded him to conform within three months on pain of deprivation, as appears by the records of our council. Every process or writing done in this matter is to be exhibited before you; and, finding the bishop to continue in his former contempt or not conformed to our pleasure and warnings given by our council, &c.

SP 10/10, no. 14

**448.**    July 24. Royal foundation of a German church in London.

It is the duty of a Christian prince to relieve fugitives from papal tyranny, many of whom come to England from Germany and remoter parts and have no certain place in which to meet. We therefore grant that there shall be a church in London to be called the Temple of Jesus, in which the meetings of Germans and other foreigners may be held by themselves according to the word of God and apostolic observance. We found a corporation of one superintendent and four ministers by name of the superintendent and ministers of the church of the Germans and other foreigners of the foundation of King Edward VI in the city of London, to hold the late church of Austin friars, London (save the quire) in frankalmoin. The superintendent and ministers shall have power to appoint other ministers and under ministers. John à Lasco, Pole, shall be the first superintendent and Walter Deleen, Martin Flandrus [Micronius], Francis Rivière and Richard Gallus [Vauville] the first four ministers. Their successors shall be elected by them and presented to the king for institution. We order the mayor, sheriffs and aldermen of London and all archbishops, bishops, justices and officers to allow the superintendent freely to conduct their services although they do not accord with the usual rites in our

realm.
*8 pp.*
*Latin.*
*Copy*: made in 1634 by Joshua Manet, notary public, from C 66/830, m. 42 (*CPR 1549–50*, 317).
*Printed*: Rymer, xv, 242–4. Burnet, v, 305–8.                          SP 10/10, no. 15

**449.**  French translation of the above.
*7 pp.*
*Copy*: made in 1696; said to have been printed by E[dward] Allde in London in 1607 (untraced).
*Printed*: J. Collier, *An ecclesiastical history of Great Britain*, (1708–14), ii, *Records*, no. LXV, pp. 74–5.                                                                SP 10/10, no. 16

**450.**  July 24. Grant to Sir Thomas Wroth, one of the principal gentlemen of the privy chamber, of the lordship, manor and borough of Bardfield, Essex, great and little parks there, the lordships and manors of Chigwell and West Hatch, Essex, and all their appurtenances, late in the tenure of William Rolte, and all possessions and perquisites in Great Bardfield, Little Bardfield, Saling, Chigwell and West Hatch, Essex, which Wroth had by letters patent of 23 December 1549,* now surrendered, extended at the yearly value of £77.15.4; to him and his heirs male by service of one fortieth of a knight's fee, from Michaelmas last, and for £11.2.3 paid in augmentations. Without fine or fee.
*4 pp.*
*Latin.*
*Copy*: from C 66/834, mm. 26–7 (*CPR 1550–3*, 17).                     SP 10/10, no. 17

**451.**  On the dorse of several leaves of the preceding document are jottings in a Jacobean hand: mathematical calculations; the obligation of Hugh Justyce of London, plumber, to maintain the waterworks of the city and university of Oxford, and those laid by him at the charge of Otho Nicholson; the heading of an account of the same Nicholson as receiver from 25 June 1616 to 18 May 1618.                     SP 10/10, no. 17, dorse

**452.**  July 24. 'Lee'. John Eason to William Cecil.
Since my discharge from the council, about five days before Christmas, I wished to write to you, but I dare not for I heard you were much offended with me. But if you knew my heart and how I was handled you would bear me no ill will. When I was with you last summer on going to Kent I stayed at Ponchyon's house, where the letters you sent me were taken and delivered by him to [Sir Thomas] Chaloner. After Michaelmas, when I received the letter signed by the king and [the duke of] Somerset, I took up 352 armed men to serve the king. As we were coming towards Windsor, since I had heard tales on the way to discourage the men, I inspired them, saying I would bring them to the king. One, I think a spy for the lord warden, † asked me aloud whether the lord warden was a traitor. I answered before all men that I did not know, but was sure that the lord protector was with the king and could be no traitor, and that I heard [the earl of] Warwick, the lord warden and others had raised a power in London which should serve against the king rather than with him. I added that if the London lords had the upper hand and executed the lord protector, they would fear that the king would revenge his uncle's death on his majority. If they did not execute him they would fear he would destroy them. Although they meant the king no evil, these fears would set them against him. I then marched forward and on the way heard certainly that the lord protector had

---

\*        C 66/823, m. 1 (*CPR 1549–50*, 68).
†        Sir Thomas Cheyne, lord warden of the Cinque Ports.

yielded. I paid my men wages of my own money, distributed my victuals among them, and returned home. Within three days, I think on Monday, I was summoned to the council at Hampton Court. There [the earls of] Arundel and Southampton charged me with treason for raising the people. After about half an hour I was ordered to the lobby until they had consulted. Mr Chaloner followed me, saying he knew now all Cecil's and my inkling, had all our writings to show, and that [Richard] Palady had confessed. I was summoned back to the council and they bound me in recognisance to appear before them daily. When I came every day Mr Chaloner would be sure to record my appearance, to talk with me about your matter, commanding me in the name of Lord Warwick and the lord chancellor to write them the truth. I cannot say what he did when he saw I would write nothing. But my father, Mr Justice Hales, sent and told me that some of the council had asked him to advise me to write, or it would turn to my displeasure. I was then told by some of my friends that the two younger Chaloners and Chamberlain, John Chaloner's bedfellow, had laid watch to attack me. When I came to court to record my appearance I could not be at rest, but was pointed at. Then [Sir Nicholas] Bagnall told me in the court that you should tell Palady that he had a nest of birds and bees in his head – which I had never heard before, and which made me think that Chaloner had searched your house and found my letters, and that Palady had confessed. All these matters weighed together with my trouble and the ungentle handling of those whom I knew to be Chaloner's accusers, whom I saw daily walking with Chaloner in great friendship. Chamberlain laid things to me openly in court concerning Chaloner's matter that were never thought or done by you or me. I was so overcome that I wrote to the Lord Chancellor and put it in my bosom. When I came to court Mr Chaloner asked me whether I had written a letter according to the council's command. I said I had, but as it was not wholly true I would write another. He asked to see it and when he had read it would not return it. I cannot tell whether he delivered it to the lord chancellor or what. But I wrote no more, and was never merry since. I wish I were dead, for I have hardly ever been out of my house since my charge, which cost me £100. Unless [the duke of] Somerset is good, I will be undone, for all the friends I can make will not persuade the lord warden from taking revenge because I said openly that I thought him and the other lords traitors rather than my lord's grace. But I served the king then as faithfully as any man. Sir Anthony Aucher knows my pains and service then. After I received the letter I was never in bed until I returned home. I would be most glad to hear that you had remitted your displeasure.

*Holograph.*                                                                         SP 10/10, no. 18

**453.**    August 2. [Wells]. John Goodman, dean of Wells to [John] Berwick.
    You will receive here brief instructions lest you have lost previous letters. If ever you will do good to reform any man, hurry to [the duke of Somerset] to tell him the truth, that he may better perceive how to handle [the bishop of Bath and Wells] at his coming. If he once enters my lord's grace's favour, let his grace not look hereafter to have any pleasure at his hand. Be good to an honest poor man whom the bishop has wronged; you shall perceive by his supplication how greedy the bishop is. He has so much declared his charity in his deeds among the people that none any more comes to his sermons. Where the people used to murmur when my lord's grace should have any lordship of the bishopric, now if he should have all they would thank God.

*Impression of seal.*                                                                SP 10/10, no. 19

**454.**    [August 2. Enclosed with the above]. Unseemly reports of the bishop of Bath declared to sundry persons against the duke of Somerset, some in the time of his trouble and some since midsummer. All have been reported to me* and others of late, and [they]

*         The dean [cf. no. **453** above].

offer to prove them whenever called.

[1]. After [the duke of] Somerset was apprehended a gentleman asked the bishop how he liked my lord in his trouble. He answered that he never thought [otherwise] but that he should at length be found a rank traitor. This was spoken by Mr Hethe, whom you know, and who was present when the words were spoken.

[2]. The suffragan of Wells, * who had been long from home, at his return went to the bishop, with whom he had much communication of the writ of *praemunire* and of the palace. The bishop told him that he would not leave the palace to [the duke] unless commanded by the king and council. The duke had once made him a fool but would never do so again.

[3]. Of late I understand he is content to leave the palace with the lordship to [the duke]; after counting all his charges, it should be as profitable to him as though he had the whole manor [of Wells]. To compare this matter he has sent his wife to London. Thither he intends to come himself shortly. In the meantime he purposes to come up by Reading to obtain his purpose and my lord's grace's favour. I know he has sent one of his servants to Reading to prepare a house. He will break up his house here as you know he may do soon, and intends to lie at London with four or five servants; there he intends to make suit to the council and to surmise matters as he has been always wont to do.

Inform my lord's grace of these things with speed, if you have not done so already. The bishop will at first offer himself largely touching the palace and lordship so that he might creep into his grace's favour again. I think sure writings should be prepared, that he may be despatched out of hand and sent to his old house again, which will serve him well enough. For lack of the master in chancery to take the knowledge hereof, I will supply the room if there is none other and I may be admitted. If my lord's grace trusts him further than he sees him, he will be deceived. The *praemunire* sinks sore into his stomach now, and that is one cause which makes him sue my lord's grace's favour. Herein is no feigned or malicious word. SP 10/10, no. 19(i)

**455.** August 5. Wells. The dean of Wells to John Berwick.

Touching your letter I have desired your servant to declare your mind. It shall not be long before I am with you. The bishop has no other way to stay for the lordship of Wells, having received letters from the king and council, but to work 'colorously' by conditions – that he will not depart from it until he is sure of recompense, and will not trust [the duke of Somerset] by word or promise. He would be put out of the palace headlong, as he says, because the people would rejoice as they favour him not for his religion. The truth is that the people hate him not for religion's sake, for even those that favour the religion as well as he and better, and used to come to his sermons, have now clearly forsaken him. Where the church was too small for his audience, now they may be received in a little chapel. He has always been wont to extol with one part of his sermon and inveigh against the covetous and wavering. Since the lordship of Wells came into his hands he has used many tenants so uncharitably, contrary to his preaching, putting some from their rightful holdings. He promised many they should continue in their tenements, but has of late wrongfully expelled them – as shall appear by their suit shortly to be made to my lord's grace. Touching covetousness, he has set up a flock of sheep on Mendip common, whereby the poor tenants are hindered. If he is displeased with any man he openly revenges it in the pulpit. This is why the people hate him so that they would gladly tear him with their teeth.

*? Holograph.* SP 10/10, no. 20

**456.** August 8. Eresby. The duchess of Suffolk, from her house there, to William Cecil.

* William Finch, bishop of Taunton.

Your long expected letters called me from no great business. I have heard your ill favoured news, as ill favouredly told, and like it as ill favouredly. The best is that I shall not be unprovided whatever happens.

*Holograph.*

*Printed*: Green, 248.                                                              SP 10/10, no. 21

**457.**   August 9. Venice. Sir Robert Stafford to William Cecil.

I am glad that, since God sent you adversity since my coming out of England, He has ended it so favourably. This good news, although I could not be certain of it till now at the arrival of my fellow [Francis] Yaksley, has been as joyful to me as to him that loves you best. I understand you have received none of the letters I sent you after my arrival in Italy – the first by Mr Bamfyld, a servant of Sir Thomas Arundel, the second by a man of Antwerp. Lack of answer caused me to stay my hand from writing to you, but not my heart in thinking of you. Commendations to your wife, Sir Anthony Cooke and [John] Cheke.

*Holograph.*                                                                        SP 10/10, no. 22

**458.**   August 16. Reading. Thomas Fisher to William Cecil.

On arrival here this Saturday from Banbury I have been to oversee those in [the duke of Somerset's] mills; if I am not present there once or twice a week they would steal away and leave undone what my lord delivered in value to [the earl of] Warwick and is to be finished out of hand, I trust by Michaelmas. This causes me to be more absent from [the duchess of Somerset] than I desire. Before coming here, my lady being ridden hence, I found my wife very sick of an ague. Although I sped to wait on my lady until her meeting with my lord, I thought it best to stay to comfort my wife and take her to Warwickshire as soon as she may travel, hoping not to offend my lord, which I rather do in avoiding the excessive charges we sustain here, and trusting that after some recovery she may be better able to attend, if my lady commands her. There are other reasons for my not being over hasty to attend, as you shall know at our meeting, and doubtless understand. Experience teaches me and it is evident enough how I am regarded by my lord and my lady in their house; such reward I have for true and painful service, with which I will be content until I have better occasion to write of it. As you hear my lord, my lady and others talk of me, answer as for one of your poor assured friends; I hope you shall not be blamed. I am never ashamed for any untruth or unjust dealing; where I shall be considered better than I have been, I will attend, or my living will not maintain me in service. In the meantime I will creep into a corner and pray for my friends.

*? Holograph.*                                                                      SP 10/10, no. 23

**459.**   September 3. Stamford. The duchess of Suffolk to William Cecil.

It seems some time since I heard from or of you, so I will pull your ears by thanking you for your past gentleness to my cousin [William] Nawnton, praying you to continue it. I have desired of my lord a more liberal respect towards him; if it is true that the office rightly belongs to him, the portion is nought that he shall yearly pay out for it, not having his past charges answered. *Postscript.* [Richard] Fulmerston shall have for my lord's sake £40 a year from the office for life, which I think more than he is worth. I ask that in recompense of my cousin's charges for such carriages as the other has received of his offices, Fulmerston may give him £200.

*Holograph.*                                                                        SP 10/10, no. 24

**460.**   September 8. Eresby. The duchess of Suffolk to William Cecil.

Many thanks for your good news, which I received on the 6th. In four days I intend to send a servant of mine and will answer your letter more, and write as you have willed me. I have already bestowed one, not knowing so much as you wrote of it; I trust to do all as you would wish. You write that [the duchess of] Somerset would know if her letter came open to my hands: it came safely within three days of writing, as I intend to write to her shortly. I made no more haste in writing again because I see writing duty with everybody, and am slothful. Yet I answered it within five days. Commendations to you and your wife.

*Holograph.* SP 10/10, no. 25

**461.** September 9. London. Thomas Birkhed, vicar of Christ Church, [Newgate] to William Cecil.

I understand by your letter that my lord has offered me [a living] on such condition that it can only hinder me. If, as you say, I must be resident upon it, I shall be compelled to forego my poor living in London, granted me in recompense for St Bartholomew's by the king. Considering my age, feebleness, my charge and changes here, and my acquaintance and commodities, I should be no better but worse. In the king's books it is but £15.10.0. Consider this indifferently. I would ever be bound to you and my lord's grace if you would move him for something nearer London, as the next voidance of Westminster or Windsor.

*Holograph.* SP 10/10, no. 26

**462.** September 10. London. Charles [Stourton], Lord Stourton to William Cecil, principal secretary.*

The bearer, Robert Eton, served my father in the king's affairs at Newhaven [Ambleteuse] until he died and has since served the king under the lord admiral† at Boulogne; his painful service has deserved his wages, which I am informed are detained until the lord admiral's report is commended to the council. Please be immediate in your furtherance, without which he is utterly undone, being much in debt. Move the lord admiral to be his good lord respecting the request of [the duke of] Somerset's former letters to him. I am glad of your preferment.

*Holograph.* SP 10/10, no. 27

**463.** September 14. Sir Edward North to William Cecil.

Remember Sir Arthur Darcy's lease in reversion. You have the old lease in reversion, which he also gave up in lieu of this lease. I trust Secretary Petre will help to further it if you care to open it to him. I hear you are joined with him in office. God send you comfort and grace to serve as well as any before.

*Holograph.* SP 10/10, no. 28

**464.** September 14. Reading. Sir John Thynne to William Cecil.

Being glad of your appointment, I desire you to reckon on all my friendship. If before my return to the country you commune with [the duke of Somerset] of me, use your old friendship towards me in my late suit to leave my stewardship. I shall be glad to serve you in any other service his grace will appoint. In this I can never serve with good will. Remember Lord Edward [Seymour] to Mr Loss before Michaelmas. If that matter sleeps it will be long before he has anything. His whole trust is in you. Commendations to you and your wife.

*Holograph.*
*Printed*: Tytler, i, 318–19. SP 10/10, no. 29

---

\* Since September 5.
† Lord Clinton since May 14.

**465.** [September (?15)].* The earl of Warwick to William Cecil.

I have received your letter, marvelling that upon the coming of the lord chancellor this matter of the proclamation could not have been despatched as previously agreed, but that he sought me, who can show him no more than the others privy to it. I came here yesterday to take a bath and intend to use it this morning for my health. This afternoon I intend to be at court. See what [the duke of] Somerset, the master of the horse,† you and others resolve: send me the instrument if it needs my signature and I will sign it as they do this morning. I cannot attend this morning without omitting what is necessary for my health, and do not know when I shall have opportunity again. I told the master of the horse of my being here. On Monday night I could not sweat, so [Dr George] Owen advised me to bathe. When Somerset, the lord chancellor, the master of the horse and you would have me sign anything about this proclamation, send it or bring it yourself, that I may be quiet until the afternoon.

*Holograph.*

*Printed*: Hoak, 154 (part).                                                    SP 10/10, no. 30

**466.** September 16. Ely Place. The earl of Warwick to William Cecil.

So that the matter concerning the b[ishop] of D[urham] and [Ninian] M[elville] may be discussed before my return I have sent you the abstract which you delivered to me at Oatlands. Draw out the writings which came from them, that at [the duke of] Somerset's coming to court you may deliver them to him. The bishop has been here with me: I am sure he knows perfectly why he was sent for. I said he had a good friend of Melvile, marvelling that when he had him at such advantage by the testimony of his own letters he did not send him and his letters to the council. I could not tell what to make of his reply: he seems full of perplexity and fear. No doubt the matter will touch him wonderfully, and yield the king as good a nest as the bishop of Winchester is likely to do, if the cards are true.

*Holograph.*                                                                    SP 10/10, no. 31

**467.** September 18. Grimsthorpe. The duchess of Suffolk to William Cecil.

I will call you 'so scell' now you are secretary, until you deny it. Be not idle but occupied with me. You know I wrote to [the duke of] Somerset a good while ago at my son's coming to court, for [William] Nanton's cause. Because I have had no answer he fears lest my lord should blame him for my earnest writing. Help to deliver him from that doubt. You know I cannot but be cursed or earnest when I see my friend stick with me in trifles, with whom I would not stick in great things. A good turn quickly done is twice done. Save the innocent from condemnation through my fault. She wept while I wrote it, fearing that a friend should mistake anything well meant. Commendations to Mistress Mildred. *Postscript.* If right is so hard to get, God help us in all adventured matter.

*Holograph.*

*Printed*: Green, 249–50. Read, 67 (part).                                      SP 10/10, no. 32

**468.** September 22. Ashridge. Thomas Parry to William Cecil.

[Princess Elizabeth] commanded me to send her commendations and write on behalf of her old servant John Ronyon, yeoman of her robes, suitor for the parsonage of East Harptree, Somerset, now in your disposition. If you let him be your tenant she will gratify any similar desire of yours. She sends the man to be considered, and prays for answer by letter. She has long been troubled with rheums, but is now well. You will shortly hear from her again. Owtrede is occupied very honestly in her business. I am glad to hear of your good calling.

---

*        Between September 14 and 18 according to Hoak, 153.
†        Sir William Herbert.

*Printed*: Tytler, i, 322–3.                                    SP 10/10, no. 33

**469.** September 27. London. Dr William Turner to William Cecil.

At last I appreciate your great love and your secret efforts to secure me the York living. The archbishop of York was most kind and promised he would collate me to [Thomas] Magnus's prebend on his death if it were in his gift. What he had was the wardenship of the chapel of the Holy Sepulchre in York Minster, which I hear is now in danger of being transferred to profane uses: please see it is preserved for sacred ones. Golden ministers are everywhere being supplanted by leaden; if the church is soon destitute of orthodox and sound ministers it will be in gravest danger from heretics and wild papists. The archdeaconry [of the East Riding] is now vacant by Magnus's death: would it were given to one of sincerer piety than [Owen] Oglethorpe, who now claims it because of some promise. Do not think I have spoken in order to gain the appointment, for a much smaller revenue would keep myself and my family. But if Oglethorpe is preferred, advance me to the presidency of Magdalen College. My informant is my teacher, Dr [William] Clayburgh, formerly of St John's College, Cambridge, a learned and godly man who was imprisoned for defending the renewal of religion in the same college. Now alone he treads the wine press in Yorkshire. He will tell you all.

*Latin.*

*Holograph.*

*Printed*: Pocock, *Troubles*, 131–2.                         SP 10/10, no. 34

**470.** September 28. Tickencote. Harry Dygby to William Cecil.

Pardon my boldness in moving your father to be a means to you to accept my son Jasper to be at your command, and my writing to you. I shall bear his charges and commit him to your orders. If you admit him, let him come to me to be apparelled and furnished.

*Holograph.*                                         SP 10/10, no. 35

**471.** September 30. Richard Goodrich, from his house, to William Cecil.

I have considered the state of Mr Grey's land and perceive that my lord cannot be sure of repayment unless a fine is levied, which will be such a charge to Grey that he would be better to borrow money for interest. The assurance would take so long to be completed that it would not then serve its purpose. I see no way for [the duke of Somerset] to help him unless he can find him other surety without some adventure of his life. My lord knows where and how Grey shall have so much money, and may soon help himself to repayment – the more risk my lord's grace bears, the more he binds Grey. If Grey cannot find enough sureties for repayment he must either adventure of his own bond or leave him unhelped. If you wish to buy two houses that Lord Paget had in Cannon Row I can help you. I think they will be £400 in cash. If you wish to bargain I will be broker. My matter with Matson has done nothing; tell me what you have done or will do.

*Holograph.*                                         SP 10/10, no. 36

**472.** October 1. Tattershall Castle. The duchess of Suffolk to William Cecil.

I am sued by the inhabitants of Spalding and am provoked to hear their suit for my right in Pinchbeck, my lordship adjoining them. Help end a controversy between us and Market Deeping over a waste marsh and common which we have by ancient grant and continual confirmation. East Deeping [Deeping St James] pleads a grant within the same bounds, and the matter abides proof of the elder grant. It is greater than our countrymen are able to decide, so we seek a commission from above.

*Holograph.*                                         SP 10/10, no. 37

**473.**　October 2. Tattershall. The duchess of Suffolk to William Cecil.

Help this bearer in a suit that one of Jersey has against his brother. He wishes [the duke of Somerset] to write or command his under captain in Jersey to call the matter before him to make an honest end of it. Otherwise the poor soul will be undone. Help him so that he may return to his garden, for until then I can have no salads or sweet herbs.

*Holograph.*

*Printed*: Goff, 184–5. Green, 250–1.　　　　　　　　　　　　　　SP 10/10, no. 38

**474.**　October 2. Tattershall. The duchess of Suffolk to William Cecil.

I never doubted you would live by your change, and at length change for the best and come to a good market. I have always thought your wares good and saleable – but the exchange goes high nowadays. Although it was painful to go to the Tower for it, thank the Lord in the end you are no loser. I am content to become your partner and will abide all risks in your ship. Although I cannot help with costly wares, my old stuff may serve for ballast. If you marvel how I am become so cunning in ship-works, understand that I am making one here at Boston, or rather patching an old one, which recompense I had for my wines, with which the *Honor* victualled the rebels in Norfolk last year. So I am become a merchant vintner. If I speed well I promise to divide as liberally with you as you promise me. Thank you for your good news from abroad. If [William] Nanton's cause will be no better considered I hold my peace. Commendations to Lady Mildred.

*Holograph.*

*Printed*: Tytler, i, 323–4. Goff, 186. Read, 66 (part).　　　　　　　　SP 10/10, no. 39

**475.**　October 2. [Oatlands]. The council to justices of the peace.

The insatiable avarice of ungodly men causes all grain, victuals and other commodities to increase in price, which may occasion many inconveniences and almost general famine. The king has caused remedy to be provided by proclamations now published. Not doubting you will respect the special trust reposed in you for their execution, the king requires us to charge you to observe the proclamation and punish offenders.

*Corrected draft.*　　　　　　　　　　　　　　　　　　　　　　　SP 10/10, no. 42

**476.**　October 2. [Oatlands]. The council to special persons in the shires.

*Corrected draft of the following.*　　　　　　　　　　　　　　　　SP 10/10, no. 41

**477.**　October 3. Oatlands. The council to special persons in the shires.

The king has issued a proclamation for reform of excessive prices of corn and other commodities and punishment of the greedy and uncharitable who cause dearth and high prices. For better execution we have written to the justices of the peace of the county of [*blank*]. Although we trust they will have good respect thereto, because some slackness has been found in many of them, the king desired us to write to you to act as you think best for the execution of the proclamation, and to call on the justices and other officers from time to time for doing their duties.

*Signed by*: the duke of Somerset, the marquess of Northampton, Sir Thomas Darcy, Sir William Petre and William Cecil.　　　　　　　　　　　　SP 10/10, no. 40

**478.**　October 3. Oatlands. The council to the lords lieutenant.

The king has issued a proclamation for redress of excessive prices of corn and other commodities and [punishment]* reformation of the uncharitable and greedy who are the greatest cause of dearth and high prices. For its better execution we have written to all

*　　Deleted.

justices of the peace and some special men in every shire. We have sent you copies of those letters so that you may give similar order in all shires within your commission, as soon as you can.

*Corrected draft.*                                                                SP 10/10, no. 43

**479.**   October 5. Richard Goodrich, from his house, to William Cecil.

Help to rid Mr Grey. My lord cannot stand in better surety than he shall by the debentures; all the adventure he shall give shall be £100, for which he may have his bond and Laurence Ball's. I have concluded with [Sir Thomas] Pope, of whom shortly. I could do no better than I told you. There had been a new merchant at hand with him so that if he could have shipped he would have gone from me. He is such a money man, and has daily such adventures of gain as I can do nothing with him therein. I am told Mr Inysley will be in town this week. If he is, I trust you will have some help of him, and you shall have Mr Secretary's and my credence to borrow. Because I am unable to supply your lack, for all circumstances considered, I was never so poor in my life; yet I have enough. I send the draft of the indenture between Mr Pope and you. Return it with your opinion. You should see the house, for I am told the glass is all spoiled by Lord Paget's men, as Mr Pope says. He has promised me you shall have fifteen pieces of arras.

*Holograph.*                                                                      SP 10/10, no. 44

**480.**   October 6.* Richmond. Signet warrant to Sir Edmund Peckham [high treasurer of the mints].

Whereas by indenture between us and Sir John York, [treasurer of Southwark mint]† dated [October 6]† September 30 we have promised that, for service to be done in our affairs, he shall have from time to time the coin which shall grow upon the coinage of such bullion as he shall bring to the mint, you shall deliver him all money and coin in the mint upon the bullion he shall bring in from [*blank*] October until September 1 following.

*Corrected draft.*                                                                SP 10/10, no. 45

**481.**   October 8. Tattershall. The duchess of Suffolk to William Cecil.

I cannot leave [the duke of] Somerset's dealing with me in my cousin [William] Nanton's matter so little touched as in my last letter. I think you say he thinks you prevail because you have no honester excuse to help my lord's ingratitude. How could my lord not think my letter good, nor it right that [Richard] Fulmerston should restore what is not his own? Is Fulmerston such a friend of my lord that nothing else is thought of? Does money matter to my lord more than right? Let my lord choose whether it is his or Fulmerston's. My poor friend had it given him by a king, by my lord in a king's right, taken from him by my lord without trial. But if judgement lacks here, there is eventually another judge. Pardon me for writing plainly. *Postscript.* I could blame my lady for my lord's fault, but I think he has been warned too late to fall again into that evil.

*Holograph.*                                                                      SP 10/10, no. 46

**482.**   October 12. [Grantham]. William Rede, vicar of Grantham to William Cecil.

I told you that I had told my friend [Richard] Goodrich I had no house belonging to my vicarage. He purchased certain chantry houses in Grantham from the king and offered me the house I have with the orchard and yard and two other adjoining, writing to Mr Carr of Sleaford for me to have it at a reasonable price. Carr partly agreed, giving me a day of payment. After I had my deed sealed and built on my ground, Mr Armestrong

---

*       So minuted at the head, but endorsed October 8.
†       Deleted.

of Corby, an officer, viewed my house and ground, saying I had nothing to do with certain walls of burnt houses, although they were mentioned in my lease, and that Mr Goodrich and Mr Carr did not buy them. He commanded me not to occupy those wastes, four yards by thirty-five, although I had a lease of them and my house four years ago and had recently purchased them. He wished me to seek some counsel in the next audit and would be my friend. Write to him that I may enjoy the ground I bought. Dr [Edward] Crome gave me a cure or parsonage called Spitalgate besides Grantham, and to augment my vicarage I have had yearly tithes and certain land annexed to it. I ministered there all customary services – communion, wedding, burial, christening – for it has long been a parish, and without the liberty of Grantham though very near it. When your brother Lawrence Earsbye was commissioner of chantries in the town the church was presented as a parsonage by the eldest of the parish. But your letters came by Mr Armestronge that the church should be pulled down and the lead removed. All was so done. Then a parishioner and I went to London to ask Mr Ersby if the king's act took away our efficacy of the land or profits belonging to the church. Dr Crome and the previous parson came before him. We showed him that I received troth, hemp, flax, pigs, hay and all offerings at four offering days and the Easter book, which came to 13s. a year and 20s. for a hundred and six lambs in the fields. I still receive this despite the dissolution of the church. Mr Earsbye showed that the act took no effect on any of these profits. But recently Mr Armestrong commanded a woman of the parish, having the churchyard and two other yards of me for 2s. a year, not to pay me any rent. Write to him. Mr Ersby will tell you the truth. God will support my family and me, despite our poverty. Write to Mr Armestrong before the audit. I will visit you about All Hallows' Day and may speak with Mr Earsby and other friends if necessary.

*Holograph.*                                                    SP 10/10, no. 47

**483.**   October 23. Sidmanton. John Kingsmill to William Cecil.
This poor bearer obtained much displeasure from informing the council of crafty and suspicious letters. To stay his undoing the council wrote for his continuance in his cure and payment of his wages. But the parson of Broughton, who should pay him, put him from his living, all by the maintenance of John Coke the registrar and John Rychardes the ringleader of their parish. Since that letter he has had less peace than before. The bearer asked me to write to you that, the parson of Broughton now being in London, you might have order taken for his wages and the continuance of his service. Before they were displeased many of the parish gave him good report.          SP 10/10, no. 48

**484.**   October 26. Lord De La Warr, from his house, to William Cecil.
I send letters to [the duke of] Somerset and the council to answer things concerning the king's affairs. Help their delivery and answer, and credit what the bearer my servant tells you.                                                    SP 10/10, no. 49

**485.**   November 2. Pinchbeck. Richard Ogle to William Cecil.
I have sent you four marks for the fees of Toft and Gosberton for 1549, four nobles each. They were paid within these six weeks to me. The fee at Michaelmas 1551 is not yet allowed as the audit is not finished: as soon as I have it I shall send it. Mr Wyngfeld the auditor might do good there. I have written to him to show his favour. As for the marquess's courts, I have not yet a penny. I would have waited on you now to have thanked you for my daughter and your kindness to my son – but age so creeps on me that I much fear any far journeys. My wife and I greet you and yours.

*Holograph.*                                                    SP 10/11, no. 1

**486.**   November 5. John Beaumont to William Cecil.

Hearing you were informed I should claim a piece of land to be purchased from you, I determined to deliver you the truth today, as I did last Lent, since when I have never meddled therewith but suffer the priests to occupy it quietly. I have assignment of them of the same to me and my heirs. I do not meddle for myself, yet they do not cease to slander me to you and others. My desire was to have spoken with you today. Although I tarried long at court I had no time to you. Call my accuser and me together and give order, which I shall obey after I am heard.

   *Holograph.*                                   SP 10/11, no. 2

**487.** November 14. [Offington]. Lord De La Warr, from his house there, to William Cecil.

I have written to the council concerning a letter dated October 26 which I received on November 12 directed to the sheriff and justices of the peace in this shire for taking up 500 quarters of wheat, 200 quarters of rye, 500 quarters of malt and 500 quarters of barley for victualling Calais and the king's other places there for six months. Because you are privy to that letter, I certify you as I did the council that I cannot perceive how it should be done with such speed as is required. The justices of the peace are about their business in London and likely to continue there for most of this term, so that we cannot view barns according to the king's proclamation. There cannot be so much malt, barley and rye had of these parts as is demanded and the market reasonably served, for barley much failed here this year. There is yet very little malt; the old was all spent before the new came, for lack whereof great lamentation is made amongst the poor. In the hundred I dwell in I trust to make as much speed as is in my power, but cannot answer for others. Surely the justices have not before been burdened with taking up provisions, but the king's taker should do it? We have enough to do in viewing barns and making up our books how the market shall be ordered.

I understand [Henry] Foulkes, who is appointed to see the shipping of the provision and pay for it, has stayed and taken for the king 200 quarters of wheat, shipped at Chichester, but whether it went to sea I cannot tell. The carriers said it should have gone to Calais – which I think is disproved – so that 200 quarters are now ready for the king.

Thomas Thickenor, an Englishman of Beaumaris, Wales, and certain Bretons had lately loaded in Brittany ten tons of wheat and thirty-nine and a half tons of rye into a Breton balinger, of which twenty tons were Thickenor's, which he intended to have had to Beaumaris. Last Wednesday an hour before night the vessel was driven by tempest on land beside Shoreham, three miles from me. The [people of the] country, perceiving them in danger, came. The poor men, marvellously wet with sea and rain and ready to perish with cold, desired the countrymen to save their vessel and corn, saying they should have half. They went to houses to succour themselves. When they were gone the people fell to their spoil, hewed the balinger and took away the boards and nails, so that by 8 or 9 in the morning they had left nothing of the corn or vessel save the keel, two anchors, two gables, a bonnet and five or six small pieces of ordnance. The keel was taken away on Thursday. A pitiful matter, and earnestly to be looked upon. The poor men intend shortly to come and make further complaint to the council. In the meantime I will do my best to know who has the corn and other premises, and put in a stay that the corn may be bought of them at a reasonable price to serve the king now in this need. I have certified the council how it stands, according to my duty, desiring to know their pleasure, and that reformation may be had for such folks. The people grow to much disobedience in robbing, killing, hunting and other idleness without fear of execution of the king's laws.                                   SP 10/11, no. 3

**488.** November 15. Stamford. The duchess of Suffolk to William Cecil.

I have been so long in answering your letter that I am sure you look for much matter, but you shall be content with a little. Help me to have the warrant for Spilsby chantry we sued for. If it pass these ways I shall be driven to account to my son for the arrears which scarce outweigh my charges for the good will of the master and his fellows, so that I may be quit of that. I will no sooner receive it sealed than I will send it to Charles.* Thank you for not showing my hasty letter. If, as my cousin [William] Nanton writes, my lord is so good that he shall be despatched shortly, all is well and my foolish choler shall be spent. If not, I fear I shall not rule it.

    *Holograph.*                                                SP 10/11, no. 4

**489.**   November 17. The council to special men in each county.

    The king is informed that notwithstanding his command signified by two proclamations and divers letters from us for bringing grain, butter and cheese to the markets and selling them at reasonable prices, most of those who have the greatest quantities refuse to obey. This may grow to further inconvenience if not speedily remedied. The king would have the proclamations enforced and has appointed you his special commissioners for causing the justices of the peace of the county of [*blank*] to be assembled. Declaring the effect of this commission, first consult with them how the proclamations may best be executed, causing the justices and other grave gentlemen you think meetest to order the several parts of the shire. If any refuse, cause the quantities appointed to be taken from their barns or granaries and brought to the market by the constables or other honest inhabitants of the town. Send such as refuse to us in custody to be further used according to justice. You the sheriff are specially appointed to join with the rest and assemble the force of the shire if necessary. When the markets are quietly served and the proclamations obeyed the king will, upon knowledge and suit from you, order any necessary redress of prices. Although special letters have before been addressed to others of that shire for execution of the proclamation, you only shall henceforth have the chief charge, which you may signify to the others.

    *Draft.*

    *Printed*: R.W. Heinze, *The Proclamations of the Tudor Kings*, (Cambridge, 1976), 230–1 (extracts).                                           SP 10/11, no. 5

**490.**   November 18. Westminster. The council to lords lieutenant.

    By the king's appointment we write presently to special men in every shire for execution of the proclamations already set forth for bringing grain, butter and cheese to the markets, as appears by the enclosed copy of the letters. Give like order in all shires within your commission. Because many shires, namely those of Wales, have their grain mostly brought by baggers from other shires, you are by letters to the said special men to order that the baggers may be reasonably allowed for carriage of their grain, over and besides the prices limited in the proclamations.

    *Corrected draft.*                                              SP 10/11, no. 6

**491.**   November 18. List of messengers who carried letters concerning grain.

    Lord privy seal: Cornwall, Devon, Somerset, Dorset. William Fostcroft: Oxfordshire, Berkshire, Wiltshire. Cave: Kent, Surrey, Suffolk, Hampshire. Grove: Essex, Suffolk, Norfolk, Lincolnshire. Cambden: Middlesex, Hertfordshire, Huntingdonshire, Cambridgeshire. Robynson: Bedfordshire, Buckinghamshire, Northamptonshire – remember Mr Cecil – Warwickshire. Adams: Staffordshire, Rutland, Leicestershire, Nottinghamshire, Derbyshire.                                   SP 10/11, no. 7

**492.**   [Before November 19].† [Warrant for] grant to Ralph Sherman, yeoman of the

---

\*     ? Lord Charles Brandon, the duchess's younger son.

†     This date, appearing on the dorse, is that of the expedition of the grant.

king's ewery, of the rectories of Brafield [on the Green], Northamptonshire (late of the monastery of St Andrew, Northampton), Wellingborough, Northamptonshire (late of the monastery of Crowland, Lincolnshire), Woollaston and Earls Barton, Northamptonshire (late of the monastery of Delapré, Northamptonshire) and all their appurtenances, which Henry VIII granted by letters under the great seal of the court of augmentations dated 26 August 1544 to William, Lord Parr of Horton for life and eight years after his death, saving to the crown great woods and advowsons of vicarages: from the end of Lord Parr's interest for twenty-one years, paying yearly for the rectory of Brafield £12, for Wellingborough £40.6.0, for Wollaston £20 and for Earls Barton £14 at or within one month of Michaelmas and Lady Day. Quit of all other outgoings. Granting one great timber and other necessaries for repairs of buildings and sufficient housebote, hedgebote, firebote, ploughbote and cartbote.

*Latin.*

*Superscribed*: To the king.

*Sign manual.*

*Signed by*: the duke of Somerset, the archbishop of Canterbury, the earl of Wiltshire, the earl of Warwick, the earl of Bedford, the marquess of Northampton, Lord Clinton, Lord Wentworth, Sir Thomas Cheyne, Sir Richard Sackville and Richard Duke.                                                                          SP 10/11, no. 8

**493.**   November 19. Stamford. The duchess of Suffolk to William Cecil.

My thanks for what you have done for me in my cousin [William] Nanton's cause. I ask forgiveness for all my coarseness in this matter. I must write to [the duke and duchess of] Somerset to thank them for their gentleness.

*Holograph.*                                                                        SP 10/11, no. 9

**494.**   November 19. Offington. Lord De La Warr, from his house there, and Edward Shelley to William Cecil.

We received today a letter from the council dated November 16 whereby we perceive they think that we the justices of the peace in [Sussex] do not order ourselves according to the king's proclamation and our duty. I, Lord De La Warr, have written to the council that the cause of the let is lack of justices. At our assembly last Monday at my house were only myself, Sir William Goringe the sheriff, Edward Shelley and Thomas Onley – the rest of the rapes of Arundel and Bramber being at London or sick. For lack of help we could do nothing. But this Wednesday I have begun with Edward Shelley to view the barns and to proceed as far as our limits stretch, certifying their lordships that there is not enough barley or malt to serve the king and the markets here, nor is to be had here that number save of wheat, of which 250 quarters shall be shipped in the rapes of Chichester, Arundel and Bramber. We do not know what order the other three rapes – Lewes, Pevensey and Hastings – have taken. Convey the effect of this letter to the council. We will send copies of these last letters to the rest of the justices of the peace in this shire.

*Printed*: Heinze, *Proclamations*, 231 (extracts).                              SP 10/11, no. 10

**495.**   November 19. Boston. The mayor and burgesses of Boston to William Cecil, recorder of Boston, in London.

Boston is now in great distress for want of wheat and other grain which (since the last proclamation) cannot be had in this king's port. The justices of the peace in Holland have made diligent view and search from town to town in all their allotments, according to the proclamation, and have found that all Holland is not able to victual Boston or furnish the market with wheat and other necessary grain. The common bakers and brewers of the town cannot be suffered to buy any wheat or other grain in other market towns, but are answered that every country ought to victual its adjoining market. Unless you help us in soliciting the premises to the council, that we may have the king's licence for common victuallers inhabiting the town to buy in other shires and markets necessary wheat and other corn, the inhabitants and others coming to the port by water shall want victual. Certified as true by the justices of Holland – Nicholas Robartson, Blase Hollande, Anthony Robartson and John Rede.

    *Signed by*: the justices above named.

    *Printed*: Heinze, *Proclamations*, 231 (extracts).             SP 10/11, no. 11

**496.**   November 23. Beeleigh. Princess Mary to an unidentified lord.

    Thank you for your kind letters. It is not, as you and other of my friends think, the soil and air of this house which is the occasion of my sickness, but the time of year, when I have seldom escaped the same sickness. None of my household is sick. I had made provisions at Wanstead and St John's two months past, where I intended to lie all this winter. Because of one dead at Wanstead of the plague who was buried in the churchyard very near the gate, I was driven from that house. Then, my disease coming on me so sore and hearing that the air at St John's was not clear, I dare not venture so far a journey – which was a grief because my chief intent was to have seen the king. Having no house near, I thought it not meet to make any more provision in another house, but determined to rest here until Christmas was past, and caused my officers to make provision accordingly. Thank you for offering to give order for any of the king's or any other man's houses. If I do spy any suitable house I will be bold to require your favour – minding, if strength and health suffer me, to change the air and house here for its cleaning and borrow the lord chancellor's house for ten or twelve days.

    *Holograph.*

    *Printed*: Tytler, i, 345–8.                SP 10/11, no. 12

**497.**   November 28. Newark upon Trent. William Rygges to William Cecil.

    I have received your unkind letters. You say you cannot otherwise write to one whom you take to be your friend until you are better ordered. If I have mis-ordered you, as I am sure I have not willingly, I am sorry. As for the bailiwick, I never knew or heard that you were about the same either for your uncle or anybody else until now, and so I thought you would have judged of me until I had answered it or spoken with you. I trust you never heard that I ever went about to prevent any man in any matter, even my enemies, much less my friends, amongst whom I have ever taken you though I never deserved it. I am sure that he who is nearest you never bare you more good will then I have since I first knew you. There is one who is right honourable, your friend and mine, who can declare what my good will was towards you when you were in your greatest trouble. You say that the more blindness you looked for at my hand, the less you have. I would you had had occasion of my kindness and known me as you were but acquainted with me; then you would have been assured of me. So you may and shall do in this thing of which you write, and anything else. As for those quit rents which, you are informed, I will not allow to the bailiffs: I wish you had experience of a number of them as I have. Then I am sure you would not be offended with me. I am unable to control them by record in their demands of allowance. They ask too much, and I therefore [? ref]use to respect those rents of which I have no record until I have certificate from the surveyors, so that there is no disallowance or prejudice to yourself. Accept this in good part. Never a friend's letter grieved me so much. I trust your gentleness is such that, as your letter has disquieted me, so with another you will quiet me. *Postscript.* Today your servant William Amblyn was with me and has taken order that neither you nor your tenants shall be more disquieted, and the bailiffs to redeliver such money to them as they wrongfully received.

*Holograph.*                     SP 10/11, no. 13

**498.** [November]. Dr William Turner to William Cecil.

By your letter and your saying that you were weary of my matter I perceive that you were offended with my opportunity and with my letter to Master Pertryge. I have a reasonable excuse. Many about my lord promised to remind my lord's grace of my poor state. Seeing they did not, I thought best to essay what Master Pertryge would do for me.

There are no laws to depose the masters* of Magdalen College and the fellows would be forsworn if they chose me, never having been a fellow there. The king cannot (as all learned men say) put out the master* of Oriel College that I might be placed there. God forbid that I should cause perjury or wrongful deprivation. Take no more displeasure for me in labouring for either. As for the archdeaconry,† God forbid me who laboured to come into it by the window and not only for Christ. I laboured to come to it by friendship, as thieves and murderers now enter Christ's sheepfold. Let him that is most lawfully called to that office take it. Leave off labouring for it and all other benefices with cure for me. The papists will live out their time in the colleges and benefices and get yet more promotions, whether you and all other good men will or no. The law of man is so much on their side. When they are dead, perchance some Christians of the court for their long service shall succeed them, unless on the point of death they resign their offices to their brother papists, as [William] Haynes did to [John] Smith, now master of Oriel.

A benefice is no living or reward but a burden and labour. If I do my duty in my benefice I am worth my whole wage: then why should I thank any other man for that living? If I do not my duty, why should I receive of the poor and then thank a gentleman? The presentation should be freely given to the best. Is it meet that Christ's mystical body should give me £40 a year, that I should three ways feed it, and take that living for service in a gentleman's house? Therefore I intend to sue no more for any benefice. When Christ's church needs me it will lawfully call me without any of my labour. In the meantime, if I had health I would be able to get my living with my science not only in England but in Holland, Brabant and many places of Germany, although some think it would not be in England until I were better known. Seeing I cannot have health in England and am every day more vexed with the stone, help me to obtain licence of the king and council to go to Germany with two little horses, to dwell there for a time, where I may with small cost drink only Rhenish wine, and so be delivered of the stone as I was the last time I dwelt there. If I might have my poor prebend‡ yearly I will correct the whole New Testament in English and write a book of the causes of my correction of the translation. I will also finish my great herbal and my books of fishes, stones and metals. Answer at your leisure. Interpret all in the best part. You must sometimes abide other men's judgements. God grant your old divinity may bear always the chief authority.

*Holograph.*
*Printed*: Tytler, i, 333–7.                 SP 10/11, no. 14

**499.** December 6. Westminster. The king and council to justices of the peace.

We have of late set forth one proclamation for bringing all grain to the open markets and another for rating prices of all grain, butter and cheese by the judgements of experienced men. Our further pleasure has been signified to you by sundry letters from our council. This we did for the affection we bear for the profit of our subjects. We

---

\*      The heads of Magdalen and Oriel are properly called president and provost respectively.
†      Of the East Riding see no. **469** above.
‡      Botevant in York Minster.

also signified to you that, our proclamation being obeyed and the markets well served, if any prices seemed to need redress, upon suit and knowledge from you, we would order reformation. Now, understanding from Hertfordshire and other parts that our former determination touching prices cannot (because of last year's scarcity which is now found greater than at the beginning was thought, and for other considerations) take such good effect as was looked for, we signify that, upon suits from sundry parts, we revoke our later proclamation for the prices of grain, butter and cheese. Cause this our pleasure to be published as you think best, and henceforth allow these prices to be at liberty and none other than buyers and sellers can agree upon. See our former proclamation for bringing grain and victuals to the markets well observed.

*King's stamp.*

*Countersigned by*: the duke of Somerset, the archbishop of Canterbury, the earl of Wiltshire, the earl of Bedford, the marquess of Northampton, Lord Clinton, Lord Wentworth, Lord Paget, Sir Thomas Cheyne and Sir Anthony Wingfield.

SP 10/11, no. 15

**500.**   December 20. Boston. The mayor and burgesses of Boston to William Cecil, secretary of state, in London.

Thank you for your letter of November 13. We are all much bound to you for your love, not only because you have hitherto forborne to enter your lands by authority of your office (as you write for the determination of the title between the king and us) but also for divers other kindnesses to us in all our other suits to you – as yet not so thankfully recompensed as they should be. We intend to gratify your kindness without any longer contract of time. Next term Mr Mayor and others of the town will repair to you in London, and by your advice call upon the interest and title of our lands pending in star chamber for determination between the king and us, which we never intended the contrary; also to show and deliver you an abstract or book of the revenues of all our lands, with all deductions and yearly outgoings, that you may see that none of us that has the ordering thereof has had one penny's advantage (except the bailiffs and suchlike officers for their fees), although some of our enemies have otherwise reported. If any such report is made to you, we trust you will give it no credit. You are our good master, in whom is our greatest trust in all our suits. We intend to make you privy in all our matters. We send you by this bearer a poor remembrance in wildfowl, to make you merry this Christmas.

SP 10/11, no. 16

**501.**   [? December]. Parliamentary bill for better administration of justice.

The ministration of justice and determination of causes has been hindered because sheriffs and other ministers to whom execution of the king's process pertained have often neglected the same, making untrue or insufficient returns, detaining writs and by other unseemly practices. Many that have sued in the king's high court at Westminster, besides long and expensive suits, have lost their just dues by death or some other discontinuance of their suits by tract of time, and sometimes because the defendants decayed in substance and were unable to satisfy that which with long and tedious suit was recovered. For reformation be it enacted by the present parliament that the act of 23 Henry VI [c. 9] concerning sheriffs, their deputies, bailiffs and other ministers and all other former acts now in force concerning execution or return of process shall stand in all points other than shall be altered by this act. If any sheriff from November 1 next appoints any under sheriff or clerk for receipt, execution or return of process to him directed, the sheriff shall by his warrant [*in form specified*] to be put into the courts of king's bench and common pleas, besides the warrants commonly used to be put in for his deputies, authorise the under sheriff or clerk so to act in the name of the high sheriff. No high sheriff shall authorize any person to receive, execute or return any writs into either of the said courts before such warrant be so put in, on forfeit of £40. No person shall take upon himself as under sheriff or sheriff's clerk to receive, execute or return such process before such warrant be put in, on like forfeiture. One moiety of such forfeitures to be to the king, the other to the party that will sue for the same by any means. Provided that if any sheriff takes his first charge out of term time or any under sheriff or sheriff's clerk die before the discharge of the high sheriff between terms, then the high sheriff may authorize a new under sheriff or clerk without penalty, putting in the warrant within eight days after the beginning of the next term. No under sheriff or sheriff's clerk shall so act before he has taken a corporal oath [*in form specified*] before the barons of the exchequer or the justices of the peace in open general sessions or before two justices of the peace of the county, whereof one to be of the quorum, on forfeit of £40. Every such oath made in the exchequer shall be recorded there, being made at the open general sessions shall be entered of record there before the *custos rotulorum*, and being made before two justices of the peace shall be recorded at the next general sessions held in the same county on certificate of the justices or one of them. All bailiffs of liberties and franchises and all other bailiffs to whom serving and executing any precepts or warrants to be directed from any sheriff after November 20 next shall obtain, before they execute them shall take a corporal oath [*in form specified*] before the justices of the peace at the open general sessions of the county or before two justices of the peace whereof one to be of the quorum. No person after November 20 next shall as bailiff execute or serve any precept or warrant unless he be first so sworn, on forfeit of £40; the king to have one moiety and the party that will sue for the same the other. Every oath shall be recorded in form aforesaid. 4d. shall be paid for recording every oath of every under sheriff, sheriff's clerk and bailiff. All writs delivered to the under sheriff or clerk, being warranted of record in form aforesaid, shall be as effectual to bind the high sheriff or sheriffs as though they were delivered of record to the other deputies of record of the same sheriff or sheriffs. [Deputies of record are appointed by effect of 23 Henry VI. Under sheriffs were before no deputies of record].*

All sheriffs, under sheriffs and sheriffs' clerks to whom process shall be delivered to be executed shall do as much as they can to execute the process to the said sheriff directed themselves or direct his precept or warrant to the bailiff of such franchise, hundred or place where the party sued shall be supposed to be, or where it shall be by or for the plaintiff otherwise required if the process be for the arrest of any person; if the process concerns any other thing, the precept or warrant to be made to such bailiff as by whom it may be conveniently executed, on forfeit of £20. Every bailiff shall execute without fraud every precept and warrant to him directed as much as he conveniently may, and shall thereof make true and undelayed certificate, on pain of forfeitures hereafter recited. If default of not executing or untrue returning any process (not being delivered of record) shall be proved upon any averment hereafter to be grounded on this act to be in any under sheriff, sheriff's clerk or bailiff (other than bailiffs of franchises) and not in the sheriff, every one so offending shall forfeit to the high sheriff the like penalty for such offence as in this act is limited against the sheriffs, if the same under sheriff, clerk or bailiff be able to satisfy for the same to be recovered, in form hereafter recited. [If not, the high sheriff or sheriffs shall satisfy for the residue].† [An act to like effect, for false returns made by sheriffs' clerks, 26 Edward I].‡

If any writ duly delivered of record in any of the said courts shall not be returned within the time hereafter limited, the sheriff to whom it is directed shall forfeit to the king £5, to be assessed by the justices of the court where it should have been returned.

---

\*     Inserted. This and subsequently noted insertions are marginal glosses, not intended as part of the text of the bill.

†     Deleted.

‡     Inserted.

The same penalty shall be for not returning any writ although it be not delivered of record; in which case the offence to be first proved by averment as hereafter recited and then the grieved party to have the moiety. [A statute thereof, Westminster 2, and the default triable before justices of assize].*

All sheriffs and other officers having return of any writ or precept to them directed shall make true return as they shall be executed, on forfeit of £40. Provided that this and former acts [Westminster 2]* shall not bind any sheriff to return the just value of issues which by the law and former statutes ought to be returned upon every writ of distress. [More easy than the effect of Westminster 2].* So that there be returned upon every first writ of distress 5s. in issues at least, upon the second writ of distress 10s., and so upon every writ from then awarded the issues to be doubled at least. If any sheriff or other minister with return of any writ or warrant shall make any return insufficient in law he shall forfeit to the king £5, to be assessed by the justices of the court wherein the offence shall be perceived. Provided that accidental omission or mis-writing of any word shall not be reputed such an offence. [The effects of 14 Edward III (st. 1 c. 6) and 8 Henry VI (c. 12) provide for the like but not by words sufficient].* Every such default shall be amended by command of the justices. Provided also that every sheriff may cause all his insufficient returns to be amended in open court within eight days after the writs shall be returned, and save the penalty. No sheriff or other minister shall let to bail or under surety or otherwise go at liberty without lawful discharge any who by any former law be not bailable, on forfeit of £10 besides penalties provided in former statutes; the king to have one moiety and the party that will sue for the same the other, to be recovered in form first declared. [Westminster 1: the pain is loss of the sheriff's office. The justices of common pleas may punish the same: statute *de finibus*].*

Sometimes by negligence and sometimes because of diverse attorneys there have been entries in the rolls of the said courts purporting that writs were delivered of record where they were not, nor any such writ made. By reason of this judgements and outlawries were made erroneous and reversed, and sheriffs have been amerced wrongfully for not returning such writs, besides many other enormities ensuing from the imperfect order of delivery of writs of record. [By effect of 4 and 6 Henry VIII (cc. 4 and 4 respectively) all writs of proclamations upon exigents must be delivered of record, so that all such writs be entered to be delivered of record although they be not].* Be it therefore enacted that from the beginning of next Easter term there shall be in the courts of king's bench and common pleas one person named by the king, an officer or clerk of the court whereunto he shall be appointed, called the clerk of enrolment of writs, who shall enter of record all writs delivered of record in the same court and deliver the writs to the sheriffs or their deputies in form hereafter specified. If any person shall be minded to have any original writs delivered of record he shall bring them sealed to the said clerk who shall open them and note them in his book of remembrance and deliver them to the sheriff to whom they are directed, or to one of his deputies of the same court. After any writ judicial is sued forth out of either of the said courts, the party or his attorney shall bring every such writ (if it shall be delivered of record) to the said clerk and shall deliver him the fee for the seal and enrolment. The clerk shall enter the effect of every such writ in his book and cause it to be sealed. He shall with all speed deliver every such writ to the sheriff or one of his deputies in form aforesaid. He shall then make a brief entry in the rolls of the court of every such writ [*in form specified*]. The clerk shall have 4d. for every writ by him so delivered of record. All writs directed to any sheriffs out of either of the said courts being writs judicial in actions real or mixed and all writs of execution except writs of *habere facias seisinam*, *capias ad satisfaciendum* or single *capias utlagatum*, all jury writs except writs of *venire facias* and all writs of exigent, writs of proclamations upon exigents and writs of special *capias utlagatum* shall be delivered of

* Inserted.

record in form aforesaid. No other writs shall be delivered of record unless required by the party at whose suit such writs shall be awarded by his attorney; then all such writs to be delivered for the said fee of 4d. No writs in either of the said courts shall be delivered of record except by the said clerks or their deputies. Every such clerk, before he exercises the office, shall take a corporal oath before the justices of the court for the true exercise of the office, in the form used by other officers of the court. If either of the clerks appoints any deputy or clerk to enrol or deliver of record any writs, he shall first present him to the justices of the court who shall minister to him a like oath. If the justices suspect the true demeanour of any such deputy they may refuse to admit him. No person shall presume to be deputy or clerk for either of the said officers before such admission, on forfeit of £40; one moiety to the king, the other to the party that will sue for the same.

Every sheriff, or one deputy at least for every sheriff, shall be attendant in either of the courts from four days after the beginning of the next term until its end, on forfeit of £10. [They be bound thereto already but upon no such pain].* Provided that albeit any sheriff or his deputy shall default when called yet if within two days he repairs to the clerk for enrolment of writs and receives of him all such writs as then shall be directed to the same sheriff the penalty will be saved. [More beneficial to sheriffs than before].* Provided also that the clerk, immediately after the calling for every such sheriff so making default shall set upon a post in the court a brief note of the day and time when the sheriff was called. None of the clerks shall be bound to deliver any process of record except in open court. If by default of the sheriffs and their deputies any writs shall remain undelivered, the officer shall enter the amercement aforesaid to the king's use. He shall then deliver all such writs to the demandants or plaintiffs or their attorneys, if they require it, that they may have the writs otherwise delivered to the sheriffs or their deputies to be executed. [They may deliver their writs in the open county: Westminster 2].* Either of the clerks, at the days of return of all such writs (if required by the party or his attorney) shall call on the said sheriffs for return of the same writs. If at the day at or before which they ought to be returned by this act any such writ is not returned the officer or clerk is to enter the amercement heretofore limited for the same to the king's use against the offending sheriff, without taking anything for the entry of such amercements. All sheriffs to return into each of the courts all their writs within two days after the usual time of return of the same writs, except such writs as are returnable on the first day of term – all which are to be returned into the same court within eight days after the first day of term. Provided that if any writs are accidentally burned or if any sheriffs, under sheriffs or clerks, in bringing writs to be returned, fall sick or are hindered by imprisonment, floods or other impediments without fraud, so that the writs cannot be returned before the time limited in this act, and the same duly proved by examination of the justices of the court, no penalty will be incurred. All such writs (not burned or lost) to be returned as soon as possible after the said time of return. [More beneficial to sheriffs than before].* The *custos brevium* of neither court shall receive any writs after the time limited by this statute, on forfeit of £10.

Much slander has arisen concerning the *post diems* of writs because many attorneys of either court demand allowance of 4d. for the *post diem* of every or most writs which they sued forth, where in fact they caused the writs to be returned at the very days of return of the same, and so did convert the *post diems* to their own uses, whereby their clients were more charged and more offended than if a certain ordinary fee had been limited for filing every writ. Also the clerks and servants of divers officers of the same courts and others, for filing such *post diems*, which should have been paid to the *custos brevium*, have embezzled and not put in many writs, whereby many suits and recoveries have been made erroneous. Be it therefore enacted that the *custos brevium* of each of the said

*      Inserted.

courts shall not hereafter receive for filing any writs to be made after April 1 next the fee of 4d. for a *post diem* or any fee otherwise than is recited in this act. Each of the *custodes brevium* shall take for filing every writ concerning any action real or mixed 2d., for every other writ (except writs of exigent whereupon any outlawry shall be endorsed) 1d.

Sheriffs, under sheriffs and bailiffs have heretofore exacted money for execution and return of process and precepts, contrary to previous statutes, partly because of the great travail and costs wherewith sheriffs have been burdened in serving process of attendance to the king's courts and the king's affairs and with chargeable fees upon their accounts in the exchequer, and also because by former statutes no fees were limited to sheriffs and their ministers for execution of process. Be it therefore enacted that from April 1 all sheriffs and other ministers may take for execution and return of writs and precepts, besides fees allowed by former laws or lawful usages: for writs of execution in actions personal or mixed wherupon no extent shall be made by oath, whereof the debt or damages in both shall be under £10 – 2s., above £10 – 3s. 4d. [They would for the most part have 12d. for every £1 upon writs of extent].* For writs of execution whereupon extent shall be made by oath, being in debt or danger: above 40s. and under £10 – 3s. 4d., £10 and above and under £20 – 6s. 8d., £20 and above and under £40 – 10s., £40 and above – £1. For every writ of enquiry by oath – 3s. 4d. For every writ to make petition or to assign dower or suchlike – 6s. 8d. [They have exacted more in such cases].* Provided that the party at whose suit such writs of extent, writs of inquisition and writs to make petition, or to assign dower or suchlike shall be awarded shall bear the charge of writing and engrossing the inquisitions, petitions and assignments. Bailiffs and other ministers that serve precepts upon all such writs shall have the moiety of the said fees for their pains in warning the jury and other attendance; and also for all jury writs whereupon any jury shall be warned to appear 3s. 4d., whereof the sheriff to have 12d. for the precepts and the bailiff the residue. [Bailiffs have for the most part demanded 4d. for warning every juror].*

By a former statute there is limited 2s. to be taken of every person arrested, whereof the sheriff shall have 20d. and the bailiff 4d. Be it enacted that in such case the bailiff that shall arrest any person shall have the moiety of the fee and the sheriff the other. All bailiffs of franchises may have for executing every precept like fees as sheriffs, except the fee for making the sheriff's warrants. If any sheriff, under sheriff, sheriff's clerk or deputy or bailiff by himself or another exact any fee above this or former statutes or lawful usage he shall forfeit £40; one moiety to the king and the other to the party that will sue. If contention arises concerning time and order of payment of fees the justices of every court are to give order.

In all actions or suits wherein costs shall be awarded to either party the fees aforesaid shall be allowed as ordinary costs. The lord chancellor and lord treasurer shall have authority to examine within the next year all fees heretofore paid to sheriffs' accountants in the exchequer and to disallow those they consider superfluous or too great. All fees they allow are to be displayed openly in the exchequer for ever. If any officer, clerk or minister of the exchequer after April 1 next receives any fees concerning sheriffs' accounts other than ordinarily limited in the exchequer court or after this new rate, or delay the finishing of any sheriff's account, he shall forfeit £40; one moiety to the king and the other to the party that shall sue.

Many matters have been slenderly handled and much embezzling of prices and other unseemly practices frequented. Many young and unlearned persons have been admitted attorneys and others, being no attorneys, have sued forth writs and other process out of the said courts, whereby much deceit has been practised. Be it therefore enacted that no person shall be hereafter admitted attorney in any of the said courts until he is

*     Inserted.

twenty-five and examined by the justices of his honest conversation, ability in learning and experience in suit of process. Only those admitted and sworn attorneys of the courts shall sue out any writs or process returnable into the same courts, on forfeit of £10; one moiety to the king, the other to the party giving information thereof. This shall not inhibit any attorney sending his clerk or servant for any writ, process, copy, pleading or other thing required, so long as he does not set his master's name to any officer's remembrance or such like.

Divers good statutes and ordinances made concerning due execution and return of process have been smally regarded and executed because the means provided for recovery of penalties against sheriffs and others was cumbersome (being by verdict of twelve men of the county where the offence was committed, the sheriffs mostly being there so befriended and of such power that it was hard for any to prevail there in such matter). For some offences the penalties were too small and no recompense to the party grieved. [Damages only for false returns: 26 Edward I. Damages only for not returning writs: Westminster 2. Justices of assize to have power to enquire thereof: 2 Edward III (c. 8)].* For some offences no remedy was provided except action upon the case against the sheriff, which is costly and small damages are for the most part recovered. So sheriffs, under sheriffs and their other ministers have remained free to do evil without punishment. Be it therefore enacted that in all cases aforesaid where the offence concerning return or execution of writs, precepts or other process shall not appear to the justices of the said courts of record but shall depend upon further trial, the party grieved by any such offences committed after April 1 may in the same term in which the offence is committed or within two terms following make information in whichever of the two courts the writ or process shall or should have been returned [in form specified]. Although the default whereupon the averment shall be grounded shall be in the under sheriff, sheriff's clerk, deputy or sheriff's bailiff, the averment shall be made against the high sheriff. If upon process and trial made the default shall appear to be in any under sheriff, clerk, deputy or bailiff, judgement shall be given that the plaintiff shall recover the penalty, costs and damages as hereafter declared against the same sheriff. The sheriff shall recover the value against the under sheriff, clerk, deputy or bailiff. Provided that no sheriff shall have judgement to recover in value as above unless on his appearance he commits to the court his excuse that the default was in his under sheriff or other minister and prays a writ to summon the offender to be there at the day of prefixion; unless at that day the writ of summons shall be returned served, then the sheriff shall recover the value if the default is found to be in the under sheriff or other minister. Provided also that by the same writ it shall be commanded that if the sheriff or other minister to whom any such writ shall be directed cannot find the party that ought to be summoned, then he shall summon him at his house if he have one in the same county; if not he shall make open proclamation in one of the chief market towns or cities of the county that he shall be before the justices on the said day to prove what he can concerning the averment.

If any default shall be in any bailiff of any liberty or franchise having execution and return of writs or precepts, and if it is testified by return of the sheriff that he made his precept to the bailiff of the franchise for execution of the writ, then the averment shall be made against the bailiff so offending [in form specified]. [Like remedy for false returns by bailiffs of franchises as against sheriffs: 1 Edward III (st. 1 c. 4)].

If any sheriff or his minister shall return that there was made a precept to the bailiff of the liberty or franchise where in fact no such precept was made; [if the brief falsely return mandavi ballivo libertatis, &c. the lord of the franchise and the party grieved shall recover damages: Westminster 2];* or if any sheriff shall return any other answer than the bailiff of the liberty shall return or certify to him whereby any bailiff of any liberty shall be condemned in any form upon this act, then every such bailiff may have an action

* Inserted.

against the high sheriff upon this act, and shall recover against the sheriffs as much as before shall be by the false return of the sheriff recovered against him and treble damages with his ordinary costs. [The return of the bailiff of the franchise to be indented between the sheriff and him, and if the sheriff return otherwise double damages as above: statute of York].*

If any averment conceived upon this act is found true, it shall not abate because of variance or omission of words, lack of form or other misprision of the clerks or officers of the court. If at the time of making such averment against any sheriff he is not removed from office, then immediately upon the putting in of the averment the sheriff shall be solemnly demanded in the same court to answer the same. If the sheriff or any attorney for him shall within two days appear, then after the plea of the sheriff a day of prefixion shall be appointed as hereafter declared. If the sheriff or his attorney does not so appear, his under sheriff, clerk or deputy of record or as many as are present shall be called before the justices and the averment read out. If no insufficiency appears the justices shall appoint a day of prefixion in the following term to hear the [process]† proofs to be brought in upon the averment. Open proclamation shall be made in the court that both parties shall be before the justices at that day with their witnesses and proofs. No plea in bar shall be received upon such averment other than not guilty or such other special matter that shall sound to that effect. If the sheriff against whom the averment is made shall be removed before the making of the averment, immediately after its making one writ of summons importing the effect of the averment shall be directed to the new sheriff, commanding him to summon the former sheriff before the king's justices of the said courts at such day of return of the term or the next term as the plaintiff shall think good (so as there are fifteen full days before the *teste* of the writ and the day of its return) to make answer, which writ shall be delivered of record in form aforesaid. At which day, if the new sheriff return the writ sealed and the old sheriff in person or by attorney appears and pleads, the same plea shall be entered and a day of prefixion appointed by the justices for the hearing thereof next term, and so further to proceed according to the meaning of this act.

If the sheriff after his appearance and after a peremptory day of answer given him pleads no sufficient plea in bar or abatement of the averment, judgement shall be given against him by default. If upon any such writ of summons returned against the former sheriff he or his attorney shall not appear within two days after the same return, a day of prefixion shall be appointed for hearing the matter in the next term and the same openly proclaimed in court. If the writ of summons shall not be returned duly executed and served further process by summons to be awarded of record until the former sheriff shall be returned to be duly summoned. Coroners are to be proceeded against as bailiffs of liberties and sheriffs after their discharge.

No essoin, protection or wager of law shall be allowed upon any action, averment or suit conceived upon this act. If either party to such averments is in doubt that such persons as they shall require to testify will not appear at the day of prefixion without process, they may sue out against them one writ of *sub pena*. [In trials by twelve men if the witnesses would not come the party had no remedy except in special cases].* If any person to whom such writ shall in due time default with no special impediment or excuse he shall forfeit to the grieved party £10 to be demanded by action of debt and a fine to the king at the discretion of the justices of the court. If any such are sick, in prison or otherwise unable to be present, and this being by *affidavit* of two credible witnesses testified in the court, the justices shall appoint a new day of prefixion. A commission may be directed at the suit of either party to four, three or two persons named by the justices in open court in presence of both parties, if there, not objectionable to either

*　　　Inserted.
†　　　Deleted.

party, to receive depositions from impeded witnesses and certify their doings before the day of prefixion. If the commissioners, without special impediment, refuse or omit to examine the witnesses or certify their doings, they shall forfeit to the grieved party £10 to be recovered by action of debt and a fine to the king to be assessed by the justices.

At the first day of prefixion upon such averments no cause or allegation other than is declared shall stay the proceeding to the hearing of the same. No cause (death of either party excepted) shall stay the proceeding to hearing the same matter at the second day of prefixion. Justices shall have authority to award damages to the party to whom judgement is given, assessed at their discretion, and all ordinary costs (besides the penalty recovered if it is found for the plaintiff). The parties at whose denunciation or request any persons shall be examined as witnesses shall bear all reasonable expenses of their travelling to give testimony. All such expenses, being first examined by the justices, shall by their discretion be allowed as ordinary costs if the matter is found for the same party. If any person shall fraudulently procure a witness not to appear or not to testify the truth he shall forfeit to the grieved party £20 to be recovered by action of debt. These fees shall be paid for the writs and entries: for the entry of every averment 2s., for entering the day of prefixion 1s., for every writ of summons and *sub pena* 6d., for seal for entry of the commission 2s., for writing the commission 1s., for the seal 1s., for other pleading, judgement and other proceedings such fees as are used for like in either of the said courts in actions personal. If any ambiguity arises concerning the course, form, entries or other proceedings, the justices of the court where the averment is made shall order them.

If upon any such averment the default shall be found in any under sheriff, clerk or sheriff's bailiff and judgement given in form aforesaid, execution for the penalty, damages and costs recovered against the high sheriff may be awarded against the same sheriff. Like execution in value may be for the same sheriff against the under sheriff, clerk or bailiff in whom the default shall be found in form following. [By statute of 26 Edward I the sheriff shall answer for so much as the clerk shall not be able to satisfy where the fault is in the clerk].* Writs may be awarded to sheriffs or other officers in any counties in which the party against whom such execution shall be awarded is submitted to have lands, goods or chattels. All which writs shall be delivered of record and returnable at one day. By which writs all lands, goods and chattels of the party condemned shall be valued and their value returned into the court. If it appears that more goods shall be valued than shall suffice with the issues of his lands, if any be extended, for satisfaction of the condemnation, the overplus shall be awarded again to the defendant. [By common law such execution cannot be had save by *elegit* in which case execution shall be but of the moiety of the land].* If the condemned party has no lands but goods and chattels insufficient to satisfy the condemnation, or no lands, goods or chattels, a writ may be awarded into as many counties as may be required to arrest the body of the condemned party to satisfy in form abovesaid. [By common law the first *capias ad satisfaciendum* must be directed to the county where the action was sued, and none other until a *non est inventus* is there returned, and then the party cannot have two writs into two several counties].* All lands extended upon any such condemnation shall be delivered to the party in execution to hold by like tenure as tenants by *elegit* now do, until they are fully satisfied for the same condemnation. Provided that when any default shall be alleged to be in any under sheriff, sheriff's clerk or sheriff's bailiff and a writ of summons awarded and returned served, if the same under sheriff, sheriff's clerk or deputy shall not appear at the day of prefixion, but the trial shall proceed in his absence and the default tried to be in the same, then the high sheriff shall not have execution in value against him before a *scire facias* is sued out to warn him to be before the justices at a certain day to show why execution in value should not be awarded against him. The proceeding upon

---

\*      Inserted.

which writ shall be as used in other writs of *scire facias* in the same court. [Else the under sheriff might be at a great mischief, *ut antea*].* If the defendant shall appear and plead any special matter which shall declare the default whereupon the averment was conceived to be in the high sheriff, the same to be received and tried by proofs upon a day of prefixion as above, his former default notwithstanding.

All penalties limited in this act other than those wholly to the king and wholly to the party grieved, and other than such whereof one moiety is to the king and the other to the party that will sue for the same, shall be divided as follows: one fourth to the king, another fourth to be distributed to the poor at the appointment of the justices, the residue to the party grieved that shall sue for the same by averment. As much of the fines limited to the king shall be estreated by the clerk of the estreats of the same court the same term in which judgement shall be given or in which the same shall be assessed into the court of exchequer and shall be there levied as issues and amercements are usually levied, any statute, law or usage to the contrary notwithstanding. [Because this order is not generally taken the king loses much profit].*

*40¹/₂ pp.*

*Fair copy with marginal insertions (as noted above) in another hand.*                    SP 10/11, no. 17

**502.**    [1550]. Treatise by Stephen Gardiner, bishop of Winchester in answer to eucharistic and other doctrines advanced by John Hooper, bishop of Gloucester.

*65 ff. with covers from a medieval MS.*                                                              SP 10/12

**503.**    1551. January 5. Somerset Place. Dr William Turner to William Cecil.

I have been with [the archbishop of] Canterbury, who can get no perfect answer of the lawyers of the [court of] arches. Ask him to send in writing the answer he has had. He thinks that the bishop of Bath had no authority to put down the dean,† although he deserved deposition, because he was appointed by the king and was therefore best deposed by some appointed by the king. Some learned in the law should examine and depose him. I think they will grant that if he had been deposed by the king it would have been lawful, for they grant that by taking the second dignity he lost the first. The lawyers of the arches, knowing the deanery is laboured for by me, will hinder the matter as much as they can. I trust your wisdom will prevail against their malice. If this cannot be had I would be very loath to lose the other promotion of Oxford.‡ I trust you will bring me to the university again.

*Holograph.*

*Printed*: Pocock, *Troubles*, 133–4.                                                              SP 10/13, no. 1

**504.**    January 16. Westminster. Licence to the earl of Warwick to alienate in perpetuity by fine in king's bench the manor of Lydney, Gloucestershire, held of the king in chief, to Sir William Herbert and his heirs, and licence for Herbert to hold the same.

*3 pp.*

*Latin.*

*Copy*: from C 66/832, m. 12 (*CPR* 1549–50, 357).                                          SP 10/13, no. 2

**505.**    January 18. London. William Lane, merchant of London to William Cecil.

I am anxious for redress of things without which our commonwealth will run headlong into misery. Not twelve days ago I talked with [Sir John] York of the mint who was about to make a new coin of fine silver, 11 oz. fine in 2s. pieces, of which five pieces and a little more should make 1 oz. I reckoned that 1 oz. of fine silver sold to the mint

---

*          Inserted.
†          John Goodman.
‡          See no. **498** above.

at 6s. 8d., being coined, should make about 11s. to be paid out again. I said that although the silver was fine it was too dear and the money nought. He answered that it was richer than the other money lately or now made. It is well known that the exchange between us and foreign realms sets the price of almost all things of which there is no scarcity, our merchandise as well as exports. I will tell what mischief has happened since my communication with York and in these six days. The exchange for Flanders, France and Spain among the merchants is fallen about 7 in 100 because of the news of the new coin, which the people will better reckon and understand the value of now in fine silver than before in the mixture. The fall of the exchanges comes of fear of the lightness of our silver coin [the private gain of coining silver is the only cause of its long continuance]* and is [also]* the only cause that all we English merchants rob England and carry abroad all the gold in the land, because it is to more profit than the exchange. Similar mischief happened here last June, July and August when £100,000 in gold was carried out, yet silver came in as fast, all for private gain in coining, and was carried away because the pound of gold is richer than that of white money. This mischief causes our gold to be bought up at 2s. 6d. and 2s. 8d. the pound for white money. Where lately the king called the French crown from 7s. to 19 groats, they are now bought up for 7s. 3d. and 7s. 4d., to be carried away as all other gold is. Shortly we shall be quit of all our rich money for a base coin, followed by a greater fall in the exchange, the cause of dearth in almost all things.

If we should coin in six years to come so much white money as we have done in the last six, of the value that now goes, 3s. a day would not be a living wage for a poor man. Private gain in coining silver is the cause of its continuance, and what has been said will happen unless there is speedy redress. Our base coin cannot be refined without more charge than may be borne of the king or commons.

The fall of exchange within these four days has caused and will cause cloths to be bought at £66 the pack which before would not have been bought for £52. The exchange engenders dear cloth, dear cloth dear wool, dear wool many sheep, many sheep much and dear pasture, much pasture is the decay of tillage, from which springs scarcity of corn and dearth of all things.

What follows is more important. For six or eight years I have seen our commonwealth greatly charged by mostly unnecessary foreign goods. We spend more on foreign goods than the export of wool, cloth, tin, lead, leather, coals and other things can counter-balance, by a quarter part or less. We waste and consume in one year more in value of foreign goods than all the richness of our lands and the travail of our people can produce in five quarters of the year or more. By so much is our realm impoverished, in money or otherwise. But by exporting more than we import we should be enriched by foreigners and not they by us. A man who spends more than he produces necessarily decays. Yet lately I understand there is a restraint on export of lead: whoever invented this studied the commonwealth as much as he who invented that no coals should be exported from Newcastle except in a French ship. If better order were made for coals they might maintain three of our decayed towns and seats and provide work for 200 more ships and their sailors.

There are ways of redressing the latter enormity without touching the laws, intercourses or privileges between us and the house of Burgundy or the French king. But since superfluous imports cannot be remedied without parliament, in the meantime forward some remedy for the other matter, that we merchants carry not away all our rich money and leave the base money here. Once the private gain in coining is removed and our base coin of white money called down to 15s. the pound, it will do great service, keep our gold here, and stay many things which would otherwise come to misery. Do not be offended for my writing this simple judgement.

*    Deleted.

*Holograph.*
*Printed: Tudor Economic Documents*, ii, 182–6. SP 10/13, no. 3

**506.** January 20. Walter Bower, [fellow of Magdalen College, Oxford] to Dr William Turner, at Somerset House.

The president* has written to us declaring part of his trouble, desiring to know whether we will take him for our head, bear him favour, and not complain of him to the magistrates if he can retain his presidency. He promises to forego either his great benefice or his archdeaconry† to be sure of our conformity in writing. He is loath that one outside our foundation should come in – for love for the college, he says, but I think rather for lucre. He cares not to resign if we might have free election, and one that would favour the house. His friends said they cared not if he went that we might have one of our foundation and who would not give up our lands. You were named; nothing was spoken openly against you, but cloakedly. Fifteen would have the president asked to stay, for the safeguard of the college. Eight others said they were loath to hinder him and were content he should depart, trusting the house should do no worse after his departure than it did before his coming. Letters were sent to the president of what both parties said. Some fear lest [John] Harley should be preferred: he is my friend but shall never have my good will, for he is idle, not so ripe in God's truth and, worst, not much caring (I think) how religion goes forward, so that he has the pelf of the world. Stick to it lustily, as we do our will to you. We had rather keep Mr President than receive Mr Harley. Consider the state of our college, how it is provided to set forth learning for God's glory. God continue the king's favour to you and your friends; you shall have our prayers. But if it comes to election they will choose Harley, for the papists can [find] a way with him well enough. Only the king's letters must slake the stroke. The president complained in his letters that we had lately complained of him to the council. Keep it to yourself, disclosing the matter as you think good, but reserving my name to yourself. *Postscript.* He whom the president sent reported that he would be content to be president for two years without stipend until we might have free election. His friends have so handled the matter that fifteen have written to him to stay.

*Holograph.* SP 10/13, no. 4

**507.** February 8. Blankney. Thomas Husey to William Cecil.

My nephew Thorold has told me your pleasure touching the lease of Caythorpe park and my displeasure towards Nicholas Bayly. As I said to [John] Walpole I am content with you order for the lease, which this bearer shall satisfy. It is neither Caythorpe park nor the whole lease that I esteem in respect of your favour. But when Nicholas Bayly and I are heard with independent ears I trust to answer all that may be objected to me, and if I have done him one pennyworth of displeasure, to amend it with forty shillings. Although he sent word that he would complain to [the duchess of] Suffolk of me without declaring any matter, and lately his boasts in taverns and elsewhere have been that he would make my country vomit me out, and for lack of a house to place me in a cottage of his, besides that he knew how friendly my lord of Suffolk‡ and you were to me – so in mockery the matter has been so unadvisedly published that his own familiars have revealed it to me. I trust I shall never lose my lord of Suffolk or you, live without his cottage and become no stranger in Lincolnshire. These reports I have at his hands because I have done him pleasure and no harm. I shall say the rest to you at my coming

---

\* Of Magdalen [Owen Oglethorpe].

† Oglethorpe declined the archdeaconry of the East Riding. It is uncertain to which other benefice the writer alludes.

‡ Husey's master had been the duke of Norfolk; but it is as improbable that he should have written Suffolk in error as that he should seemingly refer to the late duke of Suffolk in the present tense; the young duke of Suffolk is presumably intended in the subsequent reference.

to London: this bearer will explain why I cannot come now. Credit him and satisfy your payment. SP 10/13, no. 5

**508.** February 17. Cambridge. The duchess of Suffolk to William Cecil.

At [Martin] Bucer's request and partly for my own commodity I ask you to see this his letter enclosed speedily delivered. If you cannot help, advise the bearer how it may be done. Why I require this you shall perceive from his letter, which he sends open. Considering his sickness, give it more than I am worth.

*Holograph.* SP 10/13, no. 6

**509.** March 4. Ingatestone. Sir William Petre, from his house there, to William Cecil.

Thank you for your letters which I received by this bearer, at whose sight I was first sorry because I suspected I had been sent for, and had things of my own to be done tomorrow. Your news made me sorry: God will amend this if we amend ourselves. I am glad of the likelihood of Lord Paget's placing in the room of the lord chamberlain:* so shall he that can well serve have good occasion to tarry at court. The rest I defer to our next meeting, which I intend to be next Sunday. Thank you for your book. My little ones, when they are able, shall send you some taste of their profit in those exercises. Commendations to you and your wife from me and mine.

*Holograph.*

*Printed*: F.G. Emmison, *Tudor Secretary*, (1961), 90–2. SP 10/13, no. 7

[For SP 10/13, no. 8 see no. **604** below.]

**510.** March 23. Westminster. Letters patent for the translation of John [Ponet], bishop of Rochester to the bishopric of Winchester vacant by the deprivation of Stephen [Gardiner], by virtue of an act of parliament† ordering appointment of bishops by letters patent in place of licence of *congé d'élire* and election by the dean and chapter.

*3 pp.*

*Latin.*

*Copy*: from C 66/835, m. 3 (*CPR* 1550–3, 34). SP 10/13, no. 9

[For SP 10/13, nos 10, 10(i), 11 and 12 see nos. **600, 599, 601** and **603** below respectively.]

**511.** April 17. John Hooper, bishop of Gloucester to William Cecil.

Thank you for your old friendship. God's word goes forward daily and would do so more if there were good teachers. Try to prevent any man having licence for two benefices, dangerous to the country, God, the king and the recipient. Cause order to be taken for prices, or God's wrath will punish. All things are here so dear that most people lack, and more will lack, necessary food. The body of a calf in the market is 14s. and a sheep 10s. White meat is so dear that a groat is nothing to a poor man to sow any victuals. All pasture and breeding of cattle is turned to sheep, which are not kept for the market but for wool and profit only their masters. If this continues the wealth and strength of the realm will perish. You know the tyranny of monopoly, as in Justinian, is not to the common good but to ruin. Those who have more than enough buy when things are cheap to sell afterwards dear. It is my duty to teach the people obedience, and all here love and reverence the king and the laws. But it is the magistrates and their doings which most commend them and win the people's love. You know what a perilous and unruly evil hunger is. There are many people; their cottages and poor livings decay daily, and unless they die, they must lack. God give you and the rest of my lords wisdom

---

\*      Vacant by the death of Lord Wentworth on March 3; in the event his successor was Lord Darcy.

†      1 Edward VI c. 2.

to redress it.

Ask a licence of the king for me to eat flesh on fish days. My stomach is not as it has been. A wise and sober elder of the town, John Samford, weak and sickly, asked me to be a suitor to you for him in this case. We will use the king's authority as none shall take occasion for liberty and contempt of laws. Commendations to Mistress Cecil and your father. *Postscript.* Commendations to all my friends of the robes, who have since my coming to court been friendly in all my business.

*Holograph.*

*Printed*: Tytler, i, 364–7. Townsend, *The writings of John Bradford*, ii, 395–7.

SP 10/13, no. 13

**512.** May 2. Pinchbeck. Richard Ogle to William Cecil.

Commendations to you and your wife from me and mine. I have sent you an obligation as my deed for the recordership of Boston; if anything is amiss I will reform it. I have sent you the fee of Toft and Gosberton; if Mr Wyngfeld would do anything for you the fees might be sooner paid and some allowance for paper and parchment for your clerk. It is said Anthony Irby had four marks for Toft. [The duchess of] Suffolk was never so served by him in either of the lordships as she is now, and her council will so. I know not your fee of Marquess Dorset for Moulton; last time the bailiff paid you but by geese. Thanking you for my son and daughter.

*Holograph.*                                                                                                SP 10/13, no. 14

**513.** May 14. Ratcliff. Edward [Clinton *alias* Fiennes], Lord Clinton, lord admiral to William Cecil.

I moved you to prefer to [the council] the quittance and warrant to be signed for Mr Wynbeshe, devised by the chancellor and council of augmentations, and I have acknowledged myself debtor, as appointed by my lords' letters. Let this matter take effect with speed, that the gentleman remain no longer to his charge. I am bound to him to get out all these writings, which I did upon my lords' grant and letters to the chancellor. The king has granted me the parsonage of 'Holekyrk' near Calais for a chaplain of mine, and this journey causes me to delay giving it. In case any sue for it in my absence, let it be stayed. [Sir Thomas] Wroth and [John] Cheke know the king's grant to me.

*Holograph.*                                                                                                SP 10/13, no. 15

**514.** May 14. East Horndon. Sir William Petre to William Cecil.

Thank you for sundry letters and news, especially of the recovery of your health. Whether it is this ill weather as the doctors say, or my naughty body, my fit remains, although not so sore. It gives me leave to write these few words.

*Holograph.*

*Printed*: Emmison, *Tudor Secretary*, 92.                                                    SP 10/13, no. 16

**515.** May 15. Westminster. William [Paulet], earl of Wiltshire, lord treasurer to William Cecil.

I have written to [the bishop of] Durham and the dean to be at court on Monday. Cause the other party to be there: then they made be heard as [the council] gave order. On your advertisements I have stayed the men of Carlisle and have written to [the archbishop of] Canterbury: read the letter and send it to my lord with the particulars I also send you to receive that order at your hands, and pray my lord to tell you of his doings, that order may be given and the men discharged of their trouble and charges. On Monday you shall have the treasurer of Calais and the surveyor to see their places and give order for their despatches. I have written to the lord chancellor for the commissions of lieutenants and oyer and terminer and for proclamation of the ... they were put in execution ... Saturday night. I will meet you at court. *Postscript*. Since Sir Robert Brandling is stayed at [the laird of] Ormiston's complaint it were well he were at court on Monday [that] they may be heard together.

    *Holograph.*
    *Some mutilations.*                                          SP 10/13, no. 17

**516.**    May 20. Sempringham. Lord Clinton to William Cecil.

    Remember the despatch of Mr Wynbeshe's matter of which I moved you at my departing from London. He stays in London, at great charge, only for that cause, and I am bound to him that he shall have his end according to the grant I had of [the council]. Tell me who shall come from the French king and the time set for his arrival in England.*

    *Holograph.*                                            SP 10/13, no. 18

**517.**    May 22. Wells. Dr William Turner, [dean of Wells] to William Cecil.

    John Aκανθινος,† your wife's schoolmaster, lately came desiring the schoolmastership of this town: I will do the best I can for him for your sake. We have a schoolmaster of evil judgement and naughty life, who was a year in the Marshalsea for papistry; released by the king's general pardon, he still privately defends his false doctrine. [John Taylor *alias*] Cardmaker, our chancellor, intends to put him out and receive your friend, that the king's letter be sent to the chapter that Acanthinus may be chosen, without which we shall be able to do nothing, for they are all against Mr Cardmaker and me, whom they handle as wards. I have preached eight times since Easter, but I could not make one of them preach except Mr Cardmaker, who preached once and has read often. [John] Goodman was set into a house by the chapter because it was granted him in his letters patent of the deanery; but because there is no mention of the house in my patent my belly-brethren will not admit me to it without the king's letter. Until it is done I must be pinned up in a chamber of [the bishop] with all my household, servants and children, as sheep in a pinfold. If there is any speedy remedy, help me: I cannot go to my book for the crying of children and noise in my chamber. I am unable to enter or keep a horse in the chantry lands I have by reason of the deanery; the former dean occupied thirteen closes last year. No man here helps set me in my land, and [the duke of] Somerset's chief servants are the greatest enemies I have, and no man maintains Goodman's friends, who hold me out of all possessions, as they do, namely Mr Λεπτος‡ and Mr Σαυρος,§ one all Roman, the other an atheist. Goodman was granted three quotidians and four dividends until the provostship or archdeaconry should be vacated, but he sold that both from himself and me for £160 which he received from the canons, so that I have nothing but my quotidian and not my whole dividend, and £9 a year. I pay £9 for my first fruits and £20 for entering into residence, and the tenth of my quotidians and dividends besides. I cannot therefore fulfil my obligation of hospitality, but trust to be excused.

    *Holograph.*
    *Printed*: Tytler, i, 372–4.                                    SP 10/13, no. 19

**518.**    May 22. Bourne. Sir Anthony Aucher, from his house there, to William Cecil.

    I have received your letters; you rightly think me loath to come to court, for I have been in pain in my side this quarter of the year and in one of my legs most times. I have written to the lords and pray your help. Go through with Mr Ballerde as soon as you can, for he offers the same to divers men, as I shall explain in my next letters in

---

\*      The embassy to confer the order of St Michel on the king was headed by Jacques d'Albon, seigneur de
       St André.
†      Sharp, thorny.
‡      Thin [presumably Sir John Thynne].
§      Lizard, or boy's penis.

three days. Give him twenty-five years' purchase or under if you can. Bind him to the value, and yourself to pay after the rate as you can agree, the value being as it is now let, and so you shall not be deceived in the value. If you lack money you shall find friends to pay half of it, and dare you not of one penny and yet receive their money again as money now goes, or at the price if the new coin comes. He has sent to be friend of mine for £100 to be paid him at London next Sunday, and his price to him is 1,000 marks. I have not seen the land or searched the value, but I will privily search for it and give you a narrow guess by my next letters. I would be in debt £100 that it would please you to take it for yourself. The thing stands well and is handsomely built already.                                                                                    SP 10/13, no. 20

**519.**   May 24. Bourne. Sir Anthony Aucher, from his house there, to William Cecil.

The demesne is let for £15 a year, the mill £10 and in his own hands 20 acres of meadow; the dovehouse, in indifferent repair and worth £5 a year or more, 40s.; there are also 60 acres of wood, much spoiled. This is the manor of Horton only, all which is his mother's jointure, and [she] has estate for term of her life, and he her farmer for term of years – which expired, she may put him out for term of her life. If you can get the reversion for £400, if you like it, [I] assure you the seat is fair and wholesome, and if you wish to part with it you will profit £100. The same Ballerd has adjoining land worth £6.13.4 in partialty between him and his brother; take them together if you can.
                                                                                    SP 10/13, no. 21

**520.**   May 24. Leighs. Lord Rich, lord chancellor, from his house there, to [the earl of Wiltshire], lord high treasurer.

Upon receipt of letters from you and other lords I took such immediate order with the sealing of the commissions for the marquess as the messenger was despatched by 3 p.m. yesterday, also signing the instructions, so that before now he will have delivered them. By the same messenger I received the commission of lieutenancy for Kent to be made to the lord warden* only, which herewith I have addressed to you. Return it signed and I shall seal it with expedition. I sent letters to you yesterday by the same messenger; when you have seen them, consider my desire. *Postscript.* Commendations to [the earl of] Warwick.
*Holograph.*                                                                        SP 10/13, no. 22

**521.**   May 25. Bourne, Sir Anthony Aucher, from his house there, to William Cecil.

I intend to be with you at court by next Thursday, but would be glad to know before then how your purchase proceeds, for I hear the matter is to be opened to others. I would have been with you today, but the marquess was at my house yesterday, and I must discharge two ships to Calais before I come. Let me know how your purchase goes, by tomorrow or Wednesday noon.                                          SP 10/13, no. 23

**522.**   May 25. Gloucester. John Hooper, bishop of Gloucester to William Cecil.

I sent a copy of articles [*which follow*] subscribed by Thomas Penne, a forward man who has to the unquietness and danger of many here maintained that the humanity of Christ is everywhere. Help benefices in this county to be assigned to convenient men, and God shall have His honour and the king due obedience, as you will understand if you talk with this wise and learned bearer [John] Restell, alderman of this town, whom you will not dislike in civil matters or religion.
*Holograph.*
*Printed*: Townsend, *The writings of John Bradford*, ii, 397–8.          SP 10/13, no. 24

---

\*      Sir Thomas Cheyne, lord warden of the Cinque Ports.

**523.** [May 25 or before. Enclosed with the above]. Articles upheld by Thomas Penne.

[1]. I believe in one God [2] of three persons [3] being one divine nature. [4]. I believe in Christ born of Mary, of two natures, God and man. [5]. Touching His divine nature, scripture teaches that He received the nature of man uncorrupt, having in it all natural desires, but not sinful. [6]. I believe that the body of Christ, inseparably annexed to His godhead, is a true body, and whoever attributes qualities to His humanity which are due solely to His godhead does injury to His godhead and subverts the truth of His human body. Although He has put off all conditions of a mortal man and sits at the right hand of God, that does not destroy His human body, but brings it to more perfection, as ours shall be. Christ, concerning His humanity, is in one place only – heaven. Heaven I take to be not His omnipotence, which is everywhere. No thing can be everywhere but God, and I judge it an error of Marcion, Eutyches ('Evticen') and others that would take from the body and soul of Christ the properties of a true body, having flesh and blood and soul, and occupying one place only, as I believe that the body and soul does in heaven.

*3 pp.*

*Illustrated with biblical quotations and references.*

*Signatures supplied of*: the bishop of Gloucester, John Rastell, [alderman], John Samforde, John Parkhurst, [rector of Bishop's Cleeve], Guy Eton, [the bishop's chaplain], Henry Wyllys, [canon of Gloucester], Nicholas Oldysworthe, [surrogate], John Jewell, [fellow of Corpus Christi College, Oxford], John Wylliams, [canon of Gloucester] and Roger Tyler, [minor canon of Gloucester Cathedral].

SP 10/13, no. 24(i)

**524.** May 28. Sempringham. Lord Clinton, from his house there, to William Cecil.

Thank you for your letter and the despatch of Mr Wynbeshe. If the time of the French ambassador's arrival is known, let me know it and where the king will be. I intend to be at court next week.

*Holograph.*

SP 10/13, no. 25

**525.** May. Sir Richard Rede, Henry Hervie and David Lewis to William Cecil.

Being informed by this bearer John Gunwyn that you would know of his learning and conversation, we testify that he has been a diligent student in civil law at Oxford and Cambridge, and of honest life, so that we think him meet to practise in such administration as shall be committed to him by you or any other. I, Sir Richard Rede, testify that Gunwyn was counted as toward a young man as any in his house. I, Henry Hervie, testify the same for four years in Cambridge. I, David Lewis, testify that about eight years past I knew Gunwyn in Oxford to be very studious and of much towardness.

*Holographs.*

SP 10/13, no. 26

**526.** June 17. Oath of John Scory, D.D., bishop elect of Rochester before the king, renouncing the authority of the bishop of Rome and professing allegiance to the king and his heirs, by authority of acts of 25 and 28 Henry VIII* as supreme head of the churches of England and Ireland.

*3 pp.*

*Signed by*: the bishop elect.

SP 10/13, no. 27

**527.** Copy of the above.

SP 10/13, no. 28

**528.** July 1. Greenwich. The king to the sheriffs.

We send you our writ and other things devised with the advice of our council for the better order of our country, commanding you, your under sheriff and minister, not to

---

\*    25 Henry VIII c. 20 (annates) and 28 Henry VIII c. 10 (extinguishing authority of the bishop of Rome).

break the seal of the writ until the morning of the 8th of this month, within the county mentioned in the libel of the writ. Take sufficient surety at that day. Follow the tenor of the writ circumspectly and do not disclose it or the attached schedules until the time of publication except to your under sheriff or other minister who shall execute the writ, whom you shall secretly swear to follow the tenor of the same. Do all this at your uttermost peril.

*Draft.*

*On the dorse* : For the subsidy 20s. Cloth 20s. Your boat hire five times to and from court 5s. Your boat hire from the Temple to Cannon Row 2d. Your boat hire from Somerset Place to Baynard's Castle 2d. My boat hire from the court to London and back, being sent by you when you lay at court 6d. Mending your horse 8d.

SP 10/13, no. 29

**529.**   June 18. Hampton Court. The king to the bishops.

We are disquieted to see our subjects vexed with extreme and sudden plague which daily increases. The more we study to instruct them in knowledge of God and His word, the devil is more busy to alienate their hearts from godliness; he has so prevailed that the people rebel against God, Who has sent one plague after another. The only way to recover His grace is by prayer and amendment of life. You should therefore by yourself and your ministers persuade the people to resort more diligently to common prayer and refrain from the greed with which most are infected. Engender a terror to reduce them from their corrupt lives. It is no marvel that the people wander when the chief and other ministers of the church are feeble in discharging their duties. We trust you are none of those, but exhort you to reform any negligence in your jurisdiction and increase amendment already begun, that you may be worthy of your vocation.

*King's stamp.*

*Countersigned by* : the duke of Somerset, the earl of Wiltshire, the earl of Bedford, the earl of Huntingdon, Sir Thomas Cheyne, Lord Darcy, Lord Cobham and Sir John Gates.

*Printed* : Tytler, i, 404–6.

SP 10/13, no. 30

**530.**   July 20. Hampton Court. The king to the sheriffs.

Finding a number of breaches of our laws, we have also found that the greatest occasion thereof is the negligent administration of ministers who allow our laws to be violated, which is seldom seen in any other realm. We have been informed that many who should have most regard to the good order of the rest have been the greatest doers of unlawful matters, among them many justices of the peace. We marvel and therefore have determined to prove what diligence you will use in declaring your zeal to God, your obedience to us, your regard to the oath and charge you have received, and your love to the commonwealth. We send you a proclamation against regrators, forestallers and other notable oppressors of the country, according to the statutes.* If you will be such ministers as your oaths bind you, we shall not need to write again; for if any of you have incurred the dangers of our laws, reform yourselves as an example to the rest. If you will look at it none otherwise than before, we must either wax sharper than we would be, or suffer our people to perish, whom we are bound to tend.

*Draft of signet letter.*

*King's stamp.*

*Countersigned by* : the earl of Wiltshire, the earl of Bedford, the earl of Shrewsbury, the earl of Huntingdon, Lord Darcy, Sir Thomas Cheyne, Sir John Gates and Sir Ralph Sadler.

SP 10/13, no. 31

---

\*    *Tudor Royal Proclamations*, i, 526–7, no. 377.

**531.** July 31. Bonham. Roger Basyng, Roger Mawdley, Richard Samwell, Barnaby Lye, John Dyer, John Ewen and William Stacy to the council.

On request of [William] Fauntleroye that we should report the truth of his and the sheriff's demeanour, upon receipt of your letters we went to Stourton on July 31, where we found the sheriff.* He came to the manor place and found the gates barred fast, being kept by force with guns, bows and other weapons. William Hartgill, having had secret communication with the sheriff, came to the gate and disclosed his mind to the porter through a hole, whereupon Mrs [Agnes] Ryse came herself and caused the gate to be opened. The sheriff declared that he had received your letters at Fauntleroye's suit (but showing none in our sight) and was commanded upon sight of his lease to deliver him the possession. The sheriff's request was that at least Mrs Ryse should allow Fauntleroye to put servants into the ground and a keeper in the park. She answered that she would suffer no possession to be taken, but that if Fauntleroye or any for him came upon the ground for such purpose, he should never go out alive. She allowed the sheriff and his servants, with Hartgill and others, to come in peaceably, and kept Fauntleroye and all others outside for half an hour or more. Mrs Ryse, keeping the gate herself, said she would keep possession until discharged by law. Fauntleroye, having his lease in his hand, offered it to the sheriff, desiring him to execute his office according to your letters. He answered that he had already seen his lease, but Mrs Ryse said she would meddle no further without authority. Fauntleroye was offended because he saw the carcasses of deer lying in the base court, spoiled and eaten by dogs, and taken out of Stourton park. Hartgill said he should see twenty or forty deer killed there before his face within a week, and should therefore not grudge this. Then the sheriff departed.

> *Printed*: J.E. Jackson, 'Charles, Lord Stourton and the murder of the Hartgills', *The Wiltshire Archaeological and Natural History Magazine*, viii, (1864), 287–8; which also see (pp. 242–341) for background to this letter and identifications.    SP 10/13, no. 32

**532.** [August 11]. Proclamation for further debasement.

The king, minding to refine the coin, lately ordained (for reasons partly mentioned in a proclamation of April 30 last) that the silver teston or shilling should be current for 9d. and the silver groat for 3d., minding then and since to have refined the coin by such degrees as should be least burdensome to him and easiest for his subjects. He is since informed that the excessive price of victuals and other things, which should have grown less, is, by greed of men, especially traders, increased to the hindrance of the commonwealth and burden of his subjects, especially the poor. The best remedy is the speedy reduction of the coin nearer its just fineness. From August 17 the teston shall be current in England and the marches of Calais for 6d., the groat for 2d., the 2d. piece for 1d., the 1d. piece for ½d., and the ½d. piece for ¼d., on forfeit to the king of all money paid and received at other valuations, and on pain of fine and imprisonment.

> *Draft.*
>
> *On the dorse (in another hand)*: The king's godly desires before overthrown, [he] was forced to shorten the day before limited by another proclamation set forth at Greenwich last June.
>
> *Printed*: *Tudor Royal Proclamations*, i, 529–30, no. 379 [final text, dated August 16].
>
> SP 10/13, no. 33

**533.** August 12. Hampton Court. The king to the sheriffs.

Do not break open our writ with annexed matter now addressed to you until the morning of the 16th of this month, taking good testimony for your declaration at the opening; speedily do what is appointed, without disclosing the tenor of the writ or schedule, directly or indirectly, to any person until the publication, except to your under

*    Sir John Mervin.

sheriff or other minister who shall execute the writ, whom you shall swear to secrecy until the performance of the same.

*King's stamp.*

*Countersigned by*: the duke of Somerset, Lord Rich, lord chancellor, the earl of Wiltshire, the earl of Bedford, the earl of Huntingdon, Lord Darcy, Sir Thomas Cheyne, Sir Anthony Wingfield, Sir John Gates and Sir William Petre.

*Endorsed*: For proclaiming the coin down.                                    SP 10/13, no. 34

**534.** August 29. [Windsor]. Report to the privy council of the delivery of their message to Princess Mary by [Lord Rich], lord chancellor, [Sir Anthony Wingfield], comptroller of the household and Sir William Petre, secretary.

On receipt of the king's instructions we went to [Princess] Mary's house at Copped Hall, Essex, last Friday morning, August 28. I, the lord chancellor, delivered the king's letters, which she said she would kiss for the honour of his signature rather than their content. Reading the letters to herself she said that [William] Cecil had taken much pain. She prayed me be short as she was not well, and had already written to the king. We told her that the king, having unsuccessfully tried to persuade her to conform to the established service had, by the advice of the council and other nobles, resolved that she should no longer privately use any other services. She refused to hear the names of those consenting to the resolution, saying that she knew us all to be of one sort. We said that the king wished us to forbid her chaplains to say mass or any other unlawful service or her servants to attend them. She protested loyalty but said she would rather die on the block than use any services other than those in use at her father's death. She would obey the king's orders in religion only when he was old enough to judge. Her servants should be at liberty to do as they willed; her chaplains might refuse to say mass for fear of short imprisonment, but the new service would not be used in her house, or she would leave. We told her why the council had appointed [Sir Robert] Rochester, [Sir Francis] Inglefeld and [Edward] Walgrave, her servants, to open the premises to her, and how ill they had used their charge. She said it was unwise to appoint her servants to control her in her own house; they knew her mind; the lords might punish them if they saw fit. If they refused to do the message they were honester for not speaking against their consciences.

When we told her our instructions touching the promise she claims to have been made to the emperor, she answered that she was sure the promise had been made before the king in her presence and that of seven of the council, notwithstanding the denial of it at my last being with the king. She said she had the emperor's hand testifying that the promise was made, which she believed better than the council. Though we little esteemed the emperor, we should show more favour to her for her father's sake, who for the most part made us of nothing. If the emperor were dead she would still say as she does. If he now gave her other advice she would not follow it. His ambassador would know how she was used at our hands.

We mentioned the king's wish for one to attend her in Rochester's absence. She said she was old enough to appoint her own officers. If we left any such man there she would leave. She said she was sick, but would not die willingly; though if she did, she would protest that we were the cause. Our words were fair but our deeds ill. She then went to her bedchamber, giving me a ring and saying she would be loyal save in these matters of religion, but saying that this should never be told to the king.

We called her chaplains and the rest of her household before us, commanding on pain of allegiance that the priests should not say and the servants not hear any unlawful services. After some talk the chaplains promised to obey. We also commanded them to tell at least one of the council if unlawful services were said in the house. When we had left the house and were waiting for one of the chaplains who had not been with the rest, [the princess] sent to us to speak with her. We came into the court and offered to go to her chamber, but she spoke from the window, praying us to speak to the council that her comptroller* might shortly return. Since his departing she had accounted for her own expenses: her father and mother had not brought her up with baking and brewing.

*Some mutilations.*

*Late 16th cent. copy from*: PC 2/4, pp. 378–81 (*APC*, iii, 348–52).    SP 10/13, no. 35

**535.**    Another copy of the above.                               SP 10/13, no. 36

**536.**    September 3. Sempringham. Lord Clinton to William Cecil.

Some light persons who would have joined the attempted commotion are imprisoned in Stamford and have been examined by the alderman, who has sent their confessions to me. I judge they have not confessed all. Send for and examine them, and let your father also take so much pain. These men have not met so often without more matter than appears by their confession. In case your short abode will not allow you time, I will have them brought here. I have written to the alderman to take the prisoners to your father.

*Holograph.*

*Endorsed*: Haste, haste.                                     SP 10/13, no. 37

**537.**    September 7. Lincoln. Sir Francis Ayscough, John Pope, [chancellor of Lincoln Cathedral], and Nicholas Bullingham, [archdeacon of Lincoln] to William Cecil.

We and Sir Edward Dymmoke were appointed arbitrators between [John] Dyon and the vicar of Tathwell. At the request of the parties we appointed them to be with us at Market Rasen at a certain day, when Dyon with many witnesses and the vicar appeared. But for lack of time we could neither hear the parties thoroughly nor examine any of the witnesses. We understand by Mr Dyon that you are informed we heard the matter thoroughly, which is not true.

*Originally enclosed with no.* **541** *below.*                  SP 10/13, no. 38

**538.**    September 9. Putney. Richard Goodrich to William Cecil.

As I am left the only solicitor to you in [Richard] Morison's matter I can but often remind you with my letters to obtain a warrant for £600 due to him for his diet, with a warrant for licence to make over the same, with £100 more by exchange: £700 in all, which is provided for him of his own. I sent you his own letter written to show Hales by [Lawrence] Erysby, whereby you might understand his need, which I can well believe to be as much as he alleges. His trust is only in you for all his business, which hitherto has been well answered. Let it be now, especially while I shall be left his solicitor. I sent the book for Louth school by the lord chancellor to Armigil Wade to help the same to your signature. Help it if it is not done. I wish you to see at Wimbledon how lustily I shoot on the heath mounted.

*Holograph.*                                               SP 10/13, no. 39

**539.**    September 9. London. Sir William Petre to William Cecil.

I doubt not that [John] Cliff my man has told you how I have been since your departing, and so continue, but with hope of short amendment. Today in bed I was glad to hear of your return to court. This bearer says he is chosen to be master of the Savoy according to the order of the foundation, and because I was a means to the preferment of his predecessor, I have been asked to further this man. Because I could do nothing, being absent, I pray you to help. The man that is chosen I know not ... best learned of that company, and if he shall be found otherwise meet he shall be worthier to enjoy

*     Sir Robert Rochester.

it because he is chosen (as they say) according to the statutes. I can write nothing of my return, for I am uncertain when the flux of humours into my legs shall be so stayed that I may be able to work and stand. The doctors think this comes of the dregs of my long sickness and is greater because the humour falls into a weak place recently hurt.

*Holograph. Mutilated.*

*Printed*: Emmison, *Tudor Secretary*, 95.                          SP 10/13, no. 40

**540.**   September 10. Isles of Scilly. John Kyllygrew junior to William Cecil.

The warrants I have received for payment of the works at Scilly will not be able to discharge them, through the loss of money, by £260, which will be due at Michaelmas, and for which I have written by this bearer to the council. My father the surveyor has also written to know their pleasure for the discharge or keeping of any men in work this winter. I desire your furtherance for speedy answer.                          SP 10/13, no. 41

**541.**   September 13. Lincoln. J[ohn] Dyon to William Cecil.

On September 4 I received your letter dated at Windsor on August 25 and thought it convenient to signify the truth concerning its contents, and to obtain from Sir Francis Ascough, [John] Pope, chancellor of Lincoln Cathedral and [Nicholas] Bullyngham, archdeacon of Lincoln, arbitrators with Sir Edward Dymock between the vicar of Tathwell and me, a letter to you touching their proceedings, herein enclosed.* You shall see that the matter was neither thoroughly heard, any witnesses examined, nor any order taken. I am sorry that you should burden me with vexation of any person: no such matter will be proved, but I am maliciously slandered by the vicar, even as the matter in which Lord Willoughby travailed against me: that matter has since been heard before Sir Edward Dymock, scarcely my friend, Sir Robert Tirwhit and Sir Francis Ascough, deputy lieutenants of Lincolnshire, and I was adjudged my ground in variance according to my title, and £3 towards my costs. The parties pursuant against me then said openly that Lord Willoughby told them that the matter wherein they proceeded was good. Then it appeared to the deputy lieutenants no colour of matter against me, and by the confession of the party that I proffered them before any controversy began between them and me to abide the judgement in that matter of any man learned at the which they refused. So it well appears I bear no such favour to trouble as I am informed to you of, but I love it as well as any man. Being thus deformed, I will by your favour travail, although at great cost, for my honest declaration, which I trust shall stand right with you; and when it shall justly appear that I trouble any man wrongfully against God's or man's laws, be my heavy master. In the meantime, suspend judgement against me as you promised at my last being before you.

*Holograph.*                          SP 10/13, no. 42

**542.**   September 14. London. Sir William Petre to William Cecil.

Thank you for your letters and your pains for the Savoy. I doubt not that (as you write) there are many anglers for it. I wish he might have it who most desires the good of the poor men and their house. I wish all were done in order, and men called to such places by other men's vocation rather than their own labour. The apostles became fishers of men, while we now again fish for mammon. You see that lying here alone I am become a preacher. I send a note of the commission for visitation of the Savoy. W[illiam] Say was not in London, and therefore I did it myself; you put out as you think good. I have put a clause that the commissioners may reform things, that when they know my lords' pleasures, they may do them without any more commission. My leg begins to amend. Tomorrow I intend to ride to my house in a litter to comfort my weak wife,

*          No. **537** above.

who is troubled with the death of her young son.* There remains among the writings in my chamber a collection of facts and laws touching the bishop of Durham's cause. Command Cliff to seek it, that it may remain with you if it is called for. I write this because a man whom I know not was at my house in London to ask for them; it was first delivered to [the duke of] Somerset and by him in the council to me.

*Holograph.*

*Endorsed*: Post haste.

*Printed*: Tytler, i, 427 (part). Emmison, *Tudor Secretary*, 96 (without last paragraph of MS).
SP 10/13, no. 43

**543.** September 16. Fulham. Nicholas Ridley, bishop of London to William Cecil.

The mixture of gladness and sorrow in your preface, the sight you had of the bottom of your purse, and your poor house, moved me to compassion. I grant that I am blamed for plainly condemning unlawful beggary, but you have persuaded me to grant you half a dozen trees, such as I may spare and my officer shall appoint. They must be pollards, for few or none others are left from the late spoil. If you that can move men so mightily would have pity on the decay of one house; if you knew the miserable spoil that was done in vacation time by the king's officers on my woods, whereby many good houses have been previously built, and might have been hereafter, so many lame relieved, so many broken amended, I do not doubt that you would be able to move the whole country to lament such decay. I was refreshed by reading your letters, and wished you had been the proctor of a hospital.

*Printed*: Tytler, i, 430–2.
SP 10/13, no. 44

**544.** September 21. Denton. George Williams to William Cecil.

According to your command I have taken order for repair of Ewerby chancel, finding there about four fothers of lead unsold which I have put in safe keeping. The residue is sold by William Audley. The value, and how much has been bestowed, I do not yet know. [William] Rigges the auditor, now in London, has had twenty ashes felled in the king's lordship of Caythorpe; because the tenants have present occasion of allowance of timber, I have stayed the ashes until I know by what warrant he has so done, and to what use he will convert them, being secretly informed that he has sold them to Mr Hussey towards his buildings there.

*Holograph.*
SP 10/13, no. 45

**545.** September 19. Guildford. Bartholomew Traheron to William Cecil.

Two men of Chichester came to me yesterday, of whom I learned that the prebendaries there have free election. They doubt not that a letter from the king would prevail. If, on consideration, you do not think I deserve such letters, to ask too much would be impudent: you will do what seems right.†

*English and Greek.*

*Holograph.*
SP 10/13, no. 46

**546.** September 25. [Some of the council] to Sir Edmund Peckham, [high treasurer of the Mints].

On coming to court we declared our consciences to the king and the rest of the council touching the amendment of the coin and its establishing in fineness. As it is of much worthiness the king desires its furtherance. He prefers the patterns of the 12d. and 6d. with Roman numerals, with the parliament robe and the collar of the order.

---

\*     Petre's fourth son William, who lived only for a few weeks [Emmison, *Tudor Secretary*, 125n.].

†     The letter missive here requested was sent on October 23 and Traheron was elected dean of Chichester on November 23 [*APC*, iii, 377. J. Le Neve, *Fasti Ecclesiae Anglicanae 1541–1857*, ii, comp. J. M. Horn, (1971), 6].

HIBERN is written HIBEN, which must be amended. The king and we think his face should be shown in three-quarters. The agreement to have the standard of 11 oz. fine for the 12d. and 6d. pleases him, and he wishes to have coins of 5s. and 2s. 6d. of the same standard. He would see a proof. We send a pattern, noted by his hand, with the cipher of 5s. and on the other side of the 5s. the cross which shall be on the 12d. and on the 2s. 6d. the cross which shall be on the 6d. [Being the lowest pattern of 4 on the 4 of spades].* The king also likes the other standard for the 1d., ½d. and ¼d. to be of 4 oz. fine. Let all speed be had for the engraving and sinking of the irons and prints of all these coins. We would Derek [Anthony], [whom I and Sir William Herbert, master of the horse, desired to have tried]† were appointed for the engraving with John Laurence, named by you, as a common sinker. If Derek [Anthony] is unfit, tell us your opinions. The king wishes that for carriage of the fine, Sir John York and Nicholas Throkmerton's deputy, whose name you shall know shortly,‡ shall be in commission, and for the small moneys George Gale at York and Lawrence Warren at Canterbury. We also would speed were made with making the minutes of these commissions, putting into them authority for other necessary officers, taking the same men who served last unless some are thought not convenient, telling us those you think meeter, and all else necessary. The minutes being sent to us, we shall shortly return your commissions and answers to your desires. We shall shortly choose a man for receipt of moneys for the small coinage, and shall return your proofs at our next coming thither.

*Corrected draft.*                                                                SP 10/13, no. 47

**547.**   September [24 or 25]. Oatlands. The council with the king to the council in London.

We send Thomas Trowghton; cause him to be committed to the Counter or some other prison in London until the next market day and then have him pilloried, putting on his head a large notice that he seditiously put a bill under the council chamber door.

*Signed by*: the earl of Wiltshire.

*Endorsed by Cecil*: 5 November 1550. Minute to Mr Pikering from the council.

SP 10/13, no. 48

**548.**   September 26. London. Sir Richard Rede and Richard Lyell to William Cecil.

We have sent you the commision which you delivered yesterday to me, Sir Richard Rede, and trust it is now well, desiring that we may know when and where we shall execute it, and whether severally; if so, with which to begin; if we shall finish one cause before starting the other, with such other instructions as from you we may learn of the council. *Postscript [by Lyell]*. We should also know whether they should be granted learned counsel if required, in which case the king to have the like. One or more registrars must be appointed.

*Holograph.*                                                                     SP 10/13, no. 49

**549.**   [September (? 27)]. Commissioners in the causes of the bishops of Chichester and Worcester:§ Sir Roger Cholmley, chief justice, Sir Richard Rede, Dr [John Smith *alias*] Olyver, [master in chancery], [Richard] Goodrich, [John] Gosnold, Dr [Richard] Lyell. *Written apart from the other names*: Mr Chidly.

---

*         Inserted by Cecil.
†         Deleted.
‡         Probably Christopher Levens [C.E. Challis, *The Tudor Coinage*, (Manchester, 1978), 104 n. 222].
§         For the commission to try the bishops see *APC*, iii, 368–9 (28 September 1551) and Strype, *Cranmer*, ii, 256–7, and for nominations to the Irish sees Strype, *Cranmer*, ii, 369–82, 670–1; but note that the letter from Cranmer to Cecil on the subject printed there and in J.E. Cox (ed.), *Miscellaneous writings and letters of Thomas Cranmer*, (Parker Society, Cambridge, 1846), 438 is wrongly dated 1552.

Men eligible for the archbishoprics in Ireland, Armagh (£200) and Cashel (200 marks [£133.6.8]): Dr Turner of Canterbury,* Thomas Rosse, abiding in Norfolk, Mr Dethick, kinsman to Garter herald, [Thomas] Leverose, abiding in Ireland, [Hugh Whitacre *alias* ] Goodacre, chaplain to the bishop of Winchester.†

*Cecil's hand. By Turner's name is written Armagh, by Goodacre's Cashel.*

*In the king's hand*: another list of commissioners, omitting Oliver and adding the names of the bishop of London and [William Stanford *alias* ] Stamford.

*At the foot of the page, in Cecil's hand*: Mr Cox.

*Printed*: J.G. Nichols (ed.), *Literary Remains of King Edward the Sixth*, (1857), ii, 487–9.

SP 10/13, no. 50

**550.** September 27. Richard Goodrich to William Cecil.

I have too great experience of your friendship to mistrust it for any cause, and will not for this. What suit [John] Cheke made I know not but by his letters and yours. I made my suit at Farnham and had it granted there. One of the council would have moved the king, but you said it was unnecessary, having the lord treasurer's grant. I will excuse myself and him for any fraud, for knowledge of Mr Cheke's suit. I thought myself sure, two lords having made suit for the same and, being answered by the lord treasurer that it was passed to me, holding themselves content. I suspected Mr Cheke least of all men. Because of the trouble of mind I received by his unkindness I am fallen into sickness and gout. Never matter so grieved me. If he should have the whole profit I should have by him, although my need is greater, he shall have it. But I will not discharge myself by contenting to lose it; I will obtain my grant to perfection if I can. Although I have not been able to do him much pleasure, I have always been amicably disposed towards him. For the father's contentation I know not, but think there are good arguments on the contrary. I see no cause alleged to [*indecipherable*] the ward meet for him, but rather the contrary – as I would declare, but for vexing of us both. I did not give my servant commission to make you privy, nor the contrary, but sent my suit only to the lord treasurer, hoping to speed it at his hands; being at Windsor he promised me whatever was in his office if I came in time. I therefore thought it neither necessary nor honest to trouble you, whom otherwise I use in all things. If he speed it shall be against my will. Nor can hope of no profit make me content willingly to feign it, happen what may.

*Holograph.*

SP 10/13, no. 51

**551.** September 28. Richard Allen to William Cecil.

I, although unknown to you, am emboldened to ask your help because of your known kindness to all, especially the poor but scholarly, and because of your influence with the leaders of the realm. I have seen myself in parliament what I often heard about in the academic world – your graciousness to all who addressed you. For four months I have been exhausted by the hardships of this prison and am deprived because of my large debt, indeed buried alive. Speak to the council about my case, either for a pardon or a less severe sentence. Let me at least speak to my friends, that they may see how much I lack and in what debt I lie. Let me be free to use paper and ink – that with which I now write has only been obtained with difficulty and must be relinquished when I have signed this letter. I will be most bounden to you.

*Latin.*

*Holograph.*

SP 10/13, no. 52

---

\*　　Richard Turner, B.D., six preacher of Canterbury Cathedral.
†　　Appointed archbishop of Armagh on 28 October 1552.

**552.** September 30. Ingatestone. Sir William Petre, from his house there, to William Cecil.

Thank you for your letters from London. I hoped at their receipt to have been able to travel to court within a few days, for my leg was amending. About four days ago I rode four miles to see what I was able to endure. That night the humours had again such flux into my leg that next day it broke out again worse than ever. Since then I have kept to my bed, which is the only remedy. Henceforth I will learn to be more wise. At my house I received from [the countess of] Southampton the enclosed letter [*which follows* ]. If the case stands as she witnesses she has reason to seek remedy. I am loath to trouble you, but if you hear of the man about court you might open the matter. My wife, who is recovered, commends herself to you and Mistress Cecil.

*Holograph.*

*Printed*: Emmison, *Tudor Secretary*, 96 (part only).                    SP 10/13, no. 53

**553.** September 24. [Enclosed with the above]. Surbiton. Jane [Wriothesley], countess of Southampton to Sir William Petre.

Having since my husband's death sustained many injuries and unkindnesses, they are now grown so fast and lewd persons take courage thereby that I am forced to pray you to take order with my servant Colas, a Frenchman hired by my husband by indented bill to teach my children French for certain years, of which two remain. He left my house without licence for court, where I doubt not he will become servant to some other unless prevented. Have him compelled to return.

*Printed*: Green, 255–6.                    SP 10/13, no. 53(i)

**554.** September. Monday [7, 14, 21 or 28]. Grimsthorpe. The duchess of Suffolk to William Cecil.

I thank God for all His benefits, and take this last (at first sight most bitter) punishment not the least of them.* I have never been so well taught His power and love and my own weakness without Him. I would gladly talk to you of the comfort I have had of Him, but am unable quietly to behold my friends without some of those vile dregs of Adam. I will fulfil your last request by 7 a.m. tomorrow; you may use him that I send as if I stood by.

*Holograph.*

*Printed*: Goff, 201. Green, 253–4. Anderson, 336–7. G. Bertie, *Five Generations of a Loyal House*, (1845), 11.                    SP 10/13, no. 54

**555.** October 1. The king to Lord Rich, lord chancellor.

We lately signed a commission for hearing and determining the causes and contempts of the bishops of Worcester and Chichester, which our councillors then in attendance sent to you for the apposition of the great seal, with their letters to the commissioners appointed declaring our pleasure in certain points. We perceive by your letter of yesterday to the earl of Warwick, master of our household, that you with others of the council in London have subscribed the commission and affixed the great seal, but have returned the council's letter, whereby we doubt the delay of our commission, se[emi]ng to note that it has not m[ore] hands of our councillors: [eno]ugh it has indeed . . . We think our authority is such that whatever we do by the advice of our council attendant, although much fewer than eight, has more strength than to be put into question. You are not ignorant that the number of councillors does not make our authority. If you or any other should be of other opinion, as may be conjectured from your letter, that is not convenient and might be harmful where our affairs, for lack of speedy execution for expectation of other councillors, might take great detriment.

*            The duchess's two sons had died on July 14.

*Corrected draft.*
*Central section badly mutilated.*
*Printed*: Nicholas, *Remains*, ii, 347 n. 2. Hoak, 140 (part only); see also 319 nn. 137–8.

SP 10/13, no. 55

**556.** Copy of the above, made after the mutilation but supplying some words now missing in the original draft.                 SP 10/13, no. 56

**557.** October 11. Hampton Court. Ceremonial at the creation of the dukes of Suffolk and Northumberland, the marquess of Winchester and the earl of Pembroke.

After morning service their robes were brought to the king's closet whither, about 9 o'clock, the lords resorted and robed, and proceeded through the gallery and great chamber into the presence chamber where the king sat with divers nobles. First went the officers of arms, then Garter bearing the patent, Sir George Brooke, K.G., Lord Cobham bearing a golden verge, Henry Manners, earl of Rutland, bearing the cap with a coronet, John Russell, earl of Bedford, lord privy seal, bearing the sword, Henry Grey, marquess Dorset, K.G., between Edward Seymour, duke of Somerset, K.G. and William Parr, marquess of Northampton, K.G., great chamberlain. After reverences, the lords standing and the marquess kneeling, Garter delivered the letters patent to the lord chamberlain, Lord Darcy, who delivered them to the king, who gave them to Secretary Cecil to read. The king then vested him with sword, coronet and rod. The patent read, the king delivered it to him and he went to stand on the king's right until the rest were created, with £40 fee yearly for life. Then the lords and officers of arms returned for the other lords to the closet and brought before the king in like manner John Sutton, earl of Warwick, great master of the house and earl marshal, who was created duke of Northumberland with £40 fee, who afterwards stood at the king's other side with the duke of Somerset. The other lords returned to the closet for William Paulet, earl of Wiltshire and high treasurer, who was led between the marquess of Northampton and the earl of Bedford, Lord Rutland bearing his coronet, Lord Cobham his sword and Garter his patent. He was created marquess of Winchester, with 40 marks a year. The lords returned for Sir William Herbert, master of the horse, the night before made Baron Herbert and Cardiff, who was created earl of Pembroke, with £20 yearly. After obeisance the lords returned to the queen's great chamber, the trumpets sounding, disrobed and went to dinner. On the bench sat the duke of Suffolk, then the duke of Northumberland, the marquess of Winchester and last the earl of Pembroke. On the other side, a little lower, sat the duke of Somerset, the lord privy seal, the marquess of Northampton, the earl of Rutland, Lord Cobham, Lord Fitzwalter and Lord Thomas Howard. After the second course the heralds proclaimed the styles of the king and the newly created lords. These lords being departed, the king knighted his secretary, William Cecil, John Cheke, one of his schoolmasters, and Henry Sidney and Henry Nevill of his privy chamber.

*17 cent. copy.*                           SP 11/4, no. 21

**558.** October [16].* Westminster. The council to justices of the peace.

Having knowledge of heinous and detestable attempts purposed and almost executed by the duke of Somerset, with many adherents, against the realm and king, to the destruction of many nobles, seeking only his private government, we have by the king's command quietly committed him to the Tower, with Lord Grey and other adherents. Sir Ralph Vane, one of the confederates, hereupon fled, but was taken today. We are most sorry that the duke's evil heart and discontented nature prevailed in him to be so great a troubler and shame to his country that we could do none otherwise. See good

\*     The date of Somerset's arrest.

order observed in those parts committed to your charge.

*Draft in Petre's hand.*

*Printed*: Tytler, ii, 33–4.

SP 10/13, no. 57

**559.** October 19. Northampton. John Hanbie to Sir William Cecil.

Pickworth Outfield and Pickworth Infield, Rutland, part of the late attainted Lord Hussey's lands, are demised by indenture under the great seal dated 9 March 1544 to Richard Grenewaie, esq., for twenty-one years at £38.7.4 a year, as appears by the same lease made in the late court of survey.* Mr Grenewaie has made a lease of a close called Infield and another called Great Barley Close and another called Little Barley Close, with the warren of commons in Pickworth Infield to Edmund Hall at £30.7.4 a year, and another lease of all pastures in Pickworth called Pickworth Outfield for Robert Harrington, esq. for £8 a year – which two rents amount to the £38.7.4 reserved in Grenewaie's lease. Nevertheless Mr Hall yearly detains £5 of his rents under colour of certain lands called the Stoking, part of the Infield, which he affirms that Sir John Harrington claims by colour of purchase as to appertain to the late monastery of Ulverscroft, Leicestershire. Nevertheless, the matter being examined by commission from the late court of survey and certified to the same court, as I have heard, the court would not discharge the detained rent, so that Hall yearly answers but £25.7.4. The £5 remainder depends in *super* upon him. In ruling the book of arrears for the fourth year it was ordered by the chancellor and council of the court of augmentations that the bailiff should distrain from the arrears, then being £20 for four years, as appears in an enclosed paper [*which follows*]. The lands in Aunby, Lincolnshire are let by Grenewaye by indenture with the premises. Nevertheless they are not answered before me in Rutland but charged in Lincolnshire, and not included in the rent of £38.7.4. I have no particular survey of the manor of Barrowden, for among others it was granted to [Princess] Elizabeth from Michaelmas 1546 and the particulars made by [Philip] Lentall, auditor of Lord Hussey's lands, so that if Mr Hayes the surveyor has no particular survey to make the particular, the books of account of 36, 37 and 38 Henry VIII remaining in the court under the custody of [Richard] Duke will declare the just value and reprise, which the chancellor may call for and appoint Mr Duke to certify. It appears briefly in my books to be £31.8.5½d., with £1.6.0 for common fine per year. What reprise is to be declared out of the same does not appear in my book. In the surveyor's book delivered to me he has noted briefly that the manor is £21.8.2½d. clear per year, and expresses nothing further. I am sorry I cannot satisfy your expectation therein.

*Holograph.*

*With extract (also holograph) from the book of arrears to the king at Michaelmas 1551, setting out formal details of matters discussed in the letter. [Latin].*

SP 10/13, no. 58

**560.** October 20. John Chambre, Thomas Grene and William Connyngton, men of Achurch, William Byrkett and Richard Wattes of Thorpe Waterville and Robert Banester of Wadenhoe to the council.

We certify that for fifty years and more we have neither known nor heard that the close named the 'Grete Conynger' belonging to the manor place of Thorpe Waterville has paid more than 8s. a year for all tithes within the close at Easter, 4s. for the tithe of the water mill and 8d. for the dovecote.

*Five marks.*

Attestation by George Williams. The said parties and other inhabitants of Thorpe and Achurch have upon examination by me, appointed by Sir William Cecil to survey the same, confessed this bill to be true, and that the taking in before Christmas of ewes and their continuance there to Lady Day does save the tithe by their custom there used for

* I.e. general surveyors.

fifty years or more.

*Holograph.*  SP 10/13, no. 59

**561.** [October 20]. Note of timber required for the mill and repairs necessary during the summer for the water mill of Thorpe Achurch.

*So described by endorsement in Cecil's hand.*  SP 10/13, no. 60

**562.** [October 20]. Estimate of timber required for the above work, to be obtained from John Chamber of Aldwinkle; the parson of Stoke [Doyle]; Harry Abotte of Titchmarsh; Miles Byrchet; the bailiff of Aldwinkle; for timber from Aldwinkle park. All bestowed in the mill as the carpenter John Pepper can declare.  SP 10/13, no. 61

**563.** [? October]. [One of his servants] to Sir William Cecil.

I discharged a parson of Swayfield of Belton tithe over a dozen years ago, and promised it to another man in Swayfield. But the then parson (Christopher Teller) came to me with a friend and so obtained the occupation again, as he had done at the instance of the friend he brought with him, and so occupied it out his time. The next parson (Miles Clarkson) did not occupy it but during his time let it to Mr Thymelby, who was always so good a master to me that I could not say nay to him. Edward Marsh has been parson for about three years. I never received rent of him, but thought another did so to my use in the right of your farm, which he did not. Last May Day I demanded rent of the parson for two years due at Michaelmas 1550. He would have given me rent for one year and denied the other, saying he was informed he ought to pay no rent for it, being the fallow year. He said he would know further before he paid me. I told him he made a doubt I had never heard before, and that because he denied me rent I discharged him of the tithe. He made it strange to take discharge of me; nevertheless we so departed. Then I travailed to get knowledge from two old men named in my letter* of the lands out of which the tithe is due. When harvest came I heard from a friend in the town when they began to shear rye and wheat, so I repaired thither and such rye and wheat as I found tithed upon the lands I took the third sheaf, so that I received five sheaves, and had them laid up in safety in Swayfield where they remain. Then the parson went into Nottinghamshire to Mr Perpwent (who says he is his master) and obtained a letter from him and Sir John Constable to Robert Haryngton to call me before him and hear the matter. Haryngton wrote to me to meet him at Waterfall, a wood near Bytham park, where he intended to hunt. It chanced that your father came to hunt with him on August 11. There the parson and I attended and were heard. The parson reported that I did him wrong and hindered his living to discharge him of what his predecessors had occupied time out of mind, paying 1s. 8d a year to the farmer of Corby. I answered that he had denied me rent which his predecessors had only by sufferance of the farmers of Corby parsonage. Yet the lands that the tithe is due out of and the rate of the tithe are not out of mind. I declared much of the circumstances above to your father and uncle. They determined (the parson consenting) that the tithe should be gathered by an indifferent man and laid in safety until the matter was further tried. I appointed a man, with whom the parson was content, and the parson appointed the place, with which I was content. Notwithstanding, the parson usurped what was gathered and seized cocks of barley, craftily laying the fault to his servants. I have spent time with the parson to prove whether he would offer to commune, but he holds out. On September 27 I went to him with certain of his neighbours and said (as sent from you) that you wished to know if he had any composition to show between the patroness and his predecessors. He rashly answered that I would know of any such. I answered I knew none, but that he had no better knowledge of a composition (as I was sure he had not); he would have a cold end, for

---

\*  See the document following.

my master would not lose. He then started away, saying he had other business. I would have told him that my master would not lose the right of his farm for any tenant's act. I went with the neighbours and saw the corn. The following day, Michaelmas Eve, the parson craftily conveyed it to his parsonage by a back way, and has not let it continue according to the decree of my master your father and Mr Haryngton. How this will deface his claim I refer to you. I have communed with the prioresses of St Michael's* when they were in estimation of this matter of Belton tithe (with one or two of them for the time being). I remember they answered they had good evidence that would lay it out, but I could never see it. If the evidence of the house were searched I cannot say what would be found for this purpose. Doubtless there is more land of this kind if the truth were known. I am at your service.

*Unsigned.*                                                                                   SP 10/13, no. 62

**564.** May 27. [Enclosed with the above]. Declaration by Harry Laughton and Nicholas Copper, long inhabitants of Swayfield, in the presence of Richard Bachows, of the tithe of Belton in the fields of Swayfield due to the parsonage of Corby.

*Names of*: H. Laughton, John Muston, carpenter, William Tydd, Richard Backhows, Robert Whitacre, Christopher Ielyan, William Muston, Mr Colston.

*Endorsed*: Edward Marsh, parson of Swayfield.                            SP 10/13, no. 62(i)

**565.** [? October]. Proposed members of a new royal commission to visit the university of Oxford.†

The duke of Northumberland. The marquess of Northampton. The bishop of Winchester. The bishop of Lincoln. Sir William Petre. Sir William Cecil. Dr [Nicholas] Wotton. Sir John Mason. Sir Robert Bowes. Sir John Cheke. George Owen. Sir Richard Reed. Dr [Richard] Lyell. Dr [John] Warner. Dr [Richard] Cox.

In the former commission. The duke of Northumberland. The marquess of Northampton. The bishop of Lincoln. Sir Richard Morison. Dr Cox. Dr [Simon] Haynes. Richard [*recte* Christopher] Nevinson.

*In another hand*: notes that the bishop of Lincoln, Haynes and Nevinson are deceased.

SP 10/13, no. 63

**566.** November 24. The king to the lord chancellor.

The duke of Somerset and divers of his adherents remain indicted in several counties of high treasons and felonies, for trial of which we mean to administer our laws to them. Cause a commission of oyer and terminer to be made under the great seal to the marquess of Winchester, high treasurer, to be our seneschal to hear the case, in the form of the causes of the last duke of Buckingham and the marquess of Exeter, dating the commission November 28. The others to be indicted with the duke – Sir Michael Stanhope, Sir Thomas Arundel, Sir Ralph Vane, Sir Miles Partridge, John Newdigate and John Seymour – shall also be tried. Cause a commission of oyer and terminer to be directed to the chief justices of both our benches and their associates; the two chief justices and any three

---

\*        Stamford Baron, Northants.

†        A new commission was ordered by the privy council on 28 September 1551 and was apparently issued by October 2 (though no record is found in *CPR*), probably because of continuing trouble with conservatives among the senior members of the university [*APC*, iii, 371, 376]. But this draft cannot date before Dudley's elevation to the dukedom of Northumberland (October 11). Bishop Holbeach of Lincoln had died in August and his successor John Taylor was not appointed until the following June [*HBC*, 236]: it was presumably intended that the bishop of Lincoln should be an *ex officio* visitor. The notes that Holbeach, Haynes and Nevinson were dead must have been added at least twelve months later, as Haynes died between July 12 and October 24 in 1552 [PROB 11/35, ff. 228–30. *CPR* 1550–3, 270]. The writer of the draft not only erred with Nevinson's Christian name, but also credited Northampton with membership of the 1549 commission while omitting the names of Paget, Petre and Ridley from his list of the earlier visitors [see no. **218** above].

associates to be the quorum of their commission, to be dated November 29.

*Corrected draft.*                                                    SP 10/13, no. 64

**567.** [? November]. Depositions by [William] Crane, [Sir Thomas] Palmer and the earl of Arundel.

Crane affirms that the duke of Somerset bade him tell the duchess he would no further meddle with the apprehension of any of the council, and he commanded her bid [Sir Michael] Stanhope meddle no more in talk with the earl of Arundel. Arundel said he would have a parliament as soon as the apprehension was done, to establish things lest a worse evil might happen. Somerset told Crane he was sorry he had gone so far with Arundel. Somerset and Arundel talked of the apprehension of the lords of the council, including the earl of Pembroke: Arundel said he was honest and would be conformable if the others were taken. The duke and earl agreed religion should stand as now. They and the duchess were privy to the apprehension. Somerset and Arundel had great conference in the garden at Somerset House four or five days before his going west, touching reform of the realm. Arundel then promised to take the part he did. They devised to reform the state, apprehend the duke of Northumberland and the marquess of Northampton, whom they agreed should go to the Tower and be used as they were when they were there. John Seymour proves the coming of Arundel to Somerset's house, often to Somerset Place, wearing a black cloak. Crane and Palmer affirm this. Somerset told the duchess that Arundel would never confess his doings, if revealed: proved by Crane in examination before Sir Thomas Moyle, &c. Arundel refused [Sir William] Cecil and Crane, choosing Stanhope, as the duke told Crane, as messenger between the duke and earl. After the duke told Crane that Arundel would also have Pembroke apprehended, he told how Arundel devised that, before apprehending the lords, he would have Sir John York taken because he could tell many pretty things concerning the mint. Palmer says that the duke much desired to have Arundel and others assured to him. Arundel, asked what he and the duke meant to have done with the lord great master,* the lord [great] chamberlain† and Pembroke, replied he meant no harm but would have them called to answer and reform things.

*Printed*: Tytler, ii, 38–41.                                        SP 10/13, no. 65

**568.** [? November]. Report of depositions by the earl of Arundel.

At the earl's request the lord great master and the lord great chamberlain were willed by the king to repair to the Tower to him. He would not deny conferring with the duke of Somerset of the state, and misliking the order of things. He meant no harm to the great master, the great chamberlain and the earl of Pembroke had he them in his power, but would have called them to answer and reform things. He never sent Sir Michael Stanhope as messenger to the duchess, but to the duke, willing him to take care for his counsel and secrets were known. Arundel spoke similarly another time in the presence of the said lords, and of us, the lord privy seal, the earl of Pembroke and Sir Philip Hoby.

*Signed by*: the earl of Pembroke, the duke of Northumberland, the marquess of Northampton, the earl of Bedford and Sir Philip Hoby.

*Endorsed*: Sir Michael Stanhope.

*Printed*: Tytler, ii, 46–7. *Facsimiles of National MSS*, ii, 90 (facsimile no. LI).

                                                                     SP 10/13, no. 66

**569.** [? November]. Report of depositions of the earl of Arundel.

When the duke of Northumberland and the marquess of Northampton were appointed

---

*      Northumberland.
†      Northampton.

by the king to hear the confession of the earl of Arundel in the Tower, after some protestations, with much difficulty, as if loath to say anything that might touch himself, he said: I cannot deny I once talked with the duke of Somerset and determined to arrest, but not harm, you in the council. After they showed him (known by the duke's confession) that the duke and he had met many times for that purpose at Syon and Somerset Place, London, he sighed, lifted his hands and said they knew all. He was asked whether he ever sent a message to the duchess of Somerset by Sir Michael Stanhope that she and the duke should beware whom they trusted, for he had lately been at Baynard's Castle with the earl of Pembroke and perceived by his talk he had some intelligence of these matters; but if they kept their own counsel he would never confess anything to die for it. [Arundel] first swore he never sent such a message; but, being pressed by the duke and marquess, seeing they knew something, he finally confessed he warned the duke by Stanhope, but not the duchess. Afterwards when [Bernard] Hampton, one of the clerks of the council, was sent to write the whole matter he would have retracted all, especially the last, saying he did not will Stanhope to warn the duke. The duke and marquess were sent to him again with the lord privy seal and Lord Pembroke. By circumstances he confessed all, save sending Stanhope to the duke, but said he told it to Stanhope that he should warn the duke, but would not confess again he sent him.

*Signed by*: the duke of Northumberland, the marquess of Northampton, the earl of Bedford and the earl of Pembroke.

*Printed*: Tytler, ii, 43–5.                                                                SP 10/13, no. 67

**570.** [? November]. Charges against [Thomas] Kymball, mayor of Cambridge.

1. He disclosed the secrets of the council's letters to others than were chosen, perverting their sense, not to the well disposed but to the busiest brains of the town, whereby much suspicion and dissension is arisen and further inconvenience is likely in the university and town if it is not provided for. 2. He much abused the vice-chancellor and others of the university by his untrue report to the duke of Northumberland that he could not have a copy of the council's letters, where he and his brethren had the original three days. 3. He has used strange and dangerous talk, which breeds variance and trouble in the town, namely that some went about to betray the town and that he was sent for to give over it and his mayoralty. Some towards him have reported abroad to occasion the people to stir that their commons should be taken from them and given to the wealthiest of the university, which has entered into light heads and dangerous talk has already followed. 4. He leaves the advice of the gravest aldermen and follows only that of unstaid persons and worse; he goes from house to house, calls companies together and fills busy heads with untrue whisperings. 5. He is not thought so malicious himself, but follows Roger Slegge, a common practiser to overthrow all order, the firebrand of the town, poor, and living by shifts and parts. It is feared, if time served, he would enterprise some notable stir. His adherents are the gamers and lusty unthrifts of the town. In his absence it was quiet; now all is in boil. He promised when last called before the council to become a new man and move to the country. Memorandum: to peruse the depositions of the townsmen against him three or four years past. The wise and expert heads of the university and town think order and concord impossible between them unless he is disenfranchised and banished.

SP 10/13, no. 68

**571.** December 1. Wootton. Roger Leez, bailiff of Wootton under Weaver, Staffordshire, to Sir William Cecil.

I lately received your letter and am glad that the king has given you the manor of Wootton, where I am bailiff and officer. All the commands in your letter will be accomplished. Trusting you will be our good master.

*Holograph.*                                                                SP 10/13, no. 69

**572.** December 11. Valérand Poulain, [superintendent of the community of Flemish weavers at Glastonbury] to the council.

Since the superintendents of the accounts of the duchy of Somerset, recently sitting at Glastonbury, pre-occupied with other matters, have been unable to carry out your instructions to see kept the arrangement between the duke of Somerset and the Hainault merchants, I must again ask that just consideration be at last given to this important undertaking and to these men who have come in good faith from such a distance. We ask (1) that you build fifty houses suitable for their craft for these men as soon as possible, with two dyeing workshops, and that William Crouch, Hugh Bagh and Robert Heiet and other receivers and wardens of deer parks and forests should pay out the money currently available and deliver timber, stone and all materials either for homes or their equipment to our people or whomsoever you entrust. (2) Since there are no unoccupied meadows and land cannot without injustice and unrest be taken from the English, order that the whole deer park at Glastonbury (called Wirrall park) be handed over to these men according to the agreement with the duke; on condition (if it is agreed) that whenever four acres of first class meadow (enough to feed two cows for a year) are handed over to individuals, they themselves leave the deer park. The duke originally promised the deer park to our people in this way and treated with Sir Thomas Spek to recover it from him. We can prove this with suitable witnesses. The park is of moderate size, scarcely sufficient for the thirty families now in Glastonbury. However, these men prefer to be content with little until something better can be provided, rather than that anything which the English legally held before should be taken from them. (3) When the duke was in Wells he gave our people an empty garden on the north of the monastery church to harvest vegetables. Because [Henry] Cornish has up till now denied them this, we beg you to order it to be handed over to them. On this matter too we have suitable witnesses. (4) Let the money ordered by you be handed over to these men to pay for buying wool at the right time, enough for a year, for seven very large bronze cauldrons and large wooden vats for the dyers; they also need woad, madder, alum, tannin, vitriol and many other such things, and if they are not bought at a certain time for the whole year great losses will be suffered; finally, to meet the wages of six carders, more than sixty spinning women and the carpenters who make the equipment, and for living expenses for the rest of the families. They can get nothing from the sale of cloth until the dyeing workshops are finished. I have appended an account, as accurate as possible. If fields or the deer park are handed over and the houses paid for the matter might be settled for £1,200. This our people would afterwards pay off by moderate instalments, say £50 a year. If it is desired that the sum be deposited with an Englishman rather than handed over to our people, let it be one from whom they can be sure to receive the money when need arises. (5) Although it was agreed with the duke that his receiver or delegate should receive all the cloth from these men, because this is troublesome to both parties, involving greater dangers and expenses, we beg that, as the duke at Wells allowed our people to keep the cloth in their possession, these others may do the same. Let the receiver be content with £50 a year or whatever you deem just. The duke delegated so much to me that it should be sufficient that I have pledged my loyalty on behalf of all. Let not good men be harassed to no purpose by evil ones and let their wives and children be sufficient guarantee for their own persons. (6) Let the royal charter for naturalisation of our people, agreed with the duke, be no longer deferred. (7) Our people have found some men's efforts directed to private advantage, yet they themselves, refugees only for their religion, wish nothing more than to help the state so long as they can obtain a quiet dwelling here. We beg you order the superintendent to take charge of them and their affairs. If you consider an Englishman should be brought in as well, give us one who is approved by our community, just, zealous for true religion, and rather better disposed towards foreigners than those men we have so far experienced.

(8) Consideration should be given at some time to me, that an honourable salary be determined, with the promised house and land. For fifteen months I have been paying out large sums in this enterprise and have incurred incredible drudgery. (9) This undertaking is hard, and because of the negligence of the duke's servants (except [John] Newdigate) these men have been very badly treated this year, for neither are the houses ready nor the meadows assigned, as the duke often ordered. They have fallen into debt with the duke beyond original expectation. They beg you that all their debt be remitted, except the money laid out on wool. They have used up the remainder on transport of the families and goods from overseas and from London to Glastonbury, and on necessary and extremely frugal living expenses. They have spent money of their own in addition. (10) If you no longer wish to decide on these matters, at least grant the [naturalisation] charter and delegate other things to two or three men of standing who are just and godly and not harsh to foreigners. There are such men in the neighbourhood – the bishop of Bath, Sir Hugh Paulet, Sir John Seyntloo, Sir Thomas Dyer and [Alexander] Popham – who will see what is needed and will deal fairly. Meanwhile give written orders for what is necessary to be handed over to our people. We have been without wool for about eight days, and there are no means of paying the spinning women's wages. Judge what is right and this little church will continue to pray for you and the king. *Postscript.* Proofs for individual articles. The duke, in accordance with the kindness with which he has always treated these men, is not likely to reject any of them. (1) The agreement with the duke. (2) The same. Sir John Thynne, Newdigate, master of the duke's horse, William Crouch, receiver, Robert Heiet, farmer of Street, Richard Ponis, the king's servant, Cornish himself and [Humphrey] Colls. (3) The same men, Crouch, Newdigate, Cornish. (4,5,6) The same agreement. Reason, justice and common feeling. (7) The fear and experience of many. The duke allowed this practice when he was recently in Wells and has always had confidence in me. That Cornish demanded pieces of cloth on false pretences, claiming he had a letter from the council. (8,9) The same agreement, right and justice. (10) That the council's will should be carried out. When we hoped people were coming with authority to carry out the terms of the agreement we were not overmuch concerned to have [the council's] letter. Sir Thomas Dyer can give clear proof of more or less all these matters and explain how the men I mentioned are behaving.

*Latin.*

*Holograph.*                                                    SP 10/13, no. 70

**573.**   [December (? 18)]. Valérand Poulain to the council.

When last year, in answer to my request, I had obtained a letter from you to receivers [William] Crouch and [John] Berwick for paying a sum to the foreign weavers at Glastonbury, I pondered how some of this money might be extracted for building workshops and homes. I had ascertained how much was necessary for the weavers, so that I should not appear to be asking too much. But afterwards, when the council said they had no authority to order money for the workshops, I saw danger on two fronts: if I allocated the money solely for the weavers, with construction of the workshops postponed indefinitely, not only would the royal grant be ebbing away, but all the efforts and labour of honest men be lost as well. If I abstracted any of the money, the weavers were threatened with great lack of necessities when, as their money failed, they were subjected to the merchants. This, more or less, happened, to their great disadvantage. It had seemed best to me and other prudent men to ignore the second danger and guard against the first. Everyone gave me hope that this would not displease you. I threw my heart into building workshops until they were ready for production. But besides the money I had counted on, more came. When everyone was pleased with the undertaking and all was going briskly, many of the English, on my security, gave material, services, some even money, expecting that you would undertake the charges. So far they have borne with me kindly, but if you were to desert me I could only return home at once and put myself in their hands, to my utter disgrace. Already one and then another is grumbling at me. Do not allow me, after such labours and great loyalty to the realm, and considering my humiliating salary, to incur disgrace, nor allow the English to be caused loss. The whole debt is not more than £131.0.9. Write to receiver [John] Aylworth to arrange at Wells to pay this sum that, freed of all ill repute by your kindness, I may continue with this enterprise.

*Latin.*

*Holograph.*       SP 10/13, no. 72

**574.** [December (? 18)]. Valérand Poulain to Sir William Petre.

God knows how reluctantly, and with the advice of the wisest, I set about paying off the cost of the workshops, for the weavers might be in danger if any of the sum allotted them were diverted elsewhere. But it is more to be feared lest such great expenditure were wasted if the workshops are deserted and neglected. It was specially necessary for these to be completed and the work not to be postponed, as had happened before by the machinations of those who envied good men. Now, in return for my enthusiasm, devotion and energy, my livelihood and honour are in danger at the hands of those who, drawing on my credit, obtained their own work, material, and some even money, so that in this difficult negotiation we should not founder in mid course. Commend my cause and petition to the council, begging them not to wish me whom they have assisted in great matters to be abandoned now in a trivial one. I ask nothing for myself except that my standing may be restored among the good English, who have helped so generously. I shall never later ask for any of their money. I will never trouble parliament for my stipend, without which I cannot live, for I abhor greed. I would rather make satisfaction to the English by selling books and furniture. But my greatest hope is in your continuing kindness.

*Latin.*

*Holograph.*       SP 10/13, no. 73

**575.** December 18. Westminster. The council to William Crouch, receiver of the duke of Somerset's revenues in Somerset.

The king's pleasure is that of such money as is or shall come to you of the receipt of the duke of Somerset's revenues in Somerset you shall pay £340 to the superintendent and strangers at Glastonbury, at times and by order appointed by the bishop of Bath, Sir Hugh Paulet, Sir John St Loo, Sir Thomas Dyer and [Alexander] Popham or three of them; £300 to the strangers for wools and other necessaries for their occupation, £40 to the superintendent for the king's reward towards payment of his charges.

*Signed by* : the archbishop of Canterbury, the marquess of Winchester, the duke of Northumberland, the earl of Bedford, Lord Darcy, the bishop of Ely, Sir John Gates, Sir Thomas Cheyne, Dr Nicholas Wotton, Sir William Petre and Sir John Mason.

SP 10/13, no. 76

**576.** December 18. Minute of the above.

*Without signatures.*       SP 10/13, no. 77

**577.** December 18. The council to [William Barlow], bishop of Bath and Wells, Sir Hugh Paulet, Sir John St Loo, Sir Thomas Dyer and [Alexander] Popham.

The duke of Somerset caused certain strangers to repair to Glastonbury, promising houses, ground and other relief for them and their families. They are very godly and honest poor folk, ready to teach their crafts and likely soon to bring great commodity to those parts. The king, understanding they are not yet fully provided for, willed us to require you, or three of you, to take order as follows. See how every family man may be housed, with rooms for their occupations. Every household or family was promised four acres of meadow to feed two kine, which cannot now be provided without injury to others; appoint Wirrall park for them until they may be provided with meadows or other ground, and the garden north of the church for a herbary. They require much money for wools for the coming year and necessaries for their occupation, which they promise to repay; commune with them for the surety the king shall stand for repayment, and the date, the order of selling their cloths, the discipline they use and desire in their churches, and such other things as their superintendent shall open. Write of all your doings and advice, that final order may be taken. We have written to [William] Crouch, the duke of Somerset's receiver for Somerset, to deliver £340 – £300 for provisions and £40 to the superintendent in reward towards his expenses for the past year. Tell them the king grants their suit to be denizens, without charge, for which order is given here. Assist them in all reasonable suits.

*Facsimile signatures of*: the archbishop of Canterbury, the marquess of Winchester, the duke of Northumberland, the earl of Bedford, Lord Darcy, the bishop of Ely, Sir Thomas Cheyne, Sir John Gates, Sir William Petre, Dr Nicholas Wotton and Sir John Mason.                                                                                      SP 10/13, no. 74

**578.**  Corrected draft of the above.                                                          SP 10/13, no. 75

**579.**  December 24. London. The duke of Somerset to the Flemish weavers at Glastonbury.

Valérand Pouland has testified in the name of James de Cleris and Jerome Voailler, weavers, and Francis de Goiis, dyer, that they have pledged their word in the name of others, at least fourteen families occupied in weaving who, to avoid the mass and other popery, are forced, in accordance with the emperor's decree, to depart and seek a place to live with freedom for the gospel and ply their trade. As guardian of the church, and considering that no greater benefit can be conferred on any people than the introduction of crafts, of which none is more useful than weaving, we have granted Poulain a permanent habitation for these craftsmen, weavers, dyers and other refugees in Glastonbury, Somerset. Because of the importance of this undertaking, however many weavers come, together with two dyers, six carders and two carpenters, we shall give each a house which we shall have built and maintained, and enough land to support two cows, to enjoy as an inheritance for three lives. For the houses they shall pay the tax customary over the past twenty years. For the expenses of their journey and purchase of necessary tools we shall order our collector or receiver to allot such money and supply such timber and stone without charge as is needed. The only money to be debited to them in the accounts is that which they have received from the collector for the stated purposes. The weavers, or as many as we decide, shall pledge themselves to pay back the money in moderate annual instalments of 200 crowns or £50, beginning on St John's Day 1553. All the tools mentioned shall belong to them for ever; but if they sell them we or our heirs may claim them at the purchase price. Lest the craftsmen be hampered by shortages, our collector shall procure wool for them at a fair price, as among the local people. He shall provide money for all their necessities and madder, woad, alum and other requisites for dyeing. Money shall always be provided for essential living expenses and wages of the dyers, their assistants, carders and spinning women. To pay off this debt, when weavers have completed a cloth they shall hand it to our collector or commissioner who will sell it to the merchants at a price agreeable to the weavers, subtracting the amount from the total debt. We shall give this help with money and wool until our collector can enter a quarter of the sum involved in credit and the weavers are able to sell their services or cloth to the merchants. After they have ceased to use our assistance, if we require any service such as lengths of cloth they shall oblige us, understanding that we shall buy them for the same amounts as the merchants would. We shall confirm the laws of this craft by letters under our seal, and see they receive royal approval. The settlers shall elect five of their own magistrates each year in the presence of our representative who will add authority to the proceedings. So that their work and merchandise may quickly gain esteem in the realm we forbid them to admit apprentices within the first year. After that no one is to have more than one, who shall finish his apprenticeship in two years and then hire himself out. No one may obtain full rights to exercise the craft on his own until four years after the end of his apprenticeship; during these four years he is not to offer his services to anyone but his first master. After these six years he shall be free to offer his services to whomsoever he wishes; he may become a master craftsman and have a workshop wherever he likes, provided he observes the laws of the craft. Each master craftsman may have as many workers as he wishes, English or foreign. Since early provision must be made to preserve the craft, we forbid our subjects in Glastonbury, Wells and the neighbourhood to combine wool and linen in one cloth sometimes falsely called pure silk (commonly called velveteen) on pain of losing all thread, wool or flax found in their homes and a fine. [The weavers] will explain the rules observed overseas when they come to ask for our charter. Since the chief reason for their exile is their faith we grant them their own assemblies and a church in some suitable consecrated building, with the same liberty as the churches of settlers in London. They may elect a superintendent or pastor, to whom we shall give a stipend and house with some land. We have promised Poulain that we shall obtain English citizenship for those who came at the beginning as soon as he has told us their names. Their wages are to be free of constraint and they are to enjoy the same privileges as clothworkers. We promise the same to all subsequent exiles for the gospel. The superintendent shall strictly administer ecclesiastical discipline over all the craftsmen, foreign and native. Any Anabaptist, Mennonite, freethinker or other heretic or trouble maker shall be swiftly excommunicated by the superintendent and exiled by our representative. We wish these concessions to be permanent and everything to be done with equity and justice. [Poulain] may have whenever he wishes a more formal charter under our seal and confirmation by the king's letters and parliament.

*Latin.*

*Poulain's hand, testifying it to be a translation of a French document signed by the duke.*

SP 10/13, no. 71

**580.** [? December]. Notes of depositions concerning treason.

Gregory Shard, carter, of Isleworth says that on Saturday December 19 a woman came to his house saying she had been at Lady Page's, who would not speak with her, and she told him Dr Huyse, a physician, a carver and groom went about to destroy the king. [He] says he never saw the woman but once at Androo's house. He says she told him that she had once spoken to the duke of Somerset before his committing to the Tower. Elizabeth Tracye, silkwinder, in St John Walbrook by London Stone: against her house dwells a woman called Pynar. When she dwelt about Newgate, Mr Newman and his wife. She had a son, John Wyld, who dwelt with the Lady Mary. Mrs Vadye at Dowgate hired her house for her, for which she pays 6s. 8d.

*Incomplete.* SP 10/13, no. 78

[For SP 10/13, no. 79 see no. **598** below.]

**581.** [? 1551]. Petition from the merchants of the staple to the king and council.

It is manifest that [? since] the last act of retainer which was taken by the merchants of the staple of the king, because of such abundance and increase of Spanish wools as have come into Flanders and France, divers towns within both which long draped English wools and fells fell to the drapery of Spanish wools, a great decay of the vent that the staple merchants were accustomed to have there. They sustained another great hindrance that they could not go through with the act of retainer because of such licences granted to merchant strangers for shipping wools over the straits, as the wools should have been brought and shipped to the staple at Calais and there sold by the merchants of the staple to such Italian merchants as bought the wools shipped over by merchant strangers, which would have been of great help to Calais and great burden to the merchants of the staple. Doubtless the custom that the merchants of the staple pay is as beneficial to the king as that of the merchant strangers, for the strangers always clack their wools (to try out the best and fine from the coarse and refuse) and ship only the fine and best, paying five marks a sack custom and have long days of payment. But the merchants of the staple shipping to Calais middle wools and base country wools (as Kesteven, Holland and Rutland) pay as much custom and subsidy for them as for the best. Besides this they ship fells, where the strangers ship none. Though the fells are scarce worth 4d. or 5d. the king has 2d. custom of each. The merchants of the staple are always at the king's command whereas the strangers will depart when they see best profit. The act of retainer was very onerous and chargeable to the merchants of the staple; its redemption cost them over £20,000, above Staple Inn and all their properties in Calais and its marches. Many merchants were so decayed that they were never since occupied. No merchants bear so great adventure and have so small gain as those of the staple. He who buys wools or fells in England at the best fardel he can and sells them in Calais at the full price of the staple shall not gain £8 in £100. Whatever stock any merchant of the staple occupies in the staple at Calais, be it £1,000 or more, the king has the whole stock in four years for custom and subsidy. The drapery of this realm is so greatly increased that if it continues for twelve years as it has done for the past twelve there will be little enough wools to suffice the clothiers of the realm, so that the merchants of the staple shall find no wools for their money to ship to Calais. The merchants swear that the most profitable way for advancing the king's custom and the continuance of the staple is for the merchants to be at liberty and pay no more than they shall ship. Experience declares somewhat itself, for after* what time the merchants were brought to decay by the considerations rehearsed, and were unable to go through with the act of retainer, [?] fell from £12,000 to £4,000 and below. Since the king gave the merchants liberty to pay no more than they ship they have risen to 10,000 or 12,000 marks in their custom and subsidy. The merchants therefore ask that they may enjoy the liberties granted them by charters of the king's progenitors and confirmed by him, and that they may henceforth exercise their traffic of merchandise and shipping for thirty years, paying their customs and subsidies within Calais on April 6 and October 6 of such money as they shall be unfurnished and unprovided of there at the days of payment. They will give the king £1,000 in three years, 500 marks a year.†

*Corrected draft.*                                                                                    SP 10/13, no. 80

**582.** [? 1551]. Statement of the causes of the decay of the staple, with petition for redress.

A lord having tenants holding arable land must see they have sufficient cattle and seed, assuring his profits and encouraging the tenants to work for their own and their neighbours' comfort. Great decay will ensue if the stock is diminished. The staple is similar; their fellowship is but as the king's tenants and their stock only money which, if diminished, will fail to profit the king, themselves and their neighbours. The present great decay of the staple must be considered because of great extremity lately put to the

---

*        Sense lost, perhaps because a double leaf of the MS is missing.
†        The concluding section replaces an original unspecific petition to grant requests.

fellowship in paying more to the king than custom and subsidy has amounted to of such wools and fells as are yearly shipped to his staple. The fellowship has been compelled by appresting of their money to diminish greatly their stocks, to the undoing of many of them. Today the whole fellowship is so discomforted that they are minded to forsake the staple and seek some other living. A merchant cannot make less reckoning than to keep the stock whole and live by the gains. During the wars and mortality of sheep let the king grant the fellowship to be no further charged to pay him than they ship from time to time.

It is well known that great hindrance to the commodity of the king's wools and fells in his staple is grown in the past few years because of the abundance of Spanish wools that resort daily to such towns and countries as were wont to be draped by English wools and fells, which also causes much gold and silver to be left unbought in England. Let the king and council grant that all low priced wools – good and middle Holland, good and middle Rutland, middle Kesteven, middle Berkshire, Kentish and Norfolk – priced by the king to be staple wools, shall henceforth be shipped to Calais only, and the king to receive only for the custom of the same of the sack, whereby such towns and countries as have lately begun to drape Spanish wools may find at Calais as good pennyworth as they do of Spanish wools; no doubt then English wools shall have furtherance of sale, since the Spanish fleet often, by long voyage or contrary winds, disappoints the drapers. The fellowship will be more able to maintain themselves to the king's profit.

The trade in wools and fells, bought in England and leaving there much gold and silver, and yearly carried to the staple, enhancing their price among foreign merchants, has long brought to the country great treasure. This were well considered, and to encourage and revive the spirits of the king's poor subjects of the staple, let the king grant the said articles to take effect – which would be to the praise of God, profit to his grace, honour to his council and encouragement to his poor staplers. SP 10/13, no. 81

**583.** [? 1551]. Arguments against raising custom on cloths, by 'D'.

Reasons why parliament, when granting subsidies of customs in wares, always excepts cloths, to pay the old customs. 1. Most cloths and kerseys made in England to be exported were so coarse that the staplers and foreign merchants would not export them. 2. Of those coarse wools were made many western, northern and Devon kerseys, Suffolk cloths, short worsteds, castlecombes, baths, northern dozens, streets, tavistocks, penistones, long glemsfords, friezes, cottons and others. 3. The commons made and carried them to London and many thousands would otherwise beg, steal or come to destruction. 4. If of every sack of wool, 13 todds, four short cloths may be made the clothier pays the poor 40s. for making and carriage of every cloth; the merchant pays the clothier, as he supposes, towards the keeping of many servants to prepare his wools at least 13s. 4d. of every cloth, and 1s. 8d. for carriage to the water side, customs and dues – so the charge of one cloth amounts to 55s. – in four cloths £1, and in 100,000 cloths £275,000, for so many are exported by merchants, and this sum is left in the country to the relief of those who have their living by cloth making. 5. The merchant also maintains the navy and sailors, and is at other great charges abroad for gain fetched of foreigners which, if this great* custom of 6s. 8d. were raised on cloths, he would be unable to do nor remain a merchant. It is best that merchant adventurers and staplers use the accustomed trade without raising the custom. 6. The stapler pays 40s. custom and subsidy of every sack of wool, which should be 13 todds. Their allowance has long been such in weight that the cloths, if four may be made of one sack of wool, mostly made of base wools which neither foreigner nor stapler exports, should, after the rate of 6s. 8d. a cloth, be more than the foreigner or stapler pays in custom of the best wools in England, which, after

---

\* Inserted.

purchase is new shot by a sworn packer, and leaves much refuse which they sell to the clothier, of which custom is due when the cloths are shipped; otherwise no profit would grow to the prince or country if it were not put to cloth making. The poor of the country are left with no money for cloth making by the foreigner or stapler as by the adventurers. Nor does the stranger or stapler bring into the country again for his 13 todds of fine wools so much gold, fine silver or other necessaries by £6 as the adventurers for four cloths made of 13 todds of refuse or coarse wools and for four cloths of fine wools much more after the rate, so that by exporting cloths the country is more enriched by gold and silver brought in than by exporting wools. Many thousands of poor now making cloth would beg. The navy is maintained, the clothier and merchant live of it. The prince gains by loans, prests and subsidies saved more from the adventurer than the stranger or stapler. If this great custom of 6s. 8d. of every short cloth were paid, all who live by cloth making and the merchant would be undone. The inventor of the rise must have been a Burgundian who, seeing that if this custom were paid the stapler might afford his wools cheaper than the adventurer, whereby the subjects of the Low Countries would be able to make of English wools cheaper cloths than could be exported from England; the towns of the Low Countries would flourish and our subjects, towns and villages decay, many thousands beg, our navy and merchants be destroyed, and many other enormities.

Inconveniences likely if the custom of cloths were raised to 6s. 8d. 1. No custom can be raised of Burgundy and its subjects without breaking the Intercourse, which provided that nothing more should be raised of them than was fifty years before the Intercourse was confirmed – which has cost the king and the merchant adventurers many thousands of pounds. 2. If England breaks the Intercourse Burgundy will, and make English merchants pay twice for every penny raised of Burgundian subjects, so the king and people of England will be wonderfully endangered; everything they wear, eat or use from abroad will be more expensive. 3. If Burgundy will not suffer their Intercourse broken they will have double advantage of England and its merchants – they may export our cloths and afford them more cheaply than we, the custom being raised; and may make cheaper cloths of English wools than can be exported from England, so they will have the export of our cloth until their people can make enough for themselves, making many thousands in England beg who now live by cloth making. The merchants and navies of England will shortly be rooted out and consumed, weakening the king and strengthening foreigners; the gains English merchants had to maintain themselves and their navies will be in the hands of foreigners without fealty to the king. The raising of the custom will profit the king and country as the debasement of coinage did – which at first appeared great profit but experience taught otherwise.                                SP 10/13, no. 82

**584.**    1552. January 8. Ely Place. The duke of Northumberland to Sir William Cecil.
Remember the letters to be sent to Lord Conyers to repair to parliament and to Sir Ingram Clifford to repair to Carlisle and replace Conyers as captain of the town and deputy warden of the west marches until he knows the king's further pleasure. The lord deputy of Calais* has wilfully proceeded in his matter with my brother,† contrary to the council's letters, renewing unquietness between them and their retinues. To avoid further displeasure, their lordships have now good cause – considering this new trouble and his device for demanding rent arrears during the time of the late wars without first making the lords privy – to look upon such indiscreet dealing; act as you think best.
*Printed*: Tytler, ii, 103–4.                                SP 10/14, no. 1

[For SP 10/14, no. 2 see no. **587** below.]

*         Lord Willoughby of Parham.
†         Sir Andrew Dudley.

**585.** January 12. Glastonbury. The bishop of Bath and Wells, Sir John St Loo and Alexander Popham to the council.

According to your letters of December 18 to us and others touching the foreigners of Hainault now at Glastonbury, we have assembled there and taken order as appears in the enclosed articles and the foreigners' petitions [*which follow*]. Although they will grow to the king's great charges, the days of repayment are long, with no sureties but the bond of the superintendent and five of their leaders; yet since we find them so quiet, honest, diligent in bringing up their youth in labour and ready to teach the king's subjects (many English women can already spin and handle their wool as well and finely as they can themselves), this so much seems to tend to the advancement of the commonwealth, we think the money well employed. If it so appears to you, order should be taken out of hand for making ready their dye houses and other houses and things necessary for their faculties. Otherwise they must consume more than they can get with their work, as hitherto they have done.                                          SP 10/14, no. 3

**586.** [January 12. Glastonbury. Enclosed with the above]. Answers of the bishop of Bath and Wells, Sir John St Loo and Alexander Popham to the council's letters to them and others concerning the foreigners at Glastonbury.

There are now thirty-four families, and ten more are appointed to come as wind and weather serve, besides six widows and spinsters. There are only six houses complete, and twenty-two others habitable but needing much repair. Sixteen others are needed. There are some sites with walls standing, which may ease building charges. We have put off building, that the late abbey should not be spoiled of timber or stone or touched in any way until your pleasures there are known. Much more money has been spent in repairs and building houses than would have served with skilful oversight and provision: Robert Lyell of Street should join the superintendent for this. The foreigners will pay for the houses now ready and those ready before Easter the rents borne when they were last inhabited, to be charged from Lady Day; for houses ready after Easter they will pay the old rent from the next half year of their completion. Two houses must be prepared for dyeing and calendaring their worsted, for which, when it is ready and furnished with cauldrons and other necessaries (as appears in the superintendent's bill enclosed) they will pay £4 a year, half yearly. We estimate Wirrall park to be 200 acres, of which sixty acres and a great wood are herbage of little value; the rest is partly good pasture and some low meadow, but not sufficient for finding two kine for every family. Without dividing the park we have appointed the whole herbage to be occupied by the foreigners in common, as their superintendent and council appoint, paying £10 annual rent, half yearly, beginning at Michaelmas. They petition that the deer, about 140, may be bestowed by you. We have ordered the garden and void ground north of the abbey church, about two acres, to be used for their gardening, at the disposition of the superintendent and five others, to be assigned to families without gardens annexed to their houses. They desire £700 in prest besides the £300 they will now receive by your letters – £300 for wool, £500 for woad, madder, copperas, alum and other necessaries for their colours, £200 to pay loom makers, spinsters and others employed – amounting to £1,000, £100 to be repaid at Easter 1554, then £100 each Easter until all is repaid; they have no surety but the superintendent and five leaders will be bound. They desire sale of their cloths at their best commodity. They use and desire to continue the order and discipline in their churches contained in a book named *Liturgia* by the superintendent, which we enclose. The superintendent and strangers were loaned £484.14.8 by the duke of Somerset to establish their business, to be repaid at £50 a year from midsummer 1553. As they have not had the pastures, houses, instruments and other things prepared according to the duke's promise, whereby many of them have not been able to work for their livings but have lived wholly on stock of money, they desire remission of that debt save £130, the value of all the worsteds they have hitherto wrought, and that the £130 be joined to the £1,000, and they will be bound to pay the king £100 for ten years and £70 in the eleventh year. The superintendent and five bound will be bound not to leave the country without the king's special licence. If any die, they will renew their bond and replace them.                                                                SP 10/14, no. 3(i)

**587.**    [January 12. ? Enclosed with no. **585**]. Abstract of the above. Further requests of the foreigners.

   A warrant to Robert Hiet and the superintendent to repair and build forty-six houses or compound with any having convenient leases. A letter to Hiet for disparking deer. A letter to [Henry] Cornish to discharge him of the park and all other things within the abbey that may serve the foreigners. [Let him restore that which he sold piecemeal or ordered to be removed after he heard of the arrest of the duke of Somerset].* A warrant to the receivers of those parts to deliver such money thought necessary for the premises, and a letter to Hiet to receive the same. [Cash is now needed for the salaries; half the sum, £500, should be paid immediately, the rest before Pentecost].* The king's letter to confirm the superintendent in his office and licence to use the service in the *Liturgia*, and some honest stipend for the maintenance of himself and his family. [By these works and expenses he will have attended to this business for eighteen months now. Then, since he came to England, he never sought or accepted anything. Nonetheless he will have been well looked after by many other prominent men in the three years since he brought (Martin) Bucer (Paul) Fagius].* That he may have the priory house behind the church for his dwelling. To have confirmation of their craft by letters patent, with assurance of the park, houses, gardens &c. according to the commissioners' letters, with certain privileges necessary for maintenance of their craft. To have a hall for examination of the true making of their says and worsteds &c., with authority to proceed against offenders according to foreign customs, for which they desire authority to choose yearly five wardens and overseers, against whose determination there to be no appeal. That like occupation be not used elsewhere in the country for ten years, until they have satisfied the king's debt. To have all stuff pertaining to their occupation custom free and to pay English custom for exports. In all exactions to pay no more than Englishmen. To enjoy all privileges and liberties as the clothiers and dyers of the country.
   *Latin and English.*                                                     SP 10/14, no. 2

Note: SP 10/14, nos. 2, 3 and 3(i) are bound in the wrong order.

**588.**    January 23. Memorandum for acts of parliament.
   1. That no patron shall give less to the parson than the whole benefice, nor reserve any commodity to himself. 2. That no spiritual person make lease for longer than twenty-one years, nor of the demesnes of his principal house longer than for his own time. 3. Against regrating of merchandise: no man to be a merchant without having been an apprentice five years; no banker to buy of the adventurer except he sell it by retail; no merchant adventurer to buy any like ware as he brings in himself, till that is first sold.† 4. Against severing land from houses. 5. To make exporting bullion felony. 6. That no man ship at creeks, nor lie at quay, but have all his ware brought to him by lighters. 7. For preservation of timber. 8. Subsidy. 9. For apparel. 10. For treasurers and receivers. 11. Prohibiting export of horses. 12. Treaty.
   *Items 1-8 in the king's hand, 9-12 in Cecil's.*
   *Printed*: Nicholas, *Remains*, ii, 491–5.                                SP 10/14, no. 4

**589.**    Copy of the above.                                              SP 10/18, no. 13

\*        Latin insertions in hand of Poulain.
†        5 & 6 Edward VI c. 14.

**590.** January 23.* Parliamentary bill for limitation of the late duke of Somerset's lands.

At a parliament held at Westminster in 32 Henry VIII† it was enacted that all manors, lands, tenements and other hereditaments there mentioned might be appointed by common descent and remainder to Edward, late duke of Somerset, by the name of earl of Hertford, namely the manors of Muchelney, Drayton, Westover, Earnshill, [West] Camel, Downhead, Holcombe and Fivehead with their appurtenances, Somerset, of which the duke was then seised of an estate of inheritance in fee simple, from thenceforth to the duke and Anne his wife and their heirs male. It was also enacted that all his other lands and appurtenances wherein he then had estate of inheritance in fee simple might thenceforth be to him and his heirs male. In default of heirs male the said manors and other premises and all other properties in which at the time of the act the duke had any estate of inheritance in fee simple should pass to Edward Seymour, second son of the duke by Katherine his first wife, and his heirs male, then to Henry Seymour the duke's brother and his heirs male, then to Sir Thomas Seymour the duke's younger brother and his heirs male, then to the duke's heirs female, then to the right heirs of Edward Seymour, the duke's second son. It was further enacted that all other manors, lands, tenements and appurtenances which after the making of the act should come to the duke and his heirs in fee simple in possession, reversion or remainder, by descent, gift, purchase or otherwise, should be deemed and judged to the duke and his heirs male with like remainders as before. Since which act the late and present kings have by several letters patent granted the duke divers manors, lands, tenements and hereditaments, contrary to the tenor of which letters patent the duke by force of the former act was seised of and in the said manors, lands, tenements and hereditaments of an estate entail to him and his heirs male with remainder as above. By reason of which former act the estates contained in the several letters patent are clearly altered and the king, that was inheritable by the same, traduced and put to further degrees for his inheritance in that the heirs of the half blood are by the act without consideration preferred to the inheritance before his highness, being of the whole blood. As upon examination it has been proved that the act was obtained by the corrupt and sinister labour of the duke, and that contrary to the usage of all private bills neither the king's sign nor stamp was added, and as by the act much hurt and dissension has ensued to divers persons who, upon trust, have enfeoffed the duke in their lands and tenements to their uses, because contrary to their feoffments by operation of the statute their trust has been defrauded, and the duke thereof seised to his own use; and as also John Seymour, eldest son and heir of the duke has made suit to this court to be restored into such lands as were Katherine Filliol's, his mother's, late wife to the duke, being sold by the duke without her assent, as to all other lands of his mother, whereof the duke received recompense, and like suit has been made on behalf of divers others which seem to have suffered oppression and injury at the duke's hands: let it be enacted that the statute of 32 Henry VIII be consumed. The commons beseech the king that it be enacted that as the duke has sold and exchanged some part of his manors, lands and tenements that he had at the time of the act of 32 Henry VIII, that the heirs of Lady Anne his wife and all others to whom the remainders in the act are limited shall be fully recompensed of as much other land of the duke as amounts to the value of the lands alienated, to hold them of such estate expressed in the former act; the lands to be assigned by the master of the king's wards and liveries within a year of the making of this act, or it shall be lawful for the heir of Lady Anne at his majority, or any to whom the remainders are limited, to take distraint. Provided that John Seymour be by the king's order or that of his commissioners restored out of the lands that the heirs of Lady Anne have or shall have by authority of this act or that

---

\*      So dated at the head of the MS in the same hand as the text. Ascribed in *CSPD* to April 12 (the day parliament met) when it was introduced; it was passed on the following day [*CJ*, i, 19, 20, 23. Cf. Jordan, ii, 337]. HLRO, Original Act, 5 & 6 Edward VI no. 37.

†      HLRO, Original Act, 32 Henry VIII no. 74.

of 32 Henry VIII as much as shall recompense him of all lands possessed by Katherine
Filliol his mother, and whereof the duke was seised in her right and sold without her
consent, or that was given to the duke and her in special entail to them and their heirs,
or to any others to the use of the duke and Katherine and their heirs, and sold by the
duke without her consent, or whereof the duke has received any recompense in money
according to the value of the said recompense: to have and hold the same to John of
like estate as he should have had in the manors, lands and tenements that were
Katherine's. Let it be enacted that the act of 32 Henry VIII concerning all lands which
afterwards shall come to the duke shall be repealed, and that all such lands be considered
as if the former act had never been made, and stand in such estate as limited in the
letters patent or other writings to the duke solely or jointly, and all such lands whereof
any estate in fee simple was limited and expressed in any letters patent or writings to
the duke, and whereof the duke was seised at the time of his death other than such as
are by this act promised to the heir of Lady Anne with remainders as above said, shall
remain wholly to the king and his heirs. Let it be enacted that of the lands given to the
king by this act the debts of the duke be paid, all his children sustained during his
highness's pleasure, all others whose land the duke obtained by extortion, power or
contrary to justice shall be restored to such lands or their value, to be granted by the
king's commission within one year after this session of parliament. Let it be enacted that
all lands and properties that have been given since the act of 32 Henry VIII to the duke
solely or jointly shall be taken in this act to have been in the duke, but only of such
estates as were limited in the conveyance to him made to the same use and uses. Where
by this act the king is to be entitled to a great part of the ground without Temple Bar,
Middlesex, on which Somerset Place is built, because it was obtained by the duke since
the former act, which is not meet to be severed from the place, let it be enacted that
the king and his heirs shall have Somerset Place and all appurtenances and all tenements
outside Temple Bar called Somerset rents. In recompense let the heir of Lady Anne have
the residue of the duke's lands and tenements remaining in his majesty's hands, to the
same value, as formerly appointed, with the same remainders as the heir had in Somerset
Place before the making of this act, saving to all persons and corporations, their heirs
and successors, other than the heirs of Lady Anne and their heirs claiming only by the
former act or any to whom the remainders are limited by that act, and their heirs, all
rights and dues which they have or ought to have in any of the manors, lands, tenements
and other premises in such manner as though this act had never been made. Provided
that in all properties which the heir male of the duke and Lady Anne or any in the said
remainders shall receive by assignment of the master of wards and liveries, the king shall
have like benefit of wardship, livery and primer seisin as he should have had before this
act in any of the lands entailed by the former act. Let it be enacted that the duke and
his heirs male by Lady Anne shall lose for ever to the king the names of Viscount
Beauchamp, earl of Hertford and duke of Somerset and all his other titles and dignities,
and the king shall be judged in possession of the castles, manors and properties of the
duke by whatever name, which by this act or any were given to him, as though due
inquisitions had been made in every part. Where the duke and Sir Thomas Arundel, Sir
Michael Stanhope, Sir Ralph Vane and Sir Miles Partridge were lawfully attainted for
their felonies, be it enacted that the attainders shall be good and effectual in law and the
four knights shall forfeit to the king all properties, rights and dues they had of any estate
of inheritance in fee simple on the days of their felonies. The duke and four knights
shall forfeit to the king all interests and leases they had at the time of their attainders,
saving to all heirs entailed of the knights and any person claiming any interest by or
from them and the duke since the felonies committed, all rights and interests they might
have had if this act had never been made. Since it requires a long time and great cost
to have inquisitions and offices of all properties of the knights whereby the king shall

be entitled to the escheat of all the same holden of him immediately by knight service or in socage and the year day and waste of all other manors of the knights held of any other person by knight service or socage, be it enacted that all the properties, rights and dues of which the four knights at the day of their felonies were seised in fee simple shall be judged in the possession of the king and his heirs. Provided that this act shall not prejudice the mesne lords of the fee of whom the four knights hold any properties immediately by knight service or socage, and where the day and days of the felonies by them or any of them committed seised thereof in their demesne as of fee. But that after the year day and waste taken by the king and his heirs of and in the premises, the same lords of the fee may enjoy by way of escheat the premises held by them of the services foresaid. Provided that William, Lord Willoughby of Parham, his heirs and assignees, shall have and enjoy and annual rent of £30 from the manor of Cheddar, Somerset, at Lady Day and Michaelmas, according to indentures of 20 December 1548 between him, the duke and Sir Thomas Heneage, and that Lord Willoughby may distrain if the rent is unpaid fourteen days. Let it be enacted that the duke's heirs or his heirs by Lady Anne shall at all times according to the indentures save harmless Lord Willoughby and his heirs, owners of the manor of Stow, Lincolnshire, which Lord Willoughby had of the duke's grant of and from the payment of all charges heretofore granted to Anthony Foster and Thomas Smith by any of the owners of the manor of Stow. Provided that this act shall not prejudice any woman's title of dower or jointure to which they were previously entitled.

*16 pp.*
*Some marginal notes and corrections.*
*Enactment*: HLRO, Original Act, 5 & 6 Edward VI no. 37.          SP 10/14, no. 20

**591.**  January 28. The duke of Northumberland to Sir William Cecil.

The French ambassador minds to be here this afternoon, for he had no leisure, he says, the other day, to accomplish what he had to tell the lords. The lords must either come hither immediately after dinner from star chamber or his coming must be postponed till tomorrow which, if the affairs in star chamber after dinner require any time, I think best. Move this to the rest of the lords who sit there today; send me word if they will have him deferred till tomorrow and I will send one to stay him. His secretary also showed me that [George] Paris, who brought the present, desires despatch; you should come here and order these things with [Sir John] Mason.

*Printed*: Tytler, ii, 104–5.          SP 10/14, no. 5

[For SP 10/14, nos. 6, 7, 8 and 9 see nos. **792, 608, 609** and **602** respectively.]

**592.**  February 24. Complaints laid before the council by English merchants against those of the Hanse.

[1]. All liberties and privileges pretended to be granted to those of the Hanse are void by the laws of this realm, and those merchants have no sufficient corporation to take the same. [2]. Such grants and liberties they claim not to extend to any certain persons or towns, whereby it cannot be known what persons or towns should enjoy the privileges. [3]. Because of this they admit and appoint to be free with them whomever they wish, whereby the king has been deceived in his customs by about £17,000 yearly. [4]. If the pretended grants were legal, they were made on condition that they should not avow or colour any foreign goods, which they have nevertheless done, as appears in the records of the exchequer and elsewhere. [5]. For a hundred years after the pretended privileges were granted they exported no goods from the country save to their own, nor imported anything save commodities of their own countries. Now they export this country's goods to Brabant, Flanders and adjoining places, and sell them to the great damage of the

king's subjects trading there, and import here merchandise of all foreign countries, whereby the king has lost much in customs. It is contrary to a recognisance made in the time of Henry VII. [6]. In the time of Edward IV they forfeited their pretended liberties by war with England. A treaty was made by reciprocal instrument that English subjects should have liberties in Prussia and other places of the Hanse as they had or ought to have used here, and that no prices, new exactions or prests should be set on their persons other than had been for a hundred years and more. This is daily much broken, especially in Danzig, not only by prohibiting Englishmen buying and selling but in levying new exactions and impositions. Thereby the merchants of the Hanse have forfeited their pretended privileges, which they claim to have been confirmed by Edward IV.

SP 10/14, no. 10

**593.** February [? 24]. Reasons declared to the king and council why the merchants of the Steelyard or Hanse ought not to have such privileges and liberties in the realm as they claim.

[1]. They claim liberties and privileges by charter of Henry III. This gave them only such liberties as they had before, and they cannot prove they had then such privileges as they now claim. [2]. They claim by a charter of Edward I, but this was made to all foreign merchants, none of whom claims such liberties as the Hanse now does. [3]. They obtained another charter from Edward II as their former ones were not sufficient in law. By this their pretended liberties were granted to them on condition that they should not avow any foreign goods to be theirs which were not of their guild. Thereby they have forefeited their privileges by allowing the goods of others, as appears by an inquisition or office found before the escheator of London and returned into the exchequer, and also by judgement given in the same court against Anthony Male in 4 Henry VIII. [4]. They have lately imported commodities of other countries as of their own, and export this country's commodities to their own country as into others. For a hundred years after Edward I granted their liberties they only imported their own country's goods, and exported this country's goods to their own countries. Their late misuse is contrary to the intent of their privileges. [5]. In the time of Edward IV they forfeited their liberties by war with England. A treaty was made by reciprocal instrument that the English should have liberties in the places of the Hanse as they had had; and that no prices, new exactions or prests should be set on their persons or goods than had been for a hundred years or more. This has daily been much broken, especially in Danzig, in prohibiting Englishmen buying and selling freely, and in raising on them new exactions and impositions. [6]. For the great abuse of their privileges by exporting this country's goods to the Low Countries of the archduke of Austria and the duke of Burgundy, certain persons became bound to Henry VII in £20,000 that certain merchants of the Hanse, then holding the Steelyard, should no more so offend. This bond is forfeited as within these thirty-five years they have frequented the emperor's Low Countries with this country's goods, to the king's great loss. When other foreigners paid 15d. in the pound for custom inwards, and Englishmen 12d., they paid but 3d. Outwards they pay much less than other foreigners, besides subventing the good order of the king's subjects in those parts. [7]. The confirmation of their supposed privileges in the time of Edward IV was made only according to the content of their charters, and so cannot prevail since the charters are insufficient or forfeited. [8]. They cannot name how many cities or places are of the Hanse, whereby they privilege whom they like, to the king's great loss because they pay so small custom. [9]. All their privilges are void as they were never incorporated.

SP 10/14, no. 11

**594.** [? February]. Book of memoranda of government and private business kept by Sir William Cecil.

Mr Hayes. Barrowden. Sir Philip Chantery. The proclamation for wines. Vavasor's licence.

Lord Paget's matter. Bishop of Durham's. Bishop of Dublin and [Sir Anthony] St Leger. Lord Conyers's letters touching [Fergus and Richard] Greame. [Sir John] Borthwick's letters. Merchant of Dublin's warrant – £600. [James] Crofts's warrant – £1,000. A prisoner in Hertford Castle: earl of Surrey. Passport for the L. of 'Tyllebary'. Heywoode's bill: annuity £40. Sir Andrew Dudley's patent for Guînes. [John] Brigantyn's matter. Nicasius [Yetsweyrt]. Licence for wine. Tenants at Middleham. Mr Chancellor of augmentations.

Tenants of Middleham: Thomas Cecil. Mr Norrey: Stowghton £14.14.0; Appleford £14. Bishop of Gloucester: [letters to the dean of Worcester]* to the house at Worcester. Act of parliament for foreign coins. Mr Parry. Barrowden hay. Proclamation for prices of wine according to the statute. Commission for bells and plate. [Edward] Walgrave, [Anthony] Kempe, [Sir Clement] Smyth: to be sent for. George Heron's letters. Lord chancellor. [Dr John] Cox.

Lord Garrett [FitzGerald]'s suit. Ireland. Vavasor: licence to pass the realm. The goldsmith's wife [Florence, widow of Edmund Pees of London]. Marches of Wales. [*Illegible*] on Friday. Tower. [John] Bradford the preacher: unable. [Richard] Goodrich. Martin Pyrrye. Lord deputy. Calais. Laird of Ormiston: dean of Windsor. Act of parliament for divine service: prohibition for mass. Lord Garrett: earl of Kildare. The survey. Deeping men versus Spalding. Brigantyn's matter. Borthwick's matter. The king of Denmark's agent: [Thomas] Wyndham.

[John] Allerley, [yeoman] of the jewel house. Morgan Wolf: letter to him. Randall, [Sir Francis] Jobson's man: wood. [Francis] Yacksley's licence: exchange. Mr Rud. Tyrroll. Charter. Byards. St J[ohn's] Wood: trees. Barholm. Earl of Westmorland. George Williams: evidence for St Martin's. Lord Montague. Men of Deeping's evidence. H[ugh] Whithed's matter: King's Bench. John Browne. Lord Montague. Mr Solicitor. Bishop of Peterborough. Letter to the dean of Peterborough. St Martin's parish [Stamford]. Mr Parry. Barrowden hay. The lease. [Sir William] Pickering. [? John] Harolde. South Luffenham. [William] Dansell: licence for 3,000 marks of silver, 12d. for every mark (a mark weight is 8 oz.). Powder for copper: 5 or 6 [*illegible*] for the difference. Lord Conyers. Sir Ingram Percy.† Letters. [? Armigil] Wade. Commission for bells &c. Wotton under Weaver: the bailiff. A person [? parson] in the Porter's Lodge accused by Cotton. [Dr William] Tresham in the Fleet. Letters to the French king in thanks for the horses.

Laird of Ormiston. Dean of Windsor. Mr Pickering: the article in the last peace. Brigantyn's matter: his answer; warrant. Provision for the hearers of mass. [*Illegible*]. [Sir John] York's appointment. The herald in Ireland. Bill. Venetian embassy. Adding of Mr Wotton in letters for the [*illegible*]. Mr Arundel's letters. Mr Petre. [Peter] Vannes's letters. R. Wolfe. *Charta variosa*. [Sir Richard] Cotton's letters: answer. Greame. [? Sir Richard] Musgrave. Dacre. 'West Brasbrugh': lands.

Mervyn's suit: bill. Bishop of Gloucester. Mr Vane. Commission for bells. Letters of Mr Cotton. The plan of Guînes. Greame's bills. Letter to the gentlemen of Northumberland. [Sir Nicholas] Sterley. Mr Pickering's request for the article of the peace *pro oblig*. [Sir Philip] Hoby's despatch instructions; two written. Private instructions. Letter of credit. Passport unsearched. Levenish. Canterbury. Lord treasurer. Warrant. Private instructions. A private docket. Berwick: marshal [Sir John Witherington], treasurer [Richard Bunny]. [Thomas] Gower [surveyor]. Names of the commissioners for bells. Petition of Calais. For Mr Shelley's wood.

Mr Garter: herald; hatchments. Mr Baker. Dean of Wells.

Mr Pickering's letters by post or otherwise. Lord Garretts's suit. Brigantyn's matter:

---

*  Deleted.
†  Almost certainly an error for Sir Ingram *Clifford*.

warrant. Mr Crofts's warrant. Merchant of Dublin's warrant. Mr Cotton's letters from Calais. Bradford: his inability. [Walter] Haddon: Trinity Hall. Heywoode's bill. [Gregory] Lovell. Whithed. Person [? parson] of Coventry. £10 for the merchant of France. Judge of the admiralty. Lord admiral: commission of letting out old ships and selling the hulks. Writ for Mr Fosgod for Northampton. Herbeng. Emperor's ambassador. Dansell. 2 offers. 3,000 marks weight (8 oz.): 12d. for every mark. Powder for copper: 5 or 6 [illegible] the difference. Goodrich. Martin Pyrry. Bradford the preacher. Mr Haddon: master of Trinity Hall. Provision for the mass in the bill of divine service. Mr Solicitor, [Robert] Record: Steelyard. Monsieur [George] Parrys. Despatch. Sir Robert Owtred: his charges in post. Heywood's bill: request. Deeping men. Spalding. Lovel and Whithed: the dean of Durham. Letters to Mr Pickering. £40 at the amb[assador's] suit for a ship. Person [? parson] of Coventry. Sadler: suit of the French. Bishop of Worcester and Gloucester. Enclosures bill committed. Writ for Dorchester. Writ for Northampton. Writ for Mr Cobham. Mr Arundel. [Matthew] Parker. Mr Cave's information: carrying of gold. Rede. Ogle. The mayor of Bath [Edward Ludwell]. Mr Pickering's reward. Mr Owthred's warrant. Lord Garrett: his blood. Heywoode's suit. The debatable. Chart. Frenchman's warrant: £40. Ambassador. Herbengr. Emperor's ambassador.

Mr Chamber. 6d. Ragged staff.

Bishop of Durham. Lord Paget. Bishop of Dublin and Mr St Leger. Lord Conyers: west borders. Laird of Ormiston. Dean of Windsor. Mr Pickering's request. Harrold. Relief. Merchant of Dublin: warrant – £600. Mr Crofts's warrant – £1,000. Lord deputy of Calais. Sir Andrew Dudley: patent for Guînes. Brigantyn's matter: his answer. King of Denmark: Borthwick's letters. Lord Garrett's. The survey of the lands in Ireland. Vavasor's licence into France. Mr Throckmorton: stewardship. A pardon. Proclamation for wine prices. Commission for bells and plate. Lord chancellor. Mr Cox. *Custos rotulorum*. Letter to 'Strynbrie'. Letter to the boroughs. Mr Catesby's son.

Bishop of Durham. Mr Cotton. [Sir Edward] Bray. £10. Merchant. 'Bryton' [? Breedon on the Hill, Leics.]. Greame's bills. Ma[tter] of Winchester. Letters. Berwick. Gentlemen of the north. Commissions for bells. Bill for Steelyard. Borthwick. King of Denmark. Emperor's ambassador: calling to him. Mr Wynter. Baron Waldeck. Lord Garrett's case. Hollyngshed. Letters from Ireland: [Edward] Hychyngham. Letters for the ships: lord admiral. Letter for collection of debts in the counties. Commissioners' names for bell metal. [Robert] Horne, [Christopher] Morland: dean of Durham's going thither. His oath to the king. [*Illegible*].

Duke of Norfolk's writing. [Richard] Shelly: embassy. Ireland: letters. Mr Record. Fitz Garret: letters of the council. Letter to the chancellor for the lord admiral. Commission for the blockhouses. Borthwick's case. Letter to Lady Anne [of] Cleves for exchange of Bisham. Baker: licence for coats at Newcastle. Master and fellows of Christ's College, Cambridge. Mr Horne: the ma[tter] of Durham. Mr Smyth's French crowns. Lord chancellor's warrant endorsed. Commission of sewers in Lincolnshire. Bills to be signed. Heywoode's bill. Bradford: instructions. Lord Garrett's suit. Maurice Fitzgarrett. Sir Thomas Palmer's pardon. Mr Horne: the agreement for Bearpark. £20. Letters. Laird of Ormiston. Baker. Mr Hoby's man. Mayor of Canterbury. Levenish. Mr Payne's, Mr Hoby's letters. Greame's bills. [Roger] Alford's suit. Letters for certain boroughs. Lord Waldecke's suit. Lord [*sic*] Stanhope's supplication. Lord Paget's supplication.

*10 small pp.*

*Many entries crossed through or ticked off.* SP 10/5, no. 24

**595.** March 1. St Paul's Cathedral Chapter House. Indenture between William May, D.C.L., dean and the chapter of St Paul's and John Denman, D.D., parson of St Faith's, London, John Lewes, gent., one of the proctors of the arches and Robert Toye, citizen and stationer of London, churchwardens, whereby the dean and chapter leases to the other party the vault or lower east part of the church called 'crowdes', lately Jesus Chapel, under the east end of the cathedral church, together with a chapel lately called that of Our Lady and St Nicholas on the south side of the church adjoining the west end of 'crowdes' to the south, the entry leading from the south end of the steps in the cathedral leading to 'crowdes' (reserving free ingress and egress to the dean and chapter through the entry to 'crowdes' commonly called its storehouse or wine cellar) and all windows, lights and other commodities to 'crowdes', the chapel and other premises, with free egress and ingress through the cathedral by their accustomed entry as by the door on the north of 'crowdes' opening onto the north side of 'crowdes' in St Paul's churchyard commonly called Jesus Chapel door: for ninety-nine years from next Lady Day, paying 12d. a year at Whitsun, if demanded by the dean and chapter or vice-chamberlain of the cathedral. If payment is defaulted by twenty days the dean and chapter may re-enter. The lessees to convenant to maintain all windows, lights and paving, and not break any wall without prior consent of the dean and chapter, or break ground for burial without verbal licence from the dean or a residentiary canon, or in their absence from the sub-dean or clerk of the vestry. They shall pay 13s. 4d. for every burial – 6s. 8d. to the dean and chapter, 6s. 8d. to the clerk of the works, to be paid at the end of the quarter, on fine of 40s. for non payment. They may, with the chapter's licence, have a wire from the cathedral clock conveyed to a hammer to strike the bell of the parish church of St Faith, at their own expense. They convenant to occupy the vault or 'crowdes' lately known as the parish church of St Faith, at their own expense. They covenant to occupy the vault or 'crowdes' lately known as the parish church of St Faith the virgin (the bell on the north side excepted) quietly and without contradiction.

*Parchment.*

*Tags for three seals (missing).*                                   SP 10/14, no. 12

**596.** March 3. Orders taken for the foreigners at Glastonbury.

Forty-four families and six widows for whom houses must be appointed: six are finished, twenty-two others habitable except for doors, windows and other necessaries. Many houses may be had and made for them within the late monastery. In the town are walls of decayed houses which will help the building of others, at the king's charge. They are to pay the annual rent that has been paid for twenty years. Two dyehouses are appointed on the south side of the monastery where the brewhouse and bakehouse were, enclosed by a stone wall; they are to pay £4 yearly for them. Two acres north of the monastery are appointed for gardens to those who have none with their houses. As there is no meadow for their kine, according to the late duke of Somerset's promise Wirrall park is appointed for this purpose by virtue of former letters from the council to the bishop of Bath, Sir John St Loo and [Alexander] Popham, renting £10 yearly. The foreigners ask that the 140 deer remaining in the park be bestowed elsewhere. A surveyor to be appointed for assigning houses and repairing those decayed, at the king's charges. The late duke promised that they should each have a house and enough meadow to find two kine, for three lives, paying the rents paid for twenty years past. The superintendent desires the late prior's lodging and garden, with convenient stipend. Timber and stones to be assigned to them at the king's charges for setting their looms, cauldrons and other necessaries within their houses; they to bear the charges of setting them. They desire to borrow £1,000 – £300 for wool, £500 for madder, alum, copperas, brazil and other necessaries for their dyeing, and £200 for paying their spinners, loom makers and others – of which £500 in hand and the rest at Whitsuntide. The warrant for £340, dated 18 December [1551], directed to William Crouche, one of the late duke's receivers, shall be delivered. The superintendent and five others of the best offer to be bound to repay the sum in ten years at £100 a year. They had of the late duke £484.14.0 in prest towards setting up their business, to be repaid at £50 a year beginning at midsummer 1553. As they had not the houses, pastures, instruments and other necessaries prepared according to the promise, whereby they have lived of the said sum, they desire remission of it, except £130 which they are content to be bound to repay in the eleventh year. Laws, statutes and ordinances to be made by the superintendent and majority of them concerning their mysteries, faculties and occupations, to be confirmed by the king's letters patent and to be according to the late duke's device. They are to be free to bring wool and otherwise as the drapers. They desire to be charged as Englishmen in taxes, subsidies and impositions.                                                    SP 10/14, no. 13

**597.**   [? March]. Notes about the foreigners at Glastonbury.

Fifty houses for them. Two dye houses with coppers and other vessels. Wirrall park in recompense until two acres of meadow promised each provided. An empty garden north of the church for their herb garden. Money for coppers and other vessels for dyeing, and wools: for the year – £12,000. That they may have sale of their own cloths. Their letters of denization free. Stipend of their superintendent and a house. Remission of money already received, about £420. The superintendent to have oversight of them. The bishop of Bath, Sir Hugh Paulet, Sir John St Loo, Sir Thomas Dyer and [Alexander] Popham to have letters for their assistance and commission to answer their provisions.
                                                    SP 10/14, no. 14

**598.**   [? March].* Memoranda of council business.

Answer to the ambassadors of the Steelyard. Thomas Gresham's despatch. [Sir Andrew] Dudley's instructions. The strangers of Glastonbury. Answer to the earl of Tyrone's man. [Sir William] Pickering's bill and warrant. The king of Denmark's man. [Sir Nicholas] Bagnall's suit. The bishop of Durham's matter. Lord Paget's matter. [John] Beaumont's case. When the mart at Southampton shall begin. Answer to [Sir Maurice] Denys. Answer to Mr Dudley at Guînes. The mints. To write to [Sir John] York touching the stay of base moneys. The engrossers of wools.
*Petre's hand.*                                        SP 10/13, no. 79

**599.**   [March].† Memoranda of council business.

1. Appointment of some fit man in [Sir Richard] Morison's place with the emperor: named – Dr [Nicholas] Wotton, [Sir Philip] Hoby, [Richard] Shelley. 2. Deputyship of Calais. 3. Order for the mints in England: for [Sir John] York's office – [John] Freman, [Thomas] Egerton, [Martin] Pyrrye; in Ireland – [Robert] Record to be heard. 4. Answer to [Sir John] Borthwick being with the king of Denmark; his letters and instructions to be considered. 5. Appointment of special men in commission for survey of bells and church goods.                                        SP 10/13, no. 10(i)

**600.**   [March]. Memoranda of council business.

Placing some fit man in Mr Morison's room with the emperor: named – Dr Wotton, Mr Hoby, Mr Shelley. Discharge of the mints in London. Appointment in Sir John York's room: named – John Freman, Mr Egerton, Mr Pyrrye. Motion to the king for Sir Thomas Palmer's pardon and delivery: granted.‡ [The duchess of] Richmond's suit for

---

*    Ascribed to 1553 in Hoak, 283 n. 113(5), on the basis of comparison with Hatfield House, Cecil Papers, 151/98 [*HMC Salisbury MSS*, i, 120, cited in D.E. Hoak 'The King's council in the reign of Edward VI', (Ph.D. dissertation, Cambridge University, 1971), 45 n. 2(5)] which is dated 29 April 1553 – but not in a contemporary hand, and the SP 10 paper would seem clearly to belong with the seven others which follow here, nos. **599** to **605** and with no. **594** above.

†    In placing these papers I have followed the dates given by Hoak in notes on pp. 282–3 of *The King's Council* which are based on more detailed analysis in the same author's Ph.D. dissertation, pp. 41–6.

‡    In the king's hand.

licence for her father* to write to the king for mercy.

*Printed*: Nicholas, *Remains*, ii, 491.                SP 10/13, no. 10

**601.** [March]. Memoranda of council business.

Appointment of an ambassador with the emperor. Order of mints for the realm and Ireland. Deputy of Calais. Device for letting out some old ships for rent and selling hulks. Petition of Lord Abergavenny to sell for discharge of his debt £100 lands for the winter for the young lady. The certificate of the chancellor of augmentations of £58 land to be exchanged of late with the lord admiral, for which the lands delivered by the king is not assured, and an exchange of Easington. Some recompense for George Ferryse towards his living. Payment for the wines above the price of the proclamation. Surrender of Lord Rich's patent. Report to be made of the archbishop of York's case. Discharge of superfluous bulwarks in Essex, Kent and all other places. Answer to Borthwick in Denmark.                SP 10/13, no. 11

**602.** [Before March 4]. Memoranda of council business.

The matters and proceedings with the prisoners in the Tower: Lord Paget, earl of Arundel, &c. 8. The matters of Ireland: mints and mines. [Robert] Record. 9. Discharge of superfluous offices in the mints; books devised for the same. Consideration of Borthwick's message in Denmark. Proceeding with Lord Willoughby for reformation in the deputyship at Calais. Proceeding with them of the Steelyard; an act of council to be made. 10. Commission for survey of bells and plate; appointment of commissioners. 13. Appointment of new servants. Proceeding with the master of the rolls, [John] Beaumont: Lord [Grey of] Powis, Wynburne. Proceeding with the men of Hull for keeping blockhouses there. For the fee farm of Mr Sydney's lands exchanged with the king. 11. The broker's confessions touching such as have bought and sold gold above the current value. Examination of two Irishmen sent from [Sir Nicholas] Stirley: Mr Wotton, Mr Sadler. Despatch of Mr Pickering's answer and his money. 14. Answer of Courtepennyke's† request for serving the emperor. 12. Payments for Calais and Berwick. 6. Despatch of Sir Nicholas Bagnall to Ireland. His suit for lands there. Order for execution of condemned persons in the Tower; alteration of their judgement. The motion of [Michael] Wentworth of the household's suit to the king. 5. Perfection of certain warrants: the couriers into France; Mr Pickering's; Barnaby [Fitzpatrick]'s; [John] Rogers the surveyor's; the deputy of Ireland. Sir Nicholas Stirley's man to have reward for bringing the Irishmen. [Sir John] Rybault to be delivered on surety for his behaviour. Bertevile to be sent to the Fleet for a season, and to be entreated reasonably, and George to be sent for. 1. Answer to M. d'Oysel‡ touching the petition of the debatable, and commissions for the same. 2. Proceeding with the Steelyard upon the decree, and for audience to their commissaries. 3. To have or understand the instructions sent to John à Lasco from the duke of Mecklenburg. 4. Answer of Borthwick's letters remaining in Denmark; not answered since December. 15. Maurice Fitzgarrett's suit recommended by the deputy and council of Ireland.            SP 10/14, no. 9

**603.** [March]. Memoranda of council business.

Answer to M. d'Oysel touching the petition of the debatable ground. The proceeding with the Steelyard upon the decree, and for audience to their commissioners. To have or understand the instructions sent to John à Lasco from the duke of Mecklenburg. The answer of Borthwick's letters remaining in Denmark, not answered since December. Maurice Fitzgarrett's suit, recommended by the deputy and council of Ireland.

---

\*      The duke of Norfolk.
†      Conrad Pfenyng, an English agent in Germany.
‡      Henri Clutin, sieur d'Oysel, French ambassador to Scotland.

Prosecution of warrants for Mr Pickering, Mr Barnaby, Rogers the surveyor and the deputy of Ireland. Despatch of Sir Nicholas Bagnall to Ireland and his suits for land there. Sir Nicholas Stirley's man to have reward for bringing up the Irishmen. Matters of Ireland for the mints and mines there. Record. Discharge of superfluous officers in the mints; the books devised for the same. Commissioners to survey bells and plate and appointing commissioners. Brokers' confessions touching such as have bought and sold gold above the current value. Payments for Calais and Berwick. Appointing new servants. Answer of Courtpenynke's request for serving the emperor. Consideration of repair of Hornsea beck in Holderness, Yorkshire. [The earl of] Bothwell's suit for his return to Scotland and to have money in reward. The oath of those called to serve in certain commissions and their calling. The warning of Lord Wharton, Sir Thomas Chaloner and Sir Thomas Palmer. Instructions and commission for the commissions for the debatables; their diets, from what day. Letters to Sir Ingram Clifford for his departure from Carlisle. [The earl of] Westmorland. Letters of licence to Lord Wharton, Lord Conyers to depart from parliament. Commissions for the affairs of the council. Articles for the same. To move the king for [Edward] Walgrave's delivery. For John Oxleye to have the execution of the provostship of Cockermouth. Sir Thomas Palmer's suit to the king. The city of Coventry's suit for a fair three days a year.

On the dorse: rough plan of a house and some streets.                 SP 10/13, no. 12

**604.** [March 4]. Memoranda of council business.

The emperor's ambassador's coming; his answers. Courtpenny [Conrad Pfenyng]: licence to serve. Wallerdon [William Wallerthum]: licence and letters. Sir Andrew Dudley: lease in Guînes. Constable of Hull: appearance. Broxholme: appearance. Christ's College: suit; recompense. Commission of sewers in Lincolnshire. Warrants: Mr Pickering 1,000 marks, Mr Barnaby, Mr Crofts 1,000 marks, Mr Rogers £100, earl of Westmorland and his colleagues, Mr Cotton, Mr Braye, Portsmouth, Rogers, Sir John Williams, Mr Morison, Mr Shelley, Egerton, Worley.                                         SP 10/13, no. 8

**605.** March 4. Memoranda of council business.

Setting forth ships; money for them. The earl of Westmorland's expedition and his colleagues; their commissions, instructions and money. Despatch of Lord Conyers. Answers to Ireland touching mints and mines.                           SP 10/14, no. 15

**606.** [March 9].* Instructions for [the earl of Bedford], lord privy seal, the earl of Pembroke, [Lord Darcy], lord chamberlain, Sir William Petre, principal secretary, Sir John Baker, Sir Philip Hoby, Sir Robert Bowes, Sir Thomas Wroth, Edward Griffyn, solicitor general and John Gosnold, solicitor of augmentations.

They shall consider what penal laws and proclamations are most necessary, inquire of their observation in the country, and cause the most reliably informed breaches to be swiftly furthered in the ordinary courts, beginning with the greatest offenders. They shall consider how justices of the peace execute their offices, and amend or replace those found continually negligent or unfruitful. After parliament they shall assemble a few days before and after every term; at the beginning causing needful information to be furthered, and at the end seeing how it and others have proceeded. If it is necessary to expedite inquisitions in vacation they shall join their device and aid to the appropriate court. They shall see that informers are honest, encourage honest men to complain, and see them maintained and regarded in just complaints. They shall receive complaints or letters of information sent to the commissioners and the counsel for the state. After the end of term assembly they shall impart some of their doings to the privy council, that they may understand the people's obedience. If all cannot assemble, six (including one lord and

*      Date of the commission [C 66/847, m. 33d (CPR 1550–3, 352–3)].

one solicitor) will suffice. They shall not prejudice the authority of the lord chancellor
or any other court.                                                     SP 10/14, no. 17

**607.**   Summary of the above.
   *Later 16th cent. hand.*                                            SP 10/14, no. 16

**608.**   [About April].* Memoranda of council business.
   Appointment of Mr Shelley to serve in Mr Morison's room. Discharge of superfluous
offices in the mints. Some man to be in Mr York's room: named – Freman, Egerton,
Pyrrye. Consideration of Lord Willoughby for deputy of Calais. Act of parliament for
the duke of Somerset and his attainder. Act for repeal of the statute of 32 [Henry VIII].
The matter against the Steelyard. The bishop of Durham's matters. Lord Paget's case.
The causes of the rest of the prisoners. Commission to the lord admiral for selling and
letting ships. Commission for discharge of blockhouses. Taking down the duke of
Somerset's hatchments. Payment of charges at Calais; Berwick – Gower. Dissolution of
the exchange. Some prohibition of eating flesh in Lent. Some order for the men of Hull.
Constable. The two Irishmen sent from Berwick by Mr Stirley. Greame's bills to be
considered and answered. Maurice Fitzgarrett's suit from Ireland. Answer of Courtpenny's
letters. Appointing servants.                                          SP 10/14, no. 7

**609.**   [? About April]. Memoranda of council business.
   Lord Paget's cause. The bishop of Durham's cause. The bishop of Dublin and Mr St
Leger. Letters sent to Ireland for certain men. Lord Willoughby. Lord deputy of Calais.
To answer certain of his doings there. Lord Conyers's demand what shall be done if
Lord Maxwell ride the debatable. Sir Andrew Dudley, captain of Guînes, touching his
patent. Commission for bells and plate. Commissioners. Dansell's two offers. Licence
for 3,000 marks weight, 12d. per mark. Powder for copper. Commission for ecclesiastical
laws: thirty-two named by the king. Matter of the Steelyard. Mr Solicitor Goodrich.
Gosnold's report. Union of bishoprics: London, Westminster; Worcester, Gloucester;
Canterbury, Rochester. Dissolution of the duke of Somerset's house. Distribution of the
children. King of Denmark's letters. Answer to Borthwick. The bulwarks. The
hatchments.                                                            SP 10/14, no. 8

**610.**   April 7. Chelsea. The duke of Northumberland to Sir William Cecil.
   Remember the [? bill] signed for the dean of Worcester's licence for lands to the value
of £40 or more. Farewell till tomorrow, for tonight I have not . . . The weather is very
[? bad to] stir abroad in. *Postscript [? or memorandum added about a year later]*. As the
jurisdiction of the county palatine of the bishopric of Durham is now in the king's hands,
it is thought it should be used as that of Chester is. I [intend] in my absence to move
Mr Vice-Chamberlain [in that be]half, to be a means to the king that [he might give the
office of] chancellor and steward of the same . . . to me and my deputies, with such fees
and offices as the king may appoint, whereby I will be better able to serve [? his majesty]
there . . . also to despatch Lady Margaret Douglas's servant . . . here for answer to his
mistress's request [? to go] to see her father to Tantallon leaving her . . . and her husband†
here. She is young with [chil]d [and] therefore desires the surer knowledge of his [?
favour], for she would return to be . . . bed in her own house. Let her be despatched
with speed; she must have the king's own licence, for which I will appoint . . . to attend
on you today. I will be at court early tomorrow.
   *Mutilated.*                                                        SP 10/14, no. 18

---

*    Hoak, 283 n. 113 (6).
†    The earl of Lennox.

**611.** [April 8]. Clause from act of parliament [5 & 6 Edward VI c. 16, cl. 1] for restraint of the sale of offices.

If any person bargain or sell any office or the deputation or part of them, or receive any money, take any promise or bond to receive money for any office or deputation, or that any person should exercise any office or deputation, which office shall concern administration of justice or the receipt, enrolment or payment of any of the king's treasures, money, rent, revenue, account, alnage, auditorship or surveying the king's lands or customs, or keeping the king's towns, castles, &c., or clerks in the courts of record, &c., that all such persons shall lose all rights in such offices, and the persons paying money shall be immediately judged disabled in law to use such offices or deputations, and all such bargains and promises shall be void.

*Printed*: *SR*, iv, I, 151–2. SP 10/14, no. 19

[For SP 10/14, no. 20 see no. **590** above.]

**612.** April 25. St James's. The duke of Northumberland to one of the secretaries of state.

Deliver to this bearer, [the earl of] Huntingdon's servant, his warrant for wages for one half year ending last Lady Day for his band of fifty demilances. If it is not signed as the others, have it done. *Postscript.* Obtain a receipt.

*Impression of seal.* SP 10/14, no. 21

**613.** [? April]. Memoranda of council business.

To send the commissioners to Calais with money for the pays there. Their diets. Answer of the matter of Ireland and the payments there. The mines. The mints. Payment of charges at Berwick. Proceeding in the fortifications there. Commission for sale of college and chantry lands. Survey of fortifications at Portsmouth, the Isle of Wight and the coast there. Payment of [John] Rogers's warrant. Discharge of the blockhouses. Payments of their garrisons before midsummer. Answer of Captain Borthwick's letters and to consider his abode in Denmark. Discharge of the household kept for the duke of Somerset's children; sending them to the places appointed. Answer to the Steelyard's replication. The merchants of the staple's bill. Some order for the fugitives of the realm, as [Dr John] Clement, Balthazar, [Dr John] Storye, [William] Rastell and their wives. Answer upon Sir Thomas Palmer's repair with the plan of the debatable. Money for Berwick to be provided forthwith. Magdalen College. The *Saker* and the *Falcon* to be discharged. The merchant of Dublin's money. 1,000 lb. in the Tower to be coined in Ireland at 6d. the shilling. SP 10/14, no. 22

**614.** May 3. Witham. George Williams to Sir William Cecil.

Your mother is well. I have communicated with Mr Browne for his son's land at Barholm. Although he was friendly in offering the preferment, he will abate nothing of 400 marks, 100 more than it is worth. The rent is £9 a year, raised from £5.6.8 by Mr Pulvertoff who, being destitute, would rather have given 20 marks than have gone without. But as I have tried, no man can live of it giving £7 a year. The closes and commons cannot summer twenty beasts. It has but one plough land. The commons may keep but sixty sheep. It gives over 12,000 loads of hay yearly. Judge its worthiness. I have had two communications with him; at the latter, as I thought it most meet for you, yet not so meet, that you should over–buy, it. I offered him £200. My offer was rejected, and no penny of his former price abated, so I broke off. Now he perceives I have so narrowly tried out its worthiness, and spied it to be not as he reported, he says his son shall not with his good will sell it. But I do not doubt when you think best it will come, for Pulvertoft will be unable to perform his stout offer. If it never comes, it is subject to you and not you to it. I have kept your courts at Barrowden and Casterton, and shall tell you their state at my coming up. I have offered the keeping of a court at St Leonard's for Cuttberde's fee, and am denied by [John] Alyn, as he says by Robert Hawle's command, until your patent is seen. I am determined to receive no rent for it until Hawle's lease is seen, lest its receipt should be a conclusion to you. The rents I have received I have delivered to your mother.

*Holograph.*                                                            SP 10/14, no. 23

**615.**   May 10. [London]. Indenture of a lease from William May, D.C.L., dean and the chapter of St Paul's to the twelve minor canons of the cathedral, granting Pardon churchyard, with all appurtenances, from the next feast of St John Baptist for ninety-eight years, paying 2s. a year at Christmas and midsummer. The dean and chapter may repossess the property if the rent is unpaid for half a year. The minor canons will bear the cost of all repairs of the residue of the cloister between the library and the church, and the wall on the west of the churchyard adjoining the bishop of London's palace. The dean and chapter shall bear the charges of the library. The minor canons shall allow any to be buried in the cloister or the middle circuit of the churchyard or garden, to whom the dean or any residentiaries shall give licence. Any minister of the church shall be freely buried. The dean and residentiaries may have keys to enter the garden for free ingress and egress. The minor canons shall not let the churchyard, or break any wall on the east, west or north side without the consent of the dean and residentiaries.

*Parchment.*                                                           SP 10/14, no. 24

**616.**   [May 11]. Memoranda of council business.

Consideration of answer to the orators of the states of the Hanse: committed to the chancellor and others. Answer of Borthwick's letters and the king of Denmark's: devised. Setting forth ships; lack of £750 thereto. Payment of warrants, amounting to £18. Consideration of matters of Ireland: money, mints. Record to be heard. Discharge of superfluous charges in the mints at London. Perfection of the writing for the mints at York. Commissions for survey of bells and church plate. Payments for wages at Calais, Berwick. Consideration of fortifications at Portsmouth: Rogers to be sent there. Mr Shelley's despatch, his entertainment. Mr Morison's revocation. Mr Beaumont's cause to be considered. Discharge of unnecessary blockhouses.

*Marginalia in Cecil's hand.*                                          SP 10/14, no. 25

**617.**   [May 13]. Memoranda of council business.

Answer to the ambassadors of the Hanse. Order with the staple upon their bill. Full resolution for the matters of Calais for Mr Hoby and Mr Cotton's despatch. Like resolutions for Berwick, Ireland, its mints and mines, and all causes of the realm. Reports to be taken for Lord Paget's and Beaumont's causes. To send Rogers to Portsmouth and consider with [Sir Henry] Dudley and [Sir Richard] Wingfield the state of the town and the Isle of Wight. Order for Alderney and Scilly and the fortifications there.

*Petre's hand.*                                                        SP 10/14, no. 26

**618.**   May 13. Grimsthorpe. Katherine, duchess of Suffolk to Sir William Cecil.

I am so weary with writing, yet thought it would never be better to tell you I feel the lasting of your good will. I trust you mistrust not. Commend me to Mistress Mildred. *Postscript.* Monson troubles me with complaints to the lord chancellor, and therefore I have sent my lord to your lord that yours may tell him what he did between us, and rather move the lord chancellor to bear with me. I will not ask you, but remind you how Monson has used me thus no more friendly than I use my power over you, yet I think I do nothing amiss.

*Holograph.*                                                                SP10/14, no. 27

**619.** [May 20]. Signed bill for letters patent translating John Hooper to the bishopric of Worcester and annexing the bishopric of Gloucester to that of Worcester.

Since it was enacted in parliament begun at Westminster on 4 November 1547* that bishops should be appointed by letters patent in place of writs of *Congé d'élire* and capitular election, and since the bishopric of Worcester is vacant by the deprivation of Nicholas Heath, we hereby translate John Hooper, late bishop of Gloucester, to hold the bishopric of Worcester from Michaelmas last, during his good behaviour, with the palace and other temporal and spiritual properties, rights and jurisdiction. And since Henry VIII by letters patent dated at Westminster 3 September 1541† founded a cathedral church and see in the former monastery of St Peter, Gloucester, appointing John Wakeman bishop, which bishopric is vacant by the resignation of John Hooper, and because the city and county of Gloucester were formerly within the dioceses of York, Hereford and particularly Worcester, we remove the cathedral, city and county of Gloucester, with the parish and town of Kingswood, Gloucestershire, and all jurisdictions there, exempt and non exempt, and within the archdeaconry of Gloucester, from the bishopric of Gloucester and restore and transfer all to the bishopric of Worcester for ever. We hereby dissolve the bishopric of Gloucester, saving the rights and dignities of Gloucester Cathedral granted by our father and progenitors. The cathedral, city, county and archdeaconry of Gloucester, the town and parish of Kingswood, and all peculiars there, shall be free from all jurisdiction save that of the bishop of Worcester. The bishop of Worcester may confer and grant archdeaconries and canonries within the cathedrals of Worcester and Gloucester whenever they are vacant, ordain all clerks born within the diocese, institute to and deprive from all benefices, and collate to those in his gift; he shall have jurisdiction in probate and administration and all ecclesiastical causes, and the visitation of his cathedrals and diocese, and all else concerning his jurisdiction and pastoral office (especially as denoted by scripture) he shall perform, any previous royal or episcopal grant or commission notwithstanding. Bishop Hooper shall have all temporalities from Michaelmas last, during good behaviour, without account and without seeking any writ of restitution or other action, any statute, proclamation or restriction notwithstanding. These letters patent to be interpreted to the bishop's greatest commodity. The chancellor and court of augmentations and all our other officers, upon showing of these letters or their enrolment, without seeking any further royal writ or warrant, shall make full annual payment to Bishop Hooper of all revenues, and these letters shall be a warrant in exoneration. Without fine or fee, or further writ, despite no mention of the certain value of the premises.

*Sign manual.*

*Enrolment*: C 66/842, mm. 5–7 (*CPR* 1550–3, 225–6).

*Printed*: Rymer, xv, 298–333.                                              SP 10/14, no. 28

**620.** [May 28 or before]. Petition of William and George Wynter, brothers, to the duke of Northumberland.

The French king has promised restitution of goods and ships taken by his subjects from the supplicants. Sir William Petre caused George to make a book of particulars of which he and his brother were spoiled, which has been delivered to the council to take order with the French ambassador; but he has not come to court, to the lack and hindrance of the supplicants, who are also in suit before the lord chief justice for a great sum they must pay and other debts.

---

*        1 Edward VI c. 2.
†        *LP*, xvi, 1226(2).

*Jottings*: To the emperor: Sir John Mason, Sir Philip Hoby, Sir Thomas Smith. To the French king: Sir Richard Blount, Mr Shelley, Sir Thomas Chaloner.

SP 10/14, no. 29*

**621.** May 28. Otford. The duke of Northumberland to Sir William Cecil.

As Wynter knows his ship is wilfully cast away and spoilt by the French and all the goods sold openly as prizes, he desires letters from the king or council to Baron Delagard† or some other with authority in the absence of the French king for equitable recovery. I have told him that it would be vain to send or write to the baron, nor scarcely honourable, as he is the man through whose cruelty and covetousness the peace is much touched and might be violated, but to write to our own ambassador, that there may be undelayed justice in making due restitution and punishment of those who have violated and stretched the limits of amity between the princes. Let anything written be after such effect.

*Holograph.* SP 10/14, no. 30*

**622.** May 28. Otford. The duke of Northumberland to Sir William Cecil.

[Sir William] Pickering commended to me an Italian gentleman called Peche. He brought me a letter from him signifying that the Italian had showed him divers pleasures and intelligences, which I showed to the king. He has been with [Anthony] Guydote [Guidotti] at Windsor and Hampton Court. On his departing he required only a passport for two geldings, as appears by Guydot's letter, which I send. Move [the council] to let him have his despatch. My friend Mr Young has been in hand with me for the release of [Henry] Cornishe, if his suit without offence or failing his duty might be heard. Be a means to the rest of my lords to know how they have tried the matter. In case his offence has happened for zeal towards his master rather than malicious intent, he may be better borne with, seeing he has been well punished already. I have also received a letter from Mario Cardoyno who seems honestly desirous to purge himself. I doubt whether he is wrought by malice and envy or not, and wish him used as his good fame were not touched by his despatch. I therefore return his letter to be considered by your wisdom. SP 10/14, no. 31

**623.** May 28. Otford. The duke of Northumberland to Sir William Cecil.

This bearer, John Hardforde, the late bishop of Hereford's servant and now mine, has a son whom he has always kept at school and is very learned, whom he desires to send abroad to see the trade of learning there and learn other tongues. Help him to obtain the king's licence for his son to spend two or three years in Paris, Orléans or elsewhere. *Postscript.* I received today a letter from my brother at Guînes, which I send lest there be more there than in his common letter, thinking perhaps I had been at court. The point which Senarpont‡ made to my brother, that his king must use practices as the emperor had done, and that the Scots must do the deed and make the fight, should be noted – for if it comes as a practice, it should be hearkened and bets thrown abroad at least to discover their meaning. For so it may be offered and meant as it were not amiss to hear and shape an answer as the matter is worth. SP 10/14, no. 32

**624.** May 30. Otford. The duke of Northumberland to [Lord Darcy], lord chamberlain.

I have received your letters with the submissions of Lord Paget and the late master of the rolls,§ finding much variety between Paget's first and second submissions. You and other lords honourably refused the first, stuffed with subtlety and dissimulation to

---

\* Nos. 29 and 30 mis-bound.
† Antoine Escalin des Aimars, baron de la Garde.
‡ Jean de Monchy, seigneur de Senarpont, French captain of Boulogne.
§ John Beaumont.

abuse the king's clemency and your goodness, as appears by his later submission. Beaumont's first and second submissions should be better set out in articles by some of the king's learned counsel, specifying his offences, as Paget's later submission. The freeing of the countess of Sussex and [Richard] Hartypoole's wife should be better examined, for she is charged with saying one of Edward [IV]'s children was alive. I agree that [Alexander] Brette and [Thomas] Fisher have been sufficiently punished. The duke confessed to me that Brette was very evil, always seeking to irritate the duke against me. I trust this punishment will be a warning to him.

*Printed*: Tytler, ii, 108–9.                                          SP 10/14, no. 33

**625.**  May 31. Otford. The duke of Northumberland to Sir William Cecil.

I received your letters, one by [the earl of] Huntingdon, the other by a post, marvelling that you had not received mine of the 28th, enclosing a letter I then had from my brother. The learned counsel have more seriously proceeded by special articles with Lord Paget's submission than that of the late master of the rolls,* as I have partly written to the lord chamberlain. Beaumont's submission should be as particular as the other. I will see your father as I go north, if but to drink at the door; I will trouble no friend's house, for my train is and will be great, whether I will it or not. I am glad your health will allow me your company there. Commendations to Secretary Petre.

*Holograph.*

*Printed*: Tytler, ii, 110–11.                                         SP 10/14, no. 34

**626.**  May 31, 10 p.m. Otford. The duke of Northumberland to Sir William Cecil.

I return the letter from [the council] to Lord Conyers, which cannot be improved, and that which I wrote to the Greames, liked by my lords. I have none other now: trusting to see you at court some time on Saturday or Monday before dinner. The marquess has been with me, with some good fellows; we have been merry. By five tomorrow he leaves for Lord Cobham, whose life is in danger.

*Holograph.*

*Printed*: Tytler, ii, 111–12.                                         SP 10/14, no. 35

**627.**  [May 31]. Memoranda of council business.

Matters unperfected. Courtpenny [Conrad Pfenyng] and Wallerdon [William Wallerthum] – £350. Money for Borthwick – £409. The king of Denmark's agent – £230. Bishoprics void in Ireland. [Andrew] Wise's suit in consideration of a debt of £480 to purchase £50 lands in Ireland. Martin Pyrrey's despatch. 10,000 lb. to be coined after 3 oz. Himself to have the coinage of 3,000 lb. The French ambassador to be provoked for reassembling of commissioners on the debatable. Proclamation forbidding resort of suitors during the progress. Answer to be sent to the Steelyards. To have [Richard] Whalley's office of receiver in Yorkshire. Andrew Nowell. John Fysshar, pensioner, to have the office.

*Partly in Cecil's hand.*                                              SP 10/14, no. 36

**628.**  [May].† Memoranda of orders for coastal defence.

The captain of Portsmouth to attend his charge and order all captains of the isle [of Wight] to be perpetually attendant, fully furnished with good numbers and other necessaries. A letter to the sheriff and justices of the peace of Hampshire to be ready to aid the W[ight] men, as occasion serves, have their beacons, order watched, &c. For Portsmouth and Southampton. Sir Richard Wingfield to go to Portsmouth. Woodall‡ to go to his charge.

---

\*        John Beaumont.
†        Hoak, 283 n. 113(i).
‡        ? Richard Udale, captain of Yarmouth.

*Petre's hand.* SP 10/1, no. 21

**629.** June 1. Otford. The duke of Northumberland to [Lord Darcy], lord chamberlain and [Sir John Gates], vice-chamberlain.

The king has given this bearer, John Fisher, one of his pensioners, reversion of the receivership of Yorkshire in which [Richard] Whalley, for notable evil demeanours in his office as elsewhere is thought unworthy to continue; beseeching you and the rest of my lords that he my enjoy his gift. I dare be bound in all my land he will serve honestly. After the death of my son Ambrose's wife, her heir is now the son of Horwod, whose father held lands of me and was slain at Musselburgh Field. He is the king's ward for such lands as he shall have after Ambrose's wife, which he holds by courtesy of England because he had a child by her. Move the king that I may have the preferment of the child, previously my ward.

*Holograph.*
Printed: Tytler, ii, 114–15. SP 10/14, no. 37

**630.** June 2. Otford. The duke of Northumberland to the lord chamberlain and Sir William Cecil.

I perceive by your letter of this instant that unless my daughter [in-law]'s death seems dangerous or infectious, the king's pleasure is I should not absent myself nor stay my son. I shall explain what makes me suspect infection. The night before she died she was as merry as any child; she sickened about three in the morning, in a sweat; after a while she desired the stool. The indiscreet woman attending her let her rise, and she fell to swooning. With what they administered she seemed to revive until noon, still in great sweating. Then she began to alter, in continual pangs and fits until she died at six. This morning she was examined; between the shoulders and on one cheek it was very black; which, with the suddenness and her brooking nothing administered, makes me think it must be the sweat or worse. She had measles about a month before, recovered well, but a hoarseness and cough remained. I think neither I, my son, nor any in my house should repair to the king unless he commands the contrary or you think it without danger. Requiring your further answer.

*Printed*: Tytler, ii, 115–16. SP 10/14, no. 38

**631.** June 4. Otford. The duke of Northumberland to the council.

I have received your letters for staying myself and my sons until the full moon next Monday, lest there is any other infection in my house. As yet there is none among my children or family. If it so continues I intend to be at court on Tuesday with my son, [the earl of] Huntingdon, Lord Hastings and my son [in-law, Sir Henry] Sydney.

SP 10/14, no. 39

**632.** June 4. Docket of warrant for the sign manual for a licence to [John Scory], bishop of Chichester to preach and to licence or forbid others to do so in his diocese.

*Signed by*: The marquess of Winchester, Lord Darcy, Sir Thomas Cheyne, Sir William Cecil and Sir Robert Bowes. SP 38/1, f. 9

**633.** June 6. Otford. The duke of Northumberland to Sir William Cecil.

Thank the lord chamberlain and vice-chamberlain and yourself for the expedition of my warrant and that for the king's stable. I intend to be with you tomorrow to supply the rest of my thanks myself. I am sorry that the end of the old poet's verse should now be remembered, but hope it will amend if every singer does his duty. SP 10/14, no. 40

**634–50.** June 9. Dockets of warrants for the sign manual.

**634.** Grant to Sir Robert Bowes of the office of master of the rolls for life, with customary profits, from Easter.

**635.** Warrant to the four principal gentlemen of the privy chamber to pay Elizabeth Smythe, the king's laundress, £6.13.4 yearly in augmentation of her wages of £20.

**636.** Grant to Giles Forrest, groom of the chamber, of a life annuity of 12d. a day.

**637.** Lease to Sir William Cecil of the farm of Coombe Nevill *alias* Coombe park, Surrey, belonging to the late duke of Somerset, for twenty-one years at the accustomed rent of £29.5.3.

**638.** Presentation of Matthew Parker to the prebend of Corringham in Lincoln Cathedral.

**639.** Letter to the president and chapter of Lincoln Cathedral to choose and admit Matthew Parker, D.D. as dean.

**640.** Warrant to the master of the great wardrobe to deliver Thomas Mayneman, keeper of the standing wardrobe at Greenwich, stuff for the store and furniture thereof.

**641.** Warrant to the treasurer of the chamber to pay John Browne, one of the king's players of interludes, 5 marks wages and 23s. 4d. for livery yearly.

**642.** Lease to William Aylmer, gentleman pensioner, of the manor of Evercreech, Somerset, belonging to the late duke of Somerset, for twenty-one years at £49.7.4½d. rent a year, by the commissioners of requests.

**643.** Warrant to the chancellor and general surveyors of the court of augmentations and the auditors of the prests to discharge Thomas Gowre £100, part of about £200 which he owes the king, and to take bonds for payment of the rest at reasonable days. By the council.
*Not in CSPD.*

**644.** Grant to John Harleston, esq., of the lieutenantship of Ruysbank [fort] for life, with wages for himself and a man-at-arms 12d. a day each and sixteen soldiers at 8d. a day. In yearly reward to the lieutenant and man-at-arms – 20 marks each; 2d. a day reward to each soldier. For the wages of eight gunners – 8d. a day each. On surrender of the office by Sir George Somerset.
*Not in CSPD.*

**645.** Passport for John Rudilience and Francis Joseyl, ambassadors of the Steelyard to depart abroad with eight servants, £200 and their baggage.
*Not in CSPD.*

**646.** Passport for [*blank*], servant to the ambassadors, to depart abroad with four geldings.
*Not in CSPD.*

**647.** Forfeit of £36.10.0 granted to Abraham Longwel, Roger Shakespere and Thomas Best, yeomen of the chamber.

**648.** Restraint that the keepers of Eye park and the little park of Westhorpe, Suffolk shall not allow any game to be killed or any warrant served for three years.

**649.** Like restraint for Moorwood park, Gloucestershire.
*In the margin [? in the king's hand]*: Unsigned.

**650.** Grant to Bartholomew Butler *alias* York the office of king of arms of Ireland with the name of Ulster, for life, and such fee as the king puts into the book.
*Signed by*: The marquess of Winchester, the duke of Northumberland, the earl of Bedford, Lord Darcy, Sir Thomas Cheyne, Sir Philip Hoby, Sir Robert Bowes and Sir Richard Cotton. SP 38/1, ff. 12–13

**651–4.** June 10. Dockets of warrants for the sign manual.

**651.** Lease in reversion to Hugh Ellys of the manors, lands and tenements called Packhurst ('Parkers') in Shustoke, Warwickshire, late belonging to Sir James Fitzgarete, attainted of treason, for twenty-one years, paying yearly £5.14.4.

**652.** Passport for Jerome Cardanus and William Casanatus, physicians, to pass from England with their train and eight horses or geldings which they brought with them.
*Not in CSPD.*

**653.** Licence for the bishop of Lincoln\* to preach and to forbid any unable and without the king's licence to do so in his diocese.

**654.** Commission for Thomas Gowre, surveyor of the works at Berwick, to take up all manner of artificers, labourers and other necessaries at reasonable prices for finishing the king's works there.
*Not in CSPD.*
*Signed by*: The marquess of Winchester, the duke of Northumberland, the earl of Bedford, the earl of Pembroke, Lord Darcy, Sir Thomas Cheyne, Sir Philip Hoby, Sir Robert Bowes and Sir Richard Cotton. SP 38/1, f. 14

**655–62.** June 12. Dockets of warrants for the sign manual.

**655.** Letter to the lord deputy and council of Ireland for decrying the money there to the value it is in England; the minute of which remains with the council records.
*Not in CSPD.*

**656.** Commission under the great seal to Sir Richard Cotton, Sir Anthony St Leger and Thomas Mildmay for the survey of Calais and the marches, with authority to take the treasurer's account and make payments due there.
*Not in CSPD.*

**657.** Instructions to the above mentioned commissioners.
*Not in CSPD.*

**658.** Lease to Sir Thomas Wroth of the demesnes of the late monastery of Syon, paying £26.13.4 yearly, and of Isleworth mill, paying £20 yearly, both belonging to the late duke of Somerset, in Middlesex, for twenty-one years.

**659.** Grant to Sir Thomas Wroth for life of the offices of keeping the capital house of Syon and certain houses, gardens, orchards &c., Middlesex, with the 8d. a day fee; of

\*    John Taylor was appointed to the see on June 18.

the stewardship of the lordship of Isleworth, with £5 a year fee; of the bailiwick of the same, with 2d. a day fee; and of the keeping of the woods in Isleworth, Brentford, Twickenham, Heston, Whitton, Sutton and Addlestone, Middlesex, also belonging to the late duke.

**660.** Bill for the office of chief mason of Kenilworth Castle, Warwickshire, to Robert Cock, for life, with 8d. a day fee; signed before and could not pass because it was directed to the lord chancellor of England instead of the chancellor of the duchy of Lancaster.*

**661.** Letter to Sir John Borthwick, resident in Denmark, to repair here from the king of Denmark's court, and to commend to the same such suits as the king's subjects have there.
   *Not in CSPD.*

**662.** Grant to [Anthony] Bellasis, D.C.L. of a prebend in Carlisle Cathedral on the death of [William] Pyrrie, at the suit of the lord chamberlain.
   *Signed by*: The bishop of Ely, lord chancellor, the marquess of Winchester, the duke of Northumberland, the earl of Bedford, the marquess of Northampton, Lord Darcy, Sir Thomas Cheyne, Sir Anthony Wingfield, Dr Nicholas Wotton, Sir Robert Bowes and Sir Richard Cotton.                        SP 38/1, ff. 10–10v

**663.** June 18. Royston. The duke of Northumberland to [the earl of Bedford], lord privy seal and the marquess of Northampton.
   Being requested by this bearer, [Sir] Ralph Bagnold, to commend his suit for the fee farm of the late monastery of Dieulacresse, Staffordshire, in which he has twenty years to come, I could do no less, in consideration of his good service to the king, which would be better rewarded this way than with the lands his brother had in fee simple, for the king would lose no revenue. Remember John Copnold, clerk, learned and godly, meet for one of the vacant bishoprics in Ireland. I am bolder to commend him on the report of this bearer. *Postscript (holograph)*. My lord marquess, be good to Grymston, with whom, at your request and his desire, I have spoken and remitted all things past on my behalf. Hear him to an end of his reckonings.                        SP 10/14, no. 41

**664.** June 19. Sempringham. Lord Clinton to Sir William Cecil.
   Send word by this bearer when [the duke of] Northumberland will be at your father's, whether he minds to dine there, when and what way he will come to my house. Bourne is his best way, and I intend to meet him between there and your father's house; I would loath to be disappointed. I trust you will accompany him to my house. *Postscript (holograph)*. Let him be guided through Bourne, and I will be sure to meet him. If he dines anywhere by the way, send me word.
   *Printed*: Tytler, ii, 116–17.                        SP 10/14, no. 42

[For SP 10/14, no. 43 see no. **668** below.]

**665.** [June 19 or before].† Petition of Sir Nicholas le Strange to the council.
   In the late wars in Scotland he took prisoner James Stewarde, Scot, with whom he agreed to have £200 for ransom; by your command, with promise of satisfaction for his ransom, he was freed and is daily at court. Sir Nicholas asks recompense of the £200, lands worth £10 a year as are appointed to be sold by the commission, or the purchase

---

\*       Lord Paget was deprived of the chancellorship of the duchy during his imprisonment and the seals were
        delivered to Sir John Gates, but the latter was not formally appointed until 7 July 1552 [S.R. Gammon,
        *Statesman and Schemer*, (Newton Abbot, 1973), 181. *HBC*, 140].
†       See note to the following document.

of £25 yearly worth of suppressed lands, paying for half in hand and the rest within a
year.        SP 10/14, no. 44

**666.** [June 19].* Suits to be made to the king.

For some relief towards the sustenance of the late earl of Surrey's children: £100
granted. Some relief for Sir Anthony Cooke, one of the privy chamber, in consideration
of his service and charge: to enquire what he desires. For Norroy king of arms of the
north to have a commission for visitation of arms in his province. For Mr Cofferer† to
have in fee farm either the manor of West Pennard or Baltonsborough, Somerset, £100
and £102 rent respectively: one in farm. For [Richard] Chittewood of the privy chamber,
having two parks in Sussex‡ for life freely, that he may now have them in fee farm,
paying accustomed rent of £10 a year: to be considered. For Dr [Griffin] Leyson, the
fee farm of certain land and tenements in Carmarthen to the yearly value of £39.16.10
and the reversion of a lease of Manorbier farm, Pembrokeshire, of the yearly rent of
£93.6.8, in consideration of long service and upright dealing in his office: the farm of
Manorbier in lease. For Sir Thomas Dacres to have the fee farm of the parsonage of
Lanercost and other lands belonging to the house and demesne of the late priory of
Lanercost, of the yearly value of £55, paying the accustomed rent: granted. For Sir
Nicholas Strange, to know the king's pleasure touching his suits, desiring £200 in money
or £10 worth lands in recompense of a Scots prisoner he took and freed without ransom,
or the purchase of £25 worth lands, paying half in hand and half in the following year:
granted £200. For Sir Ralph Bagnall to have the fee farm of the late monastery of
Dieulacres, Staffordshire, of which he has a lease of twenty years to come: granted. For
Sir John Arundell's deliverance from recognisance to bide the order of the council and
not to leave the city of London or within [*blank*] of the same until further licenced by
the king: granted. For [the earl] of Worcester's despatch. Pardon for John Smallwell for
slaughter of George Johnson in chance mêlée.

*In Bernard Hampton's hand save date and marginalia.*        SP 10/14, no. 45

**667.** [June 19]. List of suits to be made to the king, for the earl of Surrey's children,
Chittewood, Dr Leyson, Mr Cofferer, Norroy and Sir Anthony Cooke, as in the preceding
document.

*In the hands of William Thomas, Bernard Hampton and another clerk.*        SP 10/14, no. 46

**668.** June 26. Grant by Sir John Williams, treasurer of the court of augmentations to
Richard Warde of the pastures known as Wood's grove and all their appurtenances, in
his tenure, in the parish of 'Hurst', Wiltshire, for ever. Appointment of Leonard Browne
as attorney to enter and take possession of the premises and deliver them to Warde.

*Parchment.*
*Latin.*
*Seal missing.*
*Signed by*: Williams.
*Endorsed*: Possession taken and delivered January 29 in the presence of Thomas
Hyde, Thomas Darham, Henry Wattes, gentlemen, Ralph Goswell, Thomas Mil-
warde, Robert Singe, Robert Towse, John Newberie, Edward Horwaie and many
others.        SP 10/14, no. 43

**669.** June. Wednesday, 6 a.m. Grimsthorpe. In bed. Katherine, duchess of Suffolk to

---

\*    No original date to the MS, but at the head has been added 'moved uppon Sonday xxix Junij 1552.' June
     29 was a Wednesday (and the date preferred in *CSPD*, 41). June 19, a Sunday, was suggested as more
     likely by Hoak in his Ph.D. dissertation, 41 n. 3, although he later opted for July [*The King's Council*, 282
     n. 102(5)].
†    John Ryther, cofferer of the household. See no. **682** below for the grant.
‡    Bewbush and Little Shelley (*APC*, iv, 80).

Sir William Cecil.

By the late coming of this buck you will see that wild things are not ready at command. I went out with my keeper on Saturday night after I came home (a novelty), desiring one to send after [Hugh] Latimer to his niece's churching; but she must be churched without it. Ever since you wrote for yours I have had both keepers and beaters about it, but could not prevail before this morning. I would be sorry you should leave your hunting here undone for any such requests as you spoke of. I can suffer them to come and hunt in your company, and so would wish, not for any need I have of them, but that they would hunt with my licence – for their honest behaviour, being my neighbours and the worshipful of the shire, would be more pleasant than any sport any wild beast could make me. Were it not more for the pleasures of such than my own advantage or pleasure, I would not leave one beast about me as might make any neighbour fall out with me – which were soon done, as I have not two more bucks in my park. But that must not discharge you from hunting; if you do not kill them, I will not get them unless I take them at once. You may have as good sport at the red deer. I am very glad when my friends have their pastime here. Come with whom you will. Commendations to your wife, father and mother. *Postscript.* [Richard] Bertie is at London to conclude, if he can, with the heirs. I would gladly discharge the trust my lord left me before I did anything else for any man's pleasure.

　　*Holograph.*
　　*Printed*: Tytler, ii, 118–19. Goff, 205–6, 208.　　　　　　　　　SP 10/14, no. 47

**670–81.** June. Dockets of warrants for the sign manual.

**670.**　Grant to the duke of Northumberland of the wardship and marriage of William Flamock, with an annuity of £29.11.10.

**671.**　Grant to Michael Wentworth of the wardship and marriage of Gervase Storthes.

**672.**　Grant to Thomas Welden of the wardship and marriage of Thomas, son and heir of Edward Welden, with an annuity of £9.16.5.
　　*Not in CSPD.*

**673.**　Grant to Sir Richard Lister of the wardship and marriage of Richard Lister, with an annuity of £20.
　　*Not in CSPD.*

**674.**　Grant to John Payne of the wardship and marriage of Henry Chamber, with an annuity of 4 marks.
　　*Not in CSPD.*

**675.**　Grant to the duke of Northumberland of the wardship and marriage of Margaret Whorwood, with an annuity of £20.
　　*Not in CSPD.*

**676.**　Grant to William Hellard of the wardship and marriage of John Rokeby, with an annuity of £2.3.0.

**677.**　Grant to Robert Carr of the wardship and marriage of Augustine Smythe, with an annuity of £13.10.0.

**678.**　Grant to John Holte of the wardship and marriage of Richard Seyman, with an annuity of £10.

**679.** Warrant to the chancellor and general surveyors of the court of augmentations and to the auditors of the prests for the allowance and discharge of £118.8.2¾d. which Gregory Raylton, late treasurer of the wars against Scotland, owes to the king on the determination of his account, in respect of his service and other losses of money remaining in his hand on the fall thereof.

**680.** Two warrants to the master of the great wardrobe to deliver to the master of the horse* and the clerk of the stable stuff and necessaries belonging to the same.

**681.** Grant to Sir Anthony St Leger, K.G. of the castle, manor and park of Leeds, Kent, of the yearly value of £26.13.4, in fee farm, paying yearly £10, and to keep it in repair.

    *Signed by*: The bishop of Ely, lord chancellor, the marquess of Winchester, the duke of Northumberland, the earl of Bedford, the duke of Suffolk, the earl of Huntingdon, Lord Darcy, Sir Thomas Cheyne, Sir John Mason, Sir Edward North and Sir Robert Bowes.                                        SP 38/1, ff. 16–16v

**682.** [July 12]. Particular of grant by the king to John Ryther, king's cofferer, of the manor of Baltonsborough, for ever, worth £102.1.9½d., paying the accustomed rent, which appears to be but £99.5.10½d. Certified by Sir Richard Sackville.

    Memorandum that I, John Ryther, require of the king in fee farm for ever the manor of Baltonsborough, with its appurtenances, Somerset, being of the clear yearly value expressed in the annexed particulars, paying £99.6.8.

    *17th cent copy, bearing date July 27.*

    *Enrolment*: C 66/850, m. 21 (*CPR* 1550–3, 439), dated July 12.      SP 10/14, no. 48

**683.** July 26. The Tower [of London]. Sir Philip Hoby, [master of the ordnance] to Sir William Cecil.

    Thank you for your letter of news of the 24th; being enclosed, I am unable to understand things for certain, except from you. I enclose a schedule delivered to me from the ambassador of Venice concerning the doings of the Turk, with which he is always in hand. Deliver it to the king, as he desires. He has asked me to dinner next Sunday, when I am sure to hear all the news.

    *Seal fragment.*                                                        SP 10/14, no. 49

**684.** July 27. Carlisle. The duke of Northumberland to Sir William Cecil.

    I have received your letters and news and am glad of your return to court, where you have been missing long. But since you mean to run so long a race, you needed to take a breath. Having nothing worth long advertisement from here but of persecution of thieves, I will but wish you the best. I received a letter from [Peter] Vannes worth consideration, especially his advice to send to [Sir William] Pickering for the gentle entertainment of the duke of Ferrara's son.† If he might persuade him to make a voyage to see the king, it might breed communication between him and one of the king's sisters. Under the degree of a king's son, he is the best marriage in Christendom. When you have showed the letter to the king, and if he likes it, you may work with the rest of the lords.

    *Holograph.*                                                        SP 10/14, no. 50

---

\*      Earl of Warwick.

†      Alfonso, son of Duke Ercule (Hercules) II.

**685.** July 28. The Tower. Sir Philip Hoby to Sir William Cecil.

A proportion of munition has been appointed by the council to furnish lacks at Calais and Guînes, Anthony Anthony* giving attendance for a warrant of money to provide the same; the store of this house can furnish only a little. He can get no money to make provision, despite my lords' urgency, without which nothing can be done. When the matter is called on by the council, do not let the poor officers suffer blame; they are ready to do their duties if they had the wherewithal. Let the lords take order by your furtherance. Understanding the king minds to raise certain bulwarks on the Downs and elsewhere to diminish his great charge, let me hear speedily whether the council approves my taking munition from those nearest for furnishing Calais and Guînes.

SP 10/14, no. 51

**686.** July 28. Pinchbeck. Richard Ogle to Sir William Cecil.

I have received your letters and perceive your pains for the sewers, in which I trust your father, myself and others shall take order that your work shall be remembered. For twenty years so much was not done for cleaning sewers as is and shall be done this year. You wish to know of Robert Hall's lease of St Leonard's. I kept his court two years, and saw his lease under a red seal, but whether it was the duke of Suffolk's grant of Durham's, I do not remember; I always kept the court in the king's name. I told Hall there was great doubt in his lease, as I am sure there was, but cannot remember what. He esteemed it at the time very lightly. I still have the court books. There are great liberties belonging to it. Whoever has the books of Durham can say much, for it was a cell of Durham Abbey [sic]. I think you will find in Crowland book what you have in Stamford. I cannot recompense your goodness, but would be glad of something near London towards my latter days. If any of the under barons of the exchequer fell void I think I would be able to discharge that burden. I have written to my brother [in-law, Sir Anthony] Cooke, and refer the matter to your discretion. To answer your second letter, I have sent the copy of the commission that you sued out for sewers, and a copy of the names of the commissioners in all five shires [*which follows*], which must be for the wealth of the whole shires, for in all other parts no good can be done until it is obtained. There must be good advice in suing of the general commission, that it does not hurt the special commission sued out by you and good laws made thereupon. This I refer to you and others learned. If a new general commission for the whole shire is sued, it is a discharge of all others previously sued under the great seal, so there is danger on both sides: if the general commission is not sued, great peril may follow; and if it is, what is done is in doubt. Whether so good an act shall be done again I know not. I think not during my life, unless you and such like come and see the doing as you did. Consult with learned men. If it is a *supersedeas*, let it stay till Michaelmas or after. In the meantime I trust much good shall be done on your order for placing the new commissioners.

*Printed*: Read, 476 n. 12 (extract only).                                  SP 10/14, no. 52

**687.** [July 28. Enclosed with the above]. Proposed commissioners of sewers.

Nicholas Luke, baron [of the exchequer]. Sir Clement Smyth. John Carill. John Gosnold. John Ascote. John Hasilwood.† Thomas Hutton.† Richard Ogle, &c. To have power as receivers of the bishops of Ely, Lincoln and Peterborough. Thomas, Lord Burgh.‡ Edward, Lord Clinton. William, Lord Willougby. Edward, Lord Sheffield.† Sir John Hynde.† Sir Thomas Hennege. Sir Roger Tounesend. Sir Robert Tyrwhytt junior. Sir Edward Dymmocke. Sir Francis Ayscough. Sir Nicholas Hare. Sir Nicholas Straunge.

---

*        Clerk of the ordnance.

†        Marked as deceased.

‡        Died 28 February 1550 and succeeded by William.

Sir Edmund Bedyngfeld. Sir Robert Payton. Sir Thomas Tressom. Sir Giles Alyngton. Sir John Copledyk. Sir John Candysshe. Sir Laurence Taillard. Sir William Fitzwilliam.* Sir Robert Kyrkham. William Cooke ('Coove'), serjeant-at-law. Thomas Wymbishe. John Hennege. Robert Hennege. Richard Cicill. William Cicill. William Mounson. Thomas Littilbury. Richard Godericke. Henry Bedyngfeld. Oliver Leder. Robert Apprice. Godfrey Covyle. Henry Godericke. Christopher Burgoyne. Thomas Rudston. Robert Wyngfeld. Robert Broun. Francis Quarles. George Hegard. Edward Beaupre. John Dethicke. Thomas Cotton. Miles Forest. John Laurence. Richard Bolles. Edward Forsett.* John Cotton. John Turndy. Richard Dysidy. Vincent Grantham.* Henry Portyngton. Matthew Sayntpoll. Nicholas Robertson.* George Sayntpoll. Thomas Missenden. Thomas Holland. Geoffrey Covyle. William Manby. James Smyth. Nicholas Gyrlyngton.* John Skypwith. Philip Tyrwhytt. William Dalyson. Thomas Hussey. Nicholas Pynchebek. Richard Wolmer. Robert Brokylsby.* Henry Lacy. William Tharrold. William Smythe.* Robert Carre. Augustine Porter. Richard Markham. Edward Busshe. Richard Paynell. Robert Haryngton. John Broxholme. John Bellowe. Robert Walpoll. Antony Rob[er]tson. John Bothe. Leonard Cracrofte. John Redde of Wrangle.* Edward Hall. Thomas Pulvertofte. John Hastynges.* Anthony Meres. Thomas Paynell. Athelard Welby. Anthony Tharrold. William Davy. Blaise Holland. Henry Tofte.* Simon Halt. Thomas Welby of Moulton. Commissioners of sewers in the counties of Norfolk, Northampton, Cambridge, Huntingdon and Lincoln and the isle and liberties of the bishop of Ely. Some names that seem to me good to be put into the commission. Sir John Haryngton. Sir Richard Thymolby. Laurence Bresby. Henry Savell. John Dyon. Leonard Irby. Thomas Broun. Thomas Welby of [Long] Sutton. William Adam. Robert Lyttilbury. William Derby. Thomas Whytt. John Etton. John Sheperd.

*Ogle's hand.*
*Set out with extracts (Latin) from draft commission of 27 June 1549.*    SP 10/14, no. 52(i)

**688.**   July. Notebook of Sir William Cecil.
    Answer to the duke. Licence to serve whom he will. Courtpenny [Conrad Pfenyng]: wages – £250. Wallerdon [William Wallerthum]: letters of commendation to serve – £100. [Sir John] Borthwick: letters of revocation; letters to the king of Denmark; his warrant – £409. [Thomas] Gower: his letter to the captain of Berwick; his bill for £100. . . .lanlwo. Dr [Owen] Oglethorpe: his content to surrender his college to the king's visitation; the scholars to depart home; some visitation of the house. Count [of] Mirandola. Lord admiral. Mario [Cardonio] the Italian. Merchant of Dublin. [Anthony] Guidotti's bargain: 3,000 crowns. Earl of Pembroke. Commissions for Wales. [Andrew] Wise of Ireland's suit. Commission for Calais: [Sir Richard] Cotton; [William] Berness. Suits to the king. [Sir Nicholas] Styrley's man. [George] Parish. [Richard] Jugg: licence to sell the new test[ament]: 22d. [The duchess of] Richmond's suit. Kylligrew's suit. £600 at Michaelmas. [Jacobus] Deiodane's supplication, king of Denmark's agent. [Thomas] Wyndham. [Sir Richard] Morison. Letters. Credit. 'Shorers' [? insurers]. Lōng. Mātell. Dr [Sir William] Pikeryng. Francisco. [Sir Maurice] Denny's despatch. The saymaster's commission. Instructions for the bells. Wales. Lord Grey. Lady Arundel. John Mullyns. Walter Bower. Scholars of Oxford. White's suit for a receivership. Duke of Northumberland. Letters to Winchester College for Hardyng. [Sir Robert] Bowes. Master of the rolls. Banister. [William] Crane. Lady Sussex. [Richard] Hartipoole's wife. Shaneburgh. Dux. Lat. Ireland. Leases in reversion. Leases to decay rents. Repair of boxes in the treasury at the court at Westminster. Steelyards: for so short time not to be prejudiced; occupation to and from their own cities after their old privileges. Foreign trade. The custom to be suspended. Sir Thomas Holcroft. Office. Sir John Thynne. Submission. [Richard] Grafton: to the king. £125 respite till Michaelmas. By the king to him. £410 more. [Sir

*        Marked as deceased.

John] Godsalve: pension. [Richard] Shelly: £300 for a loan. Letter to the city of Exeter. Decree for Lord Paget's fine. Letters of credit to the Fuggers. Italian 'shorers' [? insurers]. Latine. French ambassador. Debatable. Mr Vice Chamberlain. Duchy. Dowdall. Ireland. Bishop of Durham. [Sir Philip] Hoby for the Tower. Lord FitzWarine. Letter to the ambassador. Count Rhinegrave [Philip Francis, the Rhinegrave, Count of Salm]. Bishop of Dublin. Mr Cotton. Commission. Lord deputy. Sir John Baker: revocation. Berwick of Berwick. Duke of Northumberland. Mr Dudley. Captain Barbar. Edinburgh. Anthony Thompson, [groom] of the pantry. Hosyer. Letters to the French ambassador. [Sir William] Pickering. King of Denmark's letters. With Deiodane. Borthwick. Blockhouses in Essex. To move the king for some relief for the earl of Surrey's children. £10,000 for the household out of the relief. Forsett. Deputation of Boston. Recorder. My petition. £50 to pay. Bridge's man. [Christopher] Mount. Gunter. Mr Vice Chamberlain. Deeping commission. Mr Martyn. *Custos rotulorum.* Commission for the Trinity lands. Mr Villers. Langtoft. Mr Cotton. Barrowden. Lady Elizabeth. Deeping. Mr Rigges. £8 to [Sir Anthony] Auchar. Barrowden. [John] Handby. Bromley. Julius Morgan. [William] Huninges. L. of Sussex. Commission for sewers. Deeping. Stone at Syon. Mr Vice Chamberlain. Mr Heneage. Martin stone. Highgate. Byards wood. Hayman. Sir Austin Blayne. Mr Tyrwhitt: the warren of conies at Thorpe Achurch. Sir Thomas Heneage: letter for stone at Martin. [Sir John] Gates: commission for the sewers out of the duchy. Mr Hawle. Robert. For the lease of St Leonard's. For fishing the river. The dean of Durham for the evidence of St Leonard's and its liberties. The earl of Westmorland for the lease of Cranmore. To see [Richard] Grenwaye's lease of Pickworth. Mr Browne's lease of 'Woodhede'. Commission copy. Sewers. 'Fleteland' mill: 36s. 8d. Rent. *Nulla* 6s. 8d.

[*Itinerary, June-July*]. June 12: Trinity Sunday. 13: Lady Mary at court. 14: to London. 15: to Royston. 16: to Burghley. 19: duke of Northumberland at Burghley. 20: to Sempringham. 22: returned by Grimsthorpe to Burghley and Tinwell. 24: St John. At Greyfriars with [Katherine,] duchess of Suffolk. 26: Libyns preached at St Martin's. 27: to Greatford. 28: to Lyddington. 29: St Peter. At Stamford sessions. 30: to Peterborough. July 1: to Casterton and Pickworth. 3: to Pinchbeck. 4: to Boston and return to Pinchbeck. 5: to Burghley or Deeping. 8: towards London. Thorpe Waterville. Latchingdon. 9: Cambridge. Stoke [by Clare]. 10: Stoke. 11: Mr Petre's [Ingatestone Hall]. 12: Romford. 13: to London. 14: to Wimbledon. 15: [Richard] Goodrich. 16: to Croydon to the [arch]bishop of Canterbury. 17: at Wimbledon. 18: to Nonsuch. Mr Hoby. Mr Darcy. Mr Goodrich. 19: to court; at Guildford. 20: the French ambassador dined at the manor house; was answered for the debatable.

Titles of criminal deeds [*specified*]. Measures after the statutes. Weights sealed. Watch from Ascension to Michaelmas. Array in defence of the realm. Lands, goods. £40, 40 marks. Habergeon, sword, sallet, spear, horse. £20, 20 marks. All without horse. Purveyors suborned. Purprestures.* [Assignment of mounts to]: W[illiam] C[ecil], M[ildred] C[ecil], [Roger] Alford, Thomas Cecil, [Francis] Armestrong, Overton, Henry, [Thomas] Holcroft, Hieron, James, Richard, Pero, Alford's man, [George] Williams.

*16 small pp.*                                                                          SP 10/14, no. 53

**689.**    August 1. The Tower. Sir Philip Hoby to Sir William Cecil.

I received yesterday [William] Dansell's letters of July 26, saying there is much news at Antwerp that the emperor has gathered a great army, according to the enclosed billet [*which follows*]. He was lately at the queen's† camp there beyond Mons in Hainault, where he saw about 25,000 footmen and 4,000 or 5,000 horsemen. As the French king is retired with all his power, and the weather is foul, the queen has also bestowed her soldiers

*        Deleted.
†        Mary, queen dowager of Hungary, the emperor's sister.

into the towns in the frontiers of Hainault and Artois until she knows more of the French king's meaning. News is at Antwerp that Margrave Albrecht of Brandenburg has with his allies, friends to Duke Maurice [of Saxony], taken the town of Metz, leaving the burgesses and their goods unharmed but wholly sacking the priests. They are come before Frankfurt, to whom the townsmen have offered to yield upon composition, but those of Duke Maurice's party of which the margrave is the chief will not so enter but require them to surrender freely or they will attack. [Dansell] has in his custody 212 barrels of the king's gunpowder, of which he wishes to be despatched, and also wishes money to redeem the king's bullion. These requests are reasonable, and it is very requisite that the gunpowder were here. Move the council for further order, and remind them of the lack of munitions to be provided for Calais and Guînes, which cannot be done without money. *Postscript.* Command should be given for the sale of this king's gunpowder as hitherto no licence could be had for its transport hither, and that the money from the same should be used to redeem the king's bullion, the interest of which is growing to a great sum.             SP 10/14, no. 54

**690.** [July. Enclosed with the above]. News of the emperor sent through the commissioner M. Vaud.

The duke of Alba reached the emperor with 8,000 Spaniards, 6,000 Italians, with 2,400,000 ducats; other pieces to 77 ensigns; the king of the Romans – 28 ensigns; the prince and duke of Würtemberg – 8 ensigns, 600 horses. Horsemen: 2,000 Polish troopers; 200 Saxons; 3,000 Neapolitans with 800,000 ducats.

*French.*             SP 10/14, no. 54(i)

**691.** August 1. The Tower. Sir Philip Hoby to Sir William Cecil.

Last Saturday I was at Windsor with the rest of the commissioners; we could do little good because the certificate made by the dean and other masters, one of our principal things to proceed upon, was delivered to court and did not come to us until late that night, and because the dean was too sick to be there, and certain of the masters of the college were absent also. On the 8th we have appointed to meet there again, and commanded the dean and all masters to be present, when we trust at the furthest to advertise our proceedings to the content of the council. Hitherto they of the college have been very untoward in confessing the things missing out of the same. Lest our advertisement should seem to the lords long in coming, explain the premises. Mr Barkeley should be at Windsor for our meeting; I have persuaded him to stay till now, the rather as Mr Throgmorton is come to court. Let him have command to be at Windsor at the day, as one that cannot be spared. Remind my lords of the lack of munition for Calais and Guînes, impossible without money.

*Holograph.*

*Printed: Archaeologia*, xlii, I, (1869), 79.             SP 10/14, no. 55

**692.** August 3. The Tower. Sir Philip Hoby to Sir William Cecil.

For God's sake help the miseries of the ordnance office for lack of money. There are many poor men, including Charles Wolman, gunpowder maker, now in very pitiful case in the Counter as the rent of his house is unpaid for a year and a half, amounting to £13 and odd money, because no money has been paid into this office for a long time. The king is charged with his rent, being put there by his appointment for making gunpowder when there is money to set him at work, and to look to certain of the king's matters under his charge. As order has been taken by the council (as Mr Coxe can declare) that the chancellor should exchange the house that it might be the king's, and that the women who make all this business might be satisfied of the rent already due, move the council for further order by letter to the chancellor of augmentations to have the man discharged from prison, to enjoy his house and look after things committed to his custody.

*Fragment of seal.*

*Endorsed*: Haste, post haste.                                                          SP 10/14, no. 56

**693.** August 4. Wilton. The earl of Pembroke to Sir William Cecil.

Thank you for your letter. I wrote to the chancellor of augmentations on behalf of my friend James Stumpe of Malmesbury for the under stewardship and hundred there. He replied that he was restrained by letters from [the council] from granting either farm or office until they and the king should be made privy. Move the king or lords on his behalf. The chancellor has himself written to you to this effect, declaring the particulars. *Postscript.* I understand you are a suitor to the king for the wardship of [Francis] Hall's heir: at the request of my friend [Sir William] Sharington I was a means to the lord treasurer for the same in Hall's lifetime, whose grant and promise I had. Could you abandon your suit or (if you have obtained it) let Sharington have the preferment at your hands ? I would repay you with as good a turn.

*Fragment of seal.*                                                                     SP 10/14, no. 57

**694.** August 6. Indenture between Owen Oglethorpe, president of Magdalen College, Oxford and Walter Haddon, D.C.L.

In consideration of two letters from the king to the college in favour of Haddon's preferment for the presidency, and for other causes, it is agreed that (1) Haddon promises to restore Oglethorpe to such credit and reputation as he had with the king's council before the wrongful complaints made against him to certain of his own house. (2) Haddon shall obtain Oglethorpe's continuance in office until after the next audit, that he may not be seen to leave the college in haste, and that his enemies may not rejoice as they do now. (3) Oglethorpe shall have a discharge (the audit being finished and stuff remaining in the house delivered) of all his doings for the college, and a warrant under the common seal of the college that he shall not be molested for any college affairs. He will surrender all lands and tenements as he bought for the college, saving the parsonage of Evenley, which he desires to keep at his own disposal, paying such money as it cost, not minding to give it from the college, but to give it and other lands by composition to the college, if the fellows will admit the conditions. (4) Oglethorpe desires recompense from the king for his office in consideration of his long service to his grace's father and mother, because Dr [Thomas] Knowles had of him at his entry a benefice of £40 in recompense, but chiefly because he lately left an archdeaconry in York to retain his room at Oxford at the fellows' request (as appears by their letters, not unknown to the council). Haddon promises to commend this request. (5) Haddon shall sue for a non-residence for Oglethorpe, not because he intends to be much absent from his benefices, but to avoid wrongful accusation to the exchequer, and that he might sometimes resort to Oxford or London for health or medical attention. (6) Haddon will help Oglethorpe to have allowance for all his charges because of any complaints made against him by fellows of the college. (7) Haddon will befriend Oglethorpe's friends, fellows, farmers or officers of the college and not see them molested or deprived without great cause. (8) Oglethorpe gave [Robert] Bede, fellow of Magdalen, the schoolmastership of Brackley, void by the negligence of the previous occupant, and Mr Yorke the receivership now occupied by Pense. Haddon will ratify these gifts. (9) Oglethorpe shall have yearly the nomination of one demy and one chorister in the college by grant from Haddon, as Dr Knowles at his departing had of Oglethorpe. (10) Oglethorpe shall not be molested by Haddon or any of the college for his London house, and they shall not claim any interest there without his consent until he is otherwise provided for, or unless he gives the house to the college with other lands by composition.

*Unsigned.*

*On the dorse*: a child has had several attempts to write the name Edward Franciscus, finally managing 'Edwarde Franciscus is a knave'. SP 10/14, no. 58

**695.** August 14. Wilton. William Thomas, [clerk of the council] to Sir William Cecil.

As you wished at my departure I opened to [the earl of] Pembroke the consideration of the ward which you procured from your sister. He is very content, saying that though he wrote at his friend's request, he wrote to him to be considered as it might be with your own commodity. I have known him long and never saw him more bent to any man of your degree than to you. At my departure we talked of Venice; considering the stir of the world is now likely to be great there, I would like to spend a year or two there (if sent). I have not disclosed this to anyone but you, nor intend to do so. Do as you think best.

*? Holograph.* SP 10/14, no. 59

**696.** August 18. London. Gregory Raylton to Sir William Cecil.

Because of a sore ague at Chichester I had to depart from court without taking my leave of you. Although the fever is partly removed I am weak and the doctors fear consumption may follow. They have prescribed a diet, which I enclose, forbidding all fish. This bearer will further declare my state. Help me obtain the king's licence to eat flesh at prohibited times, with those in my company, whose numbers I leave at your discretion, having left a blank on my bill.

*Holograph.* SP 10/14, no. 60

**697.** August 20. Gidea Hall. Sir Anthony Cooke to Sir William Cecil.

You have heard, I suppose, my good speed in my journey. Thank you for your pains with me at court and the good relief I found at Wimbledon which was such and the air so good that although I came very weary and well wrapped, I was able to ride away in good health, though my strength is not yet as it was. I entreated my daughter* and [Richard] Goodrich to come home with me, where now we are merry. I would have them longer, but tomorrow my daughter will be at Wimbledon, whence she was loath to come save at my desire. God send you well to end this progress; in the meantime I shall be glad sometimes to hear from you. *Postscript.* Your son and mine, Thomas Cecil is here, merry, in whose towardness you have good cause to rejoice.

*Holograph.* SP 10/14, no. 61

**698.** [August (? 21)]. Sir Richard Sackvile, [chancellor of the court of augmentations] to the council.

According to your letters for hearing the titles of Lord De La Warr and Francis Shirley for the land in variance between them, I, with the rest of the council of the court of augmentations, have had before us the several patents of Lord De La Warr and Lord Admiral [Seymour], by whose grant Shirley claims the East Court lands. It appears that they legally belong to De La Warr as they are specifically granted him in his letters patent and certified by Henry Fowlkes, the king's particular surveyor, to be parcel of the manor of Knepp granted to him, where in fact the same was parcel of the manor of West Grinstead granted to the lord admiral, whose interest Shirley has in that manor, and also certified in that particular by the surveyor to be £2 less yearly rent than it is indeed, whereby De La Warr must answer to the king after twenty years' purchase £2 more rent, coming to £40. As the surveyor has wrongly certified the East Court lands to be parcel of the manor of Knepp, he has left uncertified the Parkesey rents, 60s. a year, by whose default De La Warr must also lawfully pay the king after twenty years' purchase, because

* Probably Anne, second of Cooke's five daughters.

the full value of Knepp manor was not contained in the particulars. Shirley (as he alleges) was so much more earnest in keeping possession of East Grinstead manor, which he purchased of the lord admiral, and for that De La Warr did not receive the rents of the lands in variance since the grant made to him of Knepp manor, two years ago, until last Michaelmas.

Touching the irreverent words allegedly spoken by Shirley against the king's patent and Lord De La Warr, he denies the first part, that he said he cared not a turd for my lord's patent. One of the witnesses brought in against him affirms he heard this not. But he confesses that he said that if my lord's patent would serve him no better for Knepp and Stoke park than it would do for the lands in variance, he might wipe his arse with it. He repents these rash and uncomely words. For the other matter in the articles, he denies them not, saving having kept the house with force, as you will see by his written confession enclosed [*which follows*].

Touching the rescues made to the sheriff's deputy by Shirley, who came to put Lord De La Warr in possession of the lands in variance, Shirley says that because he knew him not to be the sheriff's authorised deputy he would not allow him into the house called East Court lands, which he then kept as part of his purchase of West Grinstead manor, for which he must be recompensed of the lord admiral because he ... cannot have it, and his lordship to receive like recompense from the king for the same lands, and De La Warr to keep the same by virtue of his letters patent, but to pay the king £40 because it was not contained in his granted value, by default of the surveyor, as the omission of 60s. of Knepp manor was likewise his fault, for which De La Warr must pay the king £60 unless the king pardons him; leaving the order of the matter to your consideration.                                                                   SP 10/14, no. 62

**699.** [August (? 21). Enclosed with the above]. Articles exhibited by Francis Shirley against Lord De La Warr.

On August 10 Lord De La Warr sent his servant William Modye to take possession of a house and land called East Court in the parish of West Grinstead, Sussex, which he has by express words of the king's letters patent. Modye was withstood by Shirley and his servants. Modye came to the door and required all to leave the house that he might quietly take possession for the lord according to the king's grant. Two of Shirley's servants, John Gratweke and Stephen Cooper, answered that Modye should not enter. Modye told them they and their master would know his lord had more right; they replied that their master had bought it of the king as parcel of the lordship of West Grinstead. Modye, having a copy of the lord's patent, read it to them at a window; but they would not empty the house, and so keep it with force. Within a quarter of an hour Shirley came with William Mate, with a sword, buckler and a staple, to the door, asking Modye his business. On being told, he told Modye he would not enter, for if he were within he would make it fall about his head. Moyde said he came peaceably; but seeing he was withstood, his lord would be forced to complain. Shirley said he cared not if he did his worst. Modye said he had his lord's patent; but Shirley said he cared not a turd for it, and his lord could wipe his arse with it. Modye chastised him for his vulgarity, to which Shirley said 'tush' and would have revoked his words; then Modye left.

    *Certified by*: Edward Wolf, Thomas Haseley, William Lynfelde, William Modye, Richard Anstye *alias* Holcome and John Roberdes. Roberdes and Lynfelde did not hear the word 'turd'.

    *Four signs and six seals.*                                                                   SP 10/14, no. 62(i)

**700.** [August (? 21). Enclosed with no. **698**]. Confessions of Francis Shirley to the above articles.

1st question: agrees, save that Modye willed to leave the house save those that would keep it to his use. 1st answer, 2nd question and answer, 3rd question: agrees. 3rd answer: agrees, save that he kept it not with force but with two unarmed men, with the door shut to them. 4th question: agrees, save that his man had no buckler, nor that Shirley stepped not to the door but leant against a pail. 4th answer: agrees. 5th question: he said he should not enter. Modye answered that if he had made as much haste as he had done, he might have been in before him. Shirley answered that if he had been in, he would have come in or he would have come in at the top of his house. 5th answer: Modye answered that if he could not come in peacefully he would set the justice, who would set it whether he willed or no. 6th answer: he trusted my lord nor the justices would wrong him. 6th question: agrees. 7th answer: if the lord's patent should serve him no better for Knepp or Stoke park, he might wipe his arse with it. 7th question, 8th answer: agrees. To be certified by John Robertes, William Lyndfyld, John Goodes and William [? Mate] with others present who shall depose on oath.

*Sackvile's hand.* SP 10/14, no. 62(ii)

**701.** August 22. London. Richard Goodrich to Sir William Cecil.
I understand by your wife that you intend to go to Bath for the benefit of the baths and that you wish me with you. I cannot, for divers businesses for the king in survey of church goods in London (the burden rests chiefly on me) as for my own. Nor I think it very expedient for you for sundry causes. You have made no preparation there for your entertainment or diet, which is most necessary, especially for drink, which you must have provided in some place ten miles from Bath either at [Sir William] Sharington's or some other friend's, to be made of slow dried malt, aired and filtered to be still by your repair thither. Its lack will be so troublesome as you shall not at this time of the year take so much commodity of the baths. At this time of year, being so dangerous for fevers and so near Bristol where the pestilence rages, it will make your body too rare and apt to receive all the injury in the ague; the benefit of your legs is not to be sought with so great a hazard of your whole health. Defer your journey till the beginning of the year, when I will be glad to wait about you. You cannot be without peril at Bath, whither there is daily resort from Bristol, specially of beggars and poor folk. Remember the matter of my last letter.

*Holograph.* SP 10/14, no. 63

**702.** August 22. Cobham Hall. George [Brooke], Lord Cobham to Sir William Cecil.
Thank you for your letters and information, your remembrance of the suit of John Knight of Calais, and the final despatch of my servant Normanton. I understand you have obtained the king's grant of [Knight's] suit; procure its despatch and signature of the bill which Armigil [Waad] shall make. I intend to return shortly to court with Mr Secretary Petre. SP 10/14, no. 64

**703.** August 22. Cobham Hall. Lord Cobham to Sir William Cecil.
After enclosing my last letters I received letters from Mr Treasurer of Calais* requiring me to be means for him to the council for licence to come over to answer such points as the late commissioners beyond the seas burdened him with, and because he has written to [the duke of] Northumberland, [the earl of] Pembroke and other lords for this purpose. Prefer his suit, which is honest and reasonable. SP 10/14, no. 65

**704.** August 26. Salisbury. Memoranda of council business.
The commissioners of Calais: certificate of their commission; Sir Richard Cotton, Sir Anthony St Leger, [Thomas] Mildmay. The accord with the French ambassador for division of the debatable. Order for the commissioners' meetings. Diminution of the

---

* Sir Maurice Denys.

king's great charges. Survey of his courts. Gendarmerie. Superfluous blockhouses. Superfluous officers of revenue. Superfluous officers of works. Dover. Certificate of commissioners for the goods of Windsor church. Order to be foreseen for recovery of embezzled goods. Some fit man for the void controllership of Calais. Consideration of placing marts in the realm during the opportunity of time. Fortification of Portsmouth haven: the king has the plan devised by [John] Rogers. The bishop of Durham's case to be determined. The two vacant archbishoprics in Ireland. Execution of pirates at Calais and Dover. Bargain with John Rantzow. Order for Jacques Duke, physician, taken for suspicion of coining false money. For the controllership of Calais: Sir Thomas Palmer, Alexander Brett, Sir John Norton, Sir Edmund Grymston. For the marshalship: Sir Henry Sydney, [Sir Richard Blunt],* Sir Henry Gates, Sir Maurice Barkley.

    *Cecil's hand.*                                              SP 10/14, no. 66

**705.**  August 26. Wintney. Sir John Godsalve to Sir William Cecil.

I have obtained [Sir John] Cheke's consent to be joined with him in patent in the office of a chamberlain of the exchequer. As I cannot now be at court at Salisbury or Wilton, let me be furthered with your accustomed good report. I have made similar suit to my friend [Sir John] Mason. My suit is not to prejudice Mr Cheke a halfpenny, but to disburden him.

    *Holograph.*                                              SP 10/14, no. 67

**706.**  August 26. Richmond. The duke of Suffolk to Sir William Cecil.

My sudden departure from court was because I received letters about my wife. She has a constant burning ague, stopping of the spleen and *hypochondriaca passio*,† so it is to be feared death must follow. Commend me to the council and explain my wife's state.

    *Holograph.*                                              SP 10/14, no. 68

**707.**  August 27. Salisbury. The council to the [the bishop of Ely] lord chancellor.

As there have been piracies lately committed by Frenchmen and others about Dover and within the precinct of the five ports, the doers remaining in ward there without trial, we have thought it convenient there should immediately be sessions of oyer and terminer of piracies in the five ports, and send you a schedule of the names we think best for the commissions. Take order that the commission may forthwith be made out and sent to [the sheriff]* Dover to the deputy of the five ports, that the commissioners may proceed to the trial.

    *Draft.*

    *Signed by:* William Thomas [clerk of the council].          SP 10/14, no. 69

**708.**  August 28. Putney. Richard Goodrich to Sir William Cecil.

According to your request I have obtained particulars of divers manors in Somerset and Devon, which I enclose. As far as I can learn they are as good as are in those shires. I procured them without valuation of perquisites, and because I would wish the king's gift as beneficial to him‡ as it has been for others, for I think his service and desert equal with theirs. Besides Gidea Hall, his charge grows so much as he must crave the king's liberality. You know his worthiness better than I. Finish the enterprise as speedily as you kindly began. He is of no craving nature; his friends may use the more earnestness in his cause. If you obtain a letter from the council for him you may name the manors to be granted with all profits and commodities, and what exceeds in clear yearly rent and value £100 or such as pleases the king, to be reserved to the king in a yearly rent.

---

\*    Deleted.

†    A general term to describe illness in the lateral parts of the body below the floating rib, indigestion, or heart disease. In fact, Frances, duchess of Suffolk, was to outlive her husband.

‡    Sir Anthony Cooke.

*Holograph.*                                                                    SP 10/14, no. 70

**709.** August 28. Wimbledon. Francis Armstrong to Sir William Cecil.

Inventory seen by Richard Norwood of the goods of Dr [John] Clement remaining in Marshfoot house, Hornchurch, Essex, 18 April [1552], by command of Sir Anthony Wingfield, comptroller. [*Detailed. 4 pp.*] Witnessed by Thomas Legat, gent., Thomas Layland, and Richard Norwood, yeoman. Marshfoot house, late Dr Clement's. [*1¹/₂pp.*]

Because the bringer would not wait, I send the papers I wrote at Marshfoot house, with John Untred. There were no cattle of Clement's house there at his departure, but there are now twenty of Mr Wingfield's old kine, out of flesh. The ground will keep twenty kine and sixty sheep, in winter and summer. It is within a quarter of a mile of Rainham, and worth to be let for £12 a year. I delivered the council's letter to Robert Wingfield, his father's executor;* he will look out the intended will whereby the stuff left in Clement's house was delivered to Mr Comptroller. If you let me know where to receive the one part of the bill, I will repair with it to Mr Wingfield's to receive the stuff which was fetched away by Mr Comptroller's command last summer, so that there remains nothing in Marshfoot house but the hangings and other stuff of little value. I hear what was fetched away is worth little. Mr Comptroller's servant, who is dwelling in the same house, showed me a bill of the stuff which should be there, the copy of which I enclose. *Postscript.* Mr Wingfield says that Mr Clement made a lease of it to a farmer, reserving only the lodging to himself. Clement bought the farmer's interest, so that he claims two years by virtue of the lease. [Sir Philip] Hoby was, when I went to him concerning this, very sick of a new ague, and, sorry he could not do your pleasure, made Mr Lieutenant† privy to your letter, desiring him travail therein, from whom I learned that I could and after travailed there accordingly.

*Holograph.*                                                                    SP 10/14, no. 71

**710.** August 30. Andover. The duke of Northumberland to Sir William Cecil.

I was unable at my departure from court to tell you of the suits I had made to the king. The first was for a lease in reversion of the site and demesnes of the late monastery of Cirencester for Sir Anthony Kingston, as Basinge now occupies it, which he granted in the presence of the lord chamberlain, no years expressed; but as twenty-one years is the least after the years expired, so he being an old servant, I think ten more to him is no great matter, which I refer to you and my lord. I also sued for Sir John Abrydges to have the king's placard for retaining forty persons in his livery, as others have. Order his bill to be assigned. In your presence and that of the rest of [the council] I sued for the hospital which [Anthony] Bellasis had‡ for Sir Richard Reed. Befriend Sir Richard: I should be sorry if he lost in my absence. This bearer has an old suit before the council, for which he obtained a letter from the board to the chancellor and court of augmentations for his recompense, as all others have had. Since, the matter has been stayed, why I know not. If you think he should prosper favour him as you can. Tonight I found at my lodgings Robert Fenwyke, who was before you and my lords yesterday at the conveying of the miller, whom I return presently to my lords, thinking it meet something were done, albeit the offence for death be pardoned. The offence was heinous, therefore it requires some terror. Lord Wharton should be told of the nomination of Lord Eure ('Evers') for the east marches, Sir Richard Musgrave for Carlisle castle and Sir Thomas Dacres as deputy warden of the west marches, and a letter to Sir Nicholas Sturley of the king's pleasure concerning the east marches. Some letter should be written

*    Sir Anthony Wingfield had died on August 15.
†    Sir Arthur Darcy.
‡    Bellasis had been master of two hospitals in county Durham: St Mary Magdalene, Sherburn and St
     Edmund, Gateshead [G. Hinde (ed.), *The Registers of Cuthbert Tunstall and James Pilkington*, (Surtees Society,
     clxi, 1952), 101, 111].

to Lord Conyers from my lords marvelling that he would so suddenly surrender his office, and deeming at my departure from Carlisle to be content to remain at least until he heard from the king or council, and said he would put his life and lands in the king's hands rather than return. Such a letter with some quick words would do him good, and others of whom, perhaps, he receives counsel, rather than if he were commanded to court towards Michaelmas to answer before the council for contempt. Thereby I and all others who serve the king shall be better obeyed in that country. The party who has raised that slander of me in the country for conveying the king's coffers may be immediately delivered to [the earl of] Westmorland or [the earl of] Shrewsbury to be conveyed to court with a letter to one of the earls. Now I remember that Shrewsbury is presently in Shropshire, and will be there this month. I think Westmorland meeter to be written to. Several letters should be written to Lord Eure, Sir Richard Musgrave and Sir Thomas Dacres to repair to Lord Wharton for further knowledge of the king's pleasure concerning their placing in their office. Lord Eure is now ridden to his wife in Lincolnshire, and would be glad to receive such a letter.

*Endorsed*: With speed. At the court.                                     SP 10/14, no. 72

**711.**   September 3. Knole. The duke of Northumberland to Sir William Cecil.

Today I received your letters of August 31 with [Sir Richard] Morison's – a mass of matters which I return without having gathered much fruit. I am glad that the king, on the council's advice, cuts his superfluous progress, whereby the council may better attend to his affairs in these troublesome days. Every day I hear more of French cruelty against our subjects and merchants, so that some are desperate. The honour of the king, council and realm is marvellously touched. Let the proverb you mention be often remembered: without counsel the people fall.* Where I see grave counsel esteemed, I shall be ready to do my duty. I return the packet of letters from Christopher Mount, at my being at court forgotten to be delivered to you. *Postscript (holograph)*. As in your former packet the minute of the earl of Westmorland's letter was omitted, there was (I think) in a letter to Lord Conyers more than was meant. Your letter to me imported that it was to be delivered to Lord Conyers's man, which letter with the rest I despatched immediately to Lord Wharton with a through post, and the letter to Lord Eure to himself to be delivered in Lincolnshire.

*Endorsed*: Haste, haste, with all diligence, haste.                      SP 10/15, no. 1

**712.**   September 4. Knole. The duke of Northumberland to Sir William Cecil.

I learnt by this bearer of a suit to be made by our merchants for licence to ship cloths now for Flanders, especially meet for one great service for the king, as the bearer will explain. Tell the king, if you think it convenient, and such others as you think will be secret. If some know of it, the parties are strait warned. Stands it not with honour that the king should rather be [in]debted to his own subjects than to strangers, and as convenient that the subject should bear with him as with strangers in these two parts? I wish the matter might be well conceived and order taken accordingly, that those whom I would should not understand the ground of the matter should set forth the suit of the merchants to a ship, and it should not be denied. What must follow this bearer can instruct.

*Printed*: Hoak, 321 n. 161 (extracts).                                   SP 10/15, no. 2

**713.**   September 7. Knole. The duke of Northumberland to Sir William Cecil.

The bishop of Winchester has, partly at my request, produced a catechism in Latin and English for learners in grammar schools and others. Be a means for the king's licence

---

*        In Latin.

for its printing, that this poor man,* always a furtherer of godly things, may be authorised for the sole printing for a certain time. *Postscript (holograph)*. Thomas Stukley arrived here from the French court, having a letter to the king from the French king declaring his honest and forward service – better words, it seems, because he received no reward. But such an instrument he has brought as has not been given to any foreign subject; it seems a bare world where such presents are made to strangers. It is a placard under the great seal of France for him to have free recourse into all French havens and ports and those of the French king's ships, with four ships armed and manned for war, with liberty to take what he can of all the French king's enemies. He also brought a letter from the French king to me in his favour, which I enclose. As such plans and descriptions of all the French king's journey and conquests of this summer's progress which he has brought are not finished, I have sent him to London to finish them, and then to repair with them to the king, who I think will have pleasure seeing them. I wish the placard were as little spoken of as might be, and therefore the fewer to know of it. But it may perhaps serve the king's purpose otherwise than was meant by the givers or known to the receiver. The young man is worthy of praise that can so behave in outward parts to have an estimation. He was the duke of Somerset's servant only by my means, and desires to take pains with me for a while. When I see opportunity I will desire the king to receive him of me. I dare say there is not in Italy or Christendom a better soldier of his time. He has also told me of what estimation Portenero is now in that court, specially for an engineer, and what devotion nevertheless he bears to this realm. Whenever he may be received with any living, although but half he may have there, he is at the king's command – which, being kept secret, may in time stand to good purpose. I mind to be at court with the king on the 15th or sooner if you have anything to do. The departing of this man without leave [should not be] taken ill, for necessity and debt was the cause. *Second postscript (holograph)*. Tell the king and council [he] offers to deliver us Brian Huchesson within ten days if he is commanded.

*Endorsed*: Haste, with diligence. SP 10/15, no. 3

**714.** [September (? 8)]. Memoranda of council business.

Answer to [Sir Richard] Morison touching his abode and for money. Answer to the commissioners at Carlisle for the treaty and touching Canonbie. Letters to [Peter] Vannes at Venice. Calais: for money and order to the ports for victuals. Ireland. Berwick and the north. Answer to the ambassadors of the Steelyard. Despatch for Hull. Appointment of the mart and its order. Answer to [Sir] H[enry] Dudley. The king of Denmark's man. The French king's desire for victuals to be unladen at Calais and from thence brought to Dover. Pardon for [George] Parys. Answer to Thomas Gresham. Answer to the commissioner at Carlisle. Blockhouses. The emperor's new embassy. SP 10/15, no. 4

**715.** September 15. Wilton. The earl of Pembroke to Sir William Cecil.

My friend Thomas Gresham, who has lately travailed honestly in the king's affairs overseas, presently means to sue for some reward, and has asked me to be a means to you for him. Work what you can.

*Holograph.* SP 10/15, no. 5

**716.** September 17. Windsor. The duke of Northumberland to Sir William Cecil.

On the question moved to [Thomas] Stukley of the occasion of his first departing such matter has come forth as God is to be praised for, as at your coming, which is required with most diligence, you shall understand.

*Holograph.* SP 10/15, no. 6

---

* Raynard Wolf printed the first edition (*STC* 4807).

**717.**   September 17. Richmond. The earl of Westmorland to Sir William Cecil.

The council wrote to me concerning the slanders and rumours spoken of the duke of Northumberland. Tell the council I have thoroughly examined them. I have sent up John Burghe for the same matter, who will only confess he told Thornton he saw chests of treasure drawn out of [Peter] Osburne's house in London, some there saying it was the king's and some the duke's, and denies he ever said the duke conveyed it from the king, although the confessions are contradictory. Concerning the land you bought of me, as I said at first, if I had been able to give it, I would have. Write by my servant this bearer what you would have me do, and I will. If you take the lease of my gift I shall send for my servant and recompense him with some other thing.

SP 10/15, no. 7

**718.**   September 21. Bisham. Sir Philip Hoby to Sir William Cecil.

In your letter by this bearer you wish to know whether I have a retainer called Harbert. I have a servant called Harbert Clarvys, 60, who lives in Worcestershire and keeps my hawks. As far as I know he has behaved honestly. I never knew he was a ranger in Woodstock park, thinking rather not. *Postscript.* Account Vastern park as much yours as mine: use it as your own.

SP 10/15, no. 8

**719.**   September 28. Annuities appointed for officers in bulwarks in Essex.

Mersea house: captain – John Burley; lieutenant – Arthur Clerke; porter – William Jermyn. St Osyth house: lieutenant – John Sondon; porter – Anthony Kynwelmarshe. Middle house, Harwich: porter – Michael Cockes. House on hill, Harwich: captain – Richard Cornwalles; porter – Richard Mapull; gunner – John Dawbeney. Tower house, Harwich: captain – Richard Bowcock; lieutenant – William Thicknis; porter – William Christmas. Landguard Point house: captain – Richard Lorde; lieutenant – John Jenynges; porter – Lewes Evans. Landguard Road house: captain – Anthony Gyrling; lieutenant – William Bramforthe; porter – John Clerke. Captains – £20; lieutenants – £10; porters – £6; gunner – £9.2.6; total – £201.2.6.

> *Signed by*: The marquess of Winchester, the duke of Northumberland, the earl of Bedford, the marquess of Northampton, Lord Cobham, Sir Richard Cotton, Sir William Cecil and Sir John Mason.                          SP 10/15, no. 9

**720.**   September 29. Hampton Court. Memoranda of council business.

The French commissioners for the answer of depredations. Discharge of excessive charges in courts of revenue and blockhouses. Consideration for massing money towards the king's debts abroad and at home. Consideration of a mart now in the opportunity of time. Device to make bargains of lead for the king, and to have knowledge of his own leads. Device to stay the great waste ecclesiastical persons make of their livelihoods. Order for commissioners in every shire to muster and view the number of great horses found upon the statute.* Consideration of the admiralty for the state of the king's ships. The debt in Ireland; diminution of the king's charges there. Payments to be made at Calais; for better proceeding of the works there. Commission for heresies.

> *Cecil's hand.*                          SP 10/15, no. 10

**721.**   [? September]. Brief declaration of principal military and naval charges of Henry VIII and Edward VI, collected from accounts of high treasurers and vice-treasurers of wars, officers of ordnance, master victuallers, purveyors, paymasters of fortifications and buildings, and on conference with officers of the king's receipts and treasurers.

[1]. Henry VIII's army royal into France, the siege before Boulogne and Montreuil,

---

\*      33 Henry VIII c. 5.

maintenance and fortification of Boulogne, Newhaven [Ambleteuse] and other forts in the county, from 1 January 1544* to the surrender of the town to the French, 1 May 1550. Coats and conduct of captains, petty captains, soldiers, victuallers and other ministers and labourers: during siege – £59,028.0.8; from the conquest of the town, 13 September 1544, to Henry VIII's death, 28 January 1547 – £8,808,16.4; from Edward VI's accession to 1 May 1550 – £3,798.11.11½d.; total – £71,635.8.11½d. Diets and wages of the army royal, the king's deputies, council and officers of the town and pieces, with entertainments of captains, petty captains and garrisons, wages of servants, purveyors, clerks and other ministers of victuals, and charges of commissioners for peace treaty and other secret affairs: during siege – £353,916.19.6¾d.; temp. Henry VIII – £318,884.3.4; temp. Edward VI – £196,751.16.7¾d.; total – £869,552.16.2½d.†
Purchases. Ordnance, powder, munitions, artillery and habiliments of war: during siege – £94,000.7.5¾d.; temp. Henry VIII – £25,989.8.7; temp. Edward VI – £20,127.17.2½d.; total – £140,187.13.3¼d.‡ Horses and mares bought and provided for carriage, carts and conduct of cart[er]s and wagoners at the siege – £13,307.12.5. 7 hoys bought for transport of ordnance, with charges of the king's galley *Greihound* serving for wasting of 9 hoys laden with provisions out of Flanders by John Dymock at the siege – £1,328.17.2. Sundry provisions: wagons, ovens, mills, copper, kettles, pans, brewing vessels, casks &c.: during siege – £14,412.5.9¼d.; temp. Henry VIII – £5,166.7.11½d.; total – £19,578.13.8¾d. Total purchases – £174,402.16.7. Freight, lighterage, keelage, with other water and land charges; ordnance, powder, munitions, artillery and habiliments of war, grain, victuals, horses and other provisions, with £10,243.19.6½d. for transport of army royal's plate and treasure: during siege – £21,761.1.3½d.; temp. Henry VIII – £8,174.2.11½d.; temp. Edward VI – £1,149.14.3; total – £31,084.18.6. Deal, wainscot, timber, boards, plank, canvas, ironwork and workmanship of divers houses, tents, hales, 'shrimpes', 'priviboates', bridges, patrons and engines of war for the siege – £9,789.0.8½d. Saddles, bridles, bits, stirrups, &c., bought and provided of the saddler, silkwoman, bitmaker, stirrupmaker, wheelwright and coffer maker for the king's stable for the siege – £2,085.0.10½d. Rewards with posting charges and special money to ambassadors and others in recompense of service, hurts and losses, in recompense of prisoners: during siege – £7,995.17.1; temp. Henry VIII – £3,182.15.6; temp. Edward VI – £13,993.14.5¾d.; total – £25,172.7.0¾d. Fortifications: high and base town of Boulogne with their pieces – £82,474.13.4½d.; old haven – £12,350.5.6; Bolemberg – £5,147.6.4; Newhaven [Ambleteuse] – £15,731.7.5½d.; Blackness – £7,051.10.10½d.; viz. temp. Henry VIII – £47,166.18.3½d.; temp. Edward VI – £75,529.5.3; total – £122,696.3.6½d. Grain decayed, wasted and lost by long lying in garrets and storehouses and stolen for want of safe storage, lost by the sea and enemies, with £320.2.11 worth lost in the skirmish at the base town, with £3,535.16.11 left to the French in the pieces at the surrender: during siege – £982.16.3½d.; temp. Henry VIII – £3,663.11.3½d.; temp. Edward VI – £3,615.1.11; total – £8,261.9.6. Victuals with implements and necessaries decayed, wasted and lost as before, with £1,277.4.0 worth lost at the skirmish in the base town and £14,363.19.8 lost to the French at the surrender: during siege – £8,040.8.4; temp. Henry VIII – £5,270.15.2; temp. Edward VI – £14,560.10.2½d.; total – £27,871.13.8½d. Sum totals: during siege – £586,718.12.3¾d.; temp. Henry VIII – £426,306.19.5; temp. Edward VI – £329,526.11.11; total – £1,342,552.3.7¾d.

[2]. Calais and Guînes, 30 September 1538 to 31 July 1552. Fortifications: temp. Henry VIII – £120,675.18.11⅝d.; temp. Edward VI – £30,736.13.0½d.; total – £151,412.12.0⅛d. Wages and diets: temp. Henry VIII – £156,089.10.7; temp. Edward VI – £63,926.16.2½d.; total – £220,016.6.9½d. Sum total – £371,428.18.9⅝d.

---

*    Erroneously given as 36 Henry VIII in sub-heading.
†    Should be £869,552.19.6½d.
‡    Should be £140,117.13.3¼d.

[3]. The wars against Scotland, 9 September 1542 to 1 May 1550, with continued wages and payments until the armies and garrisons were dissolved. Coats and conduct of captains, petty captains, soldiers, victuallers, carters and other ministers and labourers: temp. Henry VIII – £38,951.13.1½d.; temp. Edward VI – £29,720.14.1; total – £68,672.7.2½d. The king's lieutenants, lords warden, councillors, with entertainment and wages of all captains, petty captains, officers of record, soldiers, horsemen and footmen, English and strangers, and all garrisons and crews serving in forts and holds won and fortified by his majesty, with wages of surveyors, purveyors, clerks and other ministers: (borders) Berwick, with invasions and camps into Scotland besides ordinary garrison – £581,942.11.0¾d.; Warke castle – £340.18.8; Holy Island – £202.10.8; Farne Island – £81.4.0; Billie tower – £52.10.0; Castlemilk – £1,370.3.8; Carlisle citadel – £3,006.2.2; Tynemouth – £1,277.10.0; (within Scotland) Broughty Craig – £16,708.0.2½d.; Haddington – £31,640.12.4; Lauder – £6,646.15.3; Roxburgh – £5,303.9.3; Eymouth – £3,598.9.1; Dunglass – £5,954.5.10; Fast castle – £170.19.0; Jedburgh – £486.18.3; Hume castle – £253.5.8; viz. temp. Henry VIII – £235,383.8.5½d.; temp. Edward VI – £423,652.17.4¼d.; total – £659,035.5.9¾d.* Purchase of necessaries, carriage horses, coppers, brewing vessels and cooper stuff for victualling armies in Scotland: temp. Henry VIII – £6,021.0.10¾d.; temp. Edward VI – £11,172.13.8½d.; total – £17,193.13.7¼d.† Freight and land carriage of grain, victuals, ordnance, munitions and other necessaries for ordnance, clapboard, hoops, shovels, spades, mattocks, soap, tar, &c., and implements for victualling royal armies at Berwick, Holy Island and Newcastle and the said forts within England: temp. Henry VIII – £10,060.8.1¼d.; temp. Edward VI – £22,962.16.3¾d.; total £33,023.4.5. Rewards to captains, petty captains and soldiers in recompense of service, hurts and losses, in recompense of prisoners, charges and rewards to nobles and gentlemen of Scotland, ambassadors and commissioners, posting and riding charges, and special money to sundry persons: temp. Henry VIII – £19,823.14.3; temp. Edward VI – £42,332.3.0½d.; total – £62,155.17.3½d. Munitions, ordnance and habiliments of war spent, lost and employed in sundry camps, invasions and in divers sorts and pieces in Scotland and on the seas: temp. Henry VIII – £5,984.10.3; temp. Edward VI – £22,079.13.4; total – £28,064.3.7. Fortifications: Berwick – £40,860.16.0¾d.; Holy Island – £980.4.4½d.; Wark castle – £2,997.14.10; Carlisle castle and citadel – £7,291.5.3½d.; Tynemouth – £2,643.10.3; Lauder – £1,583.5.7; Broughty [Craig] – £2,265.10.0; Inchcolm – £121.12.0; Haddington – £1,423.3.11; Dunglass – £2,300.16.11; Roxburgh – £1,899.8.2½d.; Dundee – £103.11.10; Eyemouth – £1,908.5.6; Hume – £733.18.5; viz. temp. Henry VIII – £27,457.14.7¾d.; temp. Edward VI – £39,685.8.6½d.; total – £67,113.3.2¼d. Grain decayed by long storage, stolen and embezzled for want of safe storage, and loss upon the seas by weather and by enemies: temp. Henry VIII – £2,784.11.11; temp. Edward VI – £1,534.18.3¾d.; total £4,319.10.2¾d. Victuals, implements and necessaries decayed, wasted and lost as before, with £4,452.6.4¼d. lost in sundry forts and convoys in Scotland: temp. Henry VIII – £3,796.0.6¼d.; temp. Edward VI – £10,761.11.9⅝d.; total – £14,557.12.3⅞d. Total losses – £18,877.2.6⅝d. Sum totals: temp. Henry VIII – £350,243.2.2; temp. Edward VI – £603,872.16.5⅞d.; total – £954,135.18.7⅞d.‡

[4]. Sea charges during the wars. Purchase of cables, hawsers, ratline, martin[ets] and other rope and tackle, poldavy, olerons, canvas, masts, timber, boards, planks, anchors, ironwork, pitch, tar, tallow, rosin, brick, tile, chalk, oakum and other provisions for new making, rigging and redubbing the king's ships: temp. Henry VIII – £45,230.18.8; temp. Edward VI – £51,152.11.5¼d.; total – £96,383.10.1¼d. Coats and conduct of captains, master gunners, mariners and soldiers in the king's royal armies and other naval

* Should be £659,036.5.9¾d.

† Should be £17,193.14.7¼d.

‡ Should be £954,115.18.7⁄8d.

enterprises: temp. Henry VIII – £2,315.13.2; temp. Edward VI – £5,070.1.5; total – £7,485.14.7. Wages of captains, masters, mariners, gunners and common soldiers in the king's ships on the Scotch and north seas, and wages and board wages of shipwrights, caulkers, carpenters, anchorsmiths, blacksmiths and other artificers and labourers, wages of clerks, purveyors, shipkeepers, and diets and wages of principal officers of the king's marine causes and affairs: temp. Henry VIII – £127,846.10.7; temp. Edward VI – £78,263.3.8½d.; total – £206,109.14.3½d. Freight with water and land carriage of provisions and necessaries bought for the king's ships and marine causes: temp. Henry VIII – £3,582.4.7; temp. Edward VI – £2,451.14.10; total – £6,033.19.5¼d.* Charges of sundry persons posting and riding about admiralty affairs, with charges and hiring of docks and storehouses at several places for the king's ships and provisions: temp. Henry VIII – £502.4.6; temp. Edward VI – £1,609.4.6; total – £2,111.9.0. Victuals, necessaries and pursers' costs: biscuit (68,088,522 lb.) – £24,733.17.2¼d.; beer (33,425 tons, 2 barrels) – £42,087.16.0; bread (17,593 doz., 3 loaves) – £1,022.17.4; sack (258½ butts) – £1,296.10.0; malmsey (4 butts) – £26.12.4; Gascony wine (5 tons) – £35; best salt (9,897 pipes, 1 barrel) – £38,986.8.1; bacon (2,507 flitches, 164,294 lb.) – £1,460.5.10¾d.; stockfish (435 lasts, 128) – £4,940.19.5; saltfish (116,378) – £2,607.1.8; white herring (251½ lasts, 523) – £2,144.3.5½d.; red herring (105 lasts, 9½ cades) – £714; butter (1,560½ barrels, 22 lb.) – £2,386.4.10½d.; cheese (3,713½ weys, 61 lb.) – £4,578.3.8¾d.; necessaries, pursers' costs with drawing of cask – £3,435.12.8.; viz. temp. Henry VIII – £65,610.10.4½d.; temp. Edward VI – £64,844.17.3½d.; total – £130,455.8.8.† *Mary Rose* sunk at Portsmouth, the weighing of which, with recovery of some tackle, anchors and ordnance, temp. Henry VIII, cost – £559.8.7. Ordnance, munitions and habiliments of war spent, lost and employed in the king's ships: temp. Henry VIII, with £1,723 worth of ordnance lost in the *Mary Rose* and £566 in the *Lyon Lubeck* – £19,276.13.10½d.; temp. Edward VI – £10,455.16.8½d.; total – £29,722.10.7. Sum totals: temp. Henry VIII – £265.024.4.3; temp. Edward VI – £213,837.10.0; total – £478.861.14.3.

[5]. The journey to Landrecies in aid of the emperor against the French king, 1544. Coats, conduct, diets, entertainment and wages of the general, his lieutenants, captains, petty captains, with their bands, transport, rewards and other charges – £36,500.

[6]. Fortifications, with wages and entertainment of garrisons from their building until Michaelmas 1552. *Kent.* Dover: bulwarks of Archcliffe super montem, below castle and black bulwark in Dover Cliff: fortifications temp. Henry VIII – £1,496.9.3¾d.; wages for 6 years ending Michaelmas 1546 – £1,058.10.0; temp. Edward VI for like time – £1,058.10.0; total – £3,613.9.3¾d.; pier: wages for 6 years ending Michaelmas 1546 – £33,600.2.10;‡ temp. Edward VI for like time – £9,279.18.8; total – £42,880.1.6; brewhouse, bakehouse and mills in the Maison Dieu: fortifications temp. Henry VIII – £3,208.7.5½d. Total (Dover) – £49,701.18.3¼d. The Downs, viz. Deal castle, Walmer and Sandhills [Sandown] by Sandwich with the 4 green bulwarks and the clay bulwark there: fortifications temp. Henry VIII – £27,092.12.1¾d.; wages for 6 years ending Michaelmas 1546 – £4,635.4.0; temp. Edward VI for like time – £4,635.4.0; total – £36,363.0.1¾d. Sandgate by Folkestone: fortifications temp. Henry VIII – £5,587.5.10⅛d.; wages for 6 years ending Michaelmas 1546 – £1,095; temp. Edward VI for like time – £1,095; total – £7,777.5.10⅛d. Queenborough castle: fortifications temp. Henry VIII – £2,702.11.10; wages 36–38 Henry VIII – £1,874.2.6; temp. Edward VI – £381.12.0; total – £4,958.6.4. Gravesend bulwarks: fortifications temp. Henry VIII – £1,072; wages for 3 years ending Michaelmas 1546 – £273.15.0; for 6 years ending Michaelmas 1552 – £547.10.0; total – £1,893.5.0. Milton bulwarks: fortifications temp. Henry VIII – £1,072; wages for 3 years ending Michaelmas 1546 – £273.15.0; for 6 years

---

\*      *Sic.*

†      Sum of items is £126,989.0.11³/4d. and of sub totals £130,455.7.8.

‡      Written xxxiij$^m$vj$^{c}$liiij$^s$x$^d$ for xxxiij$^m$vj$^{c}$ $^{li}$ij$^s$x$^d$.

ending Michaelmas 1552 – £547.10.0; total – £1,893.5.0. Higham bulwark: fortifications temp. Henry VIII – £980; wages for 3 years ending Michaelmas 1546 – £246.7.6; for 6 years ending Michaelmas 1552 – £492.15.0; total – £1,719.2.6. *Sussex.* Camber castle: fortifications temp. Henry VIII – £15,759.9.1; wages for 3 years ending Michaelmas 1546 – £921.12.6; for 6 years ending Michaelmas 1552 – £1,843.5.0; total – £18,524.6.7. *Cornwall.* Pendennis castle on west side of Falmouth haven: fortifications temp. Henry VIII – £5,614.14.2; wages for 2½ years ending Michaelmas 1546 – £387.16.3; for 6 years ending Michaelmas 1552 – £930.15.0; total – £6,933.5.5. St Mawes castle or fort: fortifications temp. Henry VIII – £5,018.12.6; wages for 3 years ending Michaelmas 1546 – £465.7.6; for 6 years ending Michaelmas 1552 – £930.15.0; total – £6,414.15.0. *Hampshire and Isle of Wight.* Fortifications. Town and isle of Portsmouth with new castle, south castle [? Southsea], Haslar ('Hasillwood point'), St Andrew's point, Calshot point, Sandown castle, green bulwark, Hurst castle, Yarmouth castle, East and West Cowes, Sconce point ('Sharpwood'), St Helen's and Carisbrooke: temp. Henry VIII – £41,176.11.5; temp. Edward VI – £11,941.5.10; total – £53,117.17.3½d.* Four brewhouses, two bakehouses, with stables and other new houses of storage for the king's provisions: temp. Henry VIII – £1,566.7.2; temp. Edward VI – £73.2.8; total – £1,639.9.10. Total for fortifications – £54,757.7.1½d. Wages and entertainments of ordinary garrisons and crews. Town and isle of Portsmouth with new castle: 3 years ending Michaelmas 1546 – 0, for garrison paid among extraordinary mentioned below; for 6 years ending·Michaelmas 1552 – £2,628. Windmill and [John] Chaderton's bulwarks: temp. Henry VIII – £328.10.0; temp. Edward VI – £657; total – £985.10.0. Portsmouth tower: temp. Henry VIII – £82.2.6; temp. Edward VI – £164.4.0; total – £246.7.6.† Spertes bulwark and blockhouse next Portsmouth: temp. Henry VIII – £82.2.6; temp. Edward VI – £164.5.0; total – £266.7.6.‡ Castle called Calshot point: temp. Henry VIII – £520.2.6; temp. Edward VI – £1,040.5.0; total – £1,560.7.6. Castle or fort at St Andrew's point: 2 years ending Michaelmas 1546 – £170.6.8; temp. Edward VI – £511; total – £681.6.8. Hurst castle: temp. Henry VIII – £793.17.6; temp. Edward VI – £1,587.15.0; total – £2,381.12.6. South castle [? Southsea]: temp. Henry VIII – £949; temp. Edward VI – £1,898; total – £2,847. West Cowes: temp. Henry VIII – £310.5.0; temp. Edward VI – £620.10.0; total – £620.10.0.§ Sandown bay: temp. Henry VIII – 0, for paid among extraordinary below; temp. Edward VI – £1,898. Yarmouth castle: temp. Henry VIII – £793.17.6; temp. Edward VI – £1,587.15.0; total – £2,381.12.6. Total for wages – £16,786.19.2. Extraordinary: captains, petty captains with their bands serving in Portsmouth, the Isle of Wight and sundry camps there: temp. Henry VIII – £1,636.14.0; temp. Edward VI – £6,556.12.10; total – £8,193.6.10. *Dorset.* Portland castle or fort: fortifications temp. Henry VIII – £4,964.10¾d.; wages for 3 years ending Michaelmas 1546 – £447.2.6; for 6 years ending Michaelmas 1552 – £894.5.0; total – £6,306.7.4/4)d. Sandsfoot castle: fortifications temp. Henry VIII – £3,887.4.1; wages for 3 years ending Michaelmas 1546 – £346.15.0; for 6 years ending Michaelmas 1552 – £693.10.0; total – £4,927.9.1. *Yorkshire.* Hull, with forts made there: fortifications temp. Henry VIII – £23,155.17.5; wages for 3 years ending Michaelmas 1546 – £1,508; for 5 years ending Michaelmas 1551 – £4,298.6.8; total – £30,033.4.1.¶ *Essex.* Harwich, Landguard point, St Osyth, Mersea and Brightlingsea: fortifications temp. Henry VIII – £2,717.18.6½d.; wages for 2 years ending Michaelmas 1546 – £1,508.7.0; for 6 years ending Michaelmas 1552 – £4,525.1.0; total – £8,751.6.6½d. East and West Tilbury: fortifications temp. Henry VIII – £506.8.10½d.; temp. Edward VI – £207.8.8½d.; wages for 1½ years

*    *Sic.*
†    Should be £246.6.6.
‡    Should be £246.7.6.
§    Should be £930.15.0.
¶    Should be £28,962.4.1.

ending Michaelmas 1546 – £246.7.6; for 6 years ending Michaelmas 1552 – £985.10.0; total – £1,965.15.1. *Islands*. Alderney: fortifications temp. Edward VI – £9,212.18.3¾d;* wages temp. Edward VI – £4,184.7.1;* total – £14,083.18.3¾d. Scilly: fortifications temp. Edward VI – £3,787.6.2½d.;* wages temp. Edward VI – £4,184.7.1; total – £7,971.13.3½d. Jersey: fortifications temp. Edward VI – £706.19.6. Totals. Fortifications: temp. Henry VIII – £181,179.12.6⅞d.; temp. Edward VI – £35,228.18.2¼d.; total – £216,408.10.9⅛d. Wages: temp. Henry VIII – £22,026.0.5; temp. Edward VI – £52,228.5.4; total – £74,254.5.9. Sum total – £290,662.16.6⅛d.

[7]. The subversion of rebels in Norfolk, Devon and Cornwall and other places, 1549. Coats and conduct £6,446.12.2. Diets and wages – £18,827.19.6. Necessary purchases – £47.11.8. Necessary charges, breaking bridges, carriages, rewards – £2,008.4.3. Total – £27,330.7.7.

Total charges: temp. Henry VIII – £2,134,784.1.0¼d.; temp. Edward VI – £1,356,687.18.5⅛d.; sum total – £3,491,471.19.5⅜d.† on this sum.

*23 pp.*                                                                   SP 10/15, no. 11

**722.** [? September]. The duke of Northumberland to Sir William Cecil.

Move [the council] to answer Lord Willoughby's letter to me requesting his tarrying at Calais, or at least more respite. I am surprised that he appears to have written only to me. Let him and others know that those weighty offices are ruled by the whole board. Mention his placards granted to couriers and others contrary to the king's laws, besides his not observing commands received at his being here and since by sundry letters.

SP 10/15, no. 12

**723.** October 3. Memorandum of the king's debts.

Foreign: 15 November 1552 – £48,100, 15 February 1553 – £21,400, 20 July 1553 – £14,000, 15 August 1553 – £26,360, [*undated*] – £1,000; total – £110,760.‡ Home: known to be due before Michaelmas – £125,000. Total – £235,700.‡ For discharge. [1]. Sale of chantry lands already passed – £12,000. [2]. Bullion remaining in Flanders – £2,000. [3]. To borrow for two or three months from the merchant adventurers upon their cloths now shipped – £30,000. [4]. To call in the church plate – [*blank*]. [5]. To take the lead which is shipped before the restraint, upon reasonable prices – [*blank*]. [6]. Sale of land: to be appointed – [*blank*]. [7]. To borrow as many cloths from the clothiers as will repay the loan of the merchants' cloths, upon gage of chantry lands or such like. [8]. To understand the diminution of superfluous charges in the courts. [9]. To procure recovery of forfeitures of penal laws.

October 3. Syon. [Memoranda of a council meeting].

The lord great master [the duke of Northumberland], the lord privy seal [the earl of Bedford], [the duke of] Suffolk, the lord great chamberlain [the marquess of Northampton], the lord chamberlain [Lord Darcy], Lord Cobham, Secretary Cecil. Upon much communication Alderman [William] Garret, Emmanuel Lucar, Thomas Gresham, Richard Mallory, Lionel Duckat, Thomas Eaton, John Calthropp, Roger Martyn, Philip Bolde and John Elliott agreed to pay in Antwerp by the end of December 20s. of every cloth they had to discharge of the king's debt, requiring repayment within three months of delivery. They required the king's agent to help them forbear some part until the end of January, that they should have their pay, considering that a great part of these cloths belong to young men who owe much there. They required aid of the king and council for redress of certain disorders against the company of merchant adventurers, which they were promised on production of written certificate.

*Cecil's hand.*                                                          SP 10/15, no. 13

*        Sums barely visible under UV light.
†        Should be £3,501,471.19.5³⁄₈d.
‡        *Sic.*

**724.**   October 4. Memoranda of suits to be moved to the king.

For the lieutenancy of the Tower: Sir Edward Warner, [*blank*].* For the new fort at Berwick: chieftain – Sir Nicholas Styrley or [*blank*]; porter – Alexander Brett; marshal – [Sir John] Norton, Rookeby. For the deputyship of Calais: Lord William Howard, Sir Anthony St Leger. For the captaincy of Guînes. Causes moving the duke of Northumberland to propose the coming of Sir Andrew Dudley from Guînes: his impoverishment in service there, whereby he shall be compelled to depart or crave succour; the satisfaction of Lord Willoughby and his friends to see him return; the placing of others there who now remain discouraged or despised: Lord Grey. Some recompense of [Valentine] Browne, auditor, who served at Berwick: the next auditorship in the exchequer.

*Mostly in Cecil's hand.*                                                                    SP 10/15, no. 14

**725.**   October 7. Lambeth. The archbishop of Canterbury to the council.

I understand by your letters that the king wishes the book of common service diligently perused and the printer's errors amended. I shall do all I can. I needed first the written book passed by parliament and sealed with the great seal, which remains with [Francis] Spilman, clerk of the parliament, who is not in London, nor can I learn where he is. I have obtained the copy which he delivered to the printers to print by, which I think shall serve well enough. I understand by your letter that some are offended with kneeling at reception of the sacrament, and you would I considered with the bishop of London and other learned men as Peter Martyr [Vermigli] whether the prescription of kneeling should remain. I shall accomplish the king's command, albeit I trust that we with just balance weighed this at the making of the book – not only we, but many bishops and others best learned in the realm appointed for that purpose. Now, the book being approved by parliament, that this should be altered again, of what importance the matter is, I refer to your wisdom. I trust you will not be moved by these glorious and unquiet spirits, which can like nothing not after their own fancy, and cease not to make trouble when things are in good order. If such should be heard, although the book were made every year anew, it would not lack faults in their opinion. They say it is not commanded in scripture to kneel, and whatever is not commanded in scripture is against scripture, utterly unlawful and ungodly. This is the foundation of the error of Anabaptists and other sects, a subversion of all order in religion and common policy. If it is true, take away the whole book of service: why travail to set order in the form of service if none can be set but what is already prescribed by scripture? I will not trouble you with many scriptures or proofs: whoever teaches such doctrine, I will set my foot by his to be tried by fire, that his doctrine is untrue and seditious. Two prayers go before the receiving of the sacrament and two follow, when the people kneel. What inconvenience there is, I know not. If for the sacrament the people should stand or sit, then kneel again, it would rather be contemptuous than reverent. It is not expressly contained in the scripture (they say) that Christ ministered the sacrament to his apostles kneeling. Nor do they find he ministered it standing or sitting. If we follow the plain words of scripture we shall receive it lying on the ground, the custom then almost everywhere, as with Tartars and Turks still. The evangelists' words import the same, as where they say Christ fed five thousand – they sat on the ground, not on stools. Take in good part this long babbling, which I write of myself, because the bishop of London is not yet come, and you required answer with speed.

*Printed*: T.W. Perry, *Some historical considerations relating to the declaration on kneeling*, (1863), 77–9. P. Lorimer, *John Knox and the Church of England*, (1875), 103–5. C. Smyth, *Cranmer and the Reformation under Edward VI*, (Cambridge, 1926), 263–5 (part only).

SP 10/15, no. 15

*          Name erased, but almost visible under UV light.

**726.** October 7. Sandwich. Sir Thomas Cheyne, [lord warden of the Cinque Ports] to Sir William Cecil.

Thank you for your letter which I received yesterday coming from Dover, with others to the customers, controllers and searchers of this town and others, which I forwarded. I doubt much [that] Margrave Albrecht will hinder the emperor more than the French king. I think fair words all we shall get of the commissioners, as you write, for any restitution our merchants shall have. For my licence I have been in hand with divers, Bartholomew Compayne and Wynter being two, but can grow to no point: I do not intend to proceed further, but thank you for your help.

*Holograph.* SP 10/15, no. 16

**727.** October 7. Sir Walter Bucler and Thomas Parry to Sir William Cecil.

[Princess Elizabeth] lately requested the dean and chapter of Worcester for the reversion of ... little farm called Ankerdine, rented at ... 8d. a year, as appears by the [enclosed] letters. Although the dean and some o[f the canons] were willing to gratify her request, others were dissenting for ... [? en]mity or some other private re[ason]. Since the intent is to benefit an honest man, have the king, in consideration of her former suit, sign the letters we have prepared, or otherwise as you think best, and then send by this her servant Mr Tresham, who has told her your good will to her requests for him and others, for which she commands us to thank you. At this audit you will be satisfied from us touching your lease – before which time it could not be conveniently.
*Postscript (Parry's holograph).* I do not forget you; you will be fully satisfied at the audit.
*Mutilated.* SP 10/15, no. 17

**728.** October 8. Byland. Henry [Nevill], earl of Westmorland to Sir William Cecil.

I received your letter by my servant. You shall have the lease of Cranmore with all speed, and all evidence in my custody concerning Stowe and Deeping, court rolls, terriers and other rentals. [The duke of] Northumberland told you I would come up shortly: I cannot, for causes I have written to him. You have always showed me friendship.
SP 10/15, no. 18

**729.** October 9. Louth. Laurence Eresbye to Sir William Cecil, at court.

I received your letters by the pursuivant. I have appointed provision for your horses from my own store of beans, uncharged of last year – every man unwilling to sell his beans at this time of year. I trust to provide 20 quarters if I may get shipping for them. I trust to speak with the minister within a few days: at my coming you shall understand my travail. My own causes now require your help. My adversary Christopher Ascough, perceiving I am likely to keep the country for a fortnight, occupied keeping courts and certifying commissions awarded out of the court of augmentations, is lately come to London to solicit [the duke of] Northumberland to speak with the lord chancellor for dissolving the injunction awarded against him, as his grace promised in his late progress. If the lord chancellor might by your help stay the same until the matter were duly examined before him, I would be much bound to you, trusting at length to find good matter against Aiscough. If he should obtain his pretended suit in my absence, I shall not be able to try the matter with him in the country, where he is so well allied and I a private man. I intend with all speed to repair to London, these commissions certified, wherein I am constrained as your deputy to serve as of quorum alone, for neither the auditor nor receiver will take pains, although appointed to serve as I am, and the matters touch the king's title. I have willed this my servant to return shortly, having no other business. I promised my lady twenty sheep for your house, but it will be past All Hallowtide before they come. In the meanwhile I trust the markets will serve your purpose indifferently. If I may understand your further need on my servant's return, I shall be glad to help as much as I may.

    *Holograph.*                                                                                    SP 10/15, no. 19

**730.**   October 11. Memoranda of council business.

    To hear the commissioners of Calais, &c. To hear [Thomas] Wayneman, [Alexander] Semar [Seymour] and the witnesses: Mr Comptroller,* master of the rolls. To examine Derek [Anthony], goldsmith: Mr Gosnold,† Mr Lieutenant.    SP 10/15, no. 20

**731.**   October 12. Denton. George Williams to Sir William Cecil.

    The escheator sat [on] the 10th at Grantham on [Francis] Hall's office. Edmund Hall was there with Mr Saintpole who, although he would not give evidence openly, wrought all mischief he could secretly. I had there for you Anthony Tharrald of Gray's Inn, whom I thought meeter than [John] Hunt, who also penned the office after I had drawn it in paper. [Laurence] Meres of the same house was there and offered his counsel, but would take no fee. Edmund Hall utterly denied that John and Francis Hall died seised of the guild lands in Baston, seeming to relinquish his title of his lease, and drove us to the proof of the seisin and dying seised both of John and Francis. He never spoke of any lease, but said because Francis never took the profits he was never seised. Your counsel answered that point. But fully to persuade the jury we were driven to show his communication with you at London, and so much of your letter sent me by Mr Lasselles, [the earl of] Rutland's man, as made for your purpose:

        Williams. I have spoken with Francis Hall's brother, who claims a lease in his Baston lands, by whose confession it appears he never had written lease from his brother, but a letter from his brother signifying he made him a lease, paying £10 yearly.‡

    On hearing this the better part of the jury were persuaded that if he had been able to have denied either the seisin of John or Francis Hall, he would have uttered it to you as the claim of his lease. Yet it was 10 p.m. before they offered their verdict, and then they required a new day. The escheator, showing himself your friend, would not grant it, and they returned to counsel. After much debate they found the office in every point as we put it in, wherein neither will, lease nor annuity is found, but only a dying seised of the whole lands; much of the best is entailed to heirs male, of which no will could be made. I have sought the value of the lands. He has a great rabblement of houses in Grantham which shall need continual repair. There will be other outgoings, as bailiffs' fees, &c. I have not found them to the uttermost value, because I knew you desired to hear of our proceedings, and was in doubt when the escheator would return the office into chancery. Not having leisure to write the paper book again, being so long, I return it, word by word as the office is found, interlined yet legible. The escheator and his son would take no fee, but only to discharge him in the exchequer when time shall come, which I promised him. The other charges – a great company tarrying all night and part of the next day, engrossing the office in parchment, other petty officers' fees – are about £7. [Andrew] Nowell, sitting as a cipher, said neither good nor bad. I have set 'lyme wandes' (?) for St Leonard's. He himself, who now sojurns at Grantham, offered that if you would get him and his heirs £10 a year that a brother of Sir John Williams has at Ropsley or £10 a year anywhere else in Lincolnshire, he would surrender his lease to you. I answered I thought you would not purchase your own so dear. Say whether this half year's rent of your woods of Pickworth shall be paid at the audit at Northampton or not. At my brother Anthony's coming down shortly I shall tell you the state of Newstead; your new purchased lands, after your courts are once kept and your rents paid and conveyed, shall be surveyed. I shall bring your money for Bassingthorpe and

---

*      Sir Robert Cotton appointed August 27.
†      Now solicitor general.
‡      On a separate sheet.

Little Bytham, Trusthorpe being 10s. a year. I neither know where it lies nor remember any such land put into your particular. Gonerby, 8s. a year, was put in, but you write nothing thereof. This bearer is a tenant of Mr Hall's of Dunsthorpe, paying £10 a year; he and his ancestors have been the Halls' tenants and servants this hundred years. [He] is now threatened with immediate expulsion by Robert Hall, without warning. He would know no other wise but repair to you. Write to Robert Hall for a lawful warning. I do not mean the expulsion of this honest man, but to curry favour with that peevish body until it will be seen what would be wrought for St Leonard's for the lease; I would be glad to know what you would do if he might be compassed. [William] Rigges, I suppose, will not be at London before Christmas; if you return your particulars of Deeping, errors will be redressed.

*Holograph.* SP 10/15, no. 21

**732.** October 13. The duke of Northumberland to Sir William Cecil.

Move the council concerning [Princess] Elizabeth's writing to me for Penn: I return her letter. Touching the office of West Tilbury, I suppose the king will give no more such. Advise my answers. Falling down of the uvula has troubled me since the king's coming to Hampton Court, and I must seek remedy. I am told it is good to keep the house warm.

*Holograph.* SP 10/15, no. 22

**733.** October 14. Stamford. The alderman and burgesses of Stamford to Sir William Cecil.

John Alen, William Capanet and others seem to have had all the order of the spoil of churches lately united within the borough and the receipt and distributing of the money. It seems they employed a very small part of the uses they ought to have done according to the act,* causing much slander and unquietness among the inhabitants, and us to be judged ill-doers. We have no hope of amendment save you and a commission to redress the premises, and that the alderman and others be commissioners. Upon certificate shall appear indiscreet handling by the said persons, who have been authorities of themselves in defacing and selling all the spoils, without making privy the alderman or commissioners appointed by the act. They can show no authority for their doings, which have been to their own advantage, not to the commonwealth, which we all desire for the town.

*Signed by*: Geoffrey Vellars, Henry Lacy, Thomas Wateson, Robert Voynwyke, Henry Ley, William Myls, Ralph Harrope, John Oldnall and Henry Tamppyon.

SP 10/15, no. 23

**734.** October 15. St James's. The duke of Northumberland to Sir William Cecil.

Write what answer I may make to [Princess] Elizabeth's letter. Move [the council] for [Sir Richard] Morison's request for his half year's diet aforehand. Troubled with falling of the uvula I am forced to keep to my chamber; it is a fortnight since it began, and [it] worsens, that I can scarcely eat. SP 10/15, no. 24

**735.** October 16. Ashridge. Thomas Parry to William Cecil.

Accept Mr Digbie's summons and the rest of the matter in good part, for Mr Benger was not privy of your grant until now. The rent and all may be paid here by your deputy in your name whenever you appoint. For your final satisfaction send [Roger] Alford or some other sufficiently instructed. We shall then confer your book and ours, that all may be answered to [Princess Elizabeth] as it is and has been; thereupon you to have your book to pass accordingly. *Postscript (holograph).* If I could have perfected your suit you

---

* 2 & 3 Edward VI, original act no. 50 (*SR*, iv, I, p. ix).

should have had it passed and sealed before this, but now [it] shall not be longer delayed.

SP 10/15, no. 25

**736.** October [18]. The duke of Northumberland to Sir William Cecil.

Let this bearer declare his meaning, touched partly in the enclosed letter [*which follows*], if you and my other lords think it to any purpose. I think it rather a fantasy. The king has seen it and would have this man communed with.

SP 10/15, no. 26

**737.** October [18]. [Enclosed with the above]. Henry Cornyshe to the duke of Northumberland.

The daily robberies and enormities of the French reminded me of a Norman gentleman of a great house, active and witty, who through my practice, was privily brought to the late duke of Somerset and then sworn to the king. He received of the duke 200 crowns and was promised a yearly stipend to confer with me from time to time. Having perfect knowledge of the strength, entries and order of Cherbourg, he promised to deliver me the town and castle, so that I would land him 500 men suddenly at place and time appointed. Cherbourg is very strong, a key to Normandy and frontier to the coast of England. The stay of this enterprise I pass over, only minding according [to] my duty to declare this privy conference, should you with the rest of the privy council think good to entertain any such thing, or that I should renew my acquaintance with this gentleman.

*Holograph.*                                                                        SP 10/15, no. 26(i)

**738.** October 20. Memoranda of council business.

Lord William [Howard]: deputy of Calais. Sir Andrew Dudley to be called home. Lord Grey: captain of Guînes. The merchant adventurers' suits. General levy of cloths at Antwerp. Merchants of the staple. Pirates at Rye and Dover. The prest to Lord Grey and Sir Anthony Aucher to be repaid to [Sir Edmund] Peckham. Discharge of blockhouses in Kent, &c. Commissioners for seizure of church goods. Brief of the dispute at Windsor for the king. Derek [Anthony's] bills. Tower. [John] Knox. Archbishop of Canterbury. The book of the bishop of Durham. Mr Petre's letter. [Thomas] Carter of the spicery. Lȳ. Chancellor of the duchy [of Lancaster]. Commission of sewers. Commendations. Judgements given by due process in law, as showed and proved by the commissioners. Yet the French king rememb[ering] the great friendship would in some part gratify the king with [Sir Henry] Syd[ney's] and Mr Wynter's ships, and the order taken for the cost.

*In the hands of Cecil and (?) Sir Thomas Chaloner.*

*Printed*: Jordan, ii, 450 n. 2.                                                   SP 10/15, no. 27

**739.** [October 20]. The forty-five articles of religion.

*12 pp.*

*Signed by*: John Harley, William Bill, Robert Horne, Andrew Perne, Edmund Grindal and John Knox [chaplains to the king].

*Printed*: C. Hardwick, *A History of the Articles of Religion*, (3rd edn., 1876), 278–349: complete text with concordance with subsequent sets of the thirty-nine articles.

SP 10/15, no. 28

**740.** October 23. Higham Park. Sir Robert Tyrwhitt to Sir William Cecil.

Accept two acres of wood I had by virtue of my lease at Wimbledon, as I am not now resident there. Mr Garlond, woodward, will deliver it.

*? Holograph.*                                                                     SP 10/15, no. 29

**741.** October 23. Burghley. George Williams to Sir William Cecil.

I received your letter by Horner and wrote to the escheator for speedy return of the office – who, I suppose, has now returned it. With search in the chancery among the clerks of the petty bag the truth may be known, who need also to have request of speedy return into the court of wards. By the death of John Hall, dwelling besides Grantham, uncle to Francis [Hall], deceased, 20 nobles' land is descended to Arthur Hall your ward. Your rents of Casterton &c. are paid at the audit; those of your woods there are unpaid, for I knew not your pleasure sooner. I have sent £66.15.1, as much as I could get of your bailiffs, by Francis Harmstrong, including your wood money, besides R. Tailore's rent of £12.13.5. The residue shall be conveyed upon receipt. Bernard Martyn, whose charge this half year would near amount to 20 marks, has bestowed it on a house by the water where he now dwells, thinking to make you pay for his pleasure. I required Mr Dudley to be at Stamford today with the rents in his collection, but he comes not. If he brings it to London he ought to pay you this Michaelmas in claiming for the whole year £16.18.10, besides £3.10.0 for strays left unclaimed for a year at Thorpe Achurch. Robert Hall this morning made title to Horner's farm from his brother Francis, which, as you shall perceive, is of no effect. He repairs to London immediately; if you mean to benefit him place him in the farm of John Hall, late departed, now without tenant. He will offer his lease of St Leonard's; if you find him reasonable, conclude, for he is fickle. Now Mr Dudley has sent £12 of his rent, part of the £66.15.1 I delivered to Harmstrong.

*Holograph.* SP 10/15, no. 30

**742.** October 25. Launde. Elizabeth, Lady Cromwell to Sir William Cecil.

I dare not think any unkindness that you and your wife did not, according to your promise, see the poor house of Launde. When you come into these parts again you shall be most welcome. The king and council willed me to take into my tuition my four nieces; I thought it my duty, being advised by your letters to satisfy the council's requests – although had I declared what charges and other cares I have, I doubt not they would have accepted my refusal. The burden of bestowing my own children and such family as my husband left unprovided for forces me to require that about Christmas next, by your means, the council may understand that when my nieces have accomplished a year with me they shall be elsewhere provided for. As I told the council I was a lone woman, not near my kin, destitute of friendly advice, now I declare so to you, having not been instructed how to use my nieces. I have in some cases thought they should not wholly be their own guides, willing them to follow my advice – which they have not taken in good part, nor according to my expectation in them.

*Printed*: Green, 260–2. SP 10/15, no. 31

**743.** October 26. Gedney. Adlard Welby to Sir William Cecil.

I have seen £10 bestowed for the king's charges on 'Gouxland' bank, much impaired by drift of cattle before I could get the bars set up. I must watch till passengers know they cannot pass that way; so I would do at Boston dyke unless you wish otherwise. Much cost is done on the sewers in Pinchbeck and Spalding – less than ought to have been, yet more than would have been without the pains of [John] Burton, whom you may further credit in these matters. There lacks a general commission of sewers in Holland, to the great hurt of the king's possessions there. I enclose a copy of the king's lease [*which follows*]; if it is not sufficient, move the chancellor of the duchy [of Lancaster].

SP 10/15, no. 32

**744.** 1549. June 1. [Enclosed with the above]. Indenture of lease from the king to Adlard Welby of 12 acres and 1 rod of pasture (8s.), 12 acres and 3 rods and a third (13s. 4d.), 12 acres 14 parcels, Hall Rigges (13s. 4d.), 17 acres 1 rod 30 parcels (15s. 8d.), 12 acres 1 rod, Hall spring (12s.), 7 acres 30 parcels (8s.), 8 acres, Hall meadow (16s.), all then or lately in his tenure in [Long] Sutton, Holland, Lincolnshire, part of the duchy of Lancaster; from Michaelmas following for twenty-one years, paying £4.16.4 a year at Easter and Michaelmas in equal portions; the farmer to do all ditching and fencing; the crown to repossess if rent in arrears by forty days.

*Latin.*

*Copy; original under seal of the duchy of Lancaster.*                    SP 10/15, no. 32(i)

**745.**   October 27. Pinchbeck. Richard Ogle to Sir William Cecil.

By force of the commission of sewers wherein you took pain such dyking has been done in the country as shall be to its universal wealth; yet some part is to be done, which I trust shall be by the pains that my friend John Burton has taken and will take, for which he has sustained displeasure, but never ceased to see things done according to the decrees. Mr Welly [Welby] and I have sent a feigned licence to the council which we took from players – a thing much to be looked to and the offenders worth punishment. This bearer shall deliver the letter and the box, or else to be ordered as you wish. A general commission of sewers, as was sued, is very requisite for the safeguard of the whole country. I have the commission and the books that you sat upon in my hands; Burton shall show you the laws devised by us upon your remembrances, referring their reform to your discretion. Credit this bearer.

*Holograph.*

*Endorsed*: In haste.                                                     SP 10/15, no. 33

**746.**   October 27, morning. St James's. The duke of Northumberland to Sir William Cecil.

[William] Hawkyns about Easter last promised to put up a bill to the king and would have spoken with him alone; he was also once before the council for a matter at Fleet bridge. He then kept a school about St Bartholomew's. He has now confessed to Sir Arthur Darcy casting abroad and setting up seditious bills done by himself and counterfeiting the archbishop of Canterbury's hand, with intent to have stirred commotion and rebellion. He says there was one a-council with him, whose name he will by no means utter to Darcy. Some discreet persons should be forthwith appointed to examine him and by fair means or foul cause him to disclose his counsellors or comforters. This to be in the meantime kept very secret. *Postscript (holograph).* He was committed at Greenwich first to the Porter's Lodge, thence to the Tower, and has been sundry times examined by [Sir Philip] Hoby and Mr Darcy, and never would confess till yesterday. He feigned himself to be a frantic, but is now come to his right wits, as Darcy says.                                                                  SP 10/15, no. 34

**747.**   October 28. The duke of Northumberland to Sir William Cecil.

I would the king might appoint [John] Knox to the bishopric of Rochester; he would be a whetstone to sharpen the archbishop of Canterbury and confound the Anabaptists lately sprung up in Kent; he would not continue the ministration in the north, contrary to this set forth here; the Scots inhabiting Newcastle for his fellowship would not continue there. Ask the lord chamberlain or vice-chamberlain to help, for God's service and the king's. If the dean of Durham is appointed bishop with 1,000 marks more than his deanery, the houses he now has in the city and country will serve honourably – so may the king receive the castle, which has a princely site, and the other stately houses the bishop had in the country. The chancellor's living to be converted to the deanery and an honest man placed in it; the vice-chancellor to be turned into the chancellor; the suffragan,* who is placed without the king's authority, and has a great living, may be removed, being neither preacher, learned, nor honest, so pernicious that the country

---

\*        Thomas Sparke, suffragan bishop of Berwick.

abhors him. The living, with a little more to its value – 100 marks – will serve the erection of a bishop of Newcastle. Thus the king may place godly ministers in these offices and receive £2,000 a year of the best lands in the north; it will be 4,000 marks a year of as good revenue as any in the realm. Order should be taken for [Thomas] Gower. Then must the treasurer* be proceeded into for abusing his office, to the king's great detriment. Scribbled in bed, as ill as I have ever been.

*Holograph.*
*Printed*: Tytler, ii, 142–3.                                                   SP 10/15, no. 35

**748.**   October 30. St James's. The duke of Northumberland to Sir William Cecil.

[Sir John] York declares to have trussed 60 lb. of groats and 200 lb. of bullion for Ireland for furniture of [Martin] Pery's wife's licence, wherein he thought no offence, seeing the groats are not current. He has forthwith sent to return the whole, which I think good. I would have declared this had you come to dinner. I would beseech the king's licence to appoint some honest learned man to a benefice which [John] Harley had of my preferment when he was with me. [*Marginal note by Cecil*: Kidderminster]. My kinsman [Arthur], Lord Dudley's younger brother, a priest, has only the precentorship of Lichfield; if the king gives him a prebend in Worcester which he gave Harley at my suit, he shall gain a true subject. The ground belonging to Strouthar, of which you have the plan, would be the key of defence to all Glendale and most of the east marches. The king may have the inheritance, £10 a year, and a wood three quarters of a mile long, for a parsonage worth £15 or £16 yearly – no evil bargain, wherein the poor gentleman, here these three weeks, would be answered. The chancellor of Durham is not chancellor of the church, only the bishop's chancellor; he has no promotion belonging to that office of certainty. There is no other chancellor or vice-chancellor for the house was newly erected from a monastery. The living of the suffragan is not above 200 marks a year; the better part is the hospital† which the bishop gave him, not admitted or confirmed by the king. So my reckoning for elevating the king's charges will not hold; some other device must be had. Lord Wharton declares that Litster, a merchant tailor dwelling near the Pavement, York, uses a very lewd book of prophecy and expounds it to many people. Wharton thinks if he were suddenly taken and his house searched, many matters would appear. Move my lords to know their pleasure.

*Holograph.*                                                                     SP 10/15, no. 36

**749.**   October. The duke of Northumberland to Sir William Cecil.

The restraint lately taken for stay of lead throughout the realm should be substantially considered; the clamour grows great and may breed more damage than can now be seen. I have since being in the council chamber heard of that matter which makes me sorry I was ever a meddler in it. Princes' affairs, especially touching government and trade, are of two natures: though they are full of devices with appearance of profit, they must be weighed with other consequences, as in this case, for such reasons as were rehearsed today.

*Holograph.*                                                                     SP 10/15, no. 37

**750.**   October. The duke of Northumberland to Sir William Cecil.

The French ambassador's secretary was with me from his master this morning, seeming to excuse the lack of imparting to the rest of [the council] what he told the king from his king. He said nothing declared friendship more than the princely handling of [Thomas] Stukley's false reports, but as his master knew not how many of the privy council were privy to it, he forbore to open at the board what he told the king. Nevertheless he had

*        Of Berwick.
†        Greatham.

commission to tell me and others of the privy council that this kind of princely dealing should never be forgotten by his king, and to desire me and others named to help maintain amity between our master and his. He desired the immediate punishment of such a false man. This was uttered with plenty of good words, renewing his request that I and so many of my lords as wished would dine with him; I answered that I was so ill that I could not promise to come. Show this to the king at your leisure.

*Holograph.*    SP 10/15, no. 38

**751.**    October. The duke of Northumberland to Sir William Cecil.

I send a priest who would declare slanderous words spoken by [Edmund] Foorde against me and my brother, as appears by his enclosed bill. Because the matter touches none other of the council I have refused to hear it, referring it to the rest of my lords. Foorde was once punished in the Porter's Lodge for similar matter: I was then content to remit his offence towards me. He is not a little favoured with some folks. Let the matter be used indifferently.

*Holograph.*
*Endorsed*: With speed.    SP 10/15, no. 39

**752.**    [? October]. Memoranda of council business.

[George] Paris's return to England. Declaration of the state of the king's ships. Stay of cloths in all other hanses besides London. Proceedings with French pirates and Flemings at Rye. Advancement of a prest to Lord Grey. To treat with the merchants of the staple for a loan of money due to them in Flanders. Fentzler's suit for 4,000 raw cloths to be exported. To understand the king's pleasure for placing the deputy at Calais. Captain at Guînes. Letter to Lord Wharton. Seal of the princip[ality] of Durham for Paris. Sir Henry Daly. The treaty.

*Cecil's hand.*    SP 10/15, no. 40

**753.**    [? October]. Brief of all the king's debts.

External. To the Shetz – £10,700; to Lazarus Tucker – £10,700; to the Fuggers – £26,700; total – £48,100, payable 15 November 1552. To the Fuggers – £20,000; interest – £1,400; total – £21,400, payable 15 February 1553.* To the Shetz and [Conrad] Rentleger – £14,000, payable 20 July 1553. To the Fuggers – £24,000; interest – £2,360; total – £27,352.13.4 [*sic*], payable 15 August 1553. To the Shetz for the diamond – £1,000. To Francis van Hall – £17,426.13.4, payable 31 August 1553. To Sir John Rantzow – £3,093.3.4, payable 1 September 1553. Total – £132,372.10.0. Internal. To: the household – £28,000; the chamber – £20,000; the wardrobe – £6,075.18.6; the stable – £1,000; the admiralty – £5,000; the ordnance – £1,134.7.10; the surveyor of the works – £3,200; Calais – £15,000; Berwick – £6,000; the revels – £1,000; Scilly and Alderney – £1,000; Ireland – £13,128.6.8; Wynter for his voyage to Ireland – £471.4.6; Bar[tholomew] Compagni – £3,000; Portsmouth and the Isle of Wight – £1,000; men of arms – £800; lieutenant of the Tower – £1,017.2.4; total – £108,826.19.10. Sum total – £219,686.19.10.

*With a further page of calculations.*    SP 10/15, no. 41

**754.**    [? October]. Note to the king's debts with some means towards their discharge.

Total debts: external – £111,000; internal – £109,000; sum £220,000. For discharge. Thomas Gresham shall have December 1 £1,200 a week out of the sales – £12,000. Of [William] Dansell for bullion sold [at Antwerp] – £2,000. The sale of £1,000 chantry and £1,000 other lands, gathered by February 1, will discharge £40,000 borrowed from the merchants. £5,000 to be borrowed of the staplers and paid in Antwerp, which may be repaid with the sale of £500 land left of the bishop of Worcester. Of [John] Beaumont,

*    As such in the MS.

besides £9,000 to be stalled in ready money or his land to be sold – £12,000. Of Sir Thomas Arundel's lands to be sold – £4,000. Coinage of church plate – £20,000. Lord Paget's fine or sale of land for his fine – [*blank*]. Of the king's debts due to him – [*blank*].
  *Cecil's hand.*                     SP 10/15, no. 42

**755.** November 4. Pinchbeck. Richard Ogle to Sir William Cecil.
 This poor gentleman William Myddleton, who purchased land of the lord admiral in Swaton, Kesteven, Lincolnshire, at great cost, now in his age is likely to be troubled by Horseley, bailiff of the town, who has, he says, obtained a lease of ground called Cotes, part of William's farm, and would have of him 100 marks or else his hasty removal, and has discharged another poor man, Haryman, of the said town, who has a copy of his farm, on which he and his father have bestowed £20 for repairs; unless he will give Horseley 20 marks he will put him from his farm. I am sorry, being steward there, to see such extremity used to the poor, and cannot help. I cannot see so ready a help for them as to sue to you, the king's high officer in the country. If Horseley continues as he begins, he shall undo many poor men and occasion the decay of the town, as this bearer, your old servant William Hykson, can tell. Thanking you for your words to Mr Laselles, the earl of Rutland's servant, at his bringing letters to the king's council for [Thomas] Thurland, late prisoner at Grantham.      SP 10/15, no. 43

**756.** November 8. Sheen. The duke of Suffolk to Sir William Cecil.
 My servant John Walgrave, this bearer, desires to pass to Flanders in trust of some inheritance; be a means that he, his man and two horses may pass over.
 *Holograph.*                     SP 10/15, no. 44

**757.** November 9. Bisham. Sir Philip Hoby to Sir William Cecil.
 I am sorry to hear of your headache and other pains. Lady Anne of Cleves and her council misliked the books drawn up and passed for recompense of this lordship of Bisham which, as you know, the king has granted me in fee farm. According to your advice the surveyor of Berkshire valued my house today. Procure signature of those books, upon cancelling of those already signed, that that may be ended which has been almost twelve months a-doing.
 *? Holograph.*                  SP 10/15, no. 45

**758.** November 9. Wilton. The earl of Pembroke to Sir William Cecil.
 Thank you for your news. My servant, this bringer, meaning to sue all my lords, has sought my letters on his behalf; help him for my sake.    SP 10/15, no. 46

**759.** November 13. Wilton. The earl of Pembroke to Sir John Mason and Sir William Cecil.
 My friend and neighbour [Sir William] Kaylewey, having long served the king, from home as in his country, much to his charge, means now to sue you and [the council] for release from the commission of the peace and other charges to which he is daily called within the shire. He has had to sell plate and land. Knowing him to be an upright minister of justice and a great stay for the order and quiet of his country, I think some recompense for his service should be considered. It will be hard to have his like again.
 *? Holograph.*                  SP 10/15, no. 47

**760.** November 14. Denton. George Williams to Sir William Cecil.
 At the king's audit at Newark I received your letter of October 27, writing forthwith to your father for advice in appointing lands for Manthorpe. He dislikes your choice of the friars' or Sempringham lands, Henry Lee having so long a lease therein, but rather

wishes some lands about Barholm and Deeping. I have sent you a particular of lands there not much above the value of Manthorpe, mixed with your other lands there, and in my fancy very necessary for you. There is no other good choice but Tallington, part of Bourne Abbey, worth yearly £11.16.0, or farms in East and West Deeping, part of Haltemprice Abbey, £6.5.0 a year. I have written to [Henry] Lacy about your lease of East and West Deeping, and on going to Stamford shall pay him his fee and make allowance to myself according to your command. I shall shortly make a book of discharge of all sums I have received for you and return the residue, less than 20 marks, by your father. Say what shall be done with Mr Hall's rents.

*Holograph.* SP 10/15, no. 48

**761.** November 16. Rowner. Sir John Brune, from his house there, to Sir William Cecil.

I cannot find my pedigree and so am unable to accomplish your request. I have sent you a book containing much of the conveyance concerning my inheritance and a pedigree of my late ancestors with the entail concerning a title of lands for which I now sue, and the 'dosters' of Harry Brune mentioned in the pedigree had the same lands, being entailed to the heirs male of the Brunes. See the book and return it to this bearer.

*Holograph.* SP 10/15, no. 49

**762.** November [17].* The Duke of Northumberland to Sir William Cecil.

Among those appointed to be pilloried tomorrow I understand John Borroghe was brought to Windsor for telling news of me concerning certain of the king's coffers. As I understand he is of a good house and not so much in default as others, perhaps sufficiently punished by long imprisonment, be a means to the rest of [the council] to spare him the pillory and other public punishments. I trust he will amend. His brother is of the best sort for favouring the king's godly proceedings and has no heir but this young man.

*Holograph.* SP 10/15, no. 50

**763.** November [24]. Memoranda of council business.

To govern in Ireland: [duke of] Suffolk, [earl of] Shrewsbury, earl of Huntingdon, lord admiral, Lord Cobham, Lord [*blank*], Lord Strange, Lord FitzWarine, Lord Garrett [FitzGerald]. Ambassadors with the emperor – for the Low Country: [Richard] Shelley; for the emperor: Sir Philip Hoby, Sir John Mason, Sir Anthony St Leger. Captaincy of Berwick: Sir Gervase Clifton, Sir Robert Tyrwhitt. Roocksbye's placing as marshal there. To send for [the duke of] Suffolk, Lords Shrewsbury and Huntingdon and place them in the commissions. To move the king that the new hospital in London may have of his gift the linen of the churches in London. To consider the matter disclosed to [Thomas] Gresham by Treasurer Longne.† The letter from the Scots queen touching [George] Paris. [Dr Richard] Smythe's letter concerning the same. [Sir Thomas] Chamberleyn's letter and communication with [*illegible*]. That thanks may be given. That fencers practise. Intelligence of Scotland: may be advertised by Gresham. To move the king for his pleasure touching Hussy. Lord Grey's letters.

*Cecil's hand.*

*On the dorse* : draft in another hand of the opening of a letter in French.

SP 10/15, no. 51

**764.** November 27. The mayor and burgesses of Boston to Sir William Cecil.

Thank you for assisting our rightful matter to the king for redress of pulling down,

---

\* On November 13 John Burgh and others were ordered to be pilloried at Westminster on the following Friday (November 18) (*APC*, iv, 168).

† Laurens Longin, treasurer to the regent in Flanders. See Jordan, ii, 171.

selling and carrying away fair buildings and houses here. On the 24th the letter from the king's council to John Browne was delivered; after he had read it he showed a very light countenance and said he would answer it, and that our doings would be the occasion to show more extremity against us than he before thought to have done, threatening divers of us, especially the suitor thereof, with the king's laws in the exchequer, who trust to be able to defend themselves. Browne first sold a fair mansion in which before divers honest and substantial persons dwelt, at a place called the 'quoye pytt', which is carried away and its place made a yard for hogs. Browne sold another fair house, St Peter's Hall, the slate of which is carried away with part of the timber. Had the council's letter not come to us when it did there would have been little timber or brick remaining within four days. Browne is bound for £30 to one Turpyn to take it down and carry it away peaceably. Browne sold another fair house, St George's Hall, in which dwells an honest artificer, and has made a like clause of warranty to pull it down: for that intent it was bought. The courage of his evil doings has caused others to do the same; even while suit was made for redress a very fine house near the market place was taken down and carried away. If he has any comfort in his suit it is thought there will be few houses standing in the market place or elsewhere that may be sold. Also on the 24th a letter was delivered to Robert Turpyn and Nicholas Bowmer. Turpyn was asked why he took down so fair a house to deface the town; he answered that he would build it again in the town. It was answered that he has taken down a fair house in the town to build a cottage in the field, for how might he so do when he had sold two parts thereof. Would God the king's council would cause him to rebuild it where it stood, to the example of others. He is able enough, although he came simply up to London. Nicholas Bowmer first bought a fair house at St John's bridge, Boston, which he has taken down and sold, defacing that part of the town. He found such sweetness in it that since he has entered further, as in St George's Hall, which he bought and sold to Bartholomew Grantham for profit. He was of council with Robert Turpyn in buying St Peter's Hall, and so became partner in it. He is not only a broker, but a merchant in these matters. Had he not known the profits, no such things would have been practised. On the 25th a letter was delivered to John Mollett, partner at the first house Browne sold at the 'quoye pytt'. Thomas Dytton, another of the partners, is [away] from home, as is Bartholomew Grantham. If these have no comforts in their doings we trust that Grantham nor any other will be hasty to follow. As our special and only friend we beseech your aid.

SP 10/15, no. 52

**765.** November 27. Offenham. Sir Philip Hoby to Sir William Cecil.

I am grateful, as always, for your help in procuring the king's signature for my bill of Bisham.

SP 10/15, no. 53

**766.** November 27. London. John Heron, head master of the King's School, Rochester to Sir William Cecil.

For about sixteen years I have been the poor instructor of poor boys in grammar. Not long ago, while teaching at the King's School, Rochester, I became known to the then bishop, now bishop of London, Dr Nicholas Ridley. Through the offices of Sir John Cheke he obtained for me a canonry in Rochester Cathedral then vacant by the death of William Harrison – which, however, slipped from me by some inexplicable misfortune. Being thus frustrated I reflected on fate. John Wildbore, another canon, died. I approached Cheke for his aid, but he was unwilling to act without knowing your pleasure. I saw myself bereft of the help for which I hoped, but did not despair or attempt to crave your aid. I only wished the duke of Northumberland to know I had not received Wildbore's canonry, which he had promised to obtain for me. Which done, I shall quietly return to teaching. Meanwhile the duke has recalled me here – I know not why, unless to patronise a wretched nobody. If you can speak three words to him on my behalf, I, my wife and ten children will always pray for you. I have written the more boldly because your servant [George] Burden, now a canon of Rochester, remembered me kindly.

*Latin.*

*Holograph.*

*Printed*: J.R. Bloxam (ed.), *A register of ... Magdalen College ... Oxford*, (1853–85), iii, 95–6.                                                                          SP 10/15, no. 54

**767.** November 29. The council to the bishop of Bath and Wells, Sir John St Loo, Sir Ralph Hopton and Alexander Popham.

This bearer [Valérand Poulain], superintendent of the strangers at Glastonbury, has requested the removal of deer from Wirrall park, appointed to them. Henry Cornisshe, keeper of the house there during the king's pleasure, pretends some right to keeping the park also, affirming he has nothing else to live on. He nevertheless has offered before those of us to whom the matter was committed to provide before Lady Day for each of the thirty-six* strangers' households enough ground to keep two kine all year, at no higher rate than other inhabitants yield. Order for removing the deer is deferred until he performs his promise. In assigning the land both parties have agreed to stand by your judgement, provided that the strangers have pasturage of the park as heretofore, until otherwise provided for. Because the king's audit is there now, he wishes you to have the dye houses, buying of wool and other furniture for the strangers' work viewed by his officers, to see how the great sums distributed have been employed, and how they proceed to satisfy him again. Order anything further needed, seeing the king no more charged than necessary. As some of the strangers remain without houses, [we have written to]† let Sir Ralph Hopton, [surveyor of that shire]† appoint them houses falling void in the town until all forty-six* households are provided for, if of weavers, dyers, spinners, kivers [bleachers], &c. It is not meant that all strangers of whatever science should be provided for.

*Draft.*

*A contemporary endorsement gives the erroneous date 1553.*                        SP 10/15, no. 55

**768.** November 30. Stamford. John Fenton, alderman, and the burgesses of Stamford to Sir William Cecil.

We perceive by your letters you are informed of cutting down of your willows and meddling in the stream between the Blackfriars wall downwards. By command of your father and other commissioners of sewers Andrew Skarre, late alderman, commanded divers inhabitants of the town to scour and reed the Welland stream, but none of them meddled in any of your possessions from Blackfriars wall down to St Leonard's, nor from thence to a place beneath St Thomas wells, Eastward well, nor at Newstead, where divers willows extended to the water; one grew on the ground of St Leonard's, which among others was scythed inadvisedly and sold for 3s. 4d., bestowed on the labourers by Andrew. Your father, being at Walcot with Mr Browne, was informed of wrongs to your tenants; in the afternoon he came to Stamford and, taking divers with him, walked to St Leonard's. There was nothing down from Blackfriars wall till he came to the place mentioned, where he saw the tree and others cumbering the stream. He affirmed that the tree and many others must be cut down or the stream could not be cleansed, as he will report on coming to London. Andrew Skarre will recompense the value of that one tree. Do not be offended at this offence, done against our will and consent.

*Signed by*: Richard Cecil.

\*        *Sic.*

†        Deleted.

**769.** November. The duke of Northumberland to Sir William Cecil.

The auditor of the late bishop of Durham's possessions and revenues must be sent for, or it is impossible to have any perfect knowledge for proceeding with the new elected bishop,* without great prejudice to the king. As the king must commit all to the new bishop's hands in full possession, or his majesty can have no surrender, there should be no delay, but to proceed to his highness's election and all things pertaining; by that time, if the auditor is sent for by post, he may be here with his perfect book of all the revenues, out of which the lands and royalties most meet to be reserved to his highness may be appointed. The late chancellor† or [Robert] Horne can tell [the auditor's] name and dwelling. SP 10/15, no. 57

**770.** [November]. Submission by Lord Paget.

Being taxed to pay the king a fine of £8,000, the king has remitted the moiety, requiring of me £200 lands. I am most grateful to him and am willing to deliver the following lands. *Middlesex*. Harmondsworth manor; annual assize rent – £101.0.11; court perquisites – £4.13.4 *communibus annis*; wood sales – £5 *communibus annis*; total – £110.14.3; deducted for tenths paid to the king – £9.10.10½d.; rent of Hatton stayed by Lord Windsor – 9s.; total – £9.19.10½d.; clear – £100.13.4½d. Tenements in the parish of St Clement without bars: in tenure of Ralph Jackson and Eustace Ripeley, by indenture – £16.6.8; in tenure of William Neale – £1.6.8; total – £17.13.4. *Leicestershire*. Appleby [Magna] manor: annual assize rent – £17.0.4; court perquisites – 13s. 4d. *communibus annis*. *Warwickshire*. Alcester manor: annual assize rent – £52.10.4½d.; court perquisites – £1.6.8 *communibus annis*. *Derbyshire*. Ilam manor: annual assize rent – £11.4.10. Sum – £83.5.6½d. Deducted for a perpetual pension from Alcester – £1. Rents clear – £82.5.6½d. Total clear – £200.12.3.

Nevertheless, as the king created me a baron, and without land neither I nor my heirs shall be able to live as that place requires, I beseech him that the land might remain with me, and that in lieu he might take £4,000, £1,000 at Christmas and £1,000 in the following years; or £100 lands, with £1,000 at Christmas and another £1,000 a year later. Beseeching to be admitted to the king's presence and kiss his feet.

*Printed*: B.L. Beer and S.M. Jack (ed.), 'The Letters of William, Lord Paget of Beaudesert, 1547–63', *Camden Miscellany vol. XXV*, (Camden Society, 4th ser., xiii, 1974), 103–5. SP 10/15, no. 58

**771.** November. Memoranda of causes to be moved to the king.

1. Order for meeting the great inconveniences coming by coinage of base money in Ireland. To stay further coinage and defrayances presently and to make new irons with the print of the harp on one side. 2. Declaration of the earl of Arundel's cause, with the king's pleasure to be known: lord treasurer, lord privy seal, lord chamberlain, Mr Petre to go to him next Saturday afternoon. 3. Declaration of Lord Paget's answer and submission with the king's answer to be know determinately. He has but £900 in possessions, of which £200 to his younger sons. In pension £80. [To go: lord chamberlain, Lord Clinton].‡ 4. Declaration of the alteration of the commissions on the northern frontiers: a commission of oyer and terminer to the justices in Northumberland and Cumberland; a commission for march treasons to Lord Wharton and the three deputy wardens or two of them; Lord Eure to have charge in the middle marches; Thomas Graye of Chillingham in the east marches. 5. The suit of certain men for digging treasure in Buckinghamshire, Middlesex, Hertfordshire and Hampshire.

---

\*    To be Nicholas Ridley.
†    Dr Robert Hindmers.
‡    Deleted.

*Cecil's hand.*                                                    SP 10/15, no. 59

**772.**   December 2. Chelsea. The duke of Northumberland to Sir William Cecil.

At your being with me on Thursday I forgot to deliver you these writings enclosed, and to desire you to procure their signature. They are already granted by the king, I doubt not, but are in the lord chamberlain's remembrance. One is for the prebend of Worcester which [John] Harley had of the king's gift, for my cousin Arthur Dudley of Lichfield. The other is for the presentation of Kidderminster which he had of my preferment, now for Mr Kreek. The third is for [Francis] Somerset's pardon for theft, trusting he may be reconciled to a better life. By the king's pleasure I would set him forward to seek some adventure, for I suppose he is half ashamed yet to come to his friends' sight; or else I will keep him till any shall be sent to Ireland. He is hardy, somewhat too hardy. But being of so good a house it were a pity but he should be reprieved.

*Holograph.*                                                       SP 10/15, no. 60

**773.**   December 3. The duke of Northumberland to Sir William Cecil.

I received your letter by this bearer, perceiving the staplers have murmured against this licence upon private respect, although they will seem to have so done upon just ground of hurt to the commonwealth. Seeing that to be proved before you and confessed by themselves, I would be loath to use such scruple as hereafter might prejudice [the king's] like grant and licence, which is a piece of his royal prerogative and must be always defended against such crafty policies. In the meantime, so much to hinder myself as to leave such a benefit of his majesty's gift, whereupon rises a greater profit than grows otherwise by his customs, and hurt to nobody, it should not become me to refuse it now it is tried. But upon the rumour I heard I was sorry I had ever caused it to be moved. I had rather beg my bread than procure any hurt to the commonwealth. I am very sorry for my cousin Nevyl's mishap and marvel he should so much forget himself; but the way you write that the lord chancellor and other lords have taken for its correction is good. As for my presence in affairs there, my health daily worsens; neither close keeping, warm furs nor clothes can bring any natural heat to my head, and I have no hope of recovery.

*Holograph.*                                                       SP 10/15, no. 61

**774.**   December 3. The duke of Northumberland to Sir William Cecil.

The chancellor of Durham, with the auditor of the revenues of the bishopric, is ready to present a perfect value of the revenues, which should be well to receive, and to proceed with the placing of a bishop in Durham without lengthy delay, else the country will grow more and more to barbarousness. This peevish dean* should not receive what is meet for as grave a man as may be found. I am credibly informed he is loose of tongue, and lets not to talk on his ale bench that if he may not have it after his own will he will refuse it. If all is true that is reported of his conceit, condemning every man's doings and conscience but his own, I am sorry, for I have otherwise taken him, and so reported him as you can witness. But I will see better proof in them all before I judge.

*Holograph.*                                                       SP 10/15, no. 62

**775.**   December. The duke of Northumberland to Sir William Cecil.

The matter of which we talked this morning being so important, I thought good to remind you to call on [the council] concerning the election of two apt persons for the purposes you know of, on [Hans] Bruno's advice. This is not to be delayed if honour or keeping friends is to be esteemed. I received a letter from [Sir Richard] Morison: if

*          Robert Horne.

you think it worthy let the king see it. I marvel that the establishing of these vacant sees is so prolonged. Poor [John] Harley, called before all my lords, cannot yet receive despatch. Nothing increases worse opinions more than keeping such places unfurnished. *Postscript.* By a letter from [Thomas] Gresham I perceive that one of the Scots appointed to go to Spain is arrived here for the king's safe conduct; his request should be graciously used by the king. By Gresham's enclosed letter it appears that loving matter used with him was rather a practice to catch hold on the old terms than any plan meaning towards the king's purpose; otherwise the matter is answered well enough.

    *Holograph.*                                                                                    SP 10/15, no. 63

**776.**   December 3. Beeleigh. Princess Mary to the king.

    I have received your letters and am bound to you for wishing me better health. You wish to have of me in exchange for other lands the manor[s] of St Osyth, Little and Great Clacton and Weeley. Although sundry manors I have by your patent are not commodious or profitable, I never thought to trouble you or your council for obtaining better, or to leave any of them. But I will obey your pleasure in this behalf.

    *Holograph.*

    *Printed*: Green, 259–60.                                                        SP 10/15, no. 64

**777.**   December 3. Beeleigh. Princess Mary to the council.

    I understand by your letters of November 30 the king's pleasure touching money I have this year disbursed and allowed for repairs on manors and houses I have by his letters patent, thanking him for disburdening me of them. I also thank him for willing you to tell me of the proceedings between the emperor and the French king, with other foreign news, beeseching God that all may redound to His glory and the quietness of Christendom, which is likely to ensue by this overthrow of the Turk's power. Thank you for moving the king touching my charges.

    *Holograph.*

    *Printed*: Green, 258–9.                                                          SP 10/15, no. 65

**778.**   [December 7].* Names of commissioners and directions for their proceedings in the sale and exchange of crown lands.

    The lord chancellor [the bishop of Ely], the bishop of Norwich, Mr Comptroller [Sir Richard Cotton], Mr Vice-Chamberlain [Sir John Gates], Sir Walter Mildmay, [John] Lucas, Thomas Mildmay. To examine [1] how money from the sale of land is answered, as may best be found in chancery on extract of the letters patent. [2]. The particulars of sales, gifts and exchanges, that it may be known if the king is answered after the just value or not. If not he has remedy by statute to have twenty years' rate for lands given, sold or exchanged, for so much after the rate as the rest of the sum were sold for, to be found within ten years after the date of the letters patent. Two statutes were specially made for this matter, 35 Henry VIII [c. 14] and 1 Edward VI. [3]. How the king is answered for exchanges and purchases made by his father and himself, and how the revenues and bonds are performed. [4]. Recognisances and bonds taken for woods upon purchases and exchanges, of which most are not executed nor the survey of the woods certified.

    *Clerk's fair copy.*                                                                  SP 10/2, no. 30

**779.**   December 7. Chelsea. The duke of Northumberland to Sir William Cecil.

    I return [John] Knox, who said you willed him to speak with me, because I love not to deal with men neither grateful not pleasable. I mind to have no more to do with him, nor with the dean of Durham because, under colour of conscience, he can malign others.

    *     Date of the commission [C 66/848, mm. 16d–17d (*CPR* 1550–3, 397–8)].

You may see in his letter that he cannot tell whether I am a dissembler in religion – but I have stood for twenty years to one kind which I now profess. I send the letter I mind to send to the constable of France* by [the seigneur de] Vilandry, because the constable sent me one by him which the king saw; send word of his highness's pleasure by this bearer. The matter revealed by the dean of Durham should not lie secret, for it is perhaps of more importance than it is taken for; if proveable, his majesty should know the truth, with all the circumstances and adherents, *nisi forte veniant Romani*. If any peril happens by keeping silence, all we that have been privy shall be blameworthy. I remember your considerations concerning what evil people might judge of me, as though I should be procurer of the matter against the parties for displeasure, or that I would be alone, or have some of his inheritance. The king and some of the council know who revealed the matter; while it is fresh in memory he should write how he knew and for how long before he told me. Then, with the advice and consent of some other privy councillors, it shall better appear what is further to be done, chiefly for the king's surety. For our discharges confer with the lord chamberlain and others at court who were at its revealing in the king's presence. Had I sought the people's favour without respect to his highness's surety I needed not so much obloquy for some kind of men. Though my father, after his master was dead, died for doing his master's commands, I will serve without fear, seeking God's glory and his highness's surety. They can but kill the body; he that seeks to save that with impure conscience kills the soul. I would wish a difference between such as sought their own before their master's and such as for conscience sake seek advancement of their master and country before their own – as between the wilful offender and those afraid to break a law. Till this difference is better observed, subversion of the commonwealth is like to follow and endangering of the prince. Bear with my folly; let the lord chamberlain be partaker, to whom, when time serves, I will use like words.

    *Printed*: Tytler, ii, 148–50 (with omissions).          SP 10/15, no. 66

**780.**  December 8. Wilton. The earl of Pembroke to Sir William Cecil.
    You have by sundry means declared your good will towards me that I am much bound to you, and you will find me your friend in any occasion of trial.    SP 10/15, no. 67

**781.**  December 9. Chelsea. The duke of Northumberland to Sir William Cecil.
    I have received your letters from Berwick, from the captain and from Dr [Richard] Smythe out of Scotland, which I enclose with [Hans] Bruno's and the French ambassador's letters. Impart Smythe's discourses to the lord chamberlain, vice-chamberlain and such other lords as are now there, as the matters are of importance. The opinion of G[eorge] Paris written by Smythe concerning the apprehension and examination of Ockonner's men with the deputy in Ireland should be to much purpose, as also the watching of a water named in Smythe's letter. Solicit the rest of my lords for immediate order for prevention of these treasons, so far as can be foreseen and done – or, the warning we have coming more from God than our own search and care, the shame and blame will be ours. Let us be ready to spend goods, lands and lives for our master and country, and despise the flattering of ourselves with riches as the greatest pestilence in the commonwealth. Let us not be blinded and abused by those so inflicted. Though plagued in body and purse, I am rich in good will to serve my master and commonwealth. *Postscript (holograph)*. The credit committed to this bearer I refer to you and others of my lords to be further examined.    SP 10/15, no. 68

**782.**  December [9, 16, 23 or 30]. Friday. Memorandum [to the lord treasurer] that there lacks money and warrant for payment of the king's works at the mews since Michaelmas,

   \*     Anne de Montmorency.

estimated at £150.

Minute from the marquess of Winchester to one of the secretaries of state.

Cause a warrant to be made and sent to me. I will see it paid one of the wards. This money has brought the king's horse into his own stable, to his and all the officers' great pleasure.

*Holograph.*　　　　　　　　　　　　　　　　　　　　　　　SP 10/15, no. 69

**783.** December 11. Chelsea. The duke of Northumberland to Sir William Cecil.

Direct this bearer, my chaplain, where he may receive the king's presentation of the vicarage of Kidderminster, which [John] Harley, now bishop of Hereford,* had of my gift. He is witty, honest, sufficiently learned, a good preacher, a faithful Englishman though born a Scot, and has lost blood in the king's cause. Remember what I showed you concerning [the countess of] Lennox – you and I seeming to be of one mind. I hear no word of her husband, if he minds to remain here, keeping her children in the realm. Being circumspectly looked into in her absence, the danger can be nothing. Her husband dare not enter Scotland because of an old deadly feud with the governor's† blood. Also he pretends a title for lack of issue of the young queen before the governor, and has offered to prove the governor to descend of the base line. I cannot think so much danger in her going to her father‡ as I did when you and I communed it. He may tell her something worth hearing. Therefore it is to be considered by my lords. I am sure she can have no profit or part of her father's inheritance; though he would make her sure of it tomorrow, except she would refuse habitation there, as I doubt not all my lords know. It amuses me to think why her father seeks to have her come so far only to speak with her; but some mystery must be in it.

*Holograph.*　　　　　　　　　　　　　　　　　　　　　　　SP 10/15, no. 70

**784.** [December 1552 x January 1553].§ A remembrance of things worth examination for the king.

1. How the money from the sale of land is answered: best seen in extracts of letters patent. 2. How the king is answered of lead and bell metal of abbeys: what remains, and where. 3. That execution may follow the work of the recently appointed commissioners for revenue courts, so faults may be redressed and superfluous charges diminshed. 4. That all men receiving money of the king for the wars, buildings or other affairs in prest, and not yet accounted, be called to account, especially purveyors and victuallers, whose petitions are great for wastes and other allowances. 5. That all money demanded of the king for the fall [of money] be well examined, for there is thought to be much deceit therein. 6. That the particulars of sales, gifts and exchanges be examined, that it be known if the king is answered after the just value. If not, he has remedy by statute to have twenty years' rate for lands given, and for lands sold and exchanged so much after the rate as the rest were sold for, so the same to be found within ten years after the letters patent. Two statutes were made specially for this, 35 Henry VIII [c. 14] and 1 Edward VI. 7. How the king and his father were answered of exchanges and how the covenants concerning their value are performed. 8. To examine recognisances and bonds taken for woods upon purchases and exchanges, of which most are not executed or survey certified. 9. If it were examined how the king is answered of plate, jewels, ornaments, goods and chattels of monasteries, colleges and persons attainted, the king should think the work of his commissioners well employed. 10. Since the beginning of the last wars the king and his father have had of the Fuggers and others alum, fustians,

* 　　Harley did not receive warrant for letters patent until 26 March 1553 (*CPR* 1553, 3).
† 　　The earl of Arran.
‡ 　　The earl of Angus.
§ 　　Hoak, 283 n. 115.

copper and other goods, the account whereof is worth calling for.     SP 10/5, no. 25

**785.** [December 12].* Commissioners appointed for various causes.

The lord great master [the duke of Northumberland], the lord privy seal [the earl of Bedford], the lord chamberlain [Lord Darcy], the lord admiral [Lord Clinton], the comptroller [Sir Richard Cotton], Sir Ralph Sadler, Sir Philip Hoby, Sir Walter Mildmay, [Richard] Goodrich, Thomas Mildmay. How the king is answered of lead and bell metal of abbeys and his other possessions: what remains, where, or by what order any person has meddled with it. It should be examined how the king is answered of plate, jewels, ornaments, goods and chattells of monasteries, colleges, chantries and persons attainted, and of all forfeitures of gold, silver, bullion or such wares. Authority must be given that the commissioners shall proceed by way of imprisonment and fine for satisfaction of such things as they find embezzled or made away with without reasonable cause.

SP 10/15, no. 76

**786.**    [December 1552 x January 1553].† Names of commissioners and directions for their proceedings in the receipt and expenditure of public revenues.

(1) The lord great master, (2) the lord privy seal, (3) the lord great chamberlain [the marquess of Northampton], (4) the earl of Pembroke, (5) the lord chamberlain, (6) Mr Vice Chamberlain [Sir John Gates], (7) Sir Robert Bowes, (8) Sir Walter Mildmay, (9) Sir Thomas Wroth and (10) Thomas Mildmay. All men receiving money of the king for wars, buildings or other affairs in prest and not yet accounted and discharged may be called to account, especially treasurers of towns, purveyors and victuallers, whose petitions are great for wastes and other allowances. Since the beginning of the last wars the king and his father have had of the Fuggers and other foreigners alum, fustian, copper, powder and other goods, the account of which is worth calling for. They are to examine the bargains made with the foreigners for borrowing money, and how they have been discharged. All warrants for money directed by order of the privy council to be employed in the wars, towns of war or the mints to be viewed, and it is to be considered whether the money was defrayed according to the warrants, or otherwise altered and defrayed by those in charge.                                                                 SP 10/2, no. 31

**787.**    December 14. Stamford. The alderman and burgesses of Stamford to Sir William Cecil.

Our recorder [John] Hunt, having great business (as he says) cannot attend to keep our sessions, but has discharged himself of the office. Considering your previous goodness, we move you to take on the recordership. Although the fee is nothing much to be esteemed by you, we assure you of our faithful service. For keeping sessions but at your pleasure we will not trouble you. Credit our master your father, whom we have required to tell you the state of our town, which may by your counsel be better ordered.

*Signed by*: John Fenton, alderman.

*With the names of*: Geoffrey Vyllers, Henry Lacy, William Myles, Thomas Wattson, Harry Ley, Ralph Harrope, Robert Wynwyk, Henry Tampyon and other co-burgesses.

*Postscript*: by Richard Ogle. Without your good counsel those of wilful minds will undo the town. They are in such opinions for the election of Fenton as alderman, which is opposed only by John Allyn and Kampynet.                   SP 10/15, no. 71

**788.**    [December 20]. Memoranda of council business.

In Thomas Gresham's letters: answer for sale of his fustians. John Burnell: £416 for

---

\*     Cf. C 66/848, mm. 10–11d (*CPR* 1550–3, 391–2), where the earl of Huntingdon is also mentioned.
†     Seems closest to the commission of December 12 cited in the previous note.

his diets. In [Sir Thomas] Chamberlain's letters. The Venetian ambassador's coming. Pirates in the west country: to be hanged. To Lord William Howard. To be moved to the king: Lord Paget's suit to [pay]* discharge presently for the king £8,000 in the exchequer for acquittal of £1,000 due next Christmas. Lord John [Grey]'s suit for a lease of the manor of [Breedon],† part of John Beamonte's lands, to him and his heirs, surrendering £40 pension for the same.

*Cecil's hand.* SP 10/15, no. 72

**789.** December 28. The duke of Northumberland to the council.

This morning [the earl of] Shrewsbury was with me with a note of things most necessary for the next parliament, which you think should take effect very shortly. As I have told some of you I agree, as there is no other remedy for the king's great debt, partly left by his father and augmented by the late duke of Somerset, who took up the protectorship and government of his own authority. His highness, left by his father in peace with all princes, was suddenly, by that man's unskilful protectorship and less expertise in government, plunged into wars, and his charges increased to £120,000 or £140,000 a year, above the keeping and defence of Boulogne, which almost wearied his father, being nevertheless conquered with his own adventure. These things are now so onerous, having been all this time put off as best we could, that without your speedy help dishonour and peril may follow. Sale of lands must be the most honourable means; you have tried calling in debts and seeking every man's doing in office – yet you perceive this cannot salve the sore so long suffered to fester. Being continually sick I cannot but talk of cure and medicine: bear with my infirmity, for I mean as well to master and country as the fittest. I also perceive by Lord Shrewsbury that you think the collection of anything granted the king at this parliament should not be put into effect till Michaelmas; how that will answer payment of debts, one part of the cure, I know not. But in case parliament should be summoned chiefly for that intent and then not serve the purpose, the summoning were better protracted till after harvest – so shall you have received within two months the whole benefit as if you summoned it presently, and avoid the summer. If you demand now what you will not take before winter, you shall give them too much warning to defraud the king, take away every man's comfort of traffic and gain in the meantime, yet avoid little or nothing the danger of murmuring or grudging.

SP 10/15, no. 73

**790.** December 28. The duke of Northumberland to Sir William Cecil.

I marvel at the blind walking of [Sir Thomas] Chamberlain, whom I thought had little need of a guide in so plain a path. Now you may perceive I did not mistake my late letters I sent you with [Thomas] Gresham's, perceiving that their fetch was wholly to bring us within the limits of the old treaties, whereat they shut still. I perceive by your letter that the king is moved by [the council] to employ ministers abroad for the public weal of Christendom, which will be a perpetual honour to him, and bring surety, and his majesty shall much decipher the inclination of both premises. He will be better served if those sent have grace and wit to note what they see and hear. You have named my brother and my son [in-law, Sir Henry] Sydney to be appointed, not saying which goes to the French king or the emperor. God assist them. Be a means to the rest of my lords to give them favourable instructions, the shorter the better. It is to be considered whether they shall return upon their first answer or remain – which, in my opinion, will sound more to the king's honour unless their first answer is such as he looks for. The sooner you despatch them the better, lest others come before. You and I would wish few or none knew of their going till they were ready to take ship at Dover – the more open

---

*     Deleted.
†     Cf. *APC*, iv, 85, 200.

they shall find the princes. And should they return with an answer or send and wait for the conclusion of all by others more experienced – for their learning and extenuation? If you think Sydney should go to the the emperor, having more means to express his mind in Italian than French, prefer it to the king and [council]. Let them be gone with speed, with few or none but their own train. Whoever goes to the emperor should have [Cardinal] Pole's letters, to see, if opportunity serves, what evils are fostered in his dominions, and should remember the king's thanks for the matter revealed to Gresham.

    *Holograph.*                                                               SP 10/15, no. 74

**791.**   [? December]. Bartholomew Traheron to Sir William Cecil.

    Master Warner threatens Master Cornelius,* if he can prevail no further, to take his garden from his house, to thrust his deputy out, or if all fails, to be so severe a surveyor that he will soon make him weary of his office. His uncharitable dealing against so honest and quiet a man as that deputy should be bridled. Because I cannot come today I write for your help. I am determined to resign the deanery of Chichester. Because I obtained it at your procurement and [Sir John] Cheke's, I would you should appoint my successor. If you cannot think of a man fit, remember [Thomas] Sampson, a preacher in London of such integrity as I would be glad to see placed here.

    *English and Greek.*
    *Holograph.*                                                               SP 10/15, no. 75

[For SP 10/15, no. 76 see no. **785** above.]

**792.**   [December 1552 x January 1553].† List of councillors and commissioners.

    Archbishop of Canterbury, (1) lord chancellor [the bishop of Ely], lord treasurer [the marquess of Winchester], (3,2) lord great master [the duke of Northumberland], (3,1) lord privy seal [the earl of Bedford], duke of Suffolk, lord great chamberlain [the marquess of Northampton], earl of Shrewsbury, earl of Westmorland, earl of Huntingdon, (3) earl of Pembroke, Viscount Hereford, lord admiral [Lord Clinton], (3,2) lord chamberlain [Lord Darcy], Lord Rich, Lord Cobham, Mr Treasurer [Sir Thomas Cheyne], (1) Mr Comptroller [Sir Richard Cotton], (3,1) Mr Vice Chamberlain [Sir John Gates], secretaries: Sir William Petre, Sir William Cecil, (2) Sir Ralph Sadler, Dr [Nicholas] Wotton, Sir John Gage, Sir John Mason, (2) Sir Philip Hoby, (3,1) Sir Robert Bowes, Sir Edward North, Sir John Baker, Justice [Sir Edward] Montague, Justice [Sir Thomas] Bromley. *On the dorse (in another hand).* Bishop of London, Justice [Sir James] Hales, Sir Anthony St Leger, [Dr John] Cox, bishop of Norwich, Sir Richard Sackvile, Sir Thomas Moyle, Sir Thomas Wroth, [John] Lucas, (3,1,2) Sir Walter Mildmay, Sir John Cheke, (2) Richard Goodrich, Sir Anthony Cooke, (3,2,1) Thomas Mildmay.                                         SP 10/14, no. 6

**793.**   Arguments that church property, intended for the public use of the whole ministry, ought not to be converted to private uses, and a bishop ought not to consent to such alienation.

    1. The chief aims of a Christian magistrate or minister should be God's sanctification and the edification of His church. 2. Nothing promotes these aims more than Christ's sacred ministry, instituted (Ephesians 4) for edification of the body of Christ. When the ministry is abolished or corrupted religion degenerates into superstition or profanity. 3. The church's possessions and income were acquired to encourage men to enter the ministry without anxiety for their livelihood, perform their duties with joy and, not being a burden on their flocks, have more willing followers and the wherewithal to spend on

---

\*    ? John Warner and Cornelius Zifridius.

†    Hoak, Ph.D. dissertation, 90 n. 1. The numerals indicate membership of various commissions issued at this time.

the poor. 4. Scripture shows the extension of the ministry most acceptable to God, its diminution the cause of many evils. 5. Isaiah (chapter 49) prophesied that kings would nourish the church. 6. Christ (Matthew 10) promised reward to those who entertain and support the apostles. 7. All (Luke 8) praised Mary Magdalene, Joanna, Chuza's wife, Susanna and other women who ministered to Christ and His apostles. 8. Sacred ministers of all races were held in highest regard and their property left inviolate even by such as Pharoah (Genesis 47). 9. Our king would tarnish his zeal by alienation of church property when even popish princes leave inviolate the property of their priests. 10. Achan at the fall of Jericho and King Belshazzar were punished for using consecrated vessels (Joshua 6,7); in Malachi (chapter 3) God prophesies famine and sterility because He has been robbed of tithes and first fruits. 11. The Jewish rulers were rebuked by Jeremiah because the Levites, robbed of their portions, abandoned the ministry (2 Esdras [*i.e.* Nehemiah 13]). 12. We need a Nehemiah to remind our rulers of the state of our time. There is great dearth of holy ministers, preachers and teachers; the universities do not promise enough; there is much destruction of schools. Rather than being put right by transference of church income, these wrongs daily increase, the enthusiasm of many is weakened and hope of advancement removed. 13. It might be wondered how the [tenth] commandment can be dispensed with. Since by the generosity of nobles of old churches were made corporations and given possessions, they ought to be in the same position as private individuals, or better. 14. The devout are weakened by such alienation, for the papists are not silenced by well-doing. When bad bishops and enemies of the gospel are ejected the malicious might say the rulers acted for their own benefit. The bishops and those who support such grants are regarded as simoniacs, misers and trimmers (cf. 1 Timothy 3). They achieve nothing in their ministry, but put a stumbling block in the way of the gospel (cf. Luke 17). 15. Even in secular administration Christian rulers must act for God's glory ([1] Corinthians 10). 16. A Christian ruler may divide one ample portion falling vacant among those most earnest in preaching and teaching. But not a farthing must be transferred to those outside the ministry. The distributions made by Quintus Fabius Labeo (Cicero, [*De Officiis*, i, paragraph 33]) should not be approved. 17. Many Christian princes – Constantine, Jovian, Justinian, Charlemagne – enriched churches and gave ecclesiastical property legal immunities. No ruler transferred church income to laymen. Anything not supported by good example is suspect. Justinian (*Authentica* II) forbad transfer or exchange of immovable church property. 18. A ruler may take possession of such property for the state's good if he makes adequate or greater compensation. Why should he argue against making ampler return when he has received so much from God? 19. That large revenues were acquired for churches when very learned and pious bishops flourished is established by Chrysostom (*Discourses*, 67). 20. Theoderet praised Jovian for restoring corn to churches after Julian the Apostate had revoked Constantine's edict (*History of the Church*, IV, 4). 21. No German divine has approved such alienation. Bucer termed it theft from the Lord and blamed God's vengeance on Germany on the princes' interference with church goods. 22. Ambrose (*Letters*, V, against Auxentius) would not relinquish his custody of church vessels, saying it was profitable neither for him to give nor the emperor to receive them. 23. When such gifts are made, the beneficiaries first take possession and then legal deeds are completed as if the bishops transferred church property of their own accord and for most important reasons, adding a clause that they acted against their consciences; they wish a frank record for posterity but devise inaccurate causes for their deeds. 24. Although this activity is generally overlooked, that the king may more easily carry the financial burden of the state, little profit reaches him. It is remarkable that astute politicians do not realise this is clear to everyone. 25. How shall we regard the phenomenon that in a well ordered state, where all ought to have equal rights, immovable possessions are not taken from any, however wicked, except ministers of religion, who hitherto in all states,

Christian or pagan, have enjoyed privilege rather than discrimination?
*6¹/₂ pp.*
*Latin.*
*Supported by numerous scriptural references, only some of which have been included above.*
SP 10/15, no. 77

[For SP 10/15, no. 78 see no. **431** above.]

**794.**   [Lady Cecil]* to Lady Jane Grey.
   Although I am well acquainted with certain of the ancient authors learned in divine things, none is more delightful and soothing than Basil the Great, who surpasses all the bishops of his time in birth, learning and piety. Such an author would be most suitable for you, who are of noblest origin, illustrious for learning and piety. It turns the soul from earthly to divine considerations. I therefore present you with these discourses of Basil the Great as token of my respect.
   *Greek.*
   *Holograph.*
   *Printed*: *Facsimiles of National MSS*, ii, 111 (facsimile no. LXVI).    SP 10/15, no. 79

**795.**   Printed copy of the above.                                          SP 10/15, no. 79(i)

**796.**   Modern MS translation of no. **794.**                              SP 10/15, no. 79(ii)

**797.**   1552. Book of all arrears due on February 1 in the office of the treasurer of the court of first fruits and tenths [Sir William Petre].
   *Paper book, 99 ff.*                                                        SP 10/16

**798.**   1552. December 29. Statutes of the most noble order of the Garter.
   *Vellum book, 15 written ff.*                                               SP 10/17

**799.**   1553. January 2. Chelsea. The duke of Northumberland to Sir William Cecil.
   I wish the king and [council] might consider that Durham should no longer be without a pastor. If such a matter is so little regarded, notwithstanding my continual calling on it, I would some other had my office there, and then perhaps know better what it means to govern where God is neglected. I have not heard how the dean of Durham was lately ordered by my lords – whether he is gone home or remains here. I have been much deceived by him: he is greedy, malicious, and an open evil speaker of which enough now can report. Let not the see be so long destitute of some grave, good man that knows his duty to God and his king rather than one of these new obstinate doctors without humanity or honest conditions. Most of these whom the king has lately preferred are so sotted with wives and children that they forget their poor neighbours and all else pertaining to their calling – so will they so long as his majesty allows them so great possessions to maintain their idle lives.
   *Printed*: Tytler, ii, 152–3.                                              SP 10/18, no. 1

**800.**   January 3. Chelsea. The duke of Northumberland to Sir William Cecil.
   It seems by your friendly persuasions for my coming to court that some did not understand my state or wrongly judged some negligence in my long absence. If all things were considered as I can declare myself, easy enough to be judged of others, my absence might be better borne. I am reminded of the Italian proverb that a faithful servant will

---

*       Originally ascribed to one of the daughters of Sir Anthony Cooke; of these, Mildred Cecil, as translator
        of a homily of St Basil [BL Royal MS 17 B.xxviii] is almost certainly the writer.

become a perpetual ass. If I could bear the burden I trust my lords do not mind to use me once. It is time for me to live of that which God and the king have given me, and keep the multitude of crawlers from his court that hang daily at my gate for money; so long have I passed this matter in silence and credit that shame almost compels me to hide. What comfort may I have after my long and troublesome life? So long as health gave me leave I as seldom failed my attendance as any others. When they went to their suppers and pastimes after their travail I went to bed, careful and weary. Yet no man scarcely had any good opinion of me. Now, by extreme sickness and otherwise constrained to seek health and quiet, I am not without a new evil imagination of men. Why should I wish longer life – but for my few children? To satisfy you and others whom I take for friends I have entered into the bottom of my care. If God took men's evil imaginations and left them with simple judgements, they should live angels' lives – which may not be, for Adam procured that one should be in continual affliction with another.

    *Printed*: Tytler, ii, 154–6.                                    SP 10/18, no. 2

**801.**   January 6. Chelsea. The duke of Northumberland to Lord Darcy, lord chamberlain.

    Thank you for obtaining the king's letter for Ambrose [Dudley] whereby, if it takes place, he shall be more able to serve his highness and owe you good will. I return the king's books of the order:* the last I think nearest the king's mind, but as it is all in Latin I can but guess at it. Because it is not meet to confer of it with others except of the order, I require you and the chancellor of the order† to bear with my folly. In the end of the first chapter it is said there shall be twenty-six knights, of which one to be sovereign, prince or superior and head. These words are superfluous, not giving full reverence to the king, as in the beginning and end of the second chapter. The latter seems to give him authority but once in his life to change the stalls of the knights, except emperors, kings, princes and dukes. I take it that the king, by the old statutes, may at all times change the stalls of all persons, if the same attend to their advancement, without prejudice of others. In the beginning of the third chapter where it is said that when any place is void the knights, or six of them with the sovereign or his vicar, shall come together and elect by writing the names of three princes, the states &c. I mean that at no assembly, as I take it, by the old statutes, can be any election where the sovereign is not present, though the feast may be kept and all other ceremonies in any place by his majesty's deputy. In these things and in one or two other points in the book, with the king's pleasure, I would be glad to commune with the chancellor, two or three of the order being together.                                    SP 10/18, no. 4

**802.**   January 6. The duke of Northumberland to Sir William Cecil.

    I have written to the lord chamberlain concerning my gross misunderstanding of your book, wherein, with the king's pleasure, I would gladly confer with you, two or three of the company‡ being together. Our communication would be done within two hours; then I would answer your letter. I wish to you as to myself, and no less to your friend that seemed so friendly to care – whereby I am scant deceived in his honest nature. I have not heard from you whether there shall be a bishop of Durham or not, and can hear nothing of the prebend [John] Harley had in Worcester of the king's gift nor of the benefice§ he had of mine, both which the king wished I should have preferment of. Tell me what is become of the presentations, which I was informed his highness had already signed.

    *Holograph.*                                            SP 10/18, no. 3

| | |
|---|---|
| * | The Garter. |
| † | Cecil. |
| ‡ | The order of the Garter. |
| § | The vicarage of Kidderminster. |

**803.**  January 9. Chelsea. The duke of Northumberland to Sir William Cecil.

I return [Sir Richard] Morison's and Lord Wharton's letters with those I received from Wharton on the 2nd and 3rd, and one from [John] Knox. You may perceive his perplexity. Let the rest of [the council] take some order for his recomfort. I would not wish him long there,* but to come and go as the king and [council] appoint. Wharton and those of Newcastle should know his highness favours him and his doings; otherwise hindrance in religion may grow among the inconstant people. It seems Wharton suspects how Knox's doings have been taken here. Let the king's pleasure to my lords be undelayedly certified to Wharton, that none vex the poor man for setting forth the king's godly proceedings, heretofore or hereafter; for his majesty minds to employ him from time to time there and elsewhere. Something might be written to the mayor for his greedy accusation of the poor man; he might defame the king's proceedings if he saw a time to serve his purpose.

*Holograph.*

*Printed*: Tytler, ii, 158–60.                                            SP 10/18, no. 5

**804.**  January 14. Chelsea. The duke of Northumberland to Lord Darcy, lord chamberlain.

I return Mr Secretary Cecil's arguments and collections left at your late being at Chelsea. As I then partly declared my opinion, which you seemed not to mistake, I am made bolder to scribble part of my mind on the margin: which, when you† have perused and not liked, strike out, for the text remains, so as Mr Secretary can easily enough find his own. I have scribbled so much because I believe we need not imagine the objections of every forward person, but burden their minds and hearts with the king's undeniable extreme debts and necessity – and not seem to account to the commons of his liberality to nobles or good servants, lest you make them wanton and give them occasion to take hold of your own arguments. But as it shall become no subject to argue the matter so far – so, if any should, the matter will always answer itself with honour and reason, confounding their shame. I know you and Mr Secretary wished me declare my opinion.

This bearer can declare [Princess] Elizabeth's communication with Mr Chancellor‡ concerning Durham Place; it was not much from what I conjectured. She seems satisfied by Mr Chancellor's report, but not without conceiving his displeasure against me for labouring to have the house without first knowing her mind. I must appeal to the king and you whether I ever sued for it; I trust he will defend me to her, whom I would not offend willingly. She has presently sent to cause the house to be delivered; I await his majesty's further pleasure. She has also sent me word by Mr Chancellor that she intends to visit the king about Candlemas and desires to borrow St James's for the time because she cannot have her things so soon ready at the Strand house. I am sure she would have done no less had she kept Durham House still. *Postscript.* It is time the king's pleasure were known for the speaker of the house,§ that he might have secret warning as usual, the better to prepare for his preposition. It should also be considered who shall that day preach before the king; what service shall be said instead of the old service invoking the Holy Ghost; whether his majesty will have all his lords and prelates communicate; and his pleasure concerning bringing some heirs apparent to parliament by writ, whereby they may better serve him and the realm hereafter.

*Printed*: Tytler, ii, 160–3.                                            SP 10/18, no. 6

**805.**  January 15. Proposals for reorganizing the work of the privy council.

1. Suits, petitions and warrants heard on Monday to be answered on Saturday. 2. Suits

---

*      Newcastle upon Tyne.
†      Addressed to Darcy and Cecil.
‡      Of augmentations.
§      Sir James Dyer was elected when parliament met.

to be reserved to the court. 3. To make no special warrants where there are warrants dormant. 4. Warrants above £40 for reward and £100 for affairs to pass [the king's] signature. 5. A memorial to be delivered to his majesty on Saturday night by a secretary, and thereupon the matters to be appointed to several days. 6. On Friday afternoon a collection to be made of things done the week past, with a note of the principal reasons for any conclusions. 7. This collection to be presented on Saturday morning and his majesty's pleasure to be known on things concluded, and suits of importance to be moved that time. 8. On Sunday his majesty, hearing by a secretary such more matters as are arisen, will appoint days for their consideration. 9. Sunday to attend the affairs of the realm, answer letters and be at common prayer. 10. None to leave court above two days except eight of the council remain, and then also to ask licence. 11. No assembly of council to be without at least four. 12. If letters come and fewer than four are present, they may open them and come to his majesty. 13. Four assembled and under six shall consider things against the coming of more, without resolution. 14. When his majesty's pleasure is to hear the debating of any matter, warning shall be given to the council. 15. No private suit to be moved on days assigned for matters of state. 16. If the matter is long, other causes shall not be intermeddled. 17. When debate is not ended, it shall be noted how far the matter is brought, and the arguments on both sides. 18. In busy matters two or three may be appointed to hear and rough hew them as they may be more open at the next assembly. 19. When letters or other matters require present despatch, they may be considered as they come, these orders notwithstanding.

*Petre's hand.*

*Printed*: F.G. Emmison, 'A plan of Edward VI and Secretary Petre for reorganizing the privy council's work, 1552–1553', *Bulletin of the Institute of Historical Research*, xxxi, (1958), 203–7, which includes a discussion of the document.      SP 10/1, no. 15

**806.**   Later copy of the above.                                  SP 10/1, no. 16

**807.**   January 15. Kelsey. Sir Francis Ayscough to Sir William Cecil.

Sir William Ayscowghe, my late father, was bound to Henry VIII in £300 as one of the sureties for Jeffrey Chambers, for payment of which I was called before the late Lord Wriothesley and other councillors of the late king because Jeffrey was indebted to the king; although immediately before I had been at great charges in serving the king in the wars at Boulogne, and unable to pay the £300, I was forced to deliver to the king the reversion of the manor of Bishop Burton, Yorkshire, after the death of Elizabeth Horsman, my sister-in-law, for £200, part of the £300. The manor is worth £20 a year. The remaining £100 I paid to the king's receiver, and at the same time paid the king £500 as surety to him for Lord Hussey. Now Elizabeth Horsman is dead, whereby the lands are come to the king. As they are of the inheritance of my ancestors, in consideration of my war service, I intend to sue the king's council to have them again, paying the king £200 in ready money, and desire your advice.

*Holograph.*                                                         SP 10/18, no. 7

**808.**   January 19. Chelsea. The duke of Northumberland to Sir William Cecil.

At your being with me here today ... [? we discussed] the heirs apparent the king shall now or hereafter call by writ to sit and have voice in parliament as before, specially in the time of [Henry VIII]. No man's son not of blood royal can claim any place there except peers' eldest sons to sit at the back of the king's cloth of state. At Queen Anne's instance [Henry VIII] allowed Lord William Howard to stand there, never before seen. If the king calls any heirs apparent it is of his grace, to trade up youth to serve him. They should occupy their fathers' best places, or otherwise at his pleasure. The present duke of Norfolk when earl of Surrey was called by writ to the place of the barony of

Howard; when his father was created duke he was created earl of Surrey because his father was never restored to the earldom after his father's attainder. Then he sat by his own creation – he could not have sat as an earl by writ because it was not in his father; had it been, the king might rather have called him by writ to the earldom, for heirs are always called by their fathers' next best names. This is used through all the world. But an heir must not sit as he is taken abroad – a duke's son above the ancient earls, but in the place his father had being an earl.

Move my lords for placing a grave learned man in the see of Durham. His majesty should deliberate for consecrating those already nominated – for I am afraid I shall never have honesty in preferring some of them; but if I had heard before as I now hear, I would have no less done and said as I say now.

*Mutilated.* SP 10/18, no. 8

**809.** January 23. Chelsea. The duke of Northumberland to Sir William Cecil.

I perceive by your letter that the king has been moved concerning the bishop of London, with the effect of my letter to you, by continuance of which his majesty perceives my earnest care for that north part. If he knew my care for the south as for other parts, and the hearts of us all in care for his surety and that of all his dominions, he would soon know whose care was the greatest. You and others may witness of my care for all that pertains to his highness. But if the north is well provided for, the south should do no worse. My care that way should not be taken as though others need care less, or not at all. I trust I shall be found ready to serve the king, whatever his pleasure, with my life. SP 10/18, no. 9

**810.** [? January]. The duke of Northumberland to Lord Darcy, lord chamberlain and Sir William Cecil.

[The countess of] Oxford, having almost finished her suits in the town, desired me to know what she should do touching Lady [(Thomas)] Arundel's jointure. She has received a letter from one of the council for its delivery to Lady Arundel. But although she is her niece and gave 500 marks to her marriage, she will not deliver the jointure without command of the majority of the board, for it may be prejudicial to the king in claiming her thirds. She should therefore have a letter from the board for its delivery to your lordships, with thanks that she so well considered her duty and truth. It seems Lady Arundel's great labour and suit is to get the jointure out of her sight to obtain her thirds, which some have consented to that have written alone to that effect.

*Holograph.* SP 10/18, no. 10

**811.** [? January]. The duke of Northumberland to Sir William Petre and Sir William Cecil or either of them.

Among other weighty affairs, take some time for despatch of matters preferred by Thomas Gresham, seeming for the king's profit; also for [Thomas] Stukley's despatch. I fear to be sick, as I burn as hot as fire; so did I yesterday, but thought it to proceed of an accident, having great pain in the nether part of my belly. But feeling no such grief now, the heat is nevertheless fervently upon me. SP 10/18, no. 11

**812.** [? January]. List of those appointed to hear requests.

The lord privy seal [the earl of Bedford], the lord chamberlain [Lord Darcy], Lord Cobham, the bishop of London, Sir Ralph Sadler, Sir John Mason, Sir Philip Hoby, [John] Cox and [John] Lucas, masters of requests ordinary. They shall hear all private suits customarily brought to the king or his council at the table and delivered to the masters of requests, upon whose declarations they shall be appropriately answered, denying unreasonable and inconvenient suits, and distributing all suits determinable in any ordinary court to their due places, with some regard how they are there expedited, and to cause false claimers and unreasonable shameless suitors to be punished and removed from the haunt of the court. They may sit ordinarily once a week, or oftener as they shall see cause required. Now in the beginning before the abundance of causes are distributed and in term time six shall be sufficient if the lord privy seal or lord chamberlain is one; in progress time four, or otherwise as then shall be ordered, and one of the masters of requests.　　　　　　　　　　　　　　　　　SP 10/18, no. 12

[SP 10/18, no. 13 is a copy of SP 10/14, no. 4, for which see no. **588** above.]

**813.**　[February x March].* Memoranda of matters to be moved to the king.
　　The suit of [Michael] Wentworth, one of the masters of the household, in consideration of an office granted him by bill signed by the late king, by his death unperfected, to have recompense for the same. Sir Robert Ughtred's suit for reversion of the manor of Kexby, obtained from him by the cardinal very hardly and granted to his uncle and Lady Cromwell during their lives. Granted. Consideration of the repair of Hornsea beck in Holderness, Yorkshire, in the king's charge by reason of his lands, as appears by certificate of certain commissioners. Granted. Everard Everdaye, the king's lapidary, and his brother desire to be made free denizens. Granted. Everard's suit to have his house in Westminster for life, and a pension of £60, on condition that if he departs the realm without licence or ceases to serve the king both grants shall cease. Stayed. The suit of Sir Nicholas Bagnall, farmer of waste ground in the north of Ireland worth £72 a year, of which the king was never answered rent before, to have of the king's gift in fee simple £48, being the rent reserved upon his said lease, and the residue in fee farm, considering his service and travail, intending to bring the people to civility. Granted. Lord Morley's suit to have [*blank*]. Granted £0. Mr Ferres[?'s] suit. Granted £24. £2 in fee farm. Earl of Westmorland to have licence for the departing of Lord Wharton. Granted. Lord Conyers. For Mario [Cardonio] the Italian: some entertainment of 300 crowns. Granted. Mr Hayewoode's suit for Peniston's pension. Granted £40. The suit of Sir Leonard Beckwithe and Sir Thomas Gargrave, tenants of the manors of Stillingfleet and Upton, Yorkshire, to have the reversion thereof in fee in consideration of their service and [*blank*] to b e paid to the king. Stayed. Sir Nicholas Poyntes to be delivered. Granted.
　　*In the hands of Chaloner and another clerk; the comments 'granted' or 'stayed' added by Cecil.*
　　　　　　　　　　　　　　　　　　　　　　　　　　　　　　　　SP 10/18, no. 32

**814.**　[? Early 1553].† Memoranda of matters to be moved to the king.
　　For a lease in reversion of the two disparked parks of Lanteglos and St Burian ('Ellesberie'), Cornwall, sued for by Geoffrey Peryn and Richard Guye, officers of the king's cellar. Granted. For naming a sheriff for Hampshire instead of [Sir William] Kelleway, who is unable to furnish the same, brought very poor by his former service: John Norton, Thomas White. John Norton appointed. The pardon of Hussy, for whom Lord Grey has written. Granted if he brings forth the person.
　　*In the hands of Cecil and two others.*　　　　　　　　　　　　SP 10/18, no. 33

**815.**　[Early 1553].‡ Memoranda of suits to be moved to the king.
　　Instructions for the debatable. Instructions for Thomas Gresham. The Irish merchant's suit for £53 lands, of which £40 to be given him in respect of the £800 lent by him to the deputy and the rest to be paid in a rent or purchased after twenty years' purchase.

---

\*　　　Hoak, 282 n. 102(11).
†　　　Hoak, 282 n. 102(8) suggests mid 1552. But Sir William Kelway was not appointed sheriff until 1
　　　November 1552 (*CPR* 1553, 387), and later that month the earl of Pembroke wrote on his behalf for
　　　release from public offices [no. **759** above].
‡　　　Hoak, 282 n. 102(10).

Final answer of the commissioners for the Steelyard. M. de Sulpice's desire to take his leave. Philip Denys for £40 annuity. Barmarsten's suit for the release and pardon of a forfeit for a recognisance of £50, considering he was deceived by Sir John Gascoyn.

SP 10/18, no. 34

**816.** March 20. Declaration of all sums paid by receivers to the treasurer of the court of augmentations, 20 March 1552 to 20 March 1553.

Robert Gouche (Lincolnshire, Nottinghamshire, Derbyshire, Cheshire): Annunciation – £246.13.4; Michaelmas – £2,242.17.7½d.; total – £2,489.10.11½d. William Sheldon (Northamptonshire, Warwickshire, Leicestershire and others [Rutland, Staffordshire, Shropshire, Herefordshire and Worcestershire]*): Annunciation – £611.4.7; Michaelmas – £3,960.4.9½d.; total – £4,571.9.4½d. Sir Henry Gates (duchy of Cornwall): Annunciation – £370; Michaelmas – £3,125.3.7; total – £3,495.3.7. Sir John Salisbury (North Wales): Annunciation – £283; Michaelmas – £1,866.12.7½d.; total – £2,149.12.7½d. John Eye (Norfolk, Suffolk, Cambridgeshire, Huntingdonshire): Annunciation – 0, Michaelmas – £3,010.4.4¼d. John Perte and William Wightman (South Wales): Annunciation – £560; Michaelmas – £1,643.1.5¼d.; total – £2,203.1.5¼d. George Wright (Berkshire, Buckinghamshire, Oxfordshire, Bedfordshire): Annunciation – £400; Michaelmas – £2,880.10.3½d.; total – £3,280.10.3½d. Sir Robert Chester (Essex, Middlesex, Hertfordshire, London): Annunciation – 0; Michaelmas – £226.0.6. Richard Whalley (Yorkshire): Annunciation – 0; Michaelmas – £1,000. Lord Chediock Paulet (Hampshire, Wiltshire, Gloucestershire): Annunciation – £200; Michaelmas – £3,514.14.3; total – £3,714.14.3. John Ayleworthe (Somerset, Dorset, Devon, Cornwall): Annunciation – £200; Michaelmas – £2,614.0.2; total – £2,814.0.2. Sir Thomas Newneham and Richard Asheton (Northumberland, Cumberland, Westmorland): Annunciation – 0; Michaelmas – £228. John Hales, clerk of the hanaper: Annunciation – 0; Michaelmas – £1,674.3.8. Totals: Annunciation – £3,270.17.11; Michaelmas – £30,421.17.3½d.; sum – £33,692.15.2½d.†

SP 10/18, no. 14

**817.** [? March].‡ Grant by Princess Elizabeth to Sir William Cecil.

Henry VIII by letters patent dated 8 May 1537§ granted to Richard Cecil, esq., then his servant, Ladybridge close, part of the manor of Maxey, Northamptonshire, lately occupied by Robert Grenrigg, chaplain, and a great garden de la Mare by Maxey castle, late occupied by Thomas Phillipp, and one pasture, old park, occupied by John Olyver, three closes or pieces of ground by the same close in Crackholme by the river Welland, late occupied by John Gryndell and Alice his wife, late of the lands and tenements of Margaret, countess of Richmond, in Northamptonshire, with their appurtenances, reserving to him and his heirs all woods, feudal dues and advowsons, from the subsequent Michaelmas for [twenty-one] years, paying for Ladybridge close and old park with three closes 73s. 4d., with 20d. further increment. Which Richard Cecil is now dead, upon which the term of years to come comes to Sir William Cecil, [supervisor general of our lands]¶ constable of Maxey castle, son, heir and executor of Richard Cecil. Since the said manor &c. belongs to us, we, considering that William has surrendered his interest there that we should make new letters patent to him, grant it to him from Michaelmas for twenty-one years, paying 73s. 4d. and 20d. increment, by equal portions at Easter and Michaelmas.

*Latin.*
*Draft in Cecil's hand.*

SP 10/18, no. 15

*         Cf. no. **838** below.
†         Correct totals on these sums: £2,870.17.11; £27,985.13.3¹/2d.; £30,856.11.2¹/2d.
‡         Cecil's father died during this month.
§         C 66/676, m. 4 (*LP*, xii, I 1330(24)).
¶         Deleted.

**818.** [? March].* Memoranda of matters to be moved to the king.

The cause and suit of Mr Fynes answered by the king's learned counsel. The declaration of the lands of the prebend of Southcave, part of the possessions of Sir Michael Stanhope, of £73 yearly revenue. For answer of the matter contained in the letters from Dr [Richard] Smyth. To provide that 100 crowns or 50 angels may be taken up at Newcastle of [Bertram] Andersone to be sent to Sir Nicholas Styrley for redeeming G[eorge] Paris. Letter to Sir Nicholas Styrley for the order thereof. Letters to the deputy of Ireland to advertise him thereof. To examine OChonner, the earl of Ormond's man. Mr Comptroller. [Sir Robert] Bowes. [John] Cox. [John] Lucas. To examine the fellows in the Gatehouse. The surrender of the keeping of the two parts of Tiverton by the lord privy seal to the use of Sir Gawain Carew – who to have added the custody of the house there. [The earl of] Arundel's and Lord Paget's suits to come to the king's presence to give thanks for his mercy. For taking pirates on the seas: Strangwishe, Kylligrew.

*Cecil's hand.* SP 10/18, no. 16

**819.** [April or May].† Tuesday. London. The marquess of Winchester, from his house there, to Sir William Cecil [chancellor of the order of the Garter].

I and all your friends hope to hear of your recovery. Remember the king's letter for Sir John Gage's absence this time of the feast among others, that for his age and sickness cannot make the journey without great travail and charge.

*Holograph.* SP 10/18, no. 17

**820.** April 30. Declaration of all sums received by Sir Edmund Peckham, high treasurer of the mints, since April 23 upon sales of the king's lands and of all ready money remaining in his hands on his last certificate then dated – £15,994.19.0¾d.

Abbey lands, of: Thomas Holmes, gent. – £54.0.9; John Throgmerton, esq. – £6.5.0; Sir Maurice Barkeley – £944; John Wright, gent. – £142.13.4; John Wrenne, gent. – £12.19.11; William Stubbes – £30; total – £1,189.19.0. Chantry lands, of: George Cotton, gent. – £2; John Egleforde – £2.6.8; William Manbye, gent. – £66; John Wright, gent. – £3.15.0; William Doddington – £10.5.8; John Lewes, gent. – £3.10.0; total – £87.17.4. Total abbey and chantry lands – £1,277.16.4. Total with cash remaining – £17,272.15.4¾d.

*Signed as examined by*: William Hawtrey. SP 10/18, no. 18

**821.** May 6. Dartington. Nicholas Adams to Sir William Cecil.

Because of a fever I cannot personally prosecute my assumption touching the overture of the intolerable prejudice as yet sustained by the king through concealment of collegiate, chantry and obit lands in Devon and Cornwall. Love and duty to his highness compel me to open the same to some of you councillors; each of you, although I know would take things in good part, especially when they concern the profit and honour of his highness, yet I dare not be so bold with them as I may with you. The first survey of such hereditaments in these counties, taken in the life of Henry VIII when I among others was a commissioner, whereof the minutes of the presentments remain in my hands, amounted to about £200 in surplus of the survey now certified, as both these books with Sir Walter Mildmay's knowledge, to whom I refer myself, will declare. For redress, as in like cases of fraud, you should award new commissions. I humbly desire that Sir Peter Carew, Robert Fulford and John Rudgeway be chosen for their worship, learning and discretion.

*Holograph.* SP 10/18, no. 19

---

\* Hoak, 282 n. 102(9).
† Endorsed 'May' by Cecil, but appears to refer to St George's Day feast (April 23). April 11 suggested in *CSPD*, 51.

[The document originally numbered as SP 10/18, no. 20 and calendared in *CSPD*, 51 has been re-allocated to the domestic addenda of Charles I as SP 16/523, no. 119 and is calendared in *CSPD Addenda*, 1625–49, under date of 7 May 1626.]

**822.**    May 9. Greenwich. John [Tuchet], Lord Audley to Sir William Cecil.

Be of good comfort and merry and you shall overcome all diseases. Because the lord admiral lately praised my physic I have written such medicine as I wrote to him, which I have in a book of my wife's hand; I will be happy to get anything that may do you good. A good medicine for weakness or consumption. Flay and quarter a nine day old sow, put in a still with a handful of spearmint, one of red fennel, one of liverwort, half a handful of turnip, a handful of celery, nine clean picked and pared dates, a handful of great raisins, stoned, ¼ oz. of mace and two sticks of good cinnamon pressed in a mortar. Distil with soft fire; set in a glass in the sun nine days, and drink nine spoonfuls at once when you wish. A compost. Quarter a hedgehog, and put in a still with a quart of red wine, a pint of rose water, a quart of sugar, cinnamon and great raisins, one date, twelve neeps. Tell me of any disease you have and I will send you a proved remedy.

*Printed*: Tytler, ii, 169–71.                             SP 10/18, no. 21

**823.**    May 10. Greenwich. The marquess of Winchester to Sir William Cecil.

I and all your friends rejoice at your trust of recovery and hope you will shortly be with us. I have sent you a bill for your fee unpaid in the exchequer. If you name your sureties to the clerk of wards* he will shortly make ready your books for the wardship of young [Arthur] Hall.

*Holograph.*                                               SP 10/18, no. 22

**824.**    May 15. Westminster. Particulars of property granted by the king to Sir John Gates, part of the possessions of the duke of Somerset.

Doiley wood, Hampshire, in chief by service of one-twentieth of a knight's fee, in the same form as in the king's hands by the duke's attainder.

*Latin.*

*Extract from* : C 66/857, mm. 4–6 (*CPR* 1553, 143–5).          SP 10/18, no. 23

**825.**    May 17. London. Thomas Gresham to the duke of Northumberland.

Since last being with you I have spoken with my uncle Sir John Gresham, who stormed with me for the setting of the price of the exchange and said that it lies in me now to do the merchants of this realm pleasure to increase my poor name among them for ever. I told him I had moved you in the premises and that you demanded 24s. Flemish for £1 sterling, wherein I sued that they might not pay above 22s. for £1, alleging many occasions that the merchants could not give above that price, which they will gladly come to. Nevertheless the merchants have in their heads that when they were called before the council for this matter they were told they·should be no worse used than they were last. To avoid that I have persuaded divers of my friends that you meant they should be no worse paid their money than they were last, which may be your answer whenever you call them before you. I thought good to tell you for your remembrance, and that you meant nothing less of their price, considering that the exchange was at 21s. 6d. when you called them before you and now is at 21s. 8d. and at double usance at 22s., and with good handling daily like to rise. You should be thorough with the merchants for divers considerations that may hereafter ensue, perceiving by my uncle and the rest of them that they will be earnest suitors to you and the rest of the council that there may be no price made till the days of payment come, to which you must not consent. There may be such practices wrought if you should grant them that point to bring the

*     Thomas Anton.

exchange by that day to 19s. It would grieve me to see the king so gripped amongst them, which is so long a matter that I shall defer to debate with you at leisure, wherein depend many matters for the commonwealth. It is most requisite forthwith you conclude with the merchants; but by the way you must not stop them under 24s. for £1, for they will grant no price to you until they have called all the company together. It is no marvel that my uncle storms, for he has bought £4,000 or £5,000 in wools; but before we parted we drank to each other.

I have sent you the privileges granted to us in 1296 by Duke John of Brabant and confirmed by the king and his progenitors, whereby may appear what seditious and false persons these men of the new Hanse are, whereof to them pertains correction, wishing it might be such that before they should be released they should acknowledge their fault to the merchants of the old Hanse, and such amend to be made in writing that hereafter like sedition should not rise amongst their merchants, and that no more should be made free of the new Hanse but such as serve eight years for it, wherein you shall do the king service and receive great honour and credit among all the notable merchants of this realm.

Send for Oliver Dawbeney the due of the mint of Ireland. Be somewhat quick with him, for he has not accomplished the council's letter in retaining the £1,200 that Martin Pirry owes me, which I account lost unless you are good to me. Commendations to my lady.

  *Holograph.*                  SP 10/18, no. 24

**826.** June 3. Memoranda of council business.

[For Berwick].* 1. For hearing and considering Valentine Browne's account and making report, and to see the state of [Thomas] Gower and other accountants there: Mr Comptroller, [Sir John] Cheke, [Sir Robert] Bowes. 2. To speak with [Robert] Horsley. 3. To cause the surveyor of Berwick to make a book for the numbers of workmen to remain monthly, with the charges. 4. To appoint one to carry [Claude] de l'Aubespine's despatch. 5. Sir Nicholas Stirley's revocation from Berwick and the placing of [*blank*] Houton as captain of the castle. To consider how it shall be signified to Stirley. 6. Thomas Carye to be marshal of Berwick. 7. Consideration of further proceeding with the ambassadors sent to the emperor and French king. 8. [Sir Anthony] St Leger's despatch and the matters of Ireland. 9. The letters from the governor of Scotland and their request for [Henry] Balnefes, Hormand, Lisle &c. 10. The discharge of the blockhouses. 11. The new bishops. 12. The [discharge]* suit of Burghard touching the mines. 13. The office of Captain Grouge to take for his pension of £100 a year, £200 in hand and £100 before Candlemas, in full discharge of his pension. Lord Wharton's letters of May 28 and 31. The fishing of Halywell. [William] Rygewaye's coming down. The sending of Stery and Strothar denied. The keys. My. Harvie, and touching the gold in 'Crafordmore'. Mr Treasurer's gold. The town of Hexham. Thomas Ilderton's going to London without knowledge and contention ridden. T[homas] Carre, W[illiam] Drynhow to be sent home. Thomas Carleton for Gilsland. Letters from the Steelyard and the safe conduct. The studdery. Alderney. The licences for 600 ducats of leather. The French bonneters. Answer to the ambassadors with the emperor. The request of Captain [Sir John] Borthwick: from July 1 to December 18. Sir James Dyer. Sir Thomas Smith. The dean of St Paul's. Sir Richard Rede. W[illiam] Stamford, serjeant at law. Mr Cecil.

  *Part in Petre's hand.*              SP 10/18, no. 27

**827.** [June 9. Greenwich]. The king to the bishops.

Because God has revealed to this church of England of which we have, under Christ, chief charge in earth, knowledge of the gospel, we have thought it our duty (to conserve

\*  Deleted.

the gospel with uniform profession, doctrine and preaching and to [avoid] errors) to send you [certain articles signed with our hand] devised by some of our greatest learned bishops and other clergy. Subscribe and observe them in your preachings, teachings and readings, and cause them to be subscribed and observed by all who preach, teach and read in your diocese. Advise us or our council of any having benefice there who refuse to sign the articles and exhort their parishioners to withstand them and teach in any contrary way, that further order may be directed according to our laws. Before admitting any person presented to any ecclesiastical order, ministry, office or cure, confer with him in these articles, causing him to subscribe his consent in a ledger book to remain for record, and let him have a copy of the articles. Do not admit any who refuses consent to any of the articles – for which we discharge you of all penalties and danger of actions, suits or pleas such as *praemunire, quare impedit.* If any party refuses to subscribe for lack of learning, reasonably persuade him before you peremptorily judge him as unable and recusant. Give him three to six weeks to deliberate and consent. A catechism is lately set forth by our authority for instruction of young scholars in true religion, with command to all schoolmasters to teach it. Visit or have visited yearly at least every school in your diocese, to see how the schoolmaster teaches and the scholars learn the catechism, making certificate of offenders to the archbishop within three months of every offence.

   *Fair copy, without signature.*
   *Mutilated.*
   *Printed*: Strype, *Ecclesiastical Memorials*, ii, II, 105–7, from copy in Ridley's register, Guildhall Library, London MS 9531/12, f. 297, which is dated as above.
                                                                          SP 10/18, no. 25

**828.**   Copy of the above, made before some of the mutilations.
   *17th cent.*                                                            SP 10/18, no. 26

**829.**   June 11. Memoranda of council business.
   Berwick. Order to be taken with [Thomas] Gower for his debts appearing on the declaration of Valentine Browne's account. Order to be taken for the number of workmen and labourers at Berwick and for a victualler there. Money for payments at Berwick. Consideration of the matters of Ireland. [Sir Anthony] St Leger's despatch for his own suits. His instructions and commission. The private suits. Money. The discharge of blockhouses. Declaration of the king's pleasure to the new bishops: [Edmund] Grindal – London, [William] Bill – Newcastle, [Rowland] Meryk – Bangor, [John] Whitehead – Rochester. Burcharde's suit touching the mines. Boisdauphin's suits granted. For Allard. 600 ducats of leather. For the bonneters' licence. The poor men of Alderney: a commission and articles. The proceeding with the ambassadors in France and Flanders. The answer of [Sir Nicholas] Styrley for his wages at Berwick, and touching his coming away, which he stays upon lack of payment.
   *Petre's hand, save last two items by Cecil.*                          SP 10/18, no. 28

**830.**   June 27. Westminster. Particulars of a grant for good service and £400 paid to the treasurer of the court of augmentations by Lord Robert Dudley, to Lord Robert and William Glaseour, gent., of all lands and holdings in Rockingham, Northamptonshire and [Great] Easton, Leicestershire, late possessed by William Parr, late Lord Parr, and now in tenure or occupation of Edward Watson, for ever, paying 32s. 5d. in the court of augmentations annually at Michaelmas.
   *Latin.*
   *Extract from*: C 66/860, m. 23 (*CPR* 1553, 221–3).                    SP 10/18, no. 29

**831.**   [June]. Account of stipends paid to the clerks of the signet office.

July to December 1546. July 1546: to Mr SS* – £7.17.4; to every clerk – £4.8.4. August: to Mr SS – £7.8.0; to every clerk – £3.18.0. September: to Mr SS – £11.8.8; to every clerk – £4.8.8. October: to Mr SS – £11.8.8; to every clerk – £4.8.8. November: to Mr SS – £6.4.0; to every clerk – £2.14.0. December: to Mr SS – £3.9.4; to every clerk – £[illegible]14.4. Henry VIII died on January 28 following. On 18 August 1547 the council decreed that Mr Secretary Petre should keep the seal [ad] causas ecclesiasticas and might set it on all instruments brought to him in accustomed form enabling any spiritual person &c., which was some profit to him. This continued until the seventh year of the king's reign.                                                        SP 10/18, no. 30

_____

*[The following undated papers which make up the remainder of SP 10/18 were thought by the editor of CSPD to belong to the reign of Edward VI, although some are undoubtedly of later date.]*

**832.**    Notes of evidence to prove that the land called Dover down near St Dunstan in the wolds of Canterbury belongs to Dover Priory.

In [1535] the priory was dissolved and John Johnson, then farmer of the site and lands near there (afterwards of the Isle of Thanet and since of Fordwich) was made collector of the whole revenues of the priory. In his account from Michaelmas 1536–7 made to the court of augmentations and now in the exchequer is as follows:†

Rent reserved. Of the sole heir of Edward Hextall of demesnes – 6s. 10½d. Of the Abbot of St Augustine's, Canterbury from the manor of Deal – 5s. 6d. To the archbishop of Canterbury for land in 'Baverley' – 3s. 6d. To the bailiff of Dover for land called Aycliff – 13s. 4d. To the preceptor or commander of Swingfield – 20s. All as in previous years.

These rents resolute were paid by the prior out of lands held of other lords, and the like of other lands held of other lords. Payments of pensions he sets down under other titles. In an account made by the prior from Lady Day 1527–8 he charges himself with rent received at Canterbury, 'Baverley' and Cockering (f. 2). He demands allowance for rent paid the same year to the archbishop of Canterbury for lands at 'Baverley' (f. 4). So it was received for and paid in one year. The like by another prior's account, Michaelmas 1530–1 (ff. 3,4). If this were not enough to resolve reasonable men, some deed may be found for it in the ledger book. Let them show any deed for that land, or that any other man's land bounds upon it by name of Fyneux lands, or let their land be measured by their old evidence and see if they have not their quantity beside Dover down, if they have sold no parcel from it. If it had been the Fyneux lands, why need there have been a lane specially to lead to that from the highway, which begins near a stone near the foot of the hill above St Dunstan's street where Whitstable wives mount their horses? Time out of mind the Fyneux had lands, and yet have great lands in Hougham near the priory land, some lying next to it, whereof of late Mr Fyneux of Hougham received some from Leven Busskyn, esq., farmer to the priory and lands. I have been steward and kept law day and court at the manor of Westgate, where the inhabitants and tenants about 'Baverley' appear; divers ancient tenants know to whom Dover down and the way to it belong, as do tenants of Hougham appearing at the priory law days and courts for the Fyneux lands there. So it is likely that the Fyneux long had Dover down of the prior, and the prior had land for it near the priory, for the land recovered by Mr Fyneux from Mr Busskyn had been occupied with the priory land so

*         I.e. the secretaries.
†         Extract in Latin.

long as it was taken and held by Busskyn as priory land until Fyneux found writings for it. And by like means they claim Dover down. The lord chief justice of England ([Sir John] Fyneux) was a great friend to the prior and an [? arbitrator]* for him in causes. The terriers, rentals and court rolls of the manor of Westgate of Henry VIII's reign will make this matter very plain; which, if they will stand in it, the archbishop shall be made privy to it, and to pray a warrant of him to search the court rolls &c., for his grace's farmer must not lose his land without making his grace privy.                SP 10/18, no. 31

[For SP 10/18, nos. 32–4 see nos. **813–15** above.]

**833.**   Sir William Stanley's cheques.†

David Jenkyns, 9 days – 6s. Richard Owen, 11 days – 7s. 4d. Francis Barlowe, 29 days – 19s. 4d. Hugh Nicholas, 21 days – 14s. George Martyn, 33 days – £1.2.0. Robert Bostock, 2 days – 1s. 4d. William Cade, 3 days – 2s. Ryse ap John, 7 days – 4s. 8d. Ralph Mullenix, 6 days – 4s. Robert Fludd, 1 day – 8d. Morgan Hewes, 10 days – 6s. 8d. William Browne, 24 days – 16s. Farrell Swyney, 11 days – 7s. 4d. Peter Rogers, 44 days – £1.9.4. Edward Standley, 11 days – 7s. 4d. James Howell, 1 day – 8d. Hugh Marshe, 3 days – 2s. John Bostock, 200 days – £6.13.4.                                                SP 10/18, no. 35

**834.**   List of principal gentlemen of Kent.

Sir Thomas Cheyne, treasurer of the household, lord warden of the Cinque Ports, lord lieutenant of Kent. Sir James Hales. Sir Thomas Moyle. Sir Anthony Auchar. Sir William Fynche. Sir John Norton. Sir Thomas Kempe. Henry Crippes. Walter Moyle. Christopher Roper.                                                            SP 10/18, no. 36

**835.**   Notes on the officers of the mints.

The warden of the mints shall receive of every merchant bringing in bullion to be coined the part that belongs to the king, and out of that he shall pay the master of the mints what belongs to him and the king's officers what belongs to them, and retain the remainder to the king's use. If the master and merchant cannot agree the value of the gold and silver the assay masters thereunto appointed in the presence of the warden shall try the truth and the master shall be charged accordingly. Before any deliverance of monies the warden and master shall consider the sums received and the number of persons to be paid; if the sum coined may not suffice to make full payment to all, the monies shall be measured in common so as every man may have part according to the quantity of his sum, having regard to the time of the bringing in and the time of the coining of his bullion. At the deliverance the warden shall be bound to show his reckoning to every merchant. If any merchant is absent at the time of payment and has no attorney, the warden shall receive the same and keep it under the master's seal until the merchant comes. Then payment shall be made as if he had been present at the first deliverance. Before any deliverance of monies there shall be trial of its weight and fineness in the presence of the warden. After monies are made the warden shall keep them in a chest, one key to remain with him, the other with the master, until the assays are made and deliverance to the merchants. After payment the warden and master shall take of the king's part a certain quantity of the monies which shall be put in a box under two keys for trial before the king's council once a quarter in the presence of the warden and master. The warden shall receive all the profit pertaining to the king and yield account. The master shall account only to the warden. The coining irons shall be delivered by indenture in the presence of the warden. There shall be good needles and touchstones to make the assays, which shall remain in the custody of the warden. The warden shall

---

\*        Cannot be read under UV light.
†        So headed by Petre.

see that the balances and weights are put in point from time to time. The office of warden is the most ancient of the mint and continued to the end of Henry VIII's days. There has never been a master without a warden. The warden's fee is 2s. 6d. a day, £45.12.6 a year. The fee of a clerk at 9d. a day and a porter at 3d. a day – £18.5.[0].

SP 10/18, no. 37

**836.** Fees and emoluments of a groom of the privy chamber extraordinary.
*This document appears to belong to the reign of Charles I.*   SP 10/18, no. 38

**837.** Account of the yearly profits of the manor and parsonage of Boxgrove and land in Halnaker, [Sussex] leased to the late Sir John Jenyns and now in tenure and occupation of Lord John Grey, charged with a yearly rent of £89.14.5, and thereof receives in yearly rent £70, and so paid yearly £19 above. Farm of Halnaker – £132.18.4. Farm of Boxgrove – £180.13.4. Profits of the parsonage – £100.14.8. Total – £414.6.4.   SP 10/18, no. 39

**838.** Officers in various courts and departments.
*Exchequer.* Tellers of receipt: Jerome Shelton, Robert Derknall, Nicholas Brigham, Sir Thomas Chaloner. Auditors: William Rigges, Brian Taillor, John Horneolde, John Thompson, Henry Leake, deputy to Francis Southwell. Customers: London, Boston, Bridgwater, Bristol, Chichester, Ipswich, Kingston upon Hull, [King's] Lynn, Newcastle, Poole, Plymouth and Fowey, Sandwich, Southampton, [Great] Yarmouth, Exeter and Dartmouth. *Court of augmentations.* Sir John Williams, treasurer. Thomas Mildmay, auditor; John Eyre, receiver (Norfolk, Suffolk, Cambridgeshire, Huntingdonshire). Thomas Mildmay, auditor; Robert Chester, receiver (Essex, Hertfordshire, London, Middlesex). John Wiseman, auditor; John Garreway, receiver (Kent, Surrey, Sussex). John Pykarell, auditor; George Wright, receiver (Berkshire, Buckinghamshire, Oxfordshire, Bedfordshire). William Kenyet, auditor; Lord Chediock Paulet, receiver (Hampshire, Wiltshire, Gloucestershire). John Hanby, auditor; William Sheldon, receiver (Northamptonshire, Warwickshire, Leicestershire, Rutland, Staffordshire, Shropshire, Herefordshire, Worcestershire). Henry Leake, auditor; John Ayllworth, receiver (Devon, Cornwall, Somerset, Dorset). William [*recte* Thomas] Notte, auditor; Richard Whalley, receiver (Yorkshire). Richard Hochenson, auditor; Sir Thomas Newneham, receiver (Lancashire, Westmorland, Cumberland, Northumberland, archdeaconry of Richmond, bishopric of Durham, Isle of Man). William Rigges, auditor; Robert Gouche, receiver (Lincolnshire, Nottinghamshire, Derbyshire, Cheshire). William Hamerton, auditor; William Wightman, receiver (South Wales). Thomas Tindall, auditor; Sir John Salisbury, receiver (North Wales). Thomas Mildmay, auditor; Sir Henry Gates, receiver (duchy of Cornwall). *Hanaper of chancery.* Sir Ralph Sadler, John Hales, clerks; William Dyx, Gregory Richardson, auditors. *Hanaper of augmentations.* Richard Duke, clerk; William Dyx, Gregory Richardson, auditors. *Butlerage of England.* Edward Elrington, chief butler; William Dyx, Gregory Richardson, auditors. *Great wardrobe.* Sir Ralph Sadler, master; William Dyx, Gregory Richardson, auditors. *Duchy of Lancaster.* Sir Walter Mildmay, auditor of the north parts; John Purvey, auditor of the south parts; George Owen, general receiver; 23 particular receivers. *Court of first fruits and tenths.* Sir William Petre, treasurer; Thomas Leighe, John Wrothe, auditors. *Court of wards and liveries.* William Dansell, receiver-general; William Tucke, auditor. *Treasurer of the chamber*: Sir William Cavendish. *The mint.* Thomas Egerton, treasurer; Henry Coddenham, auditor. *Calais.* Sir Maurice Dennys, treasurer; John Challoner, auditor. *Admiralty.* Benjamin Gonson, treasurer; Thomas Jenyson, auditor. *Factors touching fustian, alum, copper and money taken up in Flanders*: Stephen Vaughan, Sir Thomas Chamberleyne, Thomas Locke, John Dymmocke, William Dansell, Thomas Gresham, Sir John Gresham, Francis Foxall, Henry Saxey. *Lead matters*: Sir Edward North and Sir Richard Sackvile, chancellors of augmentations, can best declare to whose hands

they have delivered the same by warrant. Divers obligations remain in the hands of the treasurer of augmentations for lead, the days in part being already due. William Watson, the king's merchant, for affairs in Danzig. Sir Anthony Auchar for the lead of St Augustine's Canterbury.

*Paper book, 12 ff. (4 blank).*                                       SP 10/18, no. 40

**839.** [Temp. Mary I or Elizabeth I]. Certificate of troops and munitions sent north from the wapentakes of Yarburgh, Walshcroft, Bradley and Haverstow [Lincolnshire].

Numbers and charges of demilances, light horsemen, gunners, bowmen and soldiers with their corsets, almain rivets, coats of plate, splints, sallets, morions, pikes, bows and arrows, conduct money (in one instance said to be from Durham by the queen's order), mustering and training, supply of shot, and note of lack of armour and weapons.

*Signed by:* Sir Robert Tyrwhit and William Maneby.

*3 ff.*

*Mutilated.*                                                          SP 10/18, no. 41

**840.** Injunctions [for New College, Oxford].

Those who have been fellows for twenty years shall give up their fellowships and leave the college at the following feast of St John Baptist. In future no-one is to be a fellow more than twenty years unless called to take up a public post. Those having some church benefice for two years only are thereafter to be fellows. If anyone from this college is summoned by royal command from the university to court we do not wish him to be deprived of his perquisites. Although the statutes bind the warden and fellows not to admit scholars except from Winchester school, we, realising that the greater the freedom in choosing, the fuller the intellects discovered, ordain that the warden and fellows may hereafter choose any from Canterbury and Coventry schools; but, other things being equal, Wykehamists shall have preference. We do not wish anyone to be supported by the college to learn grammar. Those who understand and write Latin should be elected. Fellows may leave England for foreign centres of learning, provided that not more than three are away at the same time, and that they do not stay more than six years. They are not to be deprived of their stipends and other benefits provided by the statutes, including sustenance and clothing. Since our king is also king of Ireland, and there are many centres of learning there, one fellow of that nation is always to be maintained among you for the study of the liberal arts. We forbid the customary daily offices celebrated in chapel by chaplains, clerks and choristers: no clerks, choristers or chaplains are to remain in the college except those needed in the daily morning prayers and the sacred ministry on holy days.

*Latin.*                                                              SP 10/18, no. 42

[The document originally numbered SP 10/18, no. 43, a ground plan of the law courts at Hertford Castle (*CSPD*, 53), has be re-united with another part of the same document, formerly SP 16/89, f. 85, to form MPF/161, and dated 1582 or 1592. See *VCH Hertfordshire*, iii, 503.]

**841.** Names of gentlemen who tarry at home.

*Berkshire.* Alexander Umpton. Edward Fabian. Christopher Aysshton. Richard Bridges. *Kent.* Thomas Wyatt. John Culpeper. Sir Henry Isley. Sir John Fogge. Walter Moyle. John Norton of Norwood. Anthony Aucher. *Lincolnshire.* Sir Robert Sutton. Thomas Wynbiche. Edmund Sheffeld. Richard Markham. *Leicestershire.* Thomas Nevell of Holt. John Dygby of Welby ('Quycatoly'). *Middlesex.* Sir Arthur Darcy. Jasper Fesaunt. *Oxfordshire.* Sir William Barentyn. Edward Fines. Leonard Chamberlayn. *Hampshire.* Sir Francis Dawtrye. William Thorp. [John Coke].* Thomas Hadock. John St John. John Ludlowe. [John Vernon].*

*      Deleted.

*Staffordshire.* Edward Lytleton. Sir Philip Draycot. John Vernon. Thomas Gifford. *Shropshire.* Sir John Talbot. Richard Trentham. *Wiltshire.* Sir Michael Lister. Robert Hungerford. John Marvyn. John a Barowe. *Essex.* William Alithe. Sir Clement Harleston. Sir John Rainsford. *Gloucestershire.* John Poyntz. Thomas Gyes. Richard Ligon. Sir Edmund Tame. Maurice Denys. Sir John Bridges. Sir Walter Denye. Thomas Bruges. John Williams. *Warwickshire.* Giles Foster. Sir George Griffith. George Railegh. Sir Richard Catesby. Sir Walter Smith. Sir Fulk Grevil. Robert Throgmorton. *Worcestershire.* John Walshe. *Surrey.* Richard Morgan. *Rutland.* Sir John Harington. *Herefordshire.* John a William. Sir Richard Vaughan. John Scudamor. Nicholas Fitton. *Pembrokeshire.* [John Phillips].* Owen Phillips. Henry Wyrryer. John Wogan. *Bedfordshire.* Sir John Gascoyn. Sir John St John. Sir Thomas Rotherham. *Buckinghamshire.* Sir Anthony Lee. Sir Robert Dormer. *Cornwall.* Sir John Arundel of Trerice. Degory Grenfeld. *Dorset.* Sir Thomas Poynenges. Sir Giles Strangways. Sir John Horsey. Sir John Rogers. *Devon.* Sir Richard Grenfeld. Richard Pomerey. John St Leger. Hugh Stukeley. Richard Chidley. Roger Gifford. Roger Bluet. Thomas Pomeray. Walter Railegh. John Chichestre. *Norfolk.* Sir Richard Sowthwell. Sir William Paston. Sir Edward Knevet. Sir John Clere. Sir Edmund Windeham. Sir William Fermor. Henry Bedingfeld. *Suffolk.* Sir Arthur Hopton. Sir William Drurye. John Spring. *Northamptonshire.* Sir William Newneham. Sir Thomas Tresham. Sir Robert Kirkeham. Humfrey Stafford. Sir Thomas Griffyn. *Somerset.* Sir Henry Capell. Roger Basing. Sir Hugh Pallet. John Windeham. *Nottinghamshire.* Sir John Byron. Sir Nicholas Stirly. Sir Gervase Clifton. *Hertfordshire.* Sir Henry Parker. Ralph Varney of Pendley. John Nedeham. *Glamorganshire.* William Herberd. Sir George Herberd. Walter Herberd. William Morgan.                                                         SP 10/18, no. 44

**842.**    Precedents for royal supremacy over the English church.

In the record of the exchequer. When John [le Romeyn], archbishop of York came into the exchequer on 15 November 1292 Master Robert de Wycombe, the bishop of Durham's clerk, denounced him and his associates excommunicate and forbad the treasurer, barons and others there to reverence him on pain of the same penalty. Because excommunications, interdicts and other ecclesiastical sentences should not be made within the king's palace, Robert was immediately arrested. Henry of Durham and Ralph de Broughton stood bail. On February 6 Robert was delivered to the Tower of London. By virtue of the king's letters under the privy seal dated at Garendon Abbey on March 4 to William la Marche, treasurer, Robert was brought before him and the barons on April 6 and abjured the realm. [*Latin and French*].

25 Edward III [st. 6] c. 8. Ecclesiastical judges granted cognisance of voidance of benefices. English prelates and clergy have their liberties and immunities by the laws of the realm and the king's grant, not from the pope. By common law a clerk within or without orders and any other not having impediment for priesthood should have had privilege of clergy as often as he offended in murder, rape, robbery and theft, if he had challenged the same. 4 Henry VII c. 13. A clerk without orders shall be admitted to the privileges but once. [The clergy was first given by common law; if they say it came from the pope, it appears to be restrained by parliament].†

*Natura brevium Fitzherbert,*‡ f. 66. A man demanded his clergy and read as a clerk. The ordinary called and came not. He was returned to gaol till the ordinary should sue a writ to have him delivered to him. [Clèrgy allowed without challenge of the ordinary, and in his absence, because it was common law].† A nun, however learned, should not have privilege of clergy because she could not be a priest. The law did not originally know nuns and religious.

---

*        Deleted.
†        Inserted.
‡        *La novel natura breuium,* by Sir Anthony Fitzherbert, justice of common pleas, (1534), (*STC* 10958).

*Register brevium orig.*, f. 179. Clerks not to be put in sworn assizes or recognisances while in our allegiance. [*Latin*].

*Register brevium orig.*, f. 175. Ecclesiastical persons, by reason of lands and tenements belonging to their churches, are not customarily bound to come to the view of frankpledge in our court or any other. [*Latin*].

*Natura brevium Fitzherbert*, f. 175. Clerks in orders should not be elected bailiffs or beadles. Every church and churchyard in England is a sanctuary by common law for forty days for every offender in murder, rape, robbery and theft. Kings have granted privileges of sanctuary in other places, as Westminster. The pope cannot make a sanctuary in England as it is *locus sanctus* and *locus tutus*. The pope says he can make it *sanctus* [whereas God sanctified the whole earth],* but only the king can make it *tutus*.

*Magna Carta* c. 1 or [*correctly*] 9 Henry III. The church of England shall be free and have all her rights and liberties inviolable. Confirmed by the king and Edward I, Edward II and Edward III.

13 Edward I c. 6. Fairs or markets forbidden in churchyards.

9 Edward II c. 9. Distress shall neither be taken in highways nor fees wherewith the church has been endowed.

1 Henry VII, f. 10. On February 4 in parliament the chancellor asked what should be done about the alum taken by Englishmen from Florentines in England, because the pope had ordered disclosure of all who seized the alum. Several justices said the merchants were protected by the king's safe conduct. Lord Hussey said that in the time of Edward IV a legate in Calais had been allowed to enter the country provided he swore to bring in nothing to the king's derogation, and the bishop of Ely had it done. The legate now at Calais swears he has nothing prejudicial to the crown, and that a great advantage in this country is the manufacture of cloths which cannot be completed without alum. The chief justice said that the pope wrote to Edward I that he would make peace with Scotland, which was held from him, and would submit the matter to him. The king, advised by his council, replied that he [the pope] had no share in the temporality, which is immediately under God. The lords wrote to the pope that he wished to yield his right over Scotland, for the king of England is lord of Scotland. The bishop of London recalled that in the time of Henry VI Duke Humphrey of Gloucester burnt letters from the pope in derogation of the king. In conclusion it was agreed that the goods should be returned, but they wished this advice &c. [*Law French*].

Convocation is always called by the king's writ, as by the writ of its supreme head. The king's letters to the clergy to discharge his subjects excommunicated, wherewith the spirituality [were] grieved, the king answered he would not [? have] used but where his royal liberties should be impeached. *Tit. excomm. rege*, art. 2.

The prelates and clergy of this realm derive their jurisdiction and authority to plead in the spiritual courts from the king, not the pope.

13 Edward I. *Reg. Br. Orig.*, f. 45. The clergy shall not be punished if they plead in courts christian of things merely spiritual – penance for fornication, adultery &c., if prelates punish for leaving churchyards unclosed, or if the church is uncovered (f. 48) or not conveniently decked, or (f. 50) if a parson demands of his parishioners customary oblations and tithes (9 Edward II c. 1) or if any parson plead against another over tithes, so that a quarter of the value of the benefice is not demanded (9 Edward II c. 1); if a parson demands customary mortuaries (9 Edward II c. 1); if a prelate or patron demands a due pension; for laying violent hands on a priest (9 Edward II c. 3); in cause of defamation when money is not demanded, but a thing done for punishment of sin (9 Edward II c. 4) for breaking an oath: in these cases the spiritual judge may take knowledge, notwithstanding the king's prohibition. [All which in the statute of 13 Edward I the king

*      Deleted.

might stay].*

In obventions the king's prohibition shall hold no place (9 Edward II c. 1). The king shall have cognisance of dead usurers, the ordinaries of the church of those living (15 Edward III [st. 1] c. 5. *Reg. Orig.*, f. 49). The ministers of the church, for money taken for redemption of corporal penance (15 Edward III [st. 1] c. 6, 9 Edward II c. 2), for proof and account of wills, for solemnity of marriage and other things touching the church's jurisdiction, shall not be impeached, arrested, or driven to answer before the king's judges; and thereupon the ministers of the church shall have writs in chancery to the justices and other ministers whenever they demand them. [All in 15 Edward III (st. 1) c. 6].*

1 Henry VII c. 4. All ordinaries having episcopal jurisdiction may punish priests, clerks and religious within their jurisdictions convicted before them by church law of all sexual offences. [The judge, offenders and offences were spiritual, but ordered by parliament].*

*Reg. Orig.*, f. 54. The writ of consultation from chancery to spiritual judges empowers them to proceed in the cause mentioned in the writ (24 Edward I). If the chancellor or chief justice, on sight of the libel, cannot see that the cause cannot be redressed by any chancery writ, but that the spiritual court ought to determine the matters, they shall write to the judges before whom the cause was first moved that they proceed notwithstanding the king's previous prohibition. The writ of consultation is a command to proceed.

9 Edward II c. 13. Examination of a presentee to a benefice belongs to a spiritual judge.

9 Edward II c. 15. A clerk fleeing to the church for felony, if he affirms his clergy, shall not be compelled to abjure the realm; but, yielding himself to the law of the realm, shall enjoy the privilege of the church according to the custom of the realm.

9 Edward II c. 16. Desiring to provide for the state of the church of England and the quiet of the prelates and clergy, as we may lawfully do &c. [The prince's care over his clergy and their emendation].*

14 Edward III [st. 4] c. 1. None by us nor other commission of the great seal, small seal, nor without commission, shall take the goods of any clergy without their assent, and we take the clergy and their goods into our special protection.

18 Edward III [st. 3] c. 6. Where commissions are newly made to justices to enquire whether ecclesiastical judges have made just or excessive process in testamentary or other causes, the justices have caused the ecclesiastical judges to be indicted in blemishing the franchise of the church, that such commissions be repealed and henceforth defended, saving the article in eyre such as ought to be. [The law examined new doings in spiritual causes and sought help for it].*

18 Edward III [st. 3] c. 1. No archbishop or bishop to be impeached before our justices for crime unless we specially command them till another remedy is ordained.

18 Edward III [st. 3] c. 4. In the commissions to be made upon purveyance for the king and his service the fees of the church shall be excepted in every place.

25 Edward III c. 4. The prelates have complained that secular clerks as well as religious have been drawn and hanged by award of secular justices, in oppression of the church's jurisdiction. Clerks convicted before secular justices of any treasons or felonies touching others than the king himself shall have privilege of holy church and without delay be delivered to the ordinaries demanding them.

25 Edward III c. 4 and [st. 6 c.] 9. Privilege of clergy was granted in petty treason because the king's justices take indictments of ordinaries and their ministers of extortions and oppressions and impeach them without putting in certain the manner of their extortion. They shall not henceforth do so without putting in certain the manner of their extortion.

8 Henry VI c. 1. All clergy shall henceforth be called to convocation by the king's

* Inserted.

writ; their servants and families shall enjoy the same liberties as members of parliament.
   *Latin, Law French and English.*
   *9 pp.*                                                                SP 10/18, no. 45

**843.**   List of the almsmen of Christ Church, Oxford.*
   Lawrence Lee: said to be a leper, in a London hospital. Richard Wells: an old married
man, living in Oxfordshire. William Howe: living in London with Sir Thomas White.
[*blank*] Garland: an old man living in Oxford. [*blank*] Paget: the same. John Phillipps:
the same. Thomas Phillips: a glover in Woodstock. Thomas Massye: living in Westminster.
[*blank*] Bodington: in Oxford. [*blank*] Benam: the same. [*blank*] Lawe: the same. John
Benet: the same. [*blank*] Ward: in service with Mr Fynes by Banbury. [*blank*] Holiday: in
service. [*blank*] Boyden: begging in the country. [*blank*] Avis: at his house by Amersham.
[*blank*] Huntley: at his house by Wallingford. [*blank*] Vause: in service in London. [*blank*]
Osborne: at his house in the country. [*blank*] Yarley: the same. [*blank*] Launcelot: the
same. [*blank*] Leveret: at his house in Reading. Thomas Jones: in service with the earl of
Pembroke. Walter Jones: in Wales.                                         SP 10/9, no. 59

**844.**   1547–1553. Register of all gifts, exchanges and purchases of crown lands,
specifying the purchasers or recipients, the consideration of the gift and the amount of
purchase money, the yearly value of the lands, the rents reserved, and the dates of each
patent.
   *With index of personal names.*
   *137 pp.*                                                              SP 10/19

**845.**   [Temp. Elizabeth I]. Land sold by Sir Richard Lee since the death of Henry VIII.
   To Willymote, merchant of the staple: the manor of Newent, Gloucestershire – £105.
To Sir Rowland Hyll: the manor of Maugersbury, Gloucestershire – £25. To a servant
of Lord Montague, the judge,† in Northamptonshire – £14. To the lord keeper: the
manor of Redmere, Norfolk – £4. To Richard Grace of London, goldsmith: the manor
of Newland Squillers – £30. In housing and pasture within a mile of St Albans – £51.
Total – £228.
   Lands bought by Sir Richard Lee since the death of Henry VIII. Of the queen: the
manor of Aspley Guise – £35.‡ Of Lawrence Eyton, in Aspley – £20. Of [*blank*] West:
an inn in St Albans – £6.13.4. Of [*blank*] Kylbeas of St Albans: a copyhold – £10. Of
Mr Seamer: 6 acres – £1. Total – £72.13.4.                               SP 10/5, no. 23

---

*      Ascribed to 1549 in *CSPD*, 27; but reference to the earl of Pembroke must place it after the creation of
       that dignity in October 1551.
†      Sir Edward Montague.
‡      In 1560 (*VCH Bedfordshire*, iii, 339–40).

# INDEX

The references are to entries not to pages

## A

Ακανθινος 'Acanthinus', John, schoolmaster to Mildred Cecil, 517

Λεπτος, Mr . . ., 517

Σαυρος, Mr . . ., 517

A., Henry, [London], 378

Aaron, children of, 333

A Barowe, Abarrough *see* Burgh

Abberton (Aberton), Essex, church goods of sold, 172
churchwardens, rector and another of (*named*), 172

abbeys *see* monasteries

Abbot (Abotte), Harry of Titchmarsh, Northants, 562
William, serjeant of the cellar, 171

Abell, . . ., [Essex], 137

Aberdare (Aberdaer), Glam, musters for, 96

Abergavenny (Abbergeveney, Abergaveny, Bergavenny, Burgavenny, Burgavenye), Lord *see* Nevill, Henry

Aberlady, [East Lothian], 104

Abingdon (Abendon), [Berks], abbey, properties of, 50

Abington, Great (Greate Abydon), Cambs, musters for, 85

Abington, Little (Lytle Abydon), Cambs, musters for, 85

Abington Pigotts (Abyngton), Cambs, musters for, 86

Abiram, 333

Aborough *see* Burgh

Abotte *see* Abbot

Abowroughe *see* Burgh

Abridge *see* Bridges

Abrugh *see* Burgh

Abrydges *see* Bridges

'Acanthinus' (Ακανθινος), John, schoolmaster to Mildred Cecil, 517

Acaster Malbis (Acaster Malbys), Yorks, musters for, 83

Acaster Selby [in Stillingfleet], Yorks, musters for, 83

accounts, ministers', 73
mints, 29, 30, 31, 53, 55
naval and military (temp. Henry VIII & Edward VI), 721
superintendents of, 572
*see also* rentals

Achan (Achanus), 793

Achurch (Achurche) [in Thorpe Achurch, Northants], men of (*named*), 560

Achurch, Thorpe, Northants *see* Thorpe Achurch

acid *see* vitriol

Acomb (Acome in Holegait), Yorks, and Dringhouses and Knapton in, musters for, 83

Acton, Sir Robert, justice of the peace, [Surr], 5, 137

acts *see* statutes *under* parliament

Adam, 554, 800

Adams (Adam), . . ., messenger, 491
Nicholas, former chantry commissioner, letter from, 821
William, proposed commissioner of sewers, 687

Addington (Hadington), Surr, Leigh of, *q.v.*

Addington (surname) *see* Adington

Addlestone (Aydestons) [in Chertsey], Midd [*recte* Surr], woods in, keepership of, grant of, 659

Adington, Katherine, widow, [London], 171

admirals, English, lord *see* Dudley, John; Clinton *alias* Fiennes, Edward; Seymour, Sir Thomas
of the fleet *see* Dudley, Sir Andrew
vice- (officials) *see under* admiralty
vice- (sea officers), 140, ?143
*see also* Cotton, Thomas; Dudley, Sir Henry
French, 145, 621 (*named*)
vice- (*named*), 153, 155

admiralty, 185, 720
charges (temp. Henry VIII & Edward VI), 721(4)
debt, 753
high court of, 147, 149
advocateship of, suit for, 342
judge *see* Leyson, Dr Griffin
officers (*named*), 147, 149
proctor, 342
officers, 104
auditors (*named*), 838
treasurer *see* Gonson, Benjamin
vice-admirals, 140, 142, 143, 354 (*named*)
letters to, 103, 141
of Cornwall *see* Grenefeld, John
of Devon *see* Carew, Sir Peter

admiralty of the Cinque Ports, 422

adultery *see under* crimes and offences

adventurers, merchant *see* merchant adventurers

advocates (*named*), 342
*see also* attorneys

advowsons *see under* benefices

affidavits, 501

Agag, [king of the Amalekites], 333

Agarde, Francis, 148
Thomas father of Francis, 144, 148

agents *see* ambassadors and agents

Aglionby *see* Eglyamby

Agmondesham, John, [Surr], 345

A Gulielm, A Gulielmus *see* Williams

aigue *see under* sickness

Ainderby Steeple (Aynderbie), [Yorks], church, 78

Ainsty (Aynsty, Chaynsty), Yorks, wapentake, musters for, 83

air *see under* weather

Aiscough *see* Ayscough

aisles *see under* churches

alabaster, 204

À Lasco (de Alasco), John, Pole, superintendent of the German church in London, 448, 602, 603

Alba (Alve), duke of *see* Álvarez de Toledo y Pimentel, Fernando

Albanois (*named*), 227

# E

# H

# M

Macbraier, John, Scotsman, preacher, 74

Macclesfield, deanery, churches and chapels of (*listed*), 78

Macclesfield (Macclesfeld, Macclesfelde), [Ches], and Pott in, churches or chapels, 78

mace (spice), 822

Machell, John, [London], 171

mackerel *see under* fish

Maconyll, James, of the outer isles, captain, 79

madder, 572, 579, 586, 596

Maddox, . . ., of the privy chamber, 185, [203]

Madewe, John, preacher, 74

madness, feigned, 746

Madron (Maderne), Cornw, vicarage, valuation of, 431
Penzance in, *q.v.*

Madyson, Sir Edward, [Lincs], 137

Magdalene, St Mary, 793

magistrates, 419, 506, 511, 579
*see also* justices

Magna Carta, 842

Magnus, Thomas, archdeacon of the East Riding, 469

Maie *see* May

mail, coats of *see under* armour

Maillard [de la Mailleraye, seigneur] *see* Mony, Charles de

maintenance, cap of, 557

mainprize, bills of, mentioned, 426

Maker, Cornw, Millbrook in, *q.v.*

Makerell, Henry, surgeon to the king, 199

Makeworthe, John, [Salop], 166

Malbis, Acaster, Yorks *see* Acaster Malbis

Malby, Jane daughter of John, [London], 171
John son of John, [London], 171
Nicholas son of John, [London], 171
Thomas, [London], 171

Maldon (Malden), Essex, 360
church of St Peter, goods of sold, 172
men of (*named*), 172
Beeleigh in, *q.v.*
Church of, *q.v.*

Male, Anthony, merchant, 593

Mallory (Mallorye, Malory, Malorye), Richard, merchant, 171, 172, 723
William, [Cambs], 84, 137

malls, lead *see under* weapons

Malmesbury (Maulmesbury), [Wilts], under stewardship and hundred, suit for, 693

malmsey *see under* victuals: wine

Malory, Malorye *see* Mallory

Malpas, deanery, churches and chapels of (*listed*), 78

Malpas, [Ches], church, 78

malt *see under* crops

Malton [Farm] [in Orwell], Cambs, musters for, 86

Man, Isle of, 418
auditor of the court of augmentations for (*named*), 838
lord of *see* Stanley, Edward, earl of Derby
receiver of the court of augmentations for (*named*), 838

Manby (Manbye, Maneby), William, 820
proposed commissioner of sewers, 687
signature of, 839

Manchester (Mancestrie), [Lancs], deanery, 78

Manea (Manye), Cambs, musters for, 88

Maneby *see* Manby

Manet, Joshua, notary public, 448n

Manfield (Mansfelde), [Yorks], church of St John, 78

Manhood (the Manwood), Suss, hundred, musters for, 91

Manners (Mannours), . . . [? Sir Richard], [Leics], 44
Eleanor, countess of Rutland, [mother of the following], house of, 187
Henry, earl of Rutland, 7, 137, 182, 189, 557
depositions of, 187
servant of (*named*), 733, 755
Sir Richard, [Leics], ?44, 137

Manningtree (Mauntree), Essex, church goods of sold, 172
churchwardens (*named*), 172

Mannock (Mannockes), Henry, [Surr], 89, 137

Mannours *see* Manners

Manorbier (Manerbery), Pembs, farm, grant of, 666

manslaughter, pardon for, 666

Manthorpe (Manthorp, Manthorpp) [in Witham on the Hill, Lincs], 760

Mantua, Matthew de, 266

manuals (service books), 428

Manuden, Essex, church goods of sold, 172
churchwardens (*named*), 172

manufactures, 173

manumission of villeins, 432

Manwayring, Sir Richard, [Salop], 44

Manygham, John and Edith his wife, [Yorks], 170

maps, mentioned, 188, 610, 613, 713
*see also note after* 840 (*document transferred*)

Mapull, Richard, porter of Hill House bulwark, Harwich, 719

Marazion, Cornw, St Michael's Mount in, *q.v.*

Marbury, Thomas, widow of, [London], 171

Marchaunte, John, churchwarden of Shopland, Essex, 172

March, banner of, 16 (*bis*)

March [in Doddington], Cambs, musters for, 88

marches, Scottish, ?199, 584, 594, 710, 748, 826
wardens and deputies, 584, 721(3), 771
*see also* Bowes, Sir Robert; Clifford, Sir Ingram; Conyers, John; Dacre, Sir Thomas; Evers, Sir William; Grey, Thomas; Wharton, Sir Thomas

marches, Welsh, 113, 118, 123, 594

Marcion, heretic, 523

Marden, East (Estmarden), Suss, tithing, musters for, 91

Marden, North (Northmarden), Suss, tithing, musters for, 91

Marden, Up (Upmarden) and West Marden (Westmarden), Suss, tithing, musters for, 91

mares *see under* animals

Margaretting (Margaretynge), Essex, church goods of sold, 172
men of (*named*), 172

Marianis, Angelo de, 38

Markeham *see* Markham

Markenfeld, Thomas, [Yorks], 71

market days, 547

markets, marts, 249, 426, 487, 489, 490, 494, 495, 499, 511, 598, 704, 714, 720, 729, 842

market towns *see under* towns

munitions—*contd.*

    for Calais and Guînes, 685, 689, 691

    lost, 721(3,4)

    *see also* armour; ordnance; weapons

Munnes, Richard, churchwarden of ? Chingford, Essex, 172

    *see also* Mundes

Munte, John, of Great Bromley, Essex, 172

murder *see under* crimes

murderers *see under* criminals

Murfyn *see* Marvyn

Musgrave (Mosgrave), . . ., [? Sir Richard], 594

    Cuthbert, kinsman and servant of the earl of Warwick, 132, 165

    Sir Richard, captain of Carlisle Castle, ?594, 710

musical instruments, drums, 365, 410

    harp, on Irish coinage, 771

    lute, 185

    organs, 172

    tabors, 165

    trumpets, 165, 365, 557

musicians, foreign minstrels (*named*), payments to, 38

    player of interludes (*named*), payment to, 641

    trumpeters, 338

Musselburgh (Mouscle borro, Musskelborowe), [Midlothian], 145

    battle of [Pinkie], 629

musters, mustering, 77, 107, 720

    certificates of (muster rolls), 81, 82, 83, 84, 85, 86, 87, 88, 89, 90, 91, 92, 96

    charges of (temp. Mary I or Elizabeth I), 839

    commissioners of, 34, 107, 720

        named, 81, 82, 83, 84, 85, 86, 87, 88, 89, 90, 91, 92, 96

Musthian, . . ., 381

Muston, John, carpenter, [Lincs], 564

    William, [Lincs], 564

mutineers *see under* criminals

mutinies *see under* crimes

Mutton, Piers, serjeant of arms, 16

Mychell *see* Michell

Myddelmore, Robert, [Warwicks], 137

Myddellwoodde, Marmaduke, of Prittlewell, Essex, 172

Myddleton, Mydleton *see* Middleton

Myldemaye, Myldmay, Myldmaye *see* Mildmay

Myles (Myls), John, keeper of 'Little' forest and park, Suss, 178

    William, burgess of Stamford, Lincs, letter from, 733

    signature of, 787

Myll, Mylle *see* Mylles

Myller, John, [London], 171

Mylles (Myll, Mylle), Harry, [London], 171

    John, [Hants], 44, 137, 338

Mylner, John, churchwarden of Great Sampford, Essex, 172

Myls *see* Myles

Mynors, Hugh, serjeant of arms, 16

Myssenden *see* Missenden

Mytton, Sir Adam, [Herefs], 108

    Richard, [Salop], 71

# N

Naboth, vineyard of, 237

Nalinghurst, Ralph, [Essex], 71

Nalo, Nicholas de, [London], 171

Nanton *see* Nawnton

Nantwich (vici Malban), [Ches], deanery, churches and chapels of (*listed*), 78

napery, 178, 205

Naples, [prov. Napoli, Italy], soldiers of, 690

Nashe, . . ., 418

Nassington, Northants, Great Byards Sale in, *q.v.*

naturalisation *see* denization

navigation, security of, 200

navy, royal, 720

    charges of, 285, 721(4)

    maintained by merchants, 583

    officers, clerks, wages of, 721(4)

        principal [the navy board], wages of, 721(4)

        treasurer *see* Gonson, Benjamin

    operations, 18, 21, 27, 35, 64, 65, 79, 93, 95, 98, 104, 109, 111, 113, 140, 141, 142, 143, 144, 145, 221, 224

    provisions and victuals for, 721(4)

    salvage by, 418

    state of, memorandum for, 752

    workmen &c in, wages of, 721(4)

    *see also* ships

Nawnton (Nanton, Nawneton), William, cousin of Katherine Brandon, duchess of Suffolk, 438, 459, 467, 474, 481, 488, 493

Neale, William, [London], 770

Needham (Nedham), John, [Herts], 841

    Henry, 285

    Sir Robert, [Salop], 44

needles, for assaying, 835

neep, 822

Neeson, Richard, churchwarden of Great Warley, Essex, 172

Nehemiah, 793

Neightgaill, Robert, of Scarborough, Yorks, shipowner, 94

Nell, John, of Prittlewell, Essex, 172

Nelson, Humphrey, priest, prisoner in the Tower, 161

Neston, [Ches], church, 78

Netherlands, the, regent *see* Mary, queen dowager of Hungary

    treasurer to (*named*), 763

    *see also* Low Countries

Nevell *see* Nevill

Nevendon (Nevyndon), Essex, church goods of sold, 172

    churchwardens and others (*named*), 172

Nevenson *see* Nevinson

Nevill, Lord *see* Nevill, Henry

Nevill (Nevell, Neville, Nevyl), . . . ., cousin of the duke of Northumberland, 773

    Sir Anthony, [Notts], 44

    Henry, Baron Abergavenny, 7, 16, 187, 298 (Kent)

        lands of, 601

        larderer, 7

        petition of, mentioned, 601

oyer and terminer, commissions of, mentioned, 292, 301, 353, 360, 515, 566, 707, 771
    sessions of, for piracies, 707
Ozeir *see* Hosyer

# P

Pace (Pacy), Thomas, [Hants], 137, 338
Pachet *see* Paget
packers, 583
Pacy *see* Pace
Pagat *see* Paget
Page, ..., Lady Page, 580
    Sir Richard, 171
      a governor of Edward VI, 188, 203
    William, churchwarden of Bradwell juxta Coggeshall, Essex, 172
Paget (Pachet, Pagat, Pagète, Pagett), ..., almsman of Christ Church, Oxford, 843
    James, teller of Bristol mint, 30
    Sir William, Baron Paget (of Beaudesert) (1549), principal secretary (to 29 June 1547), comptroller of the household (29 June 1547–3 Dec 1549), 10, 66, 137, 164, 165, 182, 189, 203, 218, 234, 283, 418, 421, 441, 442
      chancellor of the duchy of Lancaster, 660n
      documents drafted by, 12, 25
      executor of Henry VIII, 11
      expected to become lord chamberlain, 509
      fine of, 688, 754
      horsemen provided by, 44
      houses of in Westminster, 471, ?479
      lands of, 754
        surrendered, 770, 771, 788
      letters from, 24, 217, 301, 395, 412
      letters to, 1, 5, 8, 23, 26, 28
      men of, 479
      pardon for, 818
      proceedings against, 594 (*ter*), 598, 602, 608, 609, 617, 624, 625, 688, 754, 770, 771, 788
      seal of, 441
      signature of, as councillor, 10, 242, 336, 499
      sons of, 771
      submission by, 770, 771, 788
      visitor of Cambridge University, 164, 210
      visitor of Oxford University, 218, 565n
Pagham (Pageham), Suss, tithing, musters for, 91
Pagington, ..., [Bucks], 137
Pagrave, Clement, [Norf], 71
Paignton (Paynton), Devon, vicarage, valuation of, 431
painting, of churches, 172
Pakington, Humfrey, [London], 171
    Sir John, 44 (Worcs), 108 (Glos, Herefs, Worcs)
palaces, episcopal, 454, 455
    *see also* Bath and Wells; Durham; Fulham; Lambeth
    royal, excommunications not allowed in (temp. Edward I), 842
      *see also* Greenwich; Hampton Court; Nonsuch; Oatlands; Richmond; St James's *under* Westminster; Westminster; Whitehall *under* Westminster

Palady (Paladye), Richard, clerk of the works to the duke of Somerset, 135, 418, 452
pales (buckets), 178
pales (hedges), destroyed by rioters, 242
Pallet *see* Paulet
Palmer (Palmar, Pawmar), John, [Glos], 71
    John, [Kent], 298
    John, [Suss], 137, 298
    Richard, [Herefs], 71
    Sir Thomas, 98, 104, 139, 603, 613
      considered for the controllership of Calais, 704
      depositions of, 567
      pardon of, memoranda for, 594, 600, 603
palsy *see under* sickness
Panmure (Palmure, Panmures), laird of *see* Maule, Patrick
Pampisford (Pampisworthe), Cambs, musters for, 85
Panell *see* Paynell
pans, 178
    charges of, 721(1)
panter *see* Dudley, John, duke of Northumberland
pantry *see under* household, royal
papacy *see* pope, the
paper, 447, 512, 551
papists, papistry *see* pope, the, adherents of
Papworth, Cambs, hundred, musters for, 84
Parcey *see* Percy
parchment, 512
pardons, papal, 301
    royal, 2, 25, 149, 301, 344, 346, 359, 365, 379, 418, 517, 594, 600, 624, 666, 698, 710, 714, 770, 771, 772, 814, 815, 818
Parham (Parrham), Lord Willoughby of *see* Willoughby, Sir William
Paris (Parys), 165
    licence sought to study at, 623
    Robet of, *q.v.*
Paris (Parise, Parish, Pariss, Parrys), George, [Irishman, double agent], 591, 594, 688, 752, 763, 781, 818
    pardon for, mentioned, 714
    Marmaduke, churchwarden of Bedale, Yorks, 78
    Philip, [Cambs], 71, 137
    William, [Kent], 71
    *see also* Parry
parish churches *see* churches
parishes, 428, 482
parishioners, 827
    offerings of, statute concerning (temp. Edward II), 842
Pariss *see* Paris
Parkar *see* Parker
Parke, John, churchwarden of St Mary's, Colchester, 172
    Margaret, [London], 171
Parker (Parkar), Dr ... [? Matthew], 74
    Sir Henry, [Herts], 44, 137, 172 (*bis*), 298, 841
    Henry, Baron Morley, 16, 44, 108 (Essex, Herts), 137, 298 (Essex)
      forces of, 399
      letter from, 399
      suit of, 813
    John, [Suss], 298
    Dr Matthew, 594
      dean of Lincoln, appointment as, 639
      preacher, 74 (? *bis*)

# Y

Printed in the United Kingdom for HMSO
Dd 291121    C4    1/92